GORDON L. ADDINGTON

DISCOVERING THE BIBLE

A Daily Reading Schedule With
Accompanying Notes To Read Through
The Bible in one Year

D1516229

Bible Study Resources, Inc.
1214 Pond View Lane
White Bear Lake, MN 55110

First Printing: January, 1995
Second Printing: April, 1995

Revised Edition: July, 1999
Second Printing: November, 1999

Second Revised Edition: October, 2003

ISBN 0-9673562-4-5 (Second Revised Edition, pbk)

Printed in the U.S.A.

To my grandchildren
With deep affection and love

With the prayer that God's Word will
continue to be a vital part of their lives, not
only in understanding the message, but in
living with the same priorities as the Lord
Jesus demonstrated when He walked the
roads and paths of our planet.

Contents

Preface

The Bible is God's story of redemption. From the very beginning of Genesis to the end of Revelation, the text of the Bible contributes to this theme.

In Luke 24 there is the account of a remarkable Bible study. It occurred just after the resurrection. Two unnamed disciples, who had heard the rumor of the resurrection, but were unconvinced about the validity of the story walked toward the village of Emmaus. Jesus joined them as they walked (but "they were kept from recognizing Him"). He inquired about their conversation – which had apparently been about the loss of their leader. At that point Jesus began to explain to them how the Old Testament scriptures told of His coming. He explained His death and resurrection from the scriptures. The implication of what Jesus told the disciples is that there are many such references (cf. Luke 24:27). His explanation excited their minds and hearts (v. 32). They understood the scriptures in a new way and the Lord Jesus in a new light as well. The scriptures had, for them, become the story of redemption!

That Bible study, conducted on a dusty road in Israel, is intriguing. Many would love to have been a participant. But we do have the completed canon of the Bible. So, it is possible, as we read the Bible, to search specifically for the references that Jesus might have spoken about. We don't know which specific passages of Scripture that Jesus explained. We do know however, that when Jesus opened the Bible to the disciples that day. He covered the major portions of the Old Testament (cf. Luke 24:27).

It is of interest that so many of the references to Jesus (the Messiah) in the Old Testament speak about the Second Advent. This emphasizes what we have known – that the cross is the central point in history, but that there is a very important end point in the redemptive story that brings us to glory with Christ Jesus.

A revision of *Discovering The Bible* in 1999 made that emphasis more specific by adding icons in the text of the notes to call attention to references to the coming Messiah in the Old Testament. These icons are explained in the introduction.

Speaking in very general terms, for too long the modern church has neglected the Old Testament. It is my deep hope that many will "discover the Bible" in a new way by allowing God's Word to speak for itself. In doing this, I believe that the reader, in the same way that I have been impressed, will see that the entire Bible is the story of redemption, and that Jesus is the key and center of that redemptive story.

I am deeply indebted to Dr. John Sailhamer Professor of Hebrew and Old Testament at Southeastern Baptist Theological Seminary for reviewing the book. In going over the work as a whole, and particularly the references to the coming Messiah, he was very much in agreement with the way the book handles the central question of the Old Testament messianic hope.

The present revision (2003) incorporates an edit of the text, making a book with fewer pages that is easier and more pleasant to read. I am most grateful to Sheri Venema, Assistant Professor of Journalism at the University of Montana, for undertaking this arduous task of editing. Any remaining errors are undoubtedly because I failed to enter her corrections properly.

Gordon Addington

October, 2003

Discovering The Bible

Introduction

Congratulations! You are about to embark on a rewarding journey that
has the potential to change your life! No book can so transform our minds
and hearts as God's Word. Along with the inherent and rich benefits of
reading the Scriptures, the accompanying notes in *Discovering The Bible*
provide further enrichment and insights into the whole of the Scriptures –
both Old and New Testaments – with its seamless message of man's need
and God's plan of redemption through Jesus Christ. Reading
systematically through God's Word and applying His truth to our daily
lives is a journey worth every step – even if it involves changing your
schedule to make this possible. There are promised eternal rewards that
will come to the student – young or old – who will undertake such a
commitment. Whether you are a seasoned reader of the scriptures or are
about to embark on that journey for the first time, *Discovering The Bible*'s
reading schedule and notes will provide understanding of the Bible and
suggestions for application in life through the year.

There is something unique about this reading program which will be
helpful to understand. *Discovering The Bible* is designed to help the reader
understand and appreciate the main themes of the Bible: the promise of the
coming of the Savior; the development of the plan of redemption and how
God brought this about; the events to which all of these pieces point – the
culmination of the age with the second coming of Christ. If we understand
how the parts of the Bible fit together and how they point to a glorious
ending, we will lift our hearts in joy at what God has done and at the
prospect of the future.

Getting Started

Today is the best day to begin reading through the Bible with *DTB*. It is
not necessary to wait until January 1. Simply check the reading schedule
and begin with today's date. By setting aside about twenty to thirty
minutes each day, you will complete a reading of the entire Bible in one
year. Or, if you prefer, begin reading at the beginning of the *Discovering
the Bible* schedule regardless of when you start, and check off each day's

reading as you proceed. The relative advantage is that this option will introduce you – at the beginning of the Bible – to the developing story of redemption.

You will notice that the reading schedule follows a unique order. Rather than beginning with Genesis and proceeding straight through Revelation, *DTB* guides the reader through both the Old and New Testaments simultaneously, and includes a daily reading in the poetic books of the Bible. This allows the daily readings in the New and Old Testaments to complement each other, highlighting the theme of redemption. In addition, many events are covered in chronological order, fitting the prophetic readings into the context of the historical accounts. The Advent season readings are especially designed, substituting the poetic readings with short sections of Old Testament prophecies related to the coming Messiah, along with corresponding New Testament passages of fulfillment, leading to a richer and deeper Advent celebration.

Several helpful suggestions have emerged from many readers who have used the *DTB* reading schedule and notes for an entire year's cycle:

- *Select a Bible to use for the entire year. By reading every part of the Bible in your personal copy during the year, you will know where to find the various books of the Bible. This will make using the Bible in other settings easier and more meaningful.*

- *Read through the scheduled scripture first, and then read the corresponding notes in* Discovering The Bible. *If you find yourself short on time, try at least to read the scripture portions for the day.*

- *If possible, set aside the same time each day for your Bible reading. Many have found this helpful for staying on schedule.*

- *Keep a journal of new insights, convictions, and applications – and of questions you may have. Find a friend who knows the Bible well to speak with about these questions. Review the truths you have identified to apply to your life, and keep yourself accountable to these insights.*

- *Be accountable to others who are also reading through the Bible. If you don't know anyone else in your area who is using the* DTB *reading schedule, challenge a friend to join you. A quick phone call each week can be an effective incentive to stay on schedule. Especially valuable has been the practice of several participants meeting together weekly to discuss the reading of the previous week.*

- *Pray daily that the Holy Spirit will give insight into the truths in His Word – those which you need in life – and help you apply these truths in your daily life.*

- *If you miss reading for a day or for a few days, don't stop the reading schedule. If you are following the calendar method of reading, it is probably best to move ahead to the present day and keep reading from there. (Trying to "catch up" may be discouraging.) If you started from the beginning of the study at a time different from January 1, and are not following the calendar, take up the reading where you stopped.*

Simply reading the scripture portions bring a number of benefits to the reader. We learn, for example, about God's plan for the nations, how God views sin, how the Old and New Testaments fit together, how the death and resurrection of the Lord Jesus are the central events in history, how to obtain eternal life, how to relate to one another, and how to live in light of Jesus' Second Coming. This is vital information that God has graciously revealed to us, and the Lord will use this systematic reading of His Word to change our thought patterns and worldview.

Yet the ultimate benefits come from purposefully applying God's truth to our lives. If we are committed to faithfully building biblical truth into our lives, God can use us in ways we cannot imagine! Commit yourself in the coming twelve months to "be doers of the Word, and not hearers only" (James 1:22). Begin the enriching journey through God's Word – *today.*

Some Special Features of Discovering The Bible

<u>First</u>, *Discovering The Bible*, points out the Old Testament promises Jesus' coming – both first and second advent.. These occurrences are noted at their beginning and at their end, by the special icons ☑...⇦. These symbols also are used in the New Testament when the coming of Jesus as the Messiah is referenced to a text of the Old Testament.

Many prophetic portions of the Old Testament refer to a universal rule of God on the earth during which peace and justice will pervade relationships between people and between nations. These are understood to be referring to the time when Jesus the Messiah will rule after the second advent, and are identified with the same icons as an aspect of the promised coming of Christ.

There are numerous specific references to the regathering of Israel and Judah to the land promised to Abraham. These are also considered part of the promise of the coming of the Messiah. This promise of restoration after dispersion among the nations is stated to be a sovereign work of God, accompanied by a reuniting of Israel and Judah – to then be ruled by a Shepherd ("my servant David"...David [the Messiah] will be a prince among them," cf. Ezek 34:22-24).

Preceding this rule of justice is the proclamation of judgment on the nations – "The Day of the Lord" – and this too is identified with the above icons as one aspect of the promise of Christ's coming.

When Jesus met the disciples on the road to Emmaus just after the resurrection, He opened the meaning of the scriptures to them by explaining how Moses and the prophets – and all of the scriptures – told of His coming. If we had been able to attend that study, we probably could point to a number of additional references to Jesus' coming. Some of you will see other references as you read. It will fulfill the hope of the author if readers discover the numerous promises of Christ's coming.

A related study that which will help the reader see the development of God's plan of redemption is to look for the specific actions God took to bring about His plan. These instances have been identified with a second set of icons: →...←. Some examples of these actions by God are the call of Abraham in Genesis 12:1-3, sending Joseph to Egypt to prepare the way for the Israelites to go to Egypt (cf. Gen 45:5-7), and giving the Ten Commandments on Mount Sinai (Exod 20:1-17). Following the history of God's people in this way will help you appreciate that these events, and how God dealt with His people, are not haphazard. They are connected to give a coherent story line to scripture – culminating in the coming of Jesus in His first advent, and bringing the final events in world history when He will come again.

A third highlight is to point out where Jesus makes it clear, explicitly or implicitly, that He is the promised Messiah, the Son of God. Such text is identified with a third set of icons: ⊃...⊂. It is remarkable how many times and in how many ways the Lord Jesus made clear His divine identity. Some – usually those who are not familiar with the Bible – assert that Jesus never really claimed to be the Son of God. This is simply not true, as the text will make clear. These icons also appear in certain instances where the text declares that Jesus is God's Son. An example of this is John Chapter 1.

We confidently believe that the Bible is the account of God's intervention in human affairs to bring salvation to mankind, to bring an end to sin and sorrow in this world, and to bring a glorious ending to all of history with a new heaven and a new earth. This reading plan, is a careful effort to help those who want to understand the Bible develop a new appreciation of what God has done for us. First-time readers of the Bible will get the picture, but repeated readings of the Bible with this perspective will bring more and more blessing to the student of God's Word.

January

Bible Reading Schedule
And Notes

☙

*They are not just idle words for you – they
are your life. Deuteronomy 32:47a*

DISCOVERING THE BIBLE
READING SCHEDULE
JANUARY

1	Luke 1:1-38	Genesis 1-2	Psalm 1
2	Luke 1:39-80	Genesis 3-4	Psalm 2
3	Luke 2:1-20	Genesis 5-6	Psalm 3
4	Luke 2:21-52	Genesis 7-8	Psalm 4
5	Luke 3:1-20	Genesis 9-10	Psalm 5
6	Luke 3:21-38	Genesis 11-12	Psalm 6
7	Luke 4:1-30	Genesis 13-14	Psalm 7
8	Luke 4:31-44	Genesis 15-16	Psalm 8
9	Luke 5:1-26	Genesis 17-18	Psalm 9
10	Luke 5:27-39	Genesis 19-20	Psalm 10
11	Luke 6:1-26	Genesis 21-22	Psalm 11
12	Luke 6:27-49	Genesis 23-24	Psalm 12
13	Luke 7:1-35	Genesis 25-26	Psalm 13
14	Luke 7:36-50	Genesis 27-28	Psalm 14
15	Luke 8:1-21	Genesis 29-30	Psalm 15
16	Luke 8:22-56	Genesis 31-32	Psalm 16
17	Luke 9:1-36	Genesis 33-34	Psalm 17
18	Luke 9:37-62	Genesis 35-36	Psalm 18
19	Luke 10:1-24	Genesis 37-38	Psalm 19
20	Luke 10:25-42	Genesis 39-40	Psalm 20
21	Luke 11:1-36	Genesis 41-42	Psalm 21
22	Luke 11:37-54	Genesis 43-44	Psalm 22
23	Luke 12:1-34	Genesis 45-46	Psalm 23
24	Luke 12:35-59	Genesis 47-48	Psalm 24
25	Luke 13:1-21	Genesis 49-50	Psalm 25
26	Luke 13:22-35	Exodus 1-2	Psalm 26
27	Luke 14:1-24	Exodus 3-4	Psalm 27
28	Luke 14:25-35	Exodus 5-6	Psalm 28
29	Luke 15	Exodus 7-8	Psalm 29
30	Luke 16:1-18	Exodus 9-10	Psalm 30
31	Luke 16:19-31	Exodus 11-12	Psalm 31

JANUARY 1

The reading in the New Testament begins with Luke and will continue with Acts to give an initial overview of Jesus' birth, His ministry, and the early church. Luke wrote both Luke and Acts, and you will note in the prologue of Luke that he had carefully researched the facts. As Acts begins, he takes up the account from what he had written in his previous book.

LUKE 1:1-38 As Luke begins the account of the life of our Lord Jesus, he states that *everything he commits to writing has been carefully verified by eyewitness accounts* (vv. 1-4). Note also that the accounts of the births of John the Baptist and Jesus were tied to other historically verifiable persons and events (v. 5).

Both Elizabeth and Zechariah were godly persons. With regard to the "priestly division of Abijah," see 1 Chronicles 24:10. The angel Gabriel "from the presence of God" (v. 19) was the messenger to Zechariah and also to Mary about the coming births of John the Baptist and Jesus. Gabriel was also the angel who delivered God's message to Daniel (Dan 8:16; 9:21).

Imagine yourself in Mary's place with the angel standing before her (vv. 26-38). ☑The message of the angel was absolutely amazing for it tied the prophecy of the Scriptures to this child she would bear. Not only would He be called God's Son, but He would sit on the throne of David in a kingdom that would never end (cf. Isa 9:6-7). The message also would have been disturbing, given the implications of a child conceived outside of marriage (cf. Isa 7:14).⇦ Mary's reply in verse 38 indicates a deep trust in what God was doing in her life.

GENESIS 1-2 Genesis is the first book of Moses – the book of beginnings. It records the creation of the earth, living things, and finally man. Sin enters the human experience in Chapter 3, with the resultant expulsion from the Garden of Eden and the conflict between brothers in Chapter 4.

Through these events, however, we find that God is working in love, and the first promises of redemption are found in these chapters. These promises, and God's action early in the human experience, set the theme of the entire Bible. That theme is the holiness of God and the salvation He promises and brings to men.

History is compressed in these chapters. Momentous events are briefly told. The reading for this week in Genesis spans more years than any other part of the Bible (considering an equivalent number of chapters).

As you read the account of the creation, note that Jesus is identified as the creator in John 1:1-3 and Hebrews 1:2.

When God finished the work of creation, He rested on the seventh day and set it aside as "holy" (2:2-3). This was affirmed in the fourth commandment (Exod 20:8-11). God also established marriage and said that a permanent bond is established in marriage (2:24). Both the observance of the Sabbath and marriage are known as "creation ordinances" and antedate the Ten Commandments.

INTRODUCTION TO THE PSALMS   The psalms are voices of the heart. Many are very personal; some are connected with historical events; some are messianic; some are prophetic (foretelling future events); some are apocalyptic (concerning the end times); some are meant for use in corporate worship. Some psalms were written in despair and others at moments of mountaintop joy.

The psalms contain a great deal of theology. The writer continually draws the reader back to truth. Often this is contrasted with distortion of the truth or with the blatant lies of the Evil One – or with the work of the Evil One as expressed through the world system. Sometimes the failure to follow God is emphasized by the result of choosing a different path.

In addition, we learn about God in His power, His creative activity, His sovereignty, His mercy, His love and faithfulness, and His judgments. We see God's concern for justice and equity. As you read the psalms in this and the coming weeks, watch for these attributes of God.

The language of the psalms, and indeed the entire Old Testament, is Hebrew. A major characteristic of Hebrew is the use of "concrete" words, or "word pictures," to explain concepts. This is in contrast to the Greek of the New Testament and to our modern Western languages that are more philosophic. Note, for example, the "pictures" drawn with words in Psalm 1: a tree standing near flowing water; the fruit from the tree; leaves that are always green; chaff scattered by the wind.

If you look for them, there are many, literally hundreds, of words that bring pictures to mind in the Old Testament. This characteristic of Hebrew is helpful in understanding the nature of God and the works of God.

Think of the writer as you read. Perhaps he was sitting on a hillside while he put personal thoughts into words in Hebrew that have been carefully preserved for us and translated into our modern language. Utterly amazing!

Finally, as you read the psalms, look for specific ways in which God, through the Holy Spirit, is prompting you to change your life. This may be a needed change in attitude, way of thinking, or specific behavior.

PSALM 1   As you read this psalm, look for the blessings that come to the person who follows the will of God. This person's most important characteristic is his attention to the Word of God, which reveals his love and respect for the Lord (v. 2). This attention results in choices that protect him and lead to blessing (vv. 1, 3, 6a). In contrast, note the result in the lives of those who choose to ignore God (vv. 4-5, 6b).

Note also the attitude of this person. Verse 1 describes God's person, who refuses to find fellowship or fulfillment with the ungodly, and doesn't allow his perspective to be formed by people around him (cf. Ps 26:4-5).

JANUARY 2

LUKE 1:39-80   When Mary spoke the "Magnificat" (vv. 46-56), her words contained truth perhaps even beyond her own understanding. Without question, the Holy Spirit inspired her words. The Lord had chosen to use the humble to bring blessing to all generations – and to use Mary in such a way that all generations would call her blessed! ☑The birth of her child would be an act of mercy to Abraham and those who have followed him (vv. 54-55). Her words tie the child's birth to the promise given to Abraham (Gen 12:2-3). This very child would fulfill God's promise that all the nations of the world would be blessed (in bringing redemption).⇦

☑Read the words of Zechariah about Jesus, the Messiah, who was to be born (vv. 67-75). Just as Mary recognized that the promise given to Abraham would be fulfilled in her Son, Zechariah affirmed it (vv. 69, 72-73). His birth was also tied to redemption (vv. 68-69) and to the Scriptures (v. 70). The ministry of Zechariah's son John would be that of a prophet – going before the Savior and preaching forgiveness through repentance (vv. 76-77; cf. Isa 40:3).⇦

GENESIS 3-4   As you read about the fall, note the steps Satan used to lead Eve to sin. *(1)* Satan questioned God's word (3:1b). *(2)* Then Satan twisted God's truth (vv. 4-5). Eve listened to Satan's lie – and Adam became an accomplice in sin (v. 6). *Result: Adam and Eve now understood the meaning of sin and knew that their fellowship with the*

Lord had been broken (v. 8). What a bitter realization this must have been!

Observe the specific results of sin in the lives of Adam and Eve (vv. 16-19). Life would never be the same. Think of their sorrow when Cain killed Abel. They lost one son in death and the other son in destroyed family relationships. Sin extracts a heavy price. Remember that the devices of Satan are still the same, and the results of sin are still death and anguish.

☑The earliest promise of coming redemption is recorded in Genesis 3:15. When God spoke to Satan, He said there would be enmity between the woman and the snake (Satan), and between her offspring and the snake's offspring. Then, in the last half of the verse, God tells Satan that "he" (male gender and singular in Hebrew; a male person who is an offspring of the woman) would crush "your" head (Satan). Further, "he" (the snake, Satan) would strike "his" (the Messiah's) heel. This reference looks forward to the coming of the Savior-Redeemer, the Lord Jesus, who would defeat Satan at the cross (cf. Col 2:14-15). Compare this to 1 Peter 1:18-20 to note that Jesus as the payment for sin was in God's plan from the very beginning!⇦

The account of Cain and Abel is a lesson about how to approach God. What do you see as the sin of Cain? Note God's warning to Cain about his attitude (4:6-7). At this point Cain had the ability to repent of his sin and turn to God – but he refused to listen to the Lord. As you follow Cain's line, notice the sin in Lamech's life (4:19-24). Lamech was an evil man and violent. Note the song of hate in verses 23-24.

Jesus came through the line of Seth. Genesis 4:26 records the first account of corporate worship.

PSALM 2   ☑Psalm 2 is a "messianic" psalm. It is written about the coming Christ. Acts 13:33 quotes the psalm to show that David was speaking of Jesus. It is also quoted in Hebrews 1:5 and 5:5 to show that Jesus was sent by God with His authority.

As you read this psalm, look for how Christ is portrayed (vv. 2b, 6, 7-9, where the writer definitely identifies the Son as Christ). Note carefully that God's Son will rule the entire world (vv. 8-9; cf. Rev 2:27; 19:15). Look for the character of the kings and nations of the world. What practical reasons are given for serving God and His Son with one's whole heart (vv. 10-12)?⇦

JANUARY 3

LUKE 2:1-20   The beloved words of Luke 2 never grow old. As you read this account, focus on how each event confirms the mission of the Lord

Jesus as Savior: ☑the birth of the child in Bethlehem, as prophesied by the prophet Micah (Mic 5:2); the message of the angels to the shepherds that the Savior, Christ, had been born; the shepherds' visit to the newborn in the town of Bethlehem. All these events are a mosaic that makes the account special.⇦

Again, the text ties these events to history. We love the story because it means so much to us – but setting aside the emotion, these events happened at a verifiable moment in history (2:1-2).

GENESIS 5-6   By Noah's time, he and his family were the only righteous persons left on the earth (6:9). The truth had been handed down through each of the individuals in Seth's line mentioned in Genesis 5. But it was a very narrow line of faith. The rest of world had succumbed to the lie of the Evil One!

God's judgment on the world through the flood is presented as historical fact. God was grieved with the sin that permeated society (6:5-6; cf. Ps 14:1-3). As you read Chapter 6, the lesson is that sin is a genuine affront to God. God cares about our behavior. He cared enough to bring judgment on those who rebelled against His law. →He also cared enough to provide the grace of deliverance to Noah and his family and to representatives of all living beings of the animal world. Through Noah's family the Lord would bring redemption to the world.⇐

PSALM 3   The circumstances surrounding the writing of this psalm are recorded in 2 Samuel 15-18. David had to flee for his life when Absalom attempted to take the crown from his father.

The word was out that God would not deliver David (v. 2). Some were watching to see David destroyed. David, however, had a firm grip on the truth, believing that God was his shield (v. 3). Because of this, he was able to sleep in peace (v. 5) and to proceed without fear (v. 6). As the record in 2 Samuel shows, David was delivered, and he gave God the glory (v. 8).

JANUARY 4

LUKE 2:21-52   God has His own special people whom He places in the right place at the right time. The world may not recognize them as significant, but they are full of the Spirit. Simeon (v. 25) and Anna (v. 36) were such people.

Isn't it remarkable that the Lord had revealed to both Simeon and Anna independently that Jesus was the promised Messiah? ☑Simeon's words tied the baby Jesus to the Savior promised in the Scriptures (vv. 25-33).⇐ Their words must have been confirming and encouraging to Mary and Joseph, who brought Jesus to the temple to fulfill the requirements of the law. Put yourself in the place of Simeon and Anna, and think of their excitement as they saw and spoke about the expected Messiah. Simeon must have been thrilled as he actually held the baby Messiah!

The sacrifice required for purification (vv. 22-24) was specified in Leviticus 12 as a lamb – but if the family could not afford a lamb, two turtle doves or two pigeons would suffice. Mary and Joseph chose the latter, indicating that they could not afford a lamb.

At the age of twelve, Jesus was skilled in the use of the Scriptures (v. 47)! One can conjecture that His parents' teaching and the presence of the Holy Spirit led Jesus at an early age to an unusual (and eventually a perfect) understanding of God's Word. ⊃The degree of Jesus' understanding with regard to His own identity is reflected in His answer to His parents: He understood that His responsibility was to attend to "His Father's house" (v. 49). This is the first reference to Jesus' understanding that He was God's Son.⊂

GENESIS 7-8   Consider the preposterous instruction (from a human perspective) that God gave Noah and his family. To build the ark away from any body of water, then herd animals into the ark and close the doors, must have seemed to the watching world like an act of lunacy. Did Noah preach repentance to the people watching as he was building? Although we aren't told in the Genesis account, 2 Peter 2:5 suggests that he did. Did Noah say that God had instructed him to build the ark in preparation for a coming flood? Surely he did! Noah's action, however, was not lunacy. It was an act of obedience born of deep faith, which in turn was the channel of deliverance for Noah and his family. The application for each of us is that our obedience to what we know is God's will is a channel of blessing, no matter how it may appear.

PSALM 4   God is the speaker in verse 2. Think about this in relation to the world around you. The world *does* love delusions, and the world *is* seeking false gods! Note the blessing of the one who belongs to the Lord (v. 3: cf. Eph 1:11; Titus 2:14; 1 Peter 1:1-5).

God blesses those who trust Him, and in verse 7 we have a glimpse of the inner joy and peace that accompany a walk with the Lord. This joy is independent of external circumstances (which, in fact, were better in the past, v. 7b). This is the priceless gift from God that the world cannot match.

JANUARY 5

LUKE 3:1-20   At the time of God's choosing, and at a time tied to specific historical events (vv. 1-2), John the Baptist began his ministry. ☑Read the synopsis of John's message in verses 4-6 as it fulfilled

Isaiah's prophecy (Isa 40:3-5). Note that the words cover John's ministry as it related to the coming of the Savior, and extend to the time when Messiah will return again in glory (v. 6; cf. Matt 24:30; Rev 1:7).⇦

Carefully think about the meaning of repentance as John presented it. Repentance is not something we mutter in a prayer, merely a religious formality, but it has practical results in our lives and our relationships. Literally, it means to turn around, to go the right direction. Repentance meant that one's life would be different (v. 8). It meant sharing with the needy (v. 11). For the tax collectors, repentance required honesty (vv. 12, 13), and for soldiers, it meant they could not take advantage of their power (v. 14).

John also pointed to Jesus as Savior (vv. 15-16) and warned listeners to heed the message of repentance while there was time (vv. 17-18). The consequences of not doing so have eternal implications (v. 17).

GENESIS 9-10 As Noah and his family came out of the ark, they received God's blessing as they worshipped Him. After the flood, God changed the order of nature by adding meat to the human diet (9:3, cf. 1:29-30). This is not to suggest that until then people had not eaten meat – but now God gave His blessing to eat meat. It is interesting to note that in the future, in the time of the Messiah, the original order will be reestablished (Isa 11:1-9). Carnivorous animals will once again eat plants!

Despite God's blessing – even with God's great deliverance from the flood – sin was not far in the background. Ham's disrespect for his father brought a curse on him and his descendants (vv. 25-27). (Canaan was Ham's son, and although Canaan is named, the reference is to Ham and his descendants.) There is an important grammatical distinction in 9:27 that affects its meaning. The NIV renders the second phrase in verse 27, "may Japheth live in the tents of Shem..." The Hebrew word that is translated Japheth is "he," and an alternate reading would refer this "he" to God in the first phrase of the verse rather than to Japheth. ☑This would put God in the tents of Shem – and we shall see in Chapter 12 that it is through the line of Shem that Abraham came and to whom the promise was given. It is through Abraham (Shem) that the Savior came.⇦

In the origins of the nations described in Chapter 10, Ham was the father of the Canaanites, Shem was the father of the Semite peoples, and Japheth of those who became maritime peoples and moved westward. Probably they would become Europeans.

PSALM 5   Verses 4-6 reveal several facts about God. <u>Conclusion</u>: It is dangerous to ignore the will of God and live in evil. It is dangerous to act arrogantly before the living God.

Verse 9 tells about evil people. Find the specific facts enumerated here. Then compare them with the truth of verses 4-6. These persons are indeed guilty, their schemes are their downfall (v. 10a), and their future is separation from God (v. 10b).

Now look at the facts about the person who trusts and obeys the Lord (vv. 11-12). If we face the facts, could we sensibly choose rebellion?

JANUARY 6

LUKE 3:21-38   At the time of Jesus' baptism, God graciously gave His sign of affirmation of Jesus – the visible dove descending on Him (The Holy Spirit, v. 22).

While reading the Old Testament, it will be valuable to follow those who appear in Jesus' genealogy. Some were individuals of deep faith and devotion to God. Others were not. Matthew's and Luke's genealogies diverge after David and come together again at Jesus' birth. Luke's genealogy comes through David's son Nathan, while Matthew's genealogy comes through Solomon and follows the kings of Judah through Jeconiah (a variant of Jehoiachin) at the time of the exile to Babylon. Jeremiah's prophecy (22:24-30) speaks of Jehoiachin and states in verse 30 that "...none of his offspring will prosper, none will sit on the throne of David or rule anymore in Judah." Thus, prophecy says that no descendent of Jehoiachin would rule (on David's throne), eliminating the possibility that Jehoiachin would be the line through which Jesus would come.

It is, therefore, most likely that Luke's genealogy, from David through Nathan, is the ancestral line of Mary, while Matthew's genealogy through Jeconiah (Jehoiachin) is that of Joseph, the assumed father of Jesus (v. 23). Joseph may have been used because genealogical lines were through the father. The impact of following Jesus' line back to Adam is to show Jesus' identification with the human race.

GENESIS 11-12   As men built the tower of Babel (11:1-9), their arrogance was apparent. God was nowhere in these plans! As a result, God confused and scattered the people by changing their languages.

☑The call of Abraham (12:1-3) is significant: God was now specifically setting in motion the plan that would finally bring Jesus and salvation to the world. God promised Abraham that he would become a great nation and that his name would be great (v. 2). However, there is also a vitally important promise that concerns us all. God told Abraham that through him all the nations of the earth would be blessed (v. 3). This is the promise of the coming Messiah – who would bring the blessing of salvation to all peoples! (cf. Gal 3:8).⇦ Note Abraham's response to God's call. Abraham obeyed God (although not perfectly) and learned to trust God in difficult circumstances.

PSALM 6   Have you ever felt completely discouraged? This was the psalmist's emotion (vv. 2-3, 6-7). Note how, in the midst of this black feeling, the writer brought truth into his mind and heart (vv. 8-10). In spite of how we feel, truth about God can, and will, change our outlook if we will allow it to do so. This is important for we all, at times, face hard circumstances or feel depressed. *Think truth. Use God's word.* Allow God to change your outlook with His truth.

JANUARY 7

LUKE 4:1-30   Jesus fasted through the entire forty days of the temptation (v. 2). This indicates how deeply Jesus felt the need for complete dependence and close fellowship with the Father during this important time. It *was* an extremely important time. Think of the implications of Jesus failing just one of the temptations and thus falling into sin during this time in the desert!

Satan's temptation came in several ways. He appealed to Jesus' physical needs and appetites (v. 3) and offered Jesus a kingdom easily acquired (vv. 5-7). The kingdoms of this world would indeed be His, but in God's timing and after His death for sin. He tempted Jesus to "prove" that He was the Son of God by casting Himself down from a height (vv. 9-11). Notice that Satan used Scripture in his appeal but used it incorrectly (v. 10). Scripture promised God's protection, but it would have been wrong to deliberately put himself in harm's way to "prove" that He was God's Son. No proof was needed! In each temptation, Jesus countered Satan by correctly using appropriate Scripture.

After the temptation in the wilderness, one of the first things Jesus did was return to Nazareth and go to the synagogue on the Sabbath. ☑When Jesus read from the Scriptures, He turned to Isaiah 61:1-2a. This passage is "messianic," and Jesus' remarks after the reading clearly declared that He was the Messiah. It is significant that Jesus stopped reading after verse 2a from Isaiah 61. Verse 2b speaks about the Messiah bringing judgment. This did not happen at the first coming of Jesus but will be fulfilled at the second coming.⇦

GENESIS 13-14   Both of these chapters reveal Abraham's growing faith. It would have been easy, and to Abraham's advantage, to "pull rank" and tell his nephew Lot to take the desert land while he took the "well watered" Jordan valley. Instead, his faith and character allowed him to act generously to Lot. →After this decision the Lord again appeared to Abraham, promising him and his descendants the land of Canaan (13:14-17).←

In Chapter 14, after Abraham had rescued Lot and his family, especially note Abraham's response to the offer of payment from the king of Sodom (vv. 21-24). Abraham was truly satisfied with what the Lord had given; more importantly, he wanted all that he owned to be what God Himself had given and provided.

PSALM 7   Both the character of the world and of David's faith are portrayed here. The character of the world is seen in verse 2, the hope of God's servant in verses 10 and 17. Destructive forces, never far from the surface, are waiting to tear apart those who are vulnerable. David's faith is clear in verse 1. In God he found his strength and refuge.

There is a transparency in the way David approached the Lord. He laid his life open to God's scrutiny. Without question, the Lord sees us for what we are anyway – but David *invited* the Lord's attention to the details of his life (vv. 3-5). He said that if he were guilty in his personal relationships, he was willing to have God deal with him as he deserved.

Consider in your own life the character of your faith. Is it a faith that leads you to walk in righteousness and obedience? Or is it a faith of convenience, to be exercised (as we might suppose) as the occasion demands? There is a difference!

JANUARY 8

LUKE 4:31-44   Jesus demonstrated His authority from God in teaching (v. 32), in ordering demons out of afflicted people (vv. 35-36), and in healing (vv. 38-41). The demons recognized Him and were compelled to submit to His authority (vv. 33-34, 41). The people were delighted with the teaching (different from what they heard from the religious authorities) and with the demonstration of God's power (v. 36). They also felt God's compassion in their lives through healing.

Note that in verse 43, Jesus said He was compelled to move on to share the good news of the kingdom with others to fulfill His mission of ministry.

GENESIS 15-16   Review the comments about the call of Abraham in the notes for Genesis 12. As the Lord again appeared to Abraham, He confirmed the previous promises of His presence and care over Abraham and said He would give Abraham a son (15:1,4). Note Abraham's reaction and the result (v. 6). Verse 6 is pivotal to our understanding of the biblical concept of God's grace. ☑At this early part of the Bible, the gift of righteousness is clearly seen as dependent upon faith and not upon earning it in some other way. Genesis 15:6 previsions the redemption that Jesus brought to the world. This is the same gift of righteousness of which Paul speaks in Romans 3:21-22 and in Romans 4. God's grace came to Abraham by faith – even though Jesus had not yet paid the price of grace at the cross (cf. Rom 3:25-26). Everyone who has been saved, from the earliest times to the present day, has been saved in the same way – by faith, on the basis of Jesus' sacrifice on the cross. ⇦

The Covenant that God established to ratify His promises to Abraham in verses 9-21 was done according to ancient custom. Usually both parties to an agreement passed between the animals that had been split. In this case, the promise was the Lord's alone, He was the guarantor, and He passed between the animals alone. Notice how God told Abraham about the Egyptian enslavement in the context of His plan and care for the nation (vv. 13-16).

We aren't told how many years passed between the events of Chapter 15 and those of Chapter 16, or whether Sarah's suggestion was to help God along or because of her great desire for children. As we shall see in Chapter 17, Ishmael was not the son of the promise.

PSALM 8   Many will see immediately that this psalm inspired one of our praise choruses. This psalm praises God's creative power. Notice that the first and the ninth verses are the same – emphasizing the wonder, greatness, and majesty of God's name.

☑When the religious leaders confronted Jesus during the Triumphal Entry into Jerusalem, they rebuked Him because the children were praising Him as the son of David (the Messiah, Matt 21:15-16). Jesus responded by quoting verse 2 of this psalm. In doing so, He declared that He was the Lord – about whom the psalm was written. ⇦

The amazing thing is that God cares for us as human beings (vv. 3-4). And this is not all, for the Lord has given us an exalted position in His creation, making us only a little lower in function and importance than the heavenly beings (v. 5), and giving us authority over much of creation (vv. 6-8).

JANUARY 9

LUKE 5:1-26   Observe how Jesus used the opportunity not only to preach to the crowds who followed Him but to instruct Peter, James, and John. Jesus preached from Peter's boat and then demonstrated His power to Peter (and to James and John) by the large catch of fish (vv. 6-7). Peter was terrified at this demonstration of power – so much so that he wanted to get away from Jesus. Peter saw himself in relation to

Jesus' righteousness! He recognized the sin in his life (v. 8). Listen to Jesus' gracious words of encouragement (v.10b). At that point, Peter, James, and John left everything and followed Jesus (v. 11).

⊃When Jesus healed the leper and the paralytic, He again exercised His authority over sickness but extended this authority to the more crucial area of forgiveness of sin. Verse 21 makes it clear. No one but God can forgive sin. Thus, Jesus clearly declared that He was God's Son. Note the difference between the reactions of the common people observing this event and of the Jewish leaders.⊂

GENESIS 17-18   →As the covenant of circumcision was established, God reaffirms His promises to Abraham (17:3-8). These are the promises of the land to Abraham's descendants and of the Lord as the God of this people. Abraham's part in the covenant was to circumcise all male descendants both at that time and for all coming generations (vv. 9-14). Note that the promise of a son is made again, and specifically, a son to be born to Abraham and Sarah (17:19, 21; 18:10-15). It would be through that son (Isaac) that God's covenant would be realized (17:19).←

Does the Lord care about the sin in the world? Genesis 18 should help us understand this. The Lord's attention had specifically been drawn to the sinful practices of Sodom and Gomorrah. Abraham was greatly troubled about the immediacy of God's judgment, since Lot and his family were in Sodom. Follow carefully Abraham's prayer for the cities and the Lord's response. When God's people pray, the Lord hears and responds (James 5:16b).

☑In Genesis 18:18, the Lord once again affirmed the universal blessing that would come to the world through Abraham (Gen 12:3). This is the specific blessing of redemption through the Savior, which reaches beyond the personal and national promises God had given to Abraham in Gen 12:1-7.⇦ In the broad sense, all of the blessings to Abraham and his descendants are part of that blessing of redemption. God used the nation to demonstrate His greatness (creation and His sovereignty), reveal Himself and His standards through His dealings with men (the law and the prophets), and finally bring Jesus, the Messiah, to the world (Rom 9:4-5).

PSALM 9   The psalmist rejoiced in the wonderful attributes of God. Look for the characteristics of God – who He is and how He deals with His children and with sinners (vv. 4-6). Note the attributes of God in verses 7-10: God, who is eternal (v. 7); God, the just ruler (v. 8); God, the protector of those in need (v. 9); God, who is faithful (v. 10).

JANUARY 10

LUKE 5:27-39   As you read verses 27-32, understand that Levi (Matthew), as a tax collector, was considered a "sinner" and was not respected by the religious Jews. Often the tax collectors solicited more than the law required and kept the difference. To make matters worse, as a tax collector, this Jew was an agent of the Romans acting for a foreign government on what they considered to be Jewish soil. So Matthew was doubly "cursed." He had sold out to the foreigners (collecting Rome's taxes) and was stealing his fellow Jews' money (taking more than he should have). Jesus saw Levi with a different redemptive perspective than others.

This outreach by our Lord is the model that we need. Levi was not easy for the Jews to deal with, but he was the sort of person who needed repentance and forgiveness. In our own evangelism efforts, we find it much easier to speak to people with whom we are comfortable – but our responsibility, through Jesus' example, is much broader (vv. 31-32). The significant thing about Levi, and about the people that the Lord has for us to reach, was that he was ready for the encounter. He was ready to respond to Jesus. Think about it!

GENESIS 19-20   When the angels came into Sodom they received Lot's hospitality. This was an obligation in the ancient East, and the necessity of protection in the wicked city soon became apparent. As the wicked men of the city came to Lot's door with their demands, the angels revealed their mission to Lot. They had been sent by God to destroy the cities of the plain and to get Lot and his family out of Sodom before the destruction (for Abraham's sake, 19:29). The men who were pledged in marriage to Lot's daughters didn't believe Lot and stayed to share the Lord's judgment on the city.

Note the origin of the Moabites and the Ammonites as recorded in 19:30-38.

Abraham had faith – but it wasn't perfect (Ch. 20)! He was afraid for his life while in Gerar because Sarah was a beautiful woman, and if he admitted that she was his wife, someone might kill him and take her. Instead of acknowledging her as his wife, he said she was his sister (which was partially true, vv. 11-12). The king of this city-kingdom took her into his house intending to make her his wife. →God had other plans. He had promised Abraham and Sarah a son – the son through whom the nations would be blessed (12:3; 18:18).← God protected both Sarah and Abraham from the danger to her by communicating directly with the king!

PSALM 10   In the previous psalm, the emphasis was on the character of God. In this psalm, we have an outline of the character of wickedness. The writer sees evil around him and asks, "Where are you, God? Why don't you seem closer (v. 1)?"

Notice the characteristics of the evil man: arrogance (v. 2); boasting (v. 3); pride (v. 4); deluded into believing a Satanic lie (v. 6); evil talk (v. 7); violence (vv. 8-10); lying about God (v. 11). The strange thing is that evil men seem to get away with this behavior (v. 5).

At verse 14 there is a transition, and the writer looks at truth. This is "reality orientation." When things around us look dark, what a blessing to know the eternal and holy God – the God who cares, who is King forever and ever, and who hears and answers prayer (vv. 14-18).

JANUARY 11

LUKE 6:1-26   Read carefully Jesus' comments about the Sabbath. Although Jesus affirmed the Mosaic law (Matt 5:17-20), He treated the Sabbath differently than the observant orthodox Jews did. In short, Jesus felt free, as Lord of the Sabbath, to do the work of the kingdom on the Sabbath as well as every other day. ➲Note that by saying He was "the Lord of the Sabbath," Jesus declared Himself equal with God!☾ Observe the reaction of the leaders (vv. 2, 11). Think about the *reason* Jesus violated what the religious leaders considered proper for the Sabbath. Does our observance of the Lord's Day conform to the Jewish religious leaders' concept (rigid) or that of Jesus' (flexible but, perhaps, with limits dictated by the circumstance) – or neither? If neither, what principle do we follow?

Compare verses 20-26 with Matthew 5:1-12. Consider the "woes" that Jesus pronounced. These are difficult words in an age of affluence! How should these make us careful, and how should our lifestyle be different from that of society? Give thought to your mind-set (Rom 8:5). What is most important in your life (Matt 6:19-24)? If we are right in our relationship with the Lord (the heart), it will protect us from the sin that led Jesus to pronounce the "woes."

GENESIS 21-22   The promise of a son realized (21:1-5)! The birth of a son to a couple physically incapable of having children had happened as the Lord had promised. ☑Further, this was the son through whom the promise would come (vv. 12-13; cf. 17:19).⇐

From a human perspective, Hagar and Ishmael's banishment seems unfair. Yet the Lord had plans for Ishmael, promising that he too would become a great nation (v. 13), and God provided for the child and his mother.

The greatest test of Abraham's faith came in the command from the Lord to sacrifice Isaac on Mount Moriah (Ch. 22). Abraham was ready to obey the Lord, believing that the God who had given him the son could, and would, raise him from the dead if he were sacrificed (Heb 11:17-19). Abraham's obedience was born in the crucible of previous experience with the Lord – obeying Him and seeing His faithfulness firsthand. Significantly, it was here on Mount Moriah that David later built an altar to the Lord after buying land from Araunah the Jebusite (1 Chron 21:18ff.). Subsequently, this became the site of the temple for which David prepared and Solomon built (2 Chron 3:1-2).

PSALM 11   Think about verse 5. God hates those who love violence. SO: Don't love violence! Don't practice violence! And don't watch violence (by choice)! God sees the practices of men (v. 4).

There is little question that if those who claim Christ as their Lord were to take this seriously, the use of media in the home would change dramatically.   Think also about books your family reads.   Some publications are characterized by violence.

In contrast to the bent of sinful man to love violence, note that the Lord is righteous and just (v. 7). It is He to whom we are responsible!

JANUARY 12

LUKE 6:27-49   What Jesus teaches in verses 27-36 is a radical ethic. It was in His day, and it still is today. This radical difference in attitude and lifestyle sets the child of the kingdom apart from the rest of the world and will be one of the most powerful witnesses possible to the grace of God.

Read Jesus' comments about judging others (vv. 37-38) along with verses 43-45, where Jesus speaks about fruit. As God's children, we should not have a critical spirit and be "picky" about others (vv. 37-42), yet we must exercise discernment about others, and this should be based on the fruit they bear. What a person is on the inside will be demonstrated by how that person acts (vv. 43-45; cf. Matt 7:15-20).

Note Jesus' comments about obedience in verses 46-49. When we apply Jesus' words to our lives and obey Him, we build a solid foundation for our lives – and demonstrate that there *is* life.

GENESIS 23-24   When Sarah died, Abraham buried her in Hebron (23:19). Remember the name, for the place will come up often in the history of God's people. King David ruled from Hebron for the first seven years of his reign. The city still remains and is occupied in Israel, and the burial place is still identified.

It was Abraham's firm desire that Isaac would not marry into the pagan culture of Canaan but that his wife should come from his family. The account of the journey that Abraham's servant made and his faith in Abraham's God is impressive. Read the servant's prayer of faith with its almost impossible conditions (24:12-14). Rebekah's faith in leaving her family and traveling hundreds of miles with a strange servant to marry a man whom she had never seen is also impressive. God's hand was in the journey.

The blessing with which her family sent Rebekah off was prophetic, for her offspring did increase to "thousands upon thousands," and her offspring did (and will yet) "possess the gates of their enemies" (24:60).

PSALM 12   Society is sick! Note the dishonesty (v. 2), arrogance and pride (vv. 3-4), and oppression of the weak and needy (v. 5a). In spite of how things appear, God is not dead and will protect His people (vv. 5b-7). Think about the truth of verse 8. Think also about God's people in a sick society in relation to Matthew 5:13-16.

JANUARY 13

LUKE 7:1-35   In verses 1-17 there are two accounts of healing. In the gospel accounts, there seem to be several reasons why Jesus healed. Sometimes it was to demonstrate His authority and to authenticate that He was the promised Messiah, as when He healed the paralytic in Luke 5:17-26. Other times the healing was a response of faith, as in verses 1-10, the healing of the centurion's servant, and in Mark 7:24-30 when the Canaanite woman pleaded with Jesus to heal her daughter. At times Jesus healed without request because of His compassion, as when He raised the widow's son from the dead in verses 11-17. The common thread in each instance is the authority of the kingdom that Jesus used to bring glory to the Father.

☑Compare Jesus' answer to the disciples of John the Baptist (vv. 18-23) with Isaiah 29:18-19, 35:5-6, 42:6-7 and 61:1-2. Jesus was calling their attention to these prophecies of the Messiah in Isaiah that would validate His work as the Messiah.⇔

GENESIS 25-26   As Abraham before him, Isaac was a man of faith. When Rebekah did not have children he prayed, and God answered (25:21). →As the Lord was choosing the human line through which Jesus would come, note His message to Rebekah about the twins she would have (v. 23). The fulfillment of the Lord's prophecy about the children began when Esau sold his birthright (vv. 29-34). Note the comment about the meaning of this in verse 34b.←

☑The Lord graciously affirmed to Isaac the promise given to Abraham (26:3-4, 24). Through Isaac, these promises, including the blessing to the whole world of the Savior, would be realized.⇦ Isaac was a man of faith but was also very human, as we see in his fear of the men of Gerar (26:7). The Lord had already told Isaac He would protect and bless him (v. 3a). In spite of Isaac's lack of faith and integrity, the Lord protected him and Rebekah (26:7-29).

PSALM 13   Sometimes it seems as if God's answer will never come. That is what David's prayer sounds like in verses 1-2. Yet, in spite of how things looked, David knew that God was real and that he would see God's answer (v. 5). This conviction was so strong that he was able to rejoice and sing (v. 6) – not in his circumstances – but in the conviction that God's love, salvation and goodness were real. David's conviction had a "reality orientation." It was valid and real – based on the character of God.

JANUARY 14

LUKE 7:36-50   Notice how Jesus cut through the Pharisee's hypocrisy with regard to the woman who anointed Jesus' feet. Simon held Jesus at arm's length to guard his own "righteousness" (which was no true righteousness at all). ➲The woman, who knew her need, confessed her faith by her actions (and received true righteousness, the gift of faith, v. 48). Jesus again made it clear that He had the authority to forgive sin and to grant salvation.➲

GENESIS 27-28   The blessing was a significant event in a family. When Isaac gave the blessing to Jacob (27:27-29), there was little else he could give to Esau (vv. 39-40). These blessings were prophetic and expressed what God would do in the lives of these two brothers. In the case of Jacob, they were prophetic for his descendants. →Note that in the blessing to Jacob, Isaac included the same promise that God had given to Abraham and to him (v. 29b).⇦ In spite of the deceit of Rebekah and Jacob, God was working.

Follow Jacob as he begins the long solitary journey to Paddan Aram to the home of Abraham and Rebekah's family. ☑The Lord reaffirmed the promise of the land and the universal promise of blessing to all peoples on the earth, which included the coming of the Messiah, to Jacob in a most gracious way (28:10-15). God's appearance to him made a difference in Jacob's life (vv. 20-22).⇦

PSALM 14   Verses 1-3 are quoted in Romans 3:10-12. Who is really foolish in this world? Those who ignore the Lord or assert that there is no God (v. 1). In fact, the depth of wickedness in the world is outlined in verses 1-3. All of us share in the sinful nature, and David recognized this.

Does God see? Indeed He does (v. 2). Does God care? He is the refuge of the poor (v. 6b). As believers, we must align our efforts to conform to God's concerns.

☑Finally, take note of David's prayer in verse 7. Salvation would indeed come to God's people in the person of the Messiah.⇦

JANUARY 15

LUKE 8:1-21   In the Parable of the Sower, Jesus presented the entire span of human response to gospel truth. It is important that we look carefully at our own lives and consider once again how we personally react to truth from God's word when we hear it.

The parable includes both the human dimension of choice and the spiritual dimension of demonic opposition. Both are real, and it is hard to separate the two. Think of the seed on the path. On a well-trodden path, the soil is hard and not ready to receive a seed so that it can grow. It is like the person whose heart has become so hardened that there is no chance for a seed of truth to germinate. Not only that, but birds come and take away the seed (the work of Satan). The rocky soil is like the person who is willing to hear but easily turns away (choice) to other pursuits. The soil with thorns describes many in our society. They are too busy and too distracted by the details of life to allow the truth to grow to maturity. Of the four examples, only the seed in good soil bore fruit. The evidence of spiritual life is fruit (Matt 7:16-20).

Where do you fit? Are you "good soil?" Allow the Holy Spirit to help you think through any areas of your life that need change to develop the fruit God desires.

GENESIS 29-30   The Lord protected Jacob (28:15) on the long journey to Paddan Aram to find his mother's and grandparents' home and family. Family ties were strong, and Jacob was welcomed into the household. Remember Isaac's instruction to Jacob as he left for Paddan Aram: Go to your mother's family and find a wife from among the daughters of Laban, your mother's brother (28:1-2). Just as Abraham had strong convictions about his son not marrying into the culture of the Canaanites (24:3-4), Isaac instructed Jacob not to marry into the Canaanite culture.

During the years that Jacob spent with Laban, he married two of Laban's daughters and also the two servants Laban had given his daughters when they were married. The marriages to the daughters' servants were utilitarian – to have more children. Rachel, who was more beautiful than Leah and whom Jacob loved more than Leah, didn't have children for several years. When she did, note that it was the Lord who gave her a child (30:22).

Follow Jacob's dealings with Laban in Chapter 30. We don't understand some of the methods Jacob used, but by selective breeding he acquired greater and greater wealth as measured by his flocks.

PSALM 15   As mentioned previously, the psalms are "voices of the heart." They are intensely personal. The writer is not afraid to bare his heart and emotion. Sometimes this is from a heart full of praise and joy, but other times he speaks from discouragement or confusion. When the latter is the case, a reorientation of mind and heart brings the writer back to the reality of God and His goodness. This perspective could be properly called "reality orientation." Look for this as you read.

In this remarkable psalm, the writer asks the question, and God answers. The question is one in which we all have a vital interest – "Who can dwell with you, Lord? Who can count on fellowship with you and enjoy your blessings?"

Look carefully at the answer in verses 2-5. God desires men and women of truth and good will. This includes a person's general direction and intent (blameless walk), and also specific behavior (doing what is righteous, v. 2a). It means speaking only truth (v. 2b) and dealing with people justly and fairly (v. 3). It means standing together with God's people (v. 4a) and keeping one's word (v. 4b). It is God's desire that we have a generous spirit and deal with others justly (v. 5a).

The promise in verse 5b is that the person who lives this way will never be shaken. This should make us very careful in our own lives. As God's children, we need to *choose* God's way. Does this mean that what we "do" brings fellowship with the Lord God? That would be a salvation by works. Rather it is faith and love for God that prompts us to choose to do God's will and walk in His way. Correct behavior is the fruit of faith (John 14:23-24).

There is a similar question in Psalm 24:3-6 and in Isaiah 33:14b-16. Look also at Psalm 119:1-8 and Micah 6:8.

JANUARY 16

LUKE 8:22-56   While reading this section, think in terms of Jesus' authority. Jesus demonstrated His power (kingdom authority) over nature (vv. 22-25) and also over the demons that possessed the man (vv. 26-33). In both instances Jesus had authority to solve the problem. Jesus' power that forced the demons out of the man brought fear to the townspeople – so much fear that they asked Jesus to leave after He healed this man (v. 37). They simply did not know how to deal with this kind of power. Perhaps they were also concerned with the economic loss of the pigs. Whatever their motivation, when they asked Jesus to leave their town, He did so.

The most dramatic demonstration of authority was raising Jairus's daughter from the dead. What emotion Jairus must have felt as he anxiously waited for Jesus to come to his home (vv. 40-56). Note that the only condition Jesus placed on the daughter's healing was that of faith. Jesus recognized faith in the parent's hearts and honored that faith by restoring their daughter to life – even though they were astonished at what Jesus did! ⊃Whether it was authority over natural elements such as the storm, over spirits who harassed individuals, over physical illness, or even over death, Jesus' acts demonstrated His authority as God's Son.⊂ From these incidents, we must understand that the Lord is more powerful than any issues we will or could face.

GENESIS 31-32   It was time for Jacob to take his family and possessions back to Canaan. The Lord had promised to protect Jacob and bring him back to the land he had been promised. Relations had become strained with Laban, and the Lord told Jacob to start back (31:1-3). The manner in which Jacob left, however, was not without blame, and Laban had reason to be angry with him (31:19-21). The Lord protected Jacob, however, by telling Laban not to touch or harm him (31:24). As a result, after their confrontation, they made a formal covenant not to harm each other and parted (vv. 43-55).

As Jacob anticipated meeting Esau, he was justifiably frightened, since Esau had previously vowed to kill Jacob (27:41). Jacob thus prepared to appease his brother. Jacob's encounter with the heavenly visitor left him with a permanent limp – perhaps a reminder of the Lord's visitation (32:22-32). Remember that when Jacob left Canaan for Paddan Aram, the Lord appeared to him (28:12-15). Now upon his return, he again had assurance of God's presence and purpose for him.

PSALM 16   In verse 1, David saw God as his only place of safety. In an uncertain world, where no one can be completely aware of all of the dangers that await, we need the safety of the Lord God. Realistically, there is no other place to turn! Note the "reality orientation" that David expresses in verse 2.

The secret of contentment is in verses 5-6. David's faith and knowledge that God had assigned him his place and path gave him a "delightful inheritance." This is expressed in the NT in 1 Timothy 6:6-8. To choose to follow the Lord and be content with what He provides, is at the same time a personal initiative on the part of the believer and a gift from the Lord.

Note also the mind-set of verse 8a: "I have set the Lord always before me." This mind-set brought spiritual, emotional, and physical well-being (v. 9). Compare this with the mind-set in Romans 8:5-8.

☑In Peter's message to the crowds on the Day of Pentecost, he made reference to verses 8-11 and explained how this passage speaks about the Lord Jesus (Acts 2:25-28; also note how Paul used this passage in Acts 13:35 in speaking about the resurrection).⇦

JANUARY 17

LUKE 9:1-36   ➲When Jesus sent His disciples to represent the kingdom, He sent them with power and authority and commissioned them to preach and to heal (vv. 1-6).   Who could delegate God's authority and His power but the Son?☾ He made it clear that theirs was to be a single-minded ministry. They were not to force themselves upon anyone (v. 5) and not to let any extraneous activity divert them.

As you read verses 1-6 and 23-26, think again about Jesus' condition of discipleship: the daily choice to do God's will instead of one's own. The idea is radically different from the self-fulfillment tone of today's culture. It is exactly at this point that we need the Holy Spirit to help us change our thinking to make this our pattern (cf. Rom 12:1-2).

➲When Peter, James, and John went with Jesus to the mountain where He was transfigured, Moses and Elijah appeared and spoke to Jesus about His coming Passion (vv. 29-31). This was no mistake. Moses represented the law and Elijah the prophets. Jesus' coming death and resurrection would fulfill the prophecies of the Old Testament (Luke 24:27).☾ Think how Peter, James and John must have looked back on the Transfiguration and seen the whole picture – understanding it in light of God's plan of redemption and of the Scriptures.

GENESIS 33-34   The meeting between the brothers could not have gone better!   Esau received his brother graciously, and their relationship was healed.   →God's hand is evident in this restored relationship, as He had promised Jacob He would bring him back safely (cf. Gen 28:15).⇐

The events of Chapter 34 occurred after at least some of Jacob's sons had reached adulthood. Simeon and Levi were the second and third of Jacob's sons. The family's emotions surrounding the rape of Dinah were intense. →Although the family probably did not understand this, the Shechemites' plan to assimilate Jacob's family did not fit God's plan to make Abraham's descendants separate from the Canaanites (34:21-23; cf. Deut 7:1-6).⇐ Read Simeon and Levi's response to Jacob in verse 31.

PSALM 17   It is apparent that this psalm was written in distress. It was a call to God to listen to the writer's prayer. He needed personal vindication. Perhaps David had been unjustly accused or was being unjustly hunted by enemies.

In this kind of situation, it is instructive for us to see how he responded. He was willing to leave vindication to God (v. 2a; cf. Rom 12:17-21). Since he had resolved to live in ways pleasing to God (v. 3b), and was instructed by God's word (v. 4), he was confident of God's answer (v. 6ff.). Contrast this attitude with how the ungodly live and deal with others (vv. 10-12).

David identified a basic difference. The reward of the person of the world is in this life – and only in this world (v. 14a). In contrast, the heritage of the believer is in this world where there is fellowship with the Lord, and also in the promises God has given about the future (vv. 14b-15). Think of the differences, and choose wisely!

JANUARY 18

LUKE 9:37-62   The intensity of spiritual battle is illustrated in the account of the child with an evil spirit in verses 37-43.   Both the destructive power and the tenacity of evil are apparent.   The disciples had been given authority over spirits, yet were unable to drive out this spirit (v. 40).   Jesus healed the boy to the amazement of the watching people (v. 43).   In the parallel accounts in Matthew (Matt 17:14-21) and Mark (Mark 9:14-29), the disciples asked Jesus why they couldn't command the demon to leave the boy.   Jesus answered that it was because of their lack of faith and prayer.   We must remember that we who are in the kingdom are given the task of confronting the power of evil.   We should not shrink from the task but must be prepared and proceed in the right way.

Jesus' comments, prompted by the disciples' discussion about which of them would be greatest in the kingdom, are significant, for they again emphasize the difference between the world system and the kingdom (vv. 46-48).   Jesus' illustration of the child brings this into focus (v. 48).   The disciples' concern was for personal position.   Jesus' point was that their concern should be for the people around them who had the least power and the greatest need for protection (as little children)!   This care for the powerless will be important in how God views us in the kingdom.

Read thoughtfully Jesus' comments on the cost of following Him (vv. 57-62).   The work of the kingdom is urgent – but the person who embarks on this work must count the cost (v. 58).   Further, decision time is now (vv. 59-60), and after beginning the course, we must stay on track (vv. 61-62).

GENESIS 35-36   The Lord again spoke to Jacob telling him to move to Bethel.   Jacob destroyed all of the false gods in his household (35:2). God protected the company from attack making the people afraid (35:5).

☑At Bethel, the Lord appeared to Jacob and confirmed the promises made to him as he left for Paddan Aram (cf. 28:10-15): the land He had promised to Abraham and to Isaac, and the great nation and great kings that would come from him (vv. 9-13). Thus, Jacob – renamed Israel – would be the person through whom the promises to Abraham would be realized.⇔ During Jacob's move from Bethel to Ephrath (Bethlehem), Rachel died as Benjamin was born (vv. 18-19). Isaac also died at Hebron (vv. 27-29) and was buried in the same cave as Abraham and Sarah (Gen 49:29-32).

PSALM 18   The prologue for this psalm explains its setting. David composed this when he had been delivered from his enemies. He describes God, His characteristics, and how He delivered David.

Think about the six metaphors that David uses to describe the God of safety in verse 2. What does this mean to you today?

Follow the ways in which David describes God in the psalm. God is powerful and awesome (vv. 7-15); a strong deliverer (vv. 16-19); one who deals justly (vv. 20-23). In verse 26b, where David states that to the crooked God is shrewd, he is saying that the ungodly will not escape God – even though they are clever! Note the comforting promise in verse 30.

Just as David affirmed his great God of strength and safety in verses 1-3, the psalm ends with an outpouring of praise to God for His mighty acts and deliverance (vv. 46-50).

JANUARY 19

LUKE 10:1-24   At this point in His ministry, Jesus sent out a larger group of disciples to present the message of the kingdom. This was partly to prepare them for the time when Jesus would no longer be with them – and ministry would be entrusted to them.

Jesus stressed the *need* for workers in the harvest (v. 2) – much to do and few to do the work! There is a real urgency to kingdom work. In addition, there is danger in the work. Note Jesus' comments in verse 3; He uses the illustration of lambs among wolves. *The danger lies in trying to use the world's methods to do kingdom work! The world will oppose the message of the gospel with slander, legal means (remember Acts and the early church), dishonest public relations techniques, and any other means that will slow the work of Christ.* The kingdom worker has no method but the power of prayer, the truth about Jesus and the cross, and love (2 Cor 10:3-5). If we leave the protection of continuing in God's will to use the world's methods, we stand in great danger!

Note also the rules of ministry that Jesus gave the workers as they went out (vv. 5-12). Jesus warned against attempting to improve their personal accommodation (vv. 5-7) and instructed them in a simple lifestyle, accepting what people offered them (v. 8). Their ministry would validate the fact that the kingdom – long awaited – had come to those who heard (v. 9). Further, He warned that although all would not accept the message, their responsibility was to present it faithfully (vv. 10-12).

⊃Think about Jesus' comments in verses 21-22, and rejoice that the Lord is still revealing Himself to humans in need.ᑕ Each of us who knows God through Christ has come through this grace. Note also the blessing of God's Word that helps us understand the gospel message (vv. 23-24). We have in hand what many in the past desired but did not understand.

GENESIS 37-38   God chose the progenitors of the Messiah from Adam, through Seth to Noah, through Noah's son Shem to Abraham, Isaac, and Jacob. Jacob's son Judah would carry the line to the Messiah, but Jacob's entire family would now become the nation (God's people) that God would love and through whom He would work.

→Joseph's dreams were from the Lord, but they made his brothers angry (Ch. 37). The dreams were prophetic concerning the place and position that Joseph would have in Egypt as they related to his family. Even Joseph's sale into slavery, however, was part of God's plan (37:28; cf. Gen 45:7-8; Ps 105:17-18). God would use Joseph in a unique way to bring the family to Egypt where they would become a strong nation, separate from other peoples. Recall that God told Abraham about this stay, which would extend for four hundred years, in Genesis 15:13-16. The time in Egypt, even the people's slavery, was part of God's plan to bring the Redeemer through His people.←

In Chapter 38, Tamar's sin is obvious. Judah, however, had sinned against Tamar by not allowing his youngest son to become her husband to give her children, as custom demanded (cf. Deut 25:5-10). Judah's two older sons had displeased God as Tamar's husbands, and God struck them dead. When Tamar disguised herself as a prostitute and became pregnant by Judah, he was ready to have her killed by burning – until she proved that he was the father of the child (children) she would have! Judah's double standard in this episode is amazing. The Bible is accurate in portraying men – even men whom God will use. No sugar coating. Nothing under the rug! It is interesting that one of the twins she bore became the one through whom Jesus would be born (cf. Matt 1:3).

PSALM 19   God has revealed Himself to mankind in two ways. The first is called "general revelation" and is what can be known about God by all who consider creation. Romans 1:19-20 speaks of this, specifically, God's eternal power and His divine nature. These, Paul states, are obvious and have been understood from what God has made. Isaiah 40:26 also affirms this truth. As we look around us, we are surrounded by the wonder of God's creation. And this is enough to convince us that there is a God. General revelation is portrayed in verses 1-6. Pick out the ways in which "God's silent proclamation" shows His greatness and speaks to the whole world in non-verbal language.

The second kind of revelation from God is specific, called "special revelation," and has come to us through the Scriptures and the person of Jesus. In this revelation, we learn things about God that can come only with His help. Verses 7-11 tell of the blessing God's child has through His word. Pick out the seven specific ways in which the special revelation of the Scriptures benefits us (vv. 7-11).

JANUARY 20

LUKE 10:25-42   As you read the Parable of the Good Samaritan, refer back to the notes on Luke 9:46-48 regarding the priorities of the kingdom. In Luke 9 the illustration was the child. Here it is an injured man. The point is that those in need are the Lord's priority. In this parable, those who should have helped the beaten man were unwilling to compromise their "purity." The Lord's message is that we need to open our eyes to needs around us – both physical and spiritual. Never mind what others think! Represent the kingdom with boldness!

Think about Jesus' message to Martha (vv. 38-42). It is tempting to be so occupied with "urgent" matters that the important things are squeezed out. If we allow this to happen, our priorities are out of "sync" with the kingdom.

GENESIS 39-40   As we read the account of Joseph after he was sold by his brothers, we see a man committed to righteous living. The text is clear that, after Potiphar had purchased Joseph from the Ishmaelites, he gave Joseph the position as chief steward in Potiphar's household because "his master saw that the Lord was with him" (39:2-6a). Joseph's character was apparent! The test he faced in Potiphar's home was an ongoing and difficult one. Yet God strengthened him to say "no" to temptation (vv. 6b-12).

Unjustly imprisoned, Joseph maintained his integrity and, in fact, was given a position of authority in prison under God's hand (vv. 20b-23). *Think about it:* How would you have responded to being sold into slavery and then being unjustly imprisoned? How would you have responded to the temptation that Joseph faced? His behavior demonstrates a deep faith in what God was doing – even though he didn't fully understand the import of what had happened to him (later, he did understand what God was doing; cf. 45:5-7). As He did with Daniel, the Lord gave Joseph the ability to interpret dreams (Ch. 40). →_All of these events were working out the Promise God gave to Abraham._←

PSALM 20   This Psalm encourages us to look for God's answer in distress. There seems to be nothing urgent at the time of writing. Rather, the psalm is an expression of faith and trust in the living God. The writer said God's people would publicly praise God for His victories (v. 5). God _is_ the hope of His people (v. 6).

Verse 7 is a lasting truth to remember personally, as a family, or a church. What is the bottom line of your "trust account"? Your bank account? Your portfolio of stocks, bonds, and real estate? Your plans for retirement fund at age sixty-five? Verse 7 is solid "reality orientation." There is nothing else worth trusting!

JANUARY 21

LUKE 11:1-36   A key section of the NT as it relates to prayer is found in this chapter. Compare this rendering of the Lord's prayer to that found in Matthew 6:9-13. When Jesus gave the model of what we know as the Lord's prayer, He taught us much about His priorities.

Consider the following. *(1)* We have the privilege of approaching God as our Father (cf. John 1:12, note the family relationship). This is the miracle of redemption! *(2)* God's name is holy. As Jesus included this truth in His model, He is praying (and we pray) that we will be careful always to treat God's name with reverence. In this regard, think about the media in your home. Is God pleased with the language you choose to listen to and, specifically, to the treatment of God's name? *(3)* We pray for God's authority on earth. ("May your kingdom come, and your will be done on earth.") How careful are we to live under God's authority (obedience!)? *(4)* We look to God for provision (our daily bread). *(5)* We look to God for forgiveness (God's work on our behalf at the cross). *(6)* We forgive others (God's work in us through the Holy Spirit), and please note that this is essential for God's continuing forgiveness to us (Matt 6:14-15). *(7)* We look to God for protection from the Evil One.

After considering these essential elements of prayer, follow Jesus' further teaching about prayer (vv. 5-13). Given these facts, our habits of prayer – both personally and corporately – may need to change.

Jesus' comments about the eye are also important (vv. 33-36). He is saying when we look at life and the world correctly (through the "eye" of the heart in faith), everything we see is different from how the world sees the same things. The Word of God and the illumination of the Holy Spirit are the keys to this perception. 1 John 1:5-7 treats the same thing when it speaks of "walking in the light." Read these verses in 1 John to see the specific blessings that come to the believer "in the light." Allow the perspective that comes with knowing Christ to shape your perception of events in your life.

GENESIS 41-42   Joseph's position took a decided turn when he interpreted Pharaoh's dreams. From prison to prime minister! Note carefully when Pharaoh called on Joseph to interpret the dream, Joseph first told the king that it would be impossible for him – but that God would give Pharaoh the meaning (41:16). →*This was God's hand on Joseph to prepare the way for Jacob and his family to come to Egypt – and to begin to fulfill the prophecy that the Lord had given Abraham in Genesis 15:13-16. As the account of God's people unfolds, it will become apparent that this move to Egypt was an integral part of the fulfillment of all of the promises given to Abraham in 12:1-3, 7.*← At about thirty years of age, Joseph had reached the pinnacle of power in one of the greatest nations on earth at the time. About one thousand years later, when Nebuchadnezzar needed someone to tell him the contents of his dream and interpret it, Daniel told the king that no man could do what he asked, but God would give him the answer he desired (Dan 2:27-28). Both young men of great character gave God the credit for the interpretation of dreams before the most powerful monarch of their respective times!

Jacob's family was in distress in Canaan because of the famine. As Joseph's brothers came to buy grain in Egypt, Joseph arranged the necessity for the brothers to bring Benjamin with them when they returned for more grain. Benjamin, you will recall, was Joseph's only true brother, the others being half-brothers. Although Jacob was loath to allow Benjamin to accompany his brothers to Egypt, necessity finally forced the issue, as we shall see in Chapter 43.

PSALM 21   ☑As David wrote this psalm, he looked far beyond his own reign to that of the Messiah. Verses 8-13 certainly speak of the second coming and the Day of the Lord – that day when God will bring judgment on the wicked nations of the world.⇔ Compare verses 9-10 with 2 Peter 3:9-10. Note the futility of attempting a stand against the Lord (v. 11), and compare this with Psalm 2:1-6. God *will* be exalted in His strength!

29

JANUARY 22

<u>LUKE 11:37-54</u>   Jesus spoke hard words to the religious elite about hypocrisy. Polishing the exterior while allowing filth on the inside is living a lie. The hard fact is that all lies are from Satan (John 8:44). The habit of "putting our best foot forward" (when it is done to obscure the real "me") is what Jesus was addressing here.

Jesus is particularly speaking of hypocrisy in religious leaders and teachers.   Those who purport to teach the truth are especially responsible to live the truth (James 3:1). Follow carefully how Jesus develops this theme. Look at the specific examples He gives. Note particularly verse 42. We also may tend to be careful about certain things (not necessarily those that are of paramount importance) but neglect even more important things because they are inconvenient. God will see through this duplicity every time! It is easy for us to see the Pharisees as "those religious leaders" and forget that we have the same heart problem!

Of all of the generations from the beginning of time, the generation that Jesus addressed had the unique privilege of listening to God's Son – which made them all the more responsible for the truth (vv. 50-51). *We share that advantage, for we have the complete record of God's word in hand!*

<u>GENESIS 43-44</u>   When the situation at home was urgent, Jacob sent Benjamin with his other sons back to Egypt (Ch. 43). The special treatment they received when they arrived (including Joseph's inquiry about their father) surprised and confused them. Why would an official of Joseph's rank be interested in their elderly father? Then there was the seating arrangement at dinner: They were seated in order of birth. How would this have been known?

It was an emotionally moving moment for Joseph when he saw Benjamin and heard about his father (43:29-30). When Joseph's silver cup was found in Benjamin's sack of grain (44:12), you can almost feel the emotion as Judah pleaded to be enslaved instead of Benjamin (vv. 18-34). Judah had guaranteed to bring Benjamin back to his father (43:8-9). Now he was ready to pay on his guarantee!

<u>PSALM 22</u>   If you have ever wondered if God knows and cares about your condition, David shared that feeling as he wrote this psalm. Even more significant, Jesus also shared this painful question. ☑Although written by David, the psalm is messianic. This remarkable psalm previews the suffering of Jesus a thousand years before the cross. The language, including specific words, so accurately mirrors the experience of Jesus as recorded in the gospels that it is amazing (Matt 27:27-50). Note the specific fulfillment of 22:18 (cf. John 19:23-24). In Hebrews

2:10-12 the author speaks of the many who have come and will yet come to the Lord through His death. In doing so, he quotes Psalm 22:22, making it clear that the redeemed are the very persons the psalmist was writing about. The psalm also looks forward to the final glory when Jesus will reign and all will acknowledge Him (v. 27; cf. Phil 2:9-11; Rev 15:3-4).⇦

We stand with a long line of men and women of faith who have been tested and have not been disappointed in God's faithfulness (vv. 4-5). We tend to think our problems are unique. God has been upholding the faithful since time's beginning. We also stand with a people who have a future (vv. 27-28). Because of redemption we look forward to worshipping God when all the families of the earth bow down before Him.

JANUARY 23

LUKE 12:1-34 This section speaks about priorities – and we all live by priorities. They set our direction in life. Even if we have never listed our priorities or even thought about them, *how we spend our time and money are determined by priorities.*

Jesus spoke about priorities in several ways. He told people to be on guard and to watch their lives. He warned about hypocrisy (v. 1, see also Ch. 11), and He gave cogent reasons to avoid it. Every single thing that we distort or conceal will be made public when Jesus comes (vv. 2-3). Make truth in speech and living a high priority! ⟳Consider carefully verses 8-9. Loyalty to Jesus must be our highest priority – because Jesus is the Son of God! This is not the time to be timid.⟲

Follow the Parable of the Rich Fool, noting the twisted priorities that caught him just when he thought his life was in order (vv. 13-21). That man is like many – perhaps most in our world: living for self, caught up in acquisitions, looking forward to leisure and plenty. The question we must face, however, is how the Lord would have us use our material goods. Verse 31 sums up how we should order our lives. If we are living for the kingdom, the rest will fall into place.

GENESIS 45-46 →In the poignant meeting with his brothers, note how Joseph gave glory to the Lord for bringing him to Egypt (45:4-8). Joseph told his brothers that the Lord had sent him to Egypt, and the reason was to preserve Jacob's family.← There was no hint of smallness in Joseph as he was united with his family. Even at that initial meeting, he was planning to bring his family to Egypt because of the famine (actually, their time in Egypt would extend for about four hundred years, cf. Gen 15:13).

→God graciously appeared once again to Jacob, assuring him that he should go to Egypt, and again affirming that God would make a great nation of his descendants *while in Egypt* (46:3; cf. 27:28-29; 35:9-13). Read again the Lord's prophecy given to Abraham concerning Egypt (Gen 15:12-16).← In all, sixty-six persons made the trip as the family moved to Egypt.

PSALM 23   This best-known and loved of all psalms should be committed to memory by all who love God. It is an expression of deep trust in God for everything in this life and for life after death.

God guides us in paths of righteousness *for His name's sake* (v. 3b). This is something to ponder, for when we take the name of God and declare that we are His, the Lord's name is at stake as we display our attitudes and behavior before the world. Note the truth: God being the shepherd, nothing that I need will be lacking (v. 1). This will include the provision for physical needs as well as quietness and restoration for our inner person (vv. 1-4). God's word provides our guidance (vv. 3-4).

The writer recognized that there are hard times in life – even times when we are close to death. The knowledge of God's presence sustains and comforts us in those times (v. 4b). Through good times and difficult, God's goodness, love, and mercy give peace. And when human life is done, we have life with the Lord (v. 6).

Think for a moment of David writing this psalm. Consider the depth of his faith. This quality of faith comes by repeatedly trusting God. *Are you building this quality of faith by repeatedly and consciously trusting God in your life?*

JANUARY 24

LUKE 12:35-59   Jesus is coming soon! (cf. Rev 22:7, 12, 20) Think of this as you read verses 35-48. Note the encouragement to watchfulness in verses 35, 37, 38, 40 and 43. Jesus repeats the admonition five times and strengthens the warnings with illustrations! That kind of emphasis should rivet our attention.

Consider the message of verse 48b. *This* is the generation to which much has been given! We have the Bible in hand and enough resources to live on. We even have leisure time. In contrast, think of the generations that didn't have these blessings. Take to heart these words of Jesus. Making it our priority to fulfill Jesus' commands for our lives will keep us prepared for His coming!

Isn't Jesus the Prince of Peace? ↄHere Jesus speaks of being one who brings division – because as God's Son He represents the kingdom (vv. 49-53). In fact, the very message of grace and forgiveness that establishes peace with God also divides us from the system of the world and its people! Jesus stated this clearly in John 17:14-19. This antagonism was implicit in Jesus' words as He sent the seventy-two on their preaching mission (10:3). If we are living for Christ, hostility will be a fact of life (John 15:20).☮

GENESIS 47-48   When the family arrived in Egypt, they followed Joseph's advice as they were received by Pharaoh. They received a place to live where they could tend cattle; since shepherds were "an abomination" to the Egyptians, they lived apart from the Egyptians (Gen 46:31-34). →This arrangement was extremely important to the family and, ultimately, part of the plan of salvation. They continued to tend cattle, prospered, grew numerous and strong, *and were never assimilated into the Egyptian culture.* When they came out of Egypt some four hundred years later, they were probably two million in number (six hundred thousand men, Exod 12:37). They went into Egypt a family; they came out a nation! God was at work, and the Promise given to Abraham was in process (Gen 12:2; 15:4-5)!←

Before he died, Jacob, now an elderly grandfather, blessed Joseph's two sons, Manasseh and Ephraim, born to Joseph before his extended family joined him in Egypt. The descendants of these two were identified as tribes known by their names, just as the descendants of their uncles (the brothers of Joseph) were known by their names. Levi was not counted as a tribe because the tribe was set apart for the Lord. Manasseh and Ephraim took the place of Joseph and Levi, making twelve tribes in all.

PSALM 24   Although all creation is the Lord's and all people are ultimately the Lord's, for He is the Lord of the universe (v. 1), not all people can claim that they know the Lord! Not everyone is welcome into God's presence. The question about who *can* come into God's presence is asked in verse 3 and answered in verse 4. But how can we have clean hands and a pure heart? Only as we receive forgiveness from the Lord Himself. Only by faith and the gift of new life! The Lord sets the standard, but the Lord makes the way for us to come to Him (through Jesus)!

JANUARY 25

LUKE 13:1-21   While reading verses 1-9, think about repentance in relation to a changed life. This parable emphasizes the need for genuine change. If there is life in the tree, fruit will come. Compare this with Matthew 3:7-10 and 7:15-20. Think about 13:8-9. Grace extends the time for fruit to appear, but there are limits.

Consider fruit in a broader sense than those you may have led to Christ. Read again Luke 3:7-14. Honesty, compassion, concern and caring for others that occur in our lives as a result of the work of the Holy Spirit are fruit! In this regard, read Galatians 5:22-26.

Note that an evil spirit caused the woman's crippled spine in verses 10-13. The destructive work of Satan comes under many guises. This pernicious influence of Satan, which we have seen several times in Luke, is truly destructive. *Eighteen years!* Satan's method is to lie and deceive (John 8:44). His object is to steal, kill, and destroy (John 10:10). Our problem often is that we don't recognize either the method or objective of Satan because we don't apply God's word (or don't know it). God's protection is ours as we walk closely with Him.

GENESIS 49-50 The blessing was important. Remember the blessing that Jacob took from Esau (Gen 27). Jacob has already given the blessing to Ephraim and Manasseh and now does so for his sons.

Reuben was the firstborn but lost dignity and full blessing because he disgraced himself and his father (vv. 3-4; cf. Gen 35:22). Simeon and Levi lost their father's wholehearted blessing because they slaughtered the men of Shechem (vv. 5-7; cf. Gen 34:25-31). ☑The blessing to Judah refers to the Promise that will come through Jesus the Messiah (49:10-12; cf. Gen 12:3). Thus, at this point in the biblical record, the Promise of the coming Messiah is identified as coming through Judah. The reference to the scepter and the ruler's staff relate to Jesus' reign as the King of all of the earth and to the fulfillment of the kingdom at the Second Coming of Christ. Compare verse 10 with Psalm 2:6-9, Psalm 110:1-3 and Revelation 19:11ff.⇦ In the blessing to Joseph, note how Jacob acknowledges the hand of God on this son (vv. 22-26).

After Jacob died and was buried at Mamre (Hebron, 50:12-14), Joseph again assured his brothers that the hand of God brought him to Egypt, and they did not need to fear him (vv. 15-21). He held no grudges.

PSALM 25 Here we see David's inner heart. There is no question that David understood integration of personality. Read through the psalm looking for David's inner motivation. Then note verses 4 and 5. His heart is open to God's leading and teaching.

Verses 14-15 contain two "pearls." In verse 14, note that God gives insight to those who fear him. (The NT parallel to this is found in John 14:21. Jesus reveals himself to those who love and obey Him.) In verse 15, obeying God is the only way to safety in this world and the only way to freedom. Compare this to John 8:31-32, 34-36.

JANUARY 26

<u>LUKE 13:22-35</u> In what sense is the door to salvation narrow (v. 24)? Jesus advises His listeners to "make every effort" to enter through the narrow door. In truth, the door of salvation is wide enough to admit people from every tribe, nation and language (Rev 5:9; 7:9), but one cannot, by effort, work one's way into the kingdom (Eph 2:8-9). Perhaps a clearer understanding of the meaning would be, "Be very careful that you enter through the right door – the door that leads to salvation."

The way is "narrow," however, in that salvation is *only* through the Lord Jesus and *only* by faith. Most people would like to use their own merit to obtain salvation. It will never be so! In addition, we must be sure ("make every effort," "be very careful") that we have the new life that comes with salvation. Jesus said it (See also Matt 7:14.). John the Baptist said it (Matt 3:8). The Apostle John said it (1 John 2:3-6). The writer to the Hebrews said it (Heb 4:11). Paul said it (Phil 2:12-13). Finally, when Jesus comes again, many tragically disappointed people will realize that they do not have what they assumed was theirs (vv. 25-30).

<u>EXODUS 1-2</u> About four hundred years have gone by. The great days of Joseph in the court have faded from memory. Kings have come and gone in Egypt, and the Pharaoh now ruling sees the Hebrew people as a threat to the country.

No wonder! Under the blessing of God, His people had become numerous, but were separate from the Egyptians while living in the Egyptians' country. They became physically strong as slaves. →The Lord, however, was preserving them and increasing their numbers for the time when they would return to Canaan (Gen 15:13-16).← That time was now approaching.

Moses' father and mother were both from the tribe of Levi (2:1). →The Lord protected Moses' life when the governmental policy was that all newborn Hebrew males were to be killed (2:1-10; cf. 1:22). He grew up privileged in Pharaoh's court but had to flee when he took the side of a Hebrew being mistreated by an Egyptian. God continued to protect Moses, and He also heard the cries of the Israelites in their oppression (2:23-25). Remember God's Promise to Abraham and the covenant with Abraham, Isaac, and Jacob (cf. Gen 12:1-3; 15:13-16).←

<u>PSALM 26</u> How open are you to the truth about your inner life? The answer to that question gives insight into character. We all tend to be defensive, but look at David's attitude and heart in verse 2. His desire was that the searchlight of God's perfect knowledge be directed to his own heart and mind (both emotion and intellect). In another psalm, he makes it clear that this examination is more than a psychological trip

(Ps 139:23-24). It is meant to change life. This is not only knowing the truth but applying it!

JANUARY 27

LUKE 14:1-24   One of the key disagreements that the religious leaders had with Jesus was with regard to His conduct on the Sabbath (vv. 1-6). Jesus affirmed the Mosaic Law (Matt 5:17-20) but did not hesitate to do the work of the kingdom on the Sabbath.

During the dinner that Jesus attended (v. 1), He used the occasion to teach about heart attitude. When He healed the man with a chronic disease, His action raised the eyebrows of the religious leaders in silent criticism.   Jesus challenged the Pharisees by pointing out that they would certainly attend to one of their children or to one of their animals in trouble on the Sabbath (vv. 5-6)! The point was that the man who was ill should have greater priority than their animals.

Jesus also called for genuine humbleness (vv. 7-11). If our priorities are correct, we will not maneuver for position. Note the principle in verse 11: Rather than seek honor for yourself, allow God to give honor as appropriate. Our concern should rather be for the disadvantaged (vv. 12-13).

As you read verses 15-24, ask yourself if there are excuses that keep you from acting upon Jesus' invitation to life. Given the real issue, is anything that important?

EXODUS 3-4   In Chapter 3, underline the words "I am" and "I have" each time the Lord says them. As the Lord stated His intentions, Moses struggled with what he saw as the reality of returning to Egypt. The Lord identified Himself as *The God Who Is* (v. 14). **HE IS THE GOD WHO IS ALIVE!** →The Lord was initiating the plan to bring His people out of Egypt to Canaan as He had promised Abraham (3:16-17; cf. Gen 15:16).← In the process, both the Israelites and the Egyptians would learn about the great power of the God of Israel (vv. 19-22).

Moses' reluctance to be the Lord's spokesman was persistent (4:1-17). The Lord answered each objection, finally becoming exasperated with Moses (vv. 11-16). God sent Aaron to meet Moses (vv. 14, 27), and the two brothers went to the elders of Israel (vv. 29-31).

PSALM 27   As you read this chapter, look at all of the ways David resolved to love and serve God. Think of his mind-set. Read verse 4 as preparation for verse 5. Days of trouble will come! If we have loved and followed God, we can then be confident of God's presence when trouble comes.

In verse 8, note that David speaks from the heart in 8a and with intellectual resolve in 8b. This accurately portrays our human makeup of emotion and intellect. We need both as we love and serve God.

Finally, take verse 14 for your life. Wait for God to act. Be strong because you trust God (intellect). Take heart (claim emotional stability) because you trust God! Do so even when the days seem dark! Wait for God to bring order into life in the face of seeming confusion.

JANUARY 28

LUKE 14:25-35   What is the cost of discipleship – the cost of deciding for Jesus? Popular appeals to decide for Christ put little emphasis on how faith affects one's "real" life. It was to that very point that Jesus made the remarks recorded here. In effect, He said we should not decide to follow Him unless we are willing to make radical changes: a shift in priorities from what "I" want to what Jesus desires (v. 33). Read Jesus' remarks in verses 25-35 carefully. If we are not willing to pay the price of loyalty to the Lord Jesus, it is not a real commitment of faith! Jesus' statements do not support a casual approach to faith. What changes in your life is faith in Christ making?

EXODUS 5-6   Sometimes God's method creates initial difficulty in order to demonstrate His greatness. Certainly this was the case when Moses and Aaron first went to Pharaoh (Ch. 5). Not only were they rebuffed, but the Israelites' oppression increased (5:2, 6-9). Their initial trust of Moses and Aaron turned to rejection and worry (vv. 20-21; 6:9).

As in Chapter 3, underline the times when the Lord uses the personal pronoun "I" followed by a verb. Did the Lord have plans for the people? Would the Lord deliver them from bondage and bring them to Canaan as He had promised long before? As you look for and recognize the ways the Lord identified Himself and announced His intentions, you will see there is no question about what God would do! →Note how the Lord relates the Israelites' deliverance from Egypt to His promises to Abraham, Isaac, and Jacob (6:8; cf. Gen 12:3, 7; 15:13-14; 22:17-18; 26:3-4; 28:13-14). Understand also that this deliverance from Egypt and the entry into the promised land was a vital link in God's plan to use His people as the channel for salvation (cf. Rom 9:4-5).←

PSALM 28   In the midst of trouble, the writer sees the Lord as his rock. As you read, look at his prayer (vv. 1-4). Note the trust in verses 6-7. God is strength for facing difficulty and is protection as the believer's shield. Rejoice in verses 8-9. God cares for His people. God really is our strength. God is our shepherd and will save His people!

JANUARY 29

LUKE 15   In the three parables in this chapter, Jesus gives insight into God's heart for the lost. We should understand how the Lord loves the lost by how far He has gone to provide salvation for them! In these parables, Jesus used illustrations that imperfectly convey the depth of His love but to which we can relate. We are concerned with lost property (vv. 3-10)! The loss of a son would be more deeply emotional (vv. 11-32). Our lesson here is that God cares for the lost. His priorities must be ours!

Look at the Parable of the Lost Son from a different perspective. Think about how the son treated his father's gifts, and compare this with the way we have treated the gifts and opportunities God has given us. There are few of us who will not be shamed! Thank God for the picture of grace and love in this parable.

EXODUS 7-8   God now sent Moses and Aaron into the presence of Pharaoh with His message. God's intention is clear in 7:1-5. →The Lord would deliver His people and would bring great glory to His name in the process. In addition, He would bring the Israelites back to the land promised to Abraham for His specific purposes of redemption. This would be a lesson to the world, and especially to the Israelites, of God's sovereign power.←

As you read the accounts of the plagues, notice that the court magicians were able to match Moses' miracles at first (7:11, 22; 8:7). But after the plagues of blood and frogs, the magicians were no longer able to duplicate the miracles and admitted to Pharaoh that it was the hand of God (8:19). This was a real "power encounter." The magicians were working with the power of Satan, which was no match for God's power. There is a humorous side to the magicians' ability to duplicate what Moses did. Although they were able to turn their staffs into snakes, they lost their staffs when Moses' snake ate them. Although they could turn water into blood and produce frogs, they only added to the calamity of the Egyptians. They couldn't make the blood or the frogs disappear!

PSALM 29   God's great power and glory is conveyed in this psalm. The writer calls his readers to acknowledge God's glory, strength, and holiness (vv. 1-2), and to worship the Lord with that in mind (v. 2b).

Verses 3-9 speak about the awesome power and majesty of the voice of God. As you read about the lightning (v. 7; cf. Exod 9:23-24) and the desert shaking (v. 8; cf. Exod 19:16-19), *understand that these verses came out of the daily lives of the Israelites!* And this remembrance moves His people to cry, "Glory!" (v. 9b).

Note the two wonderful truths in verses 10-11. The Lord is our eternal King, and He rules with majesty (v. 10). Further, this awesome God cares for His people, giving them strength and peace. What a privilege to belong to the family of God!

JANUARY 30

LUKE 16:1-18   The Parable of the Shrewd Manager is difficult to understand. The following suggestions from *The Expositor's Bible Commentary** may be of help. This draws from the culture of Jesus' time and the Jewish society:

'The master refers to the owner of the business that was selling the commodities mentioned. The manager is the person handling the accounts. The dishonesty probably is represented by an inappropriate addition to the bill by the manager for his personal gain. Thus, when he was terminated, he went back and made the accounts honest – that gained him friends among the creditors and the commendation of the master."

With this background, verses 10-15 are a call to integrity and a warning not to let money drive our decisions. God owns our possessions, and we need to serve God and not our bank account. The real question is, "Who has control of what is rightfully God's anyway? Me – you – or the Lord?"

Verses 16-17 speak of the law, which was very specific about fairness and honesty. Jesus is saying that it hasn't changed. And further, another area of the law that had not changed, but which was being carelessly observed, was that of marital fidelity (v. 18).

EXODUS 9-10   →As Egypt continued to suffer God's judgment through the plagues, the land was progressively devastated. God was using Pharaoh's refusal to let the Israelites leave to demonstrate His power to the world and especially to the Israelites. God's people needed to see firsthand what their God could, and would, do on their behalf (10:2). Remember that they had no Scripture to open and learn of Him.

As their anguish increased, Pharaoh's advisors became convinced that it was best to submit to the God of the Israelites (10:7). The economic base of the country was being ruined. The hail and the locusts destroyed an entire year's crop. More important, Pharaoh's advisors were seeing that this God was not to be tampered with. He was a God of great power. That is precisely the lesson God wanted the world to learn. God was preparing the way for the Israelites to enter Canaan,

---

*THE EXPOSITOR'S BIBLE COMMENTARY, VOL. 8, edited by Frank E. Gabelein, Copyright 1984 by the Zondervan Corporation. Used by permission of Zondervan Publishing House.

fulfilling the promise to Abraham (Gen 15:16), and making the entire region fear His power (Josh 2:9-11).←

PSALM 30   Sometimes God seems far away. The psalmist speaks of such times here (v. 7b). Catch his feeling in verses 8-10. He feels he is looking disaster directly in the face. Then observe his praise for God's delivering hand (vv. 1-3, 11-12). With this in mind, read Colossians 1:13.

The world talks about the hoped-for (but often mythical) "silver lining" or "sunshine above the clouds." God's child looks rather to the reality of the person of God and His caring. Can you join the writer in his praise for God's deliverance in verses 1-3 and 11-12?

JANUARY 31

LUKE 16:19-31   The Parable of the Rich Man and Lazarus should give us pause. Does this parable say that if the rich man had done good deeds he would have earned salvation? This would not fit with the rest of Jesus' teaching or the rest of the Bible regarding entrance into the kingdom.

Jesus and the other Scriptures do speak specifically, however, to changes in life that accompany salvation. (The good deeds are the cart, not the horse.) Giving to the needy was assumed (Matt 6:2-4). Jesus condemned an uncaring attitude about others' need (Matt 25:41-46). The whole point of loving our neighbor is to be as concerned about their needs as our own (James 2:12-17). That the rich man had not been merciful to an obviously needy person on his own step was evidence enough that he had no real relationship with the Lord. As God's children, it is essential for us to measure our lives against the Scripture regularly to be sure we are all that the Lord desires.

EXODUS 11-12   Now God prepared His people for the last of the plagues – the one that would set them free. ☑In doing so, the Lord God instituted the Passover, which previsioned how the Lamb of God (Jesus, John 1:29) would give His life to bring forgiveness and life to all who believe. On the night the lamb for the Passover was slaughtered, the Israelites smeared its blood on the doorframes of their homes. If blood was present, the angel who would bring death to the firstborn in all of the homes of Egypt would pass over that home – thus the name "Passover." In a similar way, those who have trusted Jesus for forgiveness receive that forgiveness because Jesus died for our sin (1 Peter 3:18). Jesus bought our salvation with His blood (1 Peter 1:18-19). Jesus referred to this when He spoke to the disciples during the last supper (Matt 26:27-28). Finally, remember that Jesus was crucified on the Passover.⇦

When the Israelites left on that very night, the Egyptians gave them valuable gifts – because the Lord prompted them to do so (12:36). This was God's plan for His people (3:21; cf. Gen 15:14). As the people obeyed God, asking the Egyptians for the gifts, they responded.

PSALM 31   Read through this psalm to understand David's circumstances and how he felt. Then read it again, noting the intrigue and deviousness of society (vv. 4, 13, 20).

Now notice how real God is in the life of the believer (vv. 1-3). Note the character of God and His intent for those He loves (vv. 5, 19-20, 23a). Finally, see what this does for the child of God (vv. 7-8, 15-17a, 19-20, 23). But note carefully that the assurance and safety of the believer is rooted only in the person of God (vv. 14-17). It is *because* of God! Consider the attitude and faith of the writer in verses 5, 14-15a, and 23-24. Rejoice in verse 19.

February

Bible Reading Schedule
And Notes

☙

*. . . our gospel came to you not simply
with words, but also with power, with the Holy Spirit and
with deep conviction. 1 Thessalonians 1:5*

DISCOVERING THE BIBLE
READING SCHEDULE
FEBRUARY

1	Luke 17:1-19	Exodus 13-14	Psalm 32
2	Luke 17:20-37	Exodus 15-16	Psalm 33
3	Luke 18:1-17	Exodus 17-18	Psalm 34
4	Luke 18:18-43	Exodus 19-20	Psalm 35
5	Luke 19:1-27	Exodus 21-22	Psalm 36
6	Luke 19:28-48	Exodus 23-24	Psalm 37
7	Luke 20:1-26	Exodus 25-26	Psalm 38
8	Luke 20:27-47	Exodus 27-28	Psalm 39
9	Luke 21:1-19	Exodus 29-30	Psalm 40
10	Luke 21:20-38	Exodus 31-32	Psalm 41
11	Luke 22:1-46	Exodus 33-34	Job 1
12	Luke 22:47-71	Exodus 35-36	Job 2
13	Luke 23:1-25	Exodus 37-38	Job 3
14	Luke 23:26-56	Exodus 39-40	Job 4
15	Luke 24:1-12	Leviticus 1-2	Job 5
16	Luke 24:13-53	Leviticus 3-5	Job 6
17	Acts 1	Leviticus 6-7	Job 7
18	Acts 2	Leviticus 8-9	Job 8
19	Acts 3	Leviticus 10-11	Job 9
20	Acts 4	Leviticus 12-13	Job 10
21	Acts 5	Leviticus 14-15	Job 11
22	Acts 6	Leviticus 16-17	Job 12
23	Acts 7	Leviticus 18-19	Job 13
24	Acts 8	Leviticus 20-21	Job 14
25	Acts 9	Leviticus 22-23	Job 15
26	Acts 10	Leviticus 24-25	Job 16
27	Acts 11	Leviticus 26-27	Job 17
28	Acts 12	Numbers 1-2	Job 18

FEBRUARY 1

LUKE 17:1-19   It is sobering to think of the implications of verse 1 in today's world. Many seductive messages come to almost every one of us just in the course of one day. Jesus clearly states that when these messages are successful – when they entice us to wrong behavior – the people who are responsible for those messages store up judgment from God!

Think of the billboards on our roads, the advertising in magazines on our newsstands. Think of the messages that come to the public in the media. Much of it presents wrong behavior as the normal way to live. Jesus warns that we, as His people, must have no part in what these advertisements encourage ("So watch yourselves," v. 3). Further, we must protect those for whom we are responsible, as it is possible.

Listen to Jesus when He speaks about mutual responsibility for one another as believers (vv. 3b-4; cf. Matt 18:15ff.; Gal 6:1-2). Note how this responsibility to guard one another is related to the enticements to sin mentioned above. Each of us is vulnerable in some area. We need each other!

Jesus' comments about servanthood in verses 7-10 leave little room for personal pride in our achievement as kingdom workers. In fact, it is the Lord Himself who gives the motivation and ability to do His will (Phil 2:13). The rewards will come later when the returning Master acknowledges those who have been faithful (Luke 12:35-38).

EXODUS 13-14   The Passover was established as a day to be observed in the life of the Israelite community. In addition, in remembrance of the Passover, God instructed that every firstborn male, animal or person, would be dedicated to the Lord (13:1-16).

Verses 17-18 provide a telling example of how God dealt with His people. *God led the people into experiences they could handle and through which they would learn.* He also provided the visible evidence of His presence through the pillar of cloud and the pillar of fire (vv. 21-22).

→For example, God led the people into an impossible situation with the army of Egypt at their back and the sea in front of them (14:9). Note Moses' statement to the people in verse 13. Read God's statement of intention (vv. 15-18). Visualize God's protection for His people (vv. 19-20). Then stand in awe of God's deliverance of His people (vv. 21-31).← This is one of the greatest chapters in the Bible.

PSALM 32   Most have struggled with unconfessed sin. This psalm is David's encounter with that problem. This intensely personal psalm is full of spiritual truth.

☑Verses 1-2 bring us an important principle. Blessing comes through forgiveness! The way of forgiveness is the path to peace with God! Blessing comes to those who have chosen to open themselves to God (confession) and to others (lack of deceit). Romans 4:7-8 quotes verses 1-2 and shows us that the blessing of forgiveness comes through faith in Christ. Even before Christ, forgiveness (i.e., a withholding of punishment for sin) came by faith in God (cf. Gen 15:6). The point of Romans is that Jesus has paid the price for sin, and that payment is retroactive to people of faith who lived even before the death of Christ (cf. Rom 3:21-26; Heb 9:15).⇦

In contrast, read about the burden of sin in verses 3-4. Emotional pain affects our physical well-being. *God designed us to be in fellowship with Him.* When this fellowship is broken, we pay a price. This is especially true of those who know the truth and know they are doing wrong. The answer is to get right with God! David's testimony is in verse 5, and his advice is in verse 6. Confess now while there is time (v. 6a)! Confess now before big trouble comes into your life (v. 6b)!

Follow the blessings of fellowship with God as David enumerates them: protection (v. 7); instruction and counsel from God (vv. 8-9); the promise of God's good hand and His presence (v. 10).

Take this message seriously. Go for the blessing – do it God's way by confessing known sin. Obey what you know to be God's will. Learn in this way to enjoy God's presence and blessing! Join with the psalmist in the joy of verse 11.

FEBRUARY 2

LUKE 17:20-37   The Pharisees who asked about the coming of the kingdom were looking for the visible, political kingdom they expected (v. 20). Jesus pointed to the kingdom we enter by faith; Jesus said that the kingdom was within them (v. 21). Those who gave allegiance to Jesus and lived under His authority were part of the spiritual kingdom.

➲In speaking about this to His disciples, however, Jesus makes it clear that there would indeed be a visible kingdom (v. 24). Jesus' coming in glory as the promised Messiah would be sudden and visible, but it would not happen until sometime after Jesus had been rejected by the generation then living (v. 25). When He does come, however, it will be with the promised judgment predicted in the Old Testament Scriptures (vv. 26-35).☾

Jesus warned His followers to live with care: The key is to be ready for the coming of the Master. To illustrate His point, Jesus talked about the unbelievers who scoffed at Noah and those who lived in Sodom. In both instances, life went on "as usual" with people oblivious to the danger that hung over them like a black cloud. When time was out, there was no longer opportunity to repent! In the normal course of daily living, with two people working side by side, one will be ready to go with Jesus at His return, and the other not ready (vv. 34-35). *So be ready*, anticipating the coming of the Master!

EXODUS 15-16 Time out! After the great deliverance from Egypt and the Egyptian army, the people stopped to praise the Lord under Moses' direction. From this moment on, confidence in God could be based upon His character (15:13a), His power (v. 13b), and His deliverance (v. 17).

Yet the people quickly grumbled (vv. 22-24). Note the Lord's provision (v. 25) and His instruction to the people (v. 26). *Principle: When we grumble, we really grumble about what God is doing with us (16:8b).*

As you read about God providing manna, note the Lord's instructions. This would be the Israelites' food for the next forty years until they crossed the Jordan into their promised land (16:35; cf. Josh 5:12).

PSALM 33 This remarkable psalm describes many of God's characteristics. We note God's faithfulness, truth, righteousness, justice and love (vv. 4-5). We see God's omnipotence (unlimited power) in creation (vv. 6-9). His sovereignty is revealed in His rule over men and nations (vv. 10-11, 16-17). God's omniscience (complete knowledge about everything at all times) explains His knowledge of (and interest in) the behavior and heart condition of all men (vv. 13-15, 18-19). Through all of this, God watches over those who trust in Him (vv. 18-19). This last truth should stir our hearts to cry out to God in worship! God looks for those who will trust Him (2 Chron 16:9).

The truth of this psalm also leaves us no room for complacency. God sees when we turn from Him to choose to do wrong. Knowing that God sees our hearts and what we do (even if no one else does) will help us repent of sin and choose to do right. *REMEMBER: GOD SEES! GOD CARES!*

FEBRUARY 3

LUKE 18:1-17 We must listen to Jesus' remarks about prayer in verses 1-8 and take seriously His comments that if a corrupt earthly judge will listen to a petitioner, the loving God of heaven will hear His children when they pray! Compare this with Matthew 7:7-12. Think about Jesus' question in verse 8b. We must learn and practice faith in the Lord Jesus in our prayer life (the context of this question). Remember: We learn to exercise faith in prayer by actually praying!

It is easy to criticize the Pharisee when reading verses 9-14. The Pharisee knew the scriptures and went to great lengths to "apply" them (or so he thought) to his life. He was proud that he was following God so closely. He saw himself as more righteous (confident of "personal righteousness," v. 9) and better than someone who came to God in great need. In so doing, he utterly missed repentance for his sin and failed to receive forgiveness. Consider carefully the heart and attitude of the tax collector and what Jesus added regarding humility (vv. 13-14).

It is frighteningly easy to fall into the trap of the Pharisee! We very much need to see ourselves realistically as people who continue to need God's grace while maturing spiritually, and to see those without Christ as persons whom God loves and desires to bring into the kingdom.

EXODUS 17-18 Write a small "g" in the margin of your Bible each time the Israelites grumble (17:2-3). It is impressive how slowly we learn to trust God!

The Lord gave the Israelites their first victory in battle against the Amalekites (vv. 8-15). With each new experience, the Lord taught His people that they could trust Him.

When Moses met his father-in-law and recounted their journey (18:8), he also voiced an important principle: *Hardships were the pathway to learn God's power and goodness (vv. 8b, 11).* Then his father-in-law helped Moses understand another principle: Delegation of responsibility to persons with the right qualifications is necessary (vv. 17-23).

PSALM 34 In this psalm, observe the intensely personal testimony of David. He had learned, through experience, to trust God – and on this basis, called on others to join him in praise (v. 3).

Look for the specific ways God blesses those who fear and serve Him. Verses 4-5 speak of the healing God brings to those who trust Him. Note the deliverance from fear. This is nothing less than emotional stability, and it shows (v. 5).

We must not think about this lightly. The writer provides definite steps to receive God's blessing. Verse 8 invites us to taste and see: Try trusting God! Verse 9 implores us to fear God. This means to hold God in awe and not to treat Him carelessly. Verse 13 tells us to speak truth. Verse 14 advises us to repent from wrong and choose to do right. Verse 16 is frightening! It is the flip side of verse 15.

☑When Jesus' legs were not broken at the time of the crucifixion, the gospel writer understood this as a fulfillment of the Scriptures (v. 20; cf. John 19:31-37). Recall that Jesus was the fulfillment of the Passover lamb, and the lamb's bones were not to be broken (Exod 12:46).⇦

FEBRUARY 4

LUKE 18:18-43   When the wealthy ruler came to ask Jesus about entering the kingdom, Jesus went to the heart of the matter quickly (vv. 18-22).   Adultery, murder, stealing, lying, and honoring father and mother were important (and still are).   These areas were not, however, what kept the ruler from entering the kingdom: His heart was occupied with his wealth, as is clear from his subsequent response to Jesus (v. 23; cf. Matt 6:19-24).   The "things" in the young man's life stood in the way of salvation.   Read again Jesus' comments on the cost of discipleship (14:25-35).   We must not ignore the meaning of Jesus' words or the examples that we have from His interaction with people.

We must also understand that the sins that keep us from the Lord have a tenacious hold upon us, and we need the Lord's help even to come to Him (vv. 24-27; John 6:44).   If there is anything standing in the way of your relationship with the Lord, confess the sin and look to the Lord for the ability to follow Him completely.

⊃In verses 31-33 Jesus declared that He would proceed to Jerusalem, where He would suffer and be killed, and would rise from the dead on the third day.   It is important that Jesus tied these events to the message of the prophets in the Scriptures.   This was the promise of redemption about to be fulfilled.   It was a clear statement that He was indeed the Redeemer, the Son of God.⊂

EXODUS 19-20   What happened at Sinai was awesome!   Notice the condition of God's blessing in 19:3-6 and the people's response in verse 8.   Note that the people prepared and dressed themselves properly for the Lord's presence (19:10-11).   Note also the limits that God set (19:12-13), and visualize God's meeting with the people.   Thunder, lightning, trumpet blasts, smoke billowing from the mountain, and an earthquake (vv. 16-19) all preceded the giving of the law (the Ten Commandments).   God was helping the people understand His awesome presence and the importance of the Ten Commandments.

Read the Ten Commandments.   →This is a crucially significant event in the progressive revelation of God to the Israelites and to the world.   God here declared what is of prime importance to Him.   It is a window to understand the moral character of God.   It is the standard of God's righteousness.   Jesus affirmed the law (Matt 5:17-19) as did Paul (Rom 3:31).   It is the instrument in God's hand to help us know that we are sinners and to bring us to God through Christ (Gal 3:24).   The giving of the law is a vital part of bringing redemption to the world.   It established the reality of our sin and our need of the coming Savior.←

PSALM 35   Have you ever been disappointed and hurt by the duplicity of friends, fellow workers, or employers?   This psalm brings perspective, for it speaks about the reality of hope in God (vv. 9-10, 17-18, 27-28) in the face of the deceit (vv. 15, 19-21). Here is God in the real world of our lives: at home, in school, in the marketplace, and at the shop. With the right perspective, see how the writer is able to praise God in the midst of difficulty (vv. 9-10, 28).

FEBRUARY 5

LUKE 19:1-27 Zacchaeus is a favorite subject of stories for children. If we can get beyond the little man in the big tree illustrated in children's books, however, we find a man who, as a tax collector, got little respect from the religious Jews. But Zacchaeus wanted to see and hear Jesus. We should note that Jesus ignored accepted conventions to spend time with this tax collector, and there were results. Here is a man whom we will see in the kingdom! Once again, we must learn from Jesus to see men and women in our daily experience who need God – and be ready to take advantage even of curiosity (if that is what Zacchaeus had) to introduce them to Christ.

The Parable of the Ten Minas (vv. 11-27) is a lesson about stewardship. It is reasonable for the Lord to expect us to bring a return to the kingdom by exercising the gifts He has given us. Not to do so is irresponsible. In the similar parable in Matthew 25:14-30, the servant who buried the talent is considered unfaithful and cast into outer darkness! The parable calls us to be about the Master's business. To ignore the responsibility calls into question the servant's place in the kingdom.

EXODUS 21-22 The next several chapters in Exodus are set at Mount Sinai. After the awesome manifestations of God's presence that terrified the people (Exod 19:16-19; 20:18-19), God gave Moses the Ten Commandments and the other regulations we will read. Chapters 21-23 give social laws that have a moral basis. There is a deep sense of justice and fairness in the laws, which are based on God's righteousness.

As you read, note the offenses that require the death penalty (21:12-17, 29; 22:18-20). All of these are moral crimes, deeply offensive to God. Although today's society would feel very differently about some of these crimes, we must remember God's standard.

Note how God required the individual to take responsibility for his crime. Watch for the principle of restitution (22:1, 5). Note the safeguards for the alien, widow and orphan (vv. 21-22), and for the poor (vv. 25-27). Think about how these regulations are founded in the character of God.

PSALM 36 As you read this psalm, contrast the heart of the wicked with the character and goodness of God. What distinguishes the godless is their lack of fear of God (v. 1). They do not respect God, don't understand Him, and don't care about God's truth. In addition, pride deceives them, hiding even the realization of their own sin (v. 2; cf. Eccl 5:1).

In verses 5-6, follow God's love, faithfulness, righteousness, justice, and caring. Note the "real gold" described in verse 7a and how we have life and light in verse 9.

FEBRUARY 6

LUKE 19:28-48   ☑When Jesus entered Jerusalem on the donkey, Zechariah 9:9 was fulfilled. When the people recited Psalm 118:26 (v. 38), they were acknowledging Jesus as the Messiah (Psalm 118 is messianic). The Pharisees who watched clearly understood this, for they asked Jesus to rebuke the people for what they were saying. Significantly, Jesus not only refused to do so but said that their words *needed* to be said!⇦

In reading verses 41-44, note Jesus' great compassion for the people of Jerusalem. He saw they were oblivious to their great danger. In 70 AD, the city was destroyed and the prophecy that Jesus spoke here was fulfilled. How does this relate to us today?

EXODUS 23-24   God is committed to kindness and justice (23:1-9). True justice cannot be separated from truth. Truth requires equity or equal application of the law, regardless of status. As you read these verses, think of our judicial system today. If we "think God's thoughts after Him," we must have the same concerns and work for justice in the land and in the world. *Watch for this concern for justice on the Lord's part as you continue to read.*

Read carefully the promises of 23:20-33. Underline the words "I am," "I have," and "I will" each time they occur, looking for the attached message.

In 24:4 we are told that Moses wrote down everything God had told him (for the Israelites – and for us!). Then, after offering sacrifices, Moses read the book to the people. There was a corporate response as the people promised to accept the word from God as they heard it (v. 7). As Moses proceeded up the mountain at the Lord's command, the Israelites saw the glory of the Lord appearing as a consuming fire (v. 17).

PSALM 37   Contrast the man of God with the ungodly. The writer had struggled with the success of the godless man. The wicked man ignored God, and his dealings with others were deceitful. Follow the "reality orientation" with regard to the blessings of the believer and the destiny of the ungodly.

There are six suggestions for abundant life (vv. 1, 3, 4, 5, 7, 8). Several have an attached blessing. As you ponder these suggestions, do you see any ways in which you need change? In verses 18-19, note the specific blessings that the Lord has for His own.

FEBRUARY 7

LUKE 20:1-26   ☑The crucial question of the authority of Jesus was raised by the priests and teachers of the law in verses 1-2. This was so important because if Jesus spoke with the authority of God, He was indeed the Messiah, and the leaders were obligated to listen and respond. Jesus answered the question in the Parable of the Tenants. As He told this story, with its reference to the Messiah (Ps 118:22), the priests and the teachers understood clearly what Jesus was saying.↩ Their response was to try to find a way to arrest Him.

EXODUS 25-26   God told Moses that He would dwell with the Israelites and that they were to make a tabernacle for Him (Exod 25:8-9). To do this, the people were asked to give of their resources (vv. 1-7).

The directions for the tabernacle and the articles within were very specific. These written instructions supplemented the pattern that God showed Moses on the mountain (25:40). As you read about specific items, it may be helpful to refer to Exodus 40:17-33 to visualize where these items were placed in the tabernacle.

The Most Holy Place where the ark was positioned was separated from the rest of the tent (The Holy Place) with a curtain (26:31-34). Note which items were placed in The Holy Place.

PSALM 38   The psalmist's heart is absolutely transparent here. This is the recorded prayer of his deepest emotion as he struggles with guilt (v. 4). With this in mind, note the psalmist's attitude in verse 15 and his open heart in verse 18.

Not only is the writer transparent, he is also insightful. In verse 4 he says the burden of guilt is too heavy to bear, listing six physical consequences of his emotional and spiritual suffering: non-healing sores (v. 5); a bent back (kyphosis, v. 6); back pain (v. 7); general weariness (v. 8a); depression (v. 8b); and anxiety (v. 10a). Some of these may be figurative, but there is no question that physical problems can arise from emotional and spiritual unrest.

FEBRUARY 8

LUKE 20:27-47   The Sadducees didn't believe there would be a resurrection – thus the "trick" question to Jesus about the woman who had, in succession, seven brothers as her husband.

The discussion grew out of the practice in Israel that if a woman's husband died before the couple had a son, the dead husband's brother should marry the widow to give her a son who would carry on the name of her former husband (Deut 25:5-6). The basis of this practice was the importance of children. A widow without sons was without protection and security, and further, the tribal land was passed to succeeding generations through the sons.

Jesus skillfully used their question to teach about life after human death. Relationships in heaven will not be based upon marriage and sexual union as on earth (vv. 34-36). Although people will retain their identity, they will be like angels. Jesus also told them that the resurrection had always been asserted in the Scriptures! God called Himself the God of Abraham, Isaac, and Jacob when He met Moses in the desert (Exod 3:6), and God is the God of the living (vv. 37-38).

☑Further, Jesus demonstrated that even David understood that the coming Messiah, who would be his descendent, would be greater than he was (vv. 41-44). David spoke of the Lord (God) speaking to his (David's) Lord (the Messiah). Jesus was clearly declaring that He was that Messiah!⇔

EXODUS 27-28   The garments for the priests were also very specific. To represent the people before God, they were to be dressed according to His instruction. There was a dignity to forms of worship; God could not be approached carelessly.

The ephod (28:6-14) was a reminder to the people of the special place that they, and their tribal divisions, had with the powerful God who had delivered them from Egypt. Aaron and his successors wore the two stones engraved with the twelve names of the tribes as they led in worship before the Lord.

The breastpiece (vv. 15-30) was a visual reminder that guidance and decision came from the Lord. The other specific items (in the remainder of Ch. 28) that Aaron wore were also reminders to the people of their relation to the Lord.

PSALM 39   Verse 6 is an accurate picture of today's contemporary life. There is pressure to acquire things. Security is tied to a bank account. Note, however, how worthless it all is! With all of the effort to acquire more, there is no guarantee that this man will enjoy any of the benefit (6b).

God's person looks at life in an entirely different way. Life does not go on forever (vv. 4-5); with the Lord in one's life, it is possible to look that fact in the face. Further, instead of faith in "things," the child of God has hope founded in God (v. 7). He also recognizes that he needs forgiveness from the Lord (vv. 8-10). With the mind set of verse 7, compare Psalm 16:8.

Contrast these two perspectives: the contemporary world and the person who knows the Lord. There a great difference! It is a blessing to have worthwhile goals and motives.

FEBRUARY 9

LUKE 21:1-19   How Jesus viewed giving was very different from how most of us perceive it (vv. 1-4). Clearly, Jesus saw what the widow gave as a proportion of what she had and not as a large or small amount of money. Allow this perspective to speak to your own giving.

Today, people wonder about the timing of the second coming of Christ (cf. v. 7). Jesus spoke to this in Luke 21. Although it is impossible to set specific dates for Christ's return, there are a number of reasons to suspect it will be soon. The pace of change in society has increased dramatically in the last one hundred years, and even more in the past fifty years. Travel and knowledge have increased exponentially (Dan 12:4b). Christian faith and values are under attack, and the mores of society have changed significantly (vv. 12-13; cf. 2 Tim 3:1-5). The electronic media has made it possible to communicate compromised values in a way not imagined only a few years ago. Israel is again a nation after twenty-five hundred years and is surrounded by armies (v. 20).

As you read this chapter, note the threats to Christians that the end times will bring (vv. 12-18), and think about what you need to be prepared (v. 19). We need to know God's Word to understand the issues that confront us, pray for discernment in difficult situations, and maintain a close walk with the Lord Jesus in the Spirit. As Christians, we must march to a totally different drummer than the rest of the world. That is what life in the Spirit is about (Rom 12:2)!

EXODUS 29-30   The ordination of the priests was to be done according to the Lord's instruction (Ch. 29) with sacrifices and ritual over a seven-day period. This was a formal recognition of their position before God and the people.

Consider the composite effect that the ritual and the tabernacle with its priesthood had upon the people. All of these things were reminders of God's place and presence. There were rituals, sights, smells (sacrifices), special apparel, the Sabbath, and recurring celebrations. Remember that these people didn't have the Bible in their hands. God in His grace gave them these reminders as "handles" to understand the blessing of His presence.

PSALM 40   The reality of the world around us, and also the reality of our own sin, is obvious in verse 12. Our need before the Lord is in verse 17a. All who have seriously thought about life understand the truth about the world, sin, and personal need.

The psalmist waited patiently for the Lord (v. 1). In real life, that means turning to God in trust and expectancy. Note the specific blessings that came to the writer (vv. 2-4), and also that God has pre-planned the blessings (v. 5) for His people.

Compare verse 6 with Deuteronomy 15:16-17. This writer (David) had given his life irrevocably to the Lord (vv. 6-8), which he openly acknowledged among the people (vv. 9-10).

☑Hebrews 10:5-7 links verses 6-8 of this psalm to the Lord Jesus (cf. Matt 26:39). Psalm 22:25 (a messianic psalm) also quotes Psalm 40:9. Although this psalm reflects David's heart and life, it also looks forward to the promise of redemption in the Lord Jesus Christ.↩

FEBRUARY 10

LUKE 21:20-38   In verses 20-28, Jesus spoke about the events surrounding His glorious second coming. Verses 20-24 may refer primarily to the destruction of Jerusalem in 70 AD, but they also refer to the "Tribulation" when the Antichrist will pressure God's people to serve and worship him. In contrast to pressure from the Antichrist, the "Day of the Lord" is God's great judgment on the world at Christ's coming (vv. 25-27). Isaiah 24 and Joel 1:1-2:11; 3:1-2a, 11-17 are representative of Old Testament passages that speak of the Day of the Lord. In addition to Luke 21 and other related gospel accounts, the book of Revelation tells of this coming judgment. ⊃It will be during these events that Jesus will come again in glory (v. 27). When He comes He will gather believers to be with Him, and the Day of the Lord will come (vv. 25-28; cf. Matt 24:27-31).⊂

Note verse 36. Jesus implied that His faithful followers would escape this coming catastrophe (the Day of the Lord). Those who know Christ as Savior will be protected from the wrath of God (Matt 24:30-31; cf. 1 Thess 5:9). Some, however, will be caught in the "trap," not prepared for Jesus' coming in glory (vv. 34-35; cf. 1 Thess 5:1-3), surprised, as by a thief in the night.

Most important for each of us as we await the coming of Christ is His admonition to take care (v. 34), to watch, and to pray (v. 36) so that we will not be deceived by the world. If we walk closely to the Lord Jesus, doing His will in the Spirit, we will never be surprised or lose our firm grip on the truth!

EXODUS 31-32   God gave special skills to individuals for the preparation of the tabernacle. Bezalel and Oholiab were specially empowered by the Holy Spirit for doing intricate parts of the work (31:1-11).

Reading the account of the sin of the people in Chapter 32, you might wonder how this could happen. After seeing the glory of the Lord and His awesome power and presence, how *could* this happen? How could Aaron be a part of this? This account demonstrates that men have an inner bent to evil, and it is dangerous for any of us to be careless or complacent! This was truly a black day in the history of Israel. This also underlines our built-in desire to have something to worship. Remember Exodus 20:3-6. After Moses carried the stone tablets with God's commandments written with His own hand, they lay in fragments at the base of the mountain as Moses and Joshua saw the idolatrous practice of the Israelites!

PSALM 41 Many times the Bible speaks about God's concern for the weak. Verse 1 affirms God's blessing on those who care for the weak. Specific blessings of deliverance, protection, healing, and restoration are listed in verses 2-3.

When God speaks of the widow, the orphan, and the alien, He refers to the weak. These had fewer "rights" than others in that society and had no one to protect them. The poor come under the same umbrella. Mercy is the quality of being sensitive and responsive to needs around us. With that in mind, read Micah 6:8. Look also at Proverbs 19:17. Watch for this concern of God as you continue to read through the Bible. You will be impressed at how many times it occurs.

☑Jesus called attention to verse 9 when He was with the disciples at the last Passover meal. He specifically linked this verse to His betrayal by Judas (cf. John 13:18).⇦

FEBRUARY 11

LUKE 22:1-46 The Passover had been instituted in Egypt about fifteen hundred years previously as the Lord was about to deliver His people from that land. Reread Exodus 12:1-11 along with Luke 22. A lamb was killed, roasted and eaten, and its blood smeared on the doorframes of the homes. The angel of the Lord "passed over" the homes thus marked, but the firstborn in other homes died! Jesus, knowing that He was the authentic "lamb" of atonement that the lamb of ancient times symbolized (v. 37b), prepared to eat this Passover meal for the last time on earth. The disciples, ignorant of what was coming, made the preparations with tradition in mind. ➲Jesus' comments about the bread and the wine clearly set Him apart as God's Son and as the fulfillment of the Passover imagery (vv. 17-22).☚ ☑Note Jesus' reference to Isaiah 53:12, asserting that this prophecy was written about Him and was about to be fulfilled (v. 37).⇦

Jesus discusses the basis for work in the kingdom in verses 24-30. The disciples, infected with the philosophy of the world around them, asked the question that is close to all who are climbing the ladder of success – "Which one of us is greatest?" Jesus' answer turns the world's success philosophy on end! Success is not "to be in charge," but to serve. The example is Jesus Himself (v. 27). Look at the reward for the one who is loyal in the kingdom (vv. 28-30).

EXODUS 33-34   In these chapters, observe Moses, the man of God. Consider how he was able to come to God with petitions. As we will see, he was the advocate of the people on several occasions. Consider that Moses was able to talk to God "face to face" (Exod 33:11).

Exodus 33 is a key portion of the Bible as it impresses upon us how important it is to live in God's presence. Moses understood this. When the question arose as to whether the Lord would accompany the people on their journey, Moses was convinced that if God did not go with them they should not go at all (33:1-3, 15). Further, Moses practiced an intimate relationship with the Lord. Even his face became radiant when he had been in the Lord's presence (34:33-35). In truth, we are unable to do anything of import in God's eyes without His presence and power.

Use your pen to highlight the times when God says "I will" or "I am" in these chapters. Note 34:6-7. Here God is speaking about His compassion, grace, love, patience, faithfulness, forgiveness, and justice. (This is the God of the Old Testament!)

As for foreign gods and idols, they were to be broken, smashed, and cut down (34:13). There was to be no place for other gods or the worship of idols.

How special is God in your life? Do you understand that our God is holy and awesome? Do you fear God in a reverent manner? Are there idols in your life that need to be cut down, broken, and smashed? If so, *take action*, and let God bring new joy and blessing into your life. He is the God of compassion, grace, love, faithfulness, patience, forgiveness, and justice – yet He does not ignore sin (34:6-7)!

AT THIS POINT WE WILL TAKE A BREAK FROM THE PSALMS TO CONSIDER JOB. Job is dated by most very early in history, perhaps at the time of Abraham, so this is a reasonable place to study his life. The reading schedule will return to the Psalms when Job is completed.

JOB 1   The Book of Job has some important lessons for the reader that are not readily apparent with casual reading. The record of this man of God speaks to the spiritual battle in which we are engaged as God's kingdom people here on the earth. As such, we are engaging the enemy, but in many instances we don't have the big picture of these events.

We understand in general terms that our responsibility as people of the kingdom is to bring glory to God. We don't understand, however, why bad things happen to good people (remember the book of the same title). We intuitively feel that if we obey God, His blessing will smooth our way, and we will find happiness and success. But what about those special people who work for years under adverse circumstances in a different culture, finally retiring with little material wealth to show for their efforts? We call them missionaries. What about those who never achieve financial stability but who are faithful to God, like the widow who gave all she had and earned the Lord's commendation (Mark 12:41-44)? And what about those who have died for their faith? *When we think in these terms, our intuitive feeling about what God should do for us when we love and obey Him seems flawed.*

The Book of Job addresses these questions in a manner found nowhere else in the Bible. Job endured physical suffering and misunderstanding. Job's integrity was at stake, but *the real issue was that God's integrity was at stake.* God had done a work of grace in Job's heart that was tested with the most severe suffering, both physical and emotional, that Satan could muster. Job knew nothing of this. The battle was outside Job's understanding. We read of this battle in Ephesians 6:10-18.

It seems strange to us that Satan had access to the presence of God. This is an incredible concept, and there is much about it that we don't understand, but it is also seen in Zechariah 3:1-2 and in Revelation 12:10. In the latter reference, Satan is called the accuser of the brothers and is finally banished from the presence of God, most probably after Christ's victory at the cross (cf. Col 2:13-15). Because of this spiritual conflict, it is crucial that we have Jesus to represent us before the Father (1 John 2:1-2).

Not only did Job not understand what was happening, but his friends drew what to them was the obvious conclusion – that Job must have been in sin or God would never have allowed this to happen to him. Remember their error, for it is easy to make similar judgments about people.

With these things in mind, read Chapter 1 with care. As much as it is possible, place yourself in Job's shoes and try to think of how you would react.

Satan is the father of lies and a master at distortion. Satan challenged God when he questioned the reason for Job's fidelity to God (v. 9). With God's permission, Satan destroyed all of Job's possessions and family with the exception of his wife. God knew His man! Job's reaction is an example to each of us and was a rebuke to the Evil One (vv. 20-22).

FEBRUARY 12

LUKE 22:47-71   As you read the account of the arrest and trial of Jesus, look back at Jesus' comments to Peter in verses 31-34 and compare this with verses 54-62. This was a bitter time for Peter and must be a reminder to each of us that we need to walk very closely to the Lord and depend upon Him alone.

Follow Jesus through the betrayal and trial. He displayed great dignity and command as the events proceeded. Note verses 39-44. It was in the garden in prayer before the Father where Jesus' obedience to the Father was settled. ⟳Note Jesus' statement that He indeed is the Son of God (vv. 66-71).☚

EXODUS 35-36   These are the final instructions and preparations for the building of the tabernacle. Several principles are significant.

1. The tabernacle was to be built with contributions from the people (35:5-9). The contributions were from what they had in hand (v. 5) and were from those willing to give (v. 5b). What a model this is for the support of God's work (cf. 2 Cor 8:12)! See how this worked in verses 20-24.

2. Those with skills and a willing heart were to come forward to do the work (35:10; 36:2). Note also that the skills were from the Lord (35:30-35; 36:2). We have the notion that our abilities are personal property! Not so! Abilities and skills are gifts from the Lord (cf. 1 Cor 12:4-11).

3. When God moves the hearts of His people, there is enough for the work. In fact, in this instance, contributions had to be curtailed (36:4-7).

JOB 2   Once again, Satan questioned Job's integrity before God. Again, Satan was given permission to touch Job – this time with physical problems that could extend almost to taking his life. Job was afflicted with painful lesions – on his entire body. This extremely painful condition could have been herpes zoster, commonly known as shingles. It is caused by a virus that infects nerves and causes sores on the skin in the area of the affected nerve. The condition can last for months.

It is hard for us to imagine Job's suffering. He had none of the medications that we might use to ease pain. Even his wife lost hope for his recovery and suggested that he curse God and die. Her erroneous conclusion was that God was Job's enemy.

Job's answer demonstrated that he understood the sovereignty of God – that God had control in his life, and even that God could have sent the affliction to him (not true, but God allowed it). More important than his understanding of God's control is that Job refused to see his condition as caused by "meanness" on the part of God. He seemed to understand that God had His own reasons, and he refused to turn his face from his God.

Enter Job's friends. We will follow closely Job's conversations with these men. Their comments are deeply philosophical and are much the same (though in different words) as we would hear today. Their assumptions, and therefore their resulting conclusions, are a mixture of truth and error. Because they erred about the reason for Job's problems, they were very hard on Job. We will do well to learn from Job, and from the men who visited him, to avoid the same mistakes in dealing with those in difficulty.

59

FEBRUARY 13

LUKE 23:1-25   The Jewish leaders had heard enough to convict Jesus when He declared He was God's Son (22:70-71). Since they could not execute a person under Roman rule, they had to convince the Roman authorities to carry out the execution. Verses 1-25 give this account.

Pilate saw that Jesus may have been troublesome to the Jews but was not guilty of a crime that deserved death under Roman law (vv. 4, 14-15, 22). ᗆThe Jewish leaders accused Jesus of claiming to be "Christ, a king" (i.e., the Messiah). When Pilate asked the question directly, Jesus plainly told Pilate that He was that person!ᗉ Pilate was charged to see that justice, as defined by Roman law, was carried out. Further, Pilate was disturbed by Jesus' own claim to be God's Son and His refusal to answer the false charges against Him. Faced with death, Jesus was unmoved! One can speculate that Pilate remembered these events often and thought about them – especially when the report of the resurrection came to his ears. *But his action could not later be recalled and relived.* The political pressure was too much, and Pilate capitulated to the demands of the Jewish leaders!

EXODUS 37-38   After all of the instructions and the gathering of contributions and resources, the building of the tabernacle began. It seems amazing that this could be done in the desert with resources that they had carried out of Egypt on their backs. The requisite skills came from the Lord (35:30-36:1), but note the amounts of gold, silver, and bronze that were used (38:21-31). This truly was a major undertaking.

JOB 3   In his torment, Job wished that the date of his birth could be stricken from the calendar if it could erase his birth (v. 3). He was so miserable that he longed for the peace of death (3:11-19). Every person fears that something unbearable will come to him, and Job was no exception (v. 25). *Yet, this was not cause to grumble against God (2:10).*

Job does question God's ways in not allowing him to die when he is in such misery (vv. 20-21). His assumption is that God had hedged him in (v. 23). Job, as most of us, had thought about the possibility that life would bring troubles and pain that would be hard to bear (v. 25). Life simply had no quietness or peace when he was in such pain (v. 26).

FEBRUARY 14

LUKE 23:26-56   Listen to Jesus as He was taken to be crucified. He had time to speak to those who cared about Him (vv. 27-31) and offered prayer for the very ones who drove the nails into His body (v. 34).

→This was the moment of fulfillment of Isaiah 53. Note particularly Isaiah 53:3-6. The redemption was accomplished; the price was paid for sin (cf. 1 Peter 1:18-20). Review Psalm 22 as you read verses 33-37. It is amazing how accurately Psalm 22 previsions the death of our Lord. Note verses 44-45. As Jesus died, the curtain of the temple was torn in two, symbolizing that the death of God's sinless Son atoned for sin and opened the way for persons of faith to come into the very presence of God (cf. Heb 10:19-22; 1 Peter 1:18-20).←

↻Note carefully the hope that came to the condemned criminal in verses 40-43 as Jesus offered him eternal life – which only God could do.↺ Note also the courage of Joseph of Arimathea. He was a member of the Jewish council and had not consented or agreed with the decision to seek Jesus' death, and he now honored Jesus with a burial.

EXODUS 39-40   After the tabernacle was completed, the structure was exactly what God had commanded. Follow the text and the repeated phrase, "As the Lord commanded Moses/him." This is seen nine times in Chapter 39 and eight times in Chapter 40.

When the work was done, God demonstrated His acceptance of it with His presence and glory (40:34-35). Previously, the cloud had been with the Israelites (Exod 13:21-22), but now the presence of God, in the form of the cloud, settled upon the tabernacle (40:38).   See also Numbers 9:15-23.

JOB 4   Job's friends made definite statements about the reason for Job's condition, but they, as well as Job, didn't know the facts behind Job's troubles.

As Eliphaz the Temanite speaks, look for what is true and what is not true. What he says in 4:6 is true. What he says in verses 7-11 is error. Have the innocent perished? Of course! Have they even perished innocently and before old age? Of course! Read carefully verses 12-16. This describes what sounds like a spirit encounter, and as you read verses 17-21, consider the message of the spirit. If true, there would be no hope for any living being! God's grace and forgiveness is totally missing.

FEBRUARY 15

LUKE 24:1-12   →Stand in awe as you read of the resurrection. The central point in history is the death and resurrection! The sacrifice of atonement at the cross brings forgiveness to the believer (Rom 3:21-26). The resurrection declares forever that Jesus is the sinless Son of God who *could* and *did* pay for sin (Rom 1:4). The grave could not hold the sinless Son of God. This event made a public spectacle of the evil powers of Satan (Col 2:15).←

If you place yourself with those who came to the grave on that Easter morning, it is easy to imagine their confusion in finding the heavy stone that had closed the tomb rolled away. Imagine their feeling when the angels appeared and proclaimed that Jesus was alive! It was then that events began to make sense. They remembered Jesus' words to them about the crucifixion and the resurrection (vv. 6-8). Travel with the women as they hurried back to tell the apostles the news that Jesus was alive. Imagine their frustration when no one would believe them (v. 11)! But it was so! Jesus really was alive, as the disciples would soon discover.

LEVITICUS 1-2   Leviticus is the section of the Pentateuch (the five books of Moses) in which God outlined many of the worship and social regulations that the Israelites were required to observe. These practices set the Israelites apart from the other nations among whom they lived.

The offerings were the special way God gave the Israelites to ask for forgiveness for both known and unknown sins. They also provided the opportunity to thank God for His blessings and fellowship with Him and with each other.

There were four varieties of animal sacrifices and one sacrifice that was presented without blood: the Grain Offering. Understanding these sacrifices and what they meant to the Israelites provides insight into both the Old and the New Testaments. From the perspective of the New Testament, and especially following the sacrificial death and resurrection of Jesus, we have a better understanding of the deeper meaning of the requirements.

In each of the animal sacrifices, an innocent animal was sacrificed on behalf of another living being (a person): The blood was presented at the altar, and in some instances inside the Holy Place of the tabernacle. God saw the blood sacrifice, and He forgave the sin of those on whose behalf the sacrifice was given. We now know that the blood of these animals or birds did not have the power to bring forgiveness (Heb 10:4). Only the blood of Jesus has that ability (Heb 10:8-10). God honored the faith and obedience of the people in their sacrifice until the time that Jesus, the real and perfect sacrifice, actually paid the penalty for their sins (cf. Rom 3:25-26; Heb 9:15).

As the animal was sacrificed, those making the sacrifice placed their hands on the head of the animal to symbolize transfer of their sin to the innocent animal. In every instance, the blood was poured out, and the fat was completely burned on the altar.

Here are comments about the types of sacrifices in Chapters 1-2 (today's reading).

THE BURNT OFFERING was to be made each morning and each evening on behalf of the entire people and was to be left burning at all times. An individual could also present a burnt offering. Note in 1:4 that the offering made atonement for the person who brought it. This was the only offering that was entirely burned.

THE GRAIN OFFERING was offered as a present to the Lord. It was cultivated grain, made without yeast; after the "memorial portion" was removed and burned, the rest was given to the priest to eat.

JOB 5   Note the lie of Satan in 5:1. This was Satan's direct attack (through Eliphaz) on Job at the emotional and spiritual level. Listen to the description of the human condition without grace in verses 2-7.

What Eliphaz said in verses 8-27 is generally true. What he really said, however, was that Job had sinned and needed to repent (4:8-10). If this were not true, he implied, God would not allow this difficulty. Eliphaz suggested that God was disciplining Job (v. 17) and implied that if Job would admit his sin God would deal graciously with him. In fact, neither Eliphaz nor Job understood the reason for Job's trouble, but as we shall see, Job didn't believe that it was because of sin in his life.

It is so very important that we don't draw conclusions about another person's trouble. Of course, some things are clear. A person may foolishly spend all his money and be in difficulty. Two plus two equals four! That is trouble a person brings on himself. It is true that God disciplines a person when correction is needed (Heb 12:5-6). But it is also true that God allows hard circumstances to come to help us to grow (1 Peter 1:6-7). We must not draw conclusions about God's dealings with another when we don't have the facts!

FEBRUARY 16

LUKE 24:13-53   Two disciples walked toward the city of Emmaus on that first Easter day discussing the events of the last days. Their mood was somber when Jesus joined them on the road. Interestingly, as Jesus walked with them, they didn't recognize Him as their Master. ☑When Jesus asked them what they were talking about and He began to explain the events in the light of the Scriptures, their hearts "burned" within them (v. 32). Jesus was (is) the literal fulfillment of the prophecies about the coming redemption. It wasn't until they were eating together that "their eyes were opened," and they realized that this was indeed the Lord (vv. 30-31). This is the Bible study that we would all have loved to attend! How revealing it would have been to have the Lord Himself explain the messianic portions of the Bible!

As you read this chapter, note how Jesus tied all that had happened to the Scriptures (vv. 27, 44-47). God had not skipped a beat in His plan for the ages – what had transpired had been God's holy will to redeem the world. Now, the responsibility to see that plan to the end was handed to the church (vv. 46-49), as Jesus explained that repentance and forgiveness would be preached to all nations.⇦

What had been shattered hope became the reason for worship and joy (vv. 52-53). These who had been with Jesus were changed forever – and so are we!

<u>LEVITICUS 3-5</u>   The Fellowship, Sin, and Guilt Offerings are introduced in these chapters.

THE FELLOWSHIP OFFERING was an act of thankfulness and worship. Certain portions of the animal were burned on the altar as a sacrifice to the Lord (Ch. 3). The person and his family then ate the meat before the Lord in the area of the tabernacle. The priest was to have the breast and the right thigh of the animal as his share (7:31-34).

THE SIN OFFERING was, in most instances, for unintentional sins: for priest, leader, individuals, and the assembly of people.

THE GUILT OFFERING is similar to the sin offering but also includes purposeful sin. When something had been deceitfully taken, restitution had to be made.

In the latter two sacrifices, after the pouring of the blood, the fat was burned on the altar. The hide, the head, and the intestines were burned outside the camp in a clean place (4:8-12). The meat of the animal was then given to the priest to eat in the area of the tabernacle (6:24-30). If, however, the sacrifice was for a priest (4:3-12) or for the entire community (vv. 13-21), the flesh of the animal was completely burned outside the camp.

Of the sacrifices at the tabernacle, only the Fellowship Offering could be eaten by the layperson who brought it. Leviticus 7:28-34 gives the regulation about what part of the Fellowship Offering belongs to the priest.

<u>JOB 6</u>   As Job answered his friends, his perspective was skewed. In 6:4, he mistakenly stated that the arrows of God were causing his suffering. In fact, they were the arrows of Satan! Job wanted to die (vv. 8-9) before he denied the Lord (v. 10). He had no hope and no strength to go on with life (vv. 11-13). Further, even his friends were not the encouragement he needed.

<u>FEBRUARY 17</u>

<u>ACTS 1</u>   The Book of Acts is the account of the early church. With the coming of the Holy Spirit, the church became the unique instrument to accomplish God's purpose of redemption in the world. The church under the Holy Spirit is what God will use until Jesus comes again. As you read Acts, look for the distinguishing characteristics of the church. Allow God to shape your own life and thinking through these truths. →Matthew 28:18-20 and Acts 1:8 are the marching orders and the pattern for the work of the church.←

As you read verses 9-11, put yourself with the disciples as they watched Jesus go up into heaven. Think about it. Jesus went to heaven in a cloud and will come back in the same way (cf. Rev 1:7). He ascended while a few of the disciples watched; when He returns, everyone will see Him (cf. Rev 1:7; Matt 24:30). Remember, too, that Jesus promised to return soon (Rev 22:7, 12, 20).

LEVITICUS 6-7   The principle of restitution is clear in instances of theft or extortion (6:1-7).

The priests (and their families) obtained their food from the tithes and offerings that were brought to the Lord (7:28-36). If the tithes were not brought as the law demanded, the Lord's work was compromised (cf. Neh 13:10-13).

JOB 7   Read Job's expression of misery in 7:1-6 and his complaint to the Lord in verses 7-21. Job also wondered if there was sin in his life (vv. 20-21), but if so, he was unaware of what it might be.

Job's comments to the Lord in verses 7-21 demonstrate how human he was. He lost hope (v. 7). He complained that God had him under guard and brought bad dreams to him when he was able to sleep (vv. 12-14) (and how mistaken he was, since it was Satan and not the Lord). He asked God why He had made him His target (v. 20b). The encouraging thing is that the Lord didn't castigate Job for his lack of understanding or his wrong conclusions! God understands our frailties.

FEBRUARY 18

ACTS 2   If Matthew 28:18-20 and Acts 1:8 give the marching orders and the pattern for the work of the church, the coming of the Holy Spirit enables the church for the task. Although the Holy Spirit had been present in the world previously, equipping certain persons to do particular tasks, now, with the birth of the church, every believer has the Holy Spirit (v. 38; 1 Cor 12:7).

→The timing of the Holy Spirit's coming was crucial. At Pentecost, Jews from the entire geographical region (including other countries) had come together in Jerusalem. Pentecost, known as The Feast of Weeks in the Old Testament, was one of three times yearly when all of the men of Israel were commanded to come together to worship the Lord. When the Holy Spirit came, the believers were miraculously able to speak the languages of these visitors, resulting in immediate widespread exposure of the gospel message.←

Read Peter's sermon carefully (vv. 22-41) and remember that just a few weeks earlier he had denied ever being with Jesus (Luke 22:54-62). ☑Notice how he used Old Testament Scriptures, with which the listeners could immediately relate, to validate that Jesus was indeed the coming Messiah – the one who would sit on David's throne.⇔ He spoke powerfully, calling the listeners to repentance. Note the results in verse 41.

LEVITICUS 8-9   As Aaron and his sons were ordained and set apart for the ministry of assisting in worship, the people followed the regulations given for the ordination of Aaron and his sons in Exodus 29 – lasting seven days.

The significant event when the offerings were instituted was that the Lord visibly approved by sending fire to consume the offering on the altar (9:23-24). The mighty God that delivered them from Egypt had accepted their offering. Awesome!

JOB 8   Now friend Bildad came into the conversation. Once again there was a mixture of truth and error. Bildad began by assuring Job that he (Job) was in error before God (v. 2). The assumption was that God would be unjust to allow Job's suffering unless there was wrong in his life (v. 3a). His first statement in verse 3 was absolutely true, but his conclusion about Job's children was absolutely wrong (v. 4). His statement in verses 5-7 was true, but his assumption (Job, you are in sin, and if you will get straightened out, God's blessing will come to you) was in error.

Bildad appealed to natural law to reinforce his argument (vv. 11-19). The man who forgets God is like the papyrus and the reed that needs water (God's provision) to grow but withers quickly when the water dries up. The natural law is correct and applies ultimately to men who forget God – but Job had not forgotten God!

Finally, note the truth in verses 20-22 as it applied to Job. Bildad's erroneous assumption was that the blessing would come only when Job straightened out his life and thinking.

FEBRUARY 19

ACTS 3   Imagine yourself for a few moments as the man crippled since birth. Life was not kind to a person with a significant handicap in the ancient world. He was reduced to begging for money to keep "body and soul together." Having lived in this fashion for many years, he had little or no hope of anything different. His expectation as he spoke to Peter and John was for a token of kindness from them – a small contribution.

Continue to think of yourself in his place. As Peter spoke strange words (v. 6) – most probably unintelligible to the crippled man (had he even heard of Jesus?) – and helped him to his feet, he was healed (v. 7)! Legs and ankles that hadn't functioned since birth now received strength and supported him – even to walk and leap (v. 8)! No wonder he praised God. The man had been miraculously healed in the name of Jesus of Nazareth.

The stir among the people who knew the man occasioned the opportunity for Peter to speak about the risen Lord to the crowd. ☑Follow closely his explanation to the people as he tied the death and resurrection of Jesus to the Old Testament prophecies of the Messiah (v. 18). He laid responsibility for the death of Jesus with the people (v. 15) but said he knew that they acted from ignorance (v. 17). Peter stated that Jesus was prophesied by Moses in Deuteronomy 18:15. Note also how Peter related Jesus' death and resurrection to God's will in redemption (vv. 18-19) and to the promise to Abraham (vv. 25-26; cf. Gen 12:3), and asserted that Jesus would return in fulfillment of prophecy at the end of time (v. 21).⇦ Peter then called them to repentance and faith (v. 19). Look ahead to 4:4 to see the result of the preaching. The Holy Spirit was at work.

LEVITICUS 10-11 Remember, as Chapter 9 closed, the fire from the Lord came and consumed the sacrifice. This was gracious evidence that God had accepted their offering; things were off to a good start.

→Immediately after, however, Aaron's sons Nadab and Abihu came to a bad end (10:1-2). These sons had just been ordained and set apart for the priesthood. What they did was probably not a rebellious act but simply carelessness. What they did probably seemed good to them – but went beyond God's commands. God used this to help His people understand the gravity of disobedience and the importance of doing things exactly as He had instructed them. Unless they kept the exact pattern, they would drift *from* God's plan and *toward* the practices of the pagan nations they would displace in Canaan.← At this time, just after the establishment of the priesthood, both priests and people were impressed with the importance of following the rituals of worship exactly in God's way.

The lesson for all of us is that we cannot play loose with God (cf. Acts 5:1-11). Even though we are not struck dead if we step out of line, still God cares. It is His grace that allows us to continue living, but we must not presume on His grace!

Chapter 11 and the chapters following outline many of the social laws under which the Israelites lived. These are sometimes called "Levitical ordinances."

In general, two kinds of laws were given to the Israelites. God's moral laws came directly from His character. These laws, such as the Ten Commandments and the regulations that are an extension of these commands, apply for all time. The laws about worship and the offerings grew directly out of the moral law. They were the way God provided for mankind to relate to Him and symbolized how God would finally solve the problem of sin and guilt at the cross. The offerings ceased for the church with the resurrection of Christ and the coming of the Holy Spirit: The symbolism was replaced by the reality – the sacrifice of God's holy Son, Jesus.

The second kind of laws was given to the Israelites for their social life, and these laws are not directly applicable to all times or all peoples, as are the moral laws. The laws of clean and unclean foods and of purification are examples of the social laws. These laws kept the Israelites different from the nations; as "set apart" people, the nation was the channel for lessons to us (1 Cor 10:6), for the transmission of the Scriptures (Rom 9:4), and for the coming of the Savior (Rom 9:5).

These distinctly social laws ceased to apply after the resurrection. Remember that the laws of clean and unclean meats and the law of circumcision were seen in a different way after the coming of the Holy Spirit (Acts 15). The moral laws, however, remain as a reflection of the character of God (Rom 3:31).

JOB 9   As Job answered Bildad, take note of his deep understanding about the character and work of God (9:4). As Job contemplated God, he saw Him as the creator and the sustainer of the universe (vv. 8-9). It is interesting that so long ago the constellations in the sky were recognized (v. 9), and we retain their names.

At this point, God seemed so far off to Job that it seemed impossible he could learn from God the true nature of his problem (vv. 14-16). ☑Although this is not a direct prophecy of the coming of the Savior, Job accurately anticipates the redemptive work of the Lord Jesus in his longing (vv. 33-35). Job longed for someone to arbitrate between him and God. The Lord Jesus is just such a person – He is our advocate and High Priest (cf. Heb 10:19-22; 1 John 2:1; Rom 3:21-25; 1 Tim 2:5).⇦

FEBRUARY 20

ACTS 4   Peter and John caused a stir with their strong testimony about Jesus and were arrested by the priests and the temple guard. This gave them the opportunity to bear witness to another group – the hostile religious leaders. ☑In this setting, Peter testified to Jesus as the Christ and to the fact of the resurrection. Note, in answer to the religious leaders, Peter referred to the messianic promise in Psalm 118:22 to make the point that Jesus was indeed the promised one.⇦ The courage of Peter and John was not lost on the religious leaders, especially since they knew Peter and John had been with Jesus (v. 13). In spite of the miracle, however, which they could not dispute, they very much wanted to stop the preaching about Jesus and the resurrection. Note their warning (v. 18) and Peter's and John's answer (vv. 19-20).

Read the thrilling account of their report to the church (vv. 23-31) and the remarkable prayer of the church. ☑In the church's prayer, Jesus' identity as the Messiah is again related to the Old Testament promise (vv. 25-26).⇦ Would you have prayed for continued boldness after being warned by the people who had just engineered the death of your Master? Or would you and I have suggested that perhaps we should not say much while things cooled? Note the Lord's response to their prayer (v. 31; cf. Ps 138:3). *Obviously the Holy Spirit agreed with their heart and intention.*

LEVITICUS 12-13   Recall that Mary followed the regulations of Chapter 12 after the birth of Jesus (Luke 2:22-24). An interesting detail is that Mary and Joseph could not afford a lamb so brought the birds as a sacrifice (Lev 12:8; cf. Luke 2:24).

Some of the social laws, such as isolating a person with a draining infection, were medically sound. Perhaps one day we will understand how all of these regulations had advantage for God's people.

JOB 10   It is clear that Job misunderstood his condition, attributing it to the Lord (10:3). Listen to Job as he poured out his heart to God in his prayer. Job believed he was blameless as to specific sin that would have caused his suffering (9:21) and could not understand what he assumed was God's heavy hand on his life.

Job's solution for a moment of peace was really no solution at all (vv. 20-22). But has there been any other, except for Jesus as He faced death, who felt so estranged, so cut off from contact with the living God? Job had known real fellowship with the Lord, and this was totally different.

FEBRUARY 21

ACTS 5   The church was growing. By the end of Chapter 3, the number of the men in the church had grown to five thousand (4:4). Rapid growth can cause carelessness with the basics. This happened when Ananias and Sapphira were dishonest. God used this incident to teach the church the importance of honesty. Truth reflects God's character. Anything less is from Satan (John 8:44). Notice the result of their deaths – great fear came to the entire church (5:11). The church needed the reminder and learned the lesson: *don't play games with God!*

Opposition grew, motivated by jealousy, to the message and the powerful acts of the church leaders, resulting in the third arrest of the Apostles (vv. 17-18). After their arrest, God opened the doors of the prison (vv. 19-20). Again, the Apostles spoke with power at the Lord's command. The Apostles were again arrested, answered the authorities with wisdom and courage, were warned, and this time, flogged. Note their response (vv. 29-32, 41-42).

LEVITICUS 14-15   These detailed regulations must have been difficult to follow and, at times, burdensome. Think of what it meant to be unclean! As you read 15:25-30, remember the woman who touched the robe of Jesus and was healed from bleeding that had lasted twelve years (Matt 9:20-22). She had been unclean for that long! Further, she had spent all she had in attempted cure (Mark 5:26). It is difficult to imagine her gratitude when she went away healed and forgiven.

JOB 11   Zophar now had his turn. As the conversation went on, Job's friends became more and more exasperated with his answers. Notice how Zophar opened his comments (vv. 2-6). He believed Job needed rebuke (v. 3b), and that Job was arrogant and wrong in his assertions about his faith and understanding of God (v. 4). *Yet, Job was correct (see 1:8 and 2:3).* Zophar also suggested that God hadn't punished Job enough (v. 6b).

Everything Zophar says in verses 7-11 was true. He perhaps underestimated the power of God and His word to change men (v. 12; cf. Prov 1:4). Zophar's conclusion was that Job needed to repent, and the sooner the better, if we can read between the lines (vv. 13-20).

Zophar's speech completed one round of comments by Job's friends. Each of them had assumed that he knew God's mind as it related to Job, and each had assumed that he could correctly assess Job's heart. Much of what they said was correct, but their assumptions were incorrect, and their conclusions regarding Job were wrong! In this spiritual conflict between God and Satan (1:12; 2:6), could these three men be unwittingly representing Satan's point of view in Satan's attempt to get Job to sin? Perhaps!

FEBRUARY 22

ACTS 6   Disagreement crept into the life of the early church as it was stretched with ethnic diversity. Some, it was alleged, were not being treated fairly (v. 1). To solve the problem, and to free the Apostles for prayer and ministry, seven "deacons" were selected to serve the church (vv. 1-4). The requirements for selection are instructive. These men needed to be "full of the Holy Spirit and wisdom" to serve in what seem like rather mundane tasks (v. 3). In reality, there are no mundane tasks in the work of the church. Whatever the responsibility, it is a spiritual undertaking.

One of these men was Stephen, who besides helping in church administration was also busy with outreach ministry (v. 8). Note how the Jews reacted to his ministry (vv. 9-14; cf. 2 Cor 10:3-4).

LEVITICUS 16-17   As you read 16:1-2, think of the lessons just learned in the deaths of Nadab and Abihu. God's warning could not have fallen on deaf ears this time!

The Day of Atonement was the most important sacrifice for the Israelites in the entire year. It was the one time in the year that the high priest carried the blood of the sacrifices into the inner room of the tabernacle to atone for himself and the people. The outer room was separated from the inner room of the tabernacle by a curtain. This pattern was followed in the temple Solomon built and in the reconstructed temple at the time of Jesus.

On the Day of Atonement, Aaron sacrificed a bull as a sin offering for himself and his household, taking some of the blood into the Most Holy Place and sprinkling it in front of the atonement cover of the ark. In addition, Aaron offered a ram for a burnt offering before the Lord. After this offering for himself and his household, Aaron took two goats as an offering for the people. The first goat was a sin offering. Once again he took the blood into the Most Holy Place and sprinkled it before the atonement cover, then sprinkled some of it on the tent of the meeting and on the altar before the entrance of the tabernacle. This was to make atonement for the sins of the people. Aaron then took the second goat – the live goat – and, with his hands on the head of the goat, Aaron confessed the sin and rebellion of the people, symbolically transferring their guilt to the goat. This goat was then led into a solitary place away from the camp and released.

These two goats are significant for each believer. Sin was paid for, and the guilt was taken away! Symbolically, the people's sin was paid for by the sin offering of the goat, with the blood being carried into God's presence (the Most Holy Place). Not only that, but the live goat symbolized the taking away of the sin – never to return again to the camp of the Israelites.

☑The Day of Atonement was to be a lasting ordinance for the Israelites. This day, remembered each year, reminded the people that they needed grace and forgiveness and that they could not find forgiveness without a substitute. That substitute would be the coming Savior, which, of course, they did not understand. Further, sin and guilt would be removed completely (cf. Ps 103:12; Mic 7:18-19). The solemnity of the observance underlined their sin and their need for cleansing, but also the total sufficiency of God's way of dealing with sin.

Remember that the curtain in the temple was torn from top to bottom at the moment Jesus died (Matt 27:51). The torn curtain symbolizes the direct access to the presence of God, which the believer now has because of Christ's death (Heb 10:9-10, 19-20). In these verses from Hebrews, note how the writer specifically relates the rituals and observance of the Day of Atonement to the sacrifice of the Lord Jesus on our behalf!⇦

JOB 12   Before looking at Chapter 12 in detail, quickly read Chapters 12-14 for an overview of Job's answer. Job, too, is exasperated (vv. 2-6). It is no fun to be misunderstood and berated by friends. It is easy to take advantage of someone who is enduring bad times (vv. 5-6). Notice that Job again affirmed that he was righteous and blameless (v. 4b).

As Job began his reply, he revealed amazing knowledge of God (Ch. 12). Test 12:10 and 13-25 with your knowledge of the Scriptures and see how well Job did! Even though he affirmed that he was righteous, Job understood correctly that God was aware of his plight (vv. 9-10). Job described the sovereign God, and did so accurately (vv. 13-25).

FEBRUARY 23

ACTS 7   Stephen became the first martyr of the church. Remember that he was arrested because of his ministry – he was full of grace and power, and worked great wonders and miraculous signs (6:8). When he stood before the Sanhedrin, his face looked angelic (6:15). Follow his reasoned defense. Beginning with Abraham, he used Joseph (v. 9), Moses (vv. 23-29, 40), the prophets (vv. 51-52), and Jesus (vv. 52-53) as examples of how the Jews had consistently rejected God's messengers. Further, they had rejected God Himself (vv. 30-40). Notice how direct and confrontational Stephen was in verses 51-53 (much as Peter and John had been) and how God was present as Stephen died (vv. 55-56).

Both Stephen's defense and his example are instructive. Often we are tempted to "sugarcoat" a difficult message from the Lord. The Apostles followed the example of the Old Testament prophets, John the Baptist, and Jesus in speaking directly.

It is dangerous to reject the message of the Lord. When the people turned away from Him, God turned from them (vv. 39-42; cf. Rom 1:24, 26, 28).

LEVITICUS 18-19   The detailed regulations regarding sexual sin refer back to Exodus 20:14 where God forbids adultery. As you read these regulations, watch for the phrase, "I am the Lord." When you see this, understand that the law God is giving is directly tied to His character. Note 18:5, which ties God's way to life itself. This is still valid. God's way is the way of life: Rejecting His way results in death.

A common practice of the ancient world was to sacrifice one's children to pagan gods. This is expressly forbidden in verse 21. Homosexuality is specifically forbidden in verse 22, and bestiality in verse 23. Also note that sexual sins corrupt both the people and the land (vv. 24-28). Does that make you fear for your country?

In Chapter 19, note God's concern for truth, fairness, respect for life, and respect for fellow man. Note God's special concern for the handicapped (v. 14). Note also the prohibition of divination and sorcery (vv. 26b, 31). Watch for the sins that were punishable by death. These capital crimes were always related to God's moral law.

JOB 13   As Job continued his reply to Zophar, he longed to speak with the Lord (v. 3). He expressed this desire with great faith (v. 15) and felt keenly the misunderstanding of his friends (vv. 4-5). Job told them they had no right to speak on God's behalf, and if the Lord were to examine them with the same criteria they had used against him, they would be in trouble (vv. 7-11). At this point, however, Job stated that even if God took his life he would still trust Him (v. 15). Although he didn't understand what was happening to him, he still maintained deep faith in the living God.

Job shifted from speaking to Zophar to speaking to the Lord in 13:20, and continued to address the Lord until the end of Chapter 14. It is obvious that Job lacked perspective, and this gave him great pain emotionally. He assumed that God's hand was against him (v. 21) and that God considered him His enemy (v. 24)!

FEBRUARY 24

ACTS 8   →The tension in Jerusalem that resulted in Stephen's death also brought "a great persecution" to the church. As a result, all the Christians except the Apostles were scattered through Judea and Samaria (v. 1). Read again Acts 1:8. The witness of the church was to begin in Jerusalem and then extend throughout Judea and Samaria. Was this persecution a setback for the church? Not at all: God was at work. God has many times used opposition to the church to extend its ministry. Those who were scattered preached the good news wherever they went – boldly (v. 4)!

Philip was another of the seven deacons (cf. Acts 6:5-6). He went to Samaria, preaching and performing miracles (vv. 4-25). As a result, Samaritans became believers for the first time – a significant extension of the church for the Jews did not accept the Samaritans. By scattering the church and by Philip's preaching among the Samaritans, the Lord was extending the church. The church was pushed out of her comfort zone, but the Lord was accomplishing His purpose.

Philip's ministry to the Ethiopian, under the direction of the Holy Spirit, was also a significant extension of the gospel (vv. 26-40). This man was a high official in Ethiopia and took the good news back with him to his country after his conversion.←

LEVITICUS 20-21   The call to holiness is seen twice (20:7, 26). God commands it because of His name and person – because of who God is and what He stands for, the people were called to a different lifestyle from the surrounding nations. Note the sins for which the death penalty was prescribed. These are moral sins and tell us how seriously God sees them.

The priests were called to a way of life that was even more stringent (Ch. 21). Again note that the call to holiness (separation to God) was on the basis of the person and character of God, whom the priests represented (vv. 6, 7, 8, 15, 23).

JOB 14   Review quickly Chapters 12-14 to fix in your mind the sequence of Job's comments. There are two significant convictions in Job's thinking as he speaks to God in Chapter 14.

First, Job believed in the resurrection from the dead at God's time of calling (vv. 10-15). If a tree is cut down, it may sprout again from the roots. Not so man. When he dies, he will not live again – *until God calls* (v. 15).

Second, ☑Job believed that his sins would be forgiven when he faced God at the resurrection (vv. 15-17). Job expressed great faith in God in these statements about the resurrection and redemption. This could only be true with the coming of the Savior! Embedded in Job's statement of faith is the promise of redemption. ⇦

FEBRUARY 25

ACTS 9   →God chose Paul (Saul) to be His witness not only to his own people but to the Gentiles (v. 15). What an unlikely choice! Saul had been persecuting believers and had been one of the consenting witnesses to the death of Stephen (8:1a). When Saul was on his way to hunt out believers, the risen Christ dramatically met him on the road (vv. 3-6). God's choice of Saul to be His spokesman significantly increased the evangelism and missionary outreach of the early church. ⇐

Saul's meeting with Jesus changed his life – from that moment on! Imagine his thoughts as he waited for the Lord's messenger to meet him in Damascus. When the Lord directed Ananias to go to Saul, Ananias had trouble believing this could be true (vv. 13-14). Yet, the Sovereign Lord told him once again to meet Saul, and he obeyed. After placing his hands on Saul (Ananias addressed him as "Brother Saul"!), Saul regained his sight (which he had lost when he saw Jesus). Note that almost immediately Saul began to minister for the Lord in the synagogues – knowing the Scriptures, he immediately understood that Jesus was indeed the promised Messiah – leaving only when his life was in danger (vv. 20-25). As you read the remainder of the book of Acts, note how God used Paul in special ways.

Miraculous power from the Holy Spirit continued to follow the Apostles. Peter healed Aeneas in Lydda (vv. 32-35) and raised Dorcas from the dead in Joppa (vv. 36-43).

LEVITICUS 22-23   The priests were told to treat the offerings brought to the Lord with respect (22:2) and to carefully observe the laws of the Lord. If they did not pay careful attention to these regulations, they were treating God's laws with contempt (22:9, i.e., with carelessness).

Consider 22:31-33. Not keeping the Lord's commands profaned His name! Keep the commands of the Lord because He is God! Live in holiness because God has called His people to live separated from the world.

→The yearly gatherings and festivals outlined in Chapter 23 reminded the people of what was important. The Sabbath reminded them of God in creation (v. 3). The Passover reminded the nation of grace in God's deliverance (vv. 4-8). The Feast of Firstfruits and the Feast of Weeks were reminders of God's hand in provision (vv. 9-22). The Day of Atonement reminded the people of their need for forgiveness (vv. 26-32), and the Feast of Tabernacles was a reminder of their sojourn in the wilderness coming out of Egypt (vv. 33-43).

The feasts were a time of rejoicing, thanksgiving, fasting and forgiveness. All of them tied the people directly to the Lord and His goodness and provision. These feasts also separated the Israelites from the other nations, preserving their identity for God's redemptive purpose.←

JOB 15   Each of the friends had opportunity to speak once. Now they began a second round of conversations. As before, Eliphaz led the way. As he began, it sounded as though it had been difficult for him to wait his turn. He told Job he was a sinner and that what he said was nothing but hot air (vv. 1-5). In fact, Job was so far off base that it was hardly worth the time of a wise man to answer (v. 2).

Eliphaz said Job's own words condemned him – Job refused to acknowledge that his sin was the reason for his suffering. Eliphaz, in effect, asked Job if he had been in the presence of God to listen to God about these things (vv. 8-9). Job did indeed know something that his friends didn't know – God Himself!

Note Eliphaz's words in verses 14-16. He has completely missed the point of God's work in a person's life. It is true that in himself no person can be pure. But Job was pure. He wasn't sinless, and he himself understood this (14:16-17), but he knew the reality of forgiveness that brought purity before God. That was the work of grace! Further, does God trust anyone (vv. 15-16)? Of course! God was trusting Job with the most difficult of assignments. Eliphaz's concept of the work of God in human life missed the point.

Eliphaz further missed how God deals with sinful men in verses 17-35. His thesis is that sinful men will reap the fruit of their sinful actions in this life. This, of course, is ultimately true, but it is certainly not always true in the earthly lifetime of the sinner. Many sinful men do very well by this world's standards. Their judgment waits for the final judgment of all men (Rev 20:11-15)!

FEBRUARY 26

ACTS 10 →God, at this time, led the church into an entirely new era. Gentiles could be saved! Notice how God prepared Peter for this (vv. 9-16). This was a significant new understanding for Peter. The Lord repeated the message three times to emphasize its validity. Note, too, that Cornelius was a God-fearing man who prayed regularly and gave to those in need. As God was dealing with Peter, He also appeared to Cornelius, telling him to send for Peter (vv. 1-8).

Peter was in Joppa when the Lord's vision came to him, and he took believers from Joppa with him to see Cornelius (v. 23b). With the new understanding from the Lord, Peter understood that this was indeed what Jesus had been teaching (v. 36). Using that insight, Peter spoke simply about Jesus as the One who brings forgiveness of sin through faith in His name (vv. 34-43).

The Holy Spirit had prepared the way, for as Peter was still explaining the truth of Jesus as the Savior, the Holy Spirit was poured out upon the hearers, to the amazement of the believers who had come with Peter from Joppa (vv. 45-46). The evidence of the Holy Spirit was compelling, as the new converts spoke in tongues, convincing Peter and his companions that now God accepted the Gentiles.←

Thus, the way was open for all to come to Christ. Salvation was no longer exclusively for Jews. In Chapter 8 the Samaritans were included among the saved. The Samaritans, although not recognized by the observant Jew as orthodox, shared beliefs and heritage with the Jews (cf. 2 Kings 17:24ff.). In a sense, the Samaritans were a halfway point between the Jew and the Gentile. Now, Gentiles too had come into the kingdom. God's plan for redemption, open to the whole world, was on schedule. This fulfilled the promise to Abraham that through him (through Jesus who came through Abraham's progeny) the whole world would be blessed (Gen 12:3). That blessing of redemption was now open to all (cf. Rev 5:9-10).

LEVITICUS 24-25 As you read 24:10-16, consider the holiness of God's name. Do you believe the punishment was harsh for the young man who blasphemed God's Name? In today's society certainly it seems so. The Lord, however, was demonstrating His emphasis on the proper and careful use of His name. The Lord's prayer also emphasizes it (cf. Matt 6:9). As we rub shoulders with people in society, we can't regulate how they treat God's name, but *we do control how we treat God and His Name.*

→Here, as in Chapter 10 in the example of Nadab and Abihu, the Lord was teaching the people an important principle: Treat God's instructions with care and respect. Do the same moral principles apply to us in this age? Check Jesus' comments about the Old Testament in Matthew 5:17-19.←

In Chapter 25, follow the instructions about interpersonal relationships. Note the emphasis on fair dealing and how this relates to our respect for God (v. 17). Observe God's concern for the disadvantaged and the poor in the land (v. 35; cf. 24:22). How should this principle affect us? Note also that God gave His people the land as a trust, but it belonged to God (vv. 23-24). In later years, the people did not follow the principles of this chapter, and Isaiah spoke to this in Isaiah 5:8.

JOB 16   As Job answered Eliphaz, he too was exasperated (vv. 1-3). He pointed out that if the tables were turned, he would try to encourage them instead of condemning them (v. 5). With the underlying spiritual outlook that Job had, this is probably true – and is a model for us in our relationships with others.

Job, because he didn't understand what was happening, assumed that God had brought this misery (vv. 6-17). It was true, of course, that God allowed it to happen. But it was Satan who brought his misery.

☑Take note of Job's remarkable statement in verses 19-21, and compare this with 1 John 2:1-2. Job was in the dark about many things, but he did have an unusual understanding that God somehow was working on his behalf. This is nothing short of a statement of Jesus' work on behalf of the believer!⇦

FEBRUARY 27

ACTS 11   When the church in Jerusalem heard about the Gentiles, they criticized Peter for having anything to do with them (vv. 2-3). However, as Peter explained in detail what had happened, they too had to accept that God was extending membership in the kingdom to Gentiles. →Next, the church at Antioch saw Gentiles coming to Christ (vv. 19-21). This was the plan of the Lord but not necessarily the plan of the church. God Himself was making a significant statement to the Apostles and the church. Barnabas was sent from Jerusalem to encourage these new believers in the faith (vv. 22-23).←

Notice the word "encourage" as it related to Barnabas in the last sentence. From Antioch, Barnabas went to Tarsus to find Saul and bring him back to Antioch (vv. 25-26). There they ministered together for a year. Barnabas had a reputation as an encourager. It was Barnabas who stood on behalf of Saul in the church when Saul first came to Jerusalem (9:26-27). Now Barnabas involved Saul in ministry at Antioch. Later Barnabas and Paul would part ways in ministry because Barnabas wanted to give a young worker a second chance in ministry (15:36-41).

It is hard for us to grasp how significant the extension of the church to the Gentiles was for the Jewish Christians. From earliest childhood the Jews had been taught that outsiders (Gentiles) were not and could not be part of the kingdom. That Gentiles could experience the grace of God was revolutionary.

LEVITICUS 26-27   The dramatic language in Chapter 26 emphasizes the importance of obeying God's commands.   Verses 3-13 describe genuine abundance of life – which God promised to the people if they would follow His commands.   Verses 14-39 describe misery and famine in the land and in the soul – a warning of what would come if they ignored the Lord's commands.   Note that each time God says, "I will," it is either a promise of blessing for obedience or as a prediction of judgment for carelessness in following the Lord.   With this in mind, how could they (or we) choose not to pay attention to God?   Note that, in spite of all this, God in His mercy promised to preserve them for the sake of the covenant (vv. 44-45).

The principle in Chapter 27 is that promises to the Lord must be respected.   The statement in 27:28-29 refers not to things vowed to the Lord by an individual, but spoils of war devoted to destruction at the Lord's command.   Examples of this are found in Joshua 6:21 and 1 Samuel 15:2-3, when the Lord commanded the Israelites to kill all of the people from a certain area.   See also Deuteronomy 7:2.

JOB 17   ☑Job made a request in verse 3 that only God could fulfill. He asked that the Lord stand for him in his need. This is the only hope for any of us, and it is remarkable that Job had this insight.   Psalm 49 makes the same point: Our need is such that no man can ever make a payment to God for his load of debt (Ps 49:7-9).   With our insight from the New Testament, we see the answer (Rom 3:21-26; 5:6-8).   Although Job did not understand the method that God would use, his request and his faith take us directly to the Lord Jesus and the cross!⇐

FEBRUARY 28

ACTS 12   James, the brother of John, who had left his nets to follow Jesus, became the church's second martyr (v. 2; cf. Matt 4:21-22).   Peter was on the way to becoming the third, securely chained and guarded by the Roman government, until God released him from prison and from the guards who had him chained (vv. 4, 6-11).

It is interesting that as the church prayed for Peter (v. 5), God answered, but the church couldn't believe that Peter was at the door (v. 15)!   *In spite of the signs and miracles they had seen, they had trouble believing God would answer their prayer for Peter.* Does this remind you of the church today?

Herod's arrogance finally brought the judgment of God (v. 23). God's patience is long, but there comes a time of reckoning. Herod's cup of iniquity was full and had run over.

NUMBERS 1-2   In the census, the Levites were not counted with the rest of the nation (1:49). They were to be in charge of the tabernacle and all of its furnishings (vv. 50-53). Note that non-Levites were not allowed to come near the tabernacle as the Levites did in the course of their work (v. 51b).

Chapter 2 includes a prescribed order regarding how the Israelites camped around the tabernacle. The sons of Joseph – Ephraim and Manasseh – were counted as tribes (cf. Gen 48:5-6), and Joseph was represented through them. Levi was not counted as a tribe because that tribe belonged to the Lord (Num 3:5-13). Dropping Joseph and Levi and adding Ephraim and Manasseh made up the Twelve Tribes. In subsequent text we will see that even the order in which they moved from one place to another was outlined.

JOB 18   Bildad's speech to Job contained much truth but an entirely wrong application. First, Bildad castigated Job for his impertinence and arrogance in affirming (by implication) his righteousness (vv. 2-4). Then, however, he went on to point out that the *unrighteousness of the wicked* will be the trap that brings the wicked what they deserve (in the end, but not always obvious during life). The general truth of his speech is valid, but the application to Job was totally inappropriate. This should be a good lesson to each of us. *It is easy to take truth and apply it wrongly to someone else when we don't understand all of the circumstances.* When that happens, we are not representing the Lord! Caution!

March

Bible Reading Schedule
And Notes

☙

Let the word of Christ dwell in you richly...
Colossians 3:16a

1	Acts 13	Numbers 3-4	Job 19
2	Acts 14	Numbers 5-6	Job 20
3	Acts 15	Numbers 7-8	Job 21
4	Acts 16	Numbers 9-10	Job 22
5	Acts 17	Numbers 11-12	Job 23
6	Acts 18	Numbers 13-14	Job 24
7	Acts 19	Numbers 15-16	Job 25
8	Acts 20	Numbers 17-18	Job 26
9	Acts 21	Numbers 19-20	Job 27
10	Acts 22	Numbers 21-22	Job 28
11	Acts 23	Numbers 23-24	Job 29
12	Acts 24	Numbers 25-26	Job 30
13	Acts 25	Numbers 27-28	Job 31
14	Acts 26	Numbers 29-30	Job 32
15	Acts 27	Numbers 31-32	Job 33
16	Acts 28	Numbers 33-34	Job 34
17	Mark 1	Numbers 35-36	Job 35
18	Mark 2	Deuteronomy 1-2	Job 36
19	Mark 3	Deuteronomy 3-4	Job 37
20	Mark 4	Deuteronomy 5-6	Job 38
21	Mark 5	Deuteronomy 7-8	Job 39
22	Mark 6:1-29	Deuteronomy 9-10	Job 40
23	Mark 6:30-56	Deuteronomy 11-12	Job 41
24	Mark 7	Deuteronomy 13-14	Job 42
25	Mark 8:1-26	Deuteronomy 15-16	Psalm 42
26	Mark 8:27-38	Deuteronomy 17-18	Psalm 43
27	Mark 9:1-32	Deuteronomy 19-20	Psalm 44
28	Mark 9:33-50	Deuteronomy 21-22	Psalm 45
29	Mark 10	Deuteronomy 23-24	Psalm 46
30	Mark 11	Deuteronomy 25-26	Psalm 47
31	Mark 12	Deuteronomy 27-28	Psalm 48

MARCH 1

ACTS 13   →Chapters 13 and 14 give the account of the first missionary enterprise of the church. While the church at Antioch in Syria was worshipping, fasting, and praying, the Holy Spirit told it to set apart Paul and Barnabas for "the work to which I have called them." Note the pattern. Paul and Barnabas were set apart for ministry by the church under the instruction of the Holy Spirit (v. 2). The church sent them out after a commissioning service with fasting and prayer (v. 3). When they returned from duty, they reported to the same local church (14:27).←

In the synagogue at Pisidian Antioch, we find Paul's first recorded sermon.   ☑He addressed the Jews on the Sabbath, powerfully presenting Jesus as the fulfillment of the Old Testament prophecies of the coming Messiah (vv. 16-41).⇐ By the next Sabbath, when almost the entire city (of Jews) gathered to hear Paul and Barnabas, the Jewish leaders became jealous (vv. 44-45) – and, when the missionaries turned to ministering among the Gentiles (v. 46), God gave the harvest (v. 48). Compare verses 49-52 with Matthew 5:11-12 and John 15:20-21.

NUMBERS 3-4   The Levites were divided into three families: the Gershonites, the Kohathites, and the Merarites. Specific responsibilities were assigned to these family groupings when the tabernacle was moved. The Gershonites took responsibility for the "soft" parts of the tabernacle, such as the curtains and the coverings (3:21-26; 4:24-28). The Kohathites would carry the holy things for worship within the tabernacle, but only after Aaron and his sons (the priests) had covered or wrapped these things for travel (3:31-32; 4:4-20). The Merarites had charge of the tabernacle frame and the frames for the curtains of the surrounding courtyard (3:33-37; 4:31-33). Moses and Aaron were Kohathites and were responsible for the sanctuary (3:38b). The Gershonites and the Merarites had oxen and carts for moving (3:25-26, 36-37; cf. 7:3-9), but the Kohathites carried the implements of worship on poles (4:15).

JOB 19   Job felt crushed by the words of Bildad (vv. 2-3). If it were true that his trouble was because of his sin, he said, then it was his concern alone! He was tired of listening to these "friends."

Job's comments in verses 7-20 about the way God was treating him are his strongest to this point. Note how he assumed that the Lord had specifically touched his life to cause his misery. God had not answered him when he called. God had (from Job's perspective) blocked his way. Job assumed things that were not true. But God had not caused Job's suffering. Satan caused the suffering (with permission from the Lord). What was at stake, what Satan had questioned, was the integrity of God's work in Job's life. Job's trial would prove to Satan that suffering could not shake God's authentic work in the life of a person of faith.

What of Job's faith? Job was confident of forgiveness and resurrection (14:14-17). ☑He again affirmed this in verses 25-27. Here was a man who knew God! His hope was in a Redeemer who had not yet come, but note the truth about Jesus the Messiah in his statement. It is exciting to realize that we will stand with Job before the risen Lord in eternity!⇔ His remarkable wish in verses 23-24 was literally fulfilled with the printing press.

MARCH 2

ACTS 14   The pattern of the church's advance under the power of the Holy Spirit and the resulting opposition from religious leaders is repeated on this missionary journey. Signs and wonders were performed by the missionaries, but plots and dangers were hatched by the unbelievers (vv. 2-5). There was even the danger that they would be proclaimed gods (vv. 11-13). It is quite probable that after Paul was stoned, it was the Lord who raised him when the crowd had left him for dead (vv. 19-20). The crowd knew when someone was alive or dead – and it was their intention to leave him dead! Contrast the glad hearts of those who believed with the intransigence of the opposition. Follow the route of the journey on the map in your Bible.

NUMBERS 5-6   Note that confession and restitution were required for wrongs committed against another person. Further, a wrong against another was "unfaithfulness to the Lord" (5:5-7). Personal relationships are important in the company of believers.

The test for unfaithfulness in Chapter 5 seems strange to our ears. There is no recorded application of this regulation in the Bible. The text states that if the woman is guilty, the curse will become evident – God's hand would make it happen. By itself, under normal circumstances, there would be no untoward effect from drinking water with a little dust and ink added.

The vow of the Nazirite set a person apart for a specified period as an act of devotion to God (Ch. 6). This was still observed at the time of Jesus and the early church (cf. Acts 21:20-24).

JOB 20 Zophar's turn. Read Chapter 20 carefully, and note that all of Zophar's speech is generally true, but again, is incorrectly applied to Job. The reasoning is something like the following: Job is undergoing intense suffering. No one can get away with wrong without ultimately suffering the consequence (true, but it may be delayed until eternity). Since Job is suffering, it must be because of his sin; therefore, he is deluded and wrong. This, of course, was incorrect.

We may ask, "Do the righteous suffer without cause?" Of course. Job is an example! Conversely, do the unrighteous prosper? Many do (cf. Ps 73:3-12), but they ultimately pay the price for their sin (cf. Ps 73:27).

MARCH 3

ACTS 15 Acts 11 recounts the criticism of Peter for going to the home of uncircumcised men and eating with them (11:2-3). This was settled in the Jerusalem church after Peter and his companions explained how God had led them, and the church discussed it (11:18). The Holy Spirit cast the deciding vote (11:15-17). No one could argue that the Holy Spirit had not come to the Gentiles.

Now the question was whether the Gentile believers should be circumcised in observance of the law. This point of view was held by the Jewish Christians who had been Pharisees (vv. 1, 5). Interestingly, Paul had been a Pharisee but would have nothing to do with such a notion. Both Paul and Barnabas argued strongly that the regulation should not be enforced (vv. 2, 12).

→The issue was taken to the Jerusalem church by several members of the Antioch church (vv. 2b-4). Read carefully the reasoning on both sides of the argument as the issue was considered in Jerusalem (vv. 6-21). Notice what Peter said. James, who summed things up, was the half brother of Jesus. (James the brother of John had been killed, Acts 12:1-2.) James used the Old Testament Scriptures to demonstrate God's promise that Gentiles would be included in salvation (vv. 16-18). This was a momentous decision, for it reiterated that salvation came by faith and faith alone, through the grace of the Lord Jesus. *The Promise to Abraham of Genesis 12:3b – that "all peoples on earth will be blessed through you" was being fulfilled!* The whole church settled the question, and the letter to the other churches in the area communicated their decision. Perhaps because it was so important, brothers from Jerusalem were chosen to return to Antioch with those who had been sent to Jerusalem – making this critical conclusion official.←

NUMBERS 7-8   The final acts in preparation for tabernacle worship were the people's offerings, the dedication of the implements of worship, and the ordination of the Levites (Ch. 7, 8).

The Levites were the "tithe" who were given to God (8:16-18). Recall that every firstborn animal of the herds and the flocks belonged to God and was offered to God.   The Levites took the place of the firstborn among the people; they were not counted as one of the tribes. Although Levi was one of the twelve sons of Jacob, neither Levi nor Joseph was named as a tribe.   Instead, the Levites were set apart for the service of God, and the two sons of Joseph (Ephraim and Manasseh) replaced Levi and Joseph, making twelve tribes.

JOB   21   Job   eloquently   answered   Zophar   from   their   common experience. It is apparent that many have no care for God but do well in life (vv. 7-15). All they do seems to prosper. They have (in their opinion) no need for God (v. 15).

Job pointed out, however, that their prosperity is really not in their hands (v. 16). Our idea of justice cannot fathom God's ways (vv. 17-21). The Lord may allow them to finish their lives without bringing judgment upon them, but God will have His day (vv. 22-26). Often the evil man finishes out life well from a human point of view and has a large funeral (vv. 27-33).

Job's point: "Look around and see the real world! Don't bother me with your nonsense."   He told them they could not, based on their incorrect reasoning, draw conclusions about his condition.

MARCH 4

ACTS 16   Follow Paul and his companions on this second missionary journey on the map in your Bible (15:40-18:22). Paul and Silas met Timothy at Lystra (v. 1) and took him along.   Although Timothy's mother was a Jew, he had not been circumcised as an infant. Before they started out together, Paul had Timothy circumcised. He did this not because it was necessary as a Christian but to avoid questions from the Jewish people to whom they would be ministering.

→In relation to Acts 1:8, a significant event changed the group's plans. The Holy Spirit specifically led the outreach group to Europe (vv. 6-10, first evangelistic effort in Europe!).← Note also that at this point the writer (Luke) wrote in the first person (16:10), indicating that he had joined the group.

Philippi was the first major city they visited. Lydia came to know the Lord and opened her home to the group of workers. She and her household were baptized (vv. 14-15).   Note how opposition came in

Philippi. When Paul faced the demons in the slave girl, delivering her from the oppression, trouble erupted (vv. 16-21). God's power in liberating this young girl from evil eliminated her owner's ability to use this girl for financial gain. It is a sad commentary on that society that her owners were angry over the girl's liberation. In the world system, money is far more important than people (cf. Luke 8:34-37); in contrast, God counts people as important. Yet God used this to bring the gospel to those jailed with Paul and Silas, as well as the jailer! When the Lord delivered Paul and Silas from jail, the jailer and his family were converted (vv. 25-34).

NUMBERS 9-10   After the tabernacle had been completed and set up, the Lord instructed the Israelites to observe the Passover according to its regulations (vv. 1-3). A problem arose when some of the Israelites, because they were ceremonially unclean, could not observe the Passover (vv. 6-7). Remember that keeping the Passover was not an option – it was a command from the Lord. Moses came to the Lord with the problem, and there was a solution. Those who were unclean could observe the Passover one month later. Note, however, that if a person was simply negligent he would be excluded from the Israelites (v. 13).

One of the Israelites' great blessings was the visible presence of the Lord – both day and night (v. 15). The cloud represented God's visible leading for the entire assembly. When the cloud moved, they moved. When the cloud settled, they camped (vv. 17-23).

In Chapter 10, the nation prepared to move. Especially note verses 35-36. Moses prayed for God's blessing as they moved and prayed for God's benediction on them when they camped.

JOB 22   As Eliphaz began his third conversation with Job, it is apparent that his position has hardened. His entire communication with Job in this chapter is based on false premises. First, a person's righteousness is no benefit to God (vv. 2-3). Second, Job's misery was the result of his sin (vv. 4-11). Third, if only Job would repent and accept the truth of God, He would restore Job (vv. 21-30). Eliphaz spoke from man's logic and from limited knowledge.

MARCH 5

ACTS 17   Follow the missionary team on the map from Thessalonica to Berea to Athens. Recall that in Philippi they were asked to leave the city after being jailed. In Thessalonica when people were converted, there again was trouble. Consider the methods of the opposition as you read verse 5. It is at this point that the Christian has a very different set of rules (cf. 2 Cor 10:3-5). We *are* in conflict, but it is very important that we engage the enemy using the power of the Holy Spirit and not techniques that compromise integrity. Jesus spoke to this in Matthew 10:16-20. Stay under the umbrella of the authority of the Lord Jesus. Don't use the methods of the world. Understand the nature of the battle (Eph 6:10-12) and be properly equipped (Eph 6:13-18).

In Berea (vv. 10-15), the missionaries found a different attitude in the synagogue. People were eager to know the truth and willing to examine the Scriptures to see if what Paul and his companions were saying could be substantiated. As a result, many came to know Christ (v. 12). Opposition came, but note how it came to Berea (v. 13).

At Berea the team split. Silas and Timothy stayed at Berea, but Paul, who was the "lightning rod" of the group, left for Athens. In Athens, Paul spoke differently to the philosophers than he did in his presentation to the Jews in the synagogue, but he did not compromise the message. He spoke to them in language they understood, but he still presented Jesus, the need for repentance, and the fact of coming judgment.

NUMBERS 11-12   Twice in Chapter 11, once at Taberah, and once at Kibroth Hattaavah, grumbling resulted in judgment from God. *Principle: If we grumble about our circumstances, we really complain about God's care (v. 20b).* Read both of the accounts carefully. Note that if we insist on something we desire, God may grant the request (i.e., the meat); but it isn't His best for us, and we suffer (11:18-20, 31-34). How much better to be content with what the Lord gives us (1 Tim 6:6).

Numbers 11 illustrates an important reason to pay attention to the Old Testament: We find vivid examples of human behavior and illustrations of how God deals with people. These principles almost always apply to us today. Paul's comments about the Old Testament Scriptures in 1 Corinthians 10:1-13 bring this into focus. See also Romans 15:4. God has included these examples so that we will not fall into the same sinful behavior.

Even Miriam and Aaron were presumptuous in their complaint (12:1-2) – and God responded! Can you feel Miriam's shame? Humanly, their complaint had a ring of validity ("Has the Lord spoken only through Moses? Hasn't He also spoken through us?" 12:2). However, they missed the fact that *it was God who had placed Moses in his position.* In both instances – when the Israelites complained about their food (Ch. 11) and when Miriam and Aaron challenged Moses (Ch. 12) – the key was discontent with God's plans and/or provisions. Even though Moses had been the object of Miriam and Aaron's criticism, Moses prayed to the Lord for Miriam's healing (12:11-13).

<u>JOB 23</u>   In response to Eliphaz, Job's confidence in God is a marvelous expression of faith: He was confident if he could meet face to face with the Lord, he would be vindicated (vv. 4-7). He was assured, even though he could not find God, He had him in His sight and knew his heart (vv. 8-10). God knew his character and that his life had been godly (v. 11). Specifically, Job had kept God's commands and followed His Word (v. 12). In spite of this confidence, however, Job could not understand God's dealings with him, and it seemed that a thick darkness covered him (v. 17).

<u>MARCH 6</u>

<u>ACTS 18</u>   Paul's time in Athens and Corinth gives us insight into the broad nature of his ministry. In Athens he spoke to the philosophers on their own terms. In Corinth he engaged in personal evangelism with Aquila and Priscilla, who later were active in ministry (vv. 1-3). Were they believers when they met? We aren't told, but probably so. Paul used the Scriptures to bring powerful witness to the Jews (vv. 4-5). When they wouldn't listen, he turned to the Gentiles and effectively brought the gospel to them (v. 6). With the encouragement of the Lord, Paul stayed in Corinth eighteen months teaching the Word (vv. 9-11).

When intimidation didn't get rid of Paul, the opposition turned to the law (vv. 12-13). Does that sound familiar?

Follow the missionaries on the map as they moved back to Asia Minor and returned to home base in Antioch (Caesarea). After a period in their home church, they once again left (third missionary journey), visited a number of places in Asia Minor, encouraged believers, and boldly presented the gospel message.

<u>NUMBERS 13-14</u>   To explore the land that God had promised to Abraham and to the Israelites, twelve leaders were selected and sent out (13:3-16). The majority report upon return told of the good land but of the impossible difficulty in facing the inhabitants (13:26-33). *This report questioned God's promise to them as a nation* (Gen 12:7; Gen 15:16; Exod 6:6-8). Caleb and Joshua strongly disagreed (13:30; 14:6-9), but the people believed the pessimistic report.

The people's discontent amounted to rebellion against the leadership and ultimately against God (14:1-4). The people even considered stoning Caleb and Joshua for their report (14:10), but as they talked, a remarkable thing happened: The glory of the Lord became visible to the assembly (v. 10)! The Israelites were in great danger of God's judgment (vv. 10-12), but Moses acted as their advocate (vv. 13-19). The Lord didn't destroy the entire company, but the ten who brought the contemptuous and unbelieving report died immediately at

God's hand (vv. 36-38). There were, however, bitter and irrevocable consequences for the rebellion (vv. 20-35). They could not retrieve their former opportunity. In their presumption, they attempted to move ahead to take the land but were beaten back by the Amalekites and the Canaanites (vv. 41-45).

JOB 24   Job wished that God had a definite time to bring judgment on the ungodly (v. 1). Why, he asked, should the people who know God have to wait in vain (seemingly) for God to act, while others get away with gross injustice? From our vantage point, with the Scripture in hand, we know that God *has* set such a time, and there will indeed be such a day (Acts 17:31).

Follow Job's list of how men oppress others in defiance of God's law and get away with it (vv. 2-4), and the plight of the poor in society (Who cares? Who is their advocate? Where is God? vv. 5-12). Then note the wicked agendas of "the people of the night" who use darkness to cover their sinful acts (vv. 13-17). In reality, however, God does see them, knows their hearts and actions, and will deal with them in His own way (vv. 18-24).

Job has asked the right question in verse 1. He has correctly assessed society in verses 2-17. His conclusion that God does see and will indeed set things right in the end in verses 18-24 reveals Job's deep faith and trust in God.

MARCH 7

ACTS 19   Paul had previously been invited to teach in Ephesus (18:19-21), and now returned and spent more than two years teaching daily in a rented hall (vv. 8-10). Both at Corinth and at Ephesus, where Paul spent extended periods teaching, the churches had a significant number of Greek converts. While the Jewish converts had a significant background in the Scriptures, the Greeks did not, and Paul had to build foundations in the Word of God.

When some attempted to imitate Paul's dealing with demons, they had a rude lesson (vv. 13-16). As people learned about this, they respected the power of Jesus even more.

The gospel affected the Ephesian society in two significant ways. Those who had been involved in sorcery burned their valuable scrolls (vv. 18-19). Because the idol-makers lost income, it caused a riot in the city (vv. 23-31). Again, Paul was the "lightning rod," but the church had been well-established and was now ready to get along without him.

NUMBERS 15-16   Defiance against God (disregarding what we know to be God's express command or will) is addressed in 15:30-31. *It is sobering to realize that such deliberate sin is the same as blasphemy* – in reality, despising the Lord's word. An example follows in verses 32-36, when a man was stoned for disobeying the Lord's command regarding the Sabbath. Today we would question the severity of this punishment. Read again the principle at the beginning of this paragraph, and remember that verses 30-31 are God's revelation to us. Compare this incident with Hebrews 10:26-31. The New Testament makes the same point!

The account of the rebellion of Korah, Dathan, and Abiram (Ch. 16) is also sobering. These men were not the "rabble" who incited the people to grumble about the food God had provided in 11:4. These men, and those who joined them, were leaders in the community. Their argument is one that could be popular today. "Doesn't each person count? Why, Moses, do you set yourself above the rest of us? It isn't right!" *They failed to appreciate one vital fact: The Lord Himself had placed Moses in his position.* Follow the confrontation that occurred and the judgment that came from the Lord. Almost fifteen thousand died as a result of wrong thinking and defiance. Lesson: Don't rebel against God!

JOB 25   Bildad expressed truth in verses 2-3 but then drew incorrect conclusions from this truth. In response to Bildad's question in verse 4, note Job's logic in 23:11-12. In support of Job's statement, see Psalm 15, Isaiah 1:16-20, and Micah 6:8. When a person loves God and places faith in Him, his lifestyle shows it. God did have His people in the world who were serving Him, and Job was one of them!

Beyond Job's behavior and actions, however, was another work of God that Job seemed to understand, at least in part. He had spoken in confidence of the reality of his living Redeemer (19:25-27). Bildad was absolutely correct in stating that man, in himself, could not be truly righteous (v. 4). Job, however, stood in a long line of men and women who, through their faith, were righteous (Gen 15:6). Although Job didn't understand what method God would use, he did understand there was a Redeemer, there was a resurrection, and God would forgive his sins (14:17). He even understood he had an advocate before God who was speaking for him as an intercessor (16:18-21).

MARCH 8

ACTS 20   When Paul left Ephesus, he again crossed the Aegean Sea to Macedonia. He apparently traveled from Philippi to Greece and then retraced his steps, again visiting believers in the cities in Greece and Macedonia (vv. 1-3). He probably sailed back to Troas from Neapolis (16:11), just west of Philippi.

As Paul began his trip back to Jerusalem, he passed through Miletus, which was close to Ephesus. From there he called for the elders of the Ephesian church to meet him. Notice carefully his message to the elders of the church in 20:17-37. Here we get insight into the pastoral heart of Paul in his concern for the church. He believed that his ministry among them had ended and that the church would face assault from Satan both from outside (v. 29) and from within (v. 30). Jude saw the same thing in verse 4 of his short letter. Look carefully at Paul's charge to the elders (vv. 28-31). He called on them to watch their own lives and the lives of those whom God had put in their care.

NUMBERS 17-18   Following the disaster of the rebellion instigated by Korah, Dathan, and Abiram, the Lord graciously gave a sign to make clear whom He had chosen to lead them (Ch. 17). A leader from each tribe gave a staff to Moses. Aaron also gave a staff for the tribe of Levi. When the twelve staffs had been before the Lord in the Tent of the Testimony for a day, Aaron's staff had blossomed and produced almonds. This was kept as a reminder that God had chosen the priesthood from Aaron and his sons. The people were filled with awe and fear (vv. 12-13).

Chapter 18 outlines Aaron's duties before the Lord. Aaron carried heavy responsibility on behalf of the people. The tithes brought by the other tribes were to be the Levites' livelihood. Note verse 20: *God Himself was to be their inheritance!* The duties were heavy – but God was their compensation.

JOB 26   When Job replied to Bildad, he asked a significant question. Where did Bildad's reasoning come from? What spirit prompted these comments (vv. 1-4)? Turn back to 4:12-21 and review the spirit encounter that Eliphaz had. We must understand that our outlook reflects either that of God (the Spirit of God) or of the world (the spirit of Antichrist, 1 John 4:1-3). Job's question was very much to the point! Satan was doing everything in his power to confuse Job and turn his heart away from the Lord.

Follow Job's comments about God in 26:6-14. Job had a thorough understanding about God's power and sustaining hand. He even added that everything he could see of God's power was only the "outer fringe" of His works!

MARCH 9

ACTS 21   As Paul and the group traveled back to Jerusalem, they met with and encouraged believers along the way. In the account of the third missionary journey, especially as Paul was returning to

Jerusalem, he seemed to understand that a change was coming (20:22-23; 21:13). The Lord also was revealing this others (vv. 10-11). Paul's response indicates that he was ready for whatever he might face (v. 13).

When Paul arrived at Jerusalem, the leaders of the church worried about how the Jewish Christians who were still zealous for the law viewed Paul. The controversies about the law as it related to Gentile believers, settled by the church in Jerusalem (Ch. 15), were still close to the surface for the Jewish converts (vv. 20-21). Paul had a reputation regarding these issues, and it was for this reason that the leaders asked Paul to take some action to show that he was not hostile to the law (vv. 20-25).

Although Paul complied (v. 26), events moved very quickly toward his arrest. Emotions in the city were explosive. This would mark the beginning of a long legal process with the Jews and the Roman government – which God would use for His purposes (23:11).

NUMBERS 19-20   The death of Miriam is recorded in 20:1. The people again grumbled at Kadesh because there was no water (vv. 2-5). This, of course, was a genuine crisis – but one that God could solve if they asked. Instead, there was near mutiny as the people gathered in opposition to Moses and Aaron.

Moses received his instruction from the Lord, but as you read Moses' reply to the people, you can almost hear his exasperation (20:10). When Moses took the staff (as God had commanded), he made one variation in obedience: *He struck the rock instead of speaking to it.* Although the Lord responded by giving water to the people, Moses was severely reprimanded (v. 12). He would not be allowed to go with the people into the land God had promised to them. *Lesson: details of obedience are important!*

The Israelites wanted to pass through land belonging to the Edomites, and when Moses addressed the Edomite king, he spoke of the Israelites as "your brother Israel" (20:14). Recall that the Edomite nation grew from Esau, Jacob's brother, so there was a fraternal relation between the two nations (cf. Gen 36).

Aaron also shared in the punishment for disobedience (vv. 23-24). He died on Mount Hor after Moses had taken his priestly garments and put them on Eleazar.

JOB 27   Job continued his answer to Bildad. We are treated to insight into both Job's character and his understanding of what is important in life.

Note Job's character in verses 3-4. He said that whatever came to him, he would continue to acknowledge God! Read his description of the wicked in verses 8-23. They have no real hope for the future and can expect only disappointment in death.

MARCH 10

ACTS 22   As Paul was arrested, the mob was so violent that the soldiers had to carry him to safety (21:35-36). At Paul's request, the commander allowed Paul to address the crowd, which had gathered and been screaming for his death.

Paul identified himself as a zealous Jew, trained under Gamaliel (v. 3; cf. 5:34), and a persecutor of Christians until his encounter with Jesus. He told about his vision of Jesus on the way to Damascus to arrest Christians under the authority of the Jewish leaders (vv. 2-11). The crowd gave Paul a hearing until he told them that the Lord had told him he would preach to the Gentiles (v. 21) – and, at this, would hear no more. The Roman military was about to flog him when Paul identified himself as a Roman citizen, after which he received more civil treatment.

NUMBERS 21-22   The conquest of the nations now began. Arad was defeated (21:1-3), as was Sihon, king of Heshbon, and Og, king of Bashan (vv. 21-35).   These areas were east of the Jordan River. Remember the names Sihon and Og, as they will be mentioned several times in the Old Testament.

The bronze snake (vv. 4-9) stayed with the Israelites until the time of Hezekiah. It had become an object of worship for the people, and Hezekiah destroyed it (2 Kings 18:4).

News about the Israelites' military prowess reached the Moabite people and filled them with fear. This prompted Balak, king of Moab, to contact Balaam to curse the Israelites. The name of Balaam appears in literature from the Middle East at the time of these events, describing him as a well-known sorcerer. God spoke to Balaam, telling him not to go to Moab (22:12), but Balaam again questioned the Lord when another offer came with an envoy to get him. God allowed him to go but gave Balaam's donkey the ability to speak to him (vv. 28-30). The angel of the Lord then told Balaam to say only what the Lord wanted him to say (v. 35). Balaam was dealing with a spiritual power foreign to him and much more powerful than anything he had encountered.

JOB 28   Read Job's comments on the lengths that men will go to find treasures (28:1-11). They are willing – even putting their lives at risk – to look for mineral ore and precious stones in black and dangerous mines. In contrast, real wisdom is worth far more than money can buy (vv. 12-22). Only God can point man to wisdom (vv. 23-28). This truth, in a capsule, is in verse 28. Job knew God. Job had listened to the Lord and had obeyed Him!

MARCH 11

ACTS 23   Paul was brought before the Sanhedrin at the command of the Roman military (22:30). The Sanhedrin had previously questioned some of the Apostles (5:27-42). At that previous hearing, the Sanhedrin could not make the Apostles agree to stop speaking in the name of Jesus.

Paul exploited the religious differences between the two factions of the group – the Pharisees and the Sadducees (the resurrection, v. 6ff.). In truth, the resurrection of Jesus was a major fact that needed to be faced. This created so much confusion within the body that it was unable to continue. The Lord graciously encouraged Paul that He was in the events that were unfolding and that Paul would take his testimony to Rome (v. 11).

The Lord protected Paul's life when there was a conspiracy to kill him (vv. 12-15, 19ff.), and Paul was transferred to Caesarea.

NUMBERS 23-24   The account of Balak, king of Moab, and Balaam is intriguing. In spite of all that Balak did to get Balaam to curse the Israelites, he could not do so.

God, nevertheless, spoke through Balaam with prophecy. Read Balaam's four oracles, and see God's promise of blessing and of the future. ☑As Balaam looks far into the future in the vision that God gave him, he quotes God's promise to Abraham from Genesis 12:3a (24:9b). God's people *will* be blessed! The Messiah is clearly mentioned in 24:17-19. The "star" and the "scepter" are clear references to Jesus. The promise of redemption would come through God's people.⇦ It is amazing that God confirmed His promise of redemption through this pagan sorcerer!

JOB 29   Job longed for the days in which God's blessing on him was apparent (29:2-6). Take note of verse 4 where Job spoke of God's intimate friendship with him. Job knew God! He had been respected (vv. 7-11). The respect was earned for he clearly was kind and just to those in need (vv. 12-17). He had expected that this respect would continue into old age and that he would die in his own house (v. 18ff.). All of that seemed to be shattered because Job didn't understand his suffering. In fact, *he was in the service of the Lord God!*

MARCH 12

ACTS 24   An extended judicial process now began for Paul. Paul was as human as you or I, and he needed to remember often the word from the Lord recorded in 23:11. God was having His way in Paul's life and was standing beside him.

Felix was the governor in the area of Caesarea where Paul had been taken for his protection by the military. With the help of legal counsel, the Jewish leaders wasted no time in presenting their case against Paul. Their case, from what we gather from the text, contained no truth. Paul, acting in his own defense, made this point and went on to speak again about the resurrection (vv. 10-16). He also clearly stated that he was a believer in the Way, understood by both the Jews present and Felix to mean he believed in the risen Lord.

Felix was well-acquainted with the Way (v. 22). As this session concluded, the outcome seemed to depend upon what information the military commander would bring to the proceeding when he arrived (v. 22b).

Later, before both Felix and his wife Drusilla, Paul spoke about life and death, faith, and judgment (vv. 24-25). The message of Christ brought fear to the heart of Felix – but it was because Felix was hoping for a bribe that he talked with Paul often (v. 26). Felix was a man with a sterling opportunity to know the truth and respond, who not only turned away, but compromised the trust placed in him to see that justice was served.

NUMBERS 25-26   The sad episode in the history of the Israelites recorded in Chapter 25 brought the deaths of twenty-four thousand. The immorality was a result of a planned seduction by the Moabite women, a strategy undertaken on the advice of Balaam (Num 31:16). This was exactly what God had warned the people about (Exod 34:10-16). Decisive action by the leaders contained the crisis.

Later, when the Lord gave victory to the Israelites over the Moabites, Balaam was killed (cf. Num 31;1-18). Although he could speak only what the Lord told him, he still caused great trouble for the Israelites.

The Israelites were now close to Canaan, and enough time had passed so that the generation of men who had failed to take the good advice of Caleb and Joshua and move into the land forty years previously had died (26:63-65).

JOB 30   In Chapter 29 we read of Job's longing for the days before his affliction. In Chapter 30 we see his perspective on what he was facing.

The sons of men whom Job would not have hired to take care of his dogs were mocking him (vv. 1-15). With his life seeming to ebb away, his cries to God were unanswered (vv. 16-20). It seemed unfair to Job for he had, when he had the power to do so, helped the afflicted (vv. 24-31).

MARCH 13

ACTS 25   Festus followed Felix as governor: Follow the "behind the scenes" attempts to influence Festus in his conduct of Paul's judicial proceedings (vv. 2-3). Note also why the Jews wanted Paul transferred to Jerusalem (v. 3b). Nothing good was transpiring in the background. Add to that Festus's desire to win favor with the Jews (v. 9). Paul, understanding the implications of Festus's question about his willingness to go to Jerusalem, refused and appealed to Rome (vv. 10-11, Paul's right of appeal as a Roman citizen – the "Supreme Court" of the Romans).

Paul said he was willing to die if that is what he deserved. Under Roman law, the Jews did have the authority to execute a person who had desecrated the temple – and that is what they had accused him of doing (21:27-29). If they could get their hands on him, that is what they intended to do.

Enter King Agrippa and his wife, Bernice. As Festus told Agrippa about the case, he presented the facts as they related to the law and which seemed technical and rather insignificant (vv. 16-21). He implied that there was not much of a case – different from what was taking place in the background.

NUMBERS 27-28   The five daughters of Zelophehad brought a legal question to Moses about their family property (27:1-11). Since there were no brothers, this required a special ruling. The situation was unusual enough so that they are mentioned three times in Numbers and also in Joshua. The Lord's answer to Moses supported the five daughters' request that they receive their father's property. To this point, property had been handed down only to sons when their fathers died.

The Lord informed Moses he would die after he went up a mountain to view the land God was giving to the Israelites (27:12-14). Moses, understanding the needs of the people, asked God to appoint a suitable person to lead the Israelites (vv. 15-17). →In response, the Lord told Moses to commission Joshua for the responsibility (vv. 18-19). Joshua was then commissioned before Eleazar the priest and the entire people for the task ahead.←

A reminder of the offerings and the feasts was now given to the Israelites shortly before they went into the land that God had promised (Ch. 28-29).

JOB 31   Chapter 31 is a powerful testimony of Job's faithfulness. His correct behavior and relationships to others were based on his decision to please God (vv. 1-4). This resulted in morality (vv. 1, 9-12), honesty (vv. 5-8, 33-34), justice (vv. 13-15, 21-23), mercy (vv. 16-20, 29-30), generosity (v. 31), and hospitality (v. 32) in his life. He also refused to trust in his wealth (vv. 24-25) and kept his heart from idolatry (vv. 26-27). Job is an unusual example of a life that brought glory to the Lord.

MARCH 14

ACTS 26   Standing before both Festus and Agrippa, Paul simply but eloquently gave witness to both his own experience and the truth of the gospel. He emphasized that what had happened fulfilled the Promise of the Scriptures (vv. 6-7, 22b-23).   Once again, he emphasized the resurrection as central (v. 8); Christ was raised, and because He lives, forgiveness and life are now available to all (v. 23). Paul asserted his own faithfulness to his call from the Lord Jesus (vv. 19-20). He also challenged these two Roman officials to admit that they knew many of these things to be facts (vv. 24-27).

The irony is that when stripped of the special interests that held the proceedings in limbo (24:9, 26-27), they recognized Paul was innocent and could have gone free, apart from his appeal to Caesar (vv. 30-32).

NUMBERS 29-30   As you read the regulations about the offerings that the Israelites made during the year (Ch. 28-29), consider how their lives were structured around these observances. The sights and smells of these observances were built into the very fabric of their lives. They were never more than twelve hours away from the regular burnt offerings, and the special observances brought all of the people together in worship, contemplation, and rejoicing.

Regarding vows in Chapter 30, note that her father's concurrence was required in the case of an unmarried woman, and the husband's approval in the case of the married. The widowed or divorced woman did not have such a "safety net" and was responsible, without qualification, for her promises.

JOB 32   Job's three friends, Eliphaz, Bildad, and Zophar, are silent. They have done their best to convince Job of his sin as a reason for his suffering. To no avail.

Enter Elihu, a younger man who had been listening. Custom forbade him to speak until those more senior were silent. By his testimony, it was difficult for him to be silent. He was frustrated when the three friends had been unable to change Job and his convictions. His rather long discourse contained truth and error (the same problem that the three friends had).

Job never answered Elihu's speech. When Elihu was finished, it was the Lord's turn to speak. It is interesting that the Lord told the three friends to go to Job, who would sacrifice burnt offerings on their behalf, but did not mention Elihu. They were to ask Job to pray for them that they might receive forgiveness.

MARCH 15

ACTS 27   Two hundred seventy-six persons shared in the blessing of deliverance from the storm because of Paul (vv. 23-24, 37). As evidence of the respect in which Paul was held, notice how the military commander listened to Paul's advice when some of the crew attempted to escape from the ship (vv. 27-32). Note too, because of Paul, the prisoners on board were not killed and were allowed to escape from the ship (vv. 42-43). Lesson: stay close to the person who knows the Lord (if you yourself don't). The last statement is slightly "tongue in cheek," for God does not always deliver us from danger, but He does give us great blessing.

NUMBERS 31-32   On God's command, Israel defeated the Midianites. The Midianites and the Moabites together had recruited Balaam to curse the Israelites (22:4-7). Recall that it was the Moabite and Midianite women who seduced the men of Israel, bringing judgment from the Lord on Israel (25:1-2, 6). Balaam was from Midian and was killed at this time (31:8). This was one of the last battles on the east side of the Jordan River before the Israelites crossed into Canaan.

The original plan had been that all of the tribes would cross the Jordan River and occupy Canaan. However, the land on the east side of the Jordan was attractive and suitable for permanent living, so the Reubenites, the Gadites, and half the tribe of Manasseh proposed to stay on the east side of the Jordan and make their home there (32:1-5). Follow their proposal, the disagreement (vv. 6-15), and the acceptable solution (vv. 16-22).

JOB 33   Elihu believed that Job was inconsistent because he said he was innocent (v. 9) but also said the Lord considered Job His enemy (vv. 10-11). This was not true – but it appeared so to Job. What Job had longed for was the opportunity to speak to God and argue his case.

In the light of the above, follow Elihu's line of thought. God speaks to a person in several ways (vv. 14-18), encouraging him to turn from sin and pride and preserve his soul (v. 18). Sometimes God chastens a person through adversity, and God's angel stands by his side, bringing joy to the person who is restored (vv. 19-28). Mercy is extended with forgiveness. While all of this is true, it did not apply to Job!

Note that Elihu also saw the need for a ransom but did not speak of a redeemer as Job did. He said an angel might find a ransom for the sinner (vv. 23-24). ☑Who could this be but the Redeemer Savior, the Lord Jesus (cf. 16:19-21; 19:25-27)? Job was a step ahead of Elihu!⇦

MARCH 16

ACTS 28 Paul used every opportunity to witness to those outside the kingdom and to encourage believers. In Malta, after the shipwreck, he ministered to those who lived there (vv. 7-9). He was also encouraged by people from the Roman church, who met him along the way (v. 15). He preached while he awaited trial (v. 23). For two years he spoke to all who would listen (vv. 30-31; cf. Acts 23:11). We get some additional information in the letter he wrote to the Philippian church from Rome (Phil 1:12-14). The characteristic that stands out in Paul is that he was single-minded and faithful. May God help us to follow this example.

NUMBERS 33-34 As you read Chapter 33, with the record of all the places the Israelites went and the number of times they moved, think for a moment of what that entailed. The families repeatedly packed their things and walked from one place to another. Consider the manual labor involved in taking down and reassembling the tabernacle. Remember also the grumbling, the rebellion of the people, and God's judgment on the people. A great deal of history is compressed in these verses.

Note the graphic warnings to the Israelites in verses 50-56. You can almost feel the pain in the eyes and the sides. Read Judges 3:5-6.

The Lord was very specific about the boundaries of the land He was giving to the people (Ch. 34). He also specified the men who would supervise the division of the land. It was important that this division be fair to all.

JOB 34 Elihu continued his speech, and he fell into the same error as the other three friends. In 34:5-6 he quoted Job as claiming innocence and saying that God was withholding justice. In fact, this was true. God was allowing a situation that did not seem just but was doing so for His own reasons. Elihu accused Job of sin in verses 7-9 and argued that if Job were righteous, God would not allow such injustice (vv. 10-12).

The irony of Job's situation is obvious in verse 21. God had indeed seen every step of Job, and that was why He allowed Satan to test Job – because of his righteousness!

Elihu's statement about Job in verse 35 is partially wrong (Job *didn't* have perfect insight, but he did speak with insight about the mercy of God). Elihu's accusation against Job is entirely untrue (v. 37).

MARCH 17

MARK 1   Mark's gospel account moves rapidly, emphasizing the confrontation between God's authority and Satan's power. As you read the text, note how many times you see God's authority in healing, casting out demons, and in the ability to forgive sin, as well as His authority over nature and death. →The beginning of the book (vv. 1-3), immediately introduces the reader to how God moved specifically to make preparation for the ministry of Jesus. John, the son of Zechariah and Elizabeth, is identified as the one who would fulfill the prophecies of both Malachi (Mal 3:1) and Isaiah (Isa 40:3). His ministry was a call to repentance that would prepare those who responded for the message Jesus would bring.←

Jesus spoke of John the Baptist as being as great as any man born (Luke 7:28). John courageously preached and shared truth that people needed to prepare their hearts to hear what Jesus would say. His work was urgent and his lifestyle was simple. He spoke with God's authority and lived under it as well. His urgency and simplicity are examples for us today. If the people around us are lost, we must urgently share the truth of Christ, and a simple lifestyle will free us for the work of the kingdom.

The account of Jesus' early ministry begins in verse 14ff. He alerted His hearers that the kingdom (authority of God) was near and called His first disciples. People recognized that His teaching had authority (v. 22), and He commanded a demon to come out of a man in the synagogue (vv. 23-26). Note how Jesus healed His listeners (vv. 29-34, 40-42) and how the demons responded to Him (vv. 23-26, 34b).

Very early in His ministry, Jesus established the practice of taking time away from the crowds and even the disciples for solitary prayer (vv. 35-37). If Jesus needed this practice, certainly we do as well!

NUMBERS 35-36   The Levites did not inherit real estate as did the other tribes – a territory that they could call their own – so were allotted towns in which to live that were scattered throughout the land (Ch. 35). Six of these towns were also designated as cities of refuge, where a person who had unintentionally killed another person could go and live in safety. Note the limitations on using these cities as refuge (35:22-28). A person could not use them as refuge unless the death was truly unintentional. Three of these cities were on the east of the Jordan and three on the west.

The leaders of the tribe of Manasseh now anticipated a problem regarding their land if Zelophehad's daughters married outside their tribe (Ch. 36; cf. 27:1-11). Read about the problem and the solution. There was a deep sense of equity in dealing with practical problems of living.

JOB 35   Elihu's statement in 35:6-7 implies that whatever Job does it makes no difference to God (wrong). If Job lives righteously (v. 7), it adds nothing to God (wrong)! Although it is true that under some circumstances God does not listen to the plea of wicked men (vv. 12-13; Isa 59:1-2; Prov 1:24-28), God was listening to Job (v. 14).

MARCH 18

MARK 2   Jesus' ministry of compassion was uncommon, and He quickly was surrounded with the needy and the curious (vv. 1-2). Jesus had demonstrated His great understanding of the Scriptures (1:21-22), authority to cast out demons (1:23-28, authority over the spirit world), and the ability to heal (1:34, authority to intervene in the physical). ●Now, Jesus boldly proclaimed that He was the Son of God by forgiving sin. He authenticated His authority to forgive by publicly healing the paralytic man (vv. 3-12). In addition, Jesus declared that He was Lord of the Sabbath – which made Him equal to the God who had established the Sabbath (v. 28).● His actions brought praise to God from the people (v. 12) but raised critical eyebrows among the teachers of the law (vv. 6-7). Battle lines were being drawn!

DEUTERONOMY 1-2   Deuteronomy is a record of Moses' final instructions to the Israelites and the final events before the Israelites crossed the Jordan. The book is rich in spiritual interpretation of the events in the life of the nation. This book, more than the other books of Moses, compiles the laws that God gave, with appropriate warnings and instruction to the people. As you read the book, look for the principles God gives to govern life. Look for what makes a difference to God.

The book begins with a recap of parts of Exodus, Leviticus, and Numbers. Some details are added that enhance our understanding – especially about what the Lord told Moses. For instance, when the time was drawing near for the company to cross the Jordan, the Lord told Moses to take the kingdom of Sihon, king of Heshbon. →What is added here is that the Lord would use this to put terror of the Israelites in the hearts of the nations (2:24-25).←

Note Deuteronomy 1:16-18. Justice comes from God. Principles of justice are rooted in God's truth. It is subverted when untruths (lies) are interjected into the judicial process. This is as true today as it was when this was written.

JOB 36   Elihu continued. His idea of how God deals with men is a mechanistic plan in which God responds automatically to the behavior of men. Because of these wrong assumptions, his conclusions are flawed. Obviously, he does not understand the suffering of Job, and this adds to his wrong conclusions about Job.

Yet Elihu's understanding of God's power – even some natural laws that God has designed – is quite remarkable. He speaks of the greatness of God (vv. 22-26), the process of rainfall (vv. 27-28), God's provision of food for the peoples of the earth (v. 31), and God's power demonstrated in the thunder and lightning (vv. 32-33).

MARCH 19

MARK 3   Technical failure to keep the law of the Sabbath (as the religious leaders interpreted that law) was an area that Jesus' critics hoped to use against Him (v. 2). Read carefully how Jesus countered this criticism. In fact, Jesus did not lack respect for the Sabbath but used the day to do the work of the kingdom. This was such a huge issue with the Pharisees that after Jesus healed the man with the dysfunctional hand, they retreated to see how they might kill Jesus (v. 6).

The common people, however, were thrilled (vv. 7-8). They saw in Jesus a person who cared about them and was able (had the authority) to meet their needs. Testimony to His authentic authority came even from the evil spirits (v. 11).

Jesus then appointed the twelve disciples (vv. 13-19). In the remainder of the book, follow Jesus' ministry to these men. It was His plan that they should have His authority in doing kingdom work (vv. 14-15). In the months that Jesus had with them, He prepared them for their ministry after the resurrection. Each day they were together, Jesus used the time for on-the-job training! Notice that they started learning immediately, facing the question of whether Jesus' authority was from Satan or from the living God (vv. 20-30)! ꙨIn Mark, Jesus' claim to God's authority is implicit (vv. 23-27). In the parallel account in Matthew, Jesus' statement is even more direct and explicit (Matt 12:22-32). Jesus stated that with this demonstration of God's authority, the disciples were witnessing the coming of the kingdom! He clearly meant that He was the promised Messiah.Ꙩ

<u>DEUTERONOMY 3-4</u>   The Book of Deuteronomy was Moses' final review and instruction to the Israelites before they crossed the Jordan into Canaan. Although Moses wanted to cross the river with them into the land promised to the nation, he could not do so because of his sin when he struck the rock instead of speaking to it (Deut 3:23-29). It may well have been because he could not cross with them that he took the time to write these final instructions. They reveal a leader who loved the people and who wanted them to avoid the trouble that would come with sin. Because of this emphasis, it is one of the most provocative and helpful parts of the Bible.

Note the emphasis on obedience to God's commands in Chapter 4. Moses says *their very life depended upon attention to these commands* (4:1). Note also that these laws and commands were unique among the nations (v. 8). *Their obligation was to remember, to obey, and to teach their children to do the same (vv. 9-10).* This emphasis about obedience is not confined to the Old Testament: Jesus taught the same thing in Matthew 5:17-20 and John 14:21. Look also at 1 John 2:3-6.

Verses 32-40 are thrilling as they recount the greatness of God and His acts. *This is the God that we serve and whom we worship!* With this in mind, look especially at verses 39-40.

<u>JOB 37</u>   Follow Elihu's speech about the power of God. From 36:27 to the end of Chapter 37, he speaks about the majesty and power of the Lord – with no particular reference to Job.

There are lessons for us in Job's conversations with his friends. We have the advantage of insight into what God and Satan were doing in the background. As with Job, our responsibility is to bring glory to the Lord whatever our circumstances. Righteous living does not necessarily bring obvious great reward. Someone who is suffering is not necessarily outside of God's will. In fact, God may be using adversity for reasons unknown to us. *We must be careful not to draw conclusions about people unless their behavior sets them apart in sin. PRAY FOR THOSE IN NEED, AND STAND WITH THEM IN SUFFERING.* By so doing, we will be doing the work of God on their behalf, whatever the reason for their problems.

<u>MARCH 20</u>

<u>MARK 4</u>   Even for those who consider themselves firmly within the Christian community and faith, the Parable of the Sower is a challenge. Are there impediments to growth of faith and fruitfulness in your life? How do you respond to verse 19? Remember that those who are walking with the Lord <u>will</u> bear fruit (John 15:5). Look at Jesus' comment in verse 9.

Consider also the illustration of the light (vv. 21-23). If life is present, there will be light! Then look at verse 24. We are responsible for what is entrusted to us. The work is serious and compelling and is the responsibility of each Christian. The parables of the kingdom (the Growing Seed, the Mustard Seed) emphasize the work of God in the growth of the kingdom. God's work is revealed in the individual (where there is life there will be light, vv. 21-22) and in the growth of the kingdom (the seed, vv. 26-29, and the size of the tree, vv. 30-32). Where there is life, there is a synergism between the work of God and the response of the individual.

Even the disciples were amazed when Jesus stilled the storm that threatened them on the Sea of Galilee (vv. 35-41). They knew the power of the wind on this body of water, and Jesus' ability (authority over nature) not only impressed them, it terrified them (v. 41)!

DEUTERONOMY 5-6   Moses gave a formula for success in spiritual life at the beginning of Chapter 5. He called on the people to *hear* God's commands, to *learn* them, and to *obey* them (v. 1). Moses also emphasized that these commands were not from the dusty archives but were current and valid for all Israelites (vv. 2-4). *All of the above is still true today.*

Remember again God's awesome presence at Sinai, reviewed in verses 22-27. God bared His heart as He shared with Moses His desire for the people and their welfare (vv. 28-29). Listen to Moses' heart in verses 32-33. Life, prosperity, and length of days are tied to respect and obedience to the Lord.

The message of Chapter 6 is one of the high points in the Bible. Embedded in this chapter is God's good will for His people and what they must do to receive blessing from His hand. If they meet these conditions, the blessings will extend for generations (v. 2). The principles for living are so important that they must take highest priority and be at the very center of life (vv. 4-9). Moses told the people to do whatever was necessary to remember them. Make it a mind-set. Compare this with life in the Spirit as described in Romans 8:5. ☑Also compare 6:25 with Romans 3:21-26. Embedded in this verse is the promise of Jesus' atonement for believers, which brings the gift of righteousness. Faith is expressed in obedience. Why would – how could – anyone who did not truly believe obey so completely?⇦

JOB 38   The test was over. God's silence was ended, and the Lord spoke to Job. As God spoke (Ch. 38-41), His words sound harsh. Job himself, as he understood more about God's power and sovereignty, repented his questioning. (Look ahead to Job's response in 40:3-5 and 42:1-6.) It is clear, however, that Job passed the test. In spite of his questioning – in spite of his longing to face the Lord and argue his case – he maintained his trust in God and his commitment to righteousness.

As your read Chapter 38 today, follow the Lord's revelation to Job about His sovereign wisdom in creation and sustaining power in nature. The way the Lord asked Job a series of questions showed Job how little he really knew about the God whom he worshipped.

MARCH 21

MARK 5 In this chapter, focus on two things. Think about the terrible condition of the spirit-possessed man who lived among the tombs and what Jesus did for him. The man had no hope, no friends, only the darkness of evil within, surrounded by death and the prospect of hell. Then think about the way Jesus changed his life (v. 15). ⊃Note carefully Jesus' specific and absolute authority over the demons – their request that they be allowed to enter the swine. They knew they were dealing with the Son of God (v. 7), and Jesus did not dispute the assertion that He was indeed the Son of God.⊂

Second, give your attention to the family in crisis with a mortally ill girl (vv. 22-24, 35-43). Jesus responded to the urgent request of Jairus but arrived at their home "too late." Yet Jesus responded to their faith (v. 36), and the girl was restored to life. (Jesus really had been "on time.")

Consider the people in this chapter whose lives were forever changed because of their contact with Jesus. The work of the kingdom is serious and compelling! It belongs to each of us!

DEUTERONOMY 7-8   →The Lord specifically and carefully told the Israelites how to relate to the nations that were then living in Canaan (7:1-4). Refer again to what the Lord told Abraham about these people (Gen 15:16).   The sin of these nations was the reason for their destruction (Lev 18:24-25). There was real danger in Israel linking with any of these nations (v. 4). Israel's continued existence depended upon their separation from these pagan nations. Note how idols were to be handled! Look at the four verbs in 7:5: *BREAK DOWN, SMASH, CUT DOWN, AND BURN* – radical action for dangerous implements!←

In 7:17, look at the question, "How can we drive them [the nations] out?" Look at the answers in verses 18-26, and note each mention of "the Lord."

Chapter 8 has a message that we need, and need often. Don't forget God and what He has done in our lives (vv. 10-11). When things are going well, it is easy to forget (vv. 12-14) and feel self-sufficient (v. 17).

Fatal mistake! Live by every word from God's mouth (8:3b). Think about and remember verses 18-20.

JOB 39   As the Lord continued His questions to Job, He now turned to His wisdom in creating diversity in the animal world. From the mountain goat to the donkey to the ostrich to the horse, the Lord has built into each the characteristics of its species. Job was made to understand how broad are the concerns and the work of the Lord.

MARCH 22

MARK 6:1-29   It was time for the disciples to begin their ministry without Jesus' presence. In the months Jesus had with the disciples, He was preparing them for the time when He would no longer be with them. As they went out at Jesus' command, they had the opportunity to put into practice what they learned and witnessed in Jesus' ministry. Jesus' instructions for ministry are significant (vv. 8-11): no extra baggage, no maneuvering for accommodation, and no wasted time if the message was rejected. Their preaching called for repentance. Their ministry with the hurting was to heal disease and deliver from demon possession (vv. 12-13).

The account of John the Baptist's death demonstrates the depth of human sin. Herodias's grudge (vv. 17-19) found opportunity with Herod's foolish promise made in front of a crowd of guests (v. 23). Herod was caught in the pincers of a promise and his unwillingness to lose face by refusing to honor what he knew was an evil act.

DEUTERONOMY 9-10   The Lord said, "Set the record straight!" He was not driving the nations from Canaan because of the Israelites' righteousness (9:5) but because those nations had sinned (vv. 4-6; cf. Gen 15:16). The task of taking the land looked overwhelming to the people, but God encouraged them in what He had called them to do (vv. 1-3).

There is a point to remembering our mistakes. It is not to wallow in the dreary mire of the past but to remember the lessons learned (9:7-29). Wisdom comes by applying those lessons to our lives.

Give careful attention to Moses' words in 10:12-22. God's commands are not designed to restrict us but for our good (v. 13; cf. 1 John 5:3). Pay special attention to verses 17-19. GOD IS ABSOLUTELY EVEN-HANDED! Any rationalizations we may devise for our own sin will not "cut it." Note how the Lord cares for the disadvantaged. Their care should also be our agenda.

JOB 40   A key question for each one of us is in 40:8. Perhaps Job came close to this. We must watch our attitude – for when we grumble, we question God's goodness and plan in our lives and ministry. The grumbling of the children of Israel as they came out of Egypt demonstrates this principle (1 Cor 10:9-10).

Our exams (from the Lord) may be difficult and even painful. In the process, we must not question God's wisdom (He sees the whole picture) or His justice (which is based on the truth of His being and character). Remember that the daily quizzes and the exams we face prepare us for the "final" exam (2 Cor 5:10). We have this opportunity to study and prepare for the final!

MARCH 23

MARK 6:30-56   When the disciples returned from their independent ministry, Jesus suggested that they get apart by themselves. The disciples were anxious to tell Jesus all that had happened. They needed time together to reinforce what they had learned (vv. 30-31). But the crowds anticipated where they would go and were waiting for them (vv. 32-33).

Jesus is a model for us in responding to the disappointment of frustrated plans. He had compassion on the people (v. 34). He saw them for what they were spiritually – sheep without a shepherd. He met their needs, teaching them about the kingdom and healing those with disease (v. 34; cf. Luke 9:11). He eased their hunger by multiplying the meager resources at hand (vv. 38, 41-42). Jesus then sent the disciples to Bethsaida by boat, sent the crowd home, and went to a place alone to pray (vv. 45-46). Most of us can walk on "hard" water, but Jesus overtook them walking on "wet" water – and continued His ministry when they arrived on shore (vv. 53-56).

DEUTERONOMY 11-12   If some of Moses' injunctions to the people seem redundant, it is because they (and we) needed the reminders. With a fine pen, underline each of the verbs that call for action in Chapter 11. You will be impressed with the number of ways Moses encouraged the people to pay attention to the important things in life. The blessing of productive fields was tied to the people's obedience (vv. 13-15). If you watch for it, you will see this principle several times in the Old Testament. God's blessing or God's curse is the choice in verses 26-28. Who in his right mind would choose the latter?

Note again what God commands for the foreign gods that the people will encounter (12:2-3): *destroy completely (v. 2), break down their altars, smash their sacred stones, burn their Asherah poles, cut down the idols, wipe out their names (v. 3)*. Without question, radical action! Still good advice! Avoid anything that may lead you or your family in the wrong direction.

The emphasis upon one place of worship was to keep the people from being enticed by the worship practices of the nations around them (Ch. 12). It was vital that the Israelites never associate the worship of God with the sacrifices of the other nations.

JOB 41   Beginning with 40:15 and continuing through Chapter 41, the Lord led Job to consider great animals He has created. The animal described in Chapter 40 could be the rhinoceros, the elephant, or the hippopotamus. That in Chapter 41 is probably the crocodile. The Lord's point is that He can approach any of them, while Job in his humanity can do no such thing. And – if we cannot stand against the creatures of His creation, how will we stand against Him (41:10b-11)? The point seems to be that Job needed to be cautious in his conclusions. He wasn't knowledgeable enough to have all the answers nor could he control the creatures of nature.

MARCH 24

MARK 7   The questions of the Pharisees and teachers of the law about ceremonial hand-washing were the occasion for Jesus to address their inconsistency and hypocrisy. In verses 6-8, Jesus came to the heart of the matter. His words were a telling commentary on those who were supposed to be teachers and models of truth. What they said did not reflect their hearts, and they had abandoned the Word of God for tradition. In fact, their religious trappings and rationalizations (v. 9) twisted the truth (v. 13).

The lesson should not be lost to us. It is easy to settle into religious practices that do not address the Lord's concerns for our own lives and for the church and society. The way to stay "on track" is to keep allowing God's word to inform our minds and to *do* what we know to be His will.

Think of the irony: While those who knew the Scriptures refused to acknowledge Jesus, the foreign woman came to Him with deep faith (vv. 24-30).

DEUTERONOMY 13-14   Get the message: Follow God, revere God, obey God, serve God, hold fast to God (13:4). Take note that in the theocracy of Israel each person was responsible for guarding pure doctrine and worship (Ch. 13).

→The regulations in 14:1-21 were designed to separate the Israelites from the other nations. The reason was that they were a people holy to the Lord. They were His possession (v. 2). The Lord would use His people as the channel through which His Word would be preserved for the world, and through whom the Redeemer would come. For these reasons, it was vitally important that God's people not lose their identity (Rom 9:4-5).← Compare this with Titus 2:14. God also has a vitally important purpose for every believer today!

JOB 42   Job answered God with a new perspective. The Lord had revealed Himself in a new way to Job, and Job was humbled (vv. 1-6). In spite of his questions, how wonderful it was that Job had passed the test the Lord had given him.

God extended grace to Job's three friends. Their sacrifice at God's command and Job's prayer opened the way for their fellowship with the Lord. Although the text does not tell us, they were undoubtedly humbled in the end.

There are two strong lessons that we need to learn from the book of Job. First, we cannot know everything that God is doing in our lives. If, however, we are walking in the light as He is in the light (1 John 1:7), we can be secure in our relationship to God and should not question what comes. The picture is larger than our understanding. Our first responsibility is to bring glory to God. A second lesson, fully as important, is that *we cannot know what God is doing in another Christian person's life.* Unless someone is obviously disobedient, we should not try to assign reasons for what happens. Job's friends failed this test miserably! Let us not do so.

Underlying these events, God's power and honor were at stake. The Lord placed great trust in Job in allowing Satan to test him. When we have taken the name of Jesus as Savior, our behavior also reflects upon Him. Learn from the insight that this book gives, and live with care before the watching world!

MARCH 25

MARK 8:1-26   Jesus reached out to people with compassion in many ways. In this instance, it was to feed four thousand who had followed Him to hear His message in a place where no food was available (vv. 1-9). We focus correctly on the miraculous feeding of the people, but think also about what drove the people to follow the Lord to a remote place in the hot sunshine of the Near East. Jesus' message and authority were compelling! People risked hunger and thirst to hear this man who spoke a different message than their religious leaders. He spoke to the heart: the message of the kingdom that changed lives!

Times have changed since Jesus walked the earth, but the hunger for real answers and the needs of life are still present. When Jesus' message is presented in the right way, there is interest! We need the Lord's discernment to understand the people around us and the courage to reach out in compassion to meet needs and share Christ.

DEUTERONOMY 15-16   The canceling of debts and the freeing of servants guaranteed that none of the Israelites would become hopelessly in debt or be slaves for life (unless they chose to be, 15:16-17). Some people are naturally gifted in accumulating money – and others are naturally perpetually needy.   These regulations didn't prevent a person from earning and spending, but in an agricultural society, they did place natural limits on how much could be earned. Further, recall that it was impossible to accumulate land permanently by purchase (in an agricultural society, land is money and power) for the land belonged to the Lord (Lev 25:23), and any purchases were returned to the original holder in the Year of Jubilee (Lev 25).

Moses makes a remarkable statement in 15:4 when he says none of the people should be poor. The year for canceling debts and the Year of the Jubilee were "safety nets," but there was more. Moses told them to be generous to the needy (15:7-11), and he said God would bless such generosity (cf. Prov 14:31, 19:17).

PSALM 42   A recurring phrase or statement often indicates importance. With this in mind, note 42:5, 42:11, and 43:5. It seems clear that the writer was suffering emotional distress. But note that during his distress he was "thinking truth" by placing his hope in God. Further, he faced his emotions honestly (5b). Because his soul was downcast, he deliberately turned his thoughts to remember the Lord.

Look carefully at the psalmist's heart in verses 1-2. Here was an individual who was "following hard after God." Is it reasonable to expect that God will answer such a cry?

MARCH 26

MARK 8:27-38   ↪Jesus' conversation with the disciples at Caesarea Philippi (vv. 27-38) was significant, as it was the first time He led the disciples to understand His identity as the Messiah. His question to them about His identity prompted Peter's reply that He was the Christ. Jesus did nothing to change this perception and, in fact, reinforced it by stating that Peter's conviction was from the Father (Matt 16:17). With this foundation, Jesus builds two key areas of further knowledge for the disciples.

First, Jesus told them He would be rejected by the religious authorities, be killed, and be raised from the dead on the third day (v. 31). This led Peter to say this could not be so (v. 32). This was a perfectly logical statement – he expected the Messiah to become their national leader as the Scriptures had predicted. What Peter didn't understand was that this would occur at the second coming of Christ. The cross and redemption needed to come first. Jesus identified this shortcut to glory (Peter's statement) as from Satan (v. 33) and similar to the previous shortcut Satan offered to Jesus (Matt 4:8-9).

Second, Jesus told the disciples that discipleship meant self-denial and the cross. Think about these conditions. Understand that only the Messiah, the Son of God, could make such conditions. Are you willing? Are you willing to give up personal ambition and gain to follow Jesus? Are you willing to stand for Jesus without compromise (vv. 34-38)?☾

DEUTERONOMY 17-18   The rules about capital punishment are important to understand. Capital punishment was mandated for certain moral sins, such as worshipping false gods. The method of punishment was also important and specified. The witnesses to the moral dereliction were obligated to cast the first stones. Then the entire company was to participate in the stoning (17:7). The intent was to have a pure assembly.

Compare 17:8-13 with Matthew 23:1-3. Authority was vested in the priests, but at the time of Christ, the priests were flawed by their sin and because they ignored the intent of the law. As for their political leaders, any king selected for the Israelites was obligated to have the Scriptures before him and read them daily (vv. 18-20). Further, note the regulations regarding lifestyle of the king (vv. 16-20). As you read 17:17, look at 1 Kings 10:14-25 and 1 Kings 11:1-6. It is significant that five years after Solomon died, the gold and treasure that David and Solomon had accumulated were gone (2 Chron 12:2, 9).

A clear prohibition against involvement with the spirit world is outlined in 18:9-13. Human sacrifices were connected to the worship of spirits. Note the warning about failing to pay attention to God's prophets and the test for true prophets in Chapter 18. ☑Verse 15 contains the promise that God would raise up a prophet like Moses and that His (i.e., the Messiah's) message would be God's own message to the people. Anyone who does not listen to Him will be accountable to God. Peter linked this promise to the Lord Jesus, calling on his listeners to understand that Jesus is the Christ and to repent (Acts 3:17-23).⇦

PSALM 43   In many Hebrew manuscripts, Psalms 42 and 43 are one psalm. Note that verse 5 repeats 42:5 and 11. The theme of depression in Psalm 42 reappears in Psalm 43.

The psalmist is thinking truth in spite of his emotions. He reminds himself that God is his protector in verse 2 and pleads for God's light and truth for guidance in verse 3. Our need is the Word of God, just as it was for the writer. The truth guides us to the presence of God (vv. 3b, 4).

MARCH 27

MARK 9:1-32   ⮑When they accompanied Jesus to the mountain and witnessed the Transfiguration, Peter, James, and John had a preview of the glory of Christ; Jesus was so dazzling they were disoriented (v. 6). This further revelation of Jesus as the Christ followed the conversation about Jesus' identity (8:27-30). The voice of God affirmed that Jesus was indeed His Son (v. 7). Further, Jesus' conversation with Moses and Elijah was about His coming death in Jerusalem (v. 4; cf. Luke 9:31).

It is significant that Moses (representing the law) and Elijah (representing the prophets) met to talk with Jesus (cf. Luke 24:26-27). Heaven's schedule to bring salvation to the world was on the countdown! This would fulfill the Promise of redemption!⮐ Although the disciples were confused, after the resurrection they recognized this as a powerful affirmation of Jesus as the Christ, bringing atonement through His death.

Consider the destructive force of evil (vv. 14-32). This boy had been tormented by an evil spirit. Today this might be diagnosed as a seizure disorder – but Jesus cast out the demon that was the cause. Notice the link to power that Jesus identifies in verse 29.

DEUTERONOMY 19-20   By providing cities of refuge, God recognized that not every killing was planned or malicious. But because of possible abuse, the cities had to be carefully regulated. Our own law follows much of the standard. For instance, "malice aforethought" (v. 4) must be present for a conviction of first-degree murder. Note also the rules for witnesses in verses 15-21. The penalty for perjury was measured and appropriate (v. 19). The intent was justice and the restraint of evil (v. 20).

Chapter 20 gave instruction about trusting God in battle. God's hand is what decides the outcome (20:4). 2 Chronicles 20:1-30 gives an account of how God answered prayer in battle when the people trusted Him.

PSALM 44   We do not always understand God's dealings with us. God had clearly been with His people in the past (vv. 1-3), and although the psalmist had not put his hope in the false god of military might (vv. 5-7), yet it seemed that God had turned His back on His people (vv. 9-16).

But their difficulty was not because of sin or rebellion (vv. 17-18). In spite of appearances, the psalmist didn't forsake his trust in God. God is big enough to allow us to ask the difficult questions. We can still trust Him (v. 26)!

If we are suffering, we should consider whether there is some sin in our life to confess, for the Lord sometimes uses adversity to remind us of disobedience. If not, we need to trust that God knows what He is doing. He will not allow situations to come that we cannot handle (Exod 13:17; 1 Cor 10:13). Adversity is the opportunity to learn more about God's faithfulness and to bring glory to God.

Paul quotes verse 22 of this psalm in Romans 8:36. Suffering was common in New Testament times. Jesus stated that this would be normal for His followers (John 15:18-21). Acts 5:41-42 states that the Apostles rejoiced because they had been counted worthy to suffer disgrace for the sake of Jesus' name.

MARCH 28

MARK 9:33-50   Jesus turned conventional wisdom upside down as He spoke about personal greatness in verse 35. Society thinks power; Jesus spoke humbleness. Society thinks authority over others; Jesus spoke servanthood. It will take great care and courage in church relationships and church organizations to follow this teaching of Jesus.

Note carefully Jesus' teaching about children (vv. 36-37, 42). Children are without power and are at the stage in life where their convictions and character are being formed. They are often neglected or ignored. Jesus cares about each one! Kindness to a child is seen by Jesus (v. 37), but judgment will follow for the person who leads a child into sin (v. 42).

Jesus also calls for radical action to avoid sinful practice in our lives (vv. 43-48). He is not calling us to literally cut off limbs but is using this illustration to show how careful we must be to avoid wrong. Those who play with sin are in danger of hell.

DEUTERONOMY 21-22   In 21:1-9, the Lord emphasized the gravity of murder – even an unsolved murder. The town nearest to the slain person was to make atonement for the crime. Carrying out the ritual was a reminder of the value of life.

There were safeguards for the woman taken captive in battle (vv. 10-14) to prevent abuse. Equity is addressed in 21:15-17. It would have been easy, and probably tempting, to bypass the true first-born for the son of a more favored wife.

In 22:1-4, 8, note the protection of property and life. In verses 21, 22 and 24 the phrase, "You must purge the evil from Israel," occurs three times in relation to sexual sins.

PSALM 45 ☑Although this is prefaced as a wedding song, verses 2-7 are also messianic. Compare these verses with Revelation 19:11-16. Also reread Psalm 2:9. Note the agenda of the Messiah in verse 4. The Lord is concerned with truth, humility, and righteousness. Hebrews 1:8-9 quotes verses 6-7 and relates them specifically to the Lord Jesus as God's Son. His rule will be everlasting (v. 6) and characterized by justice (v. 6b). He loves righteousness and hates wickedness (v. 7), and God has set Him above all others (v. 7b). Compare these verses with Ephesians 1:20-23 and Hebrews 1:1-4.⇦

MARCH 29

MARK 10 Compare Jesus' comments on divorce (10:1-9) with Malachi 2:13-16 and Matthew 5:31-32. God believes in the commitment of marriage. God designed the marriage relationship as a permanent bond, which isn't appreciated by society today (vv. 6-9).

Jesus again affirmed the importance of children (vv. 13-16). Jesus had time for little children! He had time to hold them (9:36-37; 10:16). On this occasion Jesus used a child's nature to illustrate faith that saves. Verse 15 is instructive: A small child receives from parents the necessities and joys of life, but the child does not worry about where the next meal or pair of shoes will come from. He simply believes the parents will provide. The child doesn't understand the family budget or the "bottom line" of finance (cf. Matt 6:25-34). Are you consciously trusting God for your needs?

Jesus' conversation with the rich ruler illustrates how the world can get in the way of our relationship with Christ (vv. 17-31). This young man had carefully kept the conditions of the law – but something kept him from loving God totally or trusting Him fully. Think about Jesus' answer to him (v. 21), and note what Jesus told the disciples in verse 27. We need the power of God to see things as they really are. The "things" of life can cloud our thinking (cf. Matt 13:7, 22)!

➲When Jesus again told the disciples of His coming death and resurrection, He affirmed that He was God's Son, the promised Messiah (vv. 32-34).☾

James and John came to Jesus with an unusual request (vv. 35-37). Read the entire discussion, but note especially verses 43-45. The bottom line in the kingdom is servanthood, and Jesus is our example (v. 45).

Compare verses 38-39 with Acts 12:1-2. James became the church's second martyr within a very short time.

DEUTERONOMY 23-24   Deuteronomy 23:1-6 excludes certain people from the assembly. The Moabites and the Ammonites were descendants of Lot's daughter's sons, born after the destruction of Sodom and Gomorrah. Ruth, the widow of Mahlon and daughter-in-law of Naomi, was a Moabite who married Boaz and was the great-grandmother of David and in the direct line of Jesus (Ruth 4:13-17; Matt 1:5-6). The Edomites (vv. 7-8) were descendants of Esau.

As you read 24:1-4, refer to Matthew 5:31-32; 19:1-9. In Chapter 24, look for the moral imperatives that are given as rules for life. These are matters of justice, fairness, generosity, and mercy – and, as such, concern God!

PSALM 46   This psalm describes events at the end of the age, and this and the following psalm describe the reign of the Lord on the earth. Verse 1 gives us a principle to follow during times of trouble, especially during extraordinary events (cf. vv. 2-3). *God is our refuge, strength, and help in trouble. (AND TROUBLE WILL COME!)*

Compare 46:2-3 with Revelation 8:8. The language of verses 2-3, 6, 8 is quite similar to what John saw in Revelation during the outpouring of God's wrath on the earth at the judgment on the nations when Jesus comes again.

God's dwelling within His city is described in 46:4-5 (cf. Isa 65:17ff.; Rev 21:1-4). With regard to the river flowing from the city, compare Ezekiel 47:1-12, Joel 3:18, Zechariah 14:8, and Revelation 22:1-2.

☑A time of unprecedented peace under God's rule (Christ's millennial reign) is seen in 46:8-47:9. Micah 4:1-5 and Isaiah 2:1-5 also speak of this time of peace when God will reign. See also Isaiah 9:6-7; 11:1-9.⇦

MARCH 30

MARK 11   Read the account of the last week of Jesus' life with an open heart to again be reminded of God's love for us in redemption.

The last week began with the triumphal entry into Jerusalem. ☑When the people shouted praises to Jesus, they were clearly recognizing Him as the Messiah (vv. 9-10; cf. Ps 118:25-26). The reference to the coming kingdom of David voiced their expectation that Jesus would fulfill the Old Testament prophecies of a restored, earthly kingdom at that time. They didn't realize that the first advent would fulfill Isaiah 53, with Jesus taking their sins upon Himself – and the coming in power and glory would not be until the second advent.⇦

The authorities again raised the question of Jesus' authority (v. 28). Jesus sidestepped the question by, in turn, asking the chief priests a question (vv. 29-30). This placed the Jewish leaders in an impossible position. The common people were convinced that John the Baptist was legitimate. If John was legitimate then so was Jesus, because John had clearly stated that Jesus was the coming Messiah.

DEUTERONOMY 25-26   In the regulations given here, be alert for the underlying principle of justice. With reference to the flogging in verses 2-3, recall that Paul received thirty-nine lashes five times from the Jews (2 Cor 11:24). Paul quoted verse 4, applying the principle to mean that Christian workers should be compensated for their efforts (1 Cor 9:9-10). The regulation regarding the remarriage of a widow within the family was used in the marriage of Ruth and Boaz (25:5-10; cf. Ruth 4). The "kinsman redeemer," who was a closer relative than Boaz to Ruth's former husband Mahlon, refused to marry Ruth, and a sandal changed hands in the refusal. Ruth, a Moabite, then married Boaz, and their son was in the direct line of Jesus.

Chapter 26 addresses the Israelites' offerings to the Lord in relation to His goodness in delivering and providing for them. Each time they brought the firstfruits to the Lord, they were to orally declare God's blessing to them and remember God's mighty acts in bringing them to the land (vv. 12-13). Note that the tithes were to be directed to the Levites, the alien, the fatherless, and the widow. Note also the covenant relationship declared in verses 16-19.

PSALM 47   ☑This psalm is a natural extension of the previous psalm and praises the reign of the Lord and His triumph over the nations (in The Day of the Lord). As you contemplate these verses, think of the Lord on the throne and the nations assembling before Him (cf. Isa 2:1-5; Zech 14:16).⇦

MARCH 31

MARK 12   When Jesus told the Parable of the Tenants, all of the persons in the story were correctly identified by the religious leaders. They understood that they were portrayed as those who had rented the vineyard. They saw that Jesus was the son and that the owner was God. ⊃This was a declaration from Jesus that He was the Son of God, the Messiah. The reference to Psalm 118:22-23 confirmed Jesus' intention in the parable. Note their reaction in laying plans to arrest Him.C

The question to Jesus about the greatest commandment (v. 28), posed by one of the teachers of the law, is central for all time. Jesus' answer quoted Deuteronomy 6:4-5 and Leviticus 19:18. Neither was a direct quotation from the Ten Commandments. The citation from Deuteronomy followed a call for God's people to obey all the commands He had given to them. Loving God in this way actually sets us on the course of following the entire law – in the way God intended – for if we love God and keep His commands, it affects all of our relationships. The quotation from Leviticus 19:18 follows a number of rules that call for fair dealings with those around us.

As you read verses 41-44, evaluate your level of support for God's work. The Lord's evaluation of stewardship is different from ours.

DEUTERONOMY 27-28   Moses told the Israelites to build an altar on Mount Ebal after they had crossed the Jordan into Canaan (Ch 27). A ceremony was mandated to remind the whole people to obey the Lord and keep His commands as they began life in the land God had promised them. Half of the tribes were to stand on Mount Ebal and half on Mount Gerizim; those on Mount Ebal were to pronounce curses on the people if they didn't obey God, and those on Mount Gerizim were to pronounce the blessing that would come in obedience. This was done after they crossed the Jordan and recorded in Joshua 8.

Read the blessings and the curses in Chapters 27-28. Put yourself in the place of the listening people. The contrast between the blessings of obedience and the dire consequences of disobedience is dramatic. How could anyone choose not to obey? Yet we know from the subsequent text that they did disobey and did so repeatedly. The reason, of course, is that we are sinful – the tug to do wrong is real.

The Lord brought both the blessings and the curses. We know that blessing is from the Lord and thank Him for it. It is frightening, however, to think of how God may bring the consequences of sin to His people: disease (28:21-22a), poor weather and failed crops (vv. 22b-24), defeat by enemies (v. 25), frustrated plans for marriage (v. 30), and on and on.

God does not deal with us in a mechanical way: one obedient day, blessing; one misstep, disaster. God does, however, see our path and our every action. He is aware of the direction of our lives. He does discipline us as needed (Heb 12:4-12). The principle of Deuteronomy 28 is still valid for us. God's blessing belongs to those who walk in His paths.

PSALM 48   To the Jews, Jerusalem was the center of the world – the most beautiful of all places.   This is reflected here.   There are two principles that we should consider from this psalm.

First: The Lord's house has a place in our lives (vv. 9ff.).   We fellowship with God wherever we are.   We pray wherever we are.   But we enjoy corporate fellowship with God and God's people in our place of worship.   Jewish culture was built around the Word of God and corporate worship at the temple.   Christian culture is built upon the Word of God, the Holy Spirit in our lives, our common fellowship in Christ, and corporate worship.

Second: It is important that each generation pass its heritage on to its children (vv. 12-14).   In a world that tries to seduce our children, this will happen only with specific and directed effort.

April

Bible Reading Schedule
And Notes

☙

*Blessed are they...who walk according
to the law of the Lord. Psalm 119:1*

DISCOVERING THE BIBLE
READING SCHEDULE
APRIL

1	Mark 13	Deuteronomy 29-30	Psalm 49
2	Mark 14:1-42	Deuteronomy 31-32	Psalm 50
3	Mark 14:43-72	Deuteronomy 33-34	Psalm 51
4	Mark 15:1-20	Joshua 1-2	Psalm 52
5	Mark 15:21-47	Joshua 3-4	Psalm 53
6	Mark 16	Joshua 5-6	Psalm 54
7	Romans 1:1-17	Joshua 7-8	Psalm 55
8	Romans 1:18-32	Joshua 9-10	Psalm 56
9	Romans 2:1-16	Joshua 11-12	Psalm 57
10	Romans 2:17-29	Joshua 13-14	Psalm 58
11	Romans 3:1-20	Joshua 15-16	Psalm 59
12	Romans 3:21-31	Joshua 17-18	Psalm 60
13	Romans 4	Joshua 19-20	Psalm 61
14	Romans 5:1-11	Joshua 21-22	Psalm 62
15	Romans 5:12-21	Joshua 23-24	Psalm 63
16	Romans 6:1-14	Judges 1-2	Psalm 64
17	Romans 6:15-23	Judges 3-4	Psalm 65
18	Romans 7:1-13	Judges 5-6	Psalm 66
19	Romans 8:1-17	Judges 7-8	Psalm 67
20	Romans 7:14-25	Judges 9-10	Psalm 68
21	Romans 8:18-39	Judges 11-12	Psalm 69
22	Romans 9	Judges 13-14	Psalm 70
23	Romans 10	Judges 15-16	Psalm 71
24	Romans 11:1-10	Judges 17-18	Psalm 72
25	Romans 11:11-24	Judges 19	Psalm 73
26	Romans 11:25-36	Judges 20-21	Psalm 74
27	Romans 12:1-8	Ruth 1-2	Psalm 75
28	Romans 12:9-21	Ruth 3-4	Psalm 76
29	Romans 13	1 Samuel 1-2	Psalm 77
30	Romans 14	1 Samuel 3-4	Psalm 78

APRIL 1

MARK 13   Jesus spoke to the disciples about the end of the age when He would return in glory to take His own to be with Him and judge the nations for their sin (vv. 26-27).

The Bible tells us that these days before the coming of Christ will be difficult (cf. 2 Tim 3:1-5). ⊃As Jesus explained these matters to the disciples, it was obvious that He was speaking of Himself as God's Son, the one who would return in glory. It will be a time of great pressure to denounce faith in Jesus as God's Son (vv. 9-13; cf. Matt 24:12-13), and we will need discernment to understand the true from the counterfeit (vv. 5, 22-23). As you read this chapter, note that Jesus tells the disciples seven times to be on guard (using several expressions). The way to stay on guard is to know the Word of God, be obedient, and continue in prayer, asking the Lord for strength and discernment. We must not be complacent as we face a hostile and seductive world.⊂

DEUTERONOMY 29-30   At this time, just before Joshua was to become the leader, the Covenant was renewed, and Moses gave final warnings. Notice how important it was to follow completely all that the Lord had spoken. Note especially 29:18-21. Compare verse 18 with Hebrews 3:12-15; 12:15. Note the self-deception in verse 19, and consider that the dishonest action had consequences to others as well (v. 19b). Secret rebellion is grievous sin. Compare this with Hebrews 10:26ff.

Consider that God's dealings are open (vv. 22-23), predictable (vv. 24-29), and merciful (30:1-10). Some things we just won't understand, and this should not cause us problems (29:29). God has given everything we need to know in His word. Trust God in matters we don't understand.

What we need to know from God is not complicated or distant (30:11-14). It is in the Bible that we have in hand. As you read verses 15-20, are you motivated to pay closer attention to God's Word? Are you willing to love God, listen to God, hold fast to God, and understand that this is your life (v. 20)?

PSALM 49   The question addressed here is, "What shall I trust?" Although society urges us to trust in possessions, is this ever enough?

Look at the answers. *(1)* We can't pay enough to purchase our relationship with God (vv. 7-9). This is a remarkable "pearl" of theology in the Old Testament! Yet, so many people act as if they are able to protect their future with money or possessions. *(2)* We will all die (vv. 10-14). No exceptions (unless Jesus returns before we die). *(3)* We will take none of our accumulated wealth with us when we die (vv. 16-20). *(4)* ☑The believer will be redeemed by the Lord (v. 15). This anticipates the coming of the Savior-Redeemer – and is the answer to verses 7-9. What no man can do, Jesus will do!⇦

APRIL 2

<u>MARK 14:1-42</u>   Satan was active in both Judas and the chief priests as the Passover approached (vv. 10-11). The priests and teachers of the law had been looking for a way to kill Jesus (vv. 1-2). Their perceptions of the Old Testament law were terribly distorted, and their personal lives were a violation of truth (Matt 15:1-14). A lack of integrity is an open door for Satan. The same was true of Judas. This man had spent many months with Jesus, had participated in Jesus' ministry (he had gone with another disciple when the disciples were sent out two by two), and had listened to Jesus' teaching. Yet he was dishonest at the core (John 12:4-6). Dishonesty is a "foothold" that Satan can use (cf. Eph 4:27).

Peter was a strong person, determined not to disown Jesus (vv. 29, 31). Strong as he was, this was a spiritual battle in which Satan targeted Peter (Luke 22:31). It would have been better for Peter to depend less on his own resolve and more on the power of God.

A spiritual struggle was stirring in the heart of the Lord Jesus as He prayed in the garden (vv. 32-42). Jesus was human. He faced death, which He didn't deserve, with the burden of the sin of mankind. In contrast to Judas and Peter, Jesus agonized in prayer, receiving the strength and clarity of vision He needed for the trial ahead.

⮑There are a number of ways here that Jesus declares that He is the Messiah. When the woman anointed Jesus with perfume, His words could only mean that He was God's Son (vv. 6-9). Jesus' words to the disciples at the Passover dinner had the same thrust (vv. 22-25). Finally, Jesus' prayer in the garden makes sense only as Jesus understands His role as the Redeemer (vv. 35-36, 41).⮐ ☑Note also that Jesus used the quotation from Zechariah 13:7 (a messianic prophecy), applying it to Himself and to the scattering of the disciples when He would die on the cross (v. 27).⇦

<u>DEUTERONOMY 31-32</u>   The change of command from Moses to Joshua is recorded in Chapter 31. Moses encouraged the people to trust in God's faithfulness and give attention to His word (vv. 1-6, 9-13). He encouraged Joshua to be a courageous leader (vv. 7-8). The Lord,

knowing what was coming, predicted the disobedience of the people (vv. 16-18). Read Moses' last words to them (vv. 24-29).

In the poetic message given to Moses by the Lord, he tells of God's work in the world and especially in the lives of the Israelites (Ch. 32; cf. 31:9). Note the consequences of turning from God (v. 19ff.). Note the root of evil (v. 32a) and the result of drinking of Satan's wine (vv. 32-33). In contrast, the Word of God will protect God's child and will be his life (vv. 45-47).

PSALM 50   As you read this psalm, think about God's greatness. ☑God, in the person of His Son, the Messiah, will come in power to judge the people of the earth. Note His greatness in verses 1, 2, and 4 and His power in verse 3.   Compare verse 3 with Zephaniah 3:8, Malachi 4:1, and 2 Peter 3:10. Although there will be a great judgment, God's people need not fear (vv. 5-6). God has the authority to summon the whole earth, from the East to the West (v. 1). And He will judge the earth while protecting His own people (v. 5).⇦

It is important to see, however, that God was not talking to all of Israel as the "consecrated ones" in verse 5. Rather, He was referring to those Israelites who worshipped Him in truth. In verse 7 God makes a complaint to those who were counting on their sacrifices rather than the worship of the heart (cf. v. 23). It was perfectly possible to perform the *externals* of worship and still miss the blessing of fellowship with God (vv. 7-22). This should not be lost upon us! *The externals are only important when accompanied by a heart to love God.*

Compare God's word to the people in verses 14-15 and verse 23 with Hebrews 13:15-16.

APRIL 3

MARK 14:43-72   ↪When Jesus was arrested He said it was happening because the Scriptures must be fulfilled. The Messiah's coming and His redemptive mission were predicted in both the Law and the Prophets (v. 49; cf. Isa 53:5-7; Luke 24:25-27).↩ Follow Jesus into the hall of the Sanhedrin where He was initially tried.   The plan of the religious leaders was to execute Jesus (v. 55). To do this, there had to be a semblance of justice. Peter watched as the process went forward (v. 54).

False witnesses attempted to implicate Jesus, but they could not agree (v. 56). Some testified to what Jesus *had* said but got the story wrong, and this didn't hold up (vv. 57-59; cf. John 2:19). ↪Finally, when the high priest directly questioned Jesus, He stated that He was indeed the Christ (vv. 61-62). Notice Jesus' remark to the high priest that he (the high priest) would see Jesus in glory, and compare this with

Revelation 1:7. For His truthful statement, Jesus was condemned to death (cf. Isa 53:8)!☾

Learn from Peter's experience (vv. 66-72). In the battle we face (and we *are* in the battle), our own strength simply isn't enough.

DEUTERONOMY 33-34   The blessing of the tribes is reminiscent of Jacob's blessing on his twelve sons in Genesis 49 just before his death. Certainly Moses had been as a father to the company of Israel, and these were his last words to the people.   Note particularly the concluding words of verses 26-29. There is no one like the God of Israel. He cares for His people (v. 27a) and goes before them (v. 27b).

There is sadness as Moses could not go into Canaan.   Sin has a price, even if it is forgiven.   Yet read 34:10-12, and rejoice that God uses those who aren't perfect.   Note also God's provision for Joshua and the people in verse 9.

PSALM 51   Even though David was a man after God's own heart, there was a period after his adulterous relationship with Bathsheba when he was estranged from the Lord.   Psalm 51 is his confession to the Lord of his sin.   The psalm is instructive because it tells of the agony he felt when his sin was unresolved between him and God.

After Nathan the prophet confronted David with his sin, David poured out his heart in confession to the Lord (cf. 2 Sam 12:1-12). Psalm 32:3-4 also describes the suffering that unconfessed sin brings. In Psalm 51, it is clear that David is well aware of his deep heart need, and that only the Lord could cleanse him and restore fellowship.   Open confession (David wrote his confession) takes the fear and dishonesty (hiding the sin) away.   With nothing to hide and forgiveness from the Lord, relationships are restored, both spiritual and human.

☑David needed forgiveness.   He knew that sacrifices were not the answer (v. 16).   He asked God to cleanse him, wash him, and blot out his sin (vv. 7-8).   David had faith that God would indeed do this on his behalf, and although David did not understand the method God would use, embedded in this request is the promise of Jesus' sacrifice on his behalf.⇦

APRIL 4

MARK 15:1-20   The entire collective leadership (chief priests, elders, teachers of the law, and the whole Sanhedrin) decided to seek the death penalty for Jesus, and took Him to Pilate (v. 1).   ➲Here, in answer Pilate's direct question, Jesus declared who He was, but did not answer the accusations of the priests (vv. 2-3).☾ Pilate faced a dilemma.   There was no evidence to order His execution, but the Jewish religious leaders were insistent (v. 10a). To satisfy the Jews, and against his judgment, he agreed to Jesus' death (v. 15). Although Jesus told only the truth, and the death penalty was clearly improper, Jesus was sentenced to be crucified (cf. 14:49b). This was a dark day for justice, but was the culmination of God's wonderful plan to bring salvation to the world (cf. Zech 12:10; Acts 3:18; 1 Peter 2:24). Picture the Lord Jesus in the Judgment Hall, and compare the scene with Isaiah 53:7-8a.

JOSHUA 1-2   God spoke directly to Joshua with strong words of encouragement (1:1-9). Joshua was chosen by the Lord to lead the Israelites into Canaan, where they would live as God's chosen. Verses 7-9 are powerful promises to hold close to the heart and review often. As Joshua began his leadership under God's direction, notice how the people responded (vv. 16-18). A good beginning!

The Lord told the Israelites that He would make the Canaanites afraid of them (Deut 2:25). Word had traveled to Jericho about the deliverance from Egypt and the more recent defeat of Sihon and Og (2:10-11). Rahab was another foreign woman who became a predecessor of Jesus (cf. Matt 1:5). Rahab is also mentioned in the "Hall of Fame" of faith in Hebrews 11:31. (Note her words of faith in the living God in 2:11b.) In contrast to the previous spies (Num 13), these men who examined the land delivered a positive report (2:23-24).

PSALM 52   Have you ever viewed man's pride as a disgrace to God? This is stated in verse 1. Note further that man's violence (v. 2), lack of truth (v.3), and deceit (v .4) lead to judgment (v. 5). It is so easy to seek security in the wrong place (v. 7). True security comes from somewhere else (vv. 8-9). Think truth!

APRIL 5

MARK 15:21-47   →Place yourself at the crucifixion, and follow each person who was present. Jesus' death was God's plan to bring salvation to the world. Jesus was the Lamb of God, chosen to pay the price for sin (1 Peter 1:18-20).← Listen to the insults of those who passed by (vv. 29-30), and of the religious leaders (vv. 31-32). Unusual darkness covered the land as Jesus was dying (v. 33). The news spread that the temple curtain had torn from top to bottom at the time of His death (v. 38). Think of how the religious leaders and Pilate felt. They *must* have had inner fears about this illegal death. Think of Peter's sorrow (14:72). Finally, think of Judas, who had denied Jesus in a most hideous manner, perhaps already dead by his own hand and having already faced God (cf. Matt 27:1-5). Note the bold action of Joseph of Arimathea in asking for Jesus' body and then placing Jesus in a tomb (vv. 42-46). He was a member of the ruling council who had become a believer (Matt

27:57) and had not agreed with the council's conclusion to put Jesus to death (Luke 23:50-51).

JOSHUA 3-4   →To fulfill His promise to Abraham, God was bringing His people back to the land. After more than four hundred years, the family that went to Egypt returned as a powerful nation (cf. Gen 12:7; 15:13-16)! In much the same way as the Israelites crossed the Red Sea, they crossed the Jordan (and while the flow was at flood stage). This was a message to the Israelites (3:10-13) and also to the people of the surrounding country, as the water from the river backed up to allow the people to cross (3:15-16; 4:24). God was at work! God was also affirming Joshua as their leader (3:7; 4:14).←

A permanent memorial to the crossing, built of rocks from the bed of the river, was placed on the western side of the Jordan (4:2-3, 20-24).

PSALM 53   Verses 1-3 of this psalm are quoted in Romans 3. As you read these verses, note the description of the corrupt heart of the godless, regardless of how they may appear. It is incredible that God actually sees each person on this earth! He looks for those who are committed to Him (2 Chron 16:9) but also sees the violence, idolatry, and pride of the godless (vv. 1-4).

This psalm helps us understand how badly we miss the mark of God's righteousness. We tend to think some people are good even if they don't confess faith in God. But God sees and evaluates the heart. The whole world badly needs God's work in the heart!

☑Note David's plea that salvation for Israel would come out of Zion, and his anticipation that God would act on behalf of His people (v. 6). Salvation did come out of Zion, and God has acted and will act on behalf of His people through the Lord Jesus.⇦

APRIL 6

MARK 16   →The resurrection was (is) God's seal of approval upon the redemptive work of Jesus. Note the testimony of the angel in the tomb – the gracious message from the Lord of Life directly from the gravesite (v. 6). The resurrection of Jesus is the cornerstone of the Christian faith (1Cor 15:20-23); without the resurrection, we have no viable faith (1Cor 15:17-19). In fact, five hundred eyewitnesses attested to the resurrection (1Cor 15:5-6). It is the guarantee that Jesus is indeed the Son of God, Christ our Lord (Rom 1:4). His resurrection power is our power for the Christian life (Eph 1:19-20).

The three-day period which encompasses the death and resurrection of Jesus is the central point of history. Everything from the fall in the Garden of Eden led to this event. At the cross the eternal issues were settled and the way opened for us to come to Christ by faith. At the cross, Satan was defeated (Col 2:13-15). All history since the cross looks back to that event and forward to the return of Christ.←

JOSHUA 5-6   The covenant of circumcision was reinstituted before the conquest of Canaan (5:2-3). While camped on the west side of the Jordan before taking Jericho, the people celebrated the Passover and the next day ate the produce of the land. From that time, the supply of manna stopped (5:10-12)!

The Lord had a unique way of giving Jericho to the Israelites. Put yourself in the city behind the wall. Knowing what they did about the work of God for the Israelites, think how the inhabitants felt for seven days, while the army marched around the city(Josh 2:8-11). Consider also what this did for the Israelites! Note God's specific commands with regard to the people and the plunder (6:17-19; cf. Gen 15:16). Rahab and her family were the only survivors from the city – because she had faith (vv. 22-25; cf. Heb 11:31).

PSALM 54   The events that prompted this psalm are found in 1 Samuel 23. David was fleeing from Saul who was trying to kill him. The Ziphites, from the area where David was hiding, told Saul where he was, prompting Saul to come after him. In spite of the trouble he faced, see the "reality orientation" in verse 4 and David's praise in verses 6-7. God did, in fact, deliver David from the evil plans of Saul.

APRIL 7

ROMANS 1:1-17   The book of Romans is unique. When Paul wrote it, he had not visited the city. Other epistles were directed to cities or regions that had already had the benefit of Paul's teaching. Thus, when he wrote to the Roman church, he took pains to lay the same foundations in writing that he had done in person at the other locations. This benefits us today, because nowhere else in the Bible is there such a logical presentation of the theology of salvation and the Christian life.

Verses 1-17 are an introduction. Paul states that he was set apart for the gospel (v. 1). This gospel is about Jesus who was a descendant of David (vv. 2-3, genuinely human), but certified (proven) to be the Son of God by the resurrection (v. 4, truly God). Now note that each believer is called on the basis of the above facts (vv. 5-6). We are called to obedience – and we are called to be saints (v. 7).

Each of us should memorize verses 16-17. The gospel, reveals God's righteousness. This will come up again in the book and is a key to understanding salvation. Righteousness is what each of us needs to be able to stand before God without incurring His wrath. Note that this righteousness comes to us by faith, and remember that Abraham is our example (Gen 15:6).

JOSHUA 7-8   From the heights of jubilation to the depths of despair! What confusion when the Israelites were defeated by the relatively small kingdom-city of Ai. Joshua turned to God to ask the reason for the defeat (7:6-9).

As God answered in verses 10-12, listen to His tone. This answer is instructive. Remember that one man sinned. But God spoke of sinners in the plural. What individuals do affects the entire body. God said the Israelites had *violated* the Covenant, *taken, stolen,* and put the stolen items in the camp. *No less than five verbs describe the sin!* And remember that thirty-six men died (7:4-5). This was a high price to pay for the sin of one man. Follow the resolution of the problem and the conquest of Ai. God was not dead and was not to be trifled with.

Now the Israelites were at the place mentioned in Deuteronomy 27, and Joshua carried out the Lord's instructions by reading the blessings and the curses on Mount Ebal and Mount Gerizim (8:30-35). As they entered the land that had been promised, this recitation was a strong reminder that obedience to the Lord was the key to their well-being.

PSALM 55   We live in a world of strife! David struggled with this. The ugly reality of the battle is obvious in verses 9-11. Violence, strife, malice, and abuse are about in the city. Is this real? Of course! We see this in our society today! These destructive forces (v. 11) are the work of Satan.

The most difficult thing for a believer to face is when the trouble is the result of a friend's seeming disloyalty (vv. 12-14, vv. 20-21). The answer to these difficult times is found not in human relationships but in God (vv. 16-19). Rejoice in the promise of verse 22, and look at the conscious, intelligent, purposeful decision of the writer in verse 23b.

APRIL 8

ROMANS 1:18-32   We learn here a great deal about the liberty that God has given to men, the effects of sin, and God's response to man's rebellion.

It is clear that although there is enough information in nature to understand that there is a God, many ignore this evidence and go their own way (vv. 19-21). God has allowed these people to choose their own way, but by doing so they stand under His wrath (v. 18); by turning away from God, they cloud their ability to discern right from wrong (v. 21). In their misguided liberty, they have foolishly chosen to worship things God has created, instead of the living God (vv. 22-23).

There have been dire consequences to the rebellion. Three times the text tells us that "God gave them over…" (vv. 24, 26, 28). Read the completion of the sentences in verses 24, 26, and 28. God has allowed sinful practices to run their course in the lives of those who have chosen wrong, and their lives have become more and more depraved. As human beings we have liberty, but if we use that liberty in the wrong way, the consequences are horrible.

Not only is this a dreadful state during life, but sinners will suffer God's wrath in eternal judgment (v. 18). Jesus described this judgment as conscious, eternal punishment (Matt 25:46; Mark 9:48).

JOSHUA 9-10   Panic seized the Canaanites. Notice what the Gibeonites said in 9:9. It was not the army or Joshua that they feared, but the hand of God (vv. 14-15; cf. Exod 23:31-33; 34:12-16; Deut 20:16-18). God had been very specific in His instruction to the Israelites regarding the people of Canaan. Their error was in not asking the Lord for guidance with regard to these people (v. 14b). The Gibeonites threw themselves on the mercy of the Israelites in the light of the promises the Israelites had made to them (vv. 22-27). It is significant that the leadership insisted on honoring the treaty because it was made in the name of the Lord (vv. 18b-21).

The major campaign to secure the land west of the Jordan River now began (Ch. 10). The Gibeonites were considered traitors by the other city kingdoms and were attacked by the surrounding armies. Since the Gibeonites had come under the protection of the Israelites, they called on the Israelites to defend them. Note 10:9-11: It was God's victory! And in the first major battle of the campaign, God graciously gave an additional sign of His hand by delaying the sun's movement for about a full day (vv. 12-14). Again note the glory given to God in 10:42. It was the Lord God who fought for Israel.

PSALM 56   The events that prompted this psalm may be those recorded in 1 Samuel 21:10-15. Note the duplicity of those who were after David (v. 5), perhaps his fellow countrymen who drove him away into the camp of the Philistines. Look at David's solution in verses 3-4, 10-11. Verse 13 is a picture of redemption – deliverance from death to walk in the light (cf. Col 1:13).

APRIL 9

ROMANS 2:1-16 In Chapter 1, Paul addressed the danger to those who denied God (vv. 18-32). In this portion, Paul speaks about the religious person. God evaluates people fairly. Many who are "religious" commit the same sins as those described in 1:18-32, and God will deal with them accordingly (vv. 6, 11). It is not religious profession that God recognizes, but rather spiritual life (faith) *as evidenced by a changed life* (vv. 7, 13).

Jesus warned that many who assume they have a relationship with Him will be bitterly disappointed (Matt 7:21-23). He said that those who have done the will of the Father will enter the kingdom of heaven. Compare Matthew 7:21-23 with Romans 2:10, 13. In Jesus' words, obedience to the Father's will evidences a true relationship with God. Paul said the evidence is obedience to the law (v. 13), and that is exactly what Jesus said. The law is the standard of God's will (Matt 7:21).

Does this mean we are saved by keeping the law and living by a set of rules? We will see that this is not the case. Yet, it is clear from what Jesus and Paul said that following God's way is indeed important. Living with care to obey God is the evidence that you believe in and honor God and His Son the Lord Jesus.

The key lies in the verses just before Matthew 7:21-23. In verses 17-20, Jesus points out that a good tree bears good fruit and a bad tree bad fruit. It is a law of nature, and it is a spiritual law. The root determines the fruit. The evidence of spiritual life is concern for the Father's will, the laws of God. We will see as the book of Romans unfolds that the new life through faith brings with it a new outlook, characterized by concerns that match those of God. The result is that doing the Father's will (Matt 7:21) and respecting God's law (Rom 2:13) will come naturally. It is the work of God through the Holy Spirit in conjunction with our own will. It is the evidence of new life in Christ.

As sinful humans, it is easy to rationalize our disregard God's commands. It is this that today's reading warns us about. We must be careful not to condemn those who reject God's laws while covering the same disregard in our own lives with religious sham (1:18-32)! It will be fatal!

JOSHUA 11-12   Joshua has been recognized as a great military strategist. During today's assigned reading, underline in your Bible each reference to the Lord's hand in the outcome of the battles. Understand the key to blessing in 11:15 – Joshua carried out all that the Lord had commanded him to do. Note that God had His hand in the nations' decision to fight the Israelites (11:20). Even the cooperative effort of several armies was no match for Joshua and the Lord (11:1-9).

It was also God's plan to give the cities, with all their buildings and possessions, to the Israelites (cf. Deut 6:10-11). This was fulfilled as they took the territory (11:13-14).

PSALM 57   The preface to this psalm relates it to the occasion when David hid from Saul in a cave, recorded in 1 Samuel 24. While David and his men were hiding in the cave, Saul came into the cave alone. It would have been easy for David to kill Saul, and with the king dead, David could have become king. He had the popular support among the people to do just that.

David, however, would not kill Saul. It was a measure of his character and his dependence upon God that he felt strongly that since God had made Saul king, God should remove him before David would assume the throne. Even at this time David knew he would become king of Israel.

With this in mind, read Psalm 57. Hear his cry for mercy in verse 1. David understood that his safety was not in killing Saul but in "the shadow of your wings." It was in God Himself that David took refuge. In the light of David's knowledge that God would make him king, read his words in verse 2. God would fulfill His purpose in David's life. This is working faith – faith when the reality of death was present!

Verses 5 and 11 are identical. Remember that repetition emphasizes truth. As we sing the praise song with these words, remember the danger that David faced. Note the reality of the danger in verse 6, and his mind-set in verse 7.

APRIL 10

ROMANS 2:17-29   In this section Paul is speaking not to the religious person in general, but to the practicing Jew. Paul knew the territory; he had been there! He knew one could say all the right things (vv. 18, 20, 21) and even teach others, while missing the grace of God. Everything that the first 16 verses of the chapter said about the religious person is here applied to the religious Jew. Review what Jesus said (Matt 5:20). The "righteousness" of the Pharisees and the teachers of the law was inadequate!

Granted, some of the examples in verses 17-24 may not have been acted out overtly. The intent and longing of the heart is enough (Matt 5:28). God sees us for what we really are. Rationalizations will not be enough on that last day (Matt 7:22-23). If hypocrisy has been a way of life, that will be apparent. Thank God that there is a different way – the way of new life by faith in Jesus (Rom 3:22). Each of us needs to be sure we have chosen the path that God has provided and not the self-help method of rules and false hope.

JOSHUA 13-14   Recall that the boundaries of the nation were set while Moses was still alive (Num 34). God now told Joshua how to divide the land. These boundaries would mark the territory of the tribes for the next several hundred years.

Several years had elapsed, as Joshua was now elderly (13:1). The Lord reminded Joshua that there were still large areas to acquire – land that God had designated for them. After the initial military push, the Israelites apparently relaxed their efforts. One of the nations that should have been dispossessed was that of the Philistines (v. 2). Remember this, and see how many times they are a problem to the Israelites in the years that followed.

Caleb and Joshua were the only ones who brought back a good report when Moses had sent representatives of the tribes to explore the land (Num 13). Thus, Caleb and Joshua were the only men of fighting age, when that exploratory expedition went out, who came into the land! Look at the testimony of Caleb in 14:6-12. Hebron had been promised to him, and he said he would drive out, with the Lord's help, its inhabitants. And he did (15:14-15). Even at age eighty-five he was a vigorous and courageous man. Hebron was the town where Abraham lived when he and Lot parted (Gen 13:18) and was the city from which King David ruled for seven years before going to Jerusalem nearly one thousand years after Abraham (2 Sam 5:1-5)! It still exists today!

PSALM 58   The preface of this psalm places the events in the same context as Psalm 57 and 59. Thus we can understand it in the light of the unjust pursuit of David by Saul. This explains verses 1-2, where David sees injustice in the rulers (the intent of Saul to pursue him and kill him).

In this short passage, David uses eight "word pictures" to illustrate the futility of opposing God (even a snake charmer). With these pictures in mind, note his conclusion in verse 11. There is a God in heaven who judges the earth and those in it! God is alive in spite of what appears to be overwhelming injustice supported by political systems.

APRIL 11

ROMANS 3:1-20   After the comments about religious Jews in 2:17-29, some might be tempted to ask if there was anything to be thankful about in being a Jew. There was indeed advantage (vv. 1-2). They were the channel through which the words of God had come to the world – and they had the Word of God in their hands. God also used His people to bring the Savior to the world (Rom 9:4-5). Many of them were individuals of faith and true spiritual life as they responded to God's truth.

Read carefully verses 9-18. Here is the summary of the human condition. *All* persons fall under God's condemnation. No one is good enough. Man from within (vv. 10-12a) and in his deeds (vv. 12b-18) is a failure.

Verses 19-20 are an important transition. They speak to the person who is trying to be good (as measured by the law), pointing out that, if this is how we hope to attain righteousness, it will fail! Man in his own effort is helpless.

Thus, at verse 20, Paul has established that the ungodly, the religious, the Gentile, the Jew, and the person trying to be good are all under God's condemnation. If the book were to stop at this point, there would be no hope. Thank God, He has provided the way!

JOSHUA 15-16   In spite of the great victories God had given and the land that had been occupied, some Canaanite communities remained (15:63; 16:10).

PSALM 59   This psalm also was written as Saul pursued David. Read David's prayer for God's protection and deliverance (vv. 1-2). In verses 3-5, David describes his life among individuals of evil intent. He clearly sees his need for God's protection.

Verses 6 and 14 contain a graphic description of violent men. Their actions and attitudes are an affront to God (v. 7).   Read David's conclusion in verses 16-17.

APRIL 12

ROMANS 3:21-31   To this point in Romans, Paul has logically demonstrated that *all* are sinners before God and stand under His judgment. Man, in every effort he can devise, comes up short! Now, beginning with verse 21, Paul outlines the radically different plan of God – not based upon man's impotent efforts but upon God's own solution: the death of His Son as a sacrifice for the sins of all men.

The section begins by speaking of a righteousness from God for men (v. 21). Righteousness is necessary for fellowship with a righteous and holy God. This righteousness is a gift from God, given in response to faith (v. 22) and because Jesus fully paid for our sin on the cross (v. 25). This does what we can never do; each of us, without exception, is a sinner (v. 23)! When Jesus became the atoning sacrifice for our sin, it opened the way for genuine fellowship with the living God.

Note verses 25-26. During all of history, until the death of Jesus, God overlooked (withheld judgment for) the sin of those men and women of faith *because of what Jesus would do on the cross* (there is no other basis). The death and resurrection of Jesus demonstrated God's justice (His legal basis for forgiving these sins). The forgiveness of all sin of men and women of faith *after* the cross is also covered by Jesus' death! God is just (He insists that the penalty for sin is paid) and the justifier of those who place their faith in Jesus (He gives the gift of righteousness, v. 26). The one condition is faith in Jesus the sin bearer, the Redeemer, the Savior (vv. 22, 25, 26).

JOSHUA 17-18   When the tribe of Ephraim and Manasseh complained to Joshua that they didn't have enough room (17:14-16), note Joshua's answer (vv. 15-18).

Joshua prodded the people to take the remainder of the land the Lord had given them (18:3). Their inaction must have disappointed him. At his instruction, they at least surveyed the remaining land. Seven of the tribes still had not received their land (18:2).

PSALM 60   In 2 Samuel 10, Joab faced the Arameans and the Ammonites against unfavorable odds. He was forced to enter battle on two fronts at the same time (vv. 8-10). The introductory note to the psalm mentions this event. In verses 11-12 Joab reveals his faith in God's ability and goodness in danger.

The psalm is a poetic expression of men facing battle against larger forces than their own. They recognize the danger, but also recognize God's sovereign work in His people (vv. 6-8). The other nations are like a washbasin or a sandal to be used for His purpose (v. 8). Note the prayer in verses 11-12.

APRIL 13

ROMANS 4   To help the religious Jew understand that salvation is a gift of God, Based on God's grace and obtained by faith, Paul used Abraham as an example. Abraham, as the father of the Jews, would have been acceptable to God (on his own) if anyone could have been (4:1-2)! But Paul points out that Abraham was also made right with God by faith (v. 3; cf. Gen 15:6). Further, he received the gift of righteousness before circumcision was instituted (v. 10) and not through the law (v. 13)! It is obvious that God accepted Abraham not because of these external actions upon which the observant Jew depended. Paul makes this point to demonstrate that salvation is not by working (not by doing things) but by faith (vv. 3-5).

Further, Paul makes the point that the Jews are not the only children of faith. All those who believe – Jew or Gentile – are true children of Abraham (vv. 16-17). Abraham's significance is that he believed God and received the gift of righteousness as a result (v. 3)! All of this is based on the death and resurrection of the Lord Jesus (v. 25). The gift of righteousness depended (and depends) upon the promise fulfilled in the coming of the Savior.

JOSHUA 19-20   Joshua was from the tribe of Ephraim (Num 13:8) and received the town Timnath Serah (within the area designated for the tribe of Ephraim) at his request (19:49-50).

Six cities of refuge were designated, as God had instructed the Israelites, where an individual could go who had inadvertently killed another person.   Three of these were on the east side and three on the west   side   of   the   Jordan.   It   is   interesting   that   the   terms "unintentionally" and "without malice aforethought" remain in our legal vocabulary today (20:5b).

PSALM 61   This is the Christian worker's psalm (especially the worker in a far-away place). When this was written, the king was God's worker. How wonderful to know that wherever we are – even the ends of the earth – God hears us when we call (v. 2).

Note   the   missionary's   prayer   in   verses   1-2a,   the   missionary's stronghold in verses 2b-3, the missionary's heart in verse 4 (to follow hard after God!), and the missionary's heritage in verse 5.

This psalm should encourage those who are working for the Lord in difficult, and perhaps lonely, circumstances.

APRIL 14

ROMANS 5:1-11   The first word of this chapter is "therefore." Because of what he has said – because of the facts carefully laid out in the previous chapters – Paul lists blessings that belong to the Christian. We have been justified by faith (3:21-24; 4:5; 5:1), and therefore we have the gift of peace with God (v. 1), the gift of grace and joy (v. 2), the gift of perspective that allows us to rejoice even in suffering (v. 3; cf. 1 Peter 1:6ff.). The Lord helps us grow (vv. 3-4), and we have the Holy Spirit (v. 5). God has provided redemption through the death of His Son (at just the right time, vv. 6-8), and because of His death, we have forgiveness and salvation (vv. 9-11).

JOSHUA 21-22   →Praise God for His faithfulness as you read 21:43-45. Four times in these three verses, the text emphasizes that it was the Lord who gave them the land.← God is as faithful to His children today as He was to the Israelites.

With the major campaign of conquest behind them, the tribes that had chosen to live east of the Jordan River were allowed to return to their land and families. The Jordan was a major division between them (no bridges), and Joshua gave them some special instruction before they left (22:5).

As the Reubenites, the Gadites, and the half-tribe of Manasseh left, there was a major misunderstanding between them and the nine and a half tribes on the west side of the river. Read about the problem (22:10-20) and the resolution (vv. 21-34). It is possible that even the best motives can be misunderstood and lead to conflict. Honest communication will bring resolution if both parties are open, as they were here.

PSALM 62   There are five paragraphs in this psalm. Evaluate the suggested descriptive title for each paragraph from the text. *(1)* God is the Lord in my life (rest, salvation, protection) (vv. 1-2). *(2)* Devious men trap others (note the "word picture") (vv. 3-4). *(3)* Find hope, honor, protection, and salvation in God alone (vv. 5-8). *(4)* Don't trust in substitutes (vv. 9-10). *(5)* God is strong, loving, and just (vv. 11-12).

This entire psalm is "reality orientation." How should these truths change your thinking and life?

APRIL 15

ROMANS 5:12-21   Two men had the potential of living a sinless life and bringing great blessing to the world. The first, Adam, fell into sin and brought all people with him (v. 12). The second, Jesus, brought God's gift of grace and life (potentially to all persons) through His obedience (v. 19). This summaries what Paul has been explaining in the first five chapters. All men are sinners – no exceptions. We share in the sin of Adam. Jesus is God's answer to the problem, and His sacrifice is sufficient for all.

JOSHUA 23-24   As Joshua faced the end of his life, he gave the Israelites last instructions and a challenge to follow God just as Moses had done. Last words don't represent "small talk." They express deep convictions and feelings. For Joshua, as well as for Moses, these last words were backed by a life of integrity and were consistent with how he had lived and followed God.

Joshua gave credit to God and His faithfulness for all that had happened (23:3, 9-10, 14). He told the Israelites to follow God without wavering (v. 6) and to avoid at all costs associating with the people of Canaan and their gods, which would subvert them (vv. 7, 12-13, 16). →Follow the challenge Joshua made and the renewal of the covenant in Chapter 24. As Joshua reviewed what God had done for the Israelites, note that from the time of Abraham through the history of the Patriarchs, the slavery in Egypt, and the exodus, God was working for and in His people. During the time in the desert and in the taking of Canaan, God was with His people. God was moving in history and in the lives of His people to bring about redemption!←

Joshua is a model of unswerving leadership: Note in 24:31 what a difference this one man's leadership made. God uses people! May God help us to live as Joshua called his people to live in 23:6, turning neither to right nor left but charting a straight course in loving and serving God.

PSALM 63   David wrote this psalm while hiding from Saul. Men were after him to kill him on orders from the king. This was genuine danger! In this setting, we see David's heart vividly portrayed. Here is a man who has seen and known God (v. 2) – a man who accurately evaluates the world (v. 1b, perhaps both literally and figuratively) and has chosen to "follow hard after God" (v. 1). David would give his life rather than stop worshipping God, and as long as he is alive he will continue that course (vv. 3-4). David spent his wakeful moments during the night treasuring God in his heart (v. 6). Note his trust in verses 7-8.

Is it any wonder that God called David a man after His own heart? May God do His good work in our lives to give us these same qualities!

APRIL 16

ROMANS 6:1-14   Romans 1:18-5:21 outlines the theology of salvation. That section explains why we need God's intervention to bring us peace with Him and how He has done this. Romans 6-8 that deals with the theology of the Christian walk. Here we may learn how God has provided the resources to live the Christian life victoriously.

The baptism in verses 3-4 is the spiritual baptism that takes place as we put our faith in the Lord Jesus. Note how we are identified with Christ in His death and resurrection. Water baptism symbolizes this, going down into the water (death), and rising from the water (life).

The result of this identification is further explained in verses 5-7: Our old life dies with Jesus at the cross and we have new life because He rose from the dead. That is the new life of verse 4. Look carefully at verse 7. We know from the rest of Scripture that we are not now free of sin, that we do continue to miss the mark of God's righteousness (1 John 1:8-10). What this *is* saying, however, is that *we are free from the obligation to sin in our conscious choices* (see 1 Cor 10:13, both in the message of the verse and in the context of 1 Cor 10). God, through the death and resurrection of His Son Jesus, has given us the ability to say no to sin! This sets the Christian apart from the world in a very practical way.

Just how practical is evident in verses 8-10, 11-14. Paul is not asking the impossible when he encourages each Christian to choose to say no to sin and yes to submission to the Lord Jesus. Winning this victory over sin is by conscious choice. *God has provided the way and the power* for victory – *it is up to the Christian to choose* to make verse 14 reality.

JUDGES 1-2   The book of Judges chronicles the history of the Israelites between the great leaders Moses and Joshua and the period of the kings. It narrates God's intervention for His people as they looked to Him – and the sad history of a people who often strayed from their God. This historical overview in 2:10-23 is an unhappy commentary of a people who had known God's goodness in their lives but were quick to turn away from Him. Read the book not simply as history or with a critical heart, but alert to its lessons, and mindful that we have the same problems. Sin in a society is tenacious. One generation was more corrupt than the last (2:19). If we give ground to evil practices or thinking, our children may be even more enmeshed! As you read, remember that there was no Bible for the people to pick up and read. We will be held to a higher standard than they were because of our many advantages.

There were twelve judges of Israel, covering perhaps three hundred years until the time of Samuel, who was also called a judge (1 Sam 7:15) in which case there would be thirteen judges. These judges are Othniel (nephew and son-in-law of Caleb, 3:7-11; 1 Chron 4:13; Josh 15:16-17), Ehud (3:12-30), Shamgar (3:31), Deborah (4:1-5:31), Gideon (6:1-8:35), Tola (10:1-2), Jair (10:3-5), Japhthah (11:1-12:7), Ibzan (12:8-10), Elon (12:11-12), Abdon (12:13-15), and Samson (13:1-16:31).

PSALM 64   In a sinful society, there will always be deceit and injustice. David often faced danger spawned by the intrigue that surrounded the monarchy.

There is no way to adequately protect yourself from untruth and secret plans to harm you. But God can protect. The important thing is that *the Lord is a safe haven for His child* (v. 10). The learned response of the Christian should be to trust God and rejoice in Him. *Often we will not even be aware of the danger from which we have found protection.*

In this description of wickedness and deceit, give attention to verse 9. ☑A time is coming when all men will stand before the Lord and give glory to Him (cf. Isa 40:5; Phil 2:10).⇦ How much wiser to worship and serve Him now – in spite of the drift of society around us (v. 10).

APRIL 17

ROMANS 6:15-23   The subject here is slavery. In our world today, when personal independence is a badge of honor, the idea that each of us is a slave will not be popular. However, slavery is a spiritual reality (v. 16). To put it in another way, we live either under the authority of Jesus or of Satan. *The Christian's protection is to carefully stay under the umbrella of kingdom authority.* Under that authority, to use terminology that the first century understood, one is a slave to righteousness (the agenda of the kingdom, vv. 17-18). Resurrection power makes it possible for us to choose God's agenda! Remember that slavery, one way or the other, is a reality. Spiritual independence is a myth – a lie from the Evil One.

Follow this outline from the text:

Verse 17: The way to life in the Lord is through obedience.

Verse 18: The way to freedom is slavery to righteousness.

Verse 19: Slavery to righteousness results in holiness.

Verse 22: Holiness results in eternal life.

JUDGES 3-4   The behavior that set the stage for the Israelites' difficulty during this period (and subsequently, as well) is found in 1:27-36, 2:10-19, and 3:5-6. Review Leviticus 18:1-5, Numbers 33:55-56, and Deuteronomy 7:1-6. The cycle of disobedience and worship of foreign gods, with the resulting discipline from the Lord, promptly began (3:7-11). The judges were God's instruments of help and deliverance for the Israelites during this period.

The account of Deborah (Ch. 4) is one of courage on her part, lack of bravery on the part of her army leader, and God's faithfulness. The timidity of Barak, the leader of the army, pushed Deborah to a prominent place in the account.

PSALM 65   This Psalm of praise outlines the many blessings that we regularly receive from the Lord. ☑Central is the gift of redemption. Here in the Old Testament is the declaration that the Lord atones for our transgressions, and the promise of the coming of the Savior-Redeemer (vv. 3, 5b; cf. Gen 12:3; Rom 5:6-8)! ⇦

Note the other provisions from the Lord: answered prayer (v. 2a); awesome deeds of righteousness (v. 5); God's care for the land in rain and produce (vv. 9-13). Finally, we receive good things in the house of the Lord (v. 4). True in David's day and still true today.

APRIL 18

ROMANS 7:1-13   In verses 1-6, Paul demonstrates how a death changes legal obligations and how this principle applies to our personal identification with Jesus' death on the cross.

The death of one partner in a marriage voids the marriage contract. The living spouse is no longer legally obligated to the one who has died. In our spiritual life, when we identify with Jesus' death on the cross, we are no longer legally obligated to the demands of the law for our salvation (Jesus paid the price for our transgressions of the law). The Christian is released to a new life (v. 6; cf. 6:4).

Is the law itself then bad? That might be a logical question, and the answer is "no." The law reveals God's standard of righteousness and, by so doing, makes us aware of our great need (vv. 7-8).

Paul makes a curious statement about his own relationship with the law in verse 9. When was Paul free of the law? He grew up in a home learning the law from his earliest years. Logically, this could refer to the time before he became aware of right and wrong – the "age of accountability." It would be the only time he was not aware of or attempting to keep the law (Acts 23:1; 24:16). Note the result of his awareness of the law in verses 9-12 and the conclusion to his encounter with the law in verse 13. The holy law of God produced spiritual death: Paul became aware – painfully – of spiritual death.

JUDGES 5-6   As you read Chapter 5, note how Deborah gives God glory. In verse 2, observe how good leadership and willing people bring praise to God.

The history of Gideon as God touched him is an account of courage. The condition of the people and the land is apparent in 6:1-10. Read the message of the prophet (6:7-10).

God called Gideon to bring relief to the people, and gently brought him to the place of service. After the angel appeared to him, Gideon followed the Lord's command to tear down his father's altar and make a proper sacrifice to the Lord (6:25-27). This act required extraordinary courage, as it could have led to his death (vv. 30-31).

Gideon asked for a sign that the Lord would be with him in delivering Israel from the Midianites. God was gracious in giving the sign – not once, but twice (6:36-40).

With regard to Gideon's request for the sign, remember his situation. God gave the signs to Gideon in His grace, but we should not think this is the norm for God's people. God may give a sign such as this even today, but in general, God expects us to obey Him, doing what we *know* to be His will simply because we know it *is* God's will. Gideon lived in an era when there was little to verify God's will, while we have God's word in hand. Jesus refused those who asked for a sign. Underlying His refusal was the fact that those who asked had adequate information that should have led them to the right conclusion.

PSALM 66   As you read, note the reference to the exodus in verses 5-6. This is a common theme in the Old Testament. The writer moves to God's sustaining grace and power for Israel (vv. 8-12), and then to personal testimony (vv. 16-20). Notice that the writer understands the spiritual necessity of a clean heart to open the channel of prayer (v. 18).

☑Take note of verse 4. All of the earth had not yet bowed to God. There is the promise, however, that this will happen (cf. Isa 45:23-24; Rom 14:11). These Scripture references place the time of this universal recognition as the final judgment before God. Philippians 2:6-11 makes it clear that the whole world will bow before Jesus.⇦

APRIL 19

ROMANS 8:1-17   To better grasp the context of 7:14-25, we will first consider 8:1-17. There is a triumphant note in 8:1-4. Jesus, in His death and resurrection, *has set us free from the law of sin and death (v. 2).* That law sentenced us to death because as humans we are sinners (Rom 5:17)! But note the remarkable statement in verse 4. For those who know the Lord Jesus, the righteous requirements of the law are fully met (because of our identification with Jesus on the cross, 6:2-3, 6).

Paul then contrasts the outlook of the Christian and the non-Christian (vv. 5-8). The New International Version uses the term "have their mind set," to describe the outlook. Think of the term "mind-set." It is what we think about most. It is what we live for. It is what determines our behavior. Paul is saying that those who live for themselves don't have the mind-set of the Spirit (v. 5) and, if this is the case, do not belong to Christ (v. 9b). Those who are obedient to the Spirit have a different mind-set (that of the Spirit, v. 5b) and belong to Christ (v. 9a). The contrast between the Christian and the non-Christian is based on thoughts and resulting behavior. It is an either/or contrast and is stating the same thing as the either/or of slavery (6:15-18)!

A good illustration of control by sin or by the Spirit is the operating system of a computer. The DOS, Windows, or Mac systems that make your personal computer operate controls what happens every time you touch a key. Yet it is working in the background, unseen. The Holy Spirit in our lives is like that. The mind-set of the Spirit brings both liberating freedom and control. There is freedom not to do wrong and freedom to do what is right. There is also the gentle control of the Holy Spirit to help us to know God's will and how to achieve it. This takes place in the ordinary events of every day. The consciousness of the Lord God is "up-front" in the mind of the believer, making his perspectives different from what they were before Christ came into life (v. 5).

Note again that as Christians we do not have an obligation "to the sinful nature to live according to it" (v. 12). We do, however, have an obligation to live by the Spirit (vv. 12-14), and this sets us apart as children of God. Review again 6:7. Our death with Christ on the cross has removed the obligation to follow the dictates of the sinful nature.

The result is that we have the status of sons in relation to God (v. 15), and the Spirit makes this clear to us.

JUDGES 7-8   Gideon prepared to face the Midianites with the men who had responded to his call as commander: Thirty-two thousand men were prepared to fight for Israel. God, however, pruned the army He would use to a ridiculously small number. The Lord told Gideon to excuse all of those who were frightened (v. 3). Then God sent home ninety-seven hundred more soldiers (vv. 4-8a) and used three hundred men to do the impossible (v. 22)!

Note Gideon's character as the men called upon him to rule over them (8:22-23), but also how Gideon stumbled when he collected gold for an ephod (vv. 24-27). The people had a bent to idolatry – a snare that led them into evil.

PSALM 67   One could entitle this psalm a call to corporate worship. Verses 3 and 5, are a double call for "all the peoples" to praise the Lord. There is joy in verse 4 because of the Lord's justice. The harvest is a result of correct worship in verse 6.

APRIL 20

ROMANS 7:14-25   This passage has evoked a great deal of discussion for as long as God's people have attempted to understand its implications. The problem is that verses 14-20 and 25b seem to be saying that the Christian (Paul) is helpless to resist sin. If this means that even though we consciously choose to avoid sin, sin is still in our lives (as defined by missing the mark of God's righteousness), there is no debate. If, however, it means that when faced with the choice of sinning or not sinning, we are helpless to resist the temptation (this is what the verses seem to say), then we are still slaves to sin. This is what Paul carefully ruled out in Chapters 6, 7:1-6, and 8. The resurrection gives us *freedom to choose to please God and to say no to ungodliness and worldly passions* (Rom 6:11-14; Titus 2:11-14).

We still possess the sinful nature and will until our final redemption (1 John 1:8). Jesus intended, however, that His death and resurrection would transform those who believe *in this present life* (cf. 6:5). This new life so changes us that we can, and do, bring glory to Him (Titus 2:11-14).

Consider that nowhere else does the Bible present such helplessness for the Christian. In fact, just the opposite is the case, and many passages urge care and obedience to Christ (1 Cor 10:13, 1 Peter 5:8-9).

One explanation to this apparent dilemma is to assume that Paul was giving personal testimony in 7:14-25 about his acute pain and frustration as a sincere practicing Jew trying to adequately keep the law. This of course was impossible without the cross and the resurrection (6:1-4) and the presence of the Holy Spirit. This interpretation would be consistent with his statement in verse 9 about being alive apart from the demands of the law (innocence) and how his understanding of the law brought his spiritual death (vv. 9-11). In contrast, he outlines his new freedom in Christ in 8:1-4.

Understand that good theologians differ on this passage. The one presented here seems to this writer to be most consistent with the context and theology of the whole NT, but we must be charitable to other conclusions.

JUDGES 9-10   The account of Abimelech in Chapter 9 tells us something of the times. Life was cheap. Political violence was common, and it was expedient for Abimelech to kill all his half brothers and trade on the reputation of his father. Jotham, the one brother who escaped murder, shouted to the people of Shechem that they had chosen a worthless leader (a thornbush instead of a useful tree). Follow this account to the death of Abimelech.

Note the sad state of the Israelites in 10:6-10. When the people cried out to the Lord, listen to the Lord's very logical answer in verses 11-14. Then observe God's heart of compassion in verse 16. Thank God for His mercy!

PSALM 68   God's power and deliverance is prominent in this psalm. His tenderness and compassion for those in need is also evident (vv. 5-6, 10). The ungodly are like melting wax and smoke (v. 2).

Praise God with the psalmist in the truth of verses 19-20. God saves us. The Lord bears our burdens. The Sovereign Lord delivers from death. God will judge the unrighteous. Stand in awe of God as He is portrayed in verse 35.

☑There seems to be, within this psalm, a vision of a larger and broader reign of the Lord God on the earth (vv. 24-35). This involves the kings of the earth who will bring their gifts to Jerusalem to the Lord. This seems to correspond to the reign of the Messiah after the Day of the Lord when the nations will come to seek the Lord's face and favor (cf. Isa 2:1-5; Zech 14:16-19).⇦

APRIL 21

ROMANS 8:18-39   All of creation is waiting for the time when sin will finally be banished (vv. 18-21). Sin brings consequences even to nature

(Hos 4:1-3 and many other Old Testament references). Not only nature, but all of God's people will enjoy the full blessings of redemption (vv. 22-25). Note the powerful ministry of the Holy Spirit in helping us to effective prayer (vv. 26-27).

As you read verses 28-39, rejoice in the work of Christ in our lives. If you were to choose a side in the cosmic conflict that surrounds us, isn't it wonderful to choose God? It seems impossible that anyone would choose death – slavery to sin – instead of life!

JUDGES 11-12   Jephthah was an illegitimate child, shunned by his father's family (11:1-2). In spite of his background, the people needed Jephthah's military prowess and called on him to lead (vv. 4-11). God blessed him, and the result was deliverance. Jephthah's sacrifice of his daughter was the result of a foolish promise to God (vv. 30-31, 34-39). This event must be seen in context. There was no reading of the law. There were few prophets to give instruction from the law. Jephthah did what he thought was necessary in the light of his promise, but this could not be justified from the Law of Moses.

PSALM 69   This psalm portrays a broken person. There is heartbreak in the lines of print. Note David's plea (v. 13): "In your time, O God! In your great love, O God!" In spite of the heartbreak – in spite of the brokenness – here is a man with a clear conviction about where to put his trust! The conclusion in verses 30-36 puts things in perspective. God knows. God cares. God hears those in need. We all, at times, need this encouragement!

☑Jesus related the world's hostility toward Him and His disciples to verse 4 (cf. John 15:18-25) and stated that this hostility fulfilled the scriptures. The disciples related verse 9 to Jesus' cleansing of the temple in John 2:13-17. In addition, verse 21 appears to be related to Jesus' crucifixion (cf. Matt 27:34, 48; John 19:29).⇦

APRIL 22

ROMANS 9   Many in Paul's audience were Jewish. They had the same prejudices that Paul had before he came to know Christ. These chapters were written with Jewish people in mind (Rom 9, 10, 11). Each of the three chapters begins with a comment about the Israelites.

In Chapter 9, the question has to do with God's sovereign choices. From a Jewish point of view, it could be quite simple. God chose the Israelites, and God didn't choose the Gentiles. With these two assumptions in mind, read the chapter. Paul carefully makes the point, in ways that his Jewish countrymen could not dispute, that not all of the children Abraham, or of Isaac for that matter, were chosen by God. On the other hand, Paul uses prophetic portions from Hosea and Isaiah to show that non-Jews will receive God's blessing. Finally, in the last verses of Romans 9, Paul makes it clear that it is not in keeping the law, but it is by faith that one must come to God (vv. 30-33).

JUDGES 13-14   The poignant account of an angel bringing the barren wife of Manoah a message of hope is recorded here (13:2-5). It is a message of hope not only to her, but to the Israelites who had been under the rule of the Philistines for forty years (13:1). When his wife told Manoah of the visitation, he immediately sought confirmation from the Lord. In the midst of godlessness, here was a man who knew to turn to God. God in His graciousness answered Manoah's prayer, sending the angel to confirm the message (13:9). As a Nazirite, the child would never cut his hair (vv. 5, 16:17).

When Samson told his parents he wanted to marry a Philistine woman, they were distressed, as this violated the command not to intermarry with the Canaanites (Deut 7:1-4). However, when he insisted, the parents took steps to arrange the marriage (the marriage never took place, 14:20). God used this to begin to bring deliverance to the Israelites (Ch. 15). This began twenty years of Samson's leadership (cf. 14:4; 15:20).

PSALM 70   The mind-set of God's child is found in verse 4. In spite of the humanly dismal outlook that the psalmist faced, he can rejoice in God's presence and protection. This is reality thinking! The outcome of every situation lies in the hand of the God who cares for His own.

APRIL 23

ROMANS 10   Chapter 10 continues Paul's concern about the Jews. Paul wished for nothing more than that the Jews as a whole people would see the truth. Using the Old Testament prophecies as documentation, Paul challenged the serious fellow-Hebrew to see God's plan for bringing salvation to the world.

Romans 9:30-10:4 asserts that the problem is not insincerity, but trying to come to God in the wrong way – and this is true of almost everybody. Many assume that if they try hard enough to do good and keep all the rules, it will suffice. Paul declares that this is not the case (as he also did in Rom 2-3). Jews and Gentiles must both come by faith (vv. 9-12).

Paul once again quotes Psalms, Deuteronomy, and Isaiah to make his point in a way that Jewish friends would have a difficult time disputing. The point is that although Israel rejected the message of grace, the way was opened to those who were not a part of the "nation" (v. 19), and Gentiles were brought into the assembly of faith (vv. 18-20)! This will become even more specific in the chapter that follows.

JUDGES 15-16   Following Samson's unhappy courtship of the Philistine woman, he wreaked havoc on the Philistines, ruining their crops and single-handedly defeating them in battle (Ch. 15). As a result, he was the leader and judge of the Israelites for twenty years (v. 20).

The sordid account of Chapter 16 tells of his illicit affair with Delilah. Before he was stripped of his strength, God gave him time to repent. But the cutting of his hair broke his Nazirite vow and took away his strength. He was captured and humiliated by having his eyes put out. God honored his prayer that his strength would return; in his last act, he avenged the loss of his sight as he died with the Philistines.

The lesson for us: It is foolhardy to play games with the Lord. Samson must have voiced the "if only" phrase many times in captivity after the Philistines had destroyed his eyes! How much better to live closely to the Lord and avoid the "if onlys."

PSALM 71   Verses 1-13 reveal the writer's discouragement, not only because of his advancing age (v. 9) but because danger was near. People were waiting to take advantage of him (vv. 4, 10-11, 13).

Through these dangers, however, note in verses 1-3 the writer's deep faith. God was the refuge to whom he could always go. God, on the basis of His righteousness, could rescue and deliver.

We see the writer's perspective even better in verses 14-24.   He would always have hope and always praise God for His many wonderful attributes – from the time of youth to the time of old age! In verse 18, he said his responsibility would not be over until he had taught the next generation about the great God he served.

One more matter deserves mention. In verse 20, the writer saw the hand of God and His grace even in the difficult times of life: "You have made me to see troubles, many and bitter." Actually, in difficult times we learn about God's goodness and provision (vv. 20b-21). Do you have this mind set? It is a way of thinking that allows us to be buoyant even in disappointment. God is sovereign even in disappointing times.

APRIL 24

ROMANS 11:1-10   In Chapter 10, Paul pointed out from the scriptures that most Jews had rejected God's message, but the gospel message had gone to non-Jews (vv. 18-21). Remember that the Jewish people were the chosen of the Lord. Does this mean, then, that the Lord has rejected His people? That is the question Paul poses in verse 1.

The answer is a resounding "no."   The Israelites were still the children of the Covenant. God used the Israelites to bring blessing to the whole world (Gen 12:3). It was through the Israelites that the scriptures, the prophets, and the ancestral line of Jesus came (Rom 9:4-5). All through the history of the Old Testament, however, there were those who believed and those who were far from the truth. In the time of Elijah, he thought he was the only believer left among the Israelites (1 Kings 19:10) – but there were seven thousand who had remained faithful and were known to God (1 Kings 19:18). It was the same in Paul's time. Paul points out that he is an honest-to-goodness Jew, and he is a believer. God had not abandoned His own people, but not all descendants of Abraham were recipients of grace. That blessing comes through (and only through) faith!

It is a fact: Sin hardens the heart (vv. 7-10). Once again read Romans 1:18-32. When people choose sin, there are consequences. God allows each person to choose his own way (freedom), but choosing sin results in less sensitivity to wrong (dulled conscience) and a hardening of heart (slavery to sin).

JUDGES 17-18 An example of society's drift away from the Lord is the casting of the idol in Chapter 17 and the engaging of a Levite to be "priest." For a Levite to act as a priest in worshipping a carved image was far from God's plan for the priesthood. Note verse 6 (people without leaders).

The Danites had not driven the Canaanites from the land that was allotted to them (Judg 1:34), and thus they were looking for available land to settle (Ch. 18). They stole Micah's idol, took the Levite with them (vv. 14-21; cf. 17:5), defeated Laish, and set up idol worship themselves (vv. 30-31)! Laish had probably been inhabited by the Sidonians.

PSALM 72 This Psalm is said to be written about Solomon. As you read 1 Kings and the account of Solomon's reign, you can see the blessings that came to the Israelites because of Solomon's wisdom and justice.

☑However, this psalm is also messianic in that it reaches far beyond David to the reign of Messiah. This concept that one prophetic passage can apply to two different events is called "the law of prophetic suggestion." There is one application in the persons and history of the general time of writing and another, many times more profound, in the future.

As you read this psalm, look for the blessings of righteous and just rule (v 2), the prosperity from the fertile ground (v. 3), the eternal nature of the king's rule (v. 5), and the world-wide scope of the kingdom (vv. 8-11). Note the concern for the weak and the poor and deliverance from oppression and violence (vv. 12-14). Finally, see how the reign of this king will fulfill the promise of Genesis 12:3 (v. 17). This is the promise of the coming Messiah: the promise of redemption and His righteous reign. The whole world will be filled with His glory (v. 19b).⇦

APRIL 25

ROMANS 11:11-24   →Paul introduces the concept that the "stumbling" of the Jews has brought salvation to the Gentiles (v. 11). It is clear that this was God's plan from long ago (10:19-20). Both Moses and Isaiah prophesied that Gentiles would come into the grace of God.← This does not mean, however, that Jews have been utterly rejected (vv. 15-16).

As you read these verses, stand in awe of the mystery of God's working. God, in His will and grace, has extended salvation to all by grafting Gentiles into the root of Abraham (the olive root, v. 17). Understand, however, that there is no cause for arrogance or complacency. Consider vv. 20-24 carefully. God will treat unbelief and disobedience in the lives of those "grafted" (the Gentiles) in the same way He has treated those of the native tree (the Israelites). This is why it is so important for each of us to read the Old Testament to see exactly how God did deal with His people (cf. 1 Cor 10:1-13).

JUDGES 19   As you read Chapter 19, look again at 17:6. The lamp of truth and righteousness was dim in the land! Also note 18:1 and 19:1. No one was enforcing proper standards. When the Levite set out with his concubine to return to his home, he stopped in Gibeah for the night. When a stranger came into a town, its inhabitants were honor-bound to provide a safe place for the traveler.   That no one immediately responded to their need for shelter was a breach of honor. The attack on the home of the man who did take them in was the same.

It is difficult to understand the willingness of the homeowner to send his daughter outside to these wicked men (vv. 22-24), and the Levite who did the same to his concubine (v. 25). The point of this account is not to condone this action, but to highlight the wickedness of a society that would allow such practices. The Levite was so incensed at the murder of his concubine that he made sure the other tribes of Israel knew what had happened in this Benjamite city.

PSALM 73   This psalm provides perspective when things are not going well and the godless seem to be prospering. The problem is stated in verse 2. The writer almost lost his perspective and faith. The reason is in verses 3-17. In spite of the pride (v. 6a), violence (v. 6b), sin (v. 7a), self-delusion (v. 7b), and arrogance (vv. 8, 11) of the godless, they do well (v. 12)! Where is God in all of this? That is the question in verses 13-14.

With these things in mind, understand the writer's heart in verses 15-28. The writer came close to betraying God and God's people (v. 15). It was, however, in God's presence that he regained his perspective (v. 17). In the remaining verses of the psalm, observe the dangerous position of the godless (vv. 18-20), the repentance of the writer (vv. 21-22), and his regained perspective (vv. 23-26). In fact, the attitudes in verses 23-26 are the discipline of personal decision!

APRIL 26

ROMANS 11:25-36   Here Paul gives us insight into God's sovereign working and plan for His people – the people of the Covenant. There is a timeline in God's work. ☑God in His grace is giving time for "the full number" of the Gentiles to be saved – *and then Israel as a people will be saved* (vv. 25-27). The reference in verses 26-27 is from Isaiah 59:20-21 – a messianic prophecy. The deliverer, who is Christ, will open the eyes of His people. They will come to understand that Jesus really is the Messiah (cf. Jer 31:31-34; Ezek 36:24-32; Zech 12:10). This will happen when God gives His people understanding and a heart to believe (just as He has given the Gentiles).⇦

As to the timing of these events, we will see more as we read the Old Testament prophets. In the interim, remember that the Jews, the people of the Covenant, will be saved (vv. 25-27). The majesty of the concept and the events move the Apostle Paul to an outburst of praise (vv. 33-36), as well they might. As you contemplate these verses, can you imagine how this extraordinary prophecy will be fulfilled?

JUDGES 20-21   When the tribes learned about the terrible event at Gibeah, they mustered forces and came to fight against the tribe of Benjamin. Almost all of the tribe of Benjamin was wiped out! In the attempt to reestablish the tribe, note the creative way wives were secured for the surviving men (21:15-23). As a postscript, note the repeated truth of 21:25.

PSALM 74   Sometimes it seems that everything has gone wrong and God doesn't even hear when we call. That is the background of this psalm (verses 1-11). There are no signs or prophecies to encourage the people (v. 9).

But even without an external sign of God's presence, the psalmist has faith! In verses 12ff., note the writer uses past events to remind himself that God is indeed sovereign, alive, and responsive even without external signs of His presence. It is on this basis that the writer can believe and ask the Lord to be faithful to those who call upon Him (vv. 18-23). This is a model for our lives today! God is alive and real.

APRIL 27

ROMANS 12:1-8   Chapter 12 begins a new portion of the book of Romans. Aside from the concluding remarks of parts of Chapters 15 and 16, this section is practical instruction in living the Christian life.

We should all memorize verses 1-2! As spiritual worship, we owe God our very lives (v. 1). We need the reminder not to conform to this world's way of thinking and living. And our minds must be continually transformed by the Holy Spirit through the Word of God! Follow the progression in these verses. If we are willing to follow God's way, we will be able to discern God's will.

Paul also emphasizes the fellowship of God's people, with each of us contributing our God-given gifts to the collective ministry (vv. 3-8). Compare this section with 1 Corinthians 12:4-11 and Ephesians 4:11-13. Each Christian has at least one gift for ministry – given so that the composite work of the church will be complete and balanced. Each of us must humbly give our effort where we are gifted (v. 3). This creates a beautiful mosaic of God's working in the fellowship and extending into the community.

RUTH 1-2   Think of Naomi's difficulty after losing her husband and sons! This left her essentially without income and protection during the times of the judges.

The beautiful account of Ruth's loyalty to Naomi is touching. Although a Moabite, Ruth had taken the faith of Naomi. Their return to Israel was difficult, and Ruth supported them both by gleaning. She caught the eye of Boaz, who unknown to her, was a relative of Naomi's husband.

PSALM 75   The writer of this psalm exalts the Lord for His power, justice, and righteousness. Time and justice are in the Lord's hand (v. 2). God gives stability to the world (v. 3). The Lord judges the earth (v. 7) and gives the cup of judgment to the nations (v. 8). God's people give thanks to Him for His amazing deeds (vv. 1, 9-10).

APRIL 28

ROMANS 12:9-21   List all of the verbs in verses 9-21. These action words have to do with relationships with one another and with the Lord. There are more than twenty such words. Think of how taking these actions would change your usefulness in the church and your relationships with others.

A real test of spiritual maturity is facing unfair treatment, or downright evil treatment (vv. 17-21). It is difficult to leave what we perceive to be wrong treatment for the Lord to settle – but to do so prayerfully may bring remarkable results.

RUTH 3-4   When Naomi learned that Boaz was paying attention to Ruth, she formulated a plan. Living strictly under Naomi's authority, Ruth followed the plan and became the wife of Boaz. Note that this arrangement followed the law (Lev 25:25; Deut 25:7-10). Obed was born to them, the grandfather of David. Thus, the Moabite Ruth became part of the lineage of Jesus.

PSALM 76   This psalm continues the theme of the righteous judgment of God on the wickedness of men (cf. Ps 75). God's holiness and majesty are proclaimed (v. 4). God's judgment will save the righteous (v. 9) and punish the wicked (v. 10). Note that God's wrath against men brings Him praise (v. 10). This is because exercising His wrath on the wicked demonstrates His justice and righteousness. Note verse 11: What vows would be appropriate to make to God today?

APRIL 29

ROMANS 13   As Paul spoke about the authority delegated to governments, note that the authority is from God. The conclusion he draws is that we, as Christians, are bound to honor God with our obedience to government.

Certainly there is no question about the vast majority of our laws. Taxes are specifically mentioned. There were no freeways when Paul wrote, but our urban and rural speed laws would not be a question either.

Think for a moment about the tremendous cost of sin in our society. Cheating on taxes is an example. Think of the medical costs of tobacco, alcohol and illicit drug use. Consider the crime costs associated with drugs. These costs are borne in a disproportionate way by Christians who do not contribute to the problems associated with them. Nevertheless, we are commanded to obey the laws, and as God's representatives, we must do so.

A different problem arises when it is apparent that government's laws conflict with the will of God. We must be careful about picking the issues, but in cases such as these we will have to obey God – then be willing to face the consequence of disobeying the law (cf. Acts 4:13-20; 5:27-29).

Follow the reasoning in verses 8-14. If we follow the "rule of love" in our interpersonal relationships we will please God. There is further impetus to do so because time is passing, and the coming of Christ is close (vv. 11-14).

1 SAMUEL 1-2 Samuel was the bridge between the judges and the kings of Israel. From the time he was very small, Samuel was a godly person who made a difference for righteousness in the whole nation (2:26).

Elkanah was a man who served the Lord with care. Of his two wives, Hannah was barren and suffered acutely because of this. Read her prayer in 1:10-11, and feel with her the despair of her heart. God answered her prayer, giving her a son whom she named Samuel, and, after Samuel's birth, five other children (1:20; 2:21). In due time, to fulfill her vow, Samuel came to live with Eli in the tabernacle at Shiloh (1:24-28).

Eli the priest had two sons who, although priests, were not godly. Eli had rebuked his sons for their sins – but they ignored their father (2:22-25). God sent His message to Eli because he had not adequately restrained his sons from evil (2:27-36). We might think Eli's rebuke was enough. Not so with the Lord. Eli should have taken the priestly duties away from these men. It was not only that Eli's sons were sinful but that they were carrying on the duties of the worship of God! It was to this mockery that God spoke (v. 29)!

PSALM 77 In the midst of trouble (vv. 1-3), when it seemed that there was no hope (vv. 4-9), remembering God's faithfulness (vv. 10-12) brought perspective and "reality orientation" (vv. 13-15). Note God's awesome power in verses 16-19 and the allusion to the exodus. Note also God's compassion in verse 20. All Christians should memorize verses 13-15!

APRIL 30

ROMANS 14 Paul presents concern for our fellow Christians as a spiritual principle – specifically, choosing behavior that will hurt no one.

We occasionally face gray areas of behavior: areas that are neither condoned nor censured in the Bible. In Paul's day, eating meat offered to idols in the market was an example. The mature Christian knew that the idols were dead and that the meat was not spiritually contaminated because of the ritual offering. But for someone recently converted from a life where such religious rituals were common, it might be important not to eat such meat. Paul pointed out that if the new Christian observed the more mature Christian eating the meat, the young Christian might also eat, even though it violated his conscience. This would compromise the young Christian. It is important that as God's children we never lead someone into a situation that could compromise that person (vv. 7, 13b, 15b, 20b).

Think about these three principles that can govern our choices:

1. Live so closely to God that you stay far from sinful behavior. Make behavioral choices that you are certain (insofar as possible) will please the Lord (vv. 8, 12, 17).

2. Even if you know something you do is within God's blessing, if it could be a problem to a younger Christian, defer to him or her (v. 13b).

3. If someone chooses otherwise do not criticize (vv. 3-12).

If we use these principles, we will be living within the boundaries of love for God and for our fellow Christian.

1 SAMUEL 3-4   While Samuel was still a child, God called him to be His spokesman and servant.   Certainly, God was forming Samuel's character even at this young age, and he responded not only to Eli but also to God.

The message God gave Samuel for Eli was essentially the same as that from the unnamed prophet (3:11-14; cf. 2:27-36). We aren't told the interval between the two warnings, but certainly the "double" delivery of the message emphasized its importance.   God's message to Eli was fulfilled when the ark was captured, Eli's two sons died in battle, and he himself died of a broken neck (Ch. 4).

Samuel is an example to each of us in his habit of carefully listening to all of God's words, as recorded in 3:19. The result is in verses 20-21.

PSALM 78   This psalm is a lengthy account of how God had shown His power to Israel.   The first eight verses introduce the reason for this review.   Remembering the facts would help Israel not choose rebellion as their fathers did.   The author calls on the nation to remember and to tell the present and coming generations so that they too may learn of and profit from God's dealing with the people (v. 4).

The psalm is important because it gives us a powerful reason to study the Old Testament. This account is not only for the Israelites. 1 Corinthians 10:1-13 relate these same events to us today.   In fact, without this attention to the Old Testament, we have an incomplete view of God and His way of dealing with people.   In relation to this psalm, read Deuteronomy 28.

May

Bible Reading Schedule
And Notes

❧

*I tell you the truth, until heaven and earth disappear,
not the smallest letter, not the least stroke of a pen,
will by any means disappear from the Law until
everything is accomplished. Matthew 5:18*

1	Romans 15:1-13	1 Samuel 5-7	Psalm 79
2	Romans 15:14-33	1 Samuel 8-9	Psalm 80
3	Romans 16	1 Samuel 10-11	Psalm 81
4	John 1:1-28	1 Samuel 12-13	Psalm 82
5	John 1:29-51	1 Samuel 14-15	Psalm 83
6	John 2	1 Samuel 16-17	Psalm 84
7	John 3:1-21	1 Samuel 18-19	Psalm 85
8	John 3:22-36	1 Samuel 20-21	Psalm 86
9	John 4:1-26	1 Samuel 22-23	Psalm 87
10	John 4:27-54	1 Samuel 24-25	Psalm 88
11	John 5:1-30	1 Samuel 26-27	Psalm 89
12	John 5:31-47	1 Samuel 28-29	Psalm 90
13	John 6:1-24	1 Samuel 30-31	Psalm 91
14	John 6:25-59	2 Samuel 1-2	Psalm 92
15	John 6:60-71	2 Samuel 3-4	Psalm 93
16	John 7:1-24	2 Samuel 5-6	Psalm 94
17	John 7:25-52	2 Samuel 7-8	Psalm 95
18	John 8:1-30	2 Samuel 9-10	Psalm 96
19	John 8:31-59	2 Samuel 11-12	Psalm 97
20	John 9	2 Samuel 13-14	Psalm 98
21	John 10:1-21	2 Samuel 15-16	Psalm 99
22	John 10:22-42	2 Samuel 17-18	Psalm 100
23	John 11:1-44	2 Samuel 19-20	Psalm 101
24	John 11:45-57	2 Samuel 21-22	Psalm 102
25	John 12:1-19	2 Samuel 23-24	Psalm 103
26	John 12:20-50	1 Chronicles 1-2	Psalm 104:1-9
27	John 13:1-17	1 Chronicles 3-4	Psalm 104:10-18
28	John 13:18-38	1 Chronicles 5-7	Psalm 104:19-26
29	John 14:1-14	1 Chronicles 8-10	Psalm 104:27-35
30	John 14:15-31	1 Chronicles 11-12	Psalm 105:1-11
31	John 15:1-17	1 Chronicles 13-14	Psalm 105:12-36

MAY 1

ROMANS 15:1-13   This passage continues the theme of Chapter 14. As Christians we have a mutual responsibility for one another (vv. 1-2). The example for this behavior is the Lord Jesus (v. 3). The result is a spirit of unity among believers that is truly from the Lord (v. 5). It is God's desire and will that, as Christians, we are filled with joy and peace (v. 13).

Look carefully at verse 4. When Paul speaks of "everything written in the past," he is obviously speaking of the Old Testament scriptures. The advantages of reading and applying these scriptures are instruction, endurance, encouragement, and hope.

☑Verses 7-12 affirm (from the scriptures) that the Lord Jesus fulfilled the promise to bring salvation to all peoples (remember Gen 12:3). This passage also affirms the promise that Jesus will come again to rule over the nations (v. 12; cf. Isa 11:10).⇔

1 SAMUEL 5-7   The Philistines took the ark and put it in the temple of their god (5:1-2). This custom in the ancient Near East demonstrated that the gods of the subdued people were weaker than the gods of the victors. But God gave the Philistines a message in two ways: Their god Dagon was broken by the presence of the ark, and the people fell ill (5:3-6).

The clue to the nature of the illness is in 6:4-6. The "tumors" that struck the people (5:6, 9) were connected with rats (6:4), which suggests bubonic plague. The illness is caused by the bite of fleas that are carried on rats, causing the often-fatal viral illness. The "tumors" are swollen lymph nodes, especially in the groin and under the arm.

Note God's awesome presence in 6:19-20. Remember that only the direct descendants of Aaron, the priesthood, could touch the ark. After they had prepared the ark for moving, the Kohathites carried the covered ark with poles (Num 4:15). These men at Beth Shemesh should not have touched the ark! Note Samuel's leadership in 7:2-9 and how God answered his prayer in a breathtaking way in 7:10-11.

PSALM 79   This psalm was written during great national distress, the land having been subjugated by invaders (vv. 1-4). The writer called upon the Lord to help Israel for three reasons. *First*, God's mercy was needed to forgive the people's sin (v. 8). *Second*, the Lord's name was at stake. With His people suffering under another nation's hand (vv. 9-10), the nations would conclude that the Israelites, who were supposed to be led by the God of heaven, actually had no God (v. 10)! *Third*, the writer called for the Lord's mercy because the people were suffering (v. 11). The writer reminded the Lord that these people were the sheep of His pasture, and with deliverance, they would praise God, both at that time and in future generations (v. 13).

MAY 2

ROMANS 15:14-33   Paul declared his mission and ministry to the Gentiles (vv. 14-16). There is a great deal to be learned from the focus of his ministry in verses 17-22. Although Paul could claim credit for many things, he said he would speak only about what God had accomplished through him (v. 18). What he accomplished was by the power of the Spirit – accompanied by signs and miracles (v. 19). Paul's personal ambition was completely captured by this mission (v. 20).

→Paul was a pioneer. He preached, whenever possible, to those who had not yet heard the gospel (v. 20). In so doing, Paul helped fulfill the scriptures that the ministry of Jesus would go to those who had not heard – meaning the Gentiles. They came to understand God's grace and love through the preaching of the good news (v. 21).←

We have no knowledge of any visit that Paul made to Spain (vv. 24, 28), but he did indeed visit Rome. God gave him the opportunity that he desired, but not precisely as he had envisioned.

1 SAMUEL 8-9   As Samuel grew old, it was natural for him to appoint his sons to carry on with his responsibilities. But the people's appreciation of Samuel did not extend to appreciation of his sons! It was common knowledge that his sons did not live by the same standards as Samuel had (8:3). This led the elders of Israel to ask Samuel for a king to rule over them (vv. 4-5).

It was hurtful to Samuel that the people asked for a king. God, however, told Samuel to move ahead with the selection of a king (note God's comment to Samuel that the people had rejected Him in asking for a king). Follow the leading of the Lord in Samuel's and Saul's life (in Chapter 10) that confirmed Saul's selection in Samuel's mind.

PSALM 80   This beautiful psalm is a prayer to the Lord for restoration and revival. Consider the following simple outline. *(1)* Hear us because you are a great God who leads His people (vv. 1-2). *(2)* Restore us, Lord (v. 3). We have suffered your hand of discipline and our enemies mock us (vv. 3-6). *(3)* Restore us for we are your people whom you delivered from Egypt and planted in this land (vv. 7-11). *(4)* Return to us for we are your people (vv. 14-18). ☑Note particularly the reference to the

Messianic hope in the "son you have raised up for yourself" (vv. 15b, 17).⇦ *(5)* Revive us so we can call upon your name (v. 18). *(6)* Restore us so that we will be saved (v. 19).

MAY 3

ROMANS 16   There are a number of "gems" in Paul's closing remarks. His greetings indicate a wide and deep relationship among the Christians of the first century. They truly worked together and stood with and for one another. They suffered for their Christian testimony. Note the frequency of the phrase, "they worked hard" or a variant. The church was alive and at work in the pagan world.

Read 16:17-27 carefully. It is a serious thing to cause division in the body of Christ (vv. 17-18). Even though people who cause such trouble may speak smoothly, their behavior shows that they are really not of the kingdom. Note verse 19. It is important that we *not* know about many areas of sinful behavior. But we need to be wise to understand what God considers good. Note also the hope in verse 20.

1 SAMUEL 10-11   If you were Saul, would you need some confirmation that you were really to be king? Samuel, under the Lord's direction, gave Saul three unmistakable signs to help his understanding (10:1-7). Look at the detail of the "signs" that were fulfilled. Note particularly verse 9. God changed Saul's heart to give him what he needed to lead God's people.

Life went on as usual until Samuel called the people together and identified Saul as the one the Lord had chosen to be king. And even then, Saul returned to his home and the people to their homes. Note, too, that there was not universal approval of the choice (10:27).

Saul entered the realm of leadership in the crisis of attack by the Ammonites (11:1-2) and led the people to a military victory (v. 11). The key to his courage is found in verse 6. The Spirit of God changed this young man into a leader. Without question, this was a good beginning! The result was a popular confirmation of Saul as king and a great celebration (vv. 12-15).

PSALM 81   Here is advice for the Lord's child. Remember to praise the Lord (v. 1), and remember His mighty acts on our behalf (v. 7)! Learn from those who failed to follow the Lord (vv. 8-12). Note verse 12, and relate this to Romans 1:24, 26, 28. If we ignore what we know to be God's will, we cannot presume upon God when we are in difficulty. Understand that the Lord loves His people and will work on behalf of those who follow Him (vv. 13-16).

MAY 4

JOHN 1:1-28   The Gospel of John is different from the other three gospels in that it does not always record events chronologically. The book presents Jesus as the Son of God and as the Savior. The truth of Jesus as the Christ unfolds in the synoptic gospels as the account of Jesus progresses, while in John it is more obviously present from the very beginning.

⊃In this first chapter, Jesus is presented as the Word (v. 1, see also Rev 19:13), eternal (v. 2), and the creator (vv. 3-4). He is life and light from God (vv. 4, 5, 9), the person through whom men can come into the family of God (vv. 12-13), and God who has come in the form of man (v. 14). Jesus is also identified as the Lamb of God by John the Baptist (vv. 29, 35) and the Son of God (v. 34). The truths are overwhelming.⊂

Look again at verses 12-13. Compare this with John 3:3. God's children are born into His family – by faith. Coming to Jesus by faith means that we have a spiritual family connection. This helps us understand our relationship with God as real and permanent (John 10:27-30). A child doesn't necessarily always "feel" as if he or she is in a family – but the feeling doesn't change the fact of the relationship. The same is true of the child of God. *Remember the "family connection!"*

Think about verse 18. If you want to know God, get to know Jesus. It is Jesus who reveals God! If you want to know whether Jesus is from God, follow His commands (John 7:17), then place your faith in Him (v. 12). This is God's way of letting us know Him – and there is absolutely no other way except through the Lord Jesus (John 14:6).

John the Baptist testified about Jesus. His understanding of his own special place in the redemption story is remarkable – he linked his ministry to Isaiah's prophecy concerning the one who would prepare the way for the Messiah (v. 23; cf. Isa 40:3-5).

1 SAMUEL 12-13   Just as Moses and Joshua had done, Samuel had last words for Israel. Not only words – Samuel called upon God to send thunder and rain (12:16-18)! Samuel called upon the people to serve God with their whole hearts (12:20), and he himself promised to pray for Israel (12:23).

Saul faced a test of character after his son Jonathan provoked the Philistines (13:3) and Saul prepared for battle. Samuel was to come and sacrifice to the Lord before the battle, and Saul had been told to wait for him (13:8). Seeing his men start to drift away in fear, Saul himself offered the sacrifice (vv. 5-9). Because of his disobedience and lack of faith, the Lord told Saul that the kingdom would not remain his (vv. 13-14). Although Saul was a Benjamite and could not act as a priest, kings of Israel did, on occasion, present sacrifices before the Lord (cf. 2 Sam 24:25; 1 Kings 3:15).

PSALM 82   Have you ever seen our judicial system defend the unjust and show partiality to the wicked? God speaks to this issue here.

Look at God's agenda in verses 3-4. Compare these verses with Proverbs 21:13 and 31:8-9. Genuine justice is deeply rooted in God's character (Deut 1:16-18). As we understand what is important to God, it should become important with us as well!

MAY 5

JOHN 1:29-51   John the Baptist's testimony about Jesus continues. Jesus was born *after* John the Baptist, yet he understood that Jesus *was* before he was (v. 30). This can only mean that John understood that Jesus was eternal. Then he declared that Jesus is the Son of God (v. 34).

Observe the calling of the first disciples. Jesus impressed these men so much that they left what they were doing and followed Him. Note how they told their family members and friends about Jesus (identified as the Messiah, vv. 41, 45). ☑Philip, speaking to Nathanael, related this to the Promise of the Law (Moses) and the Prophets (v. 45).⇦ Jesus was already selecting those with whom He would minister while on the earth; those to whom He would entrust the work of the kingdom when He was no longer with them. ➲In speaking to Nathanael, Jesus declared himself the promised Son of God (v. 51).☯

1 SAMUEL 14-15   Jonathan demonstrated courage when he attacked the Philistines single-handedly. His faith in God is impressive (14:6). He stepped out, and God responded by spreading panic among the Philistines (v. 15). Follow the dispute between Saul, Jonathan, and the army. Samuel had told Saul that he acted foolishly (13:13), and he acted foolishly again by decreeing that no one could eat (14:24).

In the battle with the Amalekites (Ch. 15), Saul again showed lack of character. After Saul disobeyed the Lord's command in the battle, the Lord spoke to Samuel (vv. 10-11). God was grieved, and Samuel was troubled – and in fact, spent the night in prayer (v. 11b). Further, when Samuel went to talk to Saul, the king was off building a monument to himself (v. 12). In Samuel's conversation with Saul, note the truth in verses 22-23. Follow Saul's rationalization and his concern for image rather than for righteousness (v. 30).

PSALM 83   The content of this psalm is so current that it could have been written today with a change in the names of the countries! The hostilities against Israel are still there and still volatile. Ultimately, the name of the Lord will be at stake (v. 18), and the Lord will demonstrate to the world that He is the God of heaven. Check Zechariah 2:8-13.

MAY 6

JOHN 2   At the wedding in Cana, which Jesus attended with His disciples, note that Jesus' mother, already understanding something of His power, asked Him to solve the problem of the wine shortage. ↄThe miracle that followed demonstrated His glory from God and led the disciples to place more faith in Him (v. 11). As the disciples interacted with Jesus, they were learning more about Him each day. But it was not until after the resurrection that they put the whole picture together, seeing Him as the Messiah and the fulfillment of the Scriptures (vv. 17, 22).ↄ

ↄJesus reacted to the crass commercialism in the temple by driving out the sellers (vv. 13-16). What chaos this must have been! Those who questioned his authority (v. 18), understood that only someone with authority from God could do what He did. Jesus' answer (v. 19) left the questioners confused, and it was not until after the resurrection that the disciples fully understood the answer. Yet this too affirmed that He was acting under God's authority and that He was the Messiah.ↄ

1 SAMUEL 16-17   When the Lord rejected Saul, Samuel was instructed to anoint a new king (16:1). Consider what the Lord looked for in the new king (16:7). After David was anointed, God's Spirit came on him in power (v. 13). Because God had rejected Saul, His Spirit was no longer with him (16:14). What exactly it means when the text states that an evil spirit from the Lord tormented him is not clear, but certainly Saul was depressed.   The departure of the presence of God *would* be depressing! It is in this context that David came into the service of the king (his selection to be king most probably unknown to Saul).

The chronology of Chapters 16 and 17 may not be exact, for Saul doesn't seem to know David when he offers to fight Goliath. Consider David's faith and courage as he faced the giant. As he fought, God's reputation was at stake rather than David's (17:26, 45-47)!

PSALM 84   When the writer speaks of the dwelling place of the Lord, he is referring to the temple but also his relationship with the Lord (v. 12).   The Israelites loved the temple as we love the church.   We associate the church with a building, but more significantly how the church, as a living organism, connects God's people to each other and to Him.

As you read this portion, substitute the word "presence" for the word "house," and look for the blessings that come to those who follow the Lord. Verses 4-5 describe the person who desires to stay as close to God as possible. Can you identify with the writer in verses 10-11? Would you choose less desirable employment and be aligned with God's will rather than align yourself with the ungodly (in ungodly pursuits)?

MAY 7

JOHN 3:1-21   In this chapter, Jesus used the first of several common illustrations to explain difficult truths. In John 1:12, John stated that through faith in Christ, we become children of God. Here, Jesus said the same thing: We are born into the family (v. 3). Further, it is through the work of the Holy Spirit (vv. 5-8) even though we don't completely understand the transaction. The way Jesus speaks of the Holy Spirit is instructive. We can feel the wind and certainly can see its effects – but we cannot see it. The work of the Spirit is similar. We feel the presence of the Spirit and can see the results, but we do not actually see the Holy Spirit. This is especially true of our entry into the kingdom. It is in retrospect that we can see how God, through the Spirit, has led us to faith and life.

⮑Jesus' second illustration to Nicodemus was the snake that Moses raised in the wilderness (v. 14; cf. Num 21:8-9). By looking to the snake that God had instructed Moses to make, the people were healed. The analogy to Jesus on the cross is clear. Jesus was telling Nicodemus that only by looking to Him could one find healing and spiritual life. Jesus was saying directly that He was the Savior.

Jesus then added three significant facts about man's condition and God's provision. *First*, God loves people so much that He provided a way for us to come to Him (v. 16a). *Second*, the way to God is through faith in His Son (vv. 16b-18). *Third*, men and women, by nature, love darkness rather than the light of God's truth (v. 19). With the perspective of these three facts, take careful note of verse 36.⮐

1 SAMUEL 18-19   In reading the historical books of the OT, and particularly the era of the kings, one is impressed with the intrigue, danger, and violence in the high circles of government. We see that here, as Saul's jealousy and fear of David became more pronounced. Saul seems to have had acute anxiety about David's popularity and depression with the loss of the Spirit of God (18:10).

In contrast, follow David's trust in God and his dealings with the king. God's hand was obviously on David, which in turn led to Saul's fear (18:12, 15, 29). Note how the Lord protected David from capture by Saul's agents and then by Saul himself (19:18-24). Saul was helpless to carry out his evil plans; the Lord Himself frustrated Saul's efforts.

PSALM 85   The first seven verses of the psalm are a prayer. Note the requests: "Restore us" in verse 4; "revive us" in verse 6; "show us your unfailing love" and "grant us your salvation" in verse 7.

This prayer isn't necessarily from a backslidden or decadent state. Rather, this is the prayer that we need every day – forgiveness for "missing the mark" of the Lord's righteousness and cleansing from the soiling of the world. This is the prayer for restoration to full fellowship with the Lord, the cleansing of the feet that Jesus gave to the disciples (cf. John 13:10).

Compare verse 10 with Hosea 4:1-3, where the prophet laments the condition of society. In Hosea's day there was no faithfulness, no love in the land. ☑ Note in Psalm 85:10b that "righteousness and peace kiss each other." The only way righteousness and peace (from God) come together is in the work of Christ on the cross. God's righteousness demands payment for our sin in death. God's peace (in forgiveness) comes to us through His love – redemption through the cross (Rom 5:1). He Himself paid the price! God's blessing to His people in the Old Testament era was based on what Jesus would do "in the fullness of time" (Rom 3:25-26; Heb 9:15)!⇦

MAY 8

JOHN 3:22-36   John the Baptist's remarkable testimony to the authenticity of Jesus as the Son of God tells volumes.   John acknowledged that he was not the Christ (vv. 28-30). Jesus, however, is from heaven (v. 31), speaks of heavenly things (v. 32), has the Spirit of God (v. 34), has the authority of God, is the Son of God (v. 35), and is the only way to eternal life (v. 36).

Look carefully at verse 36. Here the choices are clear: life or death, guilt for sin or deliverance from that guilt, knowing God's love or His wrath. Jesus is God's way of salvation. *Any other path will bring God's wrath and death!*

1 SAMUEL 20-21   David was in obvious danger! He trusted Jonathan, and together they devised a plan to discern Saul's intentions with regard to David's life. In the process, Jonathan incurred his father's wrath and almost died himself (20:33). It is noteworthy that Jonathan seemed to know David would become king and asked for David's protection for his family (20:14-15; 23:17). With Saul's intention crystal clear, David could only flee.

As he fled, David stopped at Nob, where there were a number of priests, and possibly the site of the tabernacle, to get supplies (21:1ff.). The priest, Ahimelech, suspecting that David was in trouble because he was alone, was frightened.   However, after David's untruthful explanation, he gave him food and Goliath's sword. Note the person Doeg, for he reported to Saul that David had been there (21:7).

The question of truth is intriguing. Could not David have told the truth and trusted God for the results? This seems quite straightforward to us today. Is God able to protect, even in the most difficult situation, His servant who obeys Him in truthfulness? We would answer yes. Keep this question in mind as we continue through the Bible.

PSALM 86   This entire psalm is a prayer during a time of trouble. Think about this: If we never faced difficulty, it would be easy to forget God. Instead, note how many ways the writer sees God's goodness in this psalm. This "reality orientation" gives us perspective; trouble in life actually keeps us looking to God.

☑Compare verses 9-10 with Revelation 15:3-4. The quotation in Revelation 15 is sung by the victorious people of God who had been faithful through the persecution by the Antichrist. With the return of Christ the Messiah, all of the nations will come and worship (Isa 2:2-5).⇦

The prayer of verse 11 describes a person who is "following hard after God." The undivided heart describes someone wholly committed to living under God's authority, seeking to do nothing to compromise that relationship. Understanding the God of verse 15, it is logical to pray the prayer of verse 11.

MAY 9

JOHN 4:1-26   Jesus' conversation with the Samaritan woman can teach us a great deal. He reached out to her as one who needed forgiveness when most would not have done so (vv. 9, 27). He began the conversation by using common ground (v. 7), then turned the conversation to the more important issue of eternity (v. 10ff.). ➲He spoke to her about her deep need (vv. 17-18, 21-24) and revealed Himself as the promised Messiah (v. 26).☾   As a result, the woman believed.

Do you know someone who always seems to turn a conversation to the things of God? When this person speaks to friends who do not understand their need of the Savior, the conversation seems to get to the significant matters of life and eternity. Jesus' method teaches us to use common ground and the "open doors" that are available. Our own reluctance (which should shame and humble us) often prevents strong witness. People around us need to know Jesus as Lord. By using the model Jesus gave us, we can reach many!

<u>1 SAMUEL 22-23</u>   Two significant things happened in Chapter 22. About four hundred malcontents (v. 2) attached themselves to David. Imagine the difficulty in keeping so many people hidden from Saul and his men! The second occurrence demonstrated how ruthless Saul was. He killed eighty-five priests, including Ahimelech (v. 6 ff.). Even Saul's men refused to carry out the command to kill the priests, but Doeg did so – although Ahimelech denied complicity in David's escape (Doeg must have known this, since he witnessed the conversation between David and Ahimelech).

While David was hiding from Saul, he and his men delivered Keilah from the Philistines but had to flee Keilah when Saul heard he was there. →Take note of how God specifically protected David (23:7-14, 19-29). Because he would be the ancestor of the coming Messiah, this was crucial.←

<u>PSALM 87</u>   This psalm is about Jerusalem and the Lord's temple on Mount Moriah, but goes beyond the earthly city to the spiritual reality of God's kingdom. Citizens of the neighboring countries – even those who had oppressed Israel – would be counted as God's people if they acknowledged Him (v. 4). God Himself keeps the record of man's behavior in His books (v. 6). Rahab, in verse 4, is a poetic reference to Egypt. Thus the nations listed that surround Israel (v. 4) will all have people who acknowledge God and are in His record (v. 6).

MAY 10

<u>JOHN 4:27-54</u>   The disciples and Jesus seemed to be in two separate worlds. The disciples thought about food – Jesus saw the harvest (vv. 31-34). Further, what gave Him energy was doing the will of the Father (v. 34); it was uppermost in His mind. As He saw the landscape, He saw people who were lost and without hope – that was the harvest (v. 35)! Note too that God's people work together. One sows, another reaps, but all who are dedicated to the task rejoice together in the harvest (vv. 36-38).

Think again about the Samaritans. The woman who had met Jesus had gone to her village and told them about the Lord. When Jesus spent two days with them, many believed – their curiosity had been aroused by the woman's testimony, but their encounter with the Lord brought them to faith (vv. 39-42).

⊃When Jesus, remote from the Roman official's home, healed the official's son, it was powerful evidence that Jesus was indeed God's Son (vv. 43-54). The official readily understood this, and he, along with his household, became believers.⊂

<u>1 SAMUEL 24-25</u> David's character became apparent in the encounter with Saul in Chapter 24. David had opportunity to kill his enemy, but he respected Saul's position as God's anointed (even though he himself had been anointed by Samuel). The truth was that God could take care of Saul and put David on the throne at His appointed time! And David was willing to wait for that to happen.

Samuel died (25:1). All Israel mourned, recognizing him as a judge and prophet. When David heard the news, it must have hurt him to be unable to show his respect for Samuel by his presence in Ramah.

In Chapter 25, we can follow the character of three key people. Nabal was churlish and mean. His wife Abigail was beautiful and wise. David was human enough to be very angry at the treatment he and his men received at Nabal's hand. Abigail's wisdom saved the lives of her family and household. When God took her husband's life, she became David's wife.

<u>PSALM 88</u> If you have ever felt deep despair, you will be able to relate to this psalm. There is no sense of hope or light in the whole psalm – *except* that the one who wrote turned to the Lord! That, in fact, is the light of hope. God is able to change the impossible, and only God can do it. Notice verse 1. Day and night the writer prays! Look at verse 9. *Every* day the writer prays. We would feel better if we could *do* something besides pray! *In prayer, however, we are doing the most effective thing to change the impossible – or rather, to allow God to change the impossible in our lives.*

Through all his despair, although the writer doesn't understand what God is doing, there is no grumbling or bitterness with God. We need to learn this response.

<u>MAY 11</u>

<u>JOHN 5:1-30</u> ➲Take note that Jesus made Himself equal with God (vv. 16-17). It was this declaration that evoked the Jewish leaders' desire to kill Jesus. This point is still an issue. Today's society reacts negatively to the idea that Jesus, as the Son of God, is the only way to God. It is still the truth.

Verses 19-30 give us remarkable information about salvation. Eternal life is a gift from Jesus (v. 21). Salvation is a definite transaction at a definite point in time (although some may not be aware of the time) and is received by faith (v. 24). Salvation means receiving life from a *spiritually* dead state now (v. 25), and will result in a final resurrection from the *physically* dead state to everlasting life (vv. 28-29).

Notice how Jesus emphasized that He was doing the will of the Father. That was Jesus' personal agenda, and it was connected to His claim to be God's Son (vv. 19, 26-27, 30). With this in mind, consider 1 John 2:5b-6. ☾

<u>1 SAMUEL 26-27</u>   David again had the opportunity to kill Saul and again refused because Saul was the Lord's anointed (26:9-11). Each time Saul was confronted with David's generous spirit, he repented and went home.

David felt the time had come to leave Israel completely (27:1). Gath was a city of the Philistines (1 Sam 6:17), and when asked about his activities (27:10), David answered that he had fought the surrounding cities in Israel, while in fact he had been destroying cities that were enemies of Israel.

<u>PSALM 89</u>   The psalm begins with the writer's firm decision to give faithful testimony to the greatness and the goodness of God. Follow in this chapter as the psalmist lists God's attributes.

Note particularly verses 14-18. Righteousness and justice are the foundations of the kingdom. Think about this in relation to truth. Neither righteousness nor justice is possible without truth (and only truth). Compare this with John 8:44-45.

☑Note how love and faithfulness are related to righteousness and justice (v. 14). The only way that God's love to man can be expressed along with His righteousness and justice is in Jesus. Faith in Jesus brings us the gift of needed righteousness; Jesus has borne the wrath of God for us at the cross (Rom 5:8).

The promise of the messianic reign is in verses 3-4, 27-29 and 35-37. Compare this with the promise to David (2 Sam 7:16).⇦

<u>MAY 12</u>

<u>JOHN 5:31-47</u>   Jesus' comment about His own testimony reflected the view of the listeners (v. 31). These were the same people who had laid plans for His death because He affirmed that He was indeed the Son of God (5:18). He referred to John the Baptist, whom the people had accepted as from God (vv. 33-35) – and who declared that Jesus was the Son of God (3:27-36).

⊃Note Jesus' comment that His message was more important than John's (v. 36). John had preached repentance – to prepare the way for Jesus' message. Now Jesus was offering life from the Father (v. 24)! Jesus said that His work testified that He was God's Son (v. 36). The scriptures that described Jesus, the scriptures that these Jewish leaders knew so well, also pointed to Jesus as God's Son, but they were a closed book to them because of their unbelief (vv. 39-40).☽

Think for a moment about the Old Testament scriptures and their message of redemption and the coming Redeemer. God had the plan and step by step brought it to fruition. Until Jesus came, it was "hidden" (1 Peter 1:10-12). Remember the "Road to Emmaus" Bible study when Jesus opened the Scriptures to the two disciples with whom He walked (Luke 24:13ff.). He explained how Moses and the prophets told about the coming Savior – and that He was that very person.

Jesus' comments to these who knew the Scriptures but rejected Him are thought provoking. He told them they were responsible to see Him as He was presented – and they would face judgment because of their unbelief (vv. 45-47). Moses would condemn them because they, like their fathers, didn't live by faith or follow principles of godly living found in the Old Testament scriptures (cf. Matt 5:17-20). When people repented after hearing John the Baptist, they prepared their hearts for the message of Jesus! *Doing the will of God opens the heart to understand further the truth about God (cf. John 7:17).* Genuine faith is always tied to obedience to God's truth (Luke 3:7-9). Faith is belief that results in action; it is different from mere intellectual affirmation.

1 SAMUEL 28-29   Saul was desperate (Ch. 28). He knew that he was displeasing God. His willingness to consult the spirit world indicates that his faith and trust in God were sadly compromised. In consulting the spirit world, it is quite probable that people called from death are not the ones who appear. However, in this instance, God sent Samuel to give Saul the final message of his life. The spirit medium immediately understood that this was not what she expected. Samuel's spirit had actually appeared!

Follow the sequence of Chapter 29. David was forced into a corner as he was accompanying the Philistines when they prepared to fight Israel (28:1-2). God's solution (29:4) allowed David and his men to avoid the battle with Israel.

PSALM 90   Several truths stand out in this psalm. God is eternal (vv. 1-2). The days of our lives are in the Lord's hand (vv. 5-6). The Lord knows everything about each of us (vv. 8-9), and it is only with His help that we are able to see life with a proper perspective (v. 12). The Lord gives meaning to our life and our work (v. 17).

It is easy for us to drift through days and weeks, months and years, not realizing that life will not go on forever! We need "reality orientation" that allows us to think truth in relation to life and our relationship to the Lord.

MAY 13

<u>JOHN 6:1-24</u> As Jesus ministered to the people who followed Him, He also ministered to His disciples. As you read this section of John 6, notice the lesson that Jesus gave the disciples while, at the same time, meeting needs of the large crowds following Him.

There was a gradual awakening among those who came to Jesus that He was the promised Messiah (v. 14). Many initially came to see Jesus because they were intrigued with His miraculous healing (v. 2). As they listened to Him and continued to observe His power and see His concern for His listeners, they began to accurately assess Him as the Messiah.

The parallel account of the feeding of the five thousand in Mark (6:30-44) tells us that Jesus responded to the need of the people for food because of His compassion for them – and taught them because they were like sheep without a shepherd (Mark 6:34-37). Place yourself among the disciples and imagine your reaction to Jesus' miracle. Note too that Jesus was concerned with practicing economy with what God gave on that day. He suggested that nothing be wasted and instructed them to gather up what was left over!

Now imagine yourself in the boat with the disciples as they rowed back toward Capernaum in rough water during the night (vv. 17-18). ⊃The lesson of the day was not completed until Jesus came to them, walking on the water – evoking terror in their hearts (v. 19) – and brought them to the shore with His power. Certainly a positive affirmation of Jesus' identity to the disciples (v. 21).⊂

<u>1 SAMUEL 30-31</u> Imagine the consternation among David and his men when they returned to Ziklag. The town was burned (v. 14b), and the people and possessions were gone. Note 30:6b. David turned to the Lord and, with specific guidance, set off to recover what had been taken.

The sad account of Saul's death in Chapter 31 should give us pause. Saul had every advantage after he was anointed. He had a good beginning. *He came to a bad end because he disregarded God's holy will.*

<u>PSALM 91</u> As you begin to read this wonderful psalm, note verse 1, verses 9-11, and verses 14-15. The promises of protection by the Lord are conditional. First, we need to continually turn to God. With this in mind, note that the thrust of the psalm is a call to trust and steadfast commitment to God.

Follow God's protection for His children: protection from traps or unseen hazards maliciously placed (v. 3a), protection from disease (v.

3b), and protection from fear (v. 5). Note the guardian angels in verse 11.

MAY 14

JOHN 6:25-59   In Chapter 4, Jesus used water to illustrate that He could, and would, satisfy the deepest needs and longings of the heart (4:14). Here (vv. 32-59) Jesus used the illustration of bread. This teaching builds upon Jesus' miraculous feeding of five thousand with bread (vv. 26-27).

⊃The core of this truth, which Jesus shared, is found in verses 35ff. Jesus is God's answer to man's estrangement from God – in Him is eternal life. Note how Jesus opened the subject by challenging the people to be concerned about eternal life, then said He could give that very thing to them (v. 27). In this section, Jesus unequivocally stated that He is the way to eternal life! He is the only way (vv. 37-40). Note how verses 47-51 support what Jesus said in verse 40. Then see how Jesus contrasted manna (those questioning Jesus had mentioned manna in v. 31) with the living bread (vv. 32-35). The key is faith in Jesus (vv. 40, 47). This is what "eating" Jesus' flesh means: It is participating in God's plan by believing in Him.⊂

2 SAMUEL 1-2   The messenger who came to David's camp with the news of Saul's death thought he was bringing good news. David's character is revealed, however, in his sorrow over the death of the Lord's anointed and the sad account of his people's defeat.

David, with God's direction, went back to Judah and was anointed as king, and he ruled for seven years in Hebron (2:1-4, 11). This is where Abraham lived after separating from Lot about eight hundred years earlier (Gen 13:18); it also was the city given to Caleb after the Israelites came into the land (Josh 14:13-14).

Abner, son of Ner, was the commander of Saul's army and, after Saul's death, the most powerful man in Israel. Family connections were crucial in the ancient world. Abner was Saul's cousin (1 Sam 14:50). Joab was the commander of David's men. He was David's nephew, the son of Zeruiah, David's sister. In the test of strength that took place at the pool of Gibeon, Asahel, Joab's brother, chased Abner, and was killed by Abner when he refused to give up the chase.

PSALM 92   This entire portion praises God for who He is, what He does, and how He watches over His own. Note the writer's focus and orientation toward God. His life is built around the truth of following God. He praises God in the morning and at night (vv. 1-2). He finds his joy in God's works and words (vv. 4-5). The promise is that such a person of faith will continue to be fresh even into old age (v. 14)!

In contrast, those who do not follow God are oblivious to the danger of coming judgment (vv. 6-7). The corollary is that God's children have insight from God (1 Cor 2:12). Satan works hard to keep people occupied with trivia and unaware of coming judgment.

MAY 15

JOHN 6:60-71   As Jesus taught, He always made the message clear. He never softened it to accommodate those who were reluctant to believe. On the other hand, Jesus went to great lengths to help those with a truly seeking heart. Think, for instance, of Nicodemus (John 3:1-21), and keep this in mind as you read, in just a few days, about the man born blind in John 9.

➲The section we are reading today presents Jesus as the only way to come to God and receive eternal life (vv. 61-65). This concept was too difficult for some followers to accept (v. 66). Note, however, that when "many of His disciples" turned away from Him on this one critical issue, Jesus did not offer to compromise. Some things are truly non-negotiable; Jesus as the only Son of God, the Savior, and the only way to come to God is at the top of the list!☾

2 SAMUEL 3-4   Conflict continued between David and the remnants of Saul's former kingdom, now nominally ruled by Ish-Bosheth. The real power, however, was in Abner, who had been consolidating his position (3:6). When the time came, he made his move by contacting David and meeting with him (3:12-21).

Although Abner had come in peace, Joab deceived him by pretending to speak peacefully and then murdered him after he had left David (vv. 22-27). Note David's comment in verse 29 and how David made Joab march in the funeral procession before the body of Abner. Ish-Bosheth may have been helpless in dealing with his army commander, but David was not! Note David's final words to Solomon in 1 Kings 2:5-6 and how Joab died in 1 Kings 2:28-35.

PSALM 93   This psalm lists many of God's attributes. Our God is the God of majesty (v. 1), the God of power (v. 1b), the God who is eternal (v. 2), the God of strength (v. 4), the God of truth (v. 5a), and the God of holiness (v. 5).

Look again at verses 3-4. These images have special meaning for anyone who has seen the sea during a typhoon or hurricane. Our God is even more powerful than the mighty waves that pound the sea walls and the piers.

MAY 16

JOHN 7:1-24 As this chapter begins, it is clear that Jesus' brothers did not understand that He was the Messiah. There is a note of sarcasm in their comments to Him about going to the feast in Jerusalem (vv. 1-5). Before He arrived, He was the topic of discussion (vv. 12-13). The underlying question was, "Is Jesus the Messiah?"

➲When Jesus did begin to teach, He quickly declared that His words were from God (v. 16). Think about Jesus' statement in verse 17. This is as valid today as it was when Jesus spoke these words! Compare this statement with John 8:31-32 and John 14:21. *Doing* God's will, as defined by Jesus, will confirm in your heart that this is indeed the right way – that Jesus is from God. This brings freedom to live in the Spirit in a hostile world and further understanding of the things of God!⊂

One issue that divided the crowd about the identity of Jesus was that He healed on the Sabbath (v. 23b). In response, Jesus pointed them to the practices of their own religious leaders. The Mosaic Law called for the circumcision of a male child on the eighth day of his life. If the eighth day fell on the Sabbath, the priest circumcised him on that day – even though it was the Sabbath and involved "work" on the part of the priest. Jesus challenged them to think about His healing on the Sabbath in the same way (vv. 23-24) and not be brittle about applying the law of the Sabbath.

2 SAMUEL 5-6 →David consolidated his authority in all of Israel and moved his administration to Jerusalem. God had promised the kingdom to David (1 Sam 16:1-13), and subsequently also promised that David's throne would be everlasting (belonging to the Messiah, 2 Sam 7:16). God now started to fulfill this promise.← The years that followed, including most of Solomon's reign, were the finest in the history of Israel. David loved and followed God, and God prospered him (5:10). Note how David continued to ask God for leading even from his position of human power (vv. 17-19).

When the ark was being brought to Jerusalem, Uzzah died trying to steady the ark when it was in danger of falling (6:1-7). The ark was being carried in the wrong way and by the wrong people. When the articles of worship were to be moved, the priests who were Aaron's descendants were to prepare them, and then the Kohathites (one of the divisions of the Levites) were to carry them on carrying poles (Num 3:27-32; Num 4:1-20; Num 7:9). The final return of the ark to Jerusalem is mentioned in 6:12, but the missing detail is in 1 Chronicles 15:1-2, 15. The lesson had been learned, and the Levites carried the ark to Jerusalem!

PSALM 94   This psalm speaks about sin in the world and looks forward to the time when God will settle all outstanding accounts. In verses 1-2, note that God Himself will avenge wrongs. It is as if the writer is saying to God, "It can't come soon enough!" (v. 2). Note also the gem buried in verse 2. Pride kills!

Society really hasn't changed. Note these characteristics: arrogance and boasting (v. 4), gross injustice and oppression of God's people (v. 5), violence and murder (v. 6), and the ultimate of arrogance in suggesting that God does not see their sin (v. 7).

This psalm warns the careless and sinners to listen to common sense and logic (v. 8)! This is rather unusual in the psalms. Usually the wicked are not addressed directly. Read verses 9-11. Is the creator of the universe unable to see? God knows even the thoughts of the wicked (v. 11).

In the face of the world's wickedness, how should the righteous react? First, if discipline is needed from the Lord, it will bring blessing (v. 12). Second, understand that God will stay near His own (v. 14). Third, judgment will come, and it will be based on God's righteousness (v. 15).

Verse 16 poses a question. Are you – are we – willing to stand up for the principles of God's truth? God looked for someone to "stand in the gap" in Ezekiel 22:30 but found no one!

MAY 17

JOHN 7:25-52   It didn't seem possible that the Messiah could be someone whose family background was so ordinary (v. 27). ⊃Jesus' answer once again asserted that He was doing God's will and speaking His message; i.e., He was God's Son (vv. 28-29)! This seems such an extraordinarily confrontational conversation!   Once again, note that Jesus never backed away from the truth that He was from God and brought God's message to His listeners. He told them that their refusal to accept Him as God's Son proved that they did not know God (vv. 28-29).   In the midst of this affirmation of His identity and authority, note His astounding statement verse 38 (it is still true today)!⊂

As the battle lines became more clearly drawn, the religious leaders planned to arrest Jesus (v. 32). It was remarkable that the temple guards didn't arrest Jesus as they had been told to do.   Their explanation for not making the arrest is extraordinary, but tells us much about how Jesus affected people (vv. 45-46).

Finally, take note of Nicodemus (vv. 50-51; cf. John 3:1-2). He made the one defense of Jesus before the religious leaders. He urged them to follow their own law and listen to Jesus before condemning Him.

2 SAMUEL 7-8   When David had been established in Jerusalem, he built a palace for himself (2 Sam 5:11; 1 Chron 14:1-2). Hiram, king of Tyre, provided (sold) David the materials and sent skilled workmen. Later, under Solomon, he did the same when it came to building the temple.

After David was settled and established in Jerusalem, he made plans to build a temple for the Lord. Notice that Nathan the prophet assumed that the Lord would approve the plan (7:3), but God appeared to Nathan with a message for David (vv. 5-16). This message reminded David that God had made him all that he was. God's hand had brought him from the pasture to the throne. Further, it was not God's will that David build the temple but instead, his son after him. Note the promises to David in this message and the conditions of continued blessing from the Lord. ☑In 7:11b-16, the Lord promised that David's kingdom would endure forever. As subsequent Old Testament prophecy will confirm (cf. Isa 11:1-5), this was the promise that the Messiah would come through David. The promise of a Savior first was given in the Garden of Eden after the fall (Gen 3:15). That this would come through Abraham is recorded in Genesis 12:1-3 and through his son Isaac in Genesis 17:19, 21:12, and 26:3-4. Of Isaac's two sons, the promise would be fulfilled through Jacob (Gen 28:12-14). From among Jacob's twelve sons, the promise would come through Judah (Gen 49:10). Now, in 2 Samuel 7:16, the fulfillment of the promise was narrowed to David.⇦

As you read David's response in 7:18-29, look for his attitude. David had a tender heart in his relation to God and saw God's greatness in his own life, as well as that of the nation. Notice David's humbleness in prayer.

PSALM 95   There are two central truths here that call for our response: God is a great God and King above all others (v. 3); we are the people of His pasture, the flock under His care (v. 7). Those two significant facts call us to praise, thanksgiving, and worship (vv. 1-2, 6). To praise and worship God, we need to know who He is. *So read and study God's Word!* To learn from history (vv. 7b-11), we need to know how God deals with men. *So read and study God's word!* And to give God thanksgiving, we need to know what God has done for us (theological truth as well as specific experiences of God's hand in our lives). *So walk with God!*

MAY 18

JOHN 8:1-30   Jesus had already used the illustrations of water that quenches thirst permanently (John 4:13-14), and bread that satisfies hunger eternally (John 6:35). Now Jesus used the illustration of light and darkness (8:12). Those who follow Jesus walk in the light.

This has meaning for our own age. How many times have you heard people say that they are trying to find themselves, trying to discover who they are? Or wondering what they should do? In this age of confusion, Jesus says that if a person will follow Him he or she will have light, i.e., life, understanding, and insight.

➲Once again Jesus addressed His identity and authority. He said He is the light of the world, the only way to know God, and the way to life (v. 12). Jesus declared that both His testimony (His words and works) and His Father's testimony (the scriptures) would show that He was from the Father (i.e., God's Son, vv. 13ff., 29). Note Jesus' explicit statement that He was from God the Father (vv. 16, 23-30). Further, anyone who would not believe in Him would die in sin without forgiveness (v. 24).☯

2 SAMUEL 9-10   David had made a covenant with Jonathan never to cut off kindness to Jonathan or his family (1 Sam 20:14-17); now David fulfilled that promise by showing kindness to Mephibosheth, Jonathan's only surviving son (Ch. 9). Mephibosheth's disability probably saved him, since he could not serve in the army.

The Ammonites were descendants of Lot's daughter from the son conceived through her incestuous scheme to have a child through Lot (Gen 19:30-38). God instructed the Israelites to leave the Ammonites alone as they approached Canaan because of the family connection with Abraham (Deut 2:17-19). David showed his friendship to the Ammonite king by sending a delegation, but they treated the delegation with contempt. Later, the Ammonites, along with the hired army of Aram, came out to do battle with David. Note Joab's strategy and his faith and courage (10:9-12). The Ammonites should be distinguished from the Amorites, who were among the Canaanite nations that the Israelites were commanded to conquer and wipe out (Gen 15:16; Deut 7:1-6).

PSALM 96   God's people, and in fact the whole earth, should sing to the Lord (v. 1). Note that we are to sing our praise to the Lord (v. 2) and declare His glory to the nations (vv. 3, 10). This is missionary outreach!

☑The heavens, the earth, the sea, the fields, and the trees all will sing for joy – because God comes to judge the world (vv. 11-13)! Romans 8:18-21 and Isaiah 55:12 speak of the liberation of nature when God sets the world right. This will occur with Jesus' second coming.⇦

MAY 19

JOHN 8:31-59 ➲Look at the promise in verses 31-32. Understanding truth comes through following Jesus (doing His commands). With truth comes freedom. Truth brings freedom from the slavery to sin (vv. 32; cf. Rom 6:16-18). When we come to know Jesus as Savior, we are free to obey Him and are delivered from our slavery to sin!➲

Jesus pointed out that the Jews to whom he spoke did not have this freedom. They said they were descendants of Abraham (v. 39) and children of God Himself (v. 41). Jesus, however, said that if they were Abraham's children, they would do as Abraham did (vv. 39-40). What marked Abraham as a person of God was that he believed God (Gen 15:6) and obeyed God (Gen 12:1-4). Even though Jesus was faithfully telling them God's message, they would not listen and, instead, planned to kill Him (v. 40).

As you read Jesus' comments in verses 42-47, look for Satan's characteristics. He is a murderer and a liar – the father of lies. Anything that shades the truth is not from God but from the father of lies! It is the "family connection" that Jesus is speaking about in this section. Note verse 42 and compare this with verse 51. If we belong to God, we will be receptive to His truth and will for our lives. If we don't know God through Christ, it is impossible to understand spiritual things (1 Cor 2:14).

➲This section contains one of the most powerful and clear declarations by Jesus that He is the Son of God. He said His teaching (and a relationship with Him) would bring true freedom (vv. 31-32, 36). He unequivocally said that He was from God (vv. 42, 49, 54-55). He said salvation will come to those who keep His word (v. 51), and affirmed that He existed before Abraham (v. 58). This confrontation with the Jewish leaders was sharp and hostile, but Jesus never backed away from His statement that He had come in fulfillment of the scriptures.

Again note verse 51. Jesus said that the person who keeps His word will never see death. In fact, we demonstrate our faith by keeping His word. *So, obey and live!*➲

2 SAMUEL 11-12 The Bible presents people as they really are. Here we see David, king of Israel and blessed by God in so many ways, falling into grievous sin. The events are recorded in stark detail – planned sexual sin as an offense against God. One can follow how sin led to lies and then to murder.

Consider how David felt – trapped by his own sin and seeing no way out except lies and plans for murder. Even his commander Joab was involved in the plot and made his own feeling obvious in telling David about Uriah's death (11:18-24).

The untruth continued until the child was born. As we read in Psalm 51, David suffered under the knowledge of his sin, yet did nothing until Nathan came to him with a message from the Lord (Ch. 12).

Now consider Nathan's responsibility in coming to David. This was not an easy message to bring. David had already killed a man to cover the tracks of sin! Nathan had no way of knowing just how David would react. Note his courage and the bluntness.

The sin brought immediate and long-lasting results to David and to others. The baby died, bringing great sorrow. God promised that this sin would have violent consequences for David and his family (12:10-12). God in grace forgave David, but that didn't change the results to David.

There are lessons we must learn from this incident. Each of us is vulnerable to temptation and can fall into wrong unless we keep our eyes on the Lord. Memorize 1 Corinthians 10:13. God provides a way if we are willing to take it. But we need to understand that sexual sin is a trap; step into the situation and the trap snaps shut (Prov 7:21-23)! *Further, if we are compromised by sin, the best way to get out is by immediate confession to the Lord and to the others affected.* We must also understand that our sin may bring irrevocable results that cannot be undone, despite forgiveness. In light of the events of these two chapters, review Psalm 51 to see how David felt as the circumstances were unfolding.

Lastly, consider God's gracious way of dealing with David. He sent a messenger to confront David with the truth. (Remember, we have the Bible in hand and don't need a special letter or messenger from God.) God forgave the sin; that is God's grace. The consequences, however, were real (12:10-12).

PSALM 97 Who is in charge in this world? Have you wondered if God is in charge? Read verse 1 and rejoice. As you read further in verses 2-7, stand in awe of the greatness and power of the Lord. Apart from His great mercy, there would be no hope. Praise God for the truth of verse 9. God is exalted above all gods!

In relation to the Lord's righteousness and justice, note the call to God's people in verse 10. Look at the many ways God's goodness touches the lives of those who love Him (vv. 10-12).

MAY 20

JOHN 9   The healing of the man who had been blind from birth was both a lesson to the disciples and an act of compassion for the man. The belief of that day would have assigned a reason, such as sin in the man's life (before birth?) or in his parents, for the blindness (v. 2). Jesus set the disciples straight by pointing out that the blindness was not because of sin but so that God's grace might be seen in his life (v. 3).

As you read this account, look carefully at what happened to the man who was healed, to his parents, and to the religious leaders. The man, when pushed by the Pharisees, stood by the facts, giving credit to Jesus and was finally put out of the temple because of his testimony (vv. 17-34). ↄJesus then found him and revealed Himself to the man as the Messiah, leading him to faith (vv. 35-38).ↄ The parents, when pushed, evaded answering the questions even though they knew the truth. They feared the Pharisees, and their cowardice is recorded forever in this chapter (vv. 20-23). The Pharisees were closed to even the obvious facts of the incident and cut themselves off from knowing the Savior.

We don't like to think of ourselves as being closed to truth, but do we ever behave as the parents did, with cowardice? We will *always* be right by standing with the truth!

2 SAMUEL 13-14   Again, the Bible presents sin in stark, believable detail. Amnon was David's first son, Absalom his third (2 Sam 3:2-3). Jonadab was Amnon's cousin and David's nephew.

Sexual experience before marriage was serious for Tamar, damaging her ability to make a good marriage. Her willingness to marry Amnon after the rape, regardless of what she may have felt for him, was an indication of how she saw her future in light of the rape (13:12-14, 16).

After Absalom murdered Amnon, he fled to his grandfather Talmai, the king of Geshur, and was there for three years (13:38; cf. 3:3). Joab, who arranged Absalom's return, was a cousin of Absalom but maintained a distance from him until Absalom provoked him by burning his grain. A meeting with David was subsequently arranged. The family connections and the intrigue and violence of the account again demonstrate that sin exacts a price! In fact, this violence in his family was exactly what the Lord had told David would be the consequence of his own sin (2 Sam 12:10-12).

PSALM 98   Look for the similarities between this psalm and Psalm 96. Notice that the joy, music, singing, and praise are based upon salvation (v. 2), God's love and faithfulness to Israel (v. 3), and the coming of God to judge the earth! (v. 9). Even all of nature will join in the praise (vv. 7-8)!

☑The first portion of the psalm speaks of the victories that the Lord accomplished on behalf of Israel. But they may extend further than that (v. 3b). Certainly verses 7-10 anticipate the coming of the Messiah to the earth with both judgment and righteous rule! Praise God for the Promise!⇦

MAY 21

JOHN 10:1-21 Who is your shepherd? To whose voice do you respond? That is the question as you read this portion of John. The fact is, sheep know the voice of their shepherd and respond to him. The true shepherd cares for and protects the sheep.

➲Look at the special relationship that Jesus has as the shepherd to His sheep. He calls the sheep (v. 3) and goes ahead of them (v. 4). The sheep listen to the shepherd's voice (vv. 3-4) and will not follow a stranger (v. 5). Jesus is the gate (v. 7). By this he meant that He is the only way into the sheepfold (salvation, v. 9a). The shepherd's mission is to see that sheep have a full and complete life (v. 10). Jesus cares enough to give His life for the sheep (vv. 11, 15) and will never abandon them (vv. 12-13).

Jesus specifically said that He was from the Father, that He would give His life for the sheep (vv. 14-15; cf. Isa 53:4-6), and that this would extend to those beyond Israel (i.e., the Gentiles, v. 16; cf. Gen 12:3b). Further, note carefully that Jesus said He had the authority to give His life – no one could take it from Him – and to take it back again (v. 18). The resurrection was within His own power as the sinless Son of God!☾

Whose voice do you follow? This is a crucial question! Look once again at 1 John 2:3-6. *Learn* to listen to and follow Jesus!

2 SAMUEL 15-16 Absalom demonstrated his true colors by attempting to wrest the kingdom from his father. Absalom's mother was Maacah, the daughter of Talmai, king of Geshur. Geshur was a kingdom in Gilead that the Israelites had failed to displace from the land God had given them (Josh 13:13).

Although it is speculation, it is interesting to think about the influence of a foreign mother in the life of Absalom. In a "multiple household" family (several wives, each with their own children), the mother wielded more influence in the lives of children than the father. It is probable that Maacah retained the worship of gods she had known in Geshur. There is no indication that David exercised any kind of restraint in Absalom's life. David should not have married a foreign woman, according to God's instruction as given to Moses. These things joined to bring trouble to David and his kingdom in Absalom's rebellion.

Look back at 2 Samuel 12:11-12 to see how literally Nathan's prophecy was being fulfilled.

PSALM 99   God's sovereignty is evident in verses 1-3. He rules over the nations, even when nations and rulers may think they are acting independently! The amazing thing is that this great God of sovereignty and justice communicates with His people. He answers prayer (v. 6) and reveals Himself through His word (v. 7). He forgives the sin of His people (v. 8). Knowing this, our response must be worship from the heart (v. 9)!

MAY 22

JOHN 10:22-42   As Jesus responded to questions at the Feast of Dedication, He again turned to the model of the shepherd and the sheep.

⊃Jesus' words on this occasion are very clear about His identity – He said He was one with the Father, that He gave eternal life to His followers, and that no one was able to disrupt that relationship (vv. 25-30).☾ What He said also brought the relationship between the believer and the Lord into sharp focus. Many alien voices are abroad today (as there have been in the past). They are seductive voices that will lure some professed believers from the fold (cf. John 6:66; Matt 24:12; 1 John 2:19). Remember that church membership doesn't guarantee kingdom membership (Matt 13:24-30; Acts 20:29-30; Jude 4). Does this lend an air of insecurity to the relationship between the believer and Jesus? Not at all – if the relationship defined in this passage is yours! Follow Jesus! Listen to His voice and His alone. Obey Him. Examine all other messages that come in relation to what God's Word says. Refuse to compromise with any untruth. Then rejoice in verse 28.

Follow how the listeners responded to His words (v. 31ff.). They admitted their intent to stone Jesus for His claim to be the Son of God (v. 33). ⊃Jesus reminded them that, according to the Scriptures, one *would* come sent by the Father (the Messiah, v. 36), and He challenged them to look at the facts about Himself (vv. 37-38). Further, He told them He was one with the Father (vv. 30, 38).☾

2 SAMUEL 17-18   As you follow the events recorded in these two chapters, understand that God had His hand in how the events played out.   God protected David from death and brought judgment on Absalom. Chapter 15 records Absalom's deceit (vv. 1-6) and his lies to his father (vv. 7-8). His arrogance and pride are evident in 18:18.

Although the other soldiers were reluctant to kill Absalom, Joab did so in spite of David's orders to the contrary (18:9-17). David felt overwhelming sorrow at the loss of his son and must have remembered Nathan's words to him (18:32-19:4; cf. 12:10).

PSALM 100   Two important facts with appropriate responses are given to us in this joyful psalm.

FACT ONE: The Lord is God. He made us; we are His. We are the sheep of His pasture (v. 3). *RESPONSE*: Shout for joy! Serve the Lord with gladness. Come before Him with joyful songs (vv. 1-2). Give this response because of *who* God is!

FACT TWO: God is good; His love and faithfulness are forever! (v. 5). *RESPONSE*:   Approach God in His sanctuary with praise and thanksgiving (v. 4). Do this because of *what* God is!

MAY 23

JOHN 11:1-44   Almost this entire chapter is given to the account of the death and resurrection of Lazarus. Lazarus and his two sisters, Mary and Martha, were close friends of the Lord.   When illness came to Lazarus, they were caught in circumstances they could not control – and although they called for Jesus, during His delay in arriving at their home, Lazarus died. Note the exchange between Martha and Jesus in verses 21-27. Martha commented that if only Jesus had been there her brother would not have died. After Jesus' remarkable statement to her in verse 23, Martha responded in faith (v. 24). Jesus had a more immediate meaning than Martha understood!

The delay was no accident (v. 6). As human beings, we are tied to this life and its limitations.   ⊃Jesus was about to teach His disciples (and many others) that life's limitations, as they understood them, did not limit Him (v. 15). Note Jesus' statement that He gave life, and those who received that life by faith would never die; i.e., they would have eternal life (vv. 25-26). Despite His plan to demonstrate His power, He mourned with the sisters (vv. 33-35).

Place yourself at the scene. Jesus called Lazarus to come out of the tomb, and he walked out – hobbled by the grave clothes (vv. 43-44)! We can surmise the joy of the sisters and the bewilderment of Lazarus. Many friends who were there placed their faith in Jesus (v. 45). Jesus is indeed the Lord of life! ☾

2 SAMUEL 19-20   With the crushing blow of the loss of his son, David lost his perspective of the victory his men had won. Joab spoke to David – perhaps too harshly and without giving the king the dignity he deserved (19:5-7). The result was that David decided to make Amasa commander of the army (v. 13). Remember, Amasa was also David's nephew, the son of David's sister Abigail (1 Chron 2:13-17), and a cousin

of Joab – but it was Amasa who had led the forces who fought for Absalom (17:24-25).

When the problem of Sheba's rebellion arose and Amasa was delayed in returning to the king, David bypassed Joab, asking Abishai (Joab's brother and also Amasa's cousin) to put down the rebellion. Joab accompanied the army, and when they met Amasa, Joab killed him in a deceitful manner, retaining control of the army himself (20:8-10).

PSALM 101   As the writer began the psalm, his thought was of God's love and justice. All that follows builds on this theme. Before you read the psalm, read Romans 12:9-10.

The psalmist reveals his decisions: He will exercise care to behave properly (v. 2), including what he looks at (v. 3). Further, he has decided to support and love those who love God (v. 6) and dissociate himself from evil people (vv. 3b-5, 7-8).

Review again Psalm 1:1. *Choose* to be influenced by godly people. *Choose* to support godly friends. Spend time with the unsaved to reach them for Christ, but take care! In the process, don't condone evil or move toward wrong yourself.

MAY 24

JOHN 11:45-57   After Jesus called Lazarus from the grave, there were two reactions to the miracle. Either people believed in Jesus as the Messiah (v. 45) or they moved against Him (vv. 46-48). It is important to see that it was neither truth nor justice that motivated the chief priests and Pharisees, but fear and jealousy. They were frustrated and angry that people believed in Jesus. Never mind the facts! They were so frustrated that they actually began to lay plans to kill Jesus (v. 53). Truth? Justice? Certainly not their highest aims. Their reaction was a sad commentary on their understanding of God and His ways. Look again at John 8:44 for the truth of what Jesus said about the leaders.

2 SAMUEL 21-22   The Gibeonites came to the Israelites desiring a treaty with them (Joshua 9). They had come with worn-out clothes and stale bread to make it look as if they had come from a long distance, when, in fact, they were living close by and would have been destroyed by the Israelites. The Israelites didn't seek God's advice and, before the leaders learned they had been deceived, made a pact with the Gibeonites, and thus could not take their land and annihilate them. Instead, they became servants to the Israelites. This text tells us that Saul broke the promise to the Gibeonites, and for this reason God had brought famine to the land (21:1). Saul's sin was avenged by the execution of seven of his male descendants.

David was not as young or as strong as he once was (21:15-17). David's nephew Abishai rescued him from imminent death.

As you read Chapter 22 (cf. Ps 18:1-50), see David's strong affirmation of his allegiance to God. Verses 22-24 are interesting because it isn't true that David was without sin as this implies. But it was true that David had a remarkably steady determination to serve and please God. When he did sin, he was quick to respond to God's message to him, and his repentance was complete.

As you read this song, note how David gives complete credit to God for all that he, as king, had accomplished. God had made David what he was and given him victory over the nations. While Saul and Absalom built monuments on their own behalf (1 Sam 15:12b; 2 Sam 18:18; cf. 22:28), David wrote psalms of praise to God!

PSALM 102   The writer faced difficulty of some kind. There is some suggestion that it may have been severe illness. The anchor in a world where each of us faces mortality is the enduring reign of the Lord (v. 12). Our days may be like smoke (v. 3), but God is real and eternal. In spite of difficulty, the writer has hope for the future – a faith in the Lord and His good work.

☑As you read verses 12-28, note the specific ways that the Lord will work. Notice the love that the Lord has for Jerusalem (vv. 13-14) and the Messianic content of verses 15-16. Note His compassion for the needy (vv. 17-20). Compare this with Isaiah 42:7, where Isaiah is speaking about the ministry of the Messiah. The millennial reign of Christ is suggested in verses 21-22. Compare these verses with Isaiah 2:2-4. All of the nations *will* come to Jerusalem to worship the Lord. Both creation and the consummation of history are mentioned in verses 25-27, and these verses are quoted in Hebrews 1:10-12, relating them to the Lord Jesus.⇦

MAY 25

JOHN 12:1-19   As Jesus was honored in the home of Mary, Martha, and Lazarus, follow the crosscurrents of emotion among those present. Mary anointed Jesus because she loved Him deeply. Judas objected because he was greedy (vv. 4-6). And the chief priests made plans to kill not only Jesus but also Lazarus because they were afraid of Jesus' popularity (12:10; compare also John 11:47-48, 12:19 and 12:37-40).

☑As Jesus rode into Jerusalem, the common people identified Him as the coming Messiah by quoting Psalm 118:26 (v. 13). John adds that it was to fulfill Zechariah 9:9 that Jesus rode into the city on a donkey (v. 15). The common people, perhaps the same ones who came to John the Baptist in repentance and for baptism, recognized Jesus as the

Messiah. Jesus didn't attempt to change their opinion (cf. Luke 19:38-40).⇦

2 SAMUEL 23-24   In David's last words, take special note of his testimony in verses 2-5. It is significant that he states that the Spirit of the Lord spoke through him (v. 2a). This is precisely what we believe when we say that the Scriptures are inspired. God spoke through the writers of the Bible in such a way that what God wanted us to understand was written.

As you read verses 3-4, think about government administered in the fear of God. Note the "word pictures," and understand how fresh, clean, and welcome such a government would be.

In Chapter 24, the counting of the men was an act of pride on David's part. Joab saw it as such and rebuked the king but was overruled. As the judgment of the Lord came on the people, David repented and prayed that any further judgment would fall on him and his own family. He bought the threshing floor of Araunah the Jebusite and sacrificed to the Lord on this site. This plot of land that David purchased is where the temple was constructed (1 Chron 21:25-22:1).

PSALM 103   The key to this psalm is the call to remember the Lord's benefits to His people (v. 2). These evoke praise to God. There are few places with such a list of reasons to praise God. The Lord cares for His own in many different ways – physically and spiritually. No matter what your circumstance, this is the psalm to read in remembering to praise the Lord. It reminds us that whether we are asleep or awake, whether aware or unaware, the Lord cares and the Lord meets every real need. Although our life here on earth is transient, the Lord's love for His own is eternal (vv. 15-18).

There are, however, conditions for the blessings in verses 17-18. *SO FEAR GOD, WALK WITH GOD, AND OBEY GOD!* Then join in praise to God with all of His created beings (vv. 21-22).

MAY 26

JOHN 12:20-50   Think about verses 23-29 as they relate to Jesus and to His followers (even today). ➲As Jesus contemplated His coming death, He was troubled (v. 27). Yet He knew that it was for this that He had come, and that only through death would glory come to the Father (vv. 27-28). His death and resurrection would fulfill the promise of redemption (cf. Col 2:14-15).☯ Consider the principle of the death of the seed in relation to those who confess Jesus. The death that Jesus spoke of in verse 25 is the death of personal ambition to do the will of God. It is to hold life with a "loose grip," following Jesus and trusting God for the result. We must love God more than anything the world has to offer. Think about how this applies to the kernel of wheat (v. 24). Purposefully doing kingdom work is death to personal ambition but will bring a harvest for the kingdom.

This death to personal ambition is more than a cute or trite thought. It can be heart-wrenching to give up what "I want." It requires a vision of this life in relation to eternity: a vision of lost people without hope, and more important, a vision of the call of the Savior to follow Him! This is very different from the current idea of self-fulfillment. It is different from the idea that if I am doing the will of God it will necessarily correspond to what "I want to do." But it is true that dying to personal ambition in order to follow Jesus is the only course that will bring true satisfaction – the contentment of a heart and soul filled with the peace of God. It also brings a life that is honored by God (v. 26b). The pursuit of personal ambition will bring only a mouthful of sawdust! It is, in reality, the pursuit of Satan's lie.

You might think that this is a "once-for-all" struggle and decision. There *are* major "once-for-all" decisions of surrender in life, but some decisions must be renewed daily (Luke 9:23-26). *It is a daily exercise of faith.* This is why it is so important to stay in God's Word – to be constantly reminded of reality and truth. *Go for the gold!*

To drive home how important this is, note that even among those who listened to Jesus, many did not take the step of faith – and are lost for eternity (vv. 37-43)! This fulfilled Isaiah's prophecy about how people would respond to the truth of the Messiah (Isa 53:1). Was their grasp of the "now" of personal will worth the ultimate loss?

1 CHRONICLES 1-2   1 and 2 Chronicles are somewhat parallel to the last portion of 1 Samuel, as well as 2 Samuel, 1 Kings and 2 Kings. There is more information in Chronicles about the genealogies of the Hebrews, information that isn't found elsewhere. Although our faith doesn't depend on these facts, they add to our understanding about the individuals of the Bible.

The books of Chronicles also add historical and spiritual information that is not in the other historical books. We will point out some of these things as we read.

In 1:13, note that the nations that occupied Canaan were descendants of Ham, the son of Noah. The land of Seir (1:38) was occupied by Edomites, descendants of Esau (Gen 32:3). In 2:13-17 the sons and daughters of Jesse are named. Zeruiah was a sister of David. Her three sons were Abishai, Joab, and Asahel. Abigail was another sister, and her son Amasa is mentioned. These four nephews of David were prominent in the military organization of David when he was king.

PSALM 104:1-9   Psalm 104 calls attention to a number of God's attributes, particularly in relation to creation. Verses 1-4 mention His majesty and power. Verse 4 is quoted in Hebrews 1:7 in relation to how angels are created to be God's servants.

As you read verses 5-9, also read Genesis 1:1-10. These verses refer to creation and the time when water covered the land – but God set boundaries for the water and separated the water from the dry land. When we contemplate the tremendous volumes of water and the mass of the mountains and land, we should be riveted by the power of the God of heaven.

MAY 27

JOHN 13:1-17   As the Passover meal was being served, Satan was at work in Judas (vv. 2, 27). Certainly Judas had made himself vulnerable by voluntarily choosing evil, apparently on a regular basis (John 12:4-6).

It was the custom in the Near East in Jesus' time for servants to wash the feet of guests coming into a home.   ◐When Jesus (as the master) undertook to wash the disciples' feet, He had a clear understanding of Himself and His relationship with God (v. 8b).◑   It was a highly unusual act, in their custom, for the master to wash his disciple's feet, which explains Peter's objection in verse 8. In assuming the role of a servant, Jesus was teaching humility and servanthood to the disciples, as He had done in the past (v. 14; Matt 20:24-28).

Peter's desire to have all the Lord could give led to his request that Jesus wash his hands and head as well as his feet (v. 9). Jesus' answer is instructive, for it contains a deeper spiritual truth.

When we place our faith in Jesus as Lord, we receive the gift of His righteousness (Rom 1:17, 3:21-22, 1 Cor 1:30). This righteousness, with forgiveness, opens the way to fellowship with God. Yet there is still the fact of sin in our lives (1 John 1:8). It is the "dust" of the world which contaminates us. Some of this "dust" we are unaware of, and the Bible promises that as we walk in the light of God's Word and the Holy Spirit. we will be cleansed (1 John 1:7). Other sin we know about and need to confess, but again, there is the promise of cleansing (1 John 1:9).

The righteousness we receive as a gift when we place our faith in Jesus is the "bath" that Jesus speaks of in verse 10. It includes forgiveness for past sins and prepares us to meet God. The needed washing of the feet that Jesus speaks of is the cleansing from daily sin that is also a gift on the basis of God's grace.

1 CHRONICLES 3-4   In 3:10-16 we find the kings of Judah from Solomon to Zedekiah, who was king when Judah went into captivity in

Babylon in 586 BC. All of the kings from Solomon to Josiah were in the genealogical line of Christ as recorded in Matthew. Josiah's son Jehoiakim and Jehoiakim's son Jehoiachin follow Josiah in the line of Christ. Jehoiachin is the same as Jeconiah as listed in Matthew 1:11.

It is significant that Jeremiah 22:24-30 states that Jehoiachin was despised by the Lord for his sin and would never have a descendant who would occupy the throne! Ezekiel 19:10-14 also speaks of Jehoiachin and states in verse 14b, "No strong branch is left on it fit for a ruler's scepter." This then rules out Johoiachin (Jeconiah) as being an ancestor of Christ. It is probable that the genealogy in Matthew is that of Joseph, Mary's husband. In Hebrew custom, the father's lineage was followed. The genealogy recorded in Luke records David's son Nathan as the progenitor of Christ rather than through the kings from Solomon to Jeconiah. This is most probably the genealogy of Mary – even though Joseph is listed as the father "so it was thought." It was Mary who genetically gave Jesus His human life.

PSALM 104:10-18   Having noted the power of the God of Creation in verses 1-9, attention is now given to the provision that God makes for His creatures (including man). There is a harmony in the way God has planned for the needs of the different animals and birds. There is water in the right places. Cattle have grass. The wild mountain goats are created to thrive and enjoy the rocky heights of the mountains.

Understanding these plans and provisions of the Lord can give us, as His children, a whole new appreciation of the plan of God in creation and how this brings blessing and enjoyment to us – and to all of the birds and animals that God cares for.

MAY 28

JOHN 13:18-38   It was a solemn moment in time when Jesus shared the last meal with the ones He loved. After the meal, He was troubled with the knowledge that He would be betrayed by one of His disciples and clearly told the disciples that this would be the case (v. 21). He even identified who that disciple would be (vv. 26-27). ☑Importantly, Jesus placed this betrayal in the context of fulfillment of Scripture (v. 18b, cf. Ps 41:9). These events were placed into the sovereign plan of God in bringing redemption to the world according to the Promise.⇦

Not only did Jesus tell of the betrayal, but He also warned Peter that he would deny Him that same night (v. 38)! Follow Peter in this chapter. He had great love for Jesus and a sense of propriety when at first he refused to allow Jesus, as his Lord, to wash his feet. Then, when he learned that the washing was necessary, he wanted his whole body washed! He was not a "half-way" sort of person. But he was self-assured when he should not have been (vv. 37-38). There was a dimension of spiritual conflict taking place that Peter knew nothing about. Later he would understand the issues clearly (1 Peter 5:8), but at this time his self-assurance was an opening for Satan to exploit this weakness. Peter learned about himself and the real nature of the battle through the experience.

1 CHRONICLES 5-7   Look at the hand of God in the lives of the Reubenites and the Gadites in 5:18-22. These were the two tribes, with the half tribe of Manasseh, who chose to settle in the land on the east side of the Jordan River, but they went with the other tribes to help in the battles with the Canaanites before they returned to their land. It was God's help that gave them victory because they trusted in God (vv. 20-22).

Now note the example of the people of the half tribe of Manasseh (vv. 23-26). They were men of strength, bravery, and stature (v. 24), *but they (with the Gadites and Reubenites) were later unfaithful to the Lord and suffered under God's hand of discipline. It is important to start well. It is even more important to end well!*

Moses and Aaron were from the Kohathite division of the tribe of Levi (6:2-3). The care of the holy implements of worship was the responsibility of the Kohathites (Num 4:4). The priests from among the Levites were Kohathites, and specifically, the descendants of Aaron (6:49). In 6:7-8 the priests during David's reign are listed. Note also that Samuel was a Kohathite (6:26-27) and that some of the Kohathite people received land in the hill country of Ephraim (6:66-67) where Elkanah, Samuel's father, was from (1 Sam 1:1).

PSALM 104:19-26   Think of how the author presents God as the author of natural order as you read these verses,. The Lord has created the day and the night. Day is the time for man to do his work. Night is perfectly designed for the nocturnal animals to be out in the dark. The moon in orbit around the earth marks off the months and the seasons. The environment of the sea matches the needs of the creatures of the sea.

When we think of this harmony, it is easy to join the author in verse 24, "How many are your works, O Lord! In wisdom you made them all...." Perhaps we should even learn not to grumble about the weather!

MAY 29

JOHN 14:1-14   The disciples were about to face the most shattering ordeal of their experience with Jesus – of their lives. In a few days He would go to the cross and to the grave. Jesus had told them, but they didn't really hear. Jesus, anticipating their troubled hearts, encouraged them to trust God and to trust Him (v. 1). Is it possible that the encouragement to trust Him seemed empty after the cross? Perhaps, but not after the resurrection!

ↄIn the first four verses of the chapter, there is also an answer to the anxiety to which we are prone. Trust God! Trust Jesus! Jesus told the disciples that he would go to the Father's house and that He would return to take them to be with Him. No one could say such a thing unless He was the Son of God.

Think about the remarkable message of verse 6. Jesus clearly says that He is the only way to come to God. He states that He is the only *way* to God, the only reliable *truth* about God, and the only *life* from God! There is no equivocation here. If one knows Jesus, he knows the Father (v. 7). If one has seen (known) Jesus, he has seen the Father (v. 9). Note carefully how Jesus relates Himself to the Father (vv. 10-11).ↄ

1 CHRONICLES 8-10   The historical and spiritual fact of 9:1 should give us pause. The tragic things that came to Judah happened precisely because of their disobedience.

Beginning with 9:2, the text speaks of the resettlement of the land after the Babylonian defeat (586 BC) under Ezra and Nehemiah. Note the re-establishment of responsibility of the people after the pattern established by David, when he was king about 500 years previously. This included the gatekeepers (vv. 22-27), those who were in charge of the worship articles (vv. 28-32), and the musicians (v. 33).

As you again read the account of the death of Saul, be reminded of the spiritual reality of the events (10:13-14). Saul died because he was unfaithful to the Lord. He was a young man of great promise who started well and had every opportunity under God of being great. But he ended badly because of his heart of disobedience.

PSALM 104:27-35   God is truly the sovereign God! He provides, and created beings receive from His hand not even realizing that the gifts are from the Lord. If, however, God turns His face, there is fear and terror, understanding that there is something not quite right with the order of things (v. 29a). Our life depends upon Him (v. 29b). Our very ability to breath, to walk another step, to live another moment is in His hand. We, along with all other created beings, are totally dependent upon the Lord. With this in mind, thanking the Lord for each meal that we eat makes good sense.

Are you content with what the Lord has given you and provided in your life? If we truly understand that God is sovereign and has the best interests of His children in His plan, can you join with the author in bringing praise to God (vv. 33-35)?

MAY 30

<u>JOHN 14:15-31</u>   It is startling to realize that Christians are able to do work that is as significant as that of Jesus (v. 12), enabled by the Holy Spirit (vv. 15-17), and through the power of prayer (v. 13). What Jesus is speaking about is the work of God in the world for each generation from the time of the cross until the Second Coming. This is the task of bringing the truth of salvation to people around us and seeing God work in their lives. God has chosen to use His people, the church, for this mission. *It is the most important thing that we can be about.* It is the final and great command that Jesus left for His believers (Matt 28:19-20; Acts 1:8). A significant question for each of us is how we have set our priorities and arranged our time to accomplish this business that Jesus has given to us.

In relation to the above comments, look at the call to obedience in verses 15, 21, 23-24. Importantly, see the relation between obedience and our love for the Lord. Note, too, the relationship between obedience and our growth in verse 21. Love for the Lord is demonstrated by our obedience. If we love the Lord, God loves us and so does Jesus. The Lord Jesus will progressively reveal Himself to us as we love and obey Him! Do you want to know the Lord better and more intimately? Here is the way for that to happen. There are no shortcuts! In this regard check Proverbs 4:25-27! ⊃Through this entire reading for today there is a strong message that Jesus and the Father are one. Even though not physically present with us, He promised not to leave us (v. 18). Because Jesus lives, believers will also live (v. 19b), and we are in Him (v. 20). Jesus was telling the disciples – and us – that He is God's Son!☉

One of the deepest needs of people in our world today is for peace – peace within themselves, peace with other people, and most of all, peace with God. Embrace and accept the gift that the Lord gives to His own in verse 27.

<u>1 CHRONICLES 11-12</u>   The account of the reign of David in Chronicles adds some detail and leaves out some material given in 2 Samuel. In this chapter, for instance, the seven-year stay in Hebron at the beginning of David's reign is not mentioned. The fact that Joab became the commander of the army by leading the attack on Jerusalem is not mentioned in 2 Samuel.

Benaiah (11:22) was the commander of the Kerethites and the Pelethites (the royal bodyguard, 2 Sam 8:18) and became commander of the army under Solomon (1 Kings 2:35).

This was a period of consolidation for David. As it became clear that David would indeed be the king, other military units joined ranks with the king. David wisely allowed the military units to decide that they wanted to align themselves with him, and when they did, David received them (Ch. 12). This was a time of instability and transition in the country, and the wise way that David allowed the country to come to him instead of taking power by force allowed a peaceful transition to a new political reality.

PSALM 105:1-11   A very strong emphasis in the Bible, a recurring theme, is to remember how the Lord has led and provided for one in the past. When we do so, it is much easier to believe that the Lord also has our present circumstance in control. This entire Psalm calls to remembrance how God delivered His people from Egypt in a most miraculous way.

The verses that we are reading today are an introduction to the psalm. They are a call to thank God (v. 1), sing to God (v. 2), give glory to His name (v. 3), look to God for His strength (v. 4), and remember what He has done for us (v. 5).

Note the strong statement of identification with the Lord in verse 7. *He is our God!* He is the one who remembers His promises (v. 8). He is the one who is faithful.

MAY 31

JOHN 15:1-17   Think about the vine and the gardener as portrayed in verses 1-17. First, note the reason that Jesus chose His own in verse 16. *His will is that we bear fruit.*

The work of the gardener is to help the vine to produce. There are two specific things that are mentioned that he does in this process of making the vine fruitful. The first is to cut off branches that do not bear (v. 2a). These are then gathered and burned (v. 6). The second task is to trim the branches that are bearing (v. 2b). This process of pruning involves cutting away growth that will impede the bearing process. Note that as we remain in the Lord, the result is fruit bearing (v. 5). In a practical sense, *the process of pruning involves the constant evaluation of our lives and schedules, under the direction of the Holy Spirit, to "cut away" whatever keeps us from fruit bearing.*

⊃Implicit in this whole section is the relationship that Jesus has with the Father and with believers. The bearing of fruit is the work of God through the gospel that brings men and women into relationship with Jesus and with the Father. Jesus, the true vine, is the channel through which the life of the Father is given to the world.⊂

Allow verse 10 to speak to your heart! The Lord Jesus calls us to remain in His love (vv. 9-17). It is possible to be very orthodox in creed and very busy with kingdom tasks without love that is warm and fervent (see Jesus' message to the Ephesian church, Rev 2:1-6). There is a foolproof way to remain in Jesus' love – to obey Him (vv. 10, 14).

<u>1 CHRONICLES 13-14</u> David's wisdom is seen in the way that he built consensus among his people (13:1-4). These suggestions were important for several reasons. It was a wise move at the right time (it was now clear that David would be king) to invite those who had initially been reluctant to cast their lot with David. Now it was safe for them to join him. This was an invitation to become part of "the team" instead of being treated as outsiders.

It was also wise to bring the priests and the Levites back into the mainstream of society (v. 2b). It was only with them integrated into life that the people could obey the mandates of the law and the sacrifices that were required.

Further, the ark of the covenant represented the presence of God in the life of the Israelites, and it was right that they should bring this back into their lives. The episode of the death of Uzzah should again remind us to treat the commands of God with great respect (see again the notes of May 16). David reacted with fear and awe when Uzzah was struck down. Notice that the Lord blessed the household of Obed-Edom while the Ark was within his home (13:14). The ark remained there until David had constructed his home and prepared a place for the ark in Jerusalem.

<u>PSALM 105:12-36</u> The call to remembrance is very specific. It is the miracle of God's care for His people from the time when they were a family in Canaan to the time when the Lord performed the great act of deliverance from Egypt.

→When one reads the historical account in Genesis and Exodus of these events, it is a narrative of consecutive events that may, at first, have no unifying theme or thread. Note here, however, that as these events are brought to mind, it is the Lord who orchestrated each event in sequence for His purpose. It was the Lord who protected His people when they were few and vulnerable (vv. 12-15). It was the Lord who brought the famine to Canaan and the Lord who arranged that Joseph would be sold into Egypt – later to become Pharaoh's "prime minister" (vv. 16-22). It was the Lord who brought the entire family to Egypt, who led a subsequent Pharaoh to enslave them, and it was the Lord who then sent Moses to be the instrument of deliverance for His people (vv. 23-26). It was the Lord who sent the plagues to Egypt to savage the land and convince the Egyptians that they really wanted the Israelites out of their land (vv. 27-36). In all of these events, God was at work to bring fulfillment to the promises made to Abraham and finally to bring the Savior through this nation.←

As the Israelites lived through the experiences, they had no perspective that the Lord was in each of these events. *But He was!* Living by faith means that even though we don't have the advantage of seeing the end result of what we are going through, we are able to trust that God is really in the events and will accomplish His good will through them. That conviction will allow us to live above even what would usually produce anxiety and frustration.

June

Bible Reading Schedule
And Notes

ℭℛ

*For everything that was written in the past was
written to teach us, so that through endurance and the
encouragement of the Scriptures, we might have hope.
Romans 15:4*

DISCOVERING THE BIBLE
READING SCHEDULE
JUNE

1	John 15:18-27	1 Chronicles 15-16	Psalm 105:37-45
2	John 16:1-16	1 Chronicles 17-18	Psalm 106:1-23
3	John 16:17-33	1 Chronicles 19-20	Psalm 106:24-48
4	John 17:1-12	1 Chronicles 21-22	Psalm 107:1-22
5	John 17:13-26	1 Chronicles 23-24	Psalm 107:23-43
6	John 18:1-27	1 Chronicles 25-26	Psalm 108
7	John 18:28-40	1 Chronicles 27-28	Psalm 109
8	John 19:1-16	1 Chronicles 29	Psalm 110
9	John 19:17-42	1 Kings 1-2	Psalm 111
10	John 20:1-18	1 Kings 3-4	Psalm 112
11	John 20:19-31	1 Kings 5-6	Psalm 113
12	John 21:1-14	1 Kings 7-8	Psalm 114
13	John 21:15-25	2 Chronicles 1-2	Psalm 115
14	1 Corinthians 1:1-17	2 Chronicles 3-4	Psalm 116-117
15	1 Corinthians 1:18-31	2 Chronicles 5-6	Psalm 118
16	1 Corinthians 2	1 Kings 9-10	Psalm 119:1-32
17	1 Corinthians 3	2 Chronicles 7-8	Psalm 119:33-64
18	1 Corinthians 4	2 Chronicles 9	Psalm 119:65-96
19	1 Corinthians 5	1 Kings 11-12	Psalm 119:97-128
20	1 Corinthians 6	1 Kings 13-14	Psalm 119:129-152
21	1 Corinthians 7	2 Chronicles 10-11	Psalm 119:153-176
22	1 Corinthians 8	2 Chronicles 12-13	Psalm 120
23	1 Corinthians 9	1 Kings 15-16	Psalm 121
24	1 Corinthians 10:1-13	2 Chronicles 14-16	Psalm 122
25	1 Corinthians 10:14-33	2 Chronicles 17-18	Psalm 123
26	1 Corinthians 11:1-16	2 Chronicles 19-20	Psalm 124
27	1 Corinthians 11:17-34	1 Kings 17-18	Psalm 125
28	1 Corinthians 12:1-11	1 Kings 19-20	Psalm 126
29	1 Corinthians 12:12-31	1 Kings 21-22	Psalm 127
30	1 Corinthians 13	2 Kings 1-2	Psalm 128

JUNE 1

JOHN 15:18-27   There is a flip side to remaining in the Savior's love (v. 9). The world will not appreciate it and, in fact, will dislike it intensely (vv. 18-25). This emphasizes that it is impossible to straddle the fence. Make your choice! Love Jesus, but don't expect the world to welcome you with adulation and open arms. Be realistic – and understand that it was so for Jesus, and He has told us that it will be so for each of us. ⊃In these comments to the disciples, note how Jesus identifies Himself with God the Father and how the world's rejection matches the scripture (vv. 21-25; cf. Ps 35:19; 69:4; 109:3).☾

There is synergism at work between the Holy Spirit and God's people in spreading the gospel message (vv. 26-27). The Holy Spirit is within the believer – but the Christian also chooses to testify to God's grace in the Lord Jesus.

1 CHRONICLES 15-16   Plans were made to bring the ark to Jerusalem; note the significance of David's instruction in 15:2. David had taken time to find out why Uzzah had died and gave special instruction to the Levites who would carry the ark (vv. 3-15). When all was in order, the ark was successfully carried to Jerusalem (15:15). Lesson learned! The arrival of the ark was accompanied with planned worship and prepared music (vv. 16-28).

David's psalm of thanks to the Lord is worship, testimony, acknowledgment of God's acts, and rejoicing. It is "reality orientation." Write the suggestions to God's people in the margin of your Bible beside the appropriate verses.

As David prepared for continued worship with sacrifices and offerings, notice that he did everything correctly, i.e., in conformity with the way revealed to Moses (16:39-42).

PSALM 105:37-45   →As this psalm concludes, the account of God's hand in deliverance is very apparent.   The Lord prompted the Egyptians to give the Israelites silver and gold as they left (v. 37; cf. Exod 12:33-36). The Lord protected them with His presence in the cloud (v. 39; cf. Exod 13:21-22). The Lord provided food for them (v. 40; cf. Exod 16:11-18). The Lord gave them water from the rock (v. 41; cf. Exod 17:1-7).   God was fulfilling His promise to Abraham to bring his descendants back to the promised land of Canaan (v. 42; cf. Gen 15:13-

16). God fulfilled every single promise He made to the Israelites (Josh 21:45).←

This is the sort of remembering we need to do! Think about how the Lord has led in your own life, first leading you to the truth, then to faith, then protecting and leading to where you are today. God allows us to experience the consequences of our disobedience and sin – but always with the safety net of His love beneath us to help us to grow. Praise God!

<u>JUNE 2</u>

<u>JOHN 16:1-16</u>   In the economy of the kingdom, it is clear that the coming of the Holy Spirit (the Counselor) was essential (v. 7). While Jesus' human body limited Him to one location, the Holy Spirit has no such restriction. Further, in the aftermath of the resurrection, when the disciples' perspective had matured, the Holy Spirit would give them all they needed for ministry and survival in a hostile world (vv. 1-4). Jesus was speaking about launching the church through the power of the Holy Spirit.

The truth of verse 11 is crucial. At the cross, the Evil One was judged and defeated. Although still in the world and hard at work to subvert God's work, the end of Satan's pernicious work is in sight (Rev 12:10; 20:10). The power of the cross and risen Lord is more than adequate to counter Satan's attacks on God's children.

Another truth is evident in verse 14. The Holy Spirit works on behalf of the Lord Jesus. He never calls attention to Himself but to Jesus. ⊃The "pearl" in verse 14b is that what we need to know from Jesus, He (the Holy Spirit) will give us! And all that belongs to the Father belongs to Jesus (vv. 14-15)!⊂ With God's Word and the indwelling Holy Spirit, each of us has all we need to face the world.

<u>1 CHRONICLES 17-18</u>   After David had consolidated his rule and built his palace, he determined to build a house for the Lord. But God said that instead of David building a house for Him, He would build a house (an enduring kingdom) for David (17:10b). As for the house that David wanted to build, God told him his son would build that house (17:11-12). Further, the Lord said He would establish the kingdom of David's descendent which would last forever (vv. 10b-14).

☑The Lord was speaking of the Messiah, who would come from David's line and who would be established forever (vv. 10b-14; cf. Isa 11-12). David, in response, understood that this was the sovereign will of God and that the most important thing was not what the promise would bring him personally, but that glory would come to the Lord in its fulfillment (vv. 23-24).⇦

PSALM 106:1-23   As the author began the psalm, he praised God for His goodness and greatness. He asked that God include him in the deliverance of His people (vv. 4-5). The psalmist then turned to how his own people failed to follow the Lord in trust and obedience.

As you read verses 6-23, note these failures despite God's faithfulness and presence. They failed to consider the miracles and to remember God's kindness to them (v. 7). Their memories were short; they loved it when God parted the sea but soon forgot what He had done (vv. 9-13). They grumbled, they complained about Moses and Aaron, they turned to idol worship (vv. 13-20).

Remember the lesson of Psalm 105. Keep thinking about how the Lord has led in the past – and avoid the pitfalls of the Israelites recorded in Psalm 106! When we grumble and complain in our hearts (or verbally) we are really concluding that the Lord does not care, does not have His good hand in our lives. That is the same sin the Israelites committed in the desert.

JUNE 3

JOHN 16:17-33   When Jesus told the disciples that He would leave them, they were confused. Even more confused when He coupled this statement with the promise they would see Him again "in a little while" (v. 17). This was something they would not really understand until after the events. How *could* they have understood the crucifixion and the resurrection before the fact?

Without the reality of the resurrection, there was no way Jesus could guard the disciples from the weeping, mourning, and grief that the crucifixion would bring (v. 20). Jesus' promise, however, was that when they did see Him, the grief would be replaced with a permanent joy. ⊃Jesus said He had come from the Father and was returning to Him (v. 28).⊂

This is similar to our own thinking about death. When anyone close to us dies, we grieve. Although we know about the resurrection and coming glory, without the perspective of experience, we cannot understand how joyful we will be when we see Jesus at His second coming! It is hope and faith – but a hope not yet realized.

Jesus gave two important promises to the disciples during this conversation. Jesus promised to answer prayer (vv. 23-24). Note in verse 24 that *our lives are impoverished if we don't pray*. If we don't see God working – if we don't see God's blessing – it may be because we don't pray! The second promise is the gift of peace (v. 33). In spite of the difficulty believers face, Jesus' peace is secured by His victory over the world and its evil forces.

1 CHRONICLES 19-20   This was Israel's highest hour. When David went into battle, God gave the victory (18:6b, 13b). Note also Joab's faith and courage as he faced the Ammonites and the Arameans (19:13).

We are tempted to think of these battles as merely a game – an exercise in which the outcome was obvious. Not so! Remember that this was real war in which men and armies were at risk and engaged in pitched battle. It is true that God gave the victory, but the outcome in the midst of battle wasn't nearly so black and white as it is to us as we read.

It was also at this time that much of Israel's wealth was collected (18:7; 20:2-3). The accumulation continued through the reign of Solomon, but because of the sin of leaders and people, the gold was gone five years after Solomon's death (1 Kings 10:23; 14:25-26)!

PSALM 106:24-48   The sad litany of the people's sin and rebellion continues in these verses. It is a commentary on the bent to sin that we all have. In spite of how the Lord had repeatedly demonstrated His goodness and caring for His people, they didn't believe Him (v. 24). They turned from Him in grumbling and disobedience (v. 25). They turned to idolatry and even sacrificed their children to idols (vv. 28, 36-37).

The sad result was to experience God's anger and oppression by their political enemies. As people turned to Him, God responded – but read verse 43 to see the depth of human sin. Read the prayer of the writer in verses 47-48. The writer prayed that God would bring His people back to the land. In a number of places in the Scriptures, God has promised to do that very thing (cf. Ezek 36:24-30).

JUNE 4

JOHN 17:1-12   Jesus' prayer in Chapter 17 has been known as the "high-priestly" prayer for Himself and His followers. It is rich in insight of Jesus' heart for the disciples and the church. There is a sense of completion of His work here on earth as He looked forward to the coming hours. The major focus of His prayer is the believers who had come to Him and those who would follow through the ages (vv. 9, 20).

Note Jesus' definition of eternal life (v. 3). ●Without the knowledge of Jesus and the Father through Jesus, there is no eternal life! This statement is consistent with the entire scope of Jesus' teaching and the identification of Jesus as God's Son (vv. 1-5, but implicit in the entire section). Note, too, that those who had come to Jesus in faith came to Jesus through the Father (v. 6; cf. John 6:44).☾ The mark of this faith in believers is their obedience to the will of the Father (v. 6).

The elements of this prayer help us understand Jesus' heart and the dangers of life in the world. We see His concern for His disciples and for all who had believed (vv. 9-10). Although Jesus loved the whole world, His concern for believers as members of the family was different (v. 9). He prayed for their protection through the power of the Father's name while they remain in the world, and for their unity with one another and with the Father and Son (vv. 11-12, 23).

One truth here that should make us live carefully but should also encourage us is the depth of Jesus' concern for His followers amidst the dangers that surround them in the world. This should concern us as well – and drive us to the protection of the Father and the power of His name (v. 11).

1 CHRONICLES 21-22   In 21:1, the text tells us that Satan incited David to number the men. In 2 Samuel 24:1 the text states that "he" (God) incited David to number the men. James 1:13-15 is clear that God does not tempt to sin and further explains the "cascade" that leads us into sin. Romans 1:24, 26, and 28 explain that when a person has chosen sin, God gives him over to that sin and the judgment that will follow. This was the case of Pharaoh during the plagues, when God "hardened" Pharaoh's heart. Pharaoh had chosen to do wrong, and, in the context of that choice, God led him to resist the message of the plagues in order to bring glory to God and judgment on the nation.

Satan, then, was the one who tempted David to take the prideful step of numbering the men. God, displeased with David's heart, made no move to hinder David once his heart had been drawn away. The judgment that came should teach us that our own sinful decisions and actions sometimes have far-reaching effects on many other people (seventy thousand died, 21:14).

Note David's specific instructions to Solomon as he was handing responsibility to his son (22:6-19).

PSALM 107:1-22   The message of this psalm is both literal and symbolic. From our perspective, it is easier to make symbolic applications, and this fits well with the truth of Scripture. We *are* lost until the Lord gives us the direction to come to Him. We *are* imprisoned until the Lord frees us through His truth. We *do* suffer when we rebel against the Lord's commands. Don't forget, however, the literal application that will fit our lives as well.

This is an expression of thanksgiving for the goodness and the mercy of the Lord (vv. 1-3). Review Ephesians 2:1-7. All of us – no exceptions – are lost until the mercy of God is applied to our lives. This psalm is about that mercy.

Now look at the three groups of people described in verses 1-22. Some were lost and had no clear idea of the way to safety (vv. 4-9). In this instance, there is no mention of specific sin as the reason for their predicament. The Lord often allows difficulty in our lives to demonstrate His response to our faith. In this way we learn to trust God. Some suffered because they had sinned (vv. 11, 17). In either circumstance, as we turn to the Lord we learn to trust Him and receive His blessing. With this in mind, review verses 1-3.

JUNE 5

JOHN 17:13-26   Review the entire chapter as you begin today's reading. Jesus' prayer for His disciples should give us strength and encouragement each day of the year! It was Jesus' last recorded prayer before His death for those who had, or would, believe in Him. *It extends to you and me* (vv. 20-21).

Think about what Jesus says about the citizenship of believers (vv. 14, 16). Each believer belongs as little to this world as Jesus! This extends to our interest in the things of this world and to our obligation to the demands of this world.

Look more specifically at the content of the prayer – what Jesus brought to the Father on behalf of believers. Those who believe in Jesus were given to Jesus by the Father; they have eternal life – and *they know God and Jesus* (vv. 2-3). They have obeyed God's Word (v. 6). They know with certainty that Jesus is from God (v. 8). This prayer is exclusively for believers (v. 9). Jesus prays for their protection – through the strong name and power of the Father (vv. 11b, 15) – from evil and hate (vv. 14-15). Jesus prays for the sanctity (setting apart for His purpose) of believers through the truth of God's Word (v. 17). Jesus prays for the unity of believers and for the final glory of the church with Him (vv. 23-24). ➲Once again see that Jesus came from the Father and identifies Himself with the Father – from before the creation (vv. 8, 16, 23-24).☾

This is overwhelming. It is a glimpse into Jesus' heart for members of the church and for the church as a whole. It crosses all boundaries of time, culture, and geography. It defines the believer's specific relationship with Christ and with the God of glory. It must, as we meditate upon these truths, change our perception of ourselves as God's children and our place in the kingdom and the world!

1 CHRONICLES 23-24   The Levites were the Israelites' gift to the Lord for doing His work.   Some of these tasks are mentioned in these two chapters.   The mundane tasks of caring for the tabernacle were important, as well as the more visible tasks of sacrificing and leading in worship.

The three branches of the Levites – with the exception of the sons and descendants of Aaron – had the task of carrying the tabernacle and the implements of worship when the Israelites moved from place to place.   Now, with the construction of the temple, that would change (23:25-32).   They were reassigned duties in the temple and in the worship of the people.

Luke 1:5 tells us that Zechariah was a priest in the division of Abijah.   In 1 Chronicles 24, the twenty-four divisions of the priesthood are listed, the division of Abijah being number eight (v. 10).   Isn't it interesting that for the one thousand years between David and the coming of Christ, these divisions had been observed, and Zechariah was in this line?

PSALM 107:23-43   If you have felt the force of the seas, either on shore or at sea, you will relate to verses 23-32.   A raging sea is fearful and awesome.   Especially in a small vessel, being in a heavy sea is like being on a high-speed elevator.   When down, one is surrounded by water.   When on the crest, the opposite is true.   Consider verses 26 and 27 to understand the predicament of these sailors in verses 23-32.   Then learn from their cry to the Lord (v. 28) and His act of mercy in calming the sea (v. 29).   The disciples had just such an experience recorded in Mark 4:35-41.

What happened to the Israelites is described in verses 33-42. The Lord tailors His dealings with people according to their needs.   He disciplines us to get our attention and correct wrong.   He blesses us when we call on Him.   Read verse 43.   Think back on the message of each part of the psalm and apply it to your life!

JUNE 6

JOHN 18:1-27   As you begin to read about the arrest and trial, compare verses 4 and 11 with 12:27.   Jesus knew what would happen to Him.   There were no surprises as the drama of the ages unfolded.   Although Jesus was arrested and bound, He was in control of the situation.   When the soldiers came to arrest Him and He identified Himself, they fell to the ground (v. 6).   When the ear of the high priest's servant was cut off, Jesus restored it (Luke 22:51).   When the high priest questioned Him, Jesus simply referred to the record of what He had openly taught (vv. 19-24).

Most of us can probably see ourselves in Peter as he faced the temptation to deny his Lord. Peter learned something about himself that night that stayed with him for the rest of his life. As the rooster crowed and Jesus turned to look at Peter (Luke 22:61), tremendous grief overtook him. He understood how vulnerable he had been and how he had denied Jesus. The answer to our own weakness – and each one of us has a weak point – is to walk closely to the Lord and trust the Lord in prayer (Luke 22:46).

1 CHRONICLES 25-26   Music was central in the worship of the assembly. All of Chapter 25 concerns this ministry, but look especially at verses 6-8. There was organization and planning, and personnel were dedicated to the ministry.

This was also true with the other ministries outlined in Chapter 26. There is no insignificant ministry or work in the kingdom!

PSALM 108   When we face difficulty, we need perspective. Without proper perspective, everything may look out of joint. David is a good model for us; he faced obvious difficulty (vv. 10-12), but he focused on the goodness and the power of the Lord. Note his personal resolve (vv. 1-3). His eyes were on the Lord, and his heart was committed to know Him. His thinking was correct (v. 4), and his desire was for the right thing (v. 5). This is the reality orientation we all need.

JUNE 7

JOHN 18:28-40   The injustice of the trial of Jesus is striking. The religious leaders had previously decided that Jesus should die. Even the high priest agreed (v. 14, see also John 11:49-50). Jesus told them to consider the facts (vv. 20-21). To Pilate's question about charges, the Jews gave an evasive non-answer (v. 30). Jesus answered Pilate's questions candidly, and Pilate knew there was no valid reason to send Him to His death. There is no question that Satan was at work in this. Review the part that the Evil One had in the betrayal. ➲Yet God was at work with His redemptive plan. Note Jesus' answer to Pilate in verses 36-37. Jesus proclaimed that He was a king, and it was for this reason He had been born. He was born to be a king, and He came into the world to die (John 12:27). The Lord God was about to lay on Him the iniquity of us all (Isa 53:6b); this was unknown to the rulers who were caught in the web of an unjust decision (1 Cor 2:7-8). As you again read this account, stand in awe and thankfulness for the majestic plan of redemption!➲

1 CHRONICLES 27-28   In 28:4-7, David said God had told him that of all his sons, Solomon would be the next king, and the Lord would establish his kingdom. ☑Thus, Solomon was now seemingly singled out

as the one through whom the Messiah would come and through whom the Promise would be fulfilled (28:4-7) – *if* Solomon was unswerving in carrying out the Lord's commands and laws (v. 7)! In fact, Solomon was in the legal line of Jesus through Joseph (by Jewish custom, always through the father, Matt 1:6), but Jesus' humanity came through Mary's line as given in Luke. There, Solomon's brother Nathan is the human ancestor of Jesus (Luke 3:31; cf. 1 Chron 3:5). David gave final words to his leaders (28:8) and to Solomon (28:9-10, 20-21).⇦ Note too that the plans for the temple were from the Lord (28:12), and David passed these on to Solomon. He also gave specific instructions about the Levites' duties in the service of the temple, and specifics about the weight of gold to be used in the articles of worship in the temple (vv. 13-18). These had been revealed to David, and he wanted to ensure that they would be carried out exactly (v. 19).

As Solomon assumed the kingship, he received the blessing of the Lord (29:25) which gave him a good start. We will follow his reign in Kings and Chronicles.

PSALM 109   David's complaints about the unfairness of his opponents are specific: They are lying about him (v. 2); they are attacking him without cause (v. 3); they repay evil for good even though they were supposed friends (v. 4). The character of these persons is evident in verses 16-18 – individuals of a reprobate mind. As a result, David feels devastated (vv. 22-25). There is, however, hope. David is a man of prayer (v. 4b), and he looks for the good hand of the Lord to uphold his cause. There is a sense of expectation as David waits for the answer he is sure will come (vv. 30-31).

JUNE 8

JOHN 19:1-16   Pilate was on trial. Read again 18:28-40 and continue through 19:16. Jesus was in control of Himself – and the entire situation. Pilate was obviously disturbed that he was being pressured to make a judgment. He tried to avoid the responsibility (18:31). His efforts to pull rank didn't help (18:35; 19:10). What concerned Pilate, who was responsible to uphold Roman law, was that he could find no reason to charge Jesus with a capital crime as the leaders insisted upon (18:38, 19:4). Finally he had to decide. Politics ruled, and in cowardice Pilate allowed the death penalty to stand (v. 16).

1 CHRONICLES 29   David had accumulated enormous amounts of gold, silver, and precious stones that were set aside for the construction of the temple (vv. 1-5a). David then challenged the people to do the same (v. 5b), and they responded by donating huge amounts of gold and silver (vv. 6-9).

As David prayed, he understood the person and power of God (vv. 10-13). Note also that he recognized where personal wealth comes from (vv. 14-16). With such a clear understanding, it is easier to give generously to the Lord!

Chronicles records the passage of the throne to Solomon as quite routine, but as we will see, details are omitted here that will be presented in Kings.

PSALM 110   ☑This psalm is messianic, prophetic about the coming Christ and His ministry. Jesus used verse 1 to demonstrate that David was writing about something more than an earthly son (Luke 20:41-44; see also Acts 2:29-36). The second coming of Jesus in battle and judgment is depicted in verses 2-3 and 5-7. Compare this with Revelation 19:11-16, where the Messiah as the King comes in battle array.

Note the reference to Melchizedek in verse 4. Hebrews 5:6 makes it clear that in speaking of Melchizedek, the psalmist refers to Christ. For the background on this see Genesis 14:18ff. Hebrews 7 also explains how Jesus is like Melchizedek and that this psalm refers to Jesus. ⇦

JUNE 9

JOHN 19:17-42   It is instructive to follow the different people present at the crucifixion. Each added to the composite picture. Other gospels give different details, but John leaves the reader with the unmistakable impression of Jesus' dignity even to the moment of death.

The soldiers, hardened by death and cruelty, simply took charge of three more prisoners sentenced to death (v. 16). ☑They gambled for Jesus' clothes (v. 24), thereby fulfilling the prophecy of Psalm 22:18. Note the fulfilled prophecy of verses 31-33. The bodies of those being crucified had to be removed before the Sabbath (Deut 21:22-23). To kill them more quickly, the legs of the victims were broken (v. 31). Jesus, however, was already dead, so His legs were not broken (v. 33; cf. Exod 12:46), but the soldiers pierced His side (vv. 34-37; cf. Zech 12:10) "...so that the scripture would be fulfilled..." (vv. 36-37). ⇦

Pilate, having given Jesus' life to the religious leaders, could not be pushed to change the sign on Jesus' cross identifying Him as the king of the Jews. It was as if, having given in to them on the more important issues of justice and life, he was proving his authority on this minor issue. Without doubt, this was a difficult day for Pilate. Having compromised his integrity as a judge, he lived with blood on his hands.

A small group of Jesus' followers near the cross included His mother and the Apostle John. Think of how different their perspective was from that of the soldiers and the priests – or even of Pilate. Did Mary remember the words of Simeon on the day Jesus was brought to the temple to be circumcised over thirty years earlier (Luke 2:34-35)? Simeon had told her that "a sword will pierce your own soul..." Note Jesus' concern for His mother as He gave the responsibility of her care to the Apostle John (vv. 26-27).

→Finally, note that it was Jesus who laid down His life (v. 30). The moment of death was His choice. Not a moment too soon or too late. All had been accomplished. Compare this with John 10:17-18. Redemption was complete, and the forces of evil were defeated at that very moment (Col 2:15).←

1 KINGS 1-2   This account in Kings of David's last days gives insight that 1 Chronicles does not give. There was intrigue and near violence when Adonijah (David's fourth son) tried to succeed his father as king. David had apparently made his choice of Solomon to be king after him (1:13, also note Nathan's understanding of the matter). Adonijah garnered the support of Joab and the priest Abiathar. Had he been successful, it would have meant death to Bathsheba and to Solomon (1:12, 21).

David, though feeble, made his choice clear, and with the help of Nathan the prophet, Zadok the priest, and Benaiah, the commander of the king's guard, Solomon was crowned.

Adonijah was now in danger of losing his life. Solomon spared his life, a measure of his good will.

Note David's final commands to Solomon (2:2-9): Trust and obey God. David also charged Solomon to see that Joab paid for the deaths of Abner and Amasa. He was to show kindness to the sons of Barzillai because Barzillai had done the same for David when Absalom led the rebellion (2 Sam 17:27-29; 19:31-37). He was also to see that Shimei received justice for his treatment of David (2 Sam 16:5-8, 13-14).

Follow how Solomon carried out these last instructions from his father. Adonijah, Joab, and Shimei all died because of their treachery.

PSALM 111   List the ways that God is good and faithful to His people. Beginning with verse 4, note the qualities for which the Lord should be remembered: His love, faithfulness, justice, compassion, and provision. His word (v. 7b), as well as salvation for His people (v. 9a). Wisdom begins with true acknowledgment of God (v. 10; cf. Prov 1:7). ☑Redemption has come to God's people through the Covenant that He ordained (v. 9; cf. Luke 1:68-69: Here Zechariah quotes this psalm and speaks about redemption and salvation coming in the person of

Christil). ⇦ Now go back to the first three verses of the psalm. How truly great, truly glorious and majestic are the Lord's works and His deeds!

JUNE 10

JOHN 20:1-18   Mary of Magdala knew intense sorrow at the crucifixion of Jesus. She had been delivered of seven demons (Luke 8:2) and loved Jesus deeply. It is significant that Jesus appeared to her in the garden. She came first to the tomb early in the morning after the Sabbath. When Jesus was not there, she told others who came, among them Peter and another disciple, probably John. After they left, Mary remained weeping.

→This woman, who had suffered under Satan, then had the privilege of receiving the message from the angels in the tomb (whom Peter did not see when he entered the tomb), and then was the first to see Jesus. It is hard to imagine her emotions. The Savior, who had delivered her from Satan, was alive! Think of the message Jesus gave to her, speaking of "my Father, and your Father; my God, and your God." What a powerful affirmation of her relationship with Jesus as Savior and with God! As we know Jesus as Savior and Lord, we are identified with Him in our relationship with the Father.⇐

1 KINGS 3-4   When the Lord appeared to Solomon, offering to give him what he wanted, Solomon asked for a discerning heart, able to distinguish between right and wrong. If you had been Solomon, is this what you would have requested? This was the finest request Solomon could have made. God answered in a marvelous way. Not only did Solomon have wisdom but also great knowledge about many things (4:29-34).

PSALM 112   Would you like a guarantee of the Lord's blessing? Then read this psalm. Notice that the condition for blessing is the fear of the Lord and delight in His commands (v. 1).

Look for this principle in the text of this psalm: generosity to those in need, justice in dealing with others, and giving to the poor (vv. 5, 9). Traditionally, these have not been high on our "evangelical" list of priorities, but they are prominent on the Lord's list. Consider the promise of verse 4. When one chooses God's agendas, "even in darkness, light dawns for the upright..."

JUNE 11

JOHN 20:19-31   The blessing of peace comes from the resurrection. When Jesus appeared to the disciples on the evening of the resurrection, His first word to them was "Peace be with you!" (v. 19). He repeated the blessing of peace (v. 21), and the next time He appeared to them He gave them peace (v. 26). This is not a casual matter. Jesus was teaching a valuable lesson. In John 14:27 and 16:33 Jesus had *promised* His followers peace. Now, with the resurrection, He had *secured* that peace! *His first, second, and third words to the disciples were to give His peace.* It is peace with God. It is freedom from the guilt of sin. It is the basis of peace with one another. It is God's great blessing to us – secured with the resurrection.

Jesus told the disciples that as the Father had sent Him, He was sending them to the world. When Jesus came from the Father, it was with a redemptive purpose (John 12:27). →When Jesus sends out believers, it is with the same redemptive purpose (v. 21). Consider how this should affect our thinking and our actions.←

1 KINGS 5-6   In the preparations and details of building, the Lord gave Solomon the wisdom He had promised (5:12). The Lord gave Solomon both promises and conditions (6:11-13). It is interesting that it took seven years to build the temple – but it took thirteen years to build Solomon's palace (6:38b-7:1)!

As magnificent as the temple was, again note the Lord's word to Solomon during the construction (6:11-13). An imposing building would not secure God's blessing. It was the obedience of Solomon and his people that the Lord required for His blessing.

PSALM 113   The writer calls on readers to praise the Lord five times in the first three verses of the psalm. The reasons are in verses 4-9: The Lord is a God of great glory (v. 4), unrivaled in heaven or earth (v. 5), who watches over the poor and needy (v. 7) and women not blessed with children (v. 9). God cares. God is to be praised!

JUNE 12

JOHN 21:1-14   Jesus appeared to the disciples a third time after they had been fishing the whole night and had caught no fish. While they were still in the boat, early in the morning, Jesus came to them on the shore. He told them to throw their net out on the right side of the boat, and they immediately caught more than the net could hold! This catch prompted them to conclude that it was the risen Lord (v. 7).

It is curious that when they came ashore and shared breakfast, they intuitively "knew" it was the Lord (v. 12). The text states that they didn't dare ask if He was Jesus. Why would this even be a question if His appearance was exactly what it had been? It seems that the disciples weren't sure about His identity simply by His physical appearance. It is possible that the resurrection body – although the same body – was changed to the spiritual body that will also be ours at the resurrection (1 Cor 15:42-44).

1 KINGS 7-8   →When the temple was finished, the furnishings were placed in their proper place along with the ark, which was brought by the priests and placed in the Most Holy Place. As a seal of God's presence, His glory, in the form of a cloud, filled the temple. Awesome! Solomon's speech provides historical background for the people (8:14-21). Read carefully Solomon's prayer for it is a model of worship and petition. Solomon asked the Lord not to forget His promise to David with regard to the permanence of the throne: the Messianic throne (8:25-26; cf. 2 Sam 7:11b-13). Notice Solomon's emphasis on repentance as he anticipates sin among the people (8:33-40). The temple worship kept the Israelites separate from the other nations. It was a constant reminder of the laws that the Lord gave His people. It was thus important in ensuring the channel through which the Savior would come.←

In the blessing that Solomon pronounced (vv. 54-61), he acknowledged God's faithfulness (v. 56), anticipated God's grace in their lives (v. 58), and expressed the hope that the lives of the Israelites would be a testimony to all the peoples of the world (v. 60).

PSALM 114   The Israelites were often commanded to remember their deliverance from Egypt. Each time it was recounted, they remembered God's greatness and His special purpose for them.

The deliverance from Egypt is one of the great miracles of all history (v. 1). The parting of the sea (v. 3), the Lord's provision for His people in the desert (v. 8), and their crossing the Jordan (v. 5) are each miraculous. God is powerful, and *all nations* should tremble before the Lord (v. 7)!

JUNE 13

JOHN 21:15-25   Consider Jesus' concern for Peter's restoration. It wasn't an easy conversation for Peter. There is no way Peter could come away from this encounter with a "ho-hum" or cavalier attitude about sin. Jesus' questions made him think carefully about what love for Jesus entailed. His denial created the question as to whether, if we deny Him, we love Jesus (Matt 10:32-33). Think about it. Jesus knew Peter's heart, and Peter was restored. He went away from that conversation, however, with a much more serious view of sin!

Jesus also emphasized that each of us is personally responsible to the Lord. Never mind how God deals with the other person. That is

God's business (vv. 20-22). Each of us has a unique personal assignment. Our responsibility is to fulfill it faithfully!

2 CHRONICLES 1-2   Solomon's success was based on God's blessing (1:1). Note how this blessing was expressed in wealth (vv. 14-17). It is fascinating that the site of the temple was the plot of ground that David bought from Araunah (2 Sam 24:18-25), which was Mount Moriah (2 Chron 3:1) where Abraham went to offer Isaac in sacrifice (Gen 22:2). This remains the site of the ruins of the temple.

When Solomon worshiped the Lord at the tabernacle before he had built the temple, the Lord appeared to him and told Solomon to ask for what he desired. The timing of both Solomon's public worship and the Lord's offer was significant, as it was early in his reign (1:2-10). When Solomon requested wisdom to lead his people, the Lord was pleased and promised to grant the request – and promised wealth and honor as well (vv. 11-12).

PSALM 115   This psalm contrasts the pagan peoples and their gods with those who worship the living and true God. At the beginning, the psalmist makes it clear that glory does not belong to the people but to the God of love and faithfulness. God is alive, sovereign, and powerful (v. 3).

The gods of the pagan nations, however, are dead idols who cannot speak, see, hear, smell, feel, walk, or talk (vv. 5-7). They are, in fact, *dead. And those who worship them will all be dead with them* (v. 8)! With this in mind, hear the strong call for God's people to trust in the living God (vv. 9-18)! See in these verses the blessings that God has brought them.

JUNE 14

1 CORINTHIANS 1:1-17   1 and 2 Corinthians are letters to the church that was established at Corinth under the ministry of Paul and his fellow missionaries. On the second missionary journey, Paul reached Europe and ministered in a number of cities in Macedonia. Some of these places were Philippi, Thessalonica, Berea, Athens, and Corinth. Corinth was a seaport; although there was a Jewish community in the city, the prevailing character of the city was pagan. On his first journey to Corinth, Paul taught there for a year and a half (Acts 18:1,11). If he followed the same pattern as in Ephesus, Paul found a meeting place and taught daily. We can assume, therefore, that many in the church had a substantial foundation in the faith.

As Paul opens the letter, he is genuinely thankful – for the response of the believers to the truth of the gospel and the work of the Holy Spirit in their lives (1:4-9).

But Paul quickly identified a serious problem in the church; divisions had occurred, with some following one person and others expressing allegiance to another (1:10-12). Follow Paul's logic in verses 13-17. As he speaks about God's wisdom in this chapter and the next, it is in the context of this problem of divided allegiances.

2 CHRONICLES 3-4   We read the stark account of the building and dedication of the temple in outline form. Think for a moment of the actual detail and planning that went into both the building and the dedication. Once construction began, it took seven years to complete, and we have that compressed into two chapters. If we could have viewed the scene from above, we would have seen workers swarming about the site (1 Kings 5:13-18; 9:20-23). This was a massive project, moving and putting into place huge blocks of stone after they had been prepared beforehand.

PSALM 116-117   The testimony of a man who has received great blessing from God in time of need is recorded in 116:1-11. Share in the praise of one who received God's goodness.

There is a turning point at verse 12. The psalmist asks how he can repay God's goodness. His answer in verses 13-19 is that he will continue to tell of God's goodness, trust God, and obey God. Good theology!

Psalm 117 is the shortest chapter in the Bible – a short psalm with a large message. The psalm is an expression of praise for two enduring qualities of the Lord: His love and faithfulness. It is a call to praise God for these qualities that are directed to His people. It is a universal call for praise from all peoples and nations.

JUNE 15

1 CORINTHIANS 1:18-31   In contrast to whatever eloquence or wisdom men may have (remember, the people in the Corinthian church were enamored with various men), God's wisdom is revealed in the cross, which brings salvation. The best that the world offers is nothing compared to God's wisdom (v. 19): It has power to change lives (v. 18). To the world the message of the crucified and risen Lord is either a stumbling block or foolishness (v. 23).

Think about the truth of verse 21. None of the philosophical systems of men (the wisdom of the world) have led people to God. The wisdom of God in the cross, however, opens the way for eternal life and fellowship with God. Further, note that God has, in His grace, chosen to use common men and women who are redeemed to be His hands and voice in this broken world (vv. 26-29). That is you and me! That is a miracle!

Finally, note that Jesus, who brings us wisdom from God, is our righteousness, holiness, and redemption (v. 30). He is everything we need for physical and spiritual life, for our temporal and eternal well-being. So – if you are going to pick someone to follow, choose the Lord Jesus and not one of the "great" or "eloquent" men in the world or even in the church.

2 CHRONICLES 5-6 The high point in the temple building project was moving the furnishings that had been prepared – all according to the instructions of the Lord – into the temple. When the ark of the covenant was placed in the Most Holy Place, the furnishing was complete, and there were sacrifices and music for the special occasion. Note in 5:12-14 that God graciously demonstrated His presence and acceptance of the worship by filling the temple with a cloud.

As you again read Solomon's praise to God and his prayer of dedication of the temple, picture him in the Near East sunshine, kneeling before the people and God and raising his voice to the Lord. Notice his high view of God and his understanding of the conditions of blessing from the Lord (6:16). Solomon also understood the conditions of forgiveness when the people would turn from God to sin.

PSALM 118 *FACT:* God is good; His love endures forever. Whoever we are, whatever the circumstance, the fact that God is real and His love endures is comfort. More than comfort, it gives hope to the believer in the most dismal circumstance. When all hope seems to be gone, God's power is real (vv. 13-14). Deliverance through the power of His intervention is also real (vv. 15-16). Let the testimony of thanks to the Lord also be on our lips (vv. 20-21). These are all valid truths.

☑There is no question that this psalm is also specifically Messianic. Jesus quoted verses 22-23 in regard to Himself (Matt 21:42). At Jesus' "Triumphal Entry" the crowds quoted verse 26 (cf. Luke 19:37-38), and Jesus affirmed them (Luke 19:39-40). *It is intriguing to relate this psalm to what Jesus said about the last days, and to Zechariah 14* (a specific prophecy of the Messiah's deliverance of Jerusalem and His people at His coming, cf. Joel 3:9-17). Compare Psalm 118:10 with Luke 21:20 and with Zechariah 14:2. Compare verses 10-16 with Zechariah 14:2-4, 12-15. Then apply verses 22-29 to the Messiah's great final deliverance of Jerusalem and God's people. There is a great day coming, when Jesus will appear with judgment and deliverance (Matt 24:30-31). ⇦

JUNE 16

1 CORINTHIANS 2   Take note of Paul's testimony in verses 1-3. We tend to think of this great apostle as fearless. When he came to Corinth, however, he was very human. He came in human weakness and fear (v. 3)! But he also came in godly wisdom and power (v. 4). God used Paul as a channel to bring His truth to the people of Corinth.

This wisdom of God through the Holy Spirit is eloquently expressed in 2:6-16. As you read, thank God for this amazing gift. There is a "pearl" in verses 7-8. The wisdom of God in Christ (1:30) was planned before time began. Compare this with 1 Peter 1:18-21 where Peter wrote that Christ, as the lamb, was chosen before the creation of the world. Further, the plan was "hidden" until it was an accomplished fact. It was God's will that Jesus, as the lamb, would die for the sins of the world. At that time, the triumph of the cross made a spectacle of Satan and his powers (Col 2:15).

Notice that it is only through the Holy Spirit that we can understand God's plan (vv. 10-12) and come to Him (vv. 14-16). The deep things of God are only understood through the Holy Spirit. Contrast the wisdom of the world (academia) in 1:18-22 with the wisdom of God (available to each of us – regardless of I.Q.) in 2:9-16.

1 KINGS 9-10   When the Lord appeared to Solomon after the dedication, conditions were attached to the promised blessings. The conditions of obedience were not only for Solomon but for the whole of Israel (9:3-9). God had promised David an everlasting throne (2 Sam 7:11b-16). This was the promise that through David the Messiah would come, and His throne would be an everlasting kingdom. This promise was not conditional. The promise to Solomon, however, did have conditions (6:12). Note that God also placed conditions on the nation, telling Solomon that if the Israelites stopped serving Him, He would remove His blessing and cut off the people from the land (9:6-9). This is exactly what happened. Jesus, however, as promised to David, came through David's line – and He will reign forever!

Forced labor was used to build the palace and the temple. Those conscripted were the aliens who had not been driven from the land and numbered over 150,000 (2 Chron 2:17-18).

Solomon's reputation for wisdom and splendor was known in the region, as evidenced by the visit from the Queen of Sheba. Note the amount of gold Solomon received, not only from the queen but also from the excursions of his ships abroad. As you read about the gold, the silver, and the other trappings of the court, also read Deuteronomy 17:16-17. The seeds of disaster were already in place!

PSALM 119:1-32   Psalm 119 is a celebration of the Word of God. Almost every verse has something to say about how the Scriptures apply to our lives. A helpful exercise is to take a fine ball-point pen and mark in the margins of your Bible the truths about the Scripture contained in the verses. Each verse will not have a comment, but it will surprise you that there is so much *specific* application and benefit from the Bible. There is a great deal of theology in the chapter. Recall the words of Jesus (Matt 5:17-20) and Paul (Rom 15:4) as they relate to the scriptures.

JUNE 17

1 CORINTHIANS 3   Paul cited division in the local church as evidence of immaturity and worldliness. Following the discussion of God's wisdom in Chapter 2, the contrast with those choosing sides in the church is dramatic! Look at how Paul ties this in with the discussion of godly wisdom in 3:18-23.

Rather than pick heroes to follow, understand that each of God's servants has a specific function in the work of the kingdom that complements another's work (vv. 5-9). They are not in competition, and each is needed. Choosing to follow one or another misses the point of how God's work is carried out.

Think carefully about verses 10-15. *Each* of us builds in the kingdom, and we are all responsible to God for how we build. There will be a final accounting as God Himself tests our work (2 Cor 5:10). There *will* be a final exam!

2 CHRONICLES 7-8   Try to picture the scene as fire came down from heaven and consumed the burnt offering after Solomon's prayer. That, with the glory of God filling the temple, was a dramatic visual confirmation that the Lord was in their midst. Look at God's message to Solomon and the people on this occasion (7:12-22). God will bless as promised (vv. 12-18), but no one plays games or manipulates God! Turning from God will bring consequences (vv. 19-22)! That principle still is the same for God has not changed. Think about the Lord's statement in 7:14-15. If God's people are not being blessed, it is not because God is unwilling!

PSALM 119:33-64   Remember to look for how the Word of God can affect your life. Highlight the ways you find. Look for how God (the Holy Spirit) works directly with the written word in our lives to make us different people. Look at the last phrase in verse 33. It is important to stay faithful to the Lord until the end (Matt 24:13). *It is important to start well, but it is essential to end well!*

God's work is evident in verses 33-40. The decrees of God are found in the Bible (v. 33). The psalmist, however, asks that God teach him to follow these precepts: the Word of God combined with the work of God in life! Note a similar pattern in verses 34-37.

There is hope (v. 49), renewal (v. 50), comfort (v. 52), discernment about the world (v. 53), and consistency of life (v. 54) through the Word. In verses 57-64, observe the psalmist's decisions based on the Word.

JUNE 18

1 CORINTHIANS 4   Because of immaturity in the church, some had not accepted Paul's message. Paul was the builder whom God had placed there to lay the foundations (3:10; Acts 18:1-11). Paul was an apostle and master builder, and the church should have followed his example in service and humility (vv. 9-13, 16). Instead, some had become arrogant (v. 19). As you consider verses 9-13, understand the life of the servant of Christ. Compare this with John 15:18-21. Paul's model in this section is important for us both for attitude and behavior.

You might think Christ's apostles would be treated with honor. Instead, Paul and his companions suffered ignominy at the hands of religious people (vv. 9-13). This was their lot as they traveled from city to city bringing the gospel message to those who would listen. This is what Jesus said would happen to His followers (John 15:18-20). We must not expect applause when we follow the Lord.

Paul argued for his place of spiritual authority in the church and urged that the church abandon factions.

2 CHRONICLES 9   The splendor of Solomon's reign and his widespread fame and are impressive. The description of his wealth is almost beyond comprehension. Solomon's ability to answer all of the Queen of Sheba's questions speaks to the genuineness of his wisdom and the wealth of his knowledge. In the reading tomorrow we will get insight into the downside of his later years.

PSALM 119:65-96   Look for the ministry of the Word of God in life. Look also for how God (through the Holy Spirit) teaches us and molds us through the Word. Verse 66 mentions both knowledge and good judgment. Knowledge is the acquisition of facts. Judgment is the ability to use those facts properly. Knowledge comes from the Word, but good judgment comes as God helps us (through the Holy Spirit) to apply our knowledge to life.

Compare verse 71 with verses 67, 75-76. Sometimes the Lord allows affliction to teach us valuable lessons. Affliction causes us to turn to the Lord and His Word (v. 71), which in turn comforts us (v. 76).

Consider the truth of verses 89-91. With this truth in mind, how can we neglect God's Word?

JUNE 19

1 CORINTHIANS 5   The second problem that Paul addressed in the church at Corinth was moral sin – in fact, the sin of incest. It seems from Paul's remarks (v. 2) that the church tolerated the situation without taking action or even feeling very exercised about it. This may not be much different from the church today, for it is difficult to face such matters.

Paul saw this as a serious problem in the church. The church is responsible for moral purity among the believers (v. 12). Such sin in the church has a deadly effect on the body of believers. Sin in the fellowship is like yeast in bread dough – it affects the entire loaf (v. 6). What we do influences the entire church.

An Old Testament example is found in Joshua 7. The sin of Achan caused suffering for all the Israelites! The New Testament principle of our interdependence as believers also appears in Romans 14:7-8. Each of us is responsible for each other and for the whole church.

What should be done, and why? Paul told the Corinthian church it must not condone careless and purposeful sin among its members. His advice for this specific problem was redemptive discipline (designed to bring the sinner back to fellowship, vv. 4-5) by putting him out of the church (vv. 5, 13). To "hand this man over to Satan" meant that he would lose the church's protective envelope of care and deal on his own with the powers of evil.

Paul gives one further principle. If a Christian is living in open sin, other believers should not fellowship with that person (vv. 9-11). Your fellowship gives the wrong message both to that person and the world (everything is fine!). These are strange words to us in the church today, when there is a spirit of permissiveness in the world. As God's people, we must listen to the truth of His word.

1 KINGS 11-12   Here is the dark side of Solomon's reign. How could this happen? The answer is that *Solomon ignored the Lord's commands at his own peril, bringing disaster to the nation.* Reading 11:4, we see Solomon in his later years as a foolish old man! This happened in spite of the fact that God had appeared to him twice (11:9).

There is a spiritual principle that we should note. We stand in the Lord's protection when we live in obedience. If we step out from under the umbrella of God's protection by willful disobedience, we open our lives to trouble and seduction by Satan. Ephesians 4:27 speaks to this. Don't be casual about this; none of us can stand up to Satan apart from the power that is in the Lord Jesus. Think about it!

Jeroboam was a man of promise. Note the gracious word of the Lord to him (11:38). Jeroboam, however, threw away this opportunity of blessing from God and instead instituted pagan worship in Israel (12:26-33). In so doing, his name became synonymous with evil.

PSALM 119:97-128   Verses 97-104 are the personal testimony of the psalmist. He is recounting what the Word of God has done in his life – and what the Lord has done through the Word. Note particularly the wisdom, insight, and understanding that he has gained. Note also how the Word has kept him from sin and made him hate what is wrong.

The dividing line between the person who loves God and one who loves the world is attention to God's truths (v. 118; cf. John 14:23-24a). Observe the psalmist's specific requests to the Lord and the attitude with which he prays (love and respect).

JUNE 20

1 CORINTHIANS 6   A third problem that reflected the church's immaturity is now addressed: the issue of one believer taking another to court. Paul said this practice is inconsistent with the nature of the church. It is inconsistent because the members of the body of Christ are competent to judge a matter with justice. After all, saints will judge the world (v. 2) and angels (v. 3), and the church should not display "dirty laundry" to the world (v. 6).

The solution, if all else fails, is to allow one's self to be defrauded (v. 7b). That would be better than to settle matters in a secular court!

Paul returns to sexual immorality again in the closing verses of the chapter. The sexual relationship is a very special one that joins two individuals in a unique way, making them "one flesh" (v. 16; cf. Gen 2:24; Matt 19:5). That is the way God planned for marriage and family. Through sexual immorality, one not only breaks God's law but also sins against his or her own body (v. 18, in our day, consider the disease consequences)! Further, as God's children, we are not our own. If we belong to the Lord, we must honor God with our bodies (vv. 19-20)!

1 KINGS 13-14   In 1 Kings 11, the prophet Ahijah appeared to Jeroboam, the son of Nebat, who was one of Solomon's officials. At that time ten of the twelve tribes were given to Jeroboam because of the sin

of Solomon (11:31-33). The Lord's message, however, had conditions attached (11:38-39). At that point, Jeroboam was a man of promise. He had every opportunity to receive God's blessing on his life and in his rule.

As the kingdom was split (1 Kings 12), Jeroboam did indeed become king of the ten tribes, thereafter called Israel, while the remaining tribe was called Judah. However, it became clear that this man had no true fear of God (12:26-33). He was afraid that if the people followed the Lord's commands to worship under the priests at the temple in Jerusalem, they would be drawn away from him and back to a unified kingdom. Because of this, he took matters in his own hand and instituted worship that violated the Lord's commands.

Jeroboam's sin elicited a warning from the Lord. A prophet was sent to Jeroboam (13:1-3), but Jeroboam's character is evident in the way he received the warning (13:4-6). He asked for prayer but for the wrong thing. He should have repented, but he only wanted his arm restored!

A second message came to Jeroboam in 14:1-18. God used an ingenious method to bring His message to the king, and note how it was confirmed (v. 17). At this point, both Israel and Judah had drifted far from the true worship of the Lord. It is significant that in each of the kingdoms, the ungodly leadership of their respective kings led the people away from the Lord.

PSALM 119:129-152   Consider the psalmist's grasp of reality. He understood that God's Word gives light and understanding (even to the simple, v. 130). The Word will guard us from sin (v. 133). It is righteous and trustworthy (v. 138). Further, the Word points the path to life itself (v. 144).

Compare verses 147-148 with Psalm 1:2b. The psalmist was up early in the morning but also meditated on God's Word during the night. And note, finally, that God's statutes are eternal (v. 152b). They are worth our attention.

JUNE 21

1 CORINTHIANS 7   The church had raised with Paul the question of marriage (v. 1). At the outset, Paul states his opinion that it is better for a man not to marry. We have some indication as to the reason in verse 26 – he says that "because of the present crisis" it would be better to remain single. Pressures upon believers when he wrote prompted this caution.

Many members of the church were recent converts and had spouses who didn't know Christ. This changed the dynamics of the marriage relationship, and thus Paul gives special instruction to them. Note the permanent nature of the relationship in verses 10-11.

Paul said we should be viewing life in light of the eternal – whether we are married or single (vv. 29-35). That should be our mind-set as we interact with the world. The major concern of life must be to please our Lord.

2 CHRONICLES 10-11   The account in Chronicles of the split in the kingdom gives some details that are not included in Kings.   King Rehoboam and his advisors are portrayed in 10:8-11 as young, arrogant, inexperienced, and unrealistic. They were spoiled young men who had not struggled with life as had the common people. The king's failure to listen to and heed the advice of better minds led directly to the division of the nation into Israel and Judah.

Notice too that many of the Levites, as well as God-fearing people from the tribes of Israel, left their land to come to Judah so they could worship in the temple in Jerusalem (11:13-17). Jeroboam appointed others as priests and instituted alternate worship forms in Israel (v. 15; 1 Kings 12:26-33). This brought the promise of judgment on Jeroboam, his family, and the nation (1 Kings 13:1-3; 14:1-11).

PSALM 119:153-176   The righteous and the wicked differ in their attitude to the Word of God. Look for this difference in verses 153-160. Observe the results of loyalty to God's laws – and the opposite.

Perhaps nowhere else in the Bible are so many reasons given to study and apply God's Word. God's Word is for all seasons of life, for all circumstances. It applies when we feel down and when we are exuberant. It brings us back into line when we stray from the Lord. And it is all in Psalm 119!

JUNE 22

1 CORINTHIANS 8   The meat for sale in the public markets may well have been offered to idols in pagan temples. When a person brought a sacrifice of meat for the gods, practice dictated that one third of the meat was burned, one third was taken to eat by the one offering the sacrifice, and one third went to the priest. The priest's portion could be sold in the market, providing income for the priest.

Paul urged that the recipients of the letter consider those who might be affected by eating such meat (v. 7). Many believers had only very recently been saved out of such pagan worship. To some it would mean mixing the worship of idols with their faith in Christ, and thus could harm them (v. 11).

In fact, Paul points out the idol is dead and the meat is unchanged, so the eating or not eating is the same – *if one understands this to be the case* (vv. 4, 8). The most important thing, and the principle that Paul is teaching, is that we must consider the impact of our behavior upon others. Although the mature Christian who understands the principle will not be harmed by eating such meat, it would be well to refrain if eating will cause problems for one who is not as mature (vv. 9-13).

2 CHRONICLES 12-13   One of the valuable lessons we have from reading the Old Testament is to see how God deals with man's behavior. In Chapter 12 we observe God's mercy as the leaders of Judah repented of their sin, but also the result of their sin that, nevertheless, still came to them. Sin does exact a price (12:8). If we are wise, we will think about this before we dabble in sin. Note that it was at this time, and in consequence of the nation's sin, that the riches of the land were taken (vv. 9-11).

In Chapter 13, because Abijah trusted God (v. 18), God gave Judah victory over the forces of Jeroboam.

PSALM 120   Psalms 120-134 are called "Songs of Ascent" and were recited by the Israelites on pilgrimage to Jerusalem. One always "went up" to Jerusalem, since the city is geographically higher than the surrounding countryside. While reading these psalms, think of the Israelites walking along dusty paths in the hot sun, singing praise to God.

Those reciting this psalm express distress – perhaps even as they walked they were thinking about difficult situations. Often these include people saying things that seem untrue and unfair (v. 2). The references to Meshach and Kedar are probably metaphorical (v. 5); they were areas outside Israel. The writer seems to be saying that such abuse as he was experiencing was what he would expect from foreigners, perhaps implying that the problem was closer at hand. When we have been unfairly treated, we need to let God settle the matter. God is well able to handle the deceit of men (v. 3) and will settle accounts in His time (v. 4).

JUNE 23

1 CORINTHIANS 9   In this chapter we gain insight into Paul's heart for ministry. We also see some of the responsibilities that believers have to those who minister.

It was usual for teachers to require payment from their pupils. The more teachers demanded, the higher their esteem. This carried over into Christian ministry from the secular world, but Paul said that although he would have the right (from Scripture, not from the secular precedent) to receive a living from the gospel ministry, he chose not to accept money. This was so the gospel would be free to those who needed to hear. The spin-off from this, however, was that some did not respect him precisely because he preached and taught without charge! Even so, the church is obligated to support those who minister to them (vv. 7-12).

Note in particular that all of us need to be "in training" (vv. 24-27), disciplining ourselves so that we aren't "spinning our wheels" in our efforts for Christ, or worse, being disqualified because of our methods.

1 KINGS 15-16   While the monarchy of Judah remained with the descendants of David, the monarchy of Israel changed families several times – always violently. In 15:29 note how the Lord's prophecy to Jeroboam (1 Kings 14:10-11) was carried out by King Baasha after he had killed Nadab, the son of Jeroboam. In Chapter 16, the monarchy changed families twice again! Note the comment about Omri in 16:25 and about Ahab in 16:30. Things went from bad to worse!

PSALM 121   One could call this a psalm with promise of protection. The hills (v. 1) probably represent the hill where Jerusalem is situated. The answer is not that help will come out of the hills, but that the God who made the hills (and the heavens as well) will be the psalmist's help (v. 2) – day and night (vv. 3-4) – through life and into eternity (v. 8).

What genuine comfort to know that our God protects those whom He loves.

JUNE 24

1 CORINTHIANS 10:1-13   Why study the Old Testament? Because we need the information! That is Paul's message to the church in this section.

It is possible to belong to a group of God's people without being God's child! Learn from the example of those who came out of Egypt (vv. 1-5). The point is that all the people had the same deliverance and received the same provisions and blessing. But most did not have faith (v. 5)!

Particularly note verses 11-13. The accounts from the Old Testament are included in the Bible to help us understand how God deals with men and how we should live today. Learn from the judgment of God on those who disobeyed. There is no room for complacency in our living (v. 12). If we trust God and look to Him, nothing will come to us that He will not help us face (v. 13).

2 CHRONICLES 14-16   As you read about Asa, king of Judah, consider what one man can accomplish! He effectively turned the people to God, reestablished proper worship, and publicly stated his faith in the Lord. As a result, the Lord was with him, and the entire nation was blessed. We will see this pattern several times as we read the accounts of the kings. The faithfulness of even one person can make a great difference.

But although God used Asa for good, he compromised his faith by turning to secular powers to solve his military problems. He did this even though previously God had blessed him in battle (16:1-6; cf. 14:9-15). Asa also failed to trust God in his illness (16:12). Note the truth that is within the message of the prophet to Asa in 16:9. *So trust God!*

PSALM 122   The Israelites loved Jerusalem! They loved the temple. It was unique to identify with God's people as they went to the temple to worship. They had the privilege of joining in the sacrifices and the joy of eating together. There was excitement in participating in the praise services (v. 4).

Notice the concern for the city in verses 6-9. Our Jewish friends still pray for the peace of Jerusalem. And we should do so as well.

One could term this a psalm for worship and fellowship with God's people. We, as part of that great company, must take our cue from the writer to love God's people and the house of the Lord in the same way.

JUNE 25

1 CORINTHIANS 10:14-33   Although worship practices now may vary from those of the first century, the central truth of verses 14-22 is unchanged. Don't allow the world to compete for your affections. As Christians, it is inconsistent to participate in the Lord's Table (the body and blood of Christ, v. 16) and have any association with idols (competing systems of worship, vv. 14, 21). Paul points out it is not that the idols themselves are anything, but that they represented demons: The sacrifices of the pagans of Paul's day were actually offered to demons (vv. 19-20).

Further, be sensitive about your testimony in the world (vv. 23-33). If any action could be misunderstood, then it is best left alone (vv. 28-29). The bottom line is that we live to please God and Him alone (v. 31).

2 CHRONICLES 17-18   Jehoshaphat trusted God and received His blessing. Have you heard of TEE used in overseas missions? TEE stands for Theological Education by Extension and is carried out by the

teacher going to students in outlying areas. Note here that Jehoshaphat was the first to use the method (17:7-9)!

The responsibility of the prophet in the ancient world was not an easy one. It often meant bringing an unwelcome message to a person in high office, as Micaiah did when he came before Jehoshaphat and Ahab (Ch. 18). Put yourself in Micaiah's position and imagine the intense pressure to give the king the message he wanted. Compare this with what Jesus said in Matthew 10:32-33. The true prophet (or Christian) never compromises his message, even under stress (remember also John the Baptist before Herod, Matt 14:3-5).

PSALM 123   This is a psalm for waiting in trust on God. Verse 2 indicates how we must wait and trust: as slaves look to their master (in total dependence), and as a maid looks to her mistress (in total obedience). Wait upon God for mercy. There is no other true mercy!

Read the prayer (vv. 3-4) and stand with those who suffer ridicule and contempt from the proud and arrogant. May we always have the wisdom and mercy to support and stand with those whom God loves.

JUNE 26

1 CORINTHIANS 11:1-16   The section through verse 16 is difficult. Certainly it was written within the context of first century Corinth, so some references are not clear. Other principles are more understand-able.

It is not clear whether the apostle is speaking about hair as a covering on the head or saying that a woman should wear some other covering on her head in church. Paul does seem clear that a woman's hair should be worn long and a man's short.

The question of authority in the church is mentioned in verses 3, 7-10. This, however, is not a question about which gender is "better" or "more important," (vv. 11-12 speak about the interdependence of men and women) but instead refers to administrative functions in the church.* (see note)

---

* The following comments may be helpful for this section. They come from W. Harold Mare's commentary on 1 Corinthians. Taken from the book, THE EXPOSITOR'S BIBLE COMMENTARY, VOL. 10 edited by Frank E. Gaebelein. Copyright 1976 by the Zondervan Corporation. Used by permission of Zondervan Publishing House.

The principles Paul presents here that are to govern the church and individual Christians in their life and conduct are as follows:
1. Christians should live as individuals and in corporate worship in the light of the perfect unity and interrelatedness of the persons of the Godhead. The Father and the Son are perfectly united (John 10:30) and yet there is a difference administratively: God is the head

<u>2 CHRONICLES 19-20</u>   Jehoshaphat took decisive action to see that justice was served in the land (19:4-11). Note the charge that he gave those who served in the countryside (19:4-7; cf. Deut 1:17).

Chapter 20 records one of the most amazing military victories in the Bible. What is even more amazing is how Jehoshaphat led the people to trust God in a dangerous situation.   In his prayer, Jehoshaphat petitioned the Lord (vv. 6-12).   God in his grace gave a message to Jehoshaphat and the people that they believed. Imagine the scene as the army marched into battle singing and praising the Lord. The king had trusted God publicly, and God had answered! Look at the result in verses 29-30.

<u>PSALM 124</u>   We could call this a psalm praising God for deliverance from danger and traps.   The psalm begins by emphasizing (by repeating) that if it had not been for the Lord, God's people would have been "swept away."

Remember that the Hebrew language is rich in "word pictures." This psalm is especially so. Look at the pictures of defeat at the hands of the enemy. "Swallowed alive" (v. 3). A "flood engulfing" (v. 4). A "torrent sweeping over" (v. 4). "Raging waters sweeping away" (v. 5). "Torn by teeth" (v. 6).   This is the language of total defeat, of annihilation!

Then note the picture of escape – a bird escaping from a broken snare (v. 7) to fly free! What a picture of deliverance. The bird could not provide the way of escape, but once out of the trap, the bird is truly free. 2 Chronicles 20 is an example of just such a deliverance. Verses

---

of Christ (1 Cor 11:3). So Christians are one, but they too have to be administratively subordinate to one another.
2. Christians are to remember that God first created man, then woman (Gen 2:21-23) and placed the man as administrative head over the woman and the woman as his helper-companion (Gen 2:18). So in the Christian community, the man is to conduct himself as a man (1 Cor 11:4) and as the head of the woman (v. 3), while the woman is to conduct herself as a woman with dignity without doing anything that would bring dishonor to her (v. 5).
3. Since Christians live in the Christian community of the home and that of the church, they are to remember that God has established the man and the woman as equal human beings: "As woman came from man, so also man is born of woman" (v. 12). So in the Christian community believers should treat one another with mutual respect and admiration as they realize each other's God-given special functions and positions.
4. Christian men and women should remember that, though God has made them equal human beings, yet he has made them distinct sexes. That distinction is not to be blurred in their realization that they are mutually dependent (v. 11) – the man on the woman and the woman on the man. It is also to be observed in their physical appearance (vv. 13-15), so that in worship the woman can be recognized as woman and the man as man.
5. God is a God of order. This means order in worship and peaceful decorum in the church (v. 16). Therefore Christian men and women should conduct themselves in a respectful, orderly way not only in worship but also in daily life.

20-23 of that chapter show how God acts when His people call on Him in trust.

Lastly, rejoice in the "reality orientation" of verse 8. Our help is in the name of the Lord, the Maker of heaven and earth. As literature, this psalm is wonderful. As truth, it is magnificent!

JUNE 27

1 CORINTHIANS 11:17-34　There was obvious disorder in the church regarding the observance of the Lord's Supper. Some in the church came with a whole meal – and enough wine to become intoxicated – while others were needy and came without anything to eat. Further, there was no order to the service: People started to eat without consideration of what others were doing (v. 21). Paul uses strong words for this kind of practice – it despised the church of God (v. 22).

How the church should observe the Lord's Supper is clear. It is a solemn remembrance of the body and blood of the Lord Jesus, broken at the cross, given for all men in love. It should be remembered in this way until Jesus comes again (vv. 23-26). Remembering the death of Jesus in the communion service brings the church back to the essentials of the faith and our complete dependence upon the grace of God each time it is observed.

Paul then adds cautions. Only those in fellowship with the Lord are qualified to participate. He is not saying that only perfect people can come to the table – for then none could come. Rather, he means to separate those living in obedience to Christ from those who are unsaved or have unconfessed sin in their lives. Note carefully the warning in verses 27-30. God may judge those who inappropriately share in the observance of the Lord's supper by bringing illness or premature death (v. 30).

1 KINGS 17-18　During the evil reign of Ahab, king of Israel, God sent Elijah to confront him. His message to Ahab was not a good one for an agricultural economy (17:1): no rain for a few years until Elijah would give the word! As the drought went on, Ahab searched for the prophet (18:10).

God commanded the ravens, and later the widow, to feed Elijah (17:5-16). The prophet proved to be a blessing in the home of the widow.

In the third year (18:1) Elijah again confronted Ahab (18:16-18). By this time it was clear that Elijah did indeed speak for the Lord for it hadn't rained since Ahab had seen him. The meeting with the heathen prophets was a powerful message to the people and to Ahab that the

God of Elijah was the God of gods. And to prove the power of God, Elijah prayed and the rain came!

PSALM 125   If you are concerned for safety and security, this psalm has an answer. Trust in the Lord. There is also a warning in verse 5. God's protection may be lost if we turn to "crooked" ways – ways that stray from the truth. This is worth thinking about. Jesus declares in John 8:42-44 that *all untruth* is from Satan. It is a fruitful exercise (not academic, but spiritual) to monitor your communication to others. Is what we say completely true, or do we imply things that stray from the truth? Trusting in God (v. 1) means trusting in His truth and living His truth.

JUNE 28

1 CORINTHIANS 12:1-11   Don't confuse the "gifts" of the Holy Spirit with the "fruit" of the Holy Spirit (Gal 5:22-25). →The gifts as listed in this chapter and in Romans 12:6-8 are given to persons individually by the Holy Spirit so that the work of the church can go on effectively and efficiently. The text does not say that one person can be given only one gift, but it does say that each Christian will have at least one gift of the Spirit (v. 7). The fruit of the Spirit, in contrast, is for all of us in its entirety.

Although the gifts are given to individuals, the purpose is the common good in the church (v. 7). One could even say that the gifts are given to the church, through individuals, so that the work of the church can go forward. Since each Christian is gifted specifically so that the work of the church will be complete, it follows that the spiritual gifts must be carefully applied in kingdom work. The gifts are for the church, held in stewardship by the individual. Further, it also follows that if each person uses the God-given gift correctly, the total mission of the church will be completed and on time. *There should be no frustration over the mission or the lack of resources to complete the assignment that God has given.*←

If we combine the gifts mentioned in this chapter with those in Romans 12, they would be as follows. From 1 Corinthians 12:7-11: (1) Wisdom: the ability through the Spirit to apply known facts in the work of the church and understand the right course of action. (2) Knowledge: primarily of the Word of God. (3) Faith: every Christian has faith, but the Holy Spirit gives to some unusual faith "that will move mountains." (4) Healing: using both the science of medicine and direct healing through the Holy Spirit. (5) Miracles. (6) Prophecy: primarily the ability to explain the truth of the Bible and move Christians to respond. (7) Spirit recognition: the ability to discern evil spirits and distinguish these from the Holy Spirit. (8) <u>Tongues</u>: probably relates to both "heavenly" tongues and the instant ability to speak in unlearned but known languages. (9) <u>Interpretation of tongues</u>: the ability to understand and interpret "heavenly" language. <u>From 1 Corinthians 12:27-31</u>. (10) <u>Apostles</u>: The office of Apostle ceased with those who were personally with Jesus. (11) <u>Teachers</u>: the ability to clearly explain the truth in the church. (12) <u>Helps</u>: whatever needed by the church or those in the church. (13) <u>Administration</u>: to make the work of the church go smoothly. <u>Additional gifts are added from Romans 12:6-8.</u> (14) <u>Service</u>: perhaps doing routine but necessary tasks in the church. (15) <u>Encouragement</u>: the ability to affirm and encourage others in the church. (16) <u>Giving</u>: Every Christian has the responsibility to give, but some have been given more to dispense. (17) <u>Leadership</u>: the ability to serve the church as deacons and elders. (18) <u>Mercy</u>: the ability to see with clarity the needs of others and to take steps to meet those needs.

<u>1 KINGS 19-20</u> As you read Chapter 19, follow Elijah's emotions. He had just seen the power of God demonstrated in miraculous ways, yet became totally discouraged when the king's wife, Jezebel, threatened his life (19:2). His reaction seems out of proportion to the threat (vv. 3ff.). Elijah had been through a very difficult time, and perhaps at this point he believed that things should fall into place and righteousness would reign. Today we might call Elijah's state "burnout." Note how God sustained and encouraged Elijah during this time.

As Ahab, king of Israel, faced the armies of Aram, God appeared to Ahab with a message of grace. In spite of the sin that Ahab had brought to Israel, God promised victory (20:13). Subsequently, God gave great victories twice. Notice the word of judgment that came to Ahab because he had incompletely followed the Lord's will (20:41-43).

<u>PSALM 126</u> One could title this psalm, "The Joy of Deliverance and Freedom." It speaks of the incredible joy of coming home after being a captive (vv. 1-2). The deliverance of the Israelites was obvious enough to be acknowledged by the nations (v. 2b). The psalm emphasizes that it indeed was the Lord who ended the captivity.

Verses 4-6 include both a prayer and the promise of harvest. God sees the tears of those who serve Him and will honor their faith and faithfulness. In the agrarian countryside of 1000 BC this may have been seen as an agricultural harvest only. But to us, it has greater meaning with regard to the planting of God's Word and the promise of a more significant harvest.

JUNE 29

1 CORINTHIANS 12:12-31   This section contains a graphic explanation of the function of the church.   Paul uses the human body to make his point.   Every part of the body has a function.   Some of the most important organs in the body are tiny, invisible, and unknown to the person, but still exert enormous influence in the delicate balance of the body's physiology.   The point is that without the function of each organ, the body cannot do all that it should.   The application to the church (local and universal) is obvious.   The model of a building is used to make the same point in Ephesians 2:19-22 and 1 Peter 2:4-6.

The obvious responsibility for each Christian is to understand the gift/s that God has given and use them so that the work of Christ will be complete and balanced.   When we are all working together as God has designed the church, the whole body will function to complete the work of the kingdom in God's timing.

1 KINGS 21-22   To understand Ahab, look at 21:25-26 before reading the chapter.   Seeing Ahab in this light makes his behavior more understandable.   The depth of Ahab's depravity is evident in how he used a religious fast to murder Naboth and illegally confiscate his property.

What happened to Naboth was, of course, not fair.   Sinful society and leadership sets the stage for unfair action.   The important thing to remember is that God will finally settle accounts.   It was in this context that Elijah again had to face Ahab.   Keep in mind the message, as we shall see how God fulfilled the prophecy.   It is also important to note that Ahab's repentance (by now Ahab knew that Elijah was really God's messenger) did make a difference in his own life.

Jehoshaphat, king of Judah, worshipped the Lord and led the nation in the right direction.   When he visited Ahab, who was related to him by marriage, the question arose as to a joint military venture against Aram (Chapter 22).   In this conversation, Micaiah, a true prophet of the Lord, was called to give advice from the Lord.   In 22:11, note the myth that the false prophet gave the kings and contrast the truth Micaiah brought from the Lord (vv. 17-23).

PSALM 127   As applied to any of our activities, it is true that unless the Lord has a hand in the building it is in vain.   What isn't done for the kingdom, directly or indirectly, ultimately is in vain!   All of life should be centered on that principle.   That is reality orientation.

How much of life is merely "spinning our wheels?"   If this is true in your life, take stock and reassess your priorities!   The principle certainly

231

applies with regard to home and church. It is also true with regard to our employment. *Integrating these areas with your faith can change your life – and your lifestyle.*

The blessing of family is affirmed in verses 3-5. Not all have this blessing. For those who are denied the opportunity, God can and will fill that place with His blessing in another way. For those blessed with children, there is joy and opportunity to trust God through the inevitable stresses that a growing family can bring.

JUNE 30

1 CORINTHIANS 13   Sandwiched between the discussion of gifts in Chapters 12 and 14 is this beautiful chapter of love. Using the term "sandwiched" is appropriate because Paul is talking about how we use the gifts entrusted to us. Love is the filling in the sandwich that makes the taste delightful. If gifts are not used in the context of God's love and our love for others, they will be useless (vv. 1-3)!

If we were to summarize the definition of love here in one sentence, it might be something like the following: *To desire the very best for the other person under every circumstance.* Note that it is not primarily a feeling but attitude and action. Our definitions often identify love with an emotional response and feeling. If this isn't present, we tend to think that love isn't real. Marriages break apart on this rocky shoal. Real love is measured in action – and the feeling usually follows. This biblical definition of love makes it possible for each Christian to love by attitude and action. That is a powerful witness to the validity of the work of Christ.

Paul makes an interesting statement in verse 13: Love is greater than either faith or hope. In fact, love will still be present (through eternity) after faith is fully realized and hope is completely fulfilled.

2 KINGS 1-2   Once again Elijah followed the Lord's command in bringing an unwelcome message to a disobedient king. In the encounters with the army, think of this as a spiritual tug of war or power struggle. Read Elijah's message to the king when they faced each other (vv. 16-17). How should this message from the Lord affect your life and decisions?

Two men recorded in the Bible were taken to heaven without dying: Enoch (Gen 5:18-24) and Elijah. Elisha somehow knew that the time for Elijah to leave the earth was near. God's blessing and power were conferred upon Elisha when Elijah was taken up, and this was quickly confirmed (2:13-14).

<u>PSALM 128</u>   There is a promise in verse 1 that can apply to everyone. Fear God, walk in His ways, and receive His blessing. Why do we live in any other way?   Is life more fun or more exciting without God's blessing? Is it more fulfilling? If you answer "yes," you have believed the lie of Satan. The Lord, who designed the human mind and spirit, designed it to relate to Him. Anything else is second best! Take God at face value. Fear God, obey Him, and receive His blessing.

July

Bible Reading Schedule
And Notes

☙

*I am the way and the truth and the life. No one
comes to the Father except through me. John 14:6*

1	1 Cor 14:1-25	2 Kings 3-4	Psalm 129
2	1 Cor 14:26-40	2 Kings 5-6	Psalm 130
3	1 Cor 15:1-34	2 Kings 7-8	Psalm 131
4	1 Cor 15:35-58	2 Kings 9-10	Psalm 132
5	1 Cor 16	2 Chron 21-22	Psalm 133
6	2 Cor 1	2 Kings 11-12	Psalm 134
7	2 Cor 2	2 Chron 23-24	Psalm 135
8	2 Cor 3	2 Kings 13-14	Psalm 136
9	2 Cor 4	Hosea 1-3	Psalm 137
10	2 Cor 5:1-10	Hosea 4-5	Psalm 138
11	2 Cor 5:11-21	Hosea 6-7	Psalm 139
12	2 Cor 6	Hosea 8-10	Psalm 140
13	2 Cor 7	Hosea 11-12	Psalm 141
14	2 Cor 8	Hosea 13-14	Psalm 142
15	2 Cor 9	2 Chron 25	Psalm 143
16	2 Cor 10	Joel 1	Psalm 144
17	2 Cor 11:1-15	Joel 2	Psalm 145
18	2 Cor 11:16-33	Joel 3	Psalm 146
19	2 Cor 12:1-10	Jonah 1-2	Psalm 147
20	2 Cor 12:11-21	Jonah 3-4	Psalm 148
21	2 Cor 13	Amos 1-2	Psalm 149
22	Matthew 1:1-17	Amos 3-4	Psalm 150
23	Matthew 1:18-25	Amos 5	Ecclesiastes 1
24	Matthew 2:1-12	Amos 6	Ecclesiastes 2
25	Matthew 2:13-23	Amos 7-8	Ecclesiastes 3
26	Matthew 3	Amos 9	Ecclesiastes 4
27	Matthew 4:1-11	Micah 1-2	Ecclesiastes 5
28	Matthew 4:12-25	Micah 3	Ecclesiastes 6
29	Matthew 5:1-12	Micah 4	Ecclesiastes 7
30	Matthew 5:13-32	Micah 5-6	Ecclesiastes 8
31	Matthew 5:33-48	Micah 7	Ecclesiastes 9

JULY 1

1 CORINTHIANS 14:1-25   Following the "love" chapter, Paul urges us to follow the way of love: concern for the other person. Prophecy is the "speaking forth" of the truth and is not restricted to the foretelling of events. "Tongues" may refer to unlearned but actual foreign languages (as was the case at Pentecost) or to speech that is not a known language but is given by the Holy Spirit for prayer and worship (vv. 16-17).

In the first section of this chapter (vv. 1-25), Paul urged the church to give priority to prophecy, which will strengthen, encourage, comfort, and edify the church (v. 4). It is interesting that in verses 2, 14, 15, and 16 Paul identified the "tongues" as a function of the speaker's spirit and not necessarily the Holy Spirit. The quotation from the Old Testament in verse 21 speaks about known languages used by foreign people.

Paul summed up the section in verses 22-25. Tongues can be a sign for unbelievers (as in Acts 2) but not for believers (they already have the Holy Spirit). On the other hand, if several are speaking in strange languages when an unbeliever arrives, the chaotic scene will lead him to conclude that the people are unbalanced (v. 23). However, through prophecy (explanation of God's message), the unbeliever will be convicted of sin and come to God in repentance (vv. 24-25).

The thrust of this section is to focus on the gift of prophecy in collective assembly to help believers build their understanding of the truth. Paul wants us to present that truth clearly. He recognized the validity of tongues but warned about their public use.

2 KINGS 3-4   God moved again on behalf of His people, specifically because of Jehoshaphat's presence with the king of Israel (3:14). God's methods are not always what we expect, but the result was a resounding victory for Israel (vv. 17-27).

Elisha's action on behalf of the Shunammite woman's son (4:8-37) is similar to that of Elijah in 1 Kings 17. In each case, God honored the prayer of the prophet, giving life again to the child.

Follow the other miraculous events that surrounded Elisha in this chapter. This was a time in Israel when the king and the civil administration were evil, but God was raising up a company of prophets who served Him. Elisha was the best known and most prominent of the prophets, and God used him in an unusual way. Perhaps the miracles validated his ministry before an unbelieving populace.

PSALM 129   If we are God's people, our dealings with the world will not always be smooth; it is the collision of two different cultures. That is what this psalm suggests.   Since early in Israel's history, the surrounding nations had been hostile. When God's people trusted and obeyed Him, He delivered them from the hostility and gave them peace. When they were unfaithful, they felt the hostility directly. In spite of the hostility, however, the psalmist affirms the Lord's goodness and protection. Note the "word picture" of those who oppose the Lord in verses 6-7.

Today we can apply the truth of this psalm to our dealings with the world and the world system. Love God. Trust God, and then see how God protects His own. Note that the Lord's deliverance kept the nation alive (vv. 2b, 4).

JULY 2

1 CORINTHIANS 14:26-40   Paul went to some length in his guidelines to ensure order in church services. It is fair to surmise from the detail given that there had been problems in this regard.

Take note of verse 32. Paul's statement that the "spirits of prophets are subject to the control of prophets" is a safeguard for the church. Preaching is open to the evaluation of other biblically trained and spiritually mature persons in the congregation. None of us should act independently, that is, without being open to the evaluation of peers among God's people.

Paul's comments on the place of women in public church meetings are difficult to hear in today's climate of equality. We should readily give every opportunity and advantage to people that they should have. But such decisions must be weighed carefully in light of the biblical text. Verse 34 seems definite. Perhaps the issue is one of authority as stated in 1 Timothy 2:11-12. If so, this would not require absolute silence by women in the church, but submission to the authority of the elders of the local congregation.

2 KINGS 5-6   In Chapter 5 we find a remarkable account of God's truth reaching a pagan army general. It is all the more remarkable because Naaman's introduction to Elisha and to the power of God came through an unnamed slave girl who had been taken captive from her family in Israel.

In verses 15 and 17-18, Naaman confessed his faith in the living God. Note the character of Elisha in verse 16. Elisha had no interest in personal gain through contact with this wealthy man. Contrast this with Gehazi, who compromised his life with a lie to Naaman, a second lie to Elisha, and suffered God's judgment (vv. 19-27).

In 6:8-23, note verses 16-17. Here was God's man with true faith in the living God and His resources for the situation. What an awesome thing to see God's horses and chariots of fire protecting Elisha and his servant (cf. 2:11-12). As this confrontation proceeded, note Elisha's charity and mercy to the hostile army! When Elisha led the blind army directly into Samaria where Israel could have killed them, he instructed the king of Israel to instead feed the army (vv. 22-23). The result was that the attacks on Israel stopped – at least temporarily (v. 23b).

PSALM 130   Have you ever waited for God to act, wondering how long it would take for the answer to come? That is how the psalmist feels here. The cry comes out of deep distress (v. 1). It comes from a heart of humbleness, understanding the reality of sin (v. 3). It comes with an understanding of grace and forgiveness (v. 4). And it comes with faith that God can, and will, act on behalf of His people (vv. 7-8).

☑It is significant that the writer relied on God's mercy and forgiveness, which the available Scriptures promised (vv. 7-8). These promises are based upon the redemptive and atoning work of Christ on the cross – although the writer had no way to foresee how God would provide these blessings.⇦

JULY 3

1 CORINTHIANS 15:1-34   This chapter gives the most reasoned and complete discussion of the resurrection in the entire Bible. The chapter is divided into three parts and then has a conclusion. The historical evidence for the resurrection is found in verses 1-11, the explanation about why the bodily resurrection is an essential part of our faith in verses 12-34, and the nature of the resurrection body (which we will consider in tomorrow's reading) in verses 35-55. Although the section is long, this cornerstone truth in the framework of our faith deserves our careful attention.

Consider the eyewitness evidence for the resurrection (vv. 3-8). The statement that over five hundred people saw the risen Savior at one time is astounding. Remember that this was written while many of those who saw Christ after the resurrection were still alive, and thus what Paul wrote was open to verification (v. 6).

As a side issue, an apostle was one who had been with Christ. Paul's office of apostle rests, therefore, on Jesus' appearance to Paul on the road to Damascus (vv. 9-11).

One concern that Paul addressed in this chapter is the resurrection of believers. Some were teaching that there was no resurrection (v. 12). Follow Paul's reasoning in verses 12-34. His discussion is not only logical (vv. 12-19) but theological (vv. 20-28). The theological cornerstone of the discussion is that without the resurrection of the Lord Jesus, there will be no resurrection for anyone (vv. 12-19).

When Paul mentioned that some baptized for the dead (v. 29), he was not justifying the practice, but pointing out its underlying conviction – that the resurrection is a fact.

2 KINGS 7-8   A city under siege was not a pleasant place. There seemed to be no hope of deliverance. Elisha's message of hope was spurned by the king's officer (v. 2); it seemed too impossible to accept. God's deliverance, however, was real. Could it be that what the Arameans heard (v. 6) were the horses and chariots of fire (6:16-17)? The entire city shared in the provisions of the Arameans except the unbelieving officer of the king!

In 8:1-6, notice how God protected the interests of the woman who had given Elisha a room to live in. It was no mere coincidence that had Gehazi speaking to the king at just the moment she came to petition for her land.

In 1 Kings 19:15-16 God told Elijah to anoint Hazael king of Aram. The account in 8:7-15 tells how this was fulfilled.

Joram, king of Israel, and Ahaziah, king of Judah, were both evil men who did not lead the people in the ways of the Lord (8:25-29). Remember these two, as we will see them again in 2 Kings 9.

PSALM 131   One could call this a psalm for perspective. It reminds us that pride is an affront to God (v. 1; Lord, deal with, and smash pride in our lives!). Note how the psalmist has chosen to be still and listen to God (v. 2). We also have this opportunity to choose serenity by placing our eyes on God and hoping in Him! Allow the Lord to shape your perspective!

JULY 4

1 CORINTHIANS 15:35-58   As Paul continues the discussion about the resurrection of Jesus and of all believers, it is obvious that questions had been raised about what the resurrection body would be like. Paul's answer is that it will be the same and it will be different (vv. 51-52)!

It will be the same because our actual body will be raised from the grave (and changed), and our identity will be the same. Just as the very body that Jesus had when He died was raised from the dead (Luke

240

24:36-43), we too will be raised (v. 52). In the sameness, however, there is the miracle of transformation – we will be changed (vv. 51-54). The physical, which was perishable, will be changed to an imperishable spiritual body (cf. 1 John 3:2).

Paul uses several analogies to explain the differences between our earthly body and our resurrected body. Remember that analogies are hardly ever perfect – they are not absolute explanations but help us understand similarities and differences. Paul uses the planted seed (the body) that dies in order to produce a new plant (vv. 37-38). The living flesh of men, animals, birds, and fish have similarities – but they are different. Look particularly at verses 42-44. These are "bottom line" facts. The blessing is that we will have the same kind of body as the risen Lord and bear His likeness (v. 49).

The facts about the resurrection are vital to our perspective about life (vv. 56-58). When we remember these truths, nothing the Lord brings us is too much! Our life and work is not "in vain" (v. 58).

2 KINGS 9-10   Chapter 9 gives us the details of how Jehu became king of Israel (the Northern Kingdom). This fulfilled the prophecy of 1 Kings 19:16. Jehu killed both Joram (king of Israel) and Ahaziah (king of Judah), then went to the capital city and killed Jezebel, the widow of Ahab (prophesied by Elijah in 1 Kings 21:23). In addition, Jehu killed all the descendants of Ahab (cf. 1 Kings 21:21) and all the evil ministers of Baal.

At this crossroad in his life, Jehu had the opportunity to choose righteousness and have God's blessing (10:30), but instead he led the people in wickedness (10:31).

PSALM 132   This psalm centers on the temple. David had planned it, and it was a high priority in his life (vv. 2-5). The Lord's glory came to the temple (v. 8a, God's resting-place), and God's people loved to come to this holy place (v. 7). Think, however, about the conditions of verses 11-12; then consider David's descendants and the destruction of the temple (destroyed by Babylon at the time of exile). ☑Yet there is the reminder of the promise of the Messiah in verse 11 and the promise of His reign in verses 17-18. God is not finished with His people!⇦

JULY 5

1 CORINTHIANS 16   In the first several verses (vv. 1-4), Paul gave guidelines for giving to the Lord and His work. Notice that our giving should be regular, systematic, without pressure ("so that when I come no collections will have to be made"), and proportional to individual income (v. 2).

When we think about the apostles, sometimes we lose sight of the fact that they were real people with real needs and relationships. Read these personal requests and greetings, which make us realize that someone as great as Paul had daily needs and concerns! Note that despite the faction that had followed Apollos (3:4ff.), Paul urged Apollos to again visit the church (v. 12). In the last words of the letter, he expressed his love for each of the believers in Corinth (v. 24)!

2 CHRONICLES 21-22   In reading Chapter 21, note Jehoram's unholy marriage and ungodly life (vv. 4-7)! God warned the king (vv. 12-15), and the judgment that Elijah prophesied became reality (vv. 16-20).

Ahaziah, king of Judah, had family connections in Israel that were an evil influence. Ahaziah's mother Athaliah was a granddaughter of Omri (22:2) and the daughter of Ahab, both wicked kings of Israel (21:6). Athaliah was one of the wives of Jehoram, king of Judah (22:2). Through these connections, agents from Israel (the "Northern Kingdom") become advisors to Judah's king Ahaziah (the "Southern Kingdom") (22:3-4).

While Ahaziah was visiting Joram, king of Israel, Jehu (vv. 7-9) killed both Ahaziah and Joram. God had designated Jehu to take the monarchy of Israel (1 Kings 19:16).

In the vacuum left in Judah by the death of King Ahaziah, his mother Athaliah seized power, killing all (she thought) of her son's male heirs. She had reason to fear for her life with the death of her son. The princes who were heirs to the throne were not her sons and would have been less open to the influence of the kings and advisors from Israel. In any event, one son, Joash, was preserved through the efforts of Ahaziah's sister and the priest Jehoiada. Watch Jehoiada as the account unfolds, and observe his influence on Judah (22:10-12).

PSALM 133   Although the illustration of verse 2 will not excite our present-day imagination, the truth of verse 1 should do so. Link verse 3b with the truth of verse 1. The Lord's blessing is the gift to any fellowship with true unity in the Lord. This is the unity of Philippians 2, where fellowship is built in common ministry and mutual servanthood. That kind of unity, with the blessing of the Lord, is an unbeatable combination.

JULY 6

2 CORINTHIANS 1   The Christian life is a combination of hardship and blessing. The sufferings that come into our lives are those of Christ (v. 5). Paul relates that in Asia he was under such great pressure that he and his companions despaired of life itself (vv. 8-9).

Out of this pressure, however, comes God's comfort and help (v. 4) which leads to growth and trust (vv. 9b-10). This helps us comfort others (vv. 4-6). This is God's design for His people. We don't live alone but in the community of God's people; it is God's design that we all are related to one another. The suffering or joy of one believer is designed to help and encourage others.

Note Paul's testimony about his conduct (v. 12). His behavior is a model for us. He displayed holiness, godly wisdom (as distinguished from worldly wisdom), and simplicity (vv. 12-14).

2 KINGS 11-12   Review the family connections outlined in the notes for July 5 on 2 Chronicles 22. Athaliah ruled Judah for six years. In the meantime the young king Joash was being prepared to rule. Follow how Jehoiada the priest was instrumental in putting Joash on the throne (11:4-12). In the print of history, this all seems almost routine and easy. However, there was great danger in what Jehoiada planned and carried out. Notice how he placed the guards and made special arrangements so that guards going off duty would stay while the rightful heir to the throne was crowned. If one detail had gone wrong and his attempt failed, he and the young heir would have been executed.

When Athaliah killed the royal line of the kings of Judah, she thought she was destroying the line of David and Solomon. This would have destroyed the "legal" line of Jesus through Joseph – and God did not allow that to happen! Not until the nation went into captivity under Nebuchadnezzar was that line to the throne disrupted – and then only because the nation ceased to exist. Even then, God preserved both the lines of Solomon and Nathan – the sons of David through whom Jesus' was reckoned (cf. Matt 1:6 and 1 Chron 3:10-16; Luke 3:31-32).

Note especially 12:2. Joash did well as long as Jehoiada was alive to direct him. Note, however, that he did not remove all of the influences of pagan worship (v. 3). Joash began to collect money to repair the temple (v. 4), and in the end he needed to prod Jehoiada to begin the repairs (vv. 6-7).

Preview 2 Chronicles 24:17-22 to see what happened after Jehoiada died. Note the amazing influence for good that one man, Jehoiada, had on the entire society.

PSALM 134   Imagine spending the night in the ancient temple. This psalm is a reminder to those workers to praise the Lord. It is possible that the hours were long and even monotonous. Take your cue from this psalm – praise the Lord. No one's work is always exciting – certainly not the work and lives of Christian workers. Praise the Lord; and may the Lord, the Maker of heaven and earth, bless you (v. 3)!

JULY 7

2 CORINTHIANS 2   Paul now came to one of the reasons for this second letter.   Remember that he had spoken directly to the church about its tolerance of sin in the fellowship, telling members to put the immoral man out of the church (1 Cor 5).   The church apparently did this, and the man repented.   Now, Paul instructed, forgive him and bring him back into the fellowship (vv. 6-8).   If not, the man may become so discouraged that Satan will snatch him away again.

The pattern of "redemptive discipline" modeled here is the biblical pattern for the church.   Discipline is exercised in love with the end of restoration, and forgiveness is extended with repentance.

Look carefully at verses 14-17.   Here is an explanation of how the witnessing Christian is received – gladly by those who receive the message (as one would enjoy the fragrance of flowers), but with disdain and hostility by those who will not hear (as one would turn away from a putrid smell)!   The deep difference between "the world" and "the faith" becomes apparent.   Refer again to 1 Corinthians 2:7, 12, 14-15.   Here is the explanation – the spiritual difference we must understand.   We belong to a triumphal procession of those who know Christ (v. 14).   We stand with those through the ages who have placed their faith in the Lord Jesus!

There is dignity in sharing the good news (v. 17).   Sharing the gospel is not for peddlers and hawkers!   Look again at Paul's methodology in 1:12.   God will use each personality as He has created it – but remember that it is a work of the Holy Spirit and does not need the world's promotional and marketing techniques.

2 CHRONICLES 23-24   We now review the reign of Joash (cf. notes for 2 Kings 11-12, July 6) from the perspective of Chronicles.   After he saved Joash from certain death at the hand of Athaliah (22:10-12), six years passed before the priest Jehoiada was ready to crown Joash.   The coup was carried off with careful planning, and Athaliah was deposed (she never should have been in power).

Jehoiada was good for the country and the king.   He encouraged the king and the people in righteousness.   With his death, however, influences of evil came out of the woodwork, drawing the king away from the truth (24:17-19).   One can almost hear the arguments: "The people should have the liberty of choice in worship."   Joash became the "pro-choice" king, and the people quickly turned to pagan worship.   Not only did this happen, but Zechariah, Jehoiada's son in the priesthood, was killed when he tried to give the king God's message (24:20-22).   As a result, God's hand was heavy on the land.   The Aramean army defeated

Judah's much larger army because God was not with Joash (v. 24). Contrast this with the victory of Jehoshaphat in 2 Chronicles 20:18-23, when God gave victory because the king and the people trusted the Lord. His own people murdered Joash after he was wounded in battle because he had killed Zechariah the priest (v. 25).

PSALM 135   We serve a great and wonderful God. But there is danger of becoming too familiar – of taking God for granted. This psalm helps put things in perspective. *The Lord* blesses us. He is also the God of power (vv. 6-7), deliverance, and provision (vv. 8-12). He struck down the Canaanites because of their sin (vv. 10-12; cf. Lev 18:24-25).

Look, too, at the "gods" of those who don't know the Lord (vv. 15-18). These "gods" are dead idols, and worshipping them leads to death (v. 18). The contrast of these with the true and living God should turn your heart in thankfulness to God. Also allow the contrast to turn your heart in mercy to bring the message of the true God to those who don't know Him. *Never, never, take God for granted!*

JULY 8

2 CORINTHIANS 3   Paul contrasts the ministry of the "old covenant" with that of the "new covenant" in verses 4-18. In technical terms, the covenant of the law brought death, since it made the reality of sin (through the law) apparent to all who were serious enough to think about it (v. 9a). The new covenant, through the Holy Spirit and the redemptive work of Christ, brings life (v. 9b). We have the privilege of bringing this message of life!   Further, God, through His grace, is transforming us into His likeness (v. 18).

Before Christ, under the old covenant, how were people saved? It was under the new covenant, even though Christ and His redemptive work had not been revealed at that time. Abraham was saved by faith (cf. Gen 15:6; Rom 4). The old covenant, with its impossible demands (the law), was God's revelation of His character and standard, preparing the hearts of men to receive the real answer in Christ.

What came through the knowledge of Christ – the understanding of a relationship with God both in this life and for eternity – made Paul "very bold" (v. 12). Freedom of the Spirit (v. 17) allows fellowship in a new way with the Lord and also frees God's people to reflect His glory to the watching world (v. 18).

2 KINGS 13-14   Chapter 13 is the account of two kings of Israel, neither of whom followed the Lord. Jehoahaz sought the Lord when he was oppressed (v. 4) and God graciously gave relief, but his repentance was half-hearted. Similarly, his son Jehoash was evil.

Amaziah was a king of Judah who followed the Lord, but he foolishly challenged Israel and was defeated (14:11-14). He suffered the indignity of coming back to Jerusalem with the victorious Jehoash, who broke down the wall of Jerusalem and took many of the national treasures. Azariah, Amaziah's son, who was also known as Uzziah, became king (14:21). Isaiah and Hosea began their prophetic ministries during the reign of Azariah.

PSALM 136   This is a psalm written for worship, with the public reader reciting the first half of the verse and the worshipers responding with the second half.

Reciting the psalm reminds people of the attributes of God. This was a strong element in the worship of the Israelites. We, too, need these reminders.

Consider God's attributes: sovereignty (vv. 2-3); creative power (vv. 4-9); deliverance (vv. 10-16); fulfilled promise (vv. 17-22); and compassion (vv. 23-26). We serve a great and caring God!

JULY 9

2 CORINTHIANS 4   Paul addressed the ministry of the new covenant (cf. Ch. 3) for the Corinthian church. It is significant that this ministry is part of the spiritual battle, and we must approach it on that basis.

First, we must be absolutely honest and above board. No tricks or distortions (vv. 1-2). In today's language, no marketing tricks or devices. Rather, God's messenger must straightforwardly present the truth.

Second, understand the power of the opposition. Satan actually blinds people (vv. 3-4)! The light of Jesus can penetrate the blindness caused by Satan (vv. 5-6), but Paul was careful not to get in the way personally – rather, he preached Jesus Christ as Lord (v. 5).

Third, understand our own imperfections and that God has the power (v. 7); it is not our personal attractiveness, skill, wisdom, or methods that are effective. Our own imperfections make the work of God through the Holy Spirit obvious.

Fourth, the eternal nature of the ministry makes whatever difficulty we may encounter inconsequential (vv. 16-18).

HOSEA 1-3   Hosea lived and prophesied in the Northern Kingdom, or Israel, at the same time Isaiah was God's messenger in Judah. His messages were given during the reign of Jeroboam (1:1; 2 Kings 14:23-29), about thirty years before the final defeat and deportation of the Israelites by Assyria in 722 BC. His ministry in Israel followed that of

Amos by a few years. He probably lived to see the destruction of the country by Assyria.

During the reign of Jeroboam, however, destruction of the country by a foreign nation seemed unlikely, for Jeroboam actually extended the borders of the country, and there was a degree of prosperity that had not been seen for years. In the account of Jeroboam's reign (2 Kings 14:23-29), the prosperity was not because of the people's righteousness or the king's goodness, but purely based on God's grace to the nation. In the light of this prosperity, of the land, Hosea's message calling for repentance probably fell largely on deaf ears.

Hosea's marriage (Chapter 1) and reconciliation with his wife (Chapter 3) require a word of explanation. Although several possibilities can explain this relationship, the most likely is that Gomer was not adulterous when they were married; Hosea 1:2-3 considers her and her character retrospectively. Her bad character became apparent after her marriage. Since God had led Hosea to marry the woman, as he looked back, he could say, "God told me to marry this adulterous woman."

The names of their three children all were significant. The first, Jezreel, referred to the killing of many people in Jezreel when Jehu became king (2 Kings 10). Although God had given him the kingdom, Jehu, probably for personal reasons, went beyond what God wanted by killing those who could have stood in his way. The name symbolized the violence common during Hosea's time. The second, Lo-Ruhamah, meant "not loved" and had the significance that God would no longer show love to the sinful nation (1:6). The third, Lo-Ammi, meant "not my people" and carried the message that God would no longer consider Israel His people. The message was that time was running out, and God's judgment would come to the nation – unless they repented.

In reading Chapter 2, you can see the Lord's message to the people in light of Hosea's marriage. Israel is the adulterous wife. She (Israel) had taken the gifts that her husband (God) had given her and offered them in a spiritually adulterous relationship to Baal (the pagan god, v. 8). Note God's grace in leading the adulterous wife back to Himself (vv. 14-23). In spite of the unfaithfulness, God was (and is) not done dealing in grace with His people. Judgment is coming, but still there is love! ☑The picture of renewal in 1:10-11 and 2:14-23 has not been realized yet. Compare these verses with Ezekiel 36:24-38, which promises restoration of God's people from their dispersion among the nations – purely because of God's grace and for His sovereign purposes. In fact, this will be fulfilled only with the return of the Messiah. Hosea 1:10-11 and 2:16-23 speak of this time of blessing – the sovereign work of God through the Messiah. Note this same promise in 3:4-5. The "David the King" whom they will recognize will be the descendant of David, the Messiah!

Gomer, Hosea's wife, had apparently left him, and Hosea took the initiative, at God's direction, to buy her back (Ch. 3). This too had symbolic meaning for the nation for it promised that the Lord, upon His own initiative, would bring the Israelites back into relationship with Him (see above). ⇦

PSALM 137   Jewish exiles in Babylon wrote this psalm. They suffered as they thought of the city (Jerusalem) now destroyed – the city that had been the center of their identity and their worship. "Sing us a song of your country," their captors demanded. How, for instance, could they sing Psalm 136, which detailed the Lord's deliverance? It would be laughable to the Babylonians. They vowed, however, never to forget the city they loved (vv. 5-6).

JULY 10

2 CORINTHIANS 5:1-10   This section of Chapter 5 gives perspective to life here on the earth. Thoughtfully read what Paul wrote about the reality of the eternal. We live in a tent – a temporary dwelling – while our permanent dwelling place (house) is prepared in heaven (v. 1). This life pales in importance as we consider the reality of the life to come. Paul gave us an important truth that takes the "sting" out of death (vv. 1-5). God has prepared a new and permanent dwelling for each of us to replace the temporary earthly existence, which we know will pass away.

This goes further than the assurance that we will have a place to live in heaven. Paul is clear that there are burdens for the Christian in this life (v. 4; 4:16). The assurance of God's presence in the Holy Spirit (v. 5) gives meaning to the present life, as well as guaranteeing the future.

This perspective of the eternal nature of our life, and of eternal values, dominates the life of the child of God. Life with the Lord is so real that even though we cannot see the future, we know it to be true by faith. The result is that Christians desire to please the Lord in all they do (vv. 6-9). Finally, we *will* appear before God for evaluation of how we have spent our time and resources (vv. 9-10). This will be the final exam! *Are you preparing for finals?* Allow this certainty of the eternal to shape your life!

HOSEA 4-5   Chapter 4 is a hard-hitting indictment of specific sins and spiritual adultery. *The books of Kings and Chronicles tell the story of the two nations. The prophets give the account of what God saw in their behavior*. What the Lord observed is seen in verses 1b-2. What a tragic picture this is, with dire results (v. 3). It included people (vv. 4-6a) and priests (vv. 6b-9). Spiritual prostitution led them to pagan worship of the worst kind (vv. 10-14). Because of this, judgment would come! Judgment as swift and devastating as a whirlwind (v. 19).

The call to listen was to religious and political leaders, as well as the people (5:1). God saw the sin (v. 3) that ensnared them and kept them from the Lord (v. 4). God had withdrawn from them (v. 6), and judgment would come (vv. 9-15).

There are several lessons here. The drift from the Lord can be slow and subtle. A slow drift from truth and holy living allows us to accommodate to society around us – without giving serious thought to our relationship to the Lord. Note the comment in 4:6 and the last phrase of verse 14. Our knowledge and understanding come in two ways. Careful attention to the Bible combined with obedience will protect us from slipping into attitudes and practices that will displease the Lord and endanger our spiritual lives.

PSALM 138   Is it any wonder that David was a man after God's heart? Praise and devotion filled his heart (v. 1). Look for the reasons David finds to praise the Lord (vv. 2-3). God, though most holy and exalted, sees the humble person (v. 6). This is an amazing truth!

Note also verse 2b. The Lord has exalted His name and His word. Why His name? The Lord's name stands for His person and His character. Remember that Jesus began His model of prayer by asking that God's name be kept holy (Matt 6:9). Remember also that God's Word is the channel through which we understand God's person and standard. It is through the Word that we understand sin and redemption. *In our day of gross irreverence, we must be careful that we are not infected with the virus of casual indifference to the holiness of God's name and His Word.*

JULY 11

2 CORINTHIANS 5:11-6:2   Beginning with verse 11, Paul writes about the Christians' ministry in the world. This is the world of people who are lost without Christ. Notice that Paul uses the insight of the previous section to introduce what he will say. The "fear" of the Lord is a deep respect that comes from the certainty that we will stand before Him (v. 10).

Living for Jesus has a reality orientation. Christ loved each of us enough to die for us (v. 14)! Having saved us, it is His will that we ("those who live," i.e., those with eternal life) should live for Him (v. 15). The "worldling" lives for Number One! The Christian lives for Christ!

The changed perspective of which Paul speaks determines how we see other people (v. 16). The reference to Christ in verse 16 is Paul's view of Jesus before he met Him on the road to Damascus. He thought of Christ as a mere man until then – a dangerous man. Now, Paul saw Christ as the Holy Son of God and all others as persons for whom Christ died! They were no longer just people to be tolerated, pushed out of the way, or used! They had unique status because of Christ's work on their behalf. In this context, verse 17 makes sense. Because of this new view of Jesus and of people, *everything* is new. Through the Holy Spirit, we see people with the compassion God has for them – through His eyes.

→What follows flows logically from this. The Lord has placed each of us here to be His representative in the world. He has made us special representatives – ambassadors (vv. 18-20) and has entrusted to us the "ministry of reconciliation" (v. 18). Christians are God's spokesmen in the world, through whom the world will hear the good news! This is the moment God has given to share and receive this good news (6:1-2). We may not have the gift of evangelism, but each of us can share what God has done for the world and for us. Read this section carefully, thinking about this assignment from the Lord.←

HOSEA 6-7   Hosea called for repentance in 6:1-3. Although Israel had suffered the Lord's discipline, the Lord promised healing if the people would acknowledge Him.

Look, however, at what God saw in verses 4-10. The people's love for God was as transient as the mist in the morning (v. 4). Although the people went through the motions of religion, their actions were empty. God desired to see mercy (human relationships) and acknowledgment of Him (obedience); these were missing in spite of the outward trappings of religion in the sacrifices (v. 6)! What God saw was violence (v. 9) and spiritual prostitution (v. 10).

In Chapter 7, the Lord continued to speak to the people about their sin and its effect on their nation. God saw deceit, stealing, and robbery (v. 1). The people had forgotten that God saw them (v. 2). Sinful intrigue and hidden personal agendas filled the royal courts (vv. 3-7), and the king and princes loved it (v. 3). Dabbling with foreign paganism had sapped the strength of the nation, but Israel was blind to it (v. 9). In looking for political alliances, they were like birds flying here and there (v. 11), when they should have been looking to the Lord (v. 13). Although they wailed, it was because of the consequences of sin and not because they were repenting (v. 14).

This was a society waiting for judgment to fall. Remember that a society is the composite of many persons – each of whom bears responsibility before God. While we may believe we can't do much about society, our own response can make a difference.

PSALM 139   Does God really see you and me? This psalm asserts that He does, without question. How well does God understand us? The answer is very well, indeed – in fact, perfectly. He knows our hearts, our thoughts, our intentions (vv. 1-4). He knows what is behind us and what is before us. He sees in the dark and the light (vv. 5-12). He knows us from the inside for He created each of us in a unique way (v. 13). *In fact, God has known the plan of our lives even before we were embryos (v. 16)!* For those who wonder whether life begins before birth, verses 13-16 are the key.

Note David's heart in verses 17-18 and how he stood for God's agenda in verses 19-22. Certainly we see into David's character in verses 23-24. David "followed hard after God." He was willing to have God show him new insights about himself so he could follow God better. This attitude is the key to genuine growth – getting beyond our defensiveness, rationalizations, and excuses and allowing God to show us our true selves so that He can help us change.

JULY 12

2 CORINTHIANS 6:3-18   Paul continues his theme from the previous chapters in verses 3-13. The Corinthians did not accept Paul as they should have, probably because of Paul's humility. As mentioned previously, teachers were respected at least partly on the basis of their fee. Teachers of distinction charged a great deal. But Paul refused to accept money for his ministry, especially when he first brought the gospel to an area. He considered it a spiritual ministry, different from the secular teachers, a distinction that some of those preaching – and many who listened – didn't understand. It was his firm policy to make the gospel free to those who would listen.

But if Paul didn't charge for teaching and preaching, he did have other more impressive credentials (vv. 3-10): sacrifice and hardship for believers and for the gospel, and maintained a ministry of love, honesty, and power. These marks of the true servant of God are an example for us! Note how Paul proved his credentials. Then, note particularly verse 7. The power of God and the weapons of righteousness accompanied these credentials (cf. 2 Cor 10:3-5).

As we will see in Chapter 7, Paul continued to speak about his relationship with the church. It would seem, then, that verses 14-18 should be seen in the context of this discussion as well. Paul calls into question the spiritual nature of the teachers who charged for their preaching. He even calls them false apostles in 11:13. His message is that the church should not be yoked to them. We often use these verses as reason not to enter into marriage or close business relationships with unbelievers, and this, too, is legitimate. Even so, we should not forget their primary meaning.

Finally, notice how Paul uses the Old Testament principle of the separation of God's people from the pagan nations and applies it to the Christian community. We *are* different! We have a different view of life (5:15) and the people around us (5:16-17). We have a different view of work for Christ (vv. 4-10). This should translate into a community that is obviously different – a redemptive community in a broken world. The further motivation for this difference is seen in 7:1 as Paul concludes this section.

HOSEA 8-10   Chapter 8 is a poignant account of Israel's condition when Hosea wrote. The people still remembered enough to give lip service to the worship of God, but the nation had no heart for the Lord (vv. 1-3). Because of this, a mighty predator was hovering over the land (v. 1, the eagle).

The reasons for the threat of imminent judgment from the Lord are outlined here. *(1)* Israel had chosen the wrong and rejected the good (v. 3). *(2)* They had chosen wrong leaders (v. 4a). *(3)* They had chosen wrong worship (v. 4b-6). *(4)* They had gone to the wrong place for help (vv. 9-10). Assyria was the nation that God would use to scatter Israel, but this refers to previous times when Israel had gone to Assyria for help. *(5)* They chose wrong guidelines – even though they had the Word of God (v. 12). *(6)* Finally, they had forgotten the Lord (v. 14)! *But remember, the forms of worship were still there!*

Chapter 9 continues the theme of imminent punishment. Sin will cause a poor harvest (v. 2) and will dispossess the people (v. 3). Punishment is near – the day when God will settle accounts (v. 7). God had sent His messengers to warn the people, but they were rejected (vv. 7b-8). The reference to Baal Peor in verse 10 concerns the seduction of the people to sexual sin and worship of idols recorded in Numbers 25. The significant thing is that the false worship destroyed the people (v. 10b). Centuries of wandering among the nations is foretold in verse 17.

The slippery slope of prosperity is described in 10:1-2. One result of sin and a society's lack of trust is the proliferation of litigation (v. 4). Verses 12-13 suggest two self-help programs, one true and the other false. Compare verse 12 with Isaiah 1:16-17. Here are four suggestions about how to implement the true self-help program: Love God's people and maintain justice (look ahead to 12:6); stand for truth and obey God; smash personal pride and arrogance; follow hard after God. Instead of these things, Israel chose the course outlined in verse 13!

PSALM 140   The world around us reflects Satan's agenda. This has become more obvious in the offerings of the entertainment industry and in the political agendas of state and national parties. The underlying agenda isn't new – that of drawing people and families away from God's righteousness.

David faced similar pressures. They were evil, devised by men of violence (vv. 1-2). One of the prime weapons was the deceitful word (v. 3). The intent was to entrap (v. 5).

The entire psalm is a prayer for protection, based upon David's relationship with the Lord and what he knows of God's character (vv. 6-7, 12). We are on strong ground when our prayer is based on the Lord's concerns.

JULY 13

2 CORINTHIANS 7   As you read verses 2-7, again note Paul's testimony as he details his ministry in Corinth. In verse 2 notice how he was able to say without reservation that his work and influence among them had only been for good. Notice also in verses 5-7 Paul's human emotions. He was afraid when he faced danger. It is significant that the Lord sent comfort through Titus, a younger brother in the Lord.

Paul again notes the sorrow the Corinthians felt because of the sin in the church (v. 8). An important principle comes out of this in verse 10. The church experienced "godly sorrow." This is contrasted with "worldly sorrow," which brings death instead of salvation. Godly sorrow comes because we understand that we have grieved God, and it accompanies repentance. Worldly sorrow comes from being found out and has little to do with repentance. God sees the difference!

HOSEA 11-12   Note that God called His Son from Egypt (v. 1). ☑It is clear that this refers to the Israelites and how the Lord delivered them from bondage. However, in Matthew 2:15 this is also referred to the Lord Jesus in His infancy. Because of the threat from Herod, the Lord directed Joseph to take Mary and the child to Egypt. The Lord brought them back again in His own timing.⇦ God's good hand brought blessing to Israel (11:1-4), but they rejected it (vv. 2, 3b). As a result, God's discipline would come (vv. 5-6). ☑But it would not be a final destruction. God still had (has) a heart for His people (vv. 8-11) and would bring them back to the land after their dispersion among the nations (vv. 10-11; cf. 9:17). Compare this with Amos 9:11-15.⇦

Notice the picture of worthless activity in 12:1. It was useless (like pursuing and eating wind!) to make treaties with Assyria (witness the destruction of Israel by Assyria just a few years later), or to look to Egypt. Their security should have been in the Lord! What God desired (and still desires) in His people is in verse 6 – but what God found is in verses 7-8. Note the self-deception in verse 8b! God reminds the people that He brought them out of Egypt and cared for them (vv. 9-13), but the nation has provoked the Lord to anger by its contempt (v. 14).

The lesson is obvious. We must never treat God's blessings lightly or forget what He has given. The moment we assume we can bring such blessing to our lives and homes, we demean the work of God on our behalf! He must be our life and our ambition!

PSALM 141 David made his allegiance unquestionably clear in this psalm. This decision is evident in verse 8. In verses 1-2 the same choice is stipulated but in a slightly different way. It is to God that he called and to God that he prayed.

Yet David understood that he needed help to stay on track. His prayer is that God would guard his mouth (v. 3) and help him avoid the activities of evil men (v. 4). He also prayed that if he needed correction, a fellow believer would be led of God to confront him (v. 5; cf. Prov 27:6; Gal 6:1). Even the hard things a righteous man says are a kindness.

As believers we need to make firm decisions, but we also need to understand our vulnerability and be open to correction.

JULY 14

2 CORINTHIANS 8 Chapters 8 and 9 address financial giving. Although Paul did not ask that the church give to him personally, he was clear that they had a responsibility to give to the Lord's work and to share with fellow believers in need. In this case it was the people in the church in Jerusalem who were in need, having undergone persecution.

To encourage the church to give liberally, Paul used two illustrations. He reminded them of the eagerness of the churches in Macedonia (Philippi, Thessalonica, Berea), north of Corinth, to share with those in need (vv. 1-5). He also reminded them of the Lord Jesus, who gave Himself for them (and all of us, v. 9).

The principle was not that a church in one city should give to another church out of its poverty but that there should be equality among God's people (vv. 13-15). When one part of the church is hard-pressed (in this case Jerusalem), another part of the church has the ability to send relief. Paul also used the illustration of manna for the

Israelites; every one of those who gathered manna had enough because God provided (v. 15)!

Paul gave one more important principle in verses 16-24. The handling of the money by those who would deliver it must be totally aboveboard to please God and raise no questions.

HOSEA 13-14   Ephraim usually refers to the ten northern tribes, or Israel. In 13:1, however, it refers to the tribe of Ephraim, which was respected among the tribes. When the men of Ephraim spoke, the rest of the nation listened. However, now the tribe's dignity and influence had been lost because of Baal worship (v. 1), and the evil practices, once begun, had continued in a downward spiral (v. 2).

Note the three illustrations of the result of this evil worship (v. 3). The people would be like the morning mist that disappears, like the chaff from the threshing floor that blows away, and like smoke that dissipates in the air. In contrast, the Lord desired single-minded worship (v. 4). Follow the Lord's warnings in this chapter of impending judgment because of the continuing spiritual adultery.

☑In 13:14 there is a parenthetical statement that interrupts the prophet's message to Israel. It is a note of grace. Within this message of God's judgment is the promise that God would ransom His people from the grave and redeem them from death! God's grace and mercy in redemption *looks forward* to the coming Savior. *Looking back* on Christ's redemptive work, Paul quotes this verse in 1 Corinthians 15:55 as a note of praise to explain our victory in Christ's death and resurrection, and our secure hope in a resurrection body that is imperishable.⇦

As Hosea closes (14:1-3), the prophet pleads with the nation to repent. Sin had been the people's downfall (v. 1). If words were coupled with deeds of repentance, then the Lord would receive the praise of their lips (v. 2). No more looking to the wrong place for help (Assyria), and no more wrong worship ("our gods")! Back to the Lord God in whom there is compassion (v. 3)!

☑The Lord's gracious and beautiful offer of healing found in verses 4-8 is a promise of restoration. God is not done with His people! This refers to the tender relationship the Messiah will have with His people upon His return.⇦

PSALM 142   This psalm recalls the period when David was fleeing from Saul and hiding in caves. What a blessing to have the confidence that the Lord knew his circumstance (v. 3).

The psalm expresses David's heart cry to God during this danger. In the confusion of the time, note how clearly David sees God (vv. 3a, 5) as the one who could free him from his "prison" (v. 7).

JULY 15

2 CORINTHIANS 9   In verses 1-5 Paul completed the arrangements for picking up the money that the church would contribute to the needy in Jerusalem. Note his sensitivity. First, Paul wrote that the men would come to get the relief offering. Then he reminded them to make their arrangements beforehand to avoid embarrassment.

A remarkable principle of giving is found in verse 6. God blesses those who give so that as God's people we are able to give even more! But, if we are unwilling to give (sow sparingly), God sees that the harvest is also sparing.

Think carefully about the message of verses 7-11. As we are generous, God is able to (and will) meet every need we have. In addition, something much more significant than financial provision will come to those who are generous: the harvest of righteousness (v. 10). The text does not say that by giving we will reap financial rewards but that our needs will be met, and the blessing of God will be ours.

2 CHRONICLES 25   Amaziah *started well*, but note in verse 2 that his devotion to the Lord was not wholehearted (an open door to compromise). Part of his failure to trust God was evident in his decision to hire Israelites to augment his own army when he faced Edom in battle (v. 6). The Lord graciously brought a prophet to challenge this decision – and to his credit – Amaziah did back down in spite of the money he had paid for the mercenaries (vv. 7-10). Amaziah, however, *ended poorly* because he turned to pagan worship after defeating Edom (vv. 14-15). God brought him down when he challenged Israel in battle and was defeated. He was assassinated, and his son Uzziah (Azariah) began his reign.

Learn the lesson: Leave a door open for compromise and one will probably use it! *We tend to hedge our commitments when we want to leave room for compromise.* It will be the open door for possible disaster.

PSALM 143   David followed hard after God. He longed for the Lord in his inner heart (v. 6). This made it natural to turn to God in trouble.

Observe the confidence that David brought to his prayer for deliverance. He remembered all that the Lord had done in the past (v. 5). On that basis alone, he could expect God to act. There is, however, more. God's unfailing love is a fact (v. 8). God's righteousness is a fact

(v. 1). God's mercy is a fact, or David would have no basis for prayer (v. 2)! With these factual bases, David prayed in confidence. So can you!

JULY 16

2 CORINTHIANS 10   Again, in Chapters 10 and 11, Paul visits the justification and legitimacy of his ministry as an apostle. He placed the argument squarely in the spiritual arena (where it belongs) – first, by the example of Christ in meekness and gentleness (which Paul demonstrated, and for which he was criticized, v. 1), and then by the reminder that the battle is different for the Christian (vv. 3-5). The Christian has an entirely different rulebook than the world when dealing with conflict. These are verses that each serious Christian would do well to memorize and review regularly.

Follow Paul's reasoning through the chapter, and then think about his conclusion in verses 17-18. Ask yourself who your primary audience is each day: the Lord Jesus – or the world that surrounds you?

JOEL 1   The message of the prophet Joel was directed to Judah and is thought to have been written about 835 BC, probably at the time of the reign of Joash and his reforms (2 Kings 12; 2 Chron 24). The theme of the book is the judgment of God on Judah and the nations, but there is clearly a message of God's compassion and mercy as well. There is a call for all levels of society to repent.

One of the key phrases of the book is "the Day of the Lord" by which is meant the day when God calls all society (the whole world) to account for sin. In Joel, there is an immediate meaning of judgment for Judah's sin, but there is also an obvious application later in the book to God's final judgment on the nations and the whole world system. Finally, there is the promise that God will restore His people and will dwell with them, bringing great blessing to the land of Israel and the people of the promise.

Chapter 1 includes the prophecy of judgment on an agricultural society and a plea for repentance. The judgment will reach every part of the land (v. 4). Crops will wither (v. 7), bringing bitter disappointment and sorrow (vv. 8-10). Their whole base of agriculture, and thus their economy, would be ruined (vv. 10-12). Note the condition of the land in verses 16-20.

In this context comes a strongly worded call to repentance (vv. 13-14). It was a call to religious and civil leaders to humble prayer and fasting. It is a call to reach beneath the religious veneer to the heart and to move toward real change.

PSALM 144   The psalm begins by extolling the greatness of God and, in comparison, the transient nature of man (vv. 1-4).   This is "reality orientation."   We like to think that our life here on earth will go on forever. Not so! In the eternal scheme, our lives here are like a vapor (v. 4; cf. James 4:14).

☑Compare verses 5-8 with Zechariah 14.   Although David was thinking of his own need for deliverance, the picture he brings to mind suggests the Lord's return. God will indeed touch the mountains and scatter his enemies, bringing blessing to His people when He comes again.   Count and name these blessings in the remainder of Psalm 144.⇦

JULY 17

2 CORINTHIANS 11:1-15   Paul had a specific vision for the church: The church must have only one loyalty. He used the model of marriage, saying the church should have only one husband: Christ (v. 2).   He worried that if the church listened to other teachers they would be drawn away from the Lord. To make the point, he used Eve as an example (v. 3). What the serpent said to Eve sounded attractive, but listening to Satan led to death!   Other teachers were preaching a different message (probably distorted in subtle ways) from what Paul had taught them (v. 4). Paul admitted that while he might not have been such a skilled speaker, he knew the truth (v. 6).

The issue that "hooked" the Corinthians was, at least partly, a cultural one; Paul didn't charge for his teaching, although it was customary to do so. *On principle*, Paul never charged for the gospel. Instead, after a church was established, he expected that church to help support the work of extending the gospel (v. 8). The result, however, was that at least some in the Corinthian church concluded that he wasn't much of a teacher – because he didn't charge for his ministry.

Finally, Paul exposed those who distorted the message of Christ as false teachers with a message from Satan (vv. 13-15). That the teachers appeared competent and the message sounded valid did not make it so! Satan is clever enough to wrap his message in attractive coverings. The crucial question is always whether what is taught squares with the Scriptures.

JOEL 2   ☑The Day of the Lord is mentioned in 1:15 and in 2:1-2. This term is often used to refer to God's judgment on the nations when Christ comes again. The calamity described in 2:1-9 speaks of this time, as do the specific references to the shaking of the earth (v. 10) and changes in the celestial bodies (v. 10b; cf. Matt 24:29-31). Note the reference to the Lord at the head of His army (v. 11; cf. Rev 19:11-16).⇦

Note, once again, the call to heart repentance (vv. 12-17). There was time for God's people to turn to Him and receive His grace. Think about how much closer we are to the Lord's coming than the Israelites were – and how that should call us to our knees in humble repentance.

☑In 2:28-29 there is reference to the coming of the Holy Spirit at Pentecost (cf. Acts 2:14-21). Here, as in other places in the Old Testament, the first and second advents of Christ are not separated. The coming of the Holy Spirit is mentioned in conjunction with the events at the end of the age (vv. 30-32; cf. Matt 24:29-31).⇦

PSALM 145   David had a heart to love and praise God. His was not, however, a blind devotion, but one based on solid facts. As you read the psalm, enumerate the attributes of God that David has on the tip of his tongue (pen). He knew God! He knew the Scriptures, and he knew God through experience. Consider his example for your own life. *Knowing God through the truth of the Bible, and through obedience, is an unbeatable combination.* It will prepare you for *any* hard time in life.

JULY 18

2 CORINTHIANS 11:16-33   One of the most eloquent parts of the New Testament is found in verses 22-29. Besides the persecution Paul endured, consider verses 28-29. Who would humanly choose to be an apostle? These conditions seem impossible! Yet Paul does not demand favorable working conditions as a condition of employment. Rather, he is concerned about the health and purity of the church. Paul was single-minded in his devotion to Christ and his love for the church. His suffering was in stark contrast (by implication) to the teachers who tried make a living with their teaching.

Thank God for those who have laid foundations for each of us. God has touched men and woman who made great sacrifices to bring the gospel to each generation. As you read the Bible this year, allow the Holy Spirit to show you that each of us shares in this great responsibility.

JOEL 3   ☑Even when God judges the nations, there will be a future for Israel (vv. 1-3). Verses 9-14 describe the Battle of Armageddon. Note that the Lord Himself will draw the nations to this great battle when the Lord will wreak judgment on the world. With 2:10-11, 30-31, and 3:15, compare Ezekiel 32:7-8, Isaiah 13:9-13, and Luke 21:25-28.

God's dealings with Israel will be tender, as described in verses 17-18. God's people will understand the identity of the Messiah (v. 17). It will be a time of blessing (v. 18a). The water flowing out of the Lord's house is also mentioned in Psalm 46:4, Ezekiel 47, Zechariah 14:8, and Revelation 22:1.⇦

PSALM 146 Where do you place your trust? Who is your champion? This psalm offers good advice and a wonderful example. *Advice*: Don't place your trust in men. They can't save, and they will die along with their plans (vv. 3-4). *Example*: The psalmist decided to trust God for his entire life (v. 2). He had reasons for doing so. The Lord created all that we see and reigns forever (vv. 6, 10). Further, the Lord's justice and liberating grace reach to all (vv. 7-9).

Allow verses 7-9 to challenge your priorities. If God has the concerns listed here, how should our personal concerns and those of the church be modified? Some of these can be seen in a spiritual sense (setting prisoners free and giving sight to the blind), but we must not forget the more literal meaning of these verses.

JULY 19

2 CORINTHIANS 12:1-10 It is widely believed that when Paul spoke of the person who had been caught up to paradise, he was speaking of himself (vv. 2-4). When could this have been? Possibly when he was stoned at Lystra, dragged outside the city, and left for dead (Acts 14:19-20). Whenever it was, the experience made a lasting impression on Paul. There will be glory that we cannot now imagine (1 Cor 2:9)!

Certainly that vision and the vision on the road to Damascus profoundly shaped his entire ministry. He was able to see beyond the present to the holiness of God and the glory that is yet to come. *Nothing* that the world offered – whether inconvenience, suffering, or even its riches – could ever compare, after seeing the Lord Jesus, with the eternal reality of God. *Our opportunity today to see that same vision is in the Word of God and our walk with Christ* (John 14:21). If we obey Christ, He has promised to reveal Himself to us! Don't long for the spectacular; follow the instructions (the Bible) and trust God!

Could God have delivered Paul from the "thorn"? Of course. But God, in His wisdom, allowed the disability (perhaps diseased eyes) to continue so Paul could better understand God's provision for him. It is legitimate to ask God to change our circumstances when we don't like them, but we need to understand that God has His own methods and purposes, *and we must learn to desire God's will more than our comfort or convenience.* Although it seems hard for us to understand, God's "no" is designed to turn our lives toward His grace!

JONAH 1-2 Jonah, son of Amittai, is mentioned in 2 Kings 14:25, so we know where his life fits into the historical context of Israel and Judah.

God gave him the remarkable assignment to go to the Assyrian capital of Nineveh. He was told to preach that the city had forty days to repent before God's judgment would fall on it (3:3-5).

The book of Jonah is unique among the prophetic books in that it is the account of Jonah's personal struggle with God's assignment, rather than the record of his message. The three verses mentioned above, in fact, are all we have of his message to Nineveh. Jonah was so human. As one of God's prophets to Israel, he was much more concerned with his own people than with the Assyrians. He would have been delighted to see God's judgment on Nineveh. Yet God's concerns for people were broader than Israel and Judah. The book of Nahum, also concerning the Ninevites, was written about one hundred years later. When Nahum preached, there was no repentance and judgment did come on the nation.

As you read these two short chapters, put yourself in Jonah's place. He heard God – no mistake. But he was very unhappy about the assignment. He was enough of a nationalist (Israelite) that he didn't want the people of Nineveh to repent and avert judgment (look ahead to 3:10-4:2)! They were enemies, and in his opinion, better suffering God's judgment than His mercy.

When Jonah boarded the ship to Tarshish, he went to his quarters and went to sleep – in spite of the heavy seas. *Lesson one:* It is possible to *feel* peaceful enough to sleep soundly even in disobedience (1:5-6). Jonah was more comfortable in the wrong place than the right one. As the storm became worse, watch what happens to Jonah and the sailors. The sailors had a good deal of compassion for Jonah and were very reluctant to throw him off the ship. Jonah, for his part, was quite honest that he was the problem. He could see that the waters would be stilled only if he were off the ship, and he convinced the sailors that this was the case. Act 2 of Jonah's adventure was about to begin.

The seas became quiet. Jonah, swallowed by the fish, was still alive. Both Jonah and the sailors now had a new vision of God's power. The men on the ship worshipped God (1:16) – and Jonah acknowledged God (2:2-9). The Lord kept Jonah alive in the black, wet, slippery darkness of the stomach of the fish (2:6b-7). Note especially verse 8 of Jonah's prayer. Jonah now had a different perspective. *Lesson two:* God has ways to bring His people to their senses (1:15-2:10). If Jonah had followed the Lord, he would have avoided such difficulty!

PSALM 147   Focus on verse 1. Consider the truth that it is pleasant and fitting to praise the Lord. It is good to sing praises to our God!

Thank God for the opportunity we have to gather in corporate praise, using both word and song.

Since the reestablishment of Israel, verses 2-3 have special meaning. Even through the subsequent wars in the Holy Land, God has protected Israel, and it remains intact. Exiles have been re-gathered to the nation from all over the world.

The truth in verses 10-11 is a special blessing to God's people. Most of God's people are not "picture perfect" – young, beautiful or handsome, and ideally proportioned. The world values these qualities, but God sees beyond them to the heart. The person who fears God and hopes in Him is the Lord's delight! This can include the young and the old, the beautiful and the not so beautiful. It can include the gifted and the ordinary person. In fact, this truth is the genius of the Bible's message. God has made it possible for all persons to be special! Praise the Lord!

JULY 20

2 CORINTHIANS 12:11-21   Note verse 12.   When Paul came to Corinth, it was with the legitimate evidence of a true apostle: signs, wonders, and miracles. Further, Paul persevered in his work. God's hand was upon him in his ministry to the Corinthians.

Read between the lines in this portion to understand Paul's fears about his intended visit to the church. He feared he would find that the church, or at least some in the church, had swerved from the truth in Christ, causing a painful confrontation. He also worried that even though he came to the church with the authority of an apostle, some in the church might be disappointed in him.

Paul had a legitimate pride in God's work of the Corinthians. If some had persisted in a wrong path, it would be painful and humbling for him (v. 21).

JONAH 3-4   Jonah went to the city of Nineveh and preached the message the Lord had entrusted to him. We often lose the import of the book as we fix our attention on Jonah's encounter with the large fish. His survival was indeed a miracle, *but the real miracle of the book is in the response of the people of Nineveh, from the king to the common man.* They repented when Jonah preached! The judgment of God was averted. Was Jonah surprised? Not really (4:1-2). He understood what God was doing. His continuing problem was that he couldn't agree with God's agenda! Watch the prophet as he sat in the sun and pouted. The amazing thing is that God was so gracious to him.

Many places in the Old Testament make it clear that God is concerned with the whole world. Genesis 12:3 demonstrates this as it previsions the work of Jesus the Messiah. Jonah was a reluctant missionary to a "foreign field." *Lesson three:* God has great compassion and mercy even for the "other people" of the world (1:1-2; 3:1-2; 4:11).

There is one more important lesson we should learn from the book of Jonah. God's servants need God's perspective (4:1ff.). Jonah could have been joyful over the work of God. He witnessed a wonderful miracle and had a part in it. He missed the joy by failing to align himself with the will of God! *So, learn all three of the lessons!*

PSALM 148   How can nature praise the Lord? The psalmist here calls on nature in varied forms to praise God. The meaning must be that the variety, forms, and strength of nature bring praise to God, who could, and did, create them.

The writer began with heavenly beings, then turned to inanimate nature, moved on to the dynamic events in nature, and from there to living things. At the pinnacle of living things, men and women of all stations in life are admonished to bring praise to God.

JULY 21

2 CORINTHIANS 13   As Paul ended the letter, he said he would deal firmly with any who were living in sin. Perhaps he had in mind those who had been into the impurity and sexual sin that he mentioned in 12:21, perhaps the false teachers, or perhaps those who were questioning Paul's legitimacy and his office of an apostle. It is possible that some of those causing trouble were not actually in the faith (v. 5). How can one test one's self in this way? 1 John 2:3 and the verses following offer such a test. *We demonstrate our "family connection" with the Lord by our attention to His desires for us.* Remember also Romans 8:5 and the mind-set of the child of God.

Take to heart Paul's admonition to "aim for perfection" (v. 11). We are not perfect and won't be until we meet Christ in glory. God is interested in the *process* of our progressive growth in Him. Peter stated the same thing in 1 Peter 1:15-16 when he quoted Leviticus, giving God's command to the Israelites: "Be holy, because I am holy."

AMOS 1-2   The prophet Amos lived at the time of Jeroboam, son of Jehoash, king of Israel and Uzziah (also known as Azariah), king of Judah (2 Kings 14:23-15:7). The date was probably 760-753 BC. Amos was from Judah and was a shepherd who also tended sycamore-fig trees (Amos 7:14). God called him and gave him a message for Israel (7:15).

None of Israel's kings had been godly. Yet God had His own in Israel (1 Kings 19:18) and had compassion for the people, who were suffering bitterly (2 Kings 14:26-27). God used Jeroboam to bring relief to Israel, and it was during his reign that Amos prophesied.

As the book opens, Amos brings a message for several of the kingdoms that surround Israel, concluding with a prophecy for Israel. The presentation is almost humorous, for as Israel would have listened to the prophecies directed to Damascus (Aram) to the north, Gaza (Philistia) to the southwest, Tyre (Phoenicia) to the northwest, Ammon to the east, Moab to the southeast, and Judah to the south, the people would have enthusiastically agreed that certainly everything God said about these places was justified. There would have been cheering from the pews as Amos preached!

For the pagan societies, the charges were lack of mercy, violence, bloodshed, greed, and, in the case of Edom, failure to remember their brotherhood with God's people. The charge against Judah was spiritual adultery (2:4).

But for Israel the charges were more detailed and included greed (2:6b), oppression and denied justice (v. 7a), incest (v. 7b), and the breaking of the mosaic law (v. 8). No more cheering from the pews!

The Lord reminds the people to learn from history. God delivered the people during the Canaanite campaigns recorded in Judges (v. 9) and from Egypt (v. 10). Although the Lord sent prophets and other dedicated people to them (v. 11), they rejected and persecuted them (v. 12). So, judgment was coming, and there would be no escape (vv. 13-16). Especially note the illustrations that Amos uses in these verses.

PSALM 149   Why should we praise the Lord? Verses 4-5 give us the reason. The Lord gives salvation to the humble; He delights in His people! This is reason for us to "sing a new song." This is an honor for which we rejoice (v. 5a). In reading verse 6a, compare Hebrews 13:15. Our praise is a sacrifice to the Lord! As you read verse 6b, compare this with Ephesians 6:17. Our sword is the Word of God. Our weapons are more powerful than those of the world (2 Cor 10:3-5).

☑Note too that a day of judgment and vengeance is coming in which the Lord will bring the nations, kings, and peoples of the world to account for sin (vv. 6-9; cf. Isa 61:2; 62:1). This, too, is a cause for praise (v. 6a). It will be the Day of the Lord! Compare verses 6-9 with Revelation 19:11-16.⇦

JULY 22

MATTHEW 1:1-17   This first chapter of Matthew traces the lineage of Jesus back to Abraham. In Hebrew convention, a person's lineage was always traced through the father. Thus, Jesus' line (legal) was through

Joseph, even though he was not Jesus' human father. Luke traces the line all the way back to Adam, also naming the individuals in Jesus' ancestry between Adam and Abraham. It is probable that Luke's genealogy is that of Mary and thus the human (genetic) genealogy of Jesus.

It is interesting to read that Rahab (Joshua 2) from Jericho was the mother of Boaz (Matt 1:5; also found in the Luke genealogy) and so is part of the human ancestry of Jesus. Boaz was the husband of Ruth (the Moabite who returned to Israel with Naomi). Thus Jesus' progenitors contained "alien" genes from Canaan and Moab.

AMOS 3-4   As Amos continued the prophecy, he used several illustrations from everyday life to strengthen his message. In 3:2, he prophesies about coming judgment and repeats it in verses 11-15. But follow Amos' reasoning. Two people walk together for a reason (v. 3). A lion roars for a reason (v. 4). A bird is caught because a trap has been set (v. 5). A trumpet sounds in a city because there is a reason to sound the alarm (v. 6). *And God has spoken for a reason* (v. 8). God doesn't bring judgment without warning (v. 7), *so listen!* Tell even the Philistines and the Egyptians (foreigners) to come and see how the people sin (v. 9). Follow the specifics of the coming judgment in verses 11-15.

In Chapter 4, Amos addressed the affluent, who maintain their lifestyle by oppression (vv. 1-3). Amos tells these decadent people to go ahead, continue to sin (v. 4a), continue even to bring sacrifices and tithes (vv. 4-5), but these empty gestures won't help (because there is no true turning to God).

In 4:6-11 Amos gives five ways in which God has tried to get the attention of His people (vv. 6, 7, 9, 10, 11). But because they have refused to respond, they had better get ready to meet God – the God of power (vv. 12-13)!

PSALM 150   This last psalm is a fitting ending to the book. It is an expression of praise for God's majesty, might, power, and greatness. It is a call to use all of our energy to praise God and for every living being to praise God.

Think back on this exquisite book. The psalms are *realistic* in that they accurately portray emotions – sometimes exuberant, sometimes discouraged. They realistically describe men in this world – some of integrity and many of deceit and untruth. And the psalms always have a "reality orientation," bringing the reader back to the truth about God and to a proper response to God. We will live better lives for the Lord if we regularly spend thoughtful time in the psalms.

JULY 23

MATTHEW 1:18-25   Think of yourself in Joseph's place when he learned of Mary's coming child. In the culture of Israel at that time, marrying a woman who wasn't pure would be most difficult. Since they were engaged to be married, to break it would require a formal dissolution of the marriage agreement that constituted the engagement. To protect Mary, he determined to do it quietly (vv. 18-19).

At this point, the Lord intervened with a special message for Joseph, telling him to proceed with the marriage and that the child she was to bear was from the Holy Spirit. →God was moving to bring the Redeemer into the world.← ☑It was absolutely evident in the angel's message that this child would be the Messiah (vv. 20-21). The way that Matthew related this to Isaiah 7:14 also confirms this fulfillment of the promise of the coming Messiah.⇔ Joseph's character is evident in how he responded to Mary and then to the message from the Lord.   He treated Mary with respect and obeyed the Lord when given direction.

AMOS 5 As this chapter begins, note the deep sadness over Israel's condition (v. 2). God's people had been reduced to a mere shadow of what they were when they followed the Lord. Things were so bad that the country would never again be a significant presence. All of this was because of their sin.

The sin that God specifically addressed in these verses is that of denied justice, both in court and in the marketplace. The people had trampled on righteousness (v. 7). Note how they did this: hate for those who tell the truth in court (v. 10); oppression of the poor (v. 11); oppression of those who try to uphold righteousness (v. 12). It was so evil that it was safer to not raise questions – it would only bring trouble (v. 13).

In the empty shell of their religious life, the people even publicly hoped for the Day of the Lord (v. 18, the day when the Lord would judge the nations). Amos correctly pointed out that they themselves would experience this great judgment! Far from being a day of deliverance, it would be a day of horror from which there would be no escape (vv. 18-20).   Note how the Lord felt about their sacrifices and religious gatherings (vv. 21-23).

Now look at God's call for change. Even at that late date in their national history, it was still worthwhile to turn to God in repentance (vv. 4-6, 14-15, 24). *Note especially the practical ways God calls for the fruit of repentance.* God was not calling for lip service, but for changed behavior! Don't leave this chapter without thinking about our society and our own lives. It is easy for our religious exercises to become empty! God is calling for our hearts. He wants us to live in truth, righteousness, and justice. Anything less misses the mark of God's desire for His children (cf. Titus 2:11-14). ☑Further, remember what the prophet said about the Day of the Lord – not only the coming judgment of God on Israel, but also the judgment when the Messiah comes (vv. 18-20). Judgment did come to Israel in 722 BC, a few years after Amos preached. The next time the Day of the Lord will come to this world will be when Jesus judges the nations. Then the prophecy of 5:24 will be literally fulfilled. God's righteousness will extend through the entire earth as Jesus, the Messiah, reigns.↩

ECCLESIASTES 1   Solomon wrote the book of Ecclesiastes, as well as the book of Proverbs. In this book, Solomon shares some of the ways in which he struggled with the meaning of life. He shares his thinking, which may not be absolute truth (as any of our thinking may not be entirely "on target").

What Solomon seems to be saying in this chapter is no matter how much we learn it ends in the frustration of meaningless existence. It seems that life is a treadmill. The cycles of nature recur again and again (vv. 3-7). Further, there is an unfulfilled longing in the soul of man (v. 8). Life is a recurring cycle (vv. 9-10). After death a person is forgotten – his life seems to have no permanent meaning (v. 11).

As king, and as a person of wisdom, Solomon considered these things deeply (vv. 12-13). What he saw is that most of life is a treadmill (v. 14). Further, we do not seem to learn from the past, and flawed character cannot humanly be corrected (v. 15).

Even great wisdom (understanding) has a down side. Understanding what is happening in the world brings discouragement and sorrow – for society seems to move in the wrong direction (vv. 17-18).

JULY 24

MATTHEW 2:1-12   This chapter is a vivid illustration of governmental opposition to the hand of God. God was bringing the blessing of salvation to the world in Christ, but Herod was attempting to find the baby and kill him! Did Herod understand that in doing so he was opposing the plan of God? Probably not (1 Cor 2:8-9), but forces of evil work through people. Herod, along with Pontius Pilate, did indeed oppose the Son of God (Acts 4:27). The Lord, however, protected the infant Jesus, telling the Magi not to go back to Herod. Note that the Jewish leaders were very specific that the Messiah would be born in Bethlehem in Judea (vv. 5-6; cf. Mic 5:2).

AMOS 6   Complacency is a terrible spiritual disease (v. 1)! It allows us to drift along with little thought of our condition or that of society. These Israelites were self-satisfied, unaware of their deficiencies or the dangers of their lifestyle. In fact, although they were comfortable, they were living on the edge of disaster. They failed to learn from God's judgment on other countries that sinned (v. 2). The condition of the Israelites is evident in verses 3-6. They were affluent, overfed, and indulgent. In verse 6 the prophet outlines their failure to see their condition from God's perspective. They had no sorrow for the sin in their society. *Therefore*, judgment was sure (v. 7)! Further, see the reference to denied justice and pride in verses 12b-13. *Therefore*, judgment was certain (v. 14)!

ECCLESIASTES 2   Solomon now considers the fleeting nature of pleasure (vv. 1-3). It was empty. He turned to great projects (vv. 4-6) and acquired riches (vv. 7-9). None of it brought inner peace (vv. 10-11).

Although Solomon came to understand that it is better to be wise than foolish, death will overtake both the wise man and the fool, and both will be forgotten (vv. 12-16). Consider his frustration in 2:17-23.

The kernel of truth that does give meaning to life, however, is found in 2:24-26. God gives us the understanding to accept the good things He gives us and helps us find satisfaction and enjoyment in our work. Here is a "word for our day." The name of the game in today's world is to work hard, save money, acquire things, and "enjoy life" (just what Solomon had tried). But the reality is that without the integration and understanding that God gives, all of these things are like sawdust in the mouth – not only meaningless, but distasteful! Peace can come only from the Lord.

JULY 25

MATTHEW 2:13-23   Note God's protection of Jesus and His family in this chapter. It seems incredible that Herod would go to such lengths to kill a small child thought to be the future king of the Jews (vv. 2-3, 16). Think of the suffering and anguish in Bethlehem over the murder of all of the boys under two years of age! →Specifically, God's protection is obvious in warning the Magi to avoid Herod after they had seen Jesus (v. 12), in directing Joseph to Egypt (v. 13), and also in the timing of the return to Israel (vv. 19-20). God's will that Jesus would be the Redeemer was a plan that no king could thwart!←

AMOS 7-8   The heart of the true prophet is one of concern for his people. Note how Amos demonstrates this in intercessory prayer in 7:1-6. God responded to Amos' prayer, but there still was a standard by which His people would be judged (the Word of God, vv. 7-9). To make this clear, God showed Amos a plumb line (a weight on a line, that, when held up, shows a true vertical – used in the construction of walls and buildings).

Amos was getting to the leaders! News about his preaching went to the top of the religious and civil governments (vv. 10-13). When Amos was told to get out of the country and go home to Judah, he answered with uncommon courage and directness – no backing down, and no abandoning his assignment from the Lord (vv. 14-17).

Time had run out (8:1-3)! Once fruit is ripe, it must be used. And Israel was like a basket of ripe fruit. It was ripe for judgment. There was no more time.

In 8:4-6 note the personal agendas of those with power (they could hardly wait until the Sabbath was over so that they could make money, v. 5) and the list of their oppressive economic practices, which trampled the needy and destroyed the poor. Note the dishonesty (v. 5b), oppression (v. 6a), and the selling of even the dirt from the floor along with the wheat ("creative dishonesty," v. 6b).

Did (does) God see? Did (does) God care? *YES!* And judgment was coming (8:7-9:10). Note with sadness that when things had gone far enough, there would even be a famine of truth (8:11).

ECCLESIASTES 3   Timing isn't everything, but timing is important. In the cycle of life, times are set for important events. As you read verses 1-8, think about your own life. Each of us has been born – but there is also a time set to die. Each of us has had times of happiness, but there will also be times of sorrow. If we think about our friends, there may even be a little humor here – do you know anyone who loves to save but never throws away (v. 6b)?

There are also more serious times. There is a time of grace with opportunity for turning to the Lord – but there is also a time when that opportunity will come to an end for each of us. There is a time when God stays His hand of judgment, but there is a time when judgment will come (v. 15b, 17a; Heb 9:27-28)!

We find in 3:11 one of the theological gems of the book. God has put "eternity in the hearts of men." God has built into our understanding that there is something after death. Interestingly, we see this in the most primitive tribes who have been untouched by "advanced" civilizations. Men long to know God and to find the meaning of life. Note that right after this statement in verse 11, Solomon restates the truth seen in 2:24-26   (vv. 12-13).   God's gift to men is to find satisfaction and happiness in their lives – in work and relationships as they are related correctly to Him.

JULY 26

MATTHEW 3 John the Baptist was an integral part of the first advent of Christ. He was foretold in the Scriptures as the one who would prepare the way for the Messiah (v. 3; cf. Isa 40:3). John's mother, Elizabeth, was a relative of Mary (Luke 1:36), and thus they knew one another (cf. Luke 1:35, 39ff.).

→John the Baptist's ministry prepared the way for the message of the kingdom by making people aware of the need for repentance. His preaching was powerful, straightforward, and never compromising. The repentance that he preached demanded more than lip service. It required fruit as demonstrated in changed lives (v. 8). Those who responded to John the Baptist were ready to receive the further message that Jesus would bring regarding the kingdom.←

Note particularly John's testimony about Jesus (vv. 11-12). Jesus would send the Holy Spirit, gather those going to heaven, and send the unrighteous to hell!

AMOS 9 In the judgment that God said was coming to Israel, there would be nowhere to hide (9:1b-4). Review again the illustrations that Amos used concerning the Day of the Lord in 5:19-20. It will be utterly futile to try to escape. Note the eye of the Lord on the people for evil and not for good (v. 4b). The power of God will be used against His people (vv. 5-10).

☑Yet there is a future for these people. After the judgment, which will leave only a remnant, God will bring His people back to their land – and it will be a permanent relocation (9:11-15). When will these events happen? We know it will be partially fulfilled in the church age with the inclusion of both Jews and Gentiles into the faith (cf. Acts 15:16-18). The full blessing described in verses 13-15 will be realized with the second advent of Jesus. Think carefully about the promise of verses 14-15. From that time forward, God's people will live on the land in safety.⇦

What lessons can we learn from Amos? Certainly that God cares about the behavior of His people. There should be no room for complacency in our lives. God is concerned with the broad strokes of righteousness and justice in society, and so must we be concerned. A time comes when judgment is due in a society (and it will come!); we must be working for the Lord and for His agenda while there is time.

ECCLESIASTES 4   The picture that Solomon paints of society here is not pretty.   Yet it is the picture of a society made up of the same ambitions, injustices, loneliness, and frustration of much of the world today.   Man has not changed!   This is a realistic picture of a secular society.

Note the description of the foolish king in verse 13, and refer to 1 Kings 11:1-6. Solomon decried the very trap into which he later fell.

JULY 27

MATTHEW 4:1-11   At the time of the temptation, Satan appealed to Jesus' human needs by challenging Him to turn the stones into bread (vv. 2-3). Remember that Jesus had been fasting for forty days! Using Scripture, Satan played upon Jesus' relationship to God by asking Jesus to demonstrate that the Scriptures were true (vv. 5-6) and at the same time prove that He was God's son.

The third temptation offered what already belonged to Jesus but would be fully realized only after the cross. The kingdoms of the world did belong to Jesus (Ps 2:8-9), and would come completely under His authority after the cross and when He comes again (Rev 11:15-18). There could be, however, no shortcut to accomplishing God's perfect will, and Jesus banished Satan from the scene.

In each instance, Satan had offered a shortcut to something that appeared desirable.   The lesson is that God gives what is good and appropriate to His children in His timing.   We get into trouble by attempting to take the wrong thing or take the right thing at the wrong time!

MICAH 1-2   The prophet Micah lived and ministered in the Southern Kingdom of Judah and was a contemporary of Isaiah and Amos.   His message concerned both Judah (Jerusalem) and Israel (Samaria).   It was a time of relative peace and economic well-being.   But underneath the fabric of the political strength and relative wealth, there was internal decay.   This was true both socially, as the wealthy used their power to the disadvantage of the poorer classes, and also in their spiritual life, which included Canaanite worship.   The messages of Micah were directed primarily to the capital cities of Samaria (Israel) and Jerusalem (Judah), where power was concentrated. They were the centers of influence.

At the very outset (1:2), the sovereignty of God is affirmed.   The prophecies that follow depend upon the fact that the Lord is speaking from His holy temple!

The picture of the Lord's coming (vv. 3-4) is reminiscent of Genesis 18:20-21 where the Lord came to see whether the sins of Sodom and Gomorrah were as bad as reported. Here, the sins of the two capitals deserve not only checking but judgment.

Chapter 2 articulates God's response to some specific sin: The sin of unfair acquisition of land (vv. 1-2); taking others' property (v. 8); unfairly taking another's home (v. 9); refusing to listen to the truth that God brings for the good of the people (vv. 6-7). In fact, if a "prophet" would come and prophesy wine and beer for the people, he would be welcomed (v. 11)!

☑Yet in the midst of the sin, God's covenant relationship with the people is not forgotten; in God's time, He will restore the people (vv. 12-13). This abrupt change from the prophecy of imminent judgment to the fulfillment of the covenant relationship in the more distant future is a reminder that the Lord's promises are certain. Note the reference to the Messiah in verse 13. He will be the one who accomplishes this remarkable promise to God's people.⇦

ECCLESIASTES 5   Observe Solomon's personal warning in verses 1-7. We need to understand God's majesty, glory, and power – and we won't get it from the society that surrounds us. Careful reading of God's word will shape our understanding of God and how He deals with people – both believers and non-believers. If we have that understanding, we will never approach God casually or carelessly. Take care! Fear God!

As you read 5:10-20, look at the contrast of meaningless wealth (vv. 8-17), with using wealth as a gift from God (vv. 18-20). For those who live for money and what it will bring, there is never enough (v. 10). Note too, the futility of things we acquire (v. 11). Remember that we will take nothing along with us to the grave (v. 15). In contrast, for the person with the peace of God, there is genuine contentment – a gift from the Lord. It is even easy to become old (v. 20). Too much of significance is going on for the child of God to be concerned about age! Compare verses 18-20 with 3:12-14.

JULY 28

MATTHEW 4:12-25   As Jesus began to preach, His message was also a call to repentance (4:17). ☑Note also that Matthew ties the beginning of Jesus' ministry to fulfillment of the Old Testament scriptures (vv. 15-16; cf. Isa 9:1-2). The "light that dawned" (v. 16b) was that of the promised Messiah.⇦

There was a note of authority in Jesus' call to Peter and Andrew and then to James and John. As He invited them to come with Him, they immediately left what they were doing to follow Him (vv. 18-22). Can you imagine someone doing that today – leaving their occupation to accompany a teacher? At the very beginning, there was something compelling about the Savior.

Jesus preached about the good news of the kingdom (v. 23). Good news because repentance and faith relate us to the living God in a new way. Along with the news of salvation, the Lord extended the grace of healing and deliverance from demon possession (vv. 23-24). It is no wonder that great crowds followed Him!

MICAH 3   This chapter concerns the results of sin in the nation. Political leaders were taking every personal advantage that their position allowed (vv. 1-4). These leaders knew better (vv. 1-2). They acted as wolves tearing apart a lamb! Gross injustice to the people was the result. As for the religious leaders, they would say whatever people wanted to hear, for a price (v. 5). Because of their sin, the Lord would not speak to them or through them (vv. 6-7).

In the midst of this sin (vv. 9-11a), these leaders had the audacity to claim that the Lord was among them and would protect them (v. 11b). This kind of presumptuous behavior, God promised, would make Jerusalem a heap of rubble (v. 12).

This chapter also applies to us today. God's standards do not flex with our whims. We need to know what God requires of us and obey Him. It is presumptuous and dangerous not to.

ECCLESIASTES 6 As you begin to read this chapter, compare verses 1-2 with 5:18-20. On the one hand, contentment and peace are identified as coming from the Lord. Verses 1-2, however, depict a person with all this world has to offer but without the contentment and peace from the Lord. What a difference, and what an empty life! As Solomon says in verses 3-6, better to be a stillborn child than to suffer the turmoil and dissatisfaction of life without God.

Without that peace of God, verse 7 is the whole story of life. Like sawdust in one's mouth! There is no nourishment of the soul, and even what looks attractive ends up giving no satisfaction and fulfillment. Without the unifying and integrating principle of forgiveness and peace through Christ, there is no peace (Rom 5:1-2, 6-11). Think of verse 11 (without God) as representing secular philosophy, and compare this with 1 Corinthians 1:19.

JULY 29

MATTHEW 5:1-12   These three chapters (Ch. 5-7) contain what has been called "The Sermon on the Mount." The name comes from the text

273

in Matthew 5:1, where it is recorded that Jesus taught the disciples while on a mountainside.

The "Beatitudes" are found in 5:3-12. These can also be called the "be attitudes." They represent character attributes that God wants in our lives. As you read these, try to identify the ungodly opposite of each. This will help you focus on what God wants to change in our lives. Here are suggestions, with the godly characteristic before the slash and the opposite after. ➤Poor in spirit/prideful; ➤mourn/uncaring about sin; ➤meek/arrogant; ➤hunger and thirst for righteousness/complacent about spiritual matters; ➤merciful/unmoved by others' trouble; ➤pure in heart/careless in mind and heart; ➤peacemakers/sowers of dissent and division; ➤persecuted because of righteousness/a friend of the world.

MICAH 4 ☑Micah 4:1-3 is identical to Isaiah 2:2-4. Remember that the two prophets were contemporaries. This is the picture of millennial peace, which the Lord will establish on earth upon His return. He will establish true worship and true justice (vv. 2-3a). God Himself will teach the people of the world (vv. 2-3; cf. Zech 14:16). There will be a reconstructed economy and industry (v. 3b), personal provision and security (v. 4), and true social spirituality (v. 5). There will be a place for all, even the weak (vv. 6-7). Israel will be restored. He will gather the scattered people of Israel and Judah (vv. 6-8). Although the more immediate future would bring judgment (vv. 9-10), God has His plan and will restore Israel in strength (v. 13).⇦

ECCLESIASTES 7 Our society thinks as little about death as possible. In 7:1-4, the writer encourages us to see death in our future. Does this sound morbid? Certainly to the man or woman without God, it would seem to be. But it is the fact of death that helps us think realistically and to consider how to live wisely. This is also the New Testament perspective (2 Cor 5:10; Heb 9:27).

For the same reason, sorrow should be a blessing, leading us to think realistically (v. 3), understanding that even sorrow is from the Lord (v. 14).

Think about the truth of verse 15. The writer of Psalm 73 struggled with this but came to the right perspective in Psalm 73:21-28. Isaiah 57:1-2 speaks to the same issue and adds the element of God's mercy and grace to what may appear to be the untimely death of one of God's children.

JULY 30

MATTHEW 5:13-32 Beginning with verse 13 and extending through Chapter 7, Jesus gives a number of short "sayings" that define the lifestyle and ethic of His disciples and of the kingdom. There is enough challenge in these three chapters of Matthew to keep most of us busy for a long time! For our purposes here, a simple title will help us focus. You may be able to think of a better title for each of these sections.

ACKNOWLEDGE GOD (vv. 13-16). Salt and light are crucial to our understanding of our place and the church's place in the world. Salt was used as a preservative (especially for meat) in an age with no refrigeration. The Christian's and the church's stand on matters of righteousness and morality do make a difference in society. Remember that if only ten righteous persons could have been found in Sodom the city would not have been destroyed (Gen 18:32). Remember that individual Christians as they comprise the church are the channels of light for the good news of Christ. Individually, and as the church, God's people must make a difference.

ACKNOWLEDGE GOD'S LAW (vv. 17-20). The fact of grace doesn't invalidate the law of God. Grace was the vehicle through which Abraham (and all others in the OT period) was given new life (Gen 15:6). Keeping the law does not bring salvation – rather, faith in the Lord Jesus and His sacrifice on the cross does. But that does not mean we shouldn't apply God's moral law to our lives. Read carefully verses 19-20 (cf. Rom 3:31).

LIVE IN PEACE WITH OTHERS (vv. 21-26). Murder is obviously a problem. So is anger (v. 22). Our relationship with the Lord depends upon a clean slate with others (vv. 23-26). Keep short accounts (vv. 25-26).

BE PURE AND FAITHFUL (vv. 27-32). Jesus here emphasizes that the mind and heart are where the action is. A pure heart will always result in pure action. Our thought life counts! In fact, it counts so much that we need radical action – not literally cutting off parts of the body – but cutting out the thoughts, sights, and actions that lead to impurity (vv. 29-30). Note also Jesus' high view of marriage (vv. 31-32).

MICAH 5-6 ☑The prophecy of the Messiah King is in 5:1-5a – the first advent when He will be born in Bethlehem (v. 2; cf. Matt 2:6) and the second advent when He will rule in majesty (vv. 3-5a). The calling of God's people from the nations is in verse 3, and the Savior's reign and caring for His people in verse 4. This prophecy is an extension of that in Chapter 4. It is clear that the one who would be the ruler is indeed the Messiah. In the rest of the chapter, note the allusion to the dispersion of the people in many nations but the purification of the society after re-gathering (vv. 10-15). This spiritual cleansing is seen as a sovereign work of the Lord. The same sovereign act of God in restoration and cleansing is seen in Ezekiel 36:24-38. ⇦

Chapter 6 gives God's assessment of the society and His gracious plea for the people to repent. This is serious business for the people – to consider God's complaint (vv. 1-2). Even the mountains are called to listen to what the Lord has to say. The Lord calls the people to remember His goodness and provision for them in the exodus and in the desert (vv. 4-5). Will sacrifices and offerings be enough (vv. 6-7)? No, the Lord wants a change of heart (v. 8)! *The Lord is calling His people to a spirituality in which the sacrifices are only the beginning of the relationship with Him and not the end!* Follow the Lord's message in the remainder of the chapter, noting His specific charges and what sin has done to the land and the people.

ECCLESIASTES 8 Wisdom – understanding the nature of life and our relationship to God – brightens man's face! (8:1). As we trust in God's goodness and power, we are able to see the world around us in a different light.

Solomon speaks about civil authority in verses 2-6. Some situations may need to be addressed. His advice about how to approach these problems is prudent and wise. Understand the issue (don't take on a bad cause, v. 3b), plan appropriate action, and then carefully pick the timing (vv. 5-6).

Consider the deep truth in 8:8b. *Wickedness will not release those who practice it.* In fact, God's power is needed for release (cf. Col 1:13; Prov 5:22).

Note that Solomon again calls on his readers to enjoy life under the hand of the Lord (v. 15; cf. 2:24-26; 3:12-13; 5:19-20). This is the step of faith that deliberately chooses to believe God and be content with what He gives.

JULY 31

MATTHEW 5:33-48 *BE HONEST* (vv. 33-37). No "ifs, ands, or buts!" No wrong impressions. No crossed fingers. No differing standards. Remember that Satan is the father of lies (John 8:44). Anything untrue, in whatever degree, is not from God or pleasing to God.

RESPOND IN A GODLY WAY TO EVIL (vv. 38-42). Evil is a fact. We are touched constantly by lies and unfairness. Here Jesus tells us to respond differently than the world would respond. This is an opportunity to demonstrate the grace of God to those who need to see how God's grace looks in action. Trust God for the results.

LOVE YOUR ENEMIES (vv. 43-48). Related to the above paragraph, Jesus calls us to see others through His eyes. He died for the ungodly – even those who hated and persecuted Him! Loving our enemies will be a powerful witness to the world. The world wants to get even. The child of God wants (or should want) to extend the love of Jesus, even when misused.

MICAH 7 Now the prophet spoke from his own perspective (7:1-7). His own heart was burdened with the sin of the people. Society was honeycombed with evil on every level so extensively that one could not trust friend or family!

☑The remainder of the chapter and the close of the book anticipate God bringing the people through the present judgment, to the day when the Lord will do a new thing in the world. Read with the same anticipation as the prophet had what God will do for His people and the world (vv. 11-20).⇦

Micah's message is not out of date! It speaks to us and our society today for the Lord is concerned for the same things now as in the day of Micah. The Lord desires more than the shell of worship and spirituality today just as He desired more than sacrifices in the day of Micah. Allow Micah 6:8 to speak to your heart. *Remember that however we may look to others, the Lord sees our heart.*

ECCLESIASTES 9 As Solomon reflected on life, he saw much to disappoint and frustrate the thinking person. The one hope (but very real) is that righteous people are in God's hands (v. 1). We all will face death (vv. 2-6), and it is here that Solomon had an incomplete understanding (or he didn't express it clearly) of the future for the child of God after death. He clearly saw man's bent to sin (v. 3b). He calls on the living to enjoy life, be content, be happy with one's spouse, and work hard to accomplish one's goals (vv. 7-10).

Think about the example of a wise person in verses 13-18 and especially about his conclusion of verse 17. Wise words spoken quietly have great power.

August

Bible Reading Schedule
And Notes

ॐ

*Do not let this book of the Law depart from
your mouth; meditate on it day and night, so that
you may be careful to do everything written it.*
Joshua 1:8

1	Matthew 6:1-18	2 Kings 15	Ecclesiastes 10
2	Matthew 6:19-34	2 Chronicles 26-27	Ecclesiastes 11
3	Matthew 7:1-14	2 Kings 16-17	Ecclesiastes 12
4	Matthew 7:15-29	2 Chronicles 28	Song of Songs 1-3
5	Matthew 8:1-17	2 Chronicles 29-30	Song of Songs 4-6
6	Matthew 8:18-34	2 Chronicles 31-32	Song of Songs 7-8
7	Matthew 9:1-17	Isaiah 1	Proverbs 1:1-7
8	Matthew 9:18-38	Isaiah 2	Proverbs 1:8-19
9	Matthew 10:1-23	Isaiah 3-4	Proverbs 1:20-33
10	Matthew 10:24-42	Isaiah 5	Proverbs 2:1-8
11	Matthew 11:1-19	Isaiah 6	Proverbs 2:9-22
12	Matthew 11:20-30	Isaiah 7	Proverbs 3:1-10
13	Matthew 12:1-21	Isaiah 8	Proverbs 3:11-18
14	Matthew 12:22-50	Isaiah 9-10	Proverbs 3:19-26
15	Matthew 13:1-30	Isaiah 11-12	Proverbs 3:27-35
16	Matthew 13:31-58	Isaiah 13-14	Proverbs 4:1-9
17	Matthew 14:1-21	Isaiah 15-16	Proverbs 4:10-19
18	Matthew 14:22-36	Isaiah 17-18	Proverbs 4:20-27
19	Matthew 15:1-20	Isaiah 19-20	Proverbs 5:1-14
20	Matthew 15:21-39	Isaiah 21-22	Proverbs 5:15-23
21	Matthew 16:1-12	Isaiah 23	Proverbs 6:1-5
22	Matthew 16:13-28	Isaiah 24	Proverbs 6:6-11
23	Matthew 17:1-13	Isaiah 25-26	Proverbs 6:12-19
24	Matthew 17:14-27	Isaiah 27	Proverbs 6:20-35
25	Matthew 18:1-14	Isaiah 28	Proverbs 7:1-5
26	Matthew 18:15-35	Isaiah 29-30	Proverbs 7:6-27
27	Matthew 19:1-15	Isaiah 31-32	Proverbs 8:1-11
28	Matthew 19:16-30	Isaiah 33	Proverbs 8:12-21
29	Matthew 20:1-16	Isaiah 34-35	Proverbs 8:22-36
30	Matthew 20:17-34	2 Kings 18, Isaiah 36	Proverbs 9:1-9
31	Matthew 21:1-22	2 Kings 19, Isaiah 37	Proverbs 9:10-18

AUGUST 1

MATTHEW 6:1-18 *LIVE IN TRUE RIGHTEOUSNESS*. Jesus speaks about our religious practices of giving, prayer, and fasting. True righteousness means doing these things for the Lord alone, out of the sight of others. A public display invariably means a desire for human recognition; this is not a pure offering to God.

Consider especially the model of prayer that Jesus gave the disciples (vv. 9-13). Notice the importance of God's name (holiness) and God's will on the earth (vv. 9-10). The simplicity of this prayer is striking. It is a prayer for the glory of God's name and His will on earth, for the necessities of life, for forgiveness (as we also forgive), and for protection from temptation and evil. God shows us His priorities in this prayer!

Think carefully about the Lord's challenge in verses 14-15. There is no provision in the faith to hold grudges against people! If we do so, our standing before the Lord – the reality of our salvation – is in question. Without His grace of forgiveness, each of us is in serious trouble!

2 KINGS 15 Azariah, son of Amaziah, king of Judah, was also known as Uzziah. Isaiah's ministry began during Azariah's reign and extended until Hezekiah was king (Isa 1:1). We will read more about Azariah tomorrow in 2 Chronicles 26. The text relates that Azariah had leprosy; the Lord afflicted him because he rashly attempted to usurp the priest's function and burn incense before the Lord (cf. 2 Chron 26:16-21).

As you read Chapter 15 and follow the succession of kings in Israel, you may wonder why anyone would want to be king. It was a dangerous occupation. It was also a dangerous time for the people in Israel. The reign of Israel's King Pekah (vv. 27-31) spanned Jotham's reign (Azariah's son) and extended into Ahaz's tenure (Azariah's grandson) in Judah.

ECCLESIASTES 10 It doesn't take much to spoil a beautiful reputation (10:1). One bad choice can call into question an unblemished life or ministry. Take care. Avoid sin. Live close to God and love truth.

Heed Solomon's warning in verse 20. It is absolutely amazing how what we say (what we think is in confidence) finds its way to other people. Be careful what you say. Add to this warning the guidelines for speech in Ephesians 4:29. Heeding these two admonitions will not only keep you out of trouble but will bring blessing to others.

AUGUST 2

MATTHEW 6:19-34   *KNOW GOD'S PRIORITIES AND LIVE THEM* (vv. 19-24). As you read these verses, where do you see the treasures of your friends? Your Christian friends? Your answer will reveal the state of the church. The bottom line, however, is where are your treasures? Jesus states unequivocally that your heart will be where your treasures are. Keep remembering that there is only one secure investment opportunity in this world (v. 20).

The perception of reality is the subject of verses 22-23. If your "eye" focuses upon wealth or the offerings of the world, your inner being will be full of darkness. If you focus on eternal values, especially obedience to Jesus, your inner being will be full of light (cf. John 8:31-32). There is no way to "straddle the fence" (v. 24), although we would like to think there is.

TRUST IN GOD'S PROTECTION AND PROVISION (vv. 25-34). These verses are so logical, yet so difficult for us to embrace. It seems hard to trust the Lord in what we think are the difficulties of life. Allow verses 31-34 to become liberating truth for you; that is God's desire! Look again at John 8:31-32.

2 CHRONICLES 26-27   Uzziah had a long reign and started well. Zechariah the priest, who taught him the way of the Lord, greatly influenced him (26:5). God gave him success as long as he followed His precepts (v. 5b); he had great fame because of His help (v. 15b). When he was well-established and powerful, however, his pride led him to try to usurp the priest's duties (26:16). God struck him with leprosy which he had until he died. *Uzziah illustrates our tendency to look to God in our weakness or need, receive His blessing, and then forget who has given us success.*

The reign of Jotham (Ch. 27) was mixed. Jotham himself followed the Lord steadfastly, but the people continued in sin (v. 2b). As king, his leadership didn't extend to societal change. In 2 Kings 15:36-37, the Lord sent trouble to the people from outside their country; undoubtedly sin was the cause of the trouble.

ECCLESIASTES 11   The author seems to be saying in verses 1-6 that although we cannot know what will succeed or what will fail, we should be generous to others (vv. 1-2) and diligent with what we undertake (vv. 4, 6).

Consider the perspective in 11:8. Enjoy life, but remember that life is not forever. Enjoy your youth – but remember to be responsible to the Lord (vv. 9-10).

AUGUST 3

<u>MATTHEW 7:1-14</u> **BE HUMBLE** (vv. 1-5). The humble person – who understands his deep-seated frailty – is careful not to criticize others. On the one hand, Jesus calls upon His followers to make judgments regarding the fruit of life (7:15-20). Not everyone who claims faith is a person of faith, and such a person can be destructive within the church. In this passage (7:1-5), however, Jesus speaks of a critical and destructive spirit – the person who finds it easy to pick at another's failings. Avoid it in your own life with great care!

BELIEVE THAT GOD ANSWERS PRAYER (vv. 7-12). Do you understand care for your own children? Then you will understand the care that the Lord feels for His children. Keep reminding yourself that God desires the best for you, as you do for your family. Then believe that God will give you the best, as you ask. But do ask (v. 7; cf. John 16:24). Finally, extend the same love as God gives to us to those around you (v. 12).

MAKE RIGHTEOUS CHOICES (vv. 13-14). What is this gate of which Jesus speaks? It is the gate of faith in Jesus – faith that is expressed in truth, integrity, and love. The startling thing about Jesus' statement is that most will not find this gate (v. 14)! In a parallel passage (Luke 13:22-30), Jesus tells us to "make every effort" to enter the narrow door. *The seductive gates that the world offers will deceive most!* Jesus is telling His hearers to be sure that the way we choose will bring us into a genuine relationship with the Lord! Know the truth of God's Word, and follow that truth.

<u>2 KINGS 16-17</u> Ahaz became king of Judah following the death of his godly father Jotham – but recall that in Jotham's time, society had moved away from worshipping the Lord (2 Chron 27:2). Ahaz followed the drift of society and adopted the pagan worship practices of the Canaanites and of Israel (16:2-4). When he was attacked by Aram and Israel, he bought military help from Assyria instead of trusting in the Lord (16:7-9). To make things worse, he imported plans for a pagan altar from Damascus and built a replica for the temple in Jerusalem (vv. 10-11)! Although God sent Isaiah with an offer of help against Aram and Israel (Isa 7:1-12), Ahaz persisted in his pagan practices.

The sad account of the deportation of the Northern Kingdom in 722 BC is recorded in Chapter 17. *The facts* of the exile are recorded in terse fashion in verses 1-6. Israel had been subservient to the king of Assyria, paying him a yearly tribute. In an attempt to be done with this obligation, Hoshea broke his word to Assyria, negotiated with Egypt to form an alliance that would free Israel from Assyria, and stopped paying the tribute to Assyria. These few verses cannot do justice to the human suffering caused by the sin of the people.

The origin of the Samaritans is seen in verses 24-41. After the Israelites were deported, the king of Assyria repopulated the land with other people. When things did not go well, priests from Israel were sent to teach these people how to worship the Lord God. This created a religion with elements of the worship of God mixed with pagan practices. These were the same people referred to in the New Testament as Samaritans.

ECCLESIASTES 12   Consider 12:1. Remember God in the prime of life. Do so before the infirmities of age set aside the vigor of youth (vv. 2-5).

Finally, take note of the book's conclusion. The goads mentioned in verse 11 give direction for change. The final conclusion is in verses 13-14. To fear God and keep His commandments, we need critical biblical thinking: the truth of the Bible in our minds and the work of the Holy Spirit to apply it to our lives. Finally, remember that we will all one day stand before God (v. 14; cf. 1 Cor 3:13; 2 Cor 5:10).

AUGUST 4

MATTHEW 7:15-29   *LEARN SPIRITUAL DISCERNMENT* (vv. 15-23). These comments are meant to guard the hearers, and subsequently the church, from false teaching. That this was important is obvious in Paul's comments to the elders of the church at Ephesus (Acts 20:28-31) and in Jude (v. 4). Our actions and our relationships always bear fruit – either good or bad. Jesus tells us to watch the fruit. This is also a good test of our own lives (cf. 2 Cor 13:5). How are you influencing other people's lives? Are those you touch brought closer to the Savior? Understand from these verses that our influence on those we touch is never neutral!

After Jesus' warning about false prophets come His thought-provoking words about those who will stand before Him on the last day believing– wrongly – that they are saved. This must be the ultimate tragedy. Two things go together with truly knowing God. The first is obedience to His commands (v. 21b; cf. John 14:21, 23-24; 1 John 2:3-6). The second is fruit (vv. 15-20). These two characteristics of the Christian life go together. If there is one, there will be the other. Remember the admonition of 2 Corinthians 13:5. A bit of self-examination is a healthy thing!

BUILD SOLID FOUNDATIONS (vv. 24-27). This means not only knowing what the truth is but using it to make daily decisions. Know

God's Word, and apply it carefully – weaving these truths into the fabric of relationships and daily activities. Allow God's will to be the center of your life. By doing so, nothing will move your foundations! Remember that we are building for eternity.

2 CHRONICLES 28   The account of King Ahaz in 2 Chronicles parallels the text of 2 Kings 16. Ahaz was the king to whom God sent a word of hope and mercy through Isaiah – which Ahaz rejected (Isa 7-8)! Ahaz was a blot on the history of Judah. He was blatantly forsaking God. Further, he led the people in false worship and idolatry (vv. 2-4). As a result, God brought him difficulty. Aram (Syria) from the north (v. 5), Israel from the north (v. 5b), and Edom from the south (v. 17) harassed him. Ahaz turned to Assyria for help instead of accepting the help from the Lord (v. 16), but Assyria was no help at all (vv. 20-21). Through this difficulty, Ahaz only became more committed to idolatry (v. 22ff.). The Valley of Ben Hinnom, where Ahaz sacrificed his sons (vv. 2-3), was immediately south of the walled city of Jerusalem.

The one bright spot in this account is the mercy that the Israelites extended to the prisoners who were brought to Israel from Judah (vv. 8-15). In the midst of Ahaz's depravity, the leaders of the people of Israel listened to Oded the prophet who said they should not take the people of Judah as slaves.

SONG OF SONGS 1-3   This short book, written in the highly poetic language of ancient Israel, is a love story of Solomon and his bride. The text is rich in "word pictures," but these may be understandable to our generation, since the language of love often is replete with such illustrations. · The text identifies the bride when she speaks as "Beloved," Solomon as "Lover."

Follow the anticipation, the delight in being together, and the longing in separation.

AUGUST 5

MATTHEW 8:1-17   At the end of Chapter 7 there is a transition from the hillside where Jesus had been teaching His disciples to His beginning ministry among the people.

The key to understanding the concept of the "kingdom" is authority. Jesus came to bring God's kingdom to men. In doing so, He demonstrated His authority in a number of ways. In the reading for today, for instance, He healed the sick (vv. 3, 13, 15-16), evidencing His authority over physical problems and demons.

Note especially verses 5-9. The Roman officer understood what it meant to give orders for he had people under his authority. Recognizing

Jesus' authority, he came to ask Jesus to heal his servant – correctly understanding that Jesus only had to say the word (give the order) and it would be done! Jesus' answer was remarkable (vv. 10-13). He acknowledged the soldier's genuine faith, then said that many – like this man – from outside the traditional Jewish faith would share in the kingdom, while many from inside, thinking they were secure, would be sadly disappointed (in hell, v. 12)! Tradition and heritage are not enough.

⊃These exercises of kingdom authority fulfilled the prophecy of Isaiah (v. 17; cf. Isa 53:4a), demonstrating that Jesus was the coming Promised Messiah – and that it is through the cross that we are healed.⊂

2 CHRONICLES 29-30   The account of Hezekiah in Chronicles is rich in detail about the king's actions to bring the nation back to the Lord. His father Ahaz had stripped the temple, its furnishings, and had finally closed the temple. Hezekiah wasted no time in beginning to turn things around, and his instruction to the Levites demonstrated remarkable understanding and insight regarding the nation's problems (29:3-11). He put legs to the rhetoric, and he himself led in both the restoration of the temple and in reestablished worship (vv. 27-36).

Hezekiah also invited the people of Israel (the northern kingdom) to come to Jerusalem to observe the Passover (30:1-9). Although the invitation was largely rejected, some responded. Read Hezekiah's prayer for those who were not purified and the result in 30:18-20. God heard their prayer (v. 27).

In spite of the depth to which Ahaz had taken Judah, *it is amazing what the leadership and influence of one man can accomplish under the Lord.*

SONG OF SONGS 4-6   One of the benefits of having this book in the canon of scripture is that it assures us that God and the Bible are not prudish about the delights of love when enjoyed in the context of marriage. This is a picture of an uninhibited couple giving to one another with the blessing of God.

AUGUST 6

MATTHEW 8:18-34   Jesus continued to demonstrate His kingdom authority. Remember that He had healed the sick (vv. 16-17). Now He calmed the storm (vv. 23-27), revealing authority over nature. He cast out demons (vv. 16, 28-34) proving His authority over the spirit world. Think of yourself in Jesus' presence with the disciples. What was happening before their eyes was so startling that they had trouble understanding its importance (v. 27).

Consider the demon-possessed men described in verse 28. Look at the result in verses 33-34. Then ponder the attitude of the townspeople. The pigs were more important than the men! They asked Jesus to leave their region. Do you see society valuing economics over people in our day?

2 CHRONICLES 31-32   After the Passover, the revival continued with the destruction of pagan worship articles (31:1) and practical plans for ongoing worship (vv. 2-19).

Review Hezekiah's specific steps to reinstitute worship of the Lord after he became king. *(1)* He repaired the temple and instructed the Levites to consecrate themselves (29:3-5). *(2)* He made sure that all defilement was removed from the sanctuary (v. 5b). *(3)* Hezekiah understood the spiritual problem that they faced, clearly articulated this to the people, and provided leadership (vv. 6-9). *(4)* He entered into a covenant with the Lord and led the people with him (vv. 10-11). *(5)* He reestablished true worship in the land (vv. 20-28). *(6)* He invited the people of Israel to join in worship (30:1-9). *(7)* He led the destruction of the pagan worship objects (31:1). *(8)* He provided for ongoing worship (vv. 2-19).

This text in Chronicles also adds detail not found in Kings about Sennacherib's threat to Judah. There is the implicit question in 32:1, "Why, God?" "After all that Hezekiah had so faithfully done," came the threat from Assyria. Note Hezekiah's hard work in preparation after the threat became known. Most importantly, notice the encouragement to his leaders and how he trusted God in the crisis (vv. 6-8).

A sad postscript to Hezekiah's faithful work before God was his pride, recorded in 32:25. His character is evident in his repentance when he understood the problem (v. 26).

SONG OF SONGS 7-8 As you read the lover's description of his beloved in 7:1-9, note his unrestrained delight in her body. He admires her feet and progresses from there to her head! His eyes miss nothing, and there is no hint of inhibition. Compare his descriptions to those in 4:1-7 and 6:4-9. Then note that she felt the same delight as she admired him (5:10-16).

In response to her lover, she gives her love to him with the same lack of restraint he has shown to her (7:9b-13). In context, one can feel the urgency of this man and woman to fulfill their physical love in sexual union. Without question, this is a gift of God – for the right time in life. Note, however, that as this young woman comes alive in response to her lover, she warns her friends not to let this happen until the right time (2:7; 3:5; 8:4). As she experiences the force of her emotions, she understands how difficult it would be to handle them if they could not legitimately be fulfilled (8:6).

AUGUST 7

MATTHEW 9:1-17 Further extension of kingdom authority is revealed as the gospel narrative continues. In the process, the religious leaders confronted Jesus with their unbelief.

➲When the paralytic was brought for healing, Jesus healed the man's soul first by declaring that his sins were forgiven. The teachers of the law correctly picked up the meaning of Jesus' words: Only God can forgive sin (v. 3; cf. Mark 2:6-7)! Only two meanings were possible: Either Jesus was the Messiah, the Son of God, or He was misrepresenting Himself and blaspheming. They immediately came to the second conclusion. Note how Jesus answered their silent question and validated Himself as God's Son (vv. 4-7).☯

Jesus again confronted the conventions of the religious leaders when He called Matthew, then went to his home for dinner (vv. 9-13). No rabbi in the system would have fellowshipped with Matthew – a tax collector. Think about Jesus' answer to them (v. 13), then how He explained that the kingdom could not be confined to their rigid interpretation (vv. 14-17).

ISAIAH 1 Isaiah prophesied and represented God to Judah during the reigns of Uzziah (Azariah), Jotham, Ahaz, and Hezekiah. His ministry came about 740-680 BC, corresponding to the period we have been reading about in Kings and Chronicles.

Isaiah, Jeremiah, Ezekiel, and Daniel are known as the "major prophets." The other twelve prophetic books, from Hosea to Malachi, are the "minor prophets," not because their messages are less important but because they are shorter in length.

The message of the prophets is extremely helpful to us because it correlates the events in Israel and Judah (Samuel, Kings and Chronicles) with how God viewed the people at that time and what He had to say about their behavior. What the prophets had to say is relevant to us, since problems in society today are remarkably similar to what they were then. Careful reading helps us understand accurately how God views us. This is precisely why God included these ancient books in the Bible (cf. Rom 15:4).

A great weakness of the church today is that we pay little attention to reading, teaching, or attempting to understand the importance of the prophets. Too many things compete for our attention. As we read through the Bible this year, we can begin to look at these messages to the people of ancient times and see how they apply to our own land, our church, and our lives.

As you read Chapter 1, look for the descriptions of God's people. Even an ox or donkey knows to whom it belongs, but the people of Judah don't even know that much! (v. 3). This in spite of the blessings that God has given to them (v. 2). Why don't they understand? Because their sin dulled their awareness (v. 4).

God, through Isaiah, asks Judah, "Why undergo more discipline? You are already bruised" (vv. 5-6). Then the nation is portrayed as a field of melons, with just the watchman's hut left in the field (vv. 8-9). The illustration refers to a country invaded, the rural areas taken, and only the fortified cities still standing.

Note how God felt about their religious practices (vv. 10-15). See also what God called them to do (vv. 16-17), His gracious promise of forgiveness and blessing (v. 19), and conversely, the consequence of not listening (v. 20). Read God's description of the nation *as He viewed the people* in verses 21-25a. ☑Verses 25b-31 contain the promise that in spite of the people's sin, God will redeem and restore the city and the land, and righteousness will be the rule. This restoration has not occurred yet. This kind of thoroughgoing change can only be a sovereign work of God described in Isaiah as occurring under the rule of the Messiah. (This vision is continued in 2:1-5, which describes the reign of Messiah)⇦

PROVERBS 1:1-7   The first nine chapters of Proverbs follow subject matter in sections, while most of the rest of the book is made up of single "proverbs" or wise sayings.

In this prologue to the book, note the purposes of the Proverbs. Look carefully at what they can mean in your own life (vv. 2-4) and the advantages of studying Proverbs in verses 5-6. Look for the principle in verse 7a and the fact in 7b. Which of us would not long for the blessings of verses 2-7?

Wisdom (vv. 2, 7) is more than knowledge. Wisdom applies knowledge to come to the best solution in a given circumstance. The promise here is that if we pay attention to this part of God's Word, wisdom will result.

AUGUST 8

MATTHEW 9:18-38 ⇒Jesus continued to demonstrate His credentials as the Son of God. He healed the woman who dared only to touch his garment (vv. 20-22). Could anyone but God do that? He raised the ruler's daughter from the dead (vv. 25-26). Could anyone but God do that? He healed the two blind men (vv. 27-30) and the man who was dumb because of demon possession (vv. 32-33).⇐

The events of Chapters 8 and 9, as a composite, present overwhelming evidence of the power of God in Jesus. Yet note the Pharisees' conclusion in verse 34. In spite of the evidence, they simply were not open to considering that Jesus was the promised Messiah. Instead, they concluded that the power Jesus displayed, which they didn't dispute, came from Satan.

In verses 35-38, we gain insight into Jesus' heart for the lost. As He observed the crowds, He saw them as harassed and helpless – sheep without a shepherd! They were without protection and without direction. Notice that God is the Lord of the harvest. Jesus asked His followers to pray that workers would be called to participate in this great harvest. Some will go into the field, but all have the call to pray! In fact, all of us participate in this harvest with our witness to God's work in our lives.

ISAIAH 2 ☑Verses 1-5 refer to end times, when the kingdom is established on the earth and the Messiah will reign. There will be a hunger to know God, and all will worship Him. These verses correspond to those in Micah 4:1-5. (cf. Ps 86:9; Zech 8:20-23, 14:16; and Rev 15:4).⇐

In the remainder of Chapter 2 (vv. 6-22), the prophet speaks about God's judgment on the nation because of their sin. Judah is described as a land of affluence (v. 7) but filled with pagan practices (vv. 6b, 8). The message from the Lord is that His judgment is coming; proud men will be humbled (vv. 11, 17), and there will be no place to hide. Note the call to repentance and trust in God (v. 22).

☑There also seems to be a more universal application known as The Day of the Lord – God's great judgment on the nations at the time of Jesus' second coming. The message of verse 11 is repeated in verse 17, emphasizing its truth. Compare verses 10 and 19 with Revelation 6:15-17 – which also speaks of the judgment on the nations when Christ returns.⇐

PROVERBS 1:8-19 Two pieces of advice: *do* learn and pay attention to what you have been taught (vv. 8-9), and *don't* allow others to entice you into sin (vv. 10-19).

We live in an age when many believe they need to break the "constraints" of what they have been taught. Those constraints, however, are often protective. Here, the writer speaks of parental instruction as something beautiful that will grace those who remember and observe what they have been taught.

The world in which we live has many ways to tempt us to do wrong (vv. 10-19). The result of choosing sin, however, is a destroyed life (vv. 18-19).

AUGUST 9

MATTHEW 10:1-23 When Jesus sent His disciples to minister, He sent them with the power and authority of the kingdom that He had been demonstrating to them (v. 1). He was giving them practical experience for the time when He would no longer be with them. The chapter is filled with insights about ministry in the world (theirs and ours) and is worth careful study and thought.

Jesus was realistic about the hostile nature of ministering in the world (vv. 16-17). The disciples are compared to sheep among wolves. Sheep are helpless among such predators unless they have protection. One of the most basic differences between the Christian and the world is that the Christian must follow a different rulebook than the world (v. 16b). The Christian must be open and honest, while the world will lie and take advantage as it suits the situation. This is what Jesus meant when he told them to be as innocent as doves (be absolutely honest as a child of the kingdom) but as shrewd as snakes (understand that the world twists the truth and uses slander and violence).

Although this disparity seems to put the Christian at a disadvantage, it isn't true. The Christian has the power of the Holy Spirit and the protection of God (the shepherd who protects). But take care! The most dangerous step a Christian worker can take is to use the rulebook of the world (power plays, distortion of truth) in the conflict. If we do, we may forfeit the protection of the shepherd! We must understand the nature of the conflict and use the methods of the Word of God in our interaction with society (cf. 2 Cor 10:3-5).

ISAIAH 3-4 Chapter 3 predicts God's discipline and judgment on the people. Observe the results when grace is withdrawn in verse 5. In verses 8-9, note the openness of sin in society and where the responsibility lies for the coming judgment. Society was so degraded that sin was paraded in the open. They had brought the coming disaster upon themselves (v. 9b). As you read the remainder of the chapter, observe God's view of the leaders (and the specific problems identified). The leaders had crushed the people and ground the faces of the poor (v. 15). It is a fearful thing to face the righteous judgment of the Lord (vv. 13-14). Note also God's comments about the women of Jerusalem in verses 16-26. Affluence has the smell of death and judgment when sin controls people!

☑Compare 4:2-6 with Ezekiel 36:24-38. God's sovereign work in His people will be a totally new thing. The old and sinful ways will be a memory and God will be present with His people. To illustrate, Isaiah uses the picture of God's presence with the Israelites in the deliverance from Egypt (vv. 4-6). This is the promise of Christ the Messiah's millennial reign upon His return (cf. 2:1-5).⇦

PROVERBS 1:20-33   Wisdom here is presented as a person – and identified as the Lord Himself (vv. 29-30). As you read, listen to the Lord speak to you. We *do* have many opportunities to listen to the wisdom of the Lord (vv. 20-21), but it is often true that we ignore what the Lord is saying. We *do* love our own ways!

Note the result of listening to the Lord (v. 23) but also the danger of ignoring what we know to be God's will for us (vv. 23-31). There is danger that we will believe that surely God is speaking to someone else! Pay attention to the way of life and safety (v. 33).

AUGUST 10

MATTHEW 10:24-42   When Jesus called the disciples (and us) to ministry, He underscored several important matters. Workers should be bold (vv. 26-31), and we should stand in awe before God (v. 28). There is no place for timidity. Eternity is at stake. Humanly we may feel timid – Paul did too (1 Cor 2:1-3), but with the presence of the Holy Spirit we *can* speak boldly (vv. 19-20; cf. 1 Cor 2:4). From an eternal perspective, how can we do otherwise than obey Him eagerly?

Loyalty to Christ is essential (vv. 32-33). How sobering when Jesus says that if we deny Him, He will deny us!

Jesus also discusses godly priorities (vv. 37-39). He does not suggest that we be disloyal to our families – but that obedience to Him must be foremost in our lives – even if it means the cross.

Certainly these three topics give us much to think about regarding our daily lives.

ISAIAH 5   In 5:1-4, Isaiah speaks about God's role in the nation's history, likening it to a vineyard that has been well-planted and tended – a vineyard where the gardener should expect a return in produce. Problem: bad fruit (v. 2b). Result: protection removed (v. 5b), directed judgment (v. 6a), and blessing withheld (v. 6b).   Note the tragic consequence of sin in verse 7b.

In 5:8-23, Isaiah outlines six specific sins that God abhors.   *(1)* Inappropriate acquisition of land (vv. 8-10). The land belonged to God and was given in trust (Lev 25:23). In an agricultural society, land was economic power. *(2)* Drunken pursuits (vv. 11-17). Note the partying lifestyle and the music (11b-12). *(3)* Sham spirituality (vv. 18-19). *(4)* Confused standards (v. 20). *(5)* Pride (v. 21). *(6)* Denied justice (vv. 22-23). The cause of these problems is evident in verse 24b. The people had rejected God's Word! (Should this give us something to think about today?) As a result, God would bring judgment on them (vv. 25-30).

PROVERBS 2:1-8   How much do you really desire to know God and His ways? A determined single-minded desire is described in verses 1-4 (cf. Jer 29:13). We need the mind-set from the Holy Spirit to want with all of our hearts to know God!

The results promised to those who seek God with their hearts are in verses 5-8. Meditate on these verses. Why would anyone settle for less?

AUGUST 11

MATTHEW 11:1-19   After John had been imprisoned, his disciples came to ask Jesus about His ministry. John may have wanted his disciples to see for themselves who Jesus was, and this was a way of shifting their attention to Him. Or it is possible that John wondered when Jesus would bring the promised kingdom with its judgment to the world and blessing to His people (Isa 35:4-7; 61:1-2). It is possible that, just as the disciples, John was looking for all of the blessings of the Messiah with His first advent, not understanding the sacrifice on the cross or the second advent.

⊃Jesus' answer to John's disciples referred them to Isaiah's prophecy about the Messiah (Isa 35:4-6; 42:1-9) and pointed out that He was literally fulfilling this Messianic prophecy.⊂ John's disciples would have immediately understood the import of what Jesus said. Then Jesus added that those who were not offended with Him would be blessed: i.e., don't be impatient, but trust Him.

Give attention to Jesus' comments about John. He wasn't indecisive or easily pushed (a reed swayed by the wind, v. 7). Nor was he debonair (dressed in prince's clothing, v. 8). But he was the greatest man born!

This praises John's character and spiritual accomplishment – and indicates that John would smooth the way for the coming of the Messiah (Mal 3:1).

ISAIAH 6   Isaiah is one of only a few people recorded in the Bible who saw the glory of the Lord. It is significant to compare Isaiah's reaction to this glory with that of others: Moses and the burning bush (Exod 3:5-6); Daniel in the presence of God's emissary, (Dan 10:4-11); Saul (Acts 9:3-9), and John (Rev 1:12-18). In each instance, when the person saw the glory of the eternal, he had a profound understanding of sinfulness! This experience changed Isaiah's life. That should also be our reaction as God touches our lives through His Word.

Isaiah responded to the Lord's call. The Lord made it clear that the assignment would not be easy – the people would not listen. In fact, the people were eager to hear but didn't apply what they heard (v. 9). The result would be hardened hearts and ears that didn't hear. God was not saying that He didn't want the people to respond to His call. He was telling Isaiah that the condition of the people was such that they would not respond, but they needed to hear nonetheless. When Isaiah asked how long he should speak to the people, the Lord replied that he should continue until judgment came (vv. 10-12)! ☑Note that the New Testament writers quote Isaiah 6:9-10, using this as a prophecy regarding Jesus' ministry and the response to His message (cf. Matt 13:13-15; Mark 4:10-12; Luke 8:9-10; John 12:37-40).⇦

PROVERBS 2:9-22   The writer continues to list the advantages of listening and responding to the Lord: increased understanding and discernment (vv. 9-11), and avoiding behavior that leads to judgment (vv. 12-19). Verse 18 suggests the deadly diseases that may follow sexual sin! Choose the way of righteousness (vv. 20-21). If there ever was a time in history when this kind of understanding, discernment, and discipline, has been needed, it is in our day!

AUGUST 12

MATTHEW 11:20-30   As you read verses 20-24, think about how to apply this to your life. Jesus asserted that society would be responsible for the truth to which it has been exposed. The cities Jesus mentioned had heard the message and seen the authority of God in Jesus. That should have been enough to bring them to repentance. But they didn't respond, and for this Jesus said that they will be judged!

With this in mind, what about our own cities? Surely it is only God's mercy that stays the hand of judgment on our society. Think too about our personal responsibility in sharing God's truth. These verses spell out how Jesus views lack of response to truth.

⟳Jesus' relationship to the Father is clearly defined in verse 27. All things were committed to Jesus by the Father. Jesus knew the Father and could reveal God to men! If we desire to know God, we need to know Jesus (John 1:18).

Sometimes the Christian life seems difficult and burdensome. Rejoice as you read verses 28-30. As we respond to the commands of Jesus, we experience peace and joy – God's peace and joy – not heavy burdens! He is truly the Savior.⟲

ISAIAH 7   Early in Ahaz's reign, with the threat of both Aram (Syria) and Israel at his doorstep (2 Kings 16:1-6), God offered him relief (vv. 1-9). The only condition was to trust God (v. 9b). Further, God offered to give Ahaz a sign of His intention. But Ahaz turned down the offer (v. 12).

Isaiah rebuked Ahaz for his arrogance and said that God Himself would give a sign to signal defeat of Israel and Aram by Assyria. The sign was the birth of a boy whose name would be Immanuel (v. 14). Before the child had grown enough to tell right from wrong, the prophecy would be completed. In fact, Assyria did very shortly overrun both Aram and Israel and a few years later devastated Judah as well.

☑We know from the message of the angel to Joseph that this sign (v. 14) applies to the coming of the Savior (Matt 1:22-23). That the prophecy in Isaiah 7 also applied to the current situation with Ahaz seems clear. So this prophecy has a double meaning, one as a sign to Ahaz, and the other foretelling the birth of Jesus over seven hundred years later.⇦

Who was this young woman who would have the child? Possibly a girl not yet married when the prophecy was uttered, who soon was married and had a child, naming him Immanuel (the prophecy unknown to her).

PROVERBS 3:1-10   This chapter is a treasury of wisdom. Read the text, and follow this simple outline: a call to attention to God's Word (i.e., seek wisdom, vv. 1-2); a call to relationships of love and faithfulness (vv. 3-4); a call to acknowledgment of God and to trust Him (vv. 5-6); a call to humbleness (vv. 7-8); a call to remember God with what He has provided (vv. 9-10).

All of this begins with attention to the words God has given us! Each admonition to a changed life flows from the principles of the Bible (if one lives in this way, it will be a different life from the world's norm). Each of these mandates to godly living is widely supported throughout Scripture.

Take time to identify specific ways in which change would bring you into line with God's standard.

AUGUST 13

MATTHEW 12:1-21 ➲ Jesus specifically challenged the religious leaders in their rigid interpretation of the Mosaic law (vv. 1-14). He maintained that He did not violate the law doing God's work on the Sabbath. Not only did He challenge the religious leaders' interpretation, but He also challenged their practice by revealing their inconsistency (vv. 11-12). Further, Jesus said He was Lord of the Sabbath, i.e., God (v. 8)!☢ Even so, the use of the Sabbath was the point of law that made the leaders decide that Jesus could not have been the Messiah.

☑Notice the characteristics of the Christ (vv. 18-21) that are here attributed to Jesus, quoted from Isaiah 42: His justice (v. 18); His quiet ministry (v. 19); His mercy and understanding (v. 20); and His coming reign (vv. 20b-21).⇦

ISAIAH 8 This chapter flows directly from Chapter 7. Is this child who was born to Isaiah and his wife the same as that predicted in 7:14? Possibly not. The birth of the child in Chapter 7 would herald the destruction of Israel and Syria. The event foretold in Chapter 8 was that trouble from God was coming to Israel and Syria (v. 4) and also to Judah (vv. 7-8), with Assyria as His tool of judgment. The name of Isaiah's child, Maher-Shalal-Hash-Baz, means "quick to the plunder, swift to the spoil," referring to the coming judgment of God through Assyria.

Follow Isaiah's thought in verses 6-10. When we reject the way of the Lord, we turn from His peace (gently flowing waters) to trouble (mighty flooding waters). This coming flood would sweep across Judah, bringing devastation. Is this what any one of us in our right mind would choose?

Further, learn what to fear (vv. 11-15). Don't be afraid of men or their alliances. The word "conspiracy" in verse 12 means a treaty, possibly referring to the alliance between Israel and Aram in Chapter 7. Instead of fearing external threats, fear and trust God (v. 13). Godly fear is not a shaking fear of disaster; it is awe of God's power and holiness. However, a legitimate fear of God should lead us to "quake in our shoes." For the ungodly, God is a rock over which they will be shattered (v. 14b-15). ☑Note that Paul quotes verse 14 and Peter quotes verse 14b, applying the passage to Jesus and the consequence of ignoring or disobeying the message of the gospel (cf. Rom 9:33; 1 Peter 2:8).⇦ *So*, make your choice, Isaiah says to Judah (and to us); fear God in awe and trust (healthy choice), or fear God because of His coming judgment!

☑Isaiah 8:17b-18a is quoted in Hebrews 2:13 regarding Jesus' relationship to the redeemed. Jesus declares His trust in the Lord God and presents the "children God has given me."⇦

PROVERBS 3:11-18   Note verses 11-12. We think of discipline as action to straighten our direction when we are off course. This is often true, but not always. Discipline may be a tool to strengthen what is correct! This is true of the athlete and of the professional learning the intricacies of his work. *The Lord brings discipline into our lives to better fit us for life* (cf. 1 Peter 1:3-7). Hard times? Perhaps. But from a hand of love. Change in direction? Of course, when we need change. Think about this when things aren't exactly as you would like them to be. Thank God for His love and care in giving us exactly what we need.

Consider verses 13-18 as a call to godly priorities. Take God's will as your standard and walk with the Lord. Note the result in verses 17-18: pleasant ways, a peaceful path, abundance, and blessing in life. If this is true, why pursue fantasies?

AUGUST 14

MATTHEW 12:22-50   Trying to explain Jesus' power and authority over demons, the Pharisees asserted that He used the power of the prince of the demons, Beelzebub (v. 24, see also 9:34). ➲Follow the logic of Jesus' answer. The heart of the kingdom is authority – and Jesus says that if the power of God drove out demons, then the kingdom of God had come to them (v. 28).☾

Now look at verse 32. What is the sin that will not be forgiven? The Pharisees had attributed the work of the Spirit of God (v. 28) to Satan (v. 24).

The real question is the fruit from the tree (vv. 33-35). Jesus said that the Pharisees demonstrated which tree they were by what they were saying (v. 34). Jesus then warned that we are each responsible for our words (vv. 36-37).

➲Jesus also said they would know His identity by the sign He would give them – the sign of the prophet Jonah (vv. 39-40). Just as Jonah was three days in the fish, Jesus said He would be three days in the grave – and by implication, after that time He would come out just as Jonah had. At the same time He proclaimed that He was greater than either Jonah or Solomon (the wisest man who had lived).☾ Each generation and each person is responsible to act upon to the truth that is given (vv. 41-42).

ISAIAH 9-10   ☑Isaiah 9:1-7 is one of the most beautiful prophetic portions of the Bible about the coming of Jesus. Some parts were fulfilled when Jesus lived during the first advent (Matt 4:15-16), but certainly there are aspects that will not be fulfilled until the second advent (v. 7). This is an important portion, as it reveals the character of the Messiah's reign.⇦

As you read 9:8-10:34, look for the reasons for God's judgment. God was offended by the people's pride, arrogance (9:9-10), confidence in their own ability (v. 10), and their wicked tongue (v. 17b). Leaders and people were willing to abandon God's way (vv. 15-16). Unjust and oppressive laws made it easy to take advantage of the poor (10:1-2).

Notice that 9:12b, 17b, 21b, and 10:4b repeat the same phrase. Look back at the verses preceding each of these phrases, and note its significance.

Is God sovereign over the nations? In Chapters 7 and 8, God promises to use Assyria to bring judgment on Israel, Syria, and Judah. In 10:5-19 the Lord (through Isaiah) speaks to this. God brought Assyria against Israel, Syria, and Judah (vv. 5-6). But this was not the understanding of the king of Assyria. To him, this was a national military venture that he thought he had planned to carry out with the strength of his troops (vv. 7-11). What the king of Assyria did not understand is that God would also deal with him (vv. 12-19).

PROVERBS 3:19-26   God created the heavens and the earth in His wisdom (vv. 19-20). If we will follow God in His revealed wisdom, we will preserve sound judgment and discernment – and blessing will follow.

With this in mind, consider verses 21-26. The Lord's way will be life for the believer (v. 22). It will be the way of safety (v. 23). It will give inner security (v. 24). God will be our protection (vv. 25-26).

AUGUST 15

MATTHEW 13:1-30, 36-43   A series of parables about the kingdom are grouped together at this point in Matthew's gospel. Each parable illustrates a different truth about the kingdom.

Jesus makes an important point in verses 11-17. The parables were only intelligible to some. It is possible to hear the truth but not apply it (vv. 13-15). Those who respond to the truth receive understanding.

The Parable of the Sower (vv. 1-9, 18-23) illustrates how different people respond to the truth of the gospel. As you read, note that the mark of spiritual life is its fruit. Fruit comes only with good ground, and a field free of thorns. Note also thorns (worries of this life and the deceit of wealth) choke the work of God (v. 22). Avoid the inhibiting work of thorns!

The Parable of the Weeds (vv. 24-30) shows how Satan has attempted to destroy the work of the kingdom. In the end, the Lord will separate the weeds and the wheat (v. 30). ➲In explaining the parable in verses 36-42, Jesus told the disciples that He (The Son of Man) would send the angels to gather the weeds for destruction and the righteous to receive glory (vv. 40-43).☾

ISAIAH 11-12   Chapters 11 and 12, which are messages to Judah and Jerusalem, finish the initial section of Isaiah. ☑The character of the Messiah and His reign is the subject of 11:1-9 (cf. 2 Peter 3:13). When referring to a person in the OT, it was common to refer to that person with his father's name. Thus, David is identified with his father's name Jesse.   However, it is the more distant descendant of David and his father Jesse – the Messiah – to whom Isaiah is referring in this passage.

Note the personal characteristics of the Messiah (11:1-3a): The Spirit of the Lord will empower His ministry, and from this will flow wisdom and understanding, righteous counsel, power, knowledge, respect for and fear of God.   His judgments and decisions will not depend on outward appearance, but on discernment of truth.   His character will be applied to His reign in practical ways (vv. 3b-5). The effect of His peace upon all of nature will be evident (vv. 6-9). Nature itself will be changed, and all will be safe. Finally, notice in verse 9b that all will understand the Lord. The knowledge of the Lord will cover the whole earth.

Can you imagine the earth as a place of safety and righteousness? This is why 2 Peter 3:13, with other references, speaks of the promise of this fulfillment as the "hope" of the believer. With the coming of Christ there will be true righteousness. In this regard, check Titus 2:11-14.

The restoration of God's people to the land is foretold and placed in the context of the reign of the Messiah (11:10-16). Note that it refers to a "second time." The "first" may refer to the Exodus or to the smaller restoration to the land under Ezra and Nehemiah at about 500 BC. Verse 13 says that under the Messiah's reign, the enmity between Israel and Judah will end. Further, Paul uses verse 10 to refer to the Gentiles who will come to Christ (Rom 15:12). Finally, Chapter 12 expresses the joy and praise of God's people when this great day comes.↩

PROVERBS 3:27-35   Walking with the Lord brings great blessing to the believer (vv. 17-26). Our reading for today shows us what to avoid in this walk – common pitfalls in the real world. To express these as positive principles, they call for good will toward others (v. 27), open-handed honesty (vv. 28-30), and saying "no" to deceit and violence (vv. 29-32). Note God's hatred of the sinful attitudes and actions we must avoid (vv. 32-34). Go for the gold (vv. 33b, 35a).

AUGUST 16

MATTHEW 13:31-35, 44-58   Remember from yesterday's reading that each of the parables in this section of Matthew teaches a different truth about the kingdom.

The parables of the mustard seed and the yeast illustrate how the kingdom will grow and penetrate society. Consider that from the time when Jesus lived on the earth, the church has grown and has penetrated societies around the world. Hostile governments have not been able to stamp it out. Where the church is weak, it is because of the lack of faith and obedience of its members.

The parables of the hidden treasure and the pearl illustrate the worth of the kingdom (vv. 44-46). Once the true value of the treasure or pearl was appreciated, the finder gave up everything to acquire the treasure. All else in life pales compared to the richness of knowing God and sharing in His life (Phil 3:7-10).

The parable of the net (vv. 47-50) teaches that God will decide the destiny of men at the final judgment. Thus, in both the Parable of the Weeds and the Parable of the Net, Jesus teaches that what we have been during life will determine whether we go to heaven (v. 43) or hell (vv. 42, 49-50). The most important matter that we, as individuals, must settle is that we know God through faith in the Lord Jesus. Many will be bitterly disappointed because they have not made the right choice (vv. 49-50; Luke 13:22-27).

ISAIAH 13-14   Chapters 13-23 contain prophecies about the nations of the world. Although there are references to Judah, the prime focus is upon other peoples.

Chapters 13-14 refer first to all of the nations at that time but also to the second coming of Christ. ☑Here again are references to the "Day of the Lord." This phrase, as used in the Old Testament, most often refers to the coming of world judgment when the Messiah comes in glory and power. Compare 13:9-10 with Matthew 24:29, where Jesus speaks of His coming in glory and power.

Babylon refers to the ancient power in the Near East, but also, in the Bible, to the governmental and world system of evil. Although the power of Babylon was broken in the days of Daniel (Dan 5), Revelation 14:8, 17:3-6, and 18:1-24 speak clearly of the last times in relation to

Babylon. Revelation 18 particularly speaks about the judgment that God will bring to the world system at the time of Christ's return, and this system is identified as "Babylon." There is, in fact, a great deal of parallel between the language of Isaiah 13 and Revelation 18.⇔

Chapter 14 tells of the peace on the earth after the judgment of Babylon. ☑Verses 1-8 speak about the Lord settling Israel once again in their land with the nations of the world deferring to them. This refers to the messianic reign of Christ during the Millennium.⇔ Verses 9-11 examine the "welcome" that the king of Babylon receives in the world of the dead. Verses 12-14 have been thought to give some clue to how Satan rebelled and to refer to the fall of Satan. As the passage is speaking about the king of Babylon, this would fit the characterization of Babylon as the "world system" in contrast to God's system of righteousness. Compare 14:15-17 with Colossians 2:14-15.

PROVERBS 4:1-9   This chapter has an important message for our day. Current "wisdom" is that children and young people need to distance themselves from the mores and instruction of their parents, and even that of the church, to find their own way. This is taught in the schools, in popular music, and in many of the books available to young people. As you read this chapter, note the contrasting emphasis.

A godly father and mother, teaching godly precepts in the home, is the pattern in verses 1-4. The writer calls on children to listen to and embrace this teaching.

In reading verses 5-9, review Proverbs 2:2-6. The wisdom called for here is a single-minded desire and discipline to follow after God. *Real wisdom, the ability to use available facts to make correct decisions, comes from the Lord.*

AUGUST 17

MATTHEW 14:1-21   The account of John the Baptist's murder is remarkable. Think about it: This man of God had the courage to tell the highest Roman official in the region that he was living in sin with his sister-in-law. It is all the more remarkable because Herod was secular. This reflects the truth that God's concern for marriage and morality extends to the secular world.

Jesus needed to withdraw from people when he heard about the death of John the Baptist (v. 13). A measure of Jesus' concern for people is that he received those who followed Him into His "alone place" with compassion and healed the sick. He also fed five thousand, multiplying five loaves of bread and two fish.

Sometimes we need to say "no" to demands upon our time, but we need discernment from the Lord to know when. In this instance, Jesus didn't turn people away, perhaps seeing them as described in Matthew 9:36, as sheep without a shepherd.

ISAIAH 15-16   The country of Moab is the prophetic subject of these two chapters. The Moabites came from the incestuous relation of Lot's daughter with Lot (Gen 19:36-38). The country was on the east side of the Dead Sea, across from Judah. Their sin – pride, conceit, and insolence – is mentioned in 16:6.

Judgment for sin in another's life or the life of another nation is never something in which we should take delight for we are all sinners. Instead, the refugees of war deserve compassion (16:4). The exception is Revelation 18:20, where the redeemed are told to rejoice over the final judgment on the wicked world system. In Isaiah, however, note how the prophet himself mourns over the coming judgment of Moab (15:5). The places mentioned were cities present in Moab at the time of Isaiah.

☑In 16:4b-5 see the promise of Messiah, coming through David, and bringing justice and righteousness. Compare this with 11:1-4.⇦

PROVERBS 4:10-19   The message of Proverbs 4 and of Romans 12:1-2 is the same. In the assigned reading today, note how many times the reader is urged not to follow the pattern of this world. The intriguing thing about this process of decision and growth is that it has little to do with formal education. The unschooled individual who will allow his mind to be informed by God's Word will demonstrate an uncommon wisdom.

AUGUST 18

MATTHEW 14:22-36   Although Jesus was truly human, as the Son of God He was not bound by the same limitations we have. The lesson is that Peter was not bound by the usual limitations either, as long as his eyes were on the Lord! Consider the implications of this and then read John 14:12-14. In our lives, do we compromise the power of the Holy Spirit? What more would God do in the world today through the fervent prayer and the faith of His people?

ISAIAH 17-18   Damascus was (and is) the capital of Syria. Aram was the southern portion of Syria. In 17:3, Ephraim (Israel, or the Northern Kingdom) is mentioned. Remember that in Chapter 7 Israel and Syria were aligned against Judah.

In 17:3-6, the prophet says that Israel will share in the judgment of Syria, but not be completely destroyed (v. 6), and that some would repent (vv. 7-8). Notice the truth in verse 10a and the consequences in verse 10b ff. It *does not pay* to forget or to ignore the God of heaven!

The country of Cush was Ethiopia. ☑This prophecy foresees a time when the people of Cush will come to Jerusalem to bring gifts to the Lord (18:7; cf. Isa 2:3).⇦

PROVERBS 4:20-27   Here again, the reader is urged to respond to a father's wisdom. In the flow of the text, this could also be identified as God's word. These words are life for those who pay attention (v. 22). Memorize verses 25-27 and keep them "up-front" in your mind.

AUGUST 19

MATTHEW 15:1-20   The question posed to Jesus at the beginning of the chapter (v. 2) highlights the difference between religion and true spiritual faith. The Pharisees and teachers of the law had a careful system of keeping the "law" that Jesus observed as inconsistent and inadequate. In fact, it supplanted the intent of God in the law (v. 3)! In verses 8-9 Jesus points out the danger of religious form without substance and fire. Jesus also says that the Heavenly Father must first plant the plant – or it will be pulled up as a fraud (v. 13).

The question of what creates our relationship with God – faith or personal works – is still relevant. The humbling act of coming to God by faith, with nothing to offer, remains the only way possible to know Him (John 3:16,36; Eph 2:8-9). It is God's method of planting life (v. 13).

ISAIAH 19-20   The remarkable prophecy about Egypt in Isaiah 19 looks forward to a time yet to come, but perhaps not in the distant future. It is a prophecy of judgment from the Lord, followed by a great turning to the Lord by the Egyptian people.

Three judgments to the country are foretold in 19:1-14. Verses 1-4 tell of civil war. That this is the hand of God is seen in the three statements, "I will stir up Egyptian against Egyptian" (v. 2), "I will bring their plans to nothing" (v. 3), and "I will hand the Egyptians over to the power of a cruel master" (v. 4). The second judgment is an economic crisis (vv. 5-10). Almost the entire economy of Egypt depended upon the Nile with its seasonal flooding. This judgment is the drying of the Nile with terrible consequences to farming and fishing. Third will be a crisis of wisdom and knowledge among the leaders of the country (vv. 11-15). Note God's hand making them confused (v. 14).

☑Five blessings will come to the land (vv. 18-25). Each of these blessings follows the phrase, "In that day," in verses 18, 19, 21, 23, and 24. Both the Egyptians and the Assyrians will turn to the Lord, and a highway will run between the two countries – perhaps through Israel!

These prophecies have not yet been fulfilled and may well refer to God's sovereign dealings with these nations at the time of Christ's return and the messianic reign in Jerusalem. ⇦

Ashdod (20:1) was the most important of five city-states of the Philistines that were subject to Assyria at that time. Ashdod (and the other Philistines) rebelled against Assyria, turning to Egypt for help. It was a mistake. With the rebellion of Ashdod, Sargon came and once again established Assyrian rule over the Philistines. Isaiah used their example to warn the Israelites not to go to Egypt or Cush for help, since Assyria would carry these countries off as well (vv. 3-6).

PROVERBS 5:1-14   The Scriptures are clear about the realities of sin – about how attractive sin appears and also about how, in the end, it turns to bite the person who indulges. Proverbs 5-7 considers sexual sin. Although the text speaks about the temptation of the man, the same principles apply to the woman.

There is a practical piece of advice in verses 7-14. Don't get close to danger. If so, you may fall into sin. Don't cruise – no window-shopping (I'm not buying, you know, just looking!). If we allow ourselves to get into the wrong place, it may lead to wrong actions with bitter results.

AUGUST 20

MATTHEW 15:21-39   Contrast the living faith of the Canaanite woman with the "faith" (lack of true faith) of the Pharisees and teachers of the law (vv. 1-20). This contrast illustrates the truth that Jesus spoke in Matthew 8:11-12. Don't trust in family background, church affiliation, or tradition! ⟳It was significant that when this Canaanite woman addressed Jesus it was as, "Lord, Son of David" (v. 22). She understood Jesus to be the promised Messiah – and Jesus didn't correct her. He let her assumption stand that He was the Messiah. Further, He responded to her faith.⟲

Jesus is a model for us in His use of time and opportunity. As He ministered to the crowds (vv. 29-30), He met their physical and spiritual needs. He demonstrated His compassion by feeding them (vv. 32-39). At the same time, Jesus was teaching the disciples, by example, to understand true ministry.

ISAIAH 21-22   Chapter 21 contains three short prophecies about Babylon, Edom, and Arabia. As Isaiah understood the prophecy about Babylon, he himself was distressed (vv. 3-4). This prophecy probably foretells the fall of Babylon to the Medes and Persians in 539 BC (cf. Dan 5).

Isaiah spoke strongly to his people in Chapter 22. These words (vv. 1-14) were written after the Lord delivered Judah and Jerusalem, probably when Sennacherib laid siege to the city (2 Kings 18:13-19:36). What was so hurtful to the prophet (and to the Lord) was the casual and unrepentant attitude of the people. Verses 9-11 show the desperate preparations for battle, but verse 11b reveals the people's heart. God had called them to repent (v. 12), but they ignored it (v. 13). Think about the meaning of verse 14. Sometimes there are irrevocable consequences to our sin!

Shebna (v. 15) was the king's secretary under Hezekiah (2 Kings 18:17ff.; Isa 36). God was looking at a proud man's heart (v. 16) and was calling him to account. Eliakim (v. 20; 2 Kings 18:18, 37) was the palace administrator whom the Lord recognized as having a different heart and whom, Isaiah states, God would put in Shebna's place.

PROVERBS 5:15-23   These verses call for fidelity in marriage. Don't share the intimacy you should reserve for your spouse with anyone else (vv. 15-17). God's pattern is strict monogamy. Although illicit relationships are usually presumed to be secret, even if no one else is aware, God knows (v. 21). Sin ensnares us (vv. 22-23). It is dangerous to sin – the personal entanglements are like a trap that snaps shut (v. 22).

AUGUST 21

MATTHEW 16:1-12   The religious leaders came to Jesus desiring a miracle to "prove" his authenticity (v. 1). He replied that they should heed the obvious (His teaching and actions) – just as they would look at signs of the weather – and draw correct conclusions (vv. 2-4). That should be enough to convince them that Jesus had His authority from God.

Consider verses 5-12. The yeast of the Pharisees and the Sadducees is their teaching (v. 12). They taught conformity to their view of the law and missed the central message of the scriptures! This conversation is a follow-up of the request for a "sign," which Jesus refused. Their unbelief and their preconceptions blocked their understanding of who Jesus was (see John 7:17). Jesus went a step further to identify the yeast of the Pharisees as hypocrisy (Luke 12:1). That definition matches what Jesus said in Matthew 15:7-9.

ISAIAH 23   Tyre and Sidon on the coast of the Mediterranean Sea were part of Phoenicia. This maritime country was just to the west of Israel.

Read God's complaint against the people in Chapter 23. One of the reasons for God's action against them was their pride (v. 9). It is of interest that even in these ancient times, economic interrelationships between nations were important (vv. 3, 5). In fact, the real princes in the land were the merchants (v. 8b). There would be, however, nowhere to escape God's lesson. They would be able to go neither to the west (v. 12b) nor to the east (v. 13).

PROVERBS 6:1-5   Sometimes we assume unwise obligations. The message of verses 1-5 is to free oneself from wrong obligations. Whether we knew about them when made, or have better insight later, take whatever steps necessary to untangle yourself from what is wrong.

AUGUST 22

MATTHEW 16:13-28   ⊃While Jesus was with His disciples in Caesarea Philippi, Peter said he believed that Jesus was the Christ (coming Messiah), the Son of God – and Jesus acknowledged that this was true! At this time, in the context of Peter's confession, Jesus first began to tell His disciples that He would be killed and raised from the dead. This new phase in His ministry came to the core of redemption – Jesus' death in our place.☯   Note that God's work in Peter allowed him to understand the truth about Jesus (v. 17). This was the truth upon which the church would be established (Jesus as the Christ, the Son of God, v. 18).

Think carefully about discipleship as Jesus defined it in verses 24-27. This doesn't describe a lukewarm acknowledgment that Jesus is the Savior. This faith goes to the very center of life. It will follow Jesus wherever the path leads (v. 24) instead of choosing safety or convenience (vv. 22-23). It places Jesus' will as the highest priority. It looks forward to Jesus' coming (v. 27). How does your faith compare?

ISAIAH 24   Chapters 24-27 have been called "The Little Apocalypse." The apocalyptic portions of the Bible speak of the judgment (The Day of the Lord) and restoration of the earth (the reign of the Messiah) in the final days. These events are related to the second coming of Christ. Read the entire section with this in mind.

☑Chapter 24 describes a worldwide destruction of unprecedented proportion. In the chronology of redemption, this will occur at the time of Christ's second coming. It will be a great leveler; status will not matter because all will be affected in the same tragic way (vv. 1-3). The reason for the devastation is the conscious rebellion against the laws of God (vv. 5-6). The economic and social fabric of society will be destroyed (vv. 7-13; cf. Rev 18:22-23). There will be no escape (vv. 17-18). The judgment of God will extend to the evil powers in the heavens (vv. 21-22; see also Eph 6:12).

Still, there will be cause to praise God (vv. 14-16a). Revelation 18 is a parallel to Isaiah 24, and in Revelation 18:20 God calls upon His people to rejoice in the judgment that has finally come to the earth. The reason is that righteousness is finally being established! God is judging sin and will establish His Kingdom of righteousness and justice! That is cause for rejoicing (Isa 24:23b).⇦

PROVERBS 6:6-11   This is one of the several places in the Bible that presents a work ethic. That the ant is our model should command our attention. One can't decide to "sleep in" very often without a prick of conscience when reading this (v. 9). And the attitude that "What I do today won't make a difference," just isn't supported (vv. 10-11).

AUGUST 23

MATTHEW 17:1-13   The experience on the Mount of Transfiguration gave further insight to those who accompanied Jesus about His identity and His coming death and resurrection (through His altered appearance and the audible voice of God). It is significant that Moses and Elijah came to speak to Jesus and that their conversation was about Jesus' death (Luke 9:30-31).

☑When Jesus explained His death and resurrection to the disciples after the events on the road to Emmaus (Luke 24:13-27), He pointed out that these things had been clearly foretold by Moses and the prophets. Think about the significance of those who conversed with Jesus on the mountain. Moses represented the law, Elijah represented the prophets, and Jesus fulfilled both the law and the prophets, redeeming all who believe.⇦

ISAIAH 25-26   ☑Remember to view Chapters 24-27 as a unit, speaking about the end times and the final judgment. Once again, this is The Day of The Lord, associated with the return of Christ in glory. Chapter 24 foretells the terrible judgment in vivid terms, similar to that of Revelation 18. Chapter 25 looks back on the event, and Chapter 26 again looks forward to God's judgment of the nations. Chapter 27 tells of Israel (Israel and Judah) in the context of that final judgment.

Isaiah 25:1-5 particularly looks back on the great judgment as an accomplished event. It is seen as a marvelous thing (v. 1; cf. Ps 46:8-11). The city (cities of the world) is a heap of rubble, and the strongholds of the pagans will rise no more (v. 2). The strong and the ruthless will be forced to honor God as the King (v. 3; see also Rev 15:3-4; Phil 2:9-11). In contrast, God's people have His protection (vv. 4-5).

In 25:6-9, Isaiah speaks of the time when the Lord God will institute the new order of the kingdom – the kingdom of Christ's reign, and finally the eternal kingdom of God. The banquet table for God's people will be set (v. 6; cf. Matt 8:11-12). Destruction of the shroud in verse 7 refers to freedom from obligatory sin and/or freedom from death that has been a shroud over mankind since the fall in Eden. In reading verse 8, compare Revelation 21:4; both passages speak of the same deliverance from the effects of sin. Finally, note the praise of God's people as they realize God's promises of life and deliverance (v. 9).

Moab (v. 10b) is an example of the judgment that God is bringing on the world. The pride of Moab will bring these people under the hand of God (v. 11b).

In Chapter 26, think of verses 1-9 as the testimony of God's people as they wait for the new order. What is spoken of here is anticipatory, for, "In that day," (v. 1) this song will be sung. Verses 3-4 and 7-9 are portions that each of us would do well to memorize! In verses 20-21, Isaiah tells his people to wait "for a little while" until all of this is accomplished.

Think about verses 10-11. God's goodness comes in many ways. Yet people do not recognize God's gifts or acknowledge His majesty and greatness (Rom 1:18-20). For this, God's judgment will come.

☑The reference in verses 19-21 to new life should be understood as Israel's renewal when Christ returns to judge the ungodly (v. 21; cf. Ezek 36:8-37:14; Zech 12:10-13)⇦

PROVERBS 6:12-19 The secret signals mentioned in verses 12-15 are used when there are covert intentions and alliances in a group or "behind the scenes" maneuvering. The text is clear about the result of such behavior. The seven sins of arrogance, deceit, violence, wicked intentions, evil deeds, lies, and dissension are listed in verses 16-19. As God's children, we need to stay as far as we can from deceit.

AUGUST 24

MATTHEW 17:14-27 In Matthew 10, Jesus sent out the disciples to minister and gave them authority to drive out evil spirits and heal the sick. However, when a man asked the disciples to heal his son, who suffered from epileptic seizures, they could not do so (vv. 15-16). Jesus healed the boy by driving out a demon that was causing the seizures. Why had the disciples been unable to heal the boy? Jesus related their inability to a lack of faith.

Think about verse 20 as it applies to our ministry of faith and prayer. Just as with the disciples, our ministry confronts the kingdom of Satan. To do this in power, we need to learn to pray with faith that moves mountains! Jesus says this is attainable and practical.

ISAIAH 27   ☑Chapter 27 concludes the section that anticipates the final judgment on the world and the setting up of the new order of the kingdom. This chapter promises the reestablishment of Israel, using the phrase "in that day" three times (vv. 1, 2, 12), and the phrase "in days to come" once (v. 6). God does intend a place for His people Israel in the end times, when all worship other than of the true God will be banished (v. 9). The Lord will graciously bring all of His people back to the land – one by one (v. 12-13). And in "that day," the foreign nations will come and worship the Lord (Messiah, King) in Jerusalem (cf. Isa 2:1-5; Zech 14:16).⇦

PROVERBS 6:20-35   In the days of sexual promiscuity and freedom in which we live, remember this truth about adultery (vv. 20-35). If you put your foot in this trap, the spring snaps shut, and the consequences are far-reaching and grave in relationships. But there is a better reason yet for the prudence of purity. God knows about us even if we think no one else does (cf. 5:21-23). We live openly before Him. Think about it.

AUGUST 25

MATTHEW 18:1-14   Jesus used the question posed by His disciples (v. 1) to teach them about what is important in the kingdom (vv. 3-4) and the worth of little children (vv. 5-7, 10).

Childlike humility is a condition of entry to the kingdom (v. 3). A small child trusts with unquestioning faith. The world's method of success is control and acquisition. The toddler knows nothing of these. Thus, Jesus says in verse 4 that such humility is considered great in the kingdom.

Note, too, the responsibility that we all share – not to be a part in leading a child into sinful behavior (vv. 6-8). Strong words, but from Jesus. Think about applying this truth in your own home.

ISAIAH 28   Chapters 28-33 show the people of Judah their condition from the Lord's perspective. Chapter 28 seems to be an exception, since it speaks about the Northern Kingdom, or Israel. However, in context, the message is applicable also to Judah, as the principles apply to them as well – and to us.

Verse 1 reveals the effect of alcohol on the nation: tremendous potential brought low by wine. Priests and prophets (so called) were drunkards (vv. 7-8). Attempting to teach, they taught rules (v. 10) rather than heart faith and commitment to God. ☑In the midst of this commentary is the promise of what God will finally do for His own, redeeming them in righteousness and judgment (vv. 5-6).⇦

In verses 10-13, God's Word becomes a death-knell when it is presented only as a set of rules. The very principles that are meant to bring us to know God become the death sentence to those who use the rules without turning to the Lord (cf. Rom 3:19-20). In verses 14-15, proud and insolent self-confidence imagines one does not need to fear death and hell. See what the people said in verse 15b and what God said about this in verse 18. ☑The cornerstone in verse 16 is identified as Christ in Romans 9:33 and in 1 Peter 2:6. Romans 10:11 quotes verse 16b, relating it to Christ. Jesus is the foundational stone of the entire redemption "building," but for those who refuse to believe, He is a rock of stumbling. Verses 16-19 present the Messiah as strength and salvation to the believer but judgment and death to the rebellious. Notice in verse 19b that understanding of the message will bring sheer terror – *and that understanding* <u>will</u> *come to each man,* but too late to change eternal destiny (cf. Matt 24:30).⇦

There is a lesson for the church, as well as Israel, in verses 23-29. There is a sequence to farming – plowing, planting, harvesting, processing – and the result is food. Some of us are like a farmer who keeps on plowing – and plowing – but doesn't plant, so gets no harvest. God intends us to be fruitful and progress along the way to maturity, bringing fruit, sheaves, and a harvest! Anything less runs the risk of being sham!

PROVERBS 7:1-5   There is a practical and foolproof (as long as we apply it) way to avoid illicit sexual involvement. Learn God's Word, obey God's Word, and keep reminding yourself of the truth (vv. 1-2). Do whatever is necessary to remember these principles (v. 3). Develop a kinship with wisdom and understanding (the message of the Bible, v. 4). This wisdom and understanding will be the protection needed for prudent living (v. 5).

AUGUST 26

MATTHEW 18:15-35   Guidelines for conflict among believers are outlined in verses 15-20. The key is direct and honest communication, first one-on-one, then with others if the matter cannot be settled alone. What Jesus outlines is a stepwise solution, including the entire congregation if necessary. Ultimately, exclusion from the fellowship is required if all else fails and the offense is clear.

The authority of the church in such matters is the meaning of verse 18. As the congregation looks to the Lord for guidance, Jesus promises to give it.

In the Parable of the Unmerciful Servant (vv. 21-35), ponder the meaning of the story and, in particular, the conclusion in verse 35. We know that forgiveness from the Lord is available for the asking, based on God's grace. 1 John 1:9 is biblical truth! The price for sin has been paid (1 Peter 1:18-19). But Matthew 18:35 and 6:14-15 are also true. Both of these references place a condition on God's forgiveness of us – our free forgiveness of others. Ephesians 4:32 fits well with this principle. 1 John 1:9, therefore, needs to be read with Matthew 6:14-15 in mind. If you have unfinished accounts that you need to settle, do it now!

ISAIAH 29-30   In Chapter 29 the focus of the prophecy turns to Judah and in particular Jerusalem (Ariel). The people observed a form of worship (the cycle of festivals in verse 1, verbal honor to the Lord in verse 13). However, this was form only. As a result, the people had a blindness and spiritual stupor (vv. 9-10).

The urgent lesson is that religious forms, by themselves, are abhorrent to God. At every step along the path of increased biblical knowledge or spiritual insight that God gives us, we must apply it if we are to grow. Further, there seems to be no middle ground. Unless we do apply it, the added knowledge or insight indicts us.

☑The Lord's deliverance for the nation in verses 5-8 reaches beyond the situation during Isaiah's day to the great deliverance of God's people when His judgment comes on the nations. At that time the Messiah will be the mighty deliverer as the nations attack God's people (cf. Zech 9:14ff.; 14:1ff.; Joel 3:14-16).⇦   The people's rejection of the Lord is addressed in Chapter 30. Instead of trusting God, the nation looked to Egypt for military help. But even more significant, they didn't want God's message (vv. 10-11). "Don't give us the truth, give us what we want to hear!" God replied to that attitude in verses 12-13. There still was a way open to them in verse 15. Repent. Trust God.

☑Again, the focus turns to the future when the Lord will return to judge the wicked and restore His people (29:18-24; 30:19-33). Compare 30:26 with Revelation 16:8-9, and verses 25-28 with Luke 21:25-28. Comparing these scriptures, it is clear that the coming judgment presented in Isaiah 30 is related to the coming of the Lord. A dramatic vision of this event is in Revelation 19:11-16.⇦

PROVERBS 7:6-27   As you read the account of the youth in verses 6-23, consider the fact that sexual attraction and drive is strongest in the young man between 16 and 20 years of age. It is a time when judgment is not fully developed (v. 7). During this time, at least for the young man, seduction is a real hazard. Add to this the elements in our society that push young people, both young men and women, to early and illicit sexual involvement. The lie is that casual sexual involvement is a perfectly normal part of growing up. The media touts this lie day and night. *The truth is that it is physically dangerous and personally devastating.* It can create lasting emotional scars. Pray for your children! Pray for the young people in your church! Encourage this application of the Word of God (vv. 1-4) in their lives at an early age. As families and as a church, we must do all that we can to build the Word of God into life when it is desperately needed.

AUGUST 27

MATTHEW 19:1-15   As you read verses 1-12, consider what Jesus said in Matthew 5:27-32. Then look at the disciples' response in 19:10. Their conclusion tells us about society in Jesus' day. Without question, Jesus was upgrading their view of God's standard of marriage.

In the world historically, children counted for little. Until recently, children were legally exploited for economic reasons. Today, children are still neglected, abused, ignored, and exploited. Note how Jesus treated children. Children counted with Jesus (vv. 13-15).

As Christian families, and as a church, we have the opportunity to treat children differently. Children are God's concern, and we owe them kindness, provision for needs, a solid preparation for adulthood, and most important, the opportunity to know Christ as Savior.

ISAIAH 31-32   Isaiah 31 was written during the threat of Assyria to Judah and Jerusalem (cf. 2 Kings 18:13-37; 2 Chron 32:9-21; Isa 36-37). In this crisis, Judah turned to Egypt for military help (cf. Isa 30:1-5). It was a mistake. This is the message from the Lord (vv. 1-3). It is the Lord Himself who would deliver the nation (vv. 4-5). The victory over the Assyrians would be accomplished without military power and with the Assyrians in panic (vv. 8-9). (We will see this fulfilled in Chapters 38-39.) Note the call for repentance in verses 6-7. God is graciously calling the people to trust Him rather than turn to an unreliable Egypt.

The present and future of Judah are the subject of Chapter 32. The situation at Isaiah's time is described in verses 6-14, while the new order is described in verses 1-5, 15-20. Particularly note the description of the people in Isaiah's day in verses 6-8 and God's warning in verses 9-14. Wickedness and complacency would bring God's discipline. ☑The contrast of the new order is striking (vv. 14-20). Righteousness, justice, peace, quietness, and confidence – the time of the Messiah's reign! *Be prepared for the coming of Christ!* ⇦

PROVERBS 8:1-11   This chapter is written as though wisdom is speaking. It is "wisdom personified." Look for the characteristics of God's wisdom. This wisdom is open to all (v. 4). Those who are not naturally quick or bright (from the world's perspective) will profit from it (v. 5). God's wisdom always seeks truth and speaks truth (vv. 6-7). It is worth more than any amount of money (v. 10), more than anything else we could desire (v. 11).

Think again about the implications of verse 5, and review 1:1-7. God's wisdom, found in the Scriptures, helps us understand our relation to God and helps us to react prudently and wisely to the world's temptations. In contrast to academic disciplines, you do not need a certain I.Q. to participate in this program. Those with no academic degrees and those with the highest degrees profit alike! *How can we afford to neglect the Scriptures?*

AUGUST 28

MATTHEW 19:16-30   The key to understanding Jesus' conversation with the rich young man is in Matthew 6:19-21. Especially note 6:21. Even though he lived carefully, it became obvious where the young man's treasure was.

Note what a tight grip possessions have on people (vv. 23-24). It takes the work of God to free us to a godly perspective (v. 26), which lets us love and serve God primarily, while holding possessions with an open hand. Referring once again to Jesus' words in Matthew 6:24, the question is, "Whom or what are you working for?" What is it that "turns your crank?" Is your relationship with the Lord Jesus the one that is most important?

This cuts through appearances to the heart. As the Lord evaluates the hearts of His people, there will be some surprises when we enter the kingdom (vv. 28-30)! ↄAlso note that Jesus said that, at the consummation of the age, He would sit as a ruler in the heavens (v. 28).ↄ

ISAIAH 33   Chapter 33 was probably written when Assyria was threatening Jerusalem, as recorded in 2 Kings 18-19, 2 Chronicles 32, and Isaiah 36-37. Verse 1 probably speaks of Sennacherib, king of Assyria.

The reality of the crisis is evident in verses 7-9. The countryside had already been conquered, and the army was at the wall of Jerusalem. The prayer of the people is recounted in verses 2-4 and Isaiah's message in verses 5-6. God is great. Trust and fear Him! This will be the answer to danger. Pause to think about the truth of verses 5-6 for your life.

Compare verses 14-16 with Psalm 15. God's person chooses God's way! And further, he receives God's blessing. Faith in the Old Testament is always tied to behavior (cf. John 14: 23-24)!

There is probably a double meaning in verses 17-24. On one level it describes the deliverance from the threat of Sennacherib and the Assyrian "ship of state" in verse 23. ☑The passage also seems to anticipate the reign of the Messiah. The contrast with the former state is dramatic (vv. 18-19, speaking of the officers of Assyria), and the permanent condition of the city and people will be glorious. The permanent peace will stand in contrast to the repeated threats to the nation during its ancient existence.⇦

PROVERBS 8:12-21   In this section, wisdom is speaking in the first person (as in 1:20-33). It is as if the Lord Himself is speaking – telling us about wisdom that is available to those who seek Him. With God's wisdom we can act on knowledge and get a godly result (v. 12). To apply this wisdom is to understand the evil nature of the world and turn away from evil behavior, pride, arrogance, and deceitful speech (not the natural thing for us to do, v. 13). Compare verse 17 with 8:4 and 8:35. *The invitation is open to all, and those who find this wisdom find salvation.*

AUGUST 29

MATTHEW 20:1-16   Compare Matthew 19:30 with 20:16. The Parable of the Workers illustrated Jesus' lesson after the rich young man turned away from Him. The point is, how God looks at men's hearts is different from how we do. We tend to be much infected with the world's view of things: money, power, influence. The final tally will include some definite surprises.

How can we have a kingdom view? *First* of all, keep working on biblical priorities. *Second,* evaluate your motives and actions by biblical standards and not by comparing yourself with others (this was the reason for the discontent among the workers who put in a full day's labor). *Third,* take literally the example of Jesus and his teaching about servanthood. This must be a disciplined decision for it goes against everything society teaches. It is, however, God's way!

ISAIAH 34-35   Chapters 34-35 together describe God's purpose in judgment and salvation. The message of Chapter 34 is to the nations of the world. ☑The language must refer to the "Day of the Lord." That this will be truly cataclysmic is evident in verse 4, (similar in language to Matt 24:29, Mark 13:24-25 and 2 Peter 3:10; cf. Heb 1:11-12 where the author relates these events to the Lord Jesus). Although Edom is prominent in the chapter, that country's fate is the prototype of what is coming to the whole world.

Isaiah 35 is a specific prophecy of the condition of the world subsequent to the coming of Christ as Messiah and during His reign. It will be a time of healing for nature (vv. 1-2, 7), men (vv. 3-6a), and society (vv. 8-10). Think of the singing and the everlasting joy (v. 10). What a day that will be!⇦

PROVERBS 8:22-36   Wisdom was at the very heart of God's creation. This wisdom of God is eternal (vv. 22-26), existing before any part of our world or universe was created. The beauty of the heavens, the seas, and the mountains are the result of this wisdom (vv. 27-31). *SO: Pay attention to this jewel that God is offering to all who will listen.* The alternative is the way of death, and there are only two choices (vv. 32-36).

AUGUST 30

MATTHEW 20:17-34   There was no lack of opportunity for Jesus to teach about the contrast between the kingdom and the world. The request of James and John's mother gave Jesus a chance to expand on what He had taught immediately before.

In the world, power is what counts (v. 25). In the kingdom, service and servanthood are what count (vv. 26-27), and Jesus Himself is the model and example (v. 28). How is this working out in your own life? Jesus does not present this as an option – it is a principle of life in the kingdom. ➲Note that Jesus said He would "give His life as a ransom..." (v. 28b). Jesus was declaring that He was indeed God's Son, the Redeemer.☾

➲It is significant that when the two blind men called to Jesus with the hope of receiving their sight (vv. 29-34), they called to Him as the Son of David – which means they recognized Him as the Messiah (vv. 30-31). If this had not been the case, as a person of truth and integrity, Jesus would have corrected them. Instead, Jesus healed them.☾

2 KINGS 18, ISAIAH 36   Hezekiah was the son of Ahaz (the message of Isaiah 7 was directed to Ahaz). Although Ahaz was an ungodly man, Hezekiah served the Lord and had great influence for good in Judah. Review 2 Chronicles 29-31. When he ascended the throne, he quickly set about reestablishing the worship of God. He invited those in Israel (the Northern Kingdom) to join Judah in worshiping the true God. They observed the Passover for the first time in many years and destroyed the altars used in pagan worship. Hezekiah was godly and led the people in the same direction (2 Chron 31:21).

It was during Hezekiah's reign that Israel fell to Assyria (2 Kings 17; 18:9-12). Seven years later, Sennacherib, king of Assyria set out to add Judah to his list of nations conquered (2 Kings 18:13ff.). Although Hezekiah attempted to appease Sennacherib with gold and silver, which Sennacherib accepted, Assyria continued with the plan of taking Judah and Jerusalem. When he came to the gates of the capital, the rest of the country had already fallen (18:13-16).

This was the setting for the confrontation that Sennacherib's officers had with the officials of Judah from the wall of Jerusalem (18:17ff.; Isa 36:4-20). The field commander read Sennacherib's letter to the people and then added his own commentary on the futility of attempting to resist the army of Assyria. Note how both the letter and the further remarks by the Assyrian officers disparage the Lord and His ability to help the people. Sennacherib even claimed that the Lord had sent him (2 Kings 18:25). Note also the offer that Assyria made to the people: Surrender to Assyria and live; you may stay where you are until I come and take you to a different land (18:31-32, Isa 36:16-17). This was a "gracious" offer of deportation. The situation was desperate as the officials of Judah took the message to King Hezekiah.

PROVERBS 9:1-9 The invitation to participate in the wisdom of God is presented here as a summons to a carefully prepared dinner. It is open to all who will listen, and the benefits are understanding and judgment. The condition: Leave your simple ways. The ultimate benefit: besides the gift of understanding and good judgment, life!

Contrast the one who responds to the invitation with the ungodly. No one gets thanks for correcting someone who is set in his ways (vv. 7-8a). A wise person, however, will not only accept the correction when it is needed but will love the one who gives the admonition.

AUGUST 31

MATTHEW 21:1-22 ☑As the final week of Jesus' ministry began, Scripture was fulfilled as Jesus entered Jerusalem (cf. Zech 9:9) and the crowds acclaimed Him as the Messiah (cf. Ps 118:26).⇦ The gospel account of this final week of Jesus' life takes us from the "high" of Matthew 21 to the "low" of the crucifixion and then to the victory of the resurrection. Certainly, one of the obvious lessons is that the crowds are an unreliable index of what is happening. The machinations of the leaders were taking place behind the scenes and would become evident later in the week.

As we read the account of Jesus' arrest, trial, and crucifixion, observing the power of evil and the consummate unfairness of the proceedings, it is vital to keep in perspective the eternal plan of God.

Acts 2:22-24, Acts 4:27-28, and 1 Corinthians 2:7-10 are significant in this regard. God was at work. The result was salvation for all who believe!

<u>2 KINGS 19, ISAIAH 37</u> From Hezekiah's point of view, this was a major crisis! Hezekiah called on the Lord both in prayer and by consulting Isaiah the prophet. Isaiah gave the king encouragement from the Lord (Isa 37:5-7), but Hezekiah received a further threatening letter from the field commander of Assyria.

Follow the steps that Hezekiah took when he received this letter. His response should be a model for us as individuals and for any country in danger. He prayed specifically about the threats from the king of Assyria and did so publicly (Isa 37:15-20). He had the right perspective: Only God can deliver (vv. 18-20). He also understood the implications of Assyria's threats (God's name was at risk) and had the right motive (v. 20). Follow God's response (vv. 22-35), God's victory (vv. 36-37), and God's final disposition of Sennacherib (v. 38).

If you can reconstruct the situation in your mind and feel the tension in the city, Hezekiah's actions are truly that of a godly man. He understood where the answer would lie, and he understood the issues. Think about his actions in relation to problems that you may face. We do best to have a plan so that panic and rash actions don't carry the day when we should be thinking and acting from faith.

<u>PROVERBS 9:10-18</u> The message and result of applying wisdom (knowing God) continues. As you read this section, review verses 1-9. The clear message of verses 10-12 is that wisdom is linked to our relationship with the Lord. The contrast is between wisdom (God's way) and folly (the world's method).

Listen to the claims of each; then make your choice. The way of wisdom offers life and understanding (v. 6). It is the way of continued learning (v. 9). It is the way of knowing God and understanding Him (v. 10). It is the way of longer life (v. 11).

Now listen to the claims of folly. There is no trouble hearing for her call is loud (v. 13). It is the way of the "quick buck" and unjust gain (v. 17). It is the way of the stolen tryst, and it is the way of death (vv. 17-18).

Listen to the claims, and make your choice. May God help us see past the allure and the glitter to evaluate the substance of each, and after deciding, keep our vision clear!

September

Bible Reading Schedule
And Notes

❧

*Open my eyes that I may see wonderful things
in your law. Psalm 119:18*

DISCOVERING THE BIBLE
READING SCHEDULE
SEPTEMBER

1	Matthew 21:23-46	2 Kings 20	Proverbs 10:1-9
2	Matthew 22:1-22	Isaiah 38-39	Proverbs 10:10-14
3	Matthew 22: 23-46	Isaiah 40	Proverbs 10:15-21
4	Matthew 23	Isaiah 41	Proverbs 10:22-27
5	Matthew 24:1-28	Isaiah 42	Proverbs 10:28-32
6	Matthew 24:29-51	Isaiah 43	Proverbs 11:1-8
7	Matthew 25:1-30	Isaiah 44	Proverbs 11:9-16
8	Matthew 25:31-46	Isaiah 45	Proverbs 11:17-21
9	Matthew 26:1-35	Isaiah 46-47	Proverbs 11:22-31
10	Matthew 26:36-75	Isaiah 48	Proverbs 12:1-7
11	Matthew 27:1-31	Isaiah 49	Proverbs 12:8-14
12	Matthew 27:32-66	Isaiah 50	Proverbs 12:15-21
13	Matthew 28	Isaiah 51-52:12	Proverbs 12:22-28
14	Galatians 1	Isaiah 52:13-53:12	Proverbs 13:1-6
15	Galatians 2	Isaiah 54	Proverbs 13:7-13
16	Galatians 3:1-14	Isaiah 55	Proverbs 13:14-19
17	Galatians 3:15-29	Isaiah 56-57	Proverbs 13:20-25
18	Galatians 4	Isaiah 58	Proverbs 14:1-9
19	Galatians 5:1-12	Isaiah 59	Proverbs 14:10-18
20	Galatians 5:13-26	Isaiah 60	Proverbs 14:19-26
21	Galatians 6	Isaiah 61	Proverbs 14:27-35
22	Ephesians 1:1-14	Isaiah 62-63	Proverbs 15:1-9
23	Ephesians 1:15-23	Isaiah 64-65	Proverbs 15:10-17
24	Ephesians 2:1-10	Isaiah 66	Proverbs 15:18-25
25	Ephesians 2:11-22	Naham 1-2	Proverbs 15:26-33
26	Ephesians 3	Naham 3	Proverbs 16:1-8
27	Ephesians 4:1-16	2 Kings 21, 2 Chron. 33	Proverbs 16:9-17
28	Ephesians 4:17-32	2 Kings 22, 2 Chron. 34	Proverbs 16:18-25
29	Ephesians 5:1-21	2 Kings 23:1-30	Proverbs 16:26-33
30	Ephesians 5:22-33	2 Chronicles 35	Proverbs 17:1-7

SEPTEMBER 1

MATTHEW 21:23-46   When Jesus' authority was questioned (v. 23), He did not answer directly. If Jesus answered that He ministered by the authority of God (which he had already said in many ways), the priests would accuse Him of blasphemy.   Rather, He asked the priests a question that placed them in a difficult position.   Both the priests' question to Jesus and His question to them went to the heart of the matter: the authority by which Jesus and John the Baptist ministered. However, if the religious authorities admitted that John the Baptist was working with God's authority, they would have had to accept the Baptist's assessment of Jesus' identity: the Son of God, the Redeemer (John 1:29).   Thus, they were unwilling to answer Jesus' question, for the people listening firmly believed that John the Baptist was from God.

Instead of answering their question directly, Jesus told two parables, each directed to the religious leaders.

In the Parable of the Two Sons, Jesus pointed out that they were like the son who said he would do the work of the father but didn't. The tax collectors and prostitutes, however, were like the other son who said he would not do the work of the father but did so in the end (they responded to the message of repentance that John the Baptist brought). Read Jesus' message to the priests in verses 31-32.

➲In the Parable of the Tenants, Jesus likened Himself to the son who was killed when he went to the vineyard to represent his father. Note that in verse 42 Jesus tied His parable to a specific reference in Psalm 118:22-23. The meaning was clear to the priests and Pharisees, but they were restrained from moving against Jesus because the people believed He was from God.☾

2 KINGS 20   Hezekiah had an infection that was life-threatening. Isaiah visited the king, telling him that he should put his affairs in order, for he would not recover (v. 1). Hezekiah turned to the Lord in prayer – an interesting prayer, reminding the Lord of his faithful service to the Lord (vv. 2-3). God instructed Isaiah to return to the king and tell him that He would heal him and add fifteen years to his life (vv. 4-11)!

We must learn to ask God for wisdom and help not only in crisis but also when things seem to be going well. Hezekiah suffered from pride (2 Chron 32:24-31; cf. v. 25), and this tripped him when he was visited by envoys from Babylon. Once again Isaiah was sent with a message – this time of impending judgment on Judah, but it would not fall until after Hezekiah's time. If he had turned to the Lord for guidance, he would have passed the Lord's test (2 Chron 32:31).

PROVERBS 10:1-9 Recall that Proverbs 10-29 are the collected sayings of wisdom that Solomon committed to writing. While Chapters 1-9 were organized by subjects, the proverbs in these chapters are, for the most part, "stand-alone" sayings. They reflect the unique and unusual wisdom that God gave Solomon (1 Kings 3:10-12).

It is difficult to "highlight" a chapter of stand-alone proverbs. One way is to look for the character traits that make a difference to God and to other people for good.

Character is shaped in a person's heart and reflects what God has done (or cannot do because of our hardness) in our lives. The New Testament explanation for these Old Testament truths is found in passages that speak to man's condition without God's intervention (for instance, Rom 3:9-18, Eph 2:1-2), and to the fundamental change when God brings new life to us through the work of Christ (as in John 5:24 and Eph 2:4-10).

Is it possible for someone who does not love God to have integrity and concern for others? It is, at least partially. But remember that God is looking at the inner man – the heart – and not how things appear to us. Conversely, do we see only good character in those who love God? We must admit with chagrin that this is not the case and understand that change in the believer is a process as the Holy Spirit applies God's truth to our lives in a progressive fashion.

Remember that these truths in Proverbs, often expressed as stark contrasts, reflect the heart. The ungodly may not seem as bad as the text implies, and the godly person undoubtedly still has traits that concern God. Look, then, at the general truths that the Lord has for us in the Proverbs, consider them, and apply them to your life. These truths are insights that we can use to identify needed changes in our lives. Think and reflect about what you read. Take action on the truth! Some truths that stand out to this writer will be mentioned, but God may speak more clearly to you about others.

Focus on verse 9. The person of integrity walks securely. With the anxiety and uncertainty in the world, what more could anyone want? This must be the greatest gift of all time! Money does not bring real security – there is always the danger of losing what we have. There is limited security in one's employment – if it is to the advantage of an employer, then jobs will be lost. Even in human relationships, things go wrong and people are hurt. But there is security in knowing the Lord.

He is faithful. His promises will not fail. Walk before Him with integrity and faith.

SEPTEMBER 2

MATTHEW 22:1-22 ⊃In the parable of the wedding banquet (vv. 1-14), Jesus spoke about the invitation to the kingdom that had been extended to the Jews. Specifically, this meant God had invited them to the banquet of His Son – the Messiah – and this was not lost to the leaders. Notice that in verses 5-6 the wicked men who refused the king's invitation killed the envoys who had invited the king's subjects to the wedding (cf. Matt 8:8-12). Because of their rejection, others were invited. ⊂

One man, however, was not allowed to stay for the banquet – and, in fact, was cast out "into the darkness where there will be weeping and gnashing of teeth." The proper wedding clothes (which the man lacked) illustrate the proper spiritual attire that we need to come before God. We need forgiveness and cleansing – and that righteousness comes through Jesus (cf. 1 Cor 1:30).

ISAIAH 38-39 As Hezekiah became ill and received word from the Lord that he would die, he again turned to the Lord (Ch. 38). God graciously extended his life and provided a miraculous sign for confirmation.

The account of the visit of the envoys from Babylon to Hezekiah in Isaiah 39 is also recorded in 2 Kings 20 and 2 Chronicles 32. After the Lord healed Hezekiah (2 Chron 32:24-25), he demonstrated his pride by exhibiting all of his treasures to the envoys (cf. 38:15). There may have been a political reason for the visit from Babylon, since Babylon was also throwing off the Assyrian yoke. Hezekiah may have been showing the Babylonians that he had something to offer in an alliance against Assyria. If this were the case, he should have known that God desired him and the nation to trust Him and Him alone!

PROVERBS 10:10-14 A proverb often contrasts one behavior or characteristic with another, as in verses 11-14. As you read, note the result of devious and violent behavior and contrast it with the heart of the one who walks with the Lord.

Think about the implication of these verses as the offerings of the media reflect our society. This passage should help us understand that the steady diet of devious behavior, violence, and dissension is not what God desires in us or in society. This should, in turn, make us think about what we watch, listen to, and read.

SEPTEMBER 3

MATTHEW 22:23-46 Ponder verses 34-40 in relation to your life. To love God with all of your heart, soul, and mind is a consuming passion that shapes your worldview – how you see other people (through God's eyes), your vocation (representing the Lord in the world), and your experiences (God's grace and love in your life). Jesus' words in verse 37 are quoted from Deuteronomy 6:5, and the verses that follow (Deut 6:6-9) emphasize the place that God and His Word deserve in our lives. Compare these verses with Joshua 1:7-9 and the man described in Psalm 1:1-3. Follow hard after God!

Is it possible to overdose on the Bible? Of course, if we don't apply what we read systematically under the Holy Spirit. If we apply it, how can we have too much of God?

Consider the second command that Jesus quoted (cf. Lev 19:18). If we love our neighbor as ourselves, we will see that his needs are met. Our love for ourselves sees to it that we have three meals a day and clothes to wear. This is a practical love that reaches out to others in their need.

⊃Jesus again used the Scriptures to demonstrate that the Messiah, the son of David, would be more than merely a human descendant of David (Ps 110:1). By using this reference (accepted as messianic), Jesus pointed out that His affirmation that He was God's Son and the Messiah (cf. Luke 19:38-40) was reasonable in light of the many ways He had acted with God's authority.⊂

ISAIAH 40 The remaining twenty-seven chapters of Isaiah are divided into three nine-chapter sections. Chapters 40-48 tell of the sovereign God in His creation, revelation, and promise. Chapters 49-57 are about the Servant of the Lord, the Messiah. The remaining chapters, 58-66, speak of the last times, the work of the Holy Spirit, and God as Judge and Savior. Note that the last verse of each of the first two sections (48:22, 57:21) is identical.

Is there hope for God's people? Indeed there is! Hope for Israel and for all who place their faith in the living God. As you read 40:1-11, note the comfort that comes from understanding God's purpose in bringing salvation, and the Lord's tenderness in caring for His own. ☑Verses 3-5 promise the first coming of Jesus in the ministry of John the Baptist (cf. Matt 3:3; Mark 1:3; Luke 3:4-5; John 1:23) and the second coming of Christ, when the entire world will witness His power and glory (v. 5; cf. Luke 3:6).⇦ In spite of man's frailty (vv. 6-8a), the truth of God is forever (v. 8b), and God will care for His own (vv. 9-11).

Look in verses 12-31 for the many ways in which God is presented as the Sovereign Lord of the universe. This is emphasized with five rhetorical questions in verses 12-14 and five illustrations in verses 15-17. God is greater than idols (v. 18ff.). God is sovereign in the affairs of men (vv. 21-24). God is the creator (v. 26a). God sustains the universe (v. 26b). And God gives strength to those who love and trust Him (vv. 29-31).

Pause as you read this chapter to appreciate its magnificent beauty. It presents God in His power and glory, but also as the God who is deeply involved in the lives of His people.

PROVERBS 10:15-21   Pay attention when the discipline of correction comes (v. 17). Not only does it make a difference in your own life, it spills over into the lives of others. Example is powerful. If we are into wrong attitudes or actions, it will make a difference in others' lives as well (v. 17b).

The Proverbs often emphasize the tongue – what we say. Follow the truths in verses 18-21, especially verse 19. It is good to listen carefully and to speak with thought and discretion. Compare these verses with Ephesians 4:29-30 and James 3:1-12. Our speech can be a blessing to those around us (vv. 20a, 21a).

SEPTEMBER 4

MATTHEW 23   Jesus saw hypocrisy in the lives and teaching of the religious leaders. *The shades of hypocrisy are so subtle and seductive that only God's grace can deliver us.* Don't assume that you and I are different from those Jesus addressed! Read carefully what Jesus said.

Verses 1-12 introduce the chapter and are followed with seven "woes" for the hypocrisy in the lives of the religious leaders. Compare verse 5 with Matthew 6:1 – where Jesus told His disciples not to do good things to be seen by men. Compare verses 8-12 with 20:25-28. Jesus cautioned against worldly thinking – the idea of position and the use of terms that describe position and power. Compare verse 16 with Matthew 5:33-37. Jesus said, "Simply let your 'yes' be 'yes' and your 'no,' 'no'; anything beyond this comes from the evil one." Compare verses 23-24 with Matthew 5:17-20. Jesus affirmed the true observance of the law. He spoke about the sin of giving a false impression of spirituality in verses 23-28. *Remember: Only God's grace can deliver us from these sins!* Allow Jesus' lessons to get into your thinking patterns and behavior.

⊃As Jesus mourned over the unbelief and hardness of the people of Jerusalem (vv. 37-39), He again affirmed that these very people would recognize Him as the Messiah (v. 39; cf. Ps 118:26).⊂

ISAIAH 41   →This portion tells of God's work in, and on behalf, of Israel. This extends from Abraham (v. 8), to the planting of God's people in the land (v. 9), to the blessing of the land itself (vv. 18-19). Take note of the assurance to Israel that God has not forsaken them and of His tender mercy in restoration.←

God challenges all who trust in idols to test their power (vv. 21-24). Have them tell the past (v. 22) or the future (v. 23) *or at least do something* (v. 23)! The idols are worthless, and those who trust them are detestable (v. 24).

PROVERBS 10:22-27   What is your delight? Does evil conduct, as a viewer or as a participant, give you pleasure? Check verse 23 for the Lord's commentary on evil conduct. Be careful what you watch and what you do.

Trouble happens. It can be a stepping stone to maturity and deep faith, or it can sweep you away (v. 25, see also 1 Peter 1:6-7). How you respond to trouble will give you a reading on your own faith! Remember that the Lord will allow nothing to come to you that you cannot handle (1 Cor 10:13). It is wise to think ahead and plan how you will trust God in various circumstances.

SEPTEMBER 5

MATTHEW 24:1-28   Jesus spoke about the end times in response to questions from the disciples. As you read this chapter, it is impossible not to be in awe of what is to come. People will be deceived by false teaching (vv. 4-5). Many will be persecuted (v. 9), and some will turn from the truth because of it (vv. 10, 12). Compare these words of Jesus with 2 Timothy 3:1-5. There will be a form of religion even in a time of great ungodliness. There will be little tolerance, however, for the teaching that Jesus is the very Son of God – the only way of salvation. Note the need for perseverance in the face of this opposition (vv. 12-13).

It is quite possible, even probable, that we are approaching this period now. How can we insure that we are prepared to face the deceptions and dangers of such a time? There are steps that we can take. Learn your Bible, and pray for discernment to understand what is false in society. Learn to obey what you know to be truth. Jesus will then reveal Himself to you progressively (John 14:21). Pray for God's protection. John 10:27-29 says it well. There is safety in the Savior's hand!

ISAIAH 42   Chapter 42 speaks of the Servant of the Lord. Messiah (the perfect servant) is described in verses 1-17. Between verses 17 and 18 there is a change, and in verses 18-25 Israel is called God's servant (the imperfect servant).

☑Follow the character and the characteristics of the Messiah. He will have the Spirit of God and will bring justice to the earth (v. 1). His work will be done quietly (v. 2). He will deal gently with the wounded (v. 3). He will carry out the Lord's work with faithfulness and persistence, accomplishing all of God's objectives for the entire earth (vv. 3b-4). All of these qualities are attributed to Jesus by Matthew (cf. Matt. 12:15-21). Note the ministry of the servant in verses 6-7. Think about how these characteristics match the ministry of the Lord Jesus. Note that some of this ministry concerns the first advent, while some will come with the second advent (universal justice in the world). ⇦

In contrast, Israel was an imperfect instrument in the Lord's hand (vv. 18-22). Israel was deaf to the Lord's message and blind to the nature of the world and God's power (v. 20). As a result, God's people felt His discipline – but even then they did not understand (vv. 23-25).

PROVERBS 10:28-32   What would most people give for real joy? Instead, most people's hopes are frustrated (v. 28). The only fulfillment is in knowing the Lord. That is reality. We were created with that in mind. Joy is what the Lord God has designed for His children; this is a state of being, not an emotion. It rides above the circumstances of the day because it is rooted in a genuine relationship with the living God. Choose to follow the Lord with all of your heart, and know that joy.

SEPTEMBER 6

MATTHEW 24:29-51   ➲After the terrible distress in the world that Jesus outlined (vv. 21-24), He spoke of His coming again in power and glory (vv. 29-31). When He comes, it will cause great sorrow for those who have been deceived (it will then be too late to turn to the Lord). *It will be the moment when all will understand the truth about Jesus, God's Son (v. 30).* (See also Isa 26:21, Isa 29:5b-6, Rev 1:7.) At this time, Jesus will gather those who know Him to be with Him (v. 31). Note Jesus' statement that His words (as God's Son) will never pass away (v. 35)!◖ Most people in the world will be totally unprepared for this event and the judgment that will follow. Think of the despair that will come with this understanding. How does this change your attitude toward the unsaved around you?

In verses 36-51, note how Jesus tells His hearers to be prepared, be alert, and be ready for what is coming.

ISAIAH 43   This portion speaks to Israel both in comfort and in accusation. The promises to Israel are listed in verses 1-13. God's strength will protect (v. 2). ☑The promise of the re-gathering of Israel from the nations of the world (after dispersion) is in verses 5-8. God's sovereign might is declared in verses 10b-13. ⇦

Judgment on Babylon is the theme of verses 14-15. God's historical deliverance from Egypt is remembered (vv. 16-17); on that basis God called the nation to trust Him for the future (vv. 18-21). But instead, and tragically, the nation had not trusted God. They had turned to sinful practices (vv. 22-24). God told them to review the evidence of His goodness (vv. 25-26) and said they would face disgrace because of their unfaithfulness (v. 28).

Think of how this chapter applies to our lives. Think of how God has been faithful in protection and provision. Note that God calls on His people to remember the goodness of the past (vv. 16-17) and to trust Him for the present and the future (vv. 18-19).

PROVERBS 11:1-8   Notice God's concern with truth (v. 1),   the importance of integrity (v. 3), and the "real gold" that will deliver us from judgment (vv. 4, 6).

Look at verse 4. Note especially that "righteousness delivers from death." Remember that Abraham received the gift of righteousness by faith (Gen 15:6). Those who turn to God in integrity and obedience (an expression of faith) walk in righteousness.

This righteousness that delivers from death (v. 4b) is the gift of God. It is given to those of faith (just as in Abraham) based on the death of the Lord Jesus (Rom 3:21-24). The Holy Spirit helps each believer live in righteousness – following and obeying Christ (1 John 2:3-6). This brings protection in the day of wrath. Review Matthew 24:30-31 from today's reading. Jesus is coming again in power and glory. He will gather the believers, but then wrath will come to the world. *Be sure that you are among the believers!*

SEPTEMBER 7

MATTHEW 25:1-30   Chapters 24 and 25 offer five tests of salvation. These are unique as they are brought together in one section of the book and are the direct teaching of Jesus.

1. Matthew 24:9-14. The test of true salvation is fidelity to God in the face of opposition and wickedness. *Mark the fact that the love of most will grow cold!*

2. Matthew 24:36-51. The test of true salvation is faithfulness to the task God gives us. Note that everything is "life as usual" when the master returns (vv. 37-39). Look especially at verses 45-51.

3. Matthew 25:1-13. The test of true salvation is being prepared for the coming of the bridegroom (Christ). Note here that while all of the

virgins were dressed for the event (appearing ready), five of the waiting virgins were unprepared.

4. Matthew 25:14-30. The test of true salvation is fruitfulness, using our resources to please God and benefit the kingdom.

5. Matthew 25:31-46. The test of true salvation is servanthood and mercy.

These qualities are not optional for the Christian. Each is present in some degree if we know Christ. But God, through the Holy Spirit, helps with areas that are deficient. Note that in the case of servanthood and mercy, the persons who passed the test were unaware of it (vv. 34-40)! If you see areas that need help in your life, make this a matter of prayer. God has promised to bring us to maturity as we look to Him in faith and obedience.

ISAIAH 44 →The establishment of Israel and the promise of blessing is presented in verses 1-5. This is a sovereign act of the Lord God.←

Contrast God (vv. 6-8) with idols (vv. 9-20). Look at the description of how an idol is made and the ludicrous position of the man who worships it. It's ludicrous on the surface because it is so illogical. But it is also tragic because it ends in infamy and terror (vv. 9-11, 20). So who in his right mind would choose an idol? Yet so many – even today – do choose idols.

→The last portion of the chapter (v. 24ff.) looks forward to the return of Israel after the exile in Babylon. Cyrus (king of Persia) is mentioned by name over three hundred years before he was in power (v. 28; cf. Ezra 1:1-4)! This has led some to conclude that Isaiah could not have written this. Is God big enough to see into the future and share His plan with Israel before it happened? Think about it.←

PROVERBS 11:9-16 Nations need righteous men and women (vv. 10-11, 14). When enough people demand truth and justice, it will inevitably make a difference. The opposite is also true. The wicked can destroy a city and bring a nation to its knees (vv. 11, 14). More than the political process is at work when righteous people make a difference. A righteous life is attractive and brings others into the camp of believers. Prayer is the quiet ministry that God uses to effect change. When these elements are present, the righteous voice in the political process is effective.

SEPTEMBER 8

MATTHEW 25:31-46 The Parable of the Sheep and Goats has a message for each of us. An unequivocal test of our salvation is whether we exhibit servanthood and mercy. Especially note that these qualities are required in the common ways we meet needs and ease suffering. God sees our responses to these needs!

➲Note Jesus' assertion that He will come in glory and will separate those who know Him from those who don't (vv. 31-33).☾

ISAIAH 45 →Even though Cyrus did not acknowledge God (vv. 4-5), God planned to use this ruler for His divine purposes. That is the theme and subject of this chapter. God will give him power (vv. 1-5, 13) – *in order to do His bidding* (vv. 9-13).← How could this be? Because there is no other God (vv. 14b, 18b, 21b)! *Further, our God has the ability to declare Himself before the fact* (vv. 19-21). This same God of sovereign power will save all who turn to Him (v. 22), and those who do not respond will bow the knee at God's command (vv. 23-24). Note that Philippians 2:10 and Romans 14:11 relate the mandatory worship in this passage to bowing the knee to Christ. Choose to worship Him now!

PROVERBS 11:17-21 Each of these verses contains a contrast between those who follow the Lord and those who follow their own way. Think about the self-destructive ways of the ungodly (v. 17). Compare verse 18b with verse 30b. Living for the Lord – living His agenda – is worth everything! Add to this verse 19, and review Psalm 15. Personal righteousness is very practical. Rejoice in the truth of verse 21 and in the life that God has given through Jesus, His death, and His resurrection.

SEPTEMBER 9

MATTHEW 26:1-35 With the Passover only two days away, Jesus explicitly told His disciples that He would be crucified (v. 2). At the same time, the chief priests and the elders gathered to plot the murder of Jesus (vv. 3-4). Events were rapidly focusing on the death of Jesus, whom the religious leaders saw as a threat to their authority.

Events, however, were not out of control. ☑Jesus knew exactly what was transpiring in God's plan. He understood the timetable (John 10:14-18; John 12:27). As Peter preached to the crowds in Jerusalem a few weeks later, he pointed out that through the death and resurrection of Jesus, God had fulfilled the Old Testament prophecies of redemption (Acts 3:18). Jesus was to become the heavenly Passover Lamb – the fulfillment of the prototype in Exodus 12.⇦

Imagine yourself in the shoes of the disciples as you read these verses. Look carefully at the people who took part in the unfolding events. Simon the Leper was the last to host Jesus in a home (v. 6). An unnamed woman anointed Him with perfume – an act of love (vv. 7-9). Judas was making wicked arrangements to betray Jesus (vv. 14-16). As the disciples gathered with Jesus, He instituted the memorial supper –

the last time He would eat with the disciples (vv. 17-30). Finally, listen to Peter say he would never deny his Lord (vv. 31-35).

ISAIAH 46-47   Bel and Nebo (46:1) were "gods" of the Babylonians. Review how they were made (vv. 6-7), and compare them with the living God (vv. 8-13). Here is God – who not only created and sustains the universe but also makes known the end from the beginning through His prophets (v. 10). →God's will and purpose is to bring righteousness and salvation to His people, and He will make it a reality (vv. 12-13)!←

God's judgment on pagan Babylon is the subject of Chapter 47. This powerful near-eastern people believed, in their arrogance, that nothing could touch them (vv. 7, 8, 10). But in their lack of mercy (v. 6b), pride (v. 7), arrogance (v. 8), witchcraft (v. 9b), wickedness (v. 10), and the ultimate arrogance of taking the place of God (v. 10), they didn't reckon with the true and living God. As we read Daniel, we will see that the message did come to them, and for a time they acknowledged God, but it didn't last. God's judgment would come! Compare this chapter with Revelation 18 for not only does this apply to the ancient nation but to the whole world at the time of Christ's second coming!

PROVERBS 11:22-31   Consider verse 22. Outward beauty with the character of a pig doesn't leave one with much. In the end, the gold ring will be lost, and then *all* one has is the pig! (Proverbs uses humor to portray truth.)

The principle of generosity is addressed in verses 24-26, 28. Holding on to what we have will not bring the Lord's blessing. Compare verse 24 with 2 Corinthians 9:8, and note the principle in verse 25. Finally, remember the truth of verse 28. The idol of money will never bring inner peace and will ultimately lead to death! It is absolutely the wrong place to put your faith.

SEPTEMBER 10

MATTHEW 26:36-75   In reading again the account of the betrayal, arrest, and trial of Jesus, understand that not everything in this world is fair! It wasn't in Jesus' life, and it won't be in yours and mine. Jesus said so (Matt 24:9). Further, the closest of friends may disappoint us (for example, Peter, in this chapter). The important thing when difficulty comes is that we are doing what the Lord wants us to do. Notice that Jesus was doing exactly what the Father wanted, yet He was overwhelmed with sorrow (v. 38). →To put things in perspective, God used the unfairness, the disappointment, and the sorrow to accomplish His purpose.← As God's people, our comfort is not paramount. The priorities of the kingdom are!

☑Note especially verse 56. Jesus said that these events were exactly those that would fulfill the Promise of the prophets!⇦ ➲Note Jesus' assertion to the religious leaders that He was indeed the Messiah and that they personally would see Him in the future when He came in glory (vv. 63-64)!☾

ISAIAH 48   Babylon's idols would not – could not – protect them from God's judgment. In contrast the Lord God is living, involved in the lives of His people, and is powerful to act. He gives fair and ample warning to the Israelites in Chapter 48. Take care. God warns – but He will also act (v. 3). God says He knows well their character and their sin (v. 8), and He has worked to bring them to obedience, but without result. Read in verses 17-19 how God had worked in grace with the Israelites. Consider the contrast between what could have been and what would be (captivity). But just as the Lord provided water from the rock in the desert (v. 21), He will also deliver Israel.

PROVERBS 12:1-7   As you read verse 1, think about what it says about discipline. Our age is one of self-fulfillment: "Follow your heart in doing what brings enjoyment in activity and relationships." Discipline, whether doing what it takes to master a subject (like the Bible), follow Christ, or defer pleasure, is in short supply in the world. In contrast, here the Lord encourages discipline that helps us to live properly and well, and to be grateful for correction.

Take note of the principle in verse 3. There is no way that wickedness will end in permanent blessing! Conversely, we may take refuge in the knowledge that righteous living will protect us.

SEPTEMBER 11

MATTHEW 27:1-31   Focus on Judas's despair (vv. 3-5) – three short verses that speak volumes about the consequence of sin. It is quite possible that Judas expected to see Jesus vindicated in the trial. There was, after all, no real evidence to convict Him. But things got out of hand and were beyond his control (the power of evil if we open the door). His life was wasted. Worse, at the end he was controlled by evil. This is all the more tragic because he had every opportunity to obey Jesus.

Stand with Jesus during the trial before Pilate. ➲Note Jesus' affirmation that He was indeed the king of the Jews – the Messiah (v. 11).☾ Watch Pilate try to give away responsibility that was his alone (vv. 24-26). Note the cruelty of the soldiers (vv. 27-31). Most important, observe how Jesus answered questions (26:63-64; 27:11) and stood in dignity before the hostile crowd.

ISAIAH 49   Chapter 49 begins the next section of Isaiah, which deals with the ministry of the Servant of the Lord, the Messiah, the Lord Christ.

Israel has been the servant of the Lord, identified as such in a number of places in the Scriptures. Since Abraham's call in Genesis 12, where the Lord promised to bless the whole world through Abraham, the Lord's hand has been on His people, bringing to the world God's message of righteousness and redemption.   Romans 9:4-5 addresses some ways in which this was realized. The covenant, the revelation of God through the events at Sinai and in the law, and the message of the prophets – all are part of this ministry. The ministry of Jonah to the Assyrians at Nineveh illustrates how God used His people to bring the message of righteousness and forgiveness to the Gentile world.   The coming of the promised Messiah, the Savior, was through God's people, Israel.

The Scriptures also speak of the servant of the Lord in a more narrow sense, referring to Christ. An illustration of how both meanings appear in juxtaposition is in Isaiah 49, where verses 1-7 refer to the servant of the Lord as the coming Messiah, while verses 8-26 refer to Israel restored to the land promised initially to Abraham.

☑Verse 3 could make it seem that this entire chapter refers to Israel as a nation (as the servant).   However, verse 5 says the servant will bring the nation of Israel back to the Lord, and verse 6 says the servant will restore Israel and bring salvation to the whole earth.   Further, verse 7 says the kings of the world will worship the servant.   This ministry and position obviously refers to the coming Messiah.

As you continue to read verses 8-26, follow how God will comfort and restore His people. The dispersion of God's people is seen as history (Israel under Assyria, Judah under Babylon, v. 19a), and the restoration as a sovereign act of the Lord (v. 13ff.). Note that this even extends to the Gentiles bringing God's people back to the land (vv. 22-23). Then all people will recognize the Lord as the redeemer, the God of Israel (v. 26). This, too, touches the ministry of the Messiah for He will be on the throne and bring justice to the world and liberation to the oppressed (42:1-7; cf. Isa 2:1-5).⇦

PROVERBS 12:8-14   Verse 11 makes a statement about the "work ethic." Many of us would like to follow an easy road to making a living. When this was written, the economy was agricultural, and there was no way to make a living without hard work. Do you know anyone who has chased fantasies and been a loser (v. 11)?

Another attribute of the wise person will also bring blessing: the prudent use of speech (vv. 13-14). Notice both sides of the coin. The foolish and evil man is trapped by what he says, while a wise man is blessed by prudent speech. Compare verse 13 with Matthew 12:36-37.

SEPTEMBER 12

MATTHEW 27:32-66   Stand with Jesus once again as you read the details of His death. →Understand that you are reading about the central event of history: God's grace in action – His sacrifice for the sins of men (cf. Isa 53:3-9).← Everything in the Old Testament looked forward to this moment. All that follows in the Bible looks back on this sacrifice.

Be aware of the people at the scene – the crowds, the soldiers, and Jesus' friends. Note the cruelty of the crucifixion and the mocking of the leaders (vv. 35-44). The soldiers were so hardened that they sat at the foot of the cross and gambled for Jesus' clothes. Compare verse 46 with Psalm 22:1 – Jesus' cry of abandonment. Feel the heartbreak of those who loved Jesus (vv. 55-56). Note the courage of Joseph of Arimathea, who lovingly buried Jesus (vv. 57-60).

Read 51-53 for powerful message of authentication.

ISAIAH 50   The banishment of the people in exile is mentioned in the past tense in 50:1, even though it had not yet taken place. Look at the reason for the captivity (v. 1b). This is a terribly sad commentary on God's people. God could have saved them from captivity (v. 2b). But, the willful sin of the people made their captivity and dispersion a foregone conclusion (Deut 28:58-68). Further, God raised up Nebuchadnezzar and the Babylonians for the very purpose of bringing judgment on Judah (Hab 1:5-11).

☑The work and ministry of the Messiah is foretold in verses 4-9. Jesus' understanding heart and listening ear during His ministry were from the Lord God (vv. 4-5). His suffering is described in verse 6 about eight hundred years before it happened. Compare verse 7b with Luke 9:51. Even in this death, however, Jesus knew He would be vindicated by the Lord God (v. 8a).⇔

Verses 10-11 offer a choice. Come to God in His way (Jesus) and receive His blessing, or make your own way and suffer the torment reserved for the rebellious.

PROVERBS 12:15-21   The truth of verse 15 seems obvious. We have all known people who were committed to a course of behavior that would bring disaster – yet they seemed oblivious to the danger and sure that it was the right course. It is obvious when it is someone else. It isn't so obvious when it is yourself! Failure to listen to trusted advisors marks the fool.

When you are sure that the Lord is leading you, proceed even if friends give different advice. (It is important, however, to listen to and consider the advice of trusted friends.) It may be a lonely journey but not the journey of a fool. The point is, be sure you have solid grounding for your action and that its not just a selfish whim. We should try to avoid such weakness of human nature!

Once again, read verses 17-19 regarding the use and misuse of the tongue.

SEPTEMBER 13

MATTHEW 28   No guard, no stone, no other security measure could keep Jesus in the grave. In the mystery of redemption, Jesus had the authority to lay down His life and to take it up again (John 10:18). The resurrection forever disarmed evil (Col 2:15) and forever opened the way to life for all who would believe. Romans 1:4 states that the resurrection is the declaration to the world that Jesus is the Son of God.

The angel's testimony to the women who went to the tomb was a powerful statement from the Lord. They needed such a message to introduce the miracle of the resurrection. After the angel's statement, Jesus Himself appeared to them (vv. 8-10).

Jesus gave the disciples (and the church) a mandate for action and a promise of His presence and His authority until He would come again (vv. 16-20). Think carefully about this instruction from the Lord for it is the assignment of each who confesses Christ. Each one of us shares in the agenda of the kingdom!

ISAIAH 51:1-52:12   The message of 51:1-52:12 is to God's people of faith. There is encouragement for those who pursue righteousness: Look to God, from whom you have life; receive the comfort of the Lord (51:1-3).

☑Messiah speaks in verses 4-8 about cataclysmic change but also comfort. The earth and heavens will be burned, righteousness and justice will be established, and there will be no more fear of those who threaten the righteous (v. 7). Judgment is coming for the unrighteous, and the Messiah's reign of righteousness will be lasting (vv. 7-8).⇦

This entire passage looks forward to the final deliverance of God's people by the power of the same God who brought the Israelites through the Red Sea on dry ground (v. 10). God's people will return to the land with great joy (v. 11). Israel, at that time, will have drained the full cup of the Lord's discipline and will have the Lord's blessing (vv. 17-23).

Follow the call to God's people (in the future at the time it was written) to shake off feeling downtrodden and know the joy of deliverance (52:1-12). ☑Note that verses 8-12 say that the Lord will come in the sight of all nations. Although this whole section has messianic overtones, this is a specific reference to the deliverance that Jesus, the Messiah, will bring (cf. Zech 14:3-5; Rev 1:7).⇦

PROVERBS 12:22-28   Consider verse 22, and compare this with John 8:44. Every untruth comes from the father of lies – Satan. Shading the truth to make yourself look better, or for any other reason, is not from the Lord. Think about this as you go through the day. We please God and honor Him with the truth. Truth and righteousness go hand in hand. Compare this, then, with verse 28. The way of righteousness is always the way of the Lord. Righteousness will bring everlasting life!

SEPTEMBER 14

GALATIANS 1   The book of Galatians was written to a group of churches in the region of Galatia in what is now the country of Turkey. Paul had visited Pisidian Antioch, Lystra, Derbe, and Iconium during his missionary journeys. The churches were established in a primarily Gentile area, with the message of salvation by grace alone without reliance on the law. After Paul had established the churches men from Jerusalem visited who claimed to be sent by James. They said that in addition to receiving the grace of God by faith, observing the law (circumcision) was necessary for salvation,. They also questioned Paul's apostleship, implying that he was a latecomer and didn't have the same credentials as the other apostles.

This background explains Chapter 1. The problem is stated in verses 6-9. The people had been drawn away from faith in the finished work of Christ by a distortion of the truth: i.e., God's grace plus elements of the law. Paul says any deviation from grace is heresy!

Remember that the earliest church was almost entirely made up of converted Jews. These people had come from the same background as Paul. The necessity of keeping the law, as they perceived it defined in the Old Testament, was of prime importance in establishing and maintaining a relationship with God. However, the Old Testament was very clear that the externals of worship without the inner commitment were an affront to God (cf. Isa 1:11-20).

The gospel of salvation by grace – through faith in the risen Lord, not through "works" or "personal merit" – was bound to collide with long-standing Jewish traditions. This collision of emotion and ideology caused trouble in the church, which this letter to the Galatian churches addresses.

The two poles of the controversy – neither of which represents Christian or biblical perspective – are legalism and antinomianism. The legalist sees the Christian life as one of carefully keeping the rules. The antinomian (meaning "against the law") sees the Christian life as one that lets us do almost whatever we want (under the umbrella of grace). The Christian life and doctrine permit neither of these polar positions. Salvation is by grace alone – it has nothing to do with our merit or how we keep the law (Rom 3:19-20). But we *do* have an obligation to the law (that is an expression of the character and will of God, Rom 3:31). Jesus made obedience to His commands the test of our love for Him (John 14:21). Obedience to Jesus' commands and conformance to His lifestyle *are the evidences* of salvation: If we are in the kingdom, it will show (1 John 2:3-6). The solution is to understand God's Word and to find answers to lifestyle questions in the Bible with the help of the Holy Spirit.

Paul goes on to defend the gospel he brought to them by outlining his apostleship. Jesus appeared to him and gave him the responsibility of taking His message to both Israel and the Gentiles (Acts 9:15).

ISAIAH 52:13-53:12   ☑The section of Isaiah we are reading today *is at the very center of the last twenty-seven chapters of Isaiah and presents the Messiah in His role of the sin bearer and Savior.* We consider the last three verses of Chapter 52 with Chapter 53 because the subject begins with these verses.

As the section begins, note the phrase in 52:13, "he will be raised and lifted up and highly exalted" (compare this with John 3:14-15). This verse in Isaiah, however, goes beyond being "lifted up" (on the cross) to being "highly exalted" (cf. Rev 5:12; 11:15b). This encompasses the entire scope of Christ's ministry from Savior, to victorious and reigning Lord.

Think about the statement that He was disfigured and marred – and that people were appalled by him (v. 14). He was not kingly in appearance in His first advent, and especially so in His suffering, but it will become evident that He was and is the Son of God (v. 15; Rev 1:7).

The *universal nature* of the Messiah's redeeming work is suggested by 52:15. "He will sprinkle many nations," portrays the priestly work of bringing atonement to the whole world and not only to Israel (cf. Rom 15:21). This text in Isaiah, compared with Jesus' role as redeemer, is absolutely astounding. It is a prophetic capsule of the redeeming work of Jesus.

Because Jesus came to earth in a humble way and grew up in a time of political oppression and spiritual dryness, there was little about Him that was attractive (53:2). John quoted verse 1 to explain from Scripture the unbelief of the people (cf. John 12:37-38; see also Rom 10:16). When He was rejected, all turned their faces from Him (v. 3).

Yet He carried our sins and sorrows, was crushed by God for us, and became our atonement (vv. 4-6; cf. Mark 15:28; Rom 3:23-26; 1 Peter 1:18-21). He heals our physical diseases (v. 4a; cf. Matt 8:16). Jesus' lack of defense as He stood before the religious and civil officials at His trial is reflected in verse 7 (cf. Acts 8:32). He was cut off and died for us (v. 8; cf. Acts 8:33). He was placed in the tomb of a rich man – just as all (sinful) men of His day were entombed (v. 9). Jesus, speaking of His imminent passion, quoted verse 12b and applied it to Himself (cf. Luke 22:37). And all of this was the will of God (v. 10; Acts 2:22-24).⇦

PROVERBS 13:1-6   Why is there so much violence presented in the media? Note verse 2b, and compare this with Psalm 11:5. To choose God's agenda, don't love violence, don't practice violence, and don't choose to watch violence!

Choosing righteousness is a safeguard to the person of integrity (v. 6; cf. 12:28). The way of righteousness is always God's agenda.

SEPTEMBER 15

GALATIANS 2   Chapter 2 details the growing pains of the early church. As the Gentiles received the gospel message, tensions arose that are outlined in the readings for yesterday. This resulted in what has been known as the first Church Council held in Jerusalem (2:1-10; cf. Acts 15:1-4ff.). Paul came to that council to outline how the Lord had revealed that the gospel would extend to the Gentiles of the world. Christianity's relationship to Jewish rituals and forms of worship were hammered out. The Council's conclusions as they applied to Gentile believers are in Acts 15:24-29.

Even Peter slipped back into the "legalistic" pattern when he visited Antioch – resulting in sharp discussions between Peter and Paul (vv. 11-13).

The crux of the truth is in verse 16. We will never be saved by keeping the law – or any set of rules. The follow-up truth is seen in verses 20-21. Our identification with Christ in His death and resurrection is the dynamic of new life (cf. Rom 6:5ff.).

ISAIAH 54   The message of triumphant hope and promise to Israel in Chapter 54 was only possible because of the finished work of redemption. Childlessness (v. 1) was a problem in the Old Testament, but now offspring are promised to the nation (vv. 2-3). This fulfills the promise of Genesis 12:1-3 to Abraham and Genesis 28:13-14 to Jacob. This was the promise of salvation to all peoples of the world.

☑Verses 4-8 promise restoration with true reconciliation to Israel, verses 9-10 reiterate the security of the covenant relationship with the

Lord, and verses 11-14 guarantee the beauty of Jerusalem (see Rev 21:10ff.). Finally, note that in verses 15-17 God promises His strength and presence to His people. Written about 800 BC, these events are still unfulfilled but will be when Jesus, the Messiah, returns. All of this is based on the healing through redemption in Isaiah 53! Jesus noted that His ministry on earth fulfilled verse 13 (John 6:45). ⇦

PROVERBS 13:7-13 Do you see the "plastic" lifestyle reflected in verse 7? Society makes it very easy for people to buy beyond their ability and become slaves to their credit cards. People may look more prosperous than they are – for a time. Prudence dictates a more realistic approach to spending.

Think about the message of verse 10. Pride blinds us and gets in the way of relationships. Listening to wise advice takes discipline but can smooth the rough spots.

SEPTEMBER 16

GALATIANS 3:1-14 Paul is incredulous that the Christians to whom he is writing have been drawn into false practice through a distortion of the truth. He used the illustration of Abraham, who received the gift of righteousness long before the law was given (cf. Gen 15:6). Those who are saved are the children of Abraham, since they receive salvation by faith, as Abraham did (cf. Rom 4:11). Paul developed this truth effectively when writing to the Roman Christians.

The facts are clear: If we try to enter the kingdom by keeping the law – by bringing our "parcel" of good works to God – we will be tragically disappointed. Read again the powerful summary of this truth in Romans 3:19-20. No one can, or will, be justified by keeping the law (v. 11). In fact, no one can *keep* the law. But Christ opened the way to God by paying the full penalty of the law on our behalf (vv. 13-14). This gift of righteousness comes to all who have faith in Christ (v. 14). Jesus redeemed us from the curse of the law by taking it upon Himself (v. 13; cf. 1 Peter 2:24).

ISAIAH 55 ☑Chapter 55 flows from the redemptive work of Messiah for it contains the Lord's gracious invitation to all – based on the way opened by the sin-bearer (Ch. 53). The entire Old Testament reflects the grace of God, but this passage is one of the most explicit and beautiful in the Bible.

God's offer does not require money and therefore is available to all (v. 1), is satisfying (v. 2), brings life to the soul (v. 3; cf. Acts 13:34), and is given through repentance and faith (vv. 6-7). How God does this may be beyond our understanding (vv. 8-9), but God's word to men will bring results (vv. 10-11). Further, God's blessing brings joy to both men and nature, and God's name will be honored (vv. 12-13).

What God offers is salvation – and this covenant of salvation comes through the promise given to David (vv. 3-5). This promise came first through Abraham (Gen 12:3) and later through David (2 Sam 7:15-16; cf. Isa 11). This passage, as does Isaiah 11, speaks both of the first and second advents of the Lord Jesus as Messiah. ⇦

PROVERBS 13:14-19   Remember that the wisdom Proverbs speaks about comes from knowing God – which we read about in the first chapters of the book. Wisdom, personified as God, called men to attention (Prov 1:20-33). Here, in verse 14, the teaching of the wise, i.e., one who knows God, will turn others from the way of death. This is the high calling of one who knows the Lord. To share the good news of salvation is to present the way of life to those who need the message.

Verse 16 tells us to pay attention to the truth we know. As we become more familiar with God's word, we will see more ways in which applying these truths will keep us out of trouble. To ignore the truth that we know exposes our foolishness.

SEPTEMBER 17

GALATIANS 3:15-29   Look back to verses 6-9 where Paul shows that Abraham came to salvation by faith. Abraham represented the father of the Jewish race – and, surely, if keeping the law was necessary for salvation, Abraham would have done so. But that didn't happen: Abraham received the gift of righteousness by faith (v. 6; cf. Gen 15:6). Paul then points out that this (the "faith" plan) was, and is, God's method – Abraham is the father of all who have faith, including the Gentiles (vv. 7-8).

The Jews knew they were the covenant people. They were the sons of Abraham, and the covenant came through Abraham (v. 16). Paul brings to their attention, however, that the promise of God was to Abraham and to his descendant (singular), and (they understood) that this descendant was the Messiah who was to come through the line of Abraham. Both Genesis 12:7 and 13:15 speak of God's promise to Abraham as to him and to his descendant! The Greek word "seed," which is singular, is translated from the Hebrew in the above references. The Hebrew can be read as either singular or plural – but the Jews saw the promise as referring to the Messiah. In any event, the promise given in Genesis came to Abraham over four hundred years before the law was given. The unmistakable conclusion is that the promise does not depend upon the law!

How then does the law fit into God's plan (vv. 19, 21)? Intimately, since the law shows us our great need for grace. In verses 23-24 and in Romans 3:20, Paul shows that the law makes us conscious of sin, preparing us to see our need before God and the grace of forgiveness through the Savior. The law shows us God's standard and leads us to Christ (v. 24).

The "mediator" in verse 19 was probably Moses. Moses was used by God to give the Israelites the law – but the law was God's alone. Angels as mediators are also mentioned in Acts 7:53 and Hebrews 2:2.

Consider one more thought about the law and faith. We know that all people, from all times, who have received the gift of God's righteousness (i.e., salvation) have done so by faith (3:9). What, then, was the function of the sacrifices in the Old Testament? We know that the blood of animals cannot take away sin (Heb 10:4). The sacrifices in themselves, therefore, did not take away a person's sin. *The person's faith in God, however, demonstrated in the sacrifices, could indeed take away sins* – and was confirmed once and for all at the time of the cross and resurrection (cf. Rom 3:25-26; Heb 9:15).

ISAIAH 56-57   In the opening verses of Chapter 56, note the Lord's agenda for His people (vv. 1-2). This portion continues the invitation of Isaiah 55 for all to come, including those normally excluded from temple worship (vv. 3-8). Some foreigners could not join with the Israelites (Deut 23:1-8), and a eunuch, for instance, was excluded from worship (Deut 23:1). Redemption opens the way for universal application of salvation. Notice the six marks of the godly foreigner in verse 6. Note, too, that the temple will be a house of prayer for all nations (v. 7).

In the last four verses of the chapter, and continuing in Chapter 57, God spells out His view of Israel's society. Look for how God describes the people. In the midst of ungodliness, God sometimes even allows the righteous to die to protect them from greater harm! Death brings peace for the believer that only God can give (57:1-2). This, of course, is beyond our knowledge, but for the righteous, it is great comfort to know that God is in control – even in extreme circumstances.

In reading 57:3-13, note how deeply the people had been infected with the pagan worship of the nations around them. They practiced sexual sins, human sacrifice, and idolatry. The result is seen in verse 13. When in trouble, God says, look to the idols and see if they will help. In contrast, the man who trusts God will have His blessing (v. 13b). In fact, up until verse 13a, it seems that there is no hope. But there is hope yet! Verses 13b-21 contrast the godly and the ungodly. God will honor the faith of those who worship Him – but there is no peace for the wicked (see also 48:22). This phrase closes this nine-chapter section of Isaiah.

PROVERBS 13:20-25   Choose your friends and mentors carefully. The character and practices of these friends rub off (v. 20). A godly friendship will be a blessing to both individuals.

Society's evil is reflected in verse 23. Experience shouts that this proverb is true. All of us know (and may have experienced) the dishonesty and scams that take hard-earned money away from people. This injustice can also be a decree of the courts. Remember that real justice belongs to the Lord (Deut 1:17). When we stand for honesty and justice, we are standing for God's agenda!

SEPTEMBER 18

GALATIANS 4   In this chapter, Paul contrasts slavery and freedom to help the Galatian Christians better understand why keeping the law does not bring salvation.

A key concept is in verses 4-5. God's Son came at the right time in history to free us from slavery to the law. The connecting link to this freedom is faith in Christ and His finished work on our behalf. Thus, we no longer need to rely on the other system to achieve salvation (keeping all the requirements of the law). Further, trying to combine other ways to achieve salvation questions the adequacy of Christ's work on the cross.

On this basis, Paul expresses his concern for the Christians in verses 8-20. He uses Hagar and Sarah to point out the difference between our own "self-help" programs and God's method. When Abraham didn't have children to fulfill God's promise to him, Sarah gave Abraham her servant to bear a child for them (Gen 16:1-3). Ishmael, however, was not the son that God had promised Abraham. The son of the promise came to Abraham and Sarah at exactly the time of God's own choosing (Gen 18:10) – as did God's Son into the world (v. 4).

The conclusion is that the Galatians (and all believers) must abandon all "self-help" methods (salvation by keeping the law) and come to God in the freedom of the promise: *salvation only and always by faith in the Son of God and His redemption through the cross!*

ISAIAH 58   As suggested in the notes for Isaiah 40 (Sept. 3), Isaiah 58 begins the section that deals with the last times, the work of the Holy Spirit, and the Lord as both Judge and Savior.

As you read Chapter 58, contrast the people's condition with what God wants them to be. Many people went through the motions of spiritual life but without a heart for the Lord. Even in the days set aside for worship, the people managed to do their own thing while observing the forms (vv. 3-5). Beginning with verse 6, the Lord is clear about what constitutes true spiritual life and the blessing that will flow from it. *Look for the word "is" as a beginning of a question, and "if" as a condition, followed by "then" to see the blessing.*

God's list should give us pause, for some items are not traditionally high on the evangelical agenda. Honoring the Lord by addressing injustice and oppression and by ministering to the poor are examples. Perhaps we don't see the results following the "then" in these verses because we don't pay attention to the right things. *The "functional atheism" of the people in verses 1-4 can invade the church as well as Israel!*

PROVERBS 14:1-9   "The wisdom of the prudent is to give thought to their ways" (v. 8). We all desire a prudent life. Here is an essential element in achieving that life: to evaluate – and reevaluate – what we are doing and how we do it, and to do so in the light of Scripture. This is the same principle as in John 15, where the gardener trims branches that are bearing. The object is to make them more fruitful. Think about what you are doing and how. Is it what God is pleased with? To spend time reflecting in this way is wisdom!

SEPTEMBER 19

GALATIANS 5:1-12   The discussion is still about slavery or freedom (v. 1). This is a crucial choice, for it determines the difference between fellowship with, or alienation from, Christ (v. 4). The one thing that matters above all others is faith that shows itself in love (v. 6).

If you would keep the law to be saved, you must go the whole way (vv. 2-3). Keep the whole law, and try for salvation that way! That, of course, is impossible. So Paul pleads for the Galatian Christians not to mix faith and works – for a little yeast (the idea of merit through the law) gets into the whole lump of dough (v. 9).

There will be a reckoning for those teachers who have confused the Galatian churches (v. 10). It is vital that any who teach are absolutely sure that their message is biblical. Differences that seem subtle on the surface may lead people from the truth in Christ.

ISAIAH 59   Man's dilemma is not God's doing! (59:1-2). And there is no question that man has a dilemma! Verses 3-15 describe violence, lies, and injustice. Man is sinful in deed (v. 6b), intention (v. 7a), thought (v. 7b), and heart (v. 8). The tragic result is no justice in the nation (v. 9a), no light for the path (v. 9b), no sight (insight) to understand the problem (v. 10a), no strength for the terrible situation (v. 10b), and no deliverance from the difficulty (v. 11b). Note the four sins of society in verse 13. *Do these strike a familiar note?*

Now look at what God will do in this impossible situation (vv. 16-21). ☑The Lord will bring salvation – in His own righteousness (vv. 16b-17a). The promise of His coming is in verses 19-20, and all will see His glory. This will be realized finally when the Messiah comes and true justice and righteousness will reign. God's judgment will come to the wicked. Only those who repent will escape (v. 20)! But those who have the Spirit (v. 21) will feel God's presence in the midst of trouble. *This passage had both a near and a far-off (from the time of the prophecy) promise. God's judgment did come in the captivity to Babylon in 586 BC, and it will also come to the world when Jesus returns (verse 19).*⇦

PROVERBS 14:10-18   Human wisdom, we have all found, is fallible. What looks like a good plan often does not prove as profitable as it appeared. Worse, if we rely on ourselves to decide moral values and goals, our fallen human nature will lead us astray – and seriously so (v. 12). As an example, if we were to shape our lives by the messages of today's world, would it lead to life or spiritual death? Isaiah spoke to this (Isa 59 above).

SEPTEMBER 20

GALATIANS 5:13-26   The contrast between life in the Spirit and life in sin is here highlighted. Paul's call to the Galatians is to live in the Spirit – and thus avoid the temptation to gratify the sinful nature (v. 16). The sinful nature and life in the Spirit don't mix – they are mutually incompatible (v. 17). They are like oil and water! To avoid living by the sinful nature, be led by the Spirit (v. 18).

Verses 19-21 outline the sinful acts to which we are prone. Sexual sins are sexual immorality, impurity, and debauchery. Wrong worship and evil demonic practices are idolatry and witchcraft. Sins in relationships are hatred, discord, jealousy, fits of rage, selfish ambition, dissentions, factions, and envy. Finally, the sins of self-indulgence are drunkenness and orgies. Note the sobering fact that Paul emphasizes in verse 21. *Those who display these types of behavior will not be part of the kingdom of God!*

In contrast, consider the fruit of the Spirit (vv. 22-23). The fruit of the Spirit is not the same as the gifts of the Spirit. The fruit of the Spirit is meant to be a composite of behavior in each Christian's life – while the gifts are selectively given to individual Christians (each Christian has at least one of the gifts, 1 Cor 12:7). Picture the person who lives out this portrait of the work of the Holy Spirit. There are laws against many of the things listed under the sinful nature – but no laws against the gentle, considerate person led by the Holy Spirit (v. 23b).

It is not only logical, but also productive, to work toward these characteristics of the fruit of the Spirit. We *have* the Holy Spirit if we are in the kingdom. These characteristics are God's will for each of His children. It is inconceivable that the Lord will not help us where we need it as we move toward this winsome composite – *if we are willing*! *KEEP IN STEP WITH THE SPIRIT (V. 25).*

ISAIAH 60   ☑Isaiah 60 describes a time yet to come when Israel will be established in righteousness. These events look forward to the second coming of Jesus the Messiah, when all people will recognize Jesus as Lord. The nations of the world will serve God's people, bringing their wealth to Israel (v. 5; remember that the Israelites left Egypt with that nation's wealth), and they will also help rebuild the land (v. 10). It will be a time of peace (v. 11). Jerusalem will be recognized as the city of the Lord (v. 14; cf. Isa 2:3). The hate that Israel has endured will be ended (v. 15). God Himself will light the land (v. 19; cf. Rev 21:23), bringing glory to His name (v. 21b). God is not done with His people yet!⇦

PROVERBS 14:19-26   The world's values are obvious in verse 20. Contrast that with verse 21. Here is God's agenda. If we are doing God's work, we will think about the needs of others, alleviating them when possible. This mercy is the work of the Lord. See this again in verse 31.

Remember also that no matter how things look, the one who trusts in the Lord has a sure fortress (v. 26). That is security! We often forget this vital truth, causing unnecessary and futile worry. Do we really believe that the Lord cares for His own?

SEPTEMBER 21

GALATIANS 6   Paul lists three marks of spiritual maturity in verses 1-5. Help to restore those caught in sin (v. 1), help and encourage those carrying heavy burdens (v. 2), and test your actions and attitudes by the standards of God's Word (v. 4). Heed the warning in verse 1 about helping those caught in sin: Take care – you can be tempted by the same sin and also by pride. ("I'm not involved in that kind of sin!")

Listen to the perspective, truth, and good advice in verses 7-10. You cannot play games with God! Get on the right track and persevere! Finally, take Paul's desire and prayer in verse 14 for your own. There is nothing else worth living for – or dying for!

ISAIAH 61   ☑Isaiah 61 continues the theme of the previous chapter. Jesus quoted verses 1-2a to describe His ministry when He spoke in the synagogue (Luke 4:18-19). He stopped reading in the middle of verse 2 because His ministry during the first advent extended only to that point in the text. When He comes again, He will judge the ungodly and comfort His people (vv. 2b-3). The land will be rebuilt and God's people will minister to the world (vv. 4-9). All of this will be Jesus' ministry at the second advent. This describes the period of Christ's reign over Israel and the nations. Read verses 10-11 as His words. ⇐

PROVERBS 14:27-35   A peaceful heart gives life to the body (v. 30). Contentment is God's will for His children (1 Tim 6:6). In fact, without contentment, there is no peace. Think about the fact that most advertising is designed to make people lack contentment and want more.

Genuine peace is a work of the Holy Spirit (Gal 5:22). It is based in the redemptive work of Christ (Rom 5:1-2), and it is present irrespective of circumstances (Rom 5:2b-5). At its heart is a right relationship with God and a deep conviction that God is looking after our interests and will give exactly what we need. Any physician will testify that the peaceful individual is subject to fewer emotional and physical symptoms than the "stressed out" person.

The other side of the coin is in 30b. Here is the "stressed out" person who envies others and whose wants are never satisfied. This discontentment creates havoc in both emotional stability and physical symptoms. Take your choice: Believe God, or follow the rest of the world in a mad and fruitless chase for contentment.

SEPTEMBER 22

EPHESIANS 1:1-14   Ephesus was a city on the coast of Asia that Paul visited on his second and third missionary journeys. Acts 19 gives the account of Paul's first visit to Ephesus. He spent three months presenting the gospel in the synagogue, and when there was opposition, he moved to a rented hall where he ministered daily for about two years. From this we can assume that the church had substantial foundations.

Ephesians 1 is packed with significant theological truth. Paul speaks about the spiritual blessings that Christians have in verses 3-14. Consider the following five blessings: *(1)* Christ chose us before He created the world (v. 4). *God knew your name before this world was formed!* God's specific purpose in choosing you, as seen here, is that you would be holy and blameless before Him. *(2)* God loved us and predestined us to become His adopted sons through Christ Jesus (v. 5). *(3)* Christ has redeemed us from sin (v. 7). *(4)* God has revealed to us the mystery of His will in bringing salvation to the world, and finally to bring all things in heaven and earth under the authority of Christ (v. 9). *(5)* God has marked each Christian with His seal – the Holy Spirit (vv. 13-14).

ISAIAH 62-63   ☑Isaiah, whose vision has shown him the future of Jerusalem and the nation, vows that he cannot keep silent (62:1). Time will drastically change its circumstances.   God will once again be delighted in the nation (v. 4; cf. 59:1-15 for its previous condition). The Savior is coming, and He brings His reward (v. 11). The people will be redeemed, and the city inhabited (vv. 10-12)! These events are related to the second advent.

The first verses of Chapter 63 speak of the Lord coming in power and strength, bringing judgment on the wicked nations (vv. 1-6). This is God's own statement. In Revelation 19:11-21, John sees the vision of the Lord Jesus at the time of the judgment of the nations. Notice the similarity in the descriptions of the avenging Lord!⇦

In spite of God's gracious acts and kindness to Israel (63:7-9), the people rebelled (v. 10). When God disciplined them, they remembered their days of blessing – and longed for God's blessing once again (vv. 11-14). Their prayer in verses 15-19 asks God to look once again with favor on them.

PROVERBS 15:1-9   What comes from the tongue that brings healing (v. 4)? Never "sweet talk" or flattery. Such a deceitful tongue will crush the spirit.   Consistent with the thrust of the Bible, the tongue that brings healing speaks truth with gentleness.

Three times, this chapter describes what the Lord detests. The Lord detests the sacrifice of the wicked (v. 8); in contrast, He is pleased with the prayer of the upright. The Lord detests the way of the wicked (v. 9); in contrast, He loves those who pursue righteousness. And, looking ahead to verse 26, the Lord detests the thoughts of the wicked; in contrast, the thoughts of the upright please Him. God sees the inner heart (v. 3).   Friends, acquaintances, and even the public can be deceived. But God sees behind what we give Him – what our life really is, even our thoughts. With God's help, go for purity!

SEPTEMBER 23

EPHESIANS 1:15-23   Look for what Paul prayed for on behalf of the Ephesians and the specific things we learn about Christ and His rule, both now and in the future (vv. 15-23).

Paul prayed that the Christians at Ephesus would have the Spirit of wisdom and understanding – as a gift from the Father – to know Him better (v. 17). He also he prayed for insight so they could understand the heritage that was theirs as Christians, and the power of the resurrection available to them as God's children (vv. 18-20). What would change in your life or outlook if you had these blessings? These are the things God wants for each of His children. We limit the work of God in our lives when our outlook is tied to this world and its concerns! Ask for these blessings (John 16:24), and consciously choose to walk in the Spirit, doing what you know to be God's will – even in the little things.

Follow carefully what Paul writes about Christ (vv. 20-23). He is the great King! Compare these verses with Hebrews 1:1-4. Capture this vision of the Lord Jesus, high and lifted up, the ruler of the entire universe. Then rejoice that He is personally concerned for you!

ISAIAH 64-65   ☑Isaiah longs for the realization of his vision of glory (64:1-2; cf. Zech 14:3ff.; Mal 4:1). When the Savior comes, the mountains *will* tremble as at Sinai (v. 3).⇦ In the present circumstance, hope is in waiting for Him (v. 4; cf. 1 Cor 2:9) and remembering that we are in His hand for His purposes (v. 8). Note Isaiah's poignant prayer on behalf of his people (vv. 8-12).

How does God feel about those who casually go about the business of being religious without substance? Read 65:2-16 for the answer. Verses 1-2 are quoted in Romans 10:20-21 as prophecy that the gospel message would be extended freely to the Gentiles, and that Israel would not respond to the Savior. Despite God's anger over Israel's rejection, still there is hope (vv. 8-10). Look, however, at what God will do to those who trust in luck (fortune, v. 11a) and fate (destiny, v. 11b) when they should have been trusting the living God (v. 12).

☑ Compare 65:17-25 with Revelation 21. Heaven and earth will be restructured following the judgment that will come on the nations (v. 17; cf. 2 Peter 3:10). People will have extended lives reminiscent of the Genesis era before the flood (v. 20). Nature will be peaceful (v. 25; cf. Isa 11:1-9). This time of restructured world order with Jerusalem at the center is also described in Isa 2:1-5.⇦

PROVERBS 15:10-17   A pointed message about priorities is in verses 16-17. How much we own – how large the bank account and estate – has little to do with quality of life. That quality comes with contentment and peace, not the accumulation of things, although Satan would have us think otherwise.

If we set our sights on following God and doing His will, paying attention to His agenda as outlined in God's word, we will have peace (cf. notes on Prov 14:27-35 for Sept. 21). Follow hard after God! Go for the real gold!

SEPTEMBER 24

<u>EPHESIANS 2:1-10</u>   Life and death are the issues here. Spiritual death is a fact for every human being (v. 1) – apart from the work of God in our lives. To be even more specific, all who are without Christ live under Satan's authority (v. 2). We give evidence of Satan's control by our sinful lives (v. 3). It is a depressing picture! Death is where we all are or have been (vv. 1-3).

If the account ended at verse 3, there would be nothing to hope for! Instead, the grace of God, outlined in the following verses, lifts our hearts with praise to God. His great love, rich mercy, and grace have made spiritual life possible (vv. 4-5). Not only that, but God has elevated believers to the same place as the Lord Jesus has in glory (v. 6).

Consider verses 8-10 as a definitive statement about faith, works, and salvation. Salvation is a gift of God to each believer (v. 8). It is made available to the sinner who is lost in sin (v. 5). Further, the nature of a gift means that one cannot pay for it or earn it (works). If so, it would be payment and not a gift. Specifically, no Christian can boast about earning salvation (v. 9). The definition of grace helps to understand this: favor given entirely without merit on the part of the recipient! Note, however, that good works follow the receipt of God's grace and are God's will for His children (v. 10). *The good works in no way bring salvation into our lives, but they reveal the change in our lives that salvation has brought!*

<u>ISAIAH 66</u>   Verse 2b offers insight into one attribute the Lord desires in His children. To be humble and contrite is one hundred eighty degrees from where the world is! Yet this was characteristic of the Lord Jesus, and was what He taught (Matt 18:1-5; 20:20-28). These qualities are a work of the Holy Spirit in the believer, which the Lord will accomplish as we are willing. Note too that careful attention to God's word indicates godliness (v. 2b).

In contrast to what the Lord desires in His people, read the description of what the Lord observed (vv. 3-6): people who sacrificed, but had hearts far from the Lord; people who didn't listen to God's message; men and women who said all of the right things, but without conviction. Judgment would come on them (v. 6).

☑The Lord will complete what He has promised (vv. 7-16). There is a future for Jerusalem and God's people. With the judgment coming on the nations (vv. 15-16, the Day of the Lord at Christ's coming), Jerusalem and God's people will be restored (vv. 12-14).

Finally, there will be judgment for the wicked (v. 17), but the world will finally see the glory of the Lord (v. 18). The Lord in the person of the Messiah will reign – and all will glorify Him (vv. 19-24)!⇦

PROVERBS 15:18-25 Some individuals seem to have a gift of causing dissension among friends. How much better to be patient, listen to others, and help calm a difficult situation (v. 18).

As you read verse 23, see how it aligns with verse 18. The timely word may be either encouragement or corrective advice. In either case, an honest word, carefully delivered, has the potential for blessing.

SEPTEMBER 25

EPHESIANS 2:11-22 God's grace in salvation brings profound change to Christians. One of the greatest is to break down cultural and social barriers.

One of the "highest and most impenetrable walls" between people was between Jews and Gentiles. Jews, sons of Abraham, were the exclusive sons of the covenant (vv. 11-12)! Christ has changed that (v. 13). God has now brought *all* believers into one fold, regardless of national, cultural, or social differences.

THIS HAS BEEN GOD'S PLAN FROM THE BEGINNING. One of the earliest Biblical promises is found in Genesis 12:3, where God promised Abraham that through him (i.e., through Jesus who was his descendent) all nations of the earth would be blessed. Paul demonstrates from the Old Testament that God's plan for salvation for all peoples is evident both in the law and the prophets (Rom 9:25-26, 30-33, 10:11-13, 19-21). Check Ephesians 1:4. God knew individual believers before time existed! Incredible.

NAHUM 1-2 The prophecy of Nahum was directed to Nineveh, the capital of Assyria, about one hundred years after Jonah's preaching and the city's repentance. Assyria had, by this time, destroyed Israel, done violence to much of Judah, and threatened Jerusalem. Hezekiah's prayer saved the city (2 Kings 19:14-19, 35-36). Still, Judah lived under Assyria's shadow until the time of Josiah, when Judah became more independent of the large nation to the east. Assyria was finally conquered by Babylon after Nahum's prophecy.

The Lord's description of Nineveh is graphic. The nation's idols were an offense to God (1:14). The nation's strength and its defenses will melt away. However Nineveh tries, her defenses will be inadequate (2:1). Although the army appears strong (2:3-4), it will stumble (2:5). The nation's former strength is ebbing away (2:6-12) and is like the mud on the bottom of a drained pond (2:8).

Notice the two principles in 1:3. These characteristics are rooted in the nature of God. Note the truth of 1:6 and the encouragement of 1:7.

PROVERBS 15:26-33   Is God "only a prayer away," as one song has put it?   Certainly not for all, according to verse 29.   Not according to Proverbs 1:23-28. Not according to Isaiah 59:1-2. You cannot ignore God and His will, and expect an immediate answer when trouble comes. Does God sometimes answer even when we have neglected him? Undoubtedly, but *none of us must presume upon God's grace and goodness*. The way of peace and answered prayer is to walk in the Spirit and obey (v. 29b).

SEPTEMBER 26

EPHESIANS 3   Have you considered how the gospel came to you?   If you are a Gentile, you will find yourself in this chapter, as Paul tells how God opened the way for all to come to Him. God gave Paul the responsibility to bear the gospel to the Gentile world (vv. 1-6).

The mystery of which Paul speaks is two-fold. First, the mystery of how God would bring salvation to the world (v. 3) is the same mystery that Peter speaks about in 1 Peter 1:10-12. The prophets, who foretold Christ's coming and His suffering, could not understand how or when their prophecies would be fulfilled. There is also the mystery of why Gentiles were included in the grand plan of salvation (v. 6). To the Jew, this was incomprehensible – a true mystery.

God's intent (vv. 10-11) is that as the church brings the message of redemption to the world, His wisdom will be clear to "rulers and authorities in the heavenly realms." This is something we know little about, but it is consistent with 6:12, and these beings probably represent forces of evil. The church demonstrates to the universe the grace and power of God! *As members of the church, our conduct as God's redeemed reflects upon God's work in our lives and upon God's reputation!*

Read Paul's prayer (vv. 14-21), especially noting his desire that the Christians at Ephesus would feel God's power to strengthen their spiritual character and to understand the vastness of God's work.

NAHUM 3   As this chapter opens, God makes His complaint: a city of blood, lies, plunder, and victims (v. 1).   The military might and the behavior of Nineveh are described in verses 2-3, and her evil worship in verse 4. This worship included both witchcraft and sorcery.

Note that in spite of its seeming might, the nation still will fall (vv. 8-13). In fact, God tells them, go ahead and do everything they can to be ready – but destruction is still on the way (vv. 14-17).

There are several lessons in this prophecy to a pagan nation. God was concerned about Nineveh (Jonah 4:11). God cared enough to send a prophet to the city a second time (Nahum). This time, however, the message was unheeded. Even though the nation seemed strong, that strength is nothing to the Lord when the "cup of iniquity" is full. The Lord's angel killed 185,000 of Assyria's soldiers in one night when they were encamped at Jerusalem (Isa 37:36), and Assyria fell to the Babylonians after Nahum's prophecy. No nation – no person – can afford to play games with the Lord!

PROVERBS 16:1-8   The book of Proverbs has much to say about self-deception. One way we fool ourselves is through rationalization. Read verse 2. The fact that we are able to rationalize our behavior does not change God's objective evaluation. This, in conjunction with Proverbs 15:3, should help us think clearly about our lives. Compare verse 2 with verse 25. Compare these two verses with Proverbs 17:3. There are ways to test many things in this world, but God tests the heart, and we will all stand before Him one day (2 Cor 5:10). *The one way we have to accurately assess thought and action is through God's word.*

A quick reading of verse 3 could lead you to believe that a hasty prayer over a business deal or stock purchases will lead to success. The principle here is much deeper: to bring all of your activity and resources under God's authority. If you are willing to bathe plans in prayer as you make them, the Lord can help you remain in His will – and succeed *from His perspective*. That may not mean financial success, but it will be success from a kingdom perspective.

SEPTEMBER 27

EPHESIANS 4:1-16   As you consider verses 1-16, remember that faith is always individual, *but it is never individualistic*. In verses 1-6, Paul pleads for careful relationships with each other based on our common faith. Note the number of "ones" in verses 4-6 that emphasize the corporate unity of the church. Can you envision a local church where all were humble, gentle, and patient with one another in love? This is God's standard!

Building upon the same theme, Paul then points out that within the church, gifts of the Spirit ensure a well-rounded, mature ministry (vv. 7-16). It is God's will that each local church will be equipped to do His work in that location. The Lord accomplishes this by giving His grace to each Christian individually (v. 7). The grace comes as differing gifts that, as a composite, equip the local church to accomplish all that God desires. The result is individual and corporate maturity that reflects the fullness of Christ (v. 13).

Observe the stability that this maturity brings to both the individual and the church (vv. 14-16). This maturity comes only as we apply the various gifts as the Holy Spirit leads (v. 16).

2 KINGS 21; 2 CHRONICLES 33   In these sections of 2 Kings and 2 Chronicles, review the leadership provided by the king in power in Judah. Jotham (2 Chron 27) walked with the Lord, but didn't bring his people to forsake their evil practices (27:2). Ahaz (2 Chron 28) was evil and led the people in that direction. His son Hezekiah (2 Chron 29-32) was committed to the Lord and helped the people make a new covenant with the Lord. He re-instituted the observance of the Passover and led the people to trust God in the face of the threat from Sennacherib, king of Assyria. But after his long reign, his son Manasseh reintroduced the pagan practices of the surrounding nations (2 Chron 33). Amon, his son, continued these practices, but Josiah again brought the people into fellowship with the Lord.

Be impressed with how much influence a leader can have. We all affect other people every day, either for good or evil. We have the opportunity to meet others' needs and to be ambassadors for Christ, but on the darker side, we can use relationships selfishly or even for outright evil. Read 2 Corinthians 5:14-21.

Manasseh was unbelievably evil and led the nation in his ways. He was a blot on the history of Judah, and piled up sin for God's final judgment in the Babylonian captivity (2 Kings 24:3-4). Read the list of his evil! Yet God in grace sent His messengers to bring him and the people back to Him, and finally used captivity to get his attention (2 Chron 33:10-11). The amazing thing is that when he repented, God gave him time to change and lead his people in better paths (2 Chron 33:12ff.). There were, however, lasting consequences of his wicked leadership (2 Kings 24:3), and his son Amon quickly led the people back into sin (2 Chron 33:21-23)!

PROVERBS 16:9-17   Justice and truth are from God (v. 11). Every time we deviate from honesty – whether in business or at home – we are moving into the agenda of Satan. That is serious. Choose God's agenda. Stay in the light of God's presence.

SEPTEMBER 28

EPHESIANS 4:17-32   This section urges a completely different lifestyle – from the inside out – as compared to the former life without Christ. As Paul outlines life without Christ (vv. 17-19), thank God for His grace in your own life!

In the remaining verses, note how the new life in Christ is different. We have a new attitude, a whole new person like Christ (vv. 23-24; cf.

Rom 8:5-8). This attitude requires action on our part, as do the suggestions that follow. *The power of God is available for transformation, but it requires decision and initiative on our part!* God desires the following in our lives: *(1)* truthfulness (v. 25); *(2)* self control (v. 26); *(3)* careful living to deny opportunity to the Evil One (v. 27); *(4)* integrity (v. 28a); *(5)* productive activity that will allow generosity (v. 28b); *(6)* careful speech that will bring blessing to those who hear – nothing questionable should come out of our mouths (v. 29); *(7)* abandoning destructive emotions such as bitterness, rage, anger, and malice (v. 31); *(8)* treating people with kindness and forgiveness, using the model of the Lord Jesus (v. 32); *(9)* encompassing all of the above, take care not to grieve the Holy Spirit with actions or words (v. 30).

Listing these changes makes clear the pervasive work of the Holy Spirit that is needed – and given – in our lives. God is not suggesting Band-Aids; He wants major and fundamental change!

2 KINGS 22; 2 CHRONICLES 34   Josiah (2 Chron 34) was only eight years old when he came to the throne, and by sixteen was actively seeking the Lord. By age twenty he was leading the people of Judah back to the Lord and ridding the land of pagan worship.

One of the most significant events of his reign was the discovery of the Word of God in the temple (2 Chron 34:14ff.). Josiah immediately sought the Lord to understand the implications of the Scripture for him and the nation (vv. 19-21). Josiah acted to bring the truth from God to all of the people (vv. 29-30) and led the nation in confession, repentance, and a renewal of the covenant. He promised the Lord that he (and the people) would faithfully keep God's Word (vv. 31-32). The king then made sure that all idols in the land were removed (v. 33). Josiah kept these promises for the rest of his life! His resolve was no "passing fancy."

PROVERBS 16:18-25   Pride is a fatal disease (v. 18). The Bible says much about pride – whole nations fell because of their pride. Edom (Obad 1:2-3) and Moab (Zeph 2:8-11) were both in trouble for their pride. Pride is listed in the several characteristics of the ungodly in the last days (2 Tim 3:1-5), and both James (4:6) and Peter (1 Peter 5:5) quote Proverbs 3:34 stating that God opposes the proud. Why are we so prone to pride?

The opposite of pride is humility – which the Lord commends (v. 19). Jesus promised the kingdom of heaven to the poor in spirit (Matt 5:3). *Allow God to work this quality into your personality.* Pride says, "I'm able on my own." A humble spirit says, "I need the Lord to accomplish what is worthwhile."

SEPTEMBER 29

EPHESIANS 5:1-21   Notice first of all the high standard that Paul sets for us as Christians (vv. 1-2). There is no higher example than God Himself and the Lord Jesus in His sacrifice for us.

However, we live in a sinful world. We see it all around us, and if we allowed, we would be swept into its wickedness. With this in mind, Paul's warning in verses 3-7 is in order. Don't be fooled, he says, for if you practice immorality, impurity, greed, or idolatry, your place in the kingdom is in question (vv. 5-7). Remember also that Jesus pointed out that our actions – including speech – come from the heart (Matt 12:33-35). What we allow to occupy our minds will come out. We must be sure that our minds and hearts are in the right place!

Follow Paul's argument into verses 8-13. We have new life and light, so we have the opportunity and obligation to live as children of light. Stay away from sin! Rather, as God's child, walk in the light (vv. 8-9), and live to please the Lord (vv. 10-11). Live wisely, taking every opportunity for Christ (vv. 15-16). Finally, minister to one another, and live with a thankful heart (vv. 19-20).

2 KINGS 23:1-30   After the book of the law had been discovered in the temple and brought to the king, Josiah called the people – the great and the small – to the temple and read the law to them (vv. 1-3). What a commitment to God's word! When they had understood the text, the king led the people in a new dedication to serve and obey the Lord. One individual can make a difference!

Even more far-reaching were the steps he took to rid the land of idol worship (vv. 4-19). These steps went right to the heart of the people's daily practices. Places of worship were designated, and the pagan priests were killed (v. 20). Read the commentary on Josiah's life in verse 25. Yet Manasseh's sin still hung like a pall over the country (vv. 26-27). These two men are models, one of dedication to wickedness and the other of righteousness and responsiveness to the Lord.

PROVERBS 16:26-33   The person who sows dissension among believers is dangerous (v. 28). A perverse person is "twisted." Something isn't right deep within – the work of the evil one. Paul tells the church to beware and to keep away from such a person (Rom 16:17-18). Some readers may know such persons within the church.

Verse 28b speaks about gossip, which can separate friends and polarize believers. One practical suggestion: Don't take part in any conversation that is not healthy. To do less will not honor God.

SEPTEMBER 30

<u>EPHESIANS 5:22-33</u>   The Lord has a high standard for relationships in the home.   These standards for husbands and wives have become controversial, perhaps because of the emphasis in today's society on the "rights" of individuals.   The section speaks of the obligations in marriage, with Christ and the church as the model.   Take careful note of the high standard Paul gives for husbands: to love and care for their wives as the Lord Jesus loves and cares for the church.   This extended to giving His life for those who would become the church!

This portion has nothing to do with the worth of either sex or the relative worth of husbands or wives.   Rather, it has to do with administration.   To use an illustration from another part of the Bible, the woman in Proverbs 31 is anything but a doormat.   She is an administrator par excellence in the home: a planner, a businesswoman, a provider, and a day-to-day manager.   1 Timothy 5:14 gives advice to young widows in the church – advising that they marry, have children, and *manage* their homes.

To borrow from the corporate world, the chief operating officer, the COO of an organization, takes responsibility for the day-to-day administration of the operation – seeing that relationships work, that things get done, that the product is made and delivered.   The chief executive officer, the CEO, on the other hand, is responsible for long-range planning and the corporation's interaction with industry.   Although the CEO is ultimately responsible, both are essential.   In a working organization, each of these officers consults the other.

Think of the function of the home from the Lord's perspective, and our relationships in the home in the same way.   If we use the model given, the home becomes the most comfortable place in the world – we gain love and harmony and, in the end, give up nothing!   More important, the home becomes a powerful witness to the world – a world that is full of failing and unhappy families.

<u>2 CHRONICLES 35</u>   It had been at least seventy-five years since the Passover had been properly observed in Hezekiah's time.   This observance was the culmination of the restoration of true worship in the nation (vv. 1-19).

Josiah died when he involved himself in a conflict between Egypt and Babylon.   Assyria had fallen to Babylon, and Josiah was interfering with Egypt's army on the way to face Babylon.   This was not the Lord's will (vv. 21-22).   Josiah should have listened to what Neco, king of Egypt, told him "at the Lord's command." **Principle:** *God does not protect us from our own bullheadedness.*   Therefore, pick issues carefully!

<u>PROVERBS 17:1-7</u>   The wisdom of contentment with what we have is seen in several places in Proverbs.   Contentment is both a choice we make and a gift from the Lord that comes with a renewed mind (1 Tim 6:6-8). Proverbs 17:1 speaks to this. Look also at Proverbs 15:16-17 and 16:8. Only the knowledge that God directs and provides for us gives us true contentment in this world which values acquisition of things so dearly.

Technology can determine the impurities of gold and silver (v. 3), but only the Lord sees the heart! We can't truly see ourselves because of the rationalizations we use to justify how we feel and what we do. That is why David asked God to search his heart to find what would offend the Lord (Ps 139:23-24). The Lord tests the heart! Take David's example and ask God to search your heart and find what needs changing. As we ask, God will answer.

October

Bible Reading Schedule
And Notes

☙

*All Scripture is God-breathed and is useful for teaching,
rebuking, correcting and training in righteousness, so that the man of
God may be thoroughly equipped
for every good work. 2 Tim 3:16-17*

DISCOVERING THE BIBLE
READING SCHEDULE
OCTOBER

1	Ephesians 6:1-9	Habakkuk 1	Proverbs 17:8-14
2	Ephesians 6:10-24	Habakkuk 2	Proverbs 17:15-21
3	Philippians 1	Habakkuk 3	Proverbs 17:22-28
4	Philippians 2	Zephaniah 1	Proverbs 18:1-5
5	Philippians 3	Zephaniah 2-3	Proverbs 18:6-12
6	Philippians 4	2 Kings 23:31-24:20	Proverbs 18:13-18
7	Colossians 1:1-14	2 Kings 25, 2 Chron 36	Proverbs 18:19-24
8	Colossians 1:15-2:5	Obadiah 1	Proverbs 19:1-7
9	Colossians 2:6-23	Jeremiah 1	Proverbs 19:8-14
10	Colossians 3:1-17	Jeremiah 2-3:5	Proverbs 19:15-22
11	Colossians 3:18-4:1	Jeremiah 3:6-4:31	Proverbs 19:23-29
12	Colossians 4:2-18	Jeremiah 5-6	Proverbs 20:1-10
13	1 Thess 1	Jeremiah 7-8	Proverbs 20:11-20
14	1 Thess 2:1-16	Jeremiah 9-10	Proverbs 20:21-30
15	1 Thess 2:17-3:13	Jeremiah 11-12	Proverbs 21:1-8
16	1 Thess 4:1-12	Jeremiah 13-14	Proverbs 21:9-15
17	1 Thess 4:13-5:11	Jeremiah 15-16	Proverbs 21:16-23
18	1 Thess 5:12-28	Jeremiah 17-18	Proverbs 21:24-31
19	2 Thess 1	Jeremiah 19-20	Proverbs 22:1-8
20	2 Thess 2	Jeremiah 21-22	Proverbs 22:9-16
21	2 Thess 3	Jeremiah 23-24	Proverbs 22:17-23
22	1 Timothy 1	Jeremiah 25-26	Proverbs 22:24-29
23	1 Timothy 2	Jeremiah 27-28	Proverbs 23:1-9
24	1 Timothy 3	Jeremiah 29-30	Proverbs 23:10-18
25	1 Timothy 4	Jeremiah 31-32	Proverbs 23:19-28
26	1 Timothy 5	Jeremiah 33-34	Proverbs 23:29-35
27	1 Timothy 6	Jeremiah 35-36	Proverbs 24:1-12
28	2 Timothy 1	Jeremiah 37-38	Proverbs 24:13-22
29	2 Timothy 2	Jeremiah 39-40	Lam 1:1-9
30	2 Timothy 3	Jeremiah 41-43	Lam 1:10-22
31	2 Timothy 4	Jeremiah 44-45	Lam 2:1-10

OCTOBER 1

EPHESIANS 6:1-9   Paul moves on to relationships between parents and children. This delicate relationship changes as a child moves into adolescence and beyond. Very early, the primary responsibility of parents is to nurture and protect. That phase is taken for granted here.

Later, the parent's task is to give guidance and to help the child learn to accept that guidance (become obedient). Part of guidance is careful modeling of, and instruction in, God's Word and ways (Deut 6:1-9; Prov 22:6). The modeling is at least as important as the formal instruction – and it is here that the fruit of the Spirit is vital (Gal 5:22-23). Think of patience, kindness, gentleness and self-control! Many, perhaps all, parents would like to do some things over again. One thing we might redo if we had the opportunity would be the *manner* in which we handled children. Living out the fruit of the Spirit will improve these relationships!

Note the Lord's standard (vv. 1-4): children who choose to obey parents, and fathers who are not unreasonable in either *what they ask or the manner in which they ask!*

It is logical for Paul to move from the home to relationships outside the home (vv. 5-9). To summarize Paul's comments, we should give good and faithful service to those for whom we are working – and be reasonable and responsible to those who work for us. In each of these roles, the influence of the Holy Spirit should be evident.

HABAKKUK 1   Habakkuk ministered in Judah about twenty-five years before the nation fell to Babylon. The prophecy is in the form of conversation between the prophet and the Lord, and a concluding prayer by the prophet.

Habakkuk had a serious question to pose to the Lord (1:2-4). In light of the nation's sin – the terrible condition of the land – Habakkuk asks, "How long will you wait, God, to do something about it?" God's apparent silence seemed inconsistent to Habakkuk (v. 3). Note how Habakkuk describes the society – violence and paralyzed courts resulting in perverted justice.

The Lord's answer (1:5-11) was not one Habakkuk felt was appropriate. The Lord said He would use the pagan Babylonians to bring His judgment upon Judah. This answer was an ethical dilemma for Habakkuk (1:12-2:1). How could the Lord use a nation more unrighteous than Judah to discipline His people? Look at the illustration (the fish net) that Habakkuk uses to describe Babylon (1:14-17). As Habakkuk finishes his question, you can almost see him fold his arms and ask, "What can the Lord say to that?" (2:1)

PROVERBS 17:8-14   How would one cover over an offense (v. 9)? Not necessarily by ignoring what is wrong, but perhaps by dealing with it privately rather than publicly. In fact, sometimes when we go to the person and speak about what has offended us, we find that we didn't have all the facts, and our feeling was inappropriate. Often the motives of the other person are really not wrong. By dealing directly with people, we have the opportunity to understand one another, and we avoid unfounded criticism.

Take seriously verse 14. Think about the battles you want to take on. Taking on issues that are not of great importance can disrupt your life – and for no good reason. Some things are better left alone.

OCTOBER 2

EPHESIANS 6:10-24   The spiritual battle that we face is real, and it is essential to understand the resources that we have in Christ. We often lose sight of those resources in the battle. The conflict that we intuitively know is there, but is difficult to define, is sketched for us in verses 11-12. There is no question about the reality of these forces. Recall in the gospels how Jesus understood these forces and faced them with the power of the kingdom. How we conduct ourselves personally and as a church is vitally important because God's reputation is at stake (3:10-11). God is demonstrating the extent of His grace and power to these rulers and authorities!

Because the battle is real, Paul admonishes Christians to use the resources that God has provided (vv. 13-18). The illustrations of battle dress come out of Paul's day – but are readily understood by readers today. Some are defensive, such as the helmet (guarding the mind), the shield (faith), and the breastplate (righteousness – both God's gift to the believer and the believer's integrity). Some are standard equipment that help the soldier function in battle, whether offensive or defensive, such as the shoes (moving with the gospel) and the belt (truth). Some are offensive weapons such as the sword (the Word of God) and the "blanket" of prayer (v. 18).

This battle must be fought in God's way. Refer again to Jesus' words to the disciples (Matt 10:16-20) and Paul's comments to the Corinthians (2 Cor 10:3-5). If we face the battle with God's methods, we are safe. If we use the same weapons that the world is using, we will be outmaneuvered, surrounded, and defeated. *TAKE THIS SECTION VERY SERIOUSLY, FOR WHETHER WE LIKE IT OR NOT, WE ARE IN THE BATTLE!*

<u>HABAKKUK 2</u>   The Lord's answer to Habakkuk is a lesson in His sovereign dealings with the nations (2:2-20). *First,* the Lord told Habakkuk that he (Habakkuk) heard correctly. The message was real, and would happen, and would come in God's time (vv. 2-3). *Second,* it was true that the Babylonians were wicked (vv. 4-5). They were proud, arrogant, and given to alcohol. *Third,* God would deal with Babylon in His time. Babylon's sin would catch up with the nation, and it too would be defeated and plundered – just as it plundered others. Note the five woes (vv. 6, 9, 12, 15, 19) pronounced about Babylon. God is alive and in His temple, and deserves man's obedience and worship (v. 20).

☑Verse 14 contains a promise for the future. The whole earth will know God – not here and there, but as the waters cover the sea. This will happen when the Lord returns, and all knees bow before Jesus as the Son of God, the King, the Messiah.⇔

<u>PROVERBS 17:15-21</u>   God is committed to genuine justice. His standards are far above ours (v. 15). We all know that our justice system sometimes acquits the guilty (get the best lawyer) and condemns the innocent. Once again, remember Deuteronomy 1:17. God seeks justice, and we must be as well.

A real friend remains loyal even in hard times (v. 17). Perhaps that is a good definition of friendship. The fellowship of God's people should be a model of loyalty. That kind of love is a dramatic witness to the world and brings glory to God. It demonstrates the power of the Holy Spirit in the lives of God's people.

<u>OCTOBER 3</u>

<u>PHILIPPIANS 1</u>   Paul wrote the book of Philippians from prison in Rome while he was awaiting trial for his faith. Review Paul's visit to Philippi in Acts 16:11-40. This brief epistle contains personal testimony, theology, encouragement, and gentle admonition.

Paul had a true pastoral heart. He prayed for the Philippian Christians faithfully and with confidence (vv. 3-6). Note his specific confidence that God would continue His work in the Christians, bringing them to maturity and to the "day of Christ Jesus" – the second coming. Compare this with John 10:28. There is protection in the hand of Christ!

Focus on Paul's testimony in verses 12-26. Even in prison, the Lord used Paul in a mighty way to reach people who would not otherwise have been touched with the gospel (vv. 12-14). Further, Paul's example encouraged others to speak more boldly and freely of their faith (v. 14). Never mind that some were preaching from wrong motives (vv. 15-18); God would sort that out in due time. Follow Paul's heart expression in verses 19ff. He was ready to follow the Lord, whatever that meant!

Notice too how Paul held life loosely (vv. 20-26), and compare this with Luke 9:23-26. Paul was truly a living example of what Jesus taught as the standard for the Christian life.

HABAKKUK 3   A chastened and humbled Habakkuk prayed to the Lord with a much different attitude than in Chapters 1-2. He approaches God humbly after understanding God's message. First note the awe he felt and the plea for mercy with which he began his prayer (vv. 1-2). He understands the power of God's sovereign acts (vv. 3-15). ☑Although these verses relate to God's judgment on Judah, the vision seems to go beyond Judah to the great judgment that God will bring on the Day of the Lord.⇦ Habakkuk was afraid of the coming judgment on Judah – yet he voices faith and trust in the Lord for whatever comes (vv. 16-19)! His faith and joy in the Lord were firm. What an example!

PROVERBS 17:22-28   "A discerning man keeps wisdom in view..." (v. 24). Keeping God's perspective – keeping God's word in hand and heart – will protect you from the pulls and temptations of the world (v. 24b).

Take special note of verses 27-28. Using words with restraint means careful choice and timing of what we say. You don't even have to know much to seem intelligent if you are slow to speak. Many could use this advice. We are often anxious to hear ourselves talk!

OCTOBER 4

PHILIPPIANS 2   Does the blessing and fellowship of the Christian life mean anything to you? This is the question Paul poses in verse 1 to encourage believers at Philippi to work together in love for their common purpose in the church. He suggests how to relate to one another (vv. 2, 3b, 4, 5), and points out pitfalls to avoid (v. 3a). Notice that Paul doesn't say they should all agree on the *methods* of the work, but on the *goal* to be achieved. Paul tells them to give up personal ambitions and pride, and consider other people "better than yourselves." If we will really listen to other's ideas, we will see that some have real merit – even more merit than what "I" had in mind.

The "clincher" in relationships is the example of the Lord Jesus (vv. 5-8). The Lord of the Universe assumed the role of a servant to accomplish God's will, and He is our role model (v. 5; 1 John 2:6). We struggle with this. Society values managers instead of servants. Being willing and able to be a servant is the work of the Holy Spirit!

Think about verse 12. "...continue to work out your salvation with fear and trembling." The passage does not mean we should live in fear as we work *for* our salvation. It does, however, refer to the awe and respect we should have for God as one of His redeemed, and as our lives reveal the work of redemption to a dark and needy world.

ZEPHANIAH 1   Zephaniah was God's messenger to Judah during the reign of King Josiah. Zephaniah's message penetrates beneath the surface of Josiah's reforms and addresses the heart of the people. A king can provide the leadership and the context for good, but spiritual integrity is a personal decision.

☑The key phrase in the book is "the day of the Lord." As in Joel, there is a more immediate meaning to the prophecy, fulfilled when Babylon swept away the nation, but also applies to judgment at Christ's return. The specific charges that the Lord brings against Judah are idolatrous worship (1:4-10) and complacency – the belief that God does not see or care about their behavior (1:12). Note the description of the Day of the Lord in 1:2-3, 14-18.⇦

PROVERBS 18:1-5   As you consider verse 2, review the notes about 17:27-28 in yesterday's reading. Many of us like to hear ourselves talk – even when we don't know much about the subject. How much better to listen and understand what the other person is saying – then speak with discernment.

OCTOBER 5

PHILIPPIANS 3   While reading verses 1-11, think back to what Paul wrote to the Galatian Christians (Gal 3:1-5, 10-14). The tension over keeping the law was not only in Galatia but also in Philippi. As far as the credentials of orthodoxy were concerned, Paul could travel with the best (vv. 4b-6). As a Christian, however, Paul's perspective was quite different. Just how different is evident in verses 7-11. His credentials as an orthodox Jew were rubbish (vv. 7-8)! His place in the kingdom was everything. His very reason for living is in verses 10-11.

There is an important message here for each of us. What is most important to you? Where is your identity? In your profession or in professional achievement? In accumulated wealth? In family? In "things"? Paul's testimony is significant. As a Jew, he had it all! But it meant nothing in light of the gospel. "Reality orientation" will lead us to conclude that *all* personal achievement pales relative to our relation to Christ. If we are able to see this reality (for that is what it is!), we can then move on to getting our act together as Christians (3:12-4:1). Getting on with serving the Lord follows logically. *This is what it means to be transformed by renewing the mind (Rom 12:2).* This is mature Biblical thinking that will change our lives and the world.

ZEPHANIAH 2-3   After the indictment from the Lord in Chapter 1, Zephaniah urges God's people to repent (2:1-3). The message is to listen and act before it is too late! This isn't an offer to avert judgment based upon this repentance – but rather a call to those people who were still godly, to seek God with all of their hearts. Perhaps these righteous people will be sheltered when the storm of the Lord's anger comes.

Judah would not be the only nation to feel the hand of the Lord (2:4-15). The Lord's charges against other nations are pride, insults, and taunts against His people (vv. 8-11), and the pride of Assyria, which believed that nothing could touch her (vv. 13-15).

God's comments about Jerusalem, however, are specific and hard-hitting (3:1-5). The political leaders, the prophets, and the priests – all the leaders bore responsibility before the Lord. Note, however, that the Lord was faithful in the deplorable situation (v. 5). He watched over His own.

☑Shift your thinking again to the Day of the Lord (3:6-20). This is the language of worldwide destruction (v. 8). There is also the promise of peace and a universal acknowledgment of God as the Lord of heaven and earth by not only Israelites but by the survivors of the nations (2:10-11). Compare this with Isaiah 2:1-5. God *will* have His day.⇦

PROVERBS 18:6-12   It is impressive how much Proverbs has to say about our words! Without further comment here, note verses 6-8, and review James 3:1-12.

We often believe we can build walls that will protect us from danger. The walls may be brick, stone, financial, or relationships. Note the illusion of safety in verse 11. Real safety is found only in the Lord. Build obedience to Him and righteousness of character (through the Holy Spirit) for real safety.

OCTOBER 6

PHILIPPIANS 4   Euodia and Syntyche were significant people in the church at Philippi (vv. 2-3). Their disagreement, whatever its nature, was known to Paul, and he took time and space in his handwritten letter to add this plea to the two women. If the difficulty was public enough for Paul to know about it, it was probably common knowledge in the church and had impeded the work. Perhaps it was with this situation in mind that Paul wrote 2:1-11. Those words certainly could be applied to the disagreement.

Give your attention to verses 4-9. If you apply these verses to your own life, how would your thinking change? You would certainly fret less and pray more. Much of our thought life would be modified if we were to ponder things that are true, noble, pure, lovely, and admirable! Check Romans 12:2. Here is the making of a transformed mind and life.

2 KINGS 23:31-24:20 The sad ending for the nation of Judah was near. There were no righteous kings after Josiah, and judgment was due. Josiah's son Jehoahaz reigned for three months, but was taken to Egypt in chains, and heavy tribute was exacted from Judah by the Egyptians (23:31-35). Jehoiakim, Josiah's second son, became king and reigned eleven years, but had no inclination to serve and follow the Lord (23:36-37). Even at this late hour in Judah's history, there was warning from the Lord as raiders from several nations chipped away at the land (24:2-4).

Finally, three months after Jehoiachin, son of Jehoiakim, became king, Babylon made Judah a vassal in 597 BC (24:8-17). The text tells us that the national treasures were carried off, and the best of the population (including Daniel) were taken to Babylon. King Jehoiachin was taken, and Nebuchadnezzar placed Zedekiah, Jehoiachin's uncle, on the throne in Jerusalem. Sadly, Zedekiah continued the sinful ways of the former rulers.

PROVERBS 18:13-18 Listening and speaking – so much a part of life and the fabric of relationships. What we say and how we say it has enormous consequence on how we affect others. How we listen and respond will tell volumes about how real or superficial our interest is in the other person.

Consider the wisdom of verse 13. Have you ever tried to speak to a subject, only to hear a quick answer before your words were considered? More to our point, have you ever been guilty of this affront yourself? It *is* an affront! For anyone to walk away believing they have not been heard undercuts our ability to minister to that person or to have effective ministry together. Now read verse 2. If we are not genuinely interested in the convictions of another person – enough to want to understand them – we are fools! Usually the second part of the verse goes with the first.

OCTOBER 7

COLOSSIANS 1:1-14 Colosse was a city in Asia between Ephesus and Antioch. There is no evidence that Paul visited the city, but 1:7 suggests that Epaphras brought the gospel there. Not much is known of Epaphras, but the text tells us that he was Paul's "dear fellow servant," and 4:12 suggests that he was from Colosse.

In the letter, Paul addresses heretical thinking in the church that had depreciated the person and work of Christ (quite probably Gnosticism). As a result, the book has a wonderful presentation of Christ's work and sufficiency.

Read Paul's prayer for the church (vv. 9-14). His conclusion in verses 13-14 is worth memorizing. As Christians we have been taken from the dominion of Satan and brought into the kingdom of Christ. *We no longer answer to the Evil One!*

2 KINGS 25; 2 CHRONICLES 36   Zedekiah, who had taken an oath of loyalty to Nebuchadnezzar in the Lord's name (2 Chron 36:13), foolishly rebelled against him, precipitating the total collapse of Jerusalem. The king and his advisors had become more hardened to sin (36:14), and the Lord used the cruel Babylonians (modern Iraq) as the hammer in His hand (see Hab 1:5-11). The final fall of the city was in 586 BC. Note in 2 Chronicles 36:15-21 the sad commentary as to why this happened.

As the Babylonians took the city they destroyed the things that were nearest to the people's hearts. Even though they had been far from the Lord, the temple remained very important to them. It is sad to read of the destruction of the temple and the removal of the metals and bronze that had been the symbol of God's presence. Yet this is precisely what the Lord had told them would happen if the nation worshipped the gods of the other nations. Sin exacts a price.

PROVERBS 18:19-24   Compare verse 19 with Matthew 5:23-26. Verse 19 gives a practical reason for handling disputes with another person when one has been at fault. It may be difficult or impossible for an offended person to be rational while there is unresolved conflict. The act of asking for forgiveness will usually take the fire out of the offended person. There is a deeper reason, however, to handle the matter. The offense against the other person is also an offense against the Lord God. Be quick to ask for forgiveness and restoration, as well as to extend forgiveness to someone who has offended you (Matt 6:14-15). Keep short accounts!

OCTOBER 8

COLOSSIANS 1:15-2:5   →Paul here presents God's grand plan of salvation. Jesus is the creator of all (v. 16). This includes the universe: the heavens, and all living things, both flesh and spirit. He predates all of these, and by His power all things continue to exist (v. 17). He heads the church (v. 18). God's will is to heal the sin-sickness that pervades the universe through the blood of Jesus (v. 20).←

All of the above is truth about God – theology. Now Paul becomes specific and personal as he applies the truth to the recipients of the letter. *Redemption through the blood of Christ has made a difference to them.* It has changed their thinking and has brought holiness into their lives (vv. 21-22). Notice the condition that Paul added in verse 23: "If you continue in your faith...." Does this mean that *staying* in the faith depends on my *effort*? Review what Jesus said in John 10:28. He made it clear that no one could take His people from His hand. Yet in Matthew 24:13 He states that "he who stands firm to the end will be saved." Perhaps the Apostle John brings these two seemingly contradictory ideas together in 1 John 2:19. He speaks about some who had left the fellowship of the church, saying they went because they never were really part of the body of Christ. Thus, continuing in the faith is the *evidence* of real life in Christ!

A gem of truth is in 2:2-3. All treasures of wisdom and knowledge are found in Christ. Compare this with 1 Corinthians 1:23-24, 30. *The Lord Jesus is the integrating truth that brings life together!* So don't let anyone deceive you with any other ideas (2:4). Stay on track with Christ in the faith.

OBADIAH 1 The book of Obadiah was written to the Edomites about 845 BC, corresponding to events in Kings and Chronicles that we have read about. 2 Kings 8:20-24 and 2 Chronicles 21:8-10 record the revolt of Edom from Judah. At the time, Edom had been subservient to Judah, paying tribute yearly to the king of Judah. Edomites were descendants of Esau (Gen 25:30; 32:3; 36:1). When the Israelites came out of Egypt, Edom was spared the judgment that came to the other nations. The Israelites were expressly forbidden to touch the land of Edom and told not to provoke them to battle (Deut 2:2-6). Numbers 20:14-21 gives the account of the Israelites asking for and being refused permission to pass through Edom, addressing their request to the king of Edom from "your brother Israel."

We have insight into the Edomites' attitude toward Israel in this short book. Although none of this is mentioned in Kings and Chronicles, God cared about the Edomites and sent His prophet to them to warn them.

Specifically, they were proud and arrogant (v. 3), violent toward "your brother Jacob" (v. 10), and showed no mercy while Israel was being ravished (v. 11; Ps 137:7). Verses 12-14 contain seven reprimands to the Edomites. The principles are universal. No nation should gloat or fail to show mercy in victory. ☑A day of judgment for all of the nations is coming (v. 15), and God will set the accounts straight. Specifically, this is the Day of the Lord that will bring God's judgment on the nations. Note that deliverance for God's people will come to Mount Zion (Jerusalem, v. 17; cf. Zech 14:3-4), and the Lord's kingdom will be established – the kingdom of the Messiah at the time of the second coming (v. 21).⇦

PROVERBS 19:1-7   We often blame God for our foolish decisions or the consequences of sin. This is expressed in verse 3. Making someone else responsible for our problem is called "scapegoating." Consider this for handling situations that seem unfair: If I am responsible for what others are saying, I should learn from it; if others are unfairly attributing responsibility to me, I can let God sort it out (Prov 20:22; Rom 12:17-21). Link this with verse 23. Those who walk in the light – in the fear of the Lord – can trust Him fully. This principle gives the basis for real peace!

OCTOBER 9

COLOSSIANS 2:6-23   Verses 8 and 16-23 give a clue about the heresy that the church was confronting. Verse 8 seems to indicate that some admixture of secular or pagan religious philosophy had crept into the church. In verses 16-23 it seems that once again the Jewish regulations had been presented as necessary for salvation.

With this in mind, give attention to verses 9-15. Jesus is God in the flesh (v. 9; cf. John 1:14,18; Heb 1:3). As in Chapter 1, Paul is focusing on the divinity and fullness of Christ. We as believers are identified with Christ (vv. 10-12; cf. Rom 6:4-5), and that has brought us life and forgiveness (v. 13).

Christ's complete and public victory at the cross is beautifully stated in verses 14-15. This was the public statement that all of the forces of Satan understood! The pivotal point in history is the death and resurrection. Allow these powerful truths to shape your view of the world and the issues of right and wrong, truth and untruth, reality and fantasy. *Choose to stand with Jesus in the victory of the cross.*

As to the Jewish regulations, Paul says they were merely a shadow of the reality that was to come – Jesus. Now that the reality has been made clear, the shadows can go (vv. 16-17). He warns them about those who would again try to lay the regulations on them (vv. 18-19). Keep to the course, and stay with liberty in Christ (vv. 20-23).

JEREMIAH 1   Jeremiah is called the weeping prophet. He lived through the reforms of Josiah to the exile and had the unpleasant assignment of telling the king and the people what God was doing. Because he was faithful in this assignment, he was viewed as a traitor. He suffered during his ministry. He often stood alone for the truth. But he was faithful!

The Lord called Jeremiah, having chosen him from before he was born (v. 5). Jeremiah argued that he couldn't speak (1:6), but the Lord rebuked him (vv. 7-10). God used two illustrations to tell Jeremiah that just as an almond tree blossoms and bears almonds (v. 11), the prophecies would come true. And they would include judgment poured out on the land from the north (the boiling pot, v. 13). Especially notice the Lord's advice and warning to the prophet (v. 17). "Stand for Me, and receive My protection," God tells him, "and don't be afraid of the people!"

PROVERBS 19:8-14   The person who knows and follows God (He who gets wisdom, v. 8) is taking care of his own soul. Nothing else is worth pursuing, for eternity depends upon our decision. It is good to think about this regularly, and to test your interests, motives, and goals. Use God's word as the standard; 1 John 2:3-6 is a good and reliable benchmark. It precisely outlines the direction of someone who follows the Lord Jesus.

Young men and women, seek the Lord's leading about whom you will marry. Although verses 13b and 14b speak about a wife, the text just as well fits a husband. We need God's help in this matter, for often someone who seems perfect proves a poor "fit." The Lord will, in His own way, make this decision clear if we seek His leading in this supremely important matter.

OCTOBER 10

COLOSSIANS 3:1-17   Paul appeals for godly living based on the facts presented. *Set your heart* on things above (v. 1). *Set your mind* on things above (v. 2). It is where Christ is – and where God has made a place for those He has redeemed (Eph 2:6). Do it because of what He has done and what is to come (vv. 3-4). **FACT**: You died with Christ at the cross and are with Him in the resurrection (v. 3; cf. Rom 6:5). **FACT**: Jesus is coming again – and you will share in His glory (v. 4). Get rid of the things that are offensive to God (vv. 5-9). The choice and initiative to act must be ours (vv. 8-9), but God gives us the ability (power) to carry through the "house cleaning" – the renewal that changes our outlook and behavior (v. 10).

Allow God to change your life and relationships to conform to His will (vv. 12-17). Compare the characteristics in verse 12 with the attitudes that Jesus displayed (cf. 1 John 2:6).

Follow the sequence of actions in relationships and the result in the fellowship. "*Bear* with each other and *forgive*..." (v. 13). "*...put on* love that binds them all together in perfect unity" (v. 14). These attitudes open the way for a level of relationship impossible in the surrounding world.

The result is revolutionary (vv. 15-17). It includes the peace of God (v. 15); thankfulness (v. 15); the blessing of ministering in the church (v. 16a); and songs of gratitude (v. 16b). Finally, all that we do is motivated by Christ (v. 17).

Is this "pie in the sky" or achievable? *It is achievable, and it is God's will for His children.* Please note that growth comes from taking one step at a time, requires choice and initiative, and brings our actions (again, by choice) under the authority of Christ.

JEREMIAH 2:1-3:5   As you read Chapter 2, note the Lord's specific complaints about the behavior of Judah. Although the people started well (v. 2), they left the true worship of the Lord, followed idols, and did not ask the Lord for help (vv. 4-6). The leaders of the country – both political and religious – were leading the people away from the Lord (v. 8), although God graciously led and protected them (v. 7). God summarizes His charge against them in verse 13. They forsook the true and living God and turned elsewhere! See God's perspective in verse 19. Through all of this, there is colossal self-deception in the people (v. 35).

The Lord compares Judah to an unfaithful wife (3:1-3), but still the nation has the audacity to assume He will respond to their prayer (vv. 4-5).

PROVERBS 19:15-22   The Lord watches over the needy (v. 17). Since this is God's agenda, it must be ours as well. Watch for this theme in the remainder of the book.

Disciplining young people in our society is a challenge for parents (v. 18). Yet here is the Lord's advice. Don't give up; stay with the course. Remember the example of Eli in 1 Samuel 2:22-25 and 3:10-14. Although Eli spoke to his sons about their sin, he could have done more. His lack of appropriate discipline led to disaster in the family. The resource for every Christian is prayer. This is one area where we had better not be found wanting!

OCTOBER 11

COLOSSIANS 3:18-4:1   This section deals with relationships in the home and workplace, and is similar to Ephesians 5:22-6:9. Titus 2:3-10 and 1 Peter 3:1-7 also are similar. The emphasis in each passage is to bring our relationships under God's will to bring glory to Him. There is a consistently high standard for husbands, wives, children, workers, and masters.

JEREMIAH 3:6-4:31   Although the Lord compares Judah to an unfaithful wife (3:1-3), the Lord actually considers Judah more sinful and decadent than Israel (vv. 6-11)! In the midst of this sin, the Lord is still anxious to receive her back – but only if repentance is genuine (vv. 12-13, 19-20 and 4:1-4). Notice the bitterness of apostasy (3:21).

☑In 3:14-18, the prophet looks forward to the Lord's return and His new work in the lives of His people (cf. Isa 2:1-4).   This is a parenthetical note of hope in the midst of God's charges against His people. It will be a time of renewed heart and the reestablishment of a unified Israel (vv. 17b-18).   The Lord God will be on the throne in Jerusalem – the Messiah (v. 17).⇦

A vision of the disaster about to overtake the land appears in 4:5-31. Here the boiling pot of 1:13-14 is spilling on the land. *In the midst of this, people persisted with beautiful clothes, jewelry, and painted eyes (v. 30)!* Self-deception convinced them that life would go on! But judgment was already on the way (v. 7; cf. Matt 24:36-44).

PROVERBS 19:23-29   Faith anchored in the Lord God brings peace (v. 23). This peace rides above circumstances – even trouble. Trouble will come! The miracle (from the world's perspective) is that trouble doesn't touch the inner peace of the believer. Anticipate your own reaction to trouble. Begin to think of how God will see you through. Train yourself to think truth.   Then, when difficulty comes, you will be genuinely prepared.

OCTOBER 12

COLOSSIANS 4:2-18   Paul's final instruction to the church is found in verses 2-6, and it regards two separate but related responsibilities. The first is prayer directed to watchfulness and thankfulness (and don't forget to pray, he says, for his own outreach ministry). The second is relationships between Christians and those outside the church. Paul puts it so well. Be wise in these relationships, and make the most of them! They are important! They are opportunities that God puts before us. Be thinking of each opportunity.

To complete the book, Paul sends greetings to and from several people. The interesting thing about these is the network of believers involved in kingdom work.   These people were concerned for one another, praying for one another, and helping each other. It was a worldwide effort, and even then they were keeping in touch with one another. Good examples for us today.

JEREMIAH 5-6   In Chapter 5, the prophet speaks about the depth of the nation's corruption. If only one person could be found who dealt honestly and in truth (v. 1), judgment would be averted. The prophet wondered if it was only the common people who were ignorant and rebellious (v. 4), but found it was the leaders as well (v. 5).

In spite of all the Lord had done for the people and the nation, they turned to sin – aggressively (v. 7ff.). They even said that what the Lord promised as a consequence of their sin wasn't true (vv. 12-13)! Read the rest of the chapter, noting their sin and unbelief. Even the sea observes the boundaries set by the Lord, but His own people did not (vv. 22-23).

In particular, note the message of verses 26-31. There were evil deeds, and the Lord noted the injustice (v. 28). The rich and powerful, who could have defended the fatherless and the poor, would not do so! For this, the Lord was calling them to account.

Chapter 6 outlines the coming siege and fall of Jerusalem. Judgment would come to the entire city: children and adults (v. 11), from the least to the greatest (v. 13a), including the prophets and priests who had spoken lies (v. 13b-14). The judgment would come, without mercy, from a nation to the north (v. 22). Its intensity would be like the fire of a foundry (vv. 27-30)! Yet, even at this late hour, the Lord called on His people to turn back to the truth and find genuine rest for their souls (v. 16).

PROVERBS 20:1-10   In verse 5, the author expresses how difficult it is to understand the heart. Even our own motivations are hard to understand. Psychologists tell us that a large part of our personality is hidden from our own perception. Where the text says that "a man of understanding draws them out," it may mean that as we grasp the truths of God's Word and allow it to change our lives, we gain insight into our own hearts. As Jesus reveals Himself to us, we see ourselves in the context of His truth (John 14:21).

OCTOBER 13

1 THESSALONIANS 1   The gospel came to Thessalonica during the second missionary journey, after the vision Paul received with the "call to Macedonia" (Acts 17:1-9). A solid witness and church was established. We learn something about Paul's ministry (vv. 4-5) and the character of the Christians and the church (vv. 6-10). Verse 8 is instructive regarding the witness of the church. Thessalonica was a seaport city. Believers were changed so profoundly that the news had spread throughout the world of the first century, probably through the channels of commerce.

To appreciate the depth of the change, note verses 9-10. These believers, who had worshipped idols, made an about face to love and serve the Lord Jesus (cf. v. 3). Part of that change was a new hope, the expectation of the second coming (v. 10). Is it any wonder that Paul was thankful to the Lord for what He had done (v. 2)?

JEREMIAH 7-8   The Lord told Jeremiah to go where the people would be – the temple gate – to tell them the truth from Him (7:1-10:25). Jeremiah's discourse is called "the Temple Gate Message." It is significant that at its outset there is a gracious invitation for the people to change, and thus avoid the consequence of sin (vv. 2-8).

As Jeremiah preached, note the Lord's specific complaints to His people. In Judah, the shell of true religion was there but not the substance (vv. 22-26). The people were sacrificing according to the regulations, but there was no obedience to the Lord's commands. This can still be the problem of religious people and the Christian church: the forms of religion without heart! No substance! Listen to the Lord through Jeremiah, and allow the message to penetrate your thinking.

The Lord saw stealing, murder, adultery, perjury, and idol worship – and then on top of it all, the hypocritical forms of worship to the Lord (vv. 9-11). To make matters worse, the people claimed that observing the forms of worship kept them safe (v. 10)! Remember this as you read the chapter, and look for the Lord's response.

Chapter 8 follows the same theme. The people asserted that they were wise because they had the law of the Lord. But without obedience to the terms of the law, they were wrong (v. 8)! Read the Lord's complaints (vv. 4-7), and look for the coming result of their sins (vv. 9-13). There is shattered hope (vv. 15, 19-20) and the prophet's own heartache in the realization of coming disaster (vv. 21-22).

PROVERBS 20:11-20   God has given us the ability to see, hear, and understand (v. 12). Jesus said about many who heard Him, "though seeing, they do not see; though hearing, they do not hear or understand" (Matt 13:13). The sad thing is that often we hear what we want to hear rather than listen to the truth. After each of the letters to the seven churches (Rev 2-3), Jesus invites those who have ears to hear to hear what He writes to them. Think for a moment about the agony of those who stand before the living God and know with crystal clarity that they did not listen to the truth – even though they heard the words! May each of us give our attention to God's word and respond in obedience!

Do you catch the deceit in verse 14? In the marketplace in many areas of the world, it is the custom to bargain for the best price, to depreciate the value of goods, then walk away believing you have "taken" the seller when he has reduced the price. The Bible calls it what it is.

When reading verse 15, realize that speaking knowledge should characterize the child of God. To speak the truth – words of encouragement that turn people to the Lord – is the high calling of the Christian.

OCTOBER 14

1 THESSALONIANS 2:1-16   One of the finest models for the Christian worker is presented here as Paul explains the Christian's responsibility to the gospel message. The heart of this task is explained in verse 4. The commission is from the Lord, and it is to Him alone that Paul answered. Attempting to please people rather than the Lord has crippled countless ministers and Christian workers. Further, the "marketing" mentality makes it important to please the "customer." Paul took a different stance, and this was the source of courage in the face of stiff opposition (vv. 2-3).

Look at how the missionaries worked with the new Christians (vv. 7-12). They were so attentive to the needs of the congregation that Paul could compare them to a mother caring for little children (v. 7). It was not only a "message" or "theology" that they shared but their lives (can a mother do less?) (v. 8). There was no forty-hour week in their vocabulary. Night and day they gave their lives (v. 9). They were without guile, giving the care that a father would give to his children (vv. 10-11). Observe the result of the work of Paul and Silas and the power of the Holy Spirit in the lives of the Thessalonian Christians (vv. 13-16).

This is the biblical model of discipleship. It was based in the gospel message and biblical truth, and that alone. People who cared enough to give their own lives in the effort met needs in other lives. The missionaries taught and modeled a new lifestyle, so that the lives of the new believers were turned 180 degrees – and their witness "rang out" from their city to the rest of the world (1:8). May God help us to be as faithful to our calling!

JEREMIAH 9-10   Today's reading continues the "Temple Gate Message" that started in Chapter 7. Jeremiah has been called the weeping prophet. He felt so burdened by how his people had gone astray that he could cry night and day (9:1)! Some reasons for his sorrow appear in verses 2-6. His people were unfaithful, deceitful, and directed their lives to sin (v. 5b). The coming result of their sin is in verses 7-11.

Look carefully at the Lord's direct statement (vv. 12-16). Note how insidiously sin enters our lives and homes (v. 21). Can you apply this to modern-day life? Look at what is really worth while in life as defined by the Lord (vv. 23-24).

Chapter 10 contrasts idols with the true God (vv. 1-16). Tragically, because the nation has been choosing the wrong object of worship, they have a terminal illness (v. 19). Think about the metaphors in verses 20-22.

PROVERBS 20:21-30   One of the worst traps that can imprison the soul is revenge (v. 22). The destructive energy and emotion expended in this effort can cripple a personality. Further, revenge diminishes our judgment. We can't accurately apprehend the other person's motivation in the perceived wrong. Letting God settle accounts is to trust Him, not only to bring justice, but to care for you in relationships. To focus on doing right is much wiser than to think you can straighten out the rest of the world, and even worse, get even. Check Romans 12:17-21.

How important is God's word in our lives? Consider verse 27, and compare this with Psalm 139:23-24 and Hebrews 4:12-13. We need this insight from the Lord every day.

OCTOBER 15

1 THESSALONIANS 2:17-3:13   Paul's pastoral relationship to the church is even more clearly defined beginning at 2:17 and continuing through Chapter 3. This is the relationship of a spiritual father with his children. Look at the language used: He felt "intense longing" to see those in the church (2:17); the church was his hope, joy, crown, and glory (2:19, 20); when he hadn't been able to go to the Thessalonians "we could stand it no longer" (3:1).

Paul's anxiety was founded in his concern for their well-being in the Lord. He didn't want them to be discouraged by persecution, or be drawn away by temptation (3:3, 5).

Paul's heart for the Christians in Thessalonica, as expressed in prayer, is recorded in verses 11-13: love for one another (and for all others), strength for holy living, and a life prepared by holy living to meet Christ.

JEREMIAH 11-12   God established His covenant with Israel after He gave them the law at Sinai (Exod 24:1-8). This was a solemn agreement that the people would follow the decrees of the Lord, confirmed with the blood of sacrifices sprinkled on the people. Deuteronomy 27-28 outlines the blessings of keeping the law and the curses for disregarding it. Here, through Jeremiah, the Lord reminds the people of the terms of the covenant. Their condition, however, was not one of inadvertent disobedience, but a planned return to idol worship (11:9-10). Because of this, the Lord planned disaster for the people (v. 17)! At that time, Jeremiah learned that there was a plan to kill him (vv. 18-20). Remember the Lord's promise to Jeremiah when he was called (1:17-19). Because Jeremiah was faithful, the Lord would protect him (vv. 21-23)!

In Chapter 12, Jeremiah raised the same ethical question that Habakkuk brought to the Lord (Hab 1:2-4). How come, Lord, the wicked prosper (v. 1)? Although they speak of the Lord, their lives and actions show that their words are merely "window dressing" (v. 2). Further, they also say the Lord doesn't see what they are doing (v. 4b)!

The Lord answered in verses 5-13. He *did* see and *would* act. Note, however, His word of mercy, for the Lord would not completely wipe out the nations or Judah. A remnant would survive and return to the land in the Lord's time (vv. 14-17; cf. 25:11-13; 29:10). As a condition of this restoration, the people must acknowledge the Lord (vv. 15-16).

PROVERBS 21:1-8   Our ability to deceive ourselves – to rationalize – is part of the human condition (v. 2). We can arrange things in our mind to explain our actions even when they are wrong.   But stop and consider! Our verdict is not the one that counts. The Lord's judgment counts (v. 2). With this in mind, apply verse 3 to your life. Forget about rationalizations. Open your heart to the light of God's word and ask the Lord for insight to see situations from His point of view. Obey God by aligning your life with His truth. It is the way of life.

OCTOBER 16

1 THESSALONIANS 4:1-12   Paul discusses the Christian lifestyle in his letter to the Thessalonians – and begins with the need to avoid sexual impurity (vv. 3-8). The culture in Thessalonica was not only lax, but encouraged immorality. Paul's comment about the passionate lust of the heathen is in light of that promiscuous society (v. 5).   The Christian standard of sexual purity required an about-face.

The word about controlling one's own body (v. 4) may mean "living with one's own wife" – contrasted with the common practice in Thessalonica of uncontrolled promiscuity. Related to this is a warning about "wronging one's brother" (v. 6). A wrong sexual relationship with another's wife obviously wrongs not only the woman but her husband. To extend the principle, a wrong relationship with an unmarried woman violates her and robs the person she will marry of her purity. Speaking only of the "brother" seems strange to our ears, since the sin is just as much against the "sister" as the "brother," but both should be understood in the context. Note the warning that God will punish such sins (v. 6).

The attention the Bible gives to sexual purity is impressive – revealing God's deep concern that this be a protected relationship in marriage. It also reveals the state of society when the gospel was extending its influence in the New Testament world. Our society must be much the same. Illicit sexual liaisons are accepted by more people in our own society than even a few years ago. Advertising and the media, *to which we are all exposed*, have done much – both subtly and overtly – to undermine values that were generally held. We need the input of God's Word to keep our own perspective and agenda the same as the Lord's.

Paul describes the "Christian work ethic" (vv. 11-12). The model is a quiet, steady, honest industry that will bear witness to a watching world. Working with one's hands also implies producing something useful. This kind of work is more than simply "making a living."

JEREMIAH 13-14   The Lord used an object lesson to bring home the gravity of the people's sin in Chapter 13. The spoiled linen belt illustrated the people spoiled by sin, and the disrupted bond between the Lord and His people that resulted. As you read verses 15-23, hear Jeremiah's sad voice as he laments over Jerusalem. This is the weeping prophet (v. 17). The people's hope was frustrated (v. 16): Sin demands a terrible price (v. 22)! Listen to the Lord's words as the chapter closes (vv. 24-27). It is easy to slip into self-deception, as the people of Jerusalem had done. Sin deceives. The one way to avoid this danger is to constantly evaluate our lives with the truth of the Bible.

Judah was stricken by a ground-cracking drought, as well as a spiritual drought (14:2-6). Jeremiah said the drought was God's work (vv. 7-9). The Lord told Jeremiah to not even pray for the people (vv. 10-12)! Jeremiah replied that false prophets lulled the people with their false messages (v. 13), and the Lord responded in verses 14-16. The Lord hadn't sent these "prophets" or told them what to say.

The last verses of the chapter (vv. 17-22) are an emotional expression that allows us to see the heart of a true prophet. Jeremiah loved his people. He suffered because of their sin.

PROVERBS 21:9-15   The text again reminds us to respond to the needs of the poor (v. 13). Review 19:17. God wants us to meet the needs of others when we can. Cornelius, the first Gentile to receive the Holy Spirit in the early church, was remembered by God for his kindness to the poor (Acts 10:4). James defines true religion, in part, as responsiveness to those who are needy and defenseless (James 1:27).

In our reading for today, verse 13 carries this one step further. If we do not respond to those in need, when we need help there will also be no response. Jesus applied this principle in a different way when He said if we will not forgive others, we will not receive forgiveness from the Lord (Matt 6:14-15). *We need to remember that this ministering to the poor is God's agenda for His people.*

OCTOBER 17

1 THESSALONIANS 4:13-5:11   Jesus is coming again (4:13-18)! Prior to His death and resurrection, Jesus promised He would come again (John 14:3, Matt 24:30-31). This was confirmed after the resurrection when Jesus was taken into heaven (Acts 1:11). The promise of the Messiah's coming in glory even appears in the Old Testament Scriptures (Zech 9:14). The promise of Jesus' return and the certainty of the resurrection change how a Christian views death. We grieve over the separation of death – but not like those who do not share the hope of redemption (v. 13).

Some had apparently been concerned that those who died before Jesus returned would miss the second coming. These words were meant to allay that fear. In fact, those who have died will be raised first and then those still alive will be caught up together with them to meet Christ (vv. 15-17). All will then be with the Lord for eternity.

The question that we all have is, "When will it happen? When will Jesus come again?" In 5:1-2, it is significant that Paul uses the term "the day of the Lord." Remember that this term is used for God's final judgment on the earth at the coming of Jesus. Review the notes for July 16 and 17 regarding Joel 1 and 2. These verses present the second coming from the perspective of the non-believer (5:1-3). A thief in the night is someone to be feared. The coming of Jesus will bring sudden destruction as sinners are judged. Note too that it will happen when the world is not expecting a cataclysmic event (v. 3), during a time of apparent peace and safety. Turn to Matthew 24:30-31, 36-41 to see Jesus' words.

For the person who is prepared, however, the day does not come with terror (like a thief, v. 4) but as the fulfillment of promise. Jesus' coming is the time to receive the promised salvation (v. 9). Our responsibility is to be ready for Jesus' coming (vv. 6, 8). In speaking about His coming recorded in Mark 13, Jesus tells His disciples *seven times* in one conversation to be alert and watching – for the times will be confusing, with many making false claims! *The protection of the Christian is to trust God, know the Bible, and carefully live for Him.*

JEREMIAH 15-16   In Chapter 15 we see the depth of the people's sin and the depth of God's anger about their rebellion (v. 1). Observe the results of sin (vv. 2-9). Notice that the wealth and freedom of the nation will be lost (vv. 13-14).

In verse 16, Jeremiah expressed his love for God's truth, and in verses 17-18 his pain and loneliness as he bore the Lord's message. Jeremiah even wondered if God would deceive and fail him (v. 18b). This was a sinful question: God would never deceive or fail His servants. The Lord called on Jeremiah to repent – and then he would continue to be the Lord's spokesman and the Lord would protect him (vv. 19-21).

The Lord commanded Jeremiah to assume a different lifestyle – one that set him apart from the people (16:1-9). This lifestyle would raise questions, which would give Jeremiah an opportunity to share the Lord's message (vv. 10-21). The nation and people were drifting along, assuming they were the Lord's people and that all would be well. Not so! Note verse 17. Then look at the cry of Jeremiah's heart as the chapter ends (vv. 19-21).

This message that we keep hearing from the Lord through Jeremiah is one that we need. The Lord wants more than the trappings of religion. The Lord, through the Holy Spirit, desires to make us His people of truth and integrity, people who are integrated in life and personality.

☑In the midst of this pronouncement of woe are two promises. God promised to bring His people back to the land (vv. 14-15). God also declared that He would bring the nations of the world to Jerusalem to worship Him (vv. 19-20). These nations will renounce their idols and false worship because they acknowledge the Lord God as the only true God (cf. Isa 2:1-5; Zech 14:16ff.). Both of these promises will be fulfilled under the Messiah and His rule.⇦

PROVERBS 21:16-23   When the Lord spoke to Joshua as he assumed leadership of the Israelites, God told him to obey all of the law that Moses received from the Lord and not stray from it to the right or the left (Josh 1:6-9). Remember these verses as you consider verse 16 of our chapter. To stray from the truth is dangerous – it is, in fact, deadly!

Consider also verse 21. There is real benefit from pursuing God's will. The word "prosperity" in verse 21 may also be rendered "righteousness." Life, prosperity, and honor by God's standard. The success guaranteed in Joshua 1:7 is from the Lord's perspective and not from the world's. Remember: Eternal reward follows success from God's point of view.

OCTOBER 18

1 THESSALONIANS 5:12-28   Allow Paul's final remarks to find a place in your mind and heart (vv. 12-28). His words give each of us, as Christians, something to work on! Paul is sending along some "family" guidelines: care and respect for those who minister (vv. 12-13) and help

for the less mature in the fellowship (vv. 14-15). *Adopt an optimistic outlook based on reality (vv. 16-18).* Respect the work of the Holy Spirit (v. 19). Finally, test what you hear with the Spirit of God and with the truth of Scripture (v. 21).

JEREMIAH 17-18   God's comment in 17:1 has been fulfilled with the printing press! Note God's reason for the loss of His blessing (v. 4). When all is lost, the fault will lie only with the people who have chosen sin. The verses that follow outline the spiritual desert in which the ungodly live and the blessing of the person who trusts God (vv. 5-8)! The theology is that of Psalm 1. The Lord does see how we live (vv. 9-10)! He understands our hearts much better than we do.

Put yourself in Jeremiah's place as he stood at the gates of the city and delivered the message about keeping the Sabbath (17:19-27). Economic considerations driven by greed had opened the gates of the city on the Sabbath to buy and sell, practices that were forbidden on the Sabbath. To deliver the Lord's message was a lonely and despised position. God promises blessing for obedience (vv. 24-26), and a curse for continued desecration of the Sabbath (v. 27). Money in hand was worth more to the people than the promise of the Lord.

When the Lord sent Jeremiah to see the potter's work at the wheel, an object lesson was in the making (18:1-17). The potter controls the work of his hands. As the vessel is taking shape, the potter can plan what he will do and can even change his mind about the final shape.

The Lord's application is in verses 5-10. Just as the potter controls the clay, the Lord is sovereign over the nations. There is a word of grace here as the Lord says that if a nation repents after He pronounces punishment, He will relent (v. 8). But there is also a word of warning. The nation that the Lord has blessed will face God's judgment if the people turn from the Lord to evil (vv. 9-10)! Applying this principle to Judah and Jerusalem (vv. 11-17), the Lord warned them that His judgment was on the way.

PROVERBS 21:24-31   Intimidation is a frequent technique in our day. Short term benefits of this technique include gaining control over a situation or people. However, in the eternal scheme it is not only useless but dangerous. Choose the course of the upright man who thinks carefully (from a biblical perspective) about his actions (v. 29).

Link the truths of verse 29 and 30. Ultimately, all our schemes to circumvent God's way will fail miserably. Make your plan so that it follows God's will.

OCTOBER 19

<u>2 THESSALONIANS 1</u>   The Christians in Thessalonica continued to face opposition and persecution, but in spite of these trials, the church was growing (vv. 3-4).

Paul again discusses the second coming of the Lord Jesus (vv. 5-10), once again primarily from the perspective of someone outside the kingdom at the moment when judgment begins (cf. Isa 26:21; 29:5b-6). Note that the judgment will come with "blazing fire" (v. 7; cf. 2 Peter 3:10). This judgment, however, is the *final solution to sin* and will bring relief to the faithful (v. 7).

Many people find it hard to believe that God will actually bring this kind of judgment on those who have not come to Christ (vv. 8-9). "Would a loving God send people to hell?" This question misses God's holiness and His deep offense at sin; most importantly, it misses how God, in His love, has provided – in Christ – a way for men to come to Him! *Jesus was very clear that eternal punishment waited for those who did not come to God in His way!* (cf. John 3:36; John 5:28-29; Matt 7:13-14, and the four parables in Matthew 24:45-25:46). Each parable ends with people either entering His kingdom or eternal punishment.

<u>JEREMIAH 19-20</u>   The Lord used a jar from the potter to teach the people another lesson (Ch. 19). This time the site of the message is the Valley of Ben Hinnom, just outside Jerusalem. Watch the Old Testament for this place, for it was used for Baal worship and human sacrifice (vv. 4-5). For these wicked practices, the Lord would smash Jerusalem just as Jeremiah smashed the clay jar in the people's presence (vv. 10-13).

Jeremiah faced danger as the Lord's servant (Ch. 20). The religious leaders, especially, were offended by the message of violence and destruction (v. 8) that Jeremiah kept bringing. After beating him, they placed him in stocks overnight (vv. 1-3a). This was a time of testing for the prophet. He wished he didn't have to preach the message God gave him, but he could not keep silent (vv. 8-9). Even his friends waited for him to slip up and do the wrong thing (v. 10). He wished he had never been born (vv. 14-18). Yet he was God's person, placed in the position for a specific task, and could not do other than the Lord's will. This is the prophet's heart!

<u>PROVERBS 22:1-8</u>   Is it wise to think ahead to avoid danger? God expects us to use the knowledge and understanding He has given (v. 3). From our New Testament perspective, we have the whole Bible and the Holy Spirit to give guidance. If we neglect these blessings, we do so at our own peril!

Consider verse 6. The principle is that if we guide our children in biblical principles and set them on their way with consideration for their gifts and abilities, they will travel a lifelong path of fruitfulness. This is more than teaching truth to children. We must also pay attention to the particular gifts and the "bent" that each individual has from God. Parents need to pray for discernment for their children and guide them carefully and humbly.

OCTOBER 20

2 THESSALONIANS 2   There was obvious concern in the church about the timing of the Lord's coming and the events surrounding it (vv. 1-2; cf. 1 Thess 4:13-18). People were afraid the Lord had already come again, and they were confused about the status of believers still in the world. Paul addresses that question in this section.

The term "the Day of the Lord" is most commonly used in the Bible to refer to God's judgment on rebellious men and nations at the end times. This is the reference, for instance, in Isaiah 13:6-13; 24. Paul speaks about this event in 1:7b-10, and as it relates to the unsaved in 1 Thessalonians 5:1-3. Paul here says that before the Day of the Lord comes, the "rebellion" will occur, and the "man of lawlessness" will be revealed (v. 3).

Paul speaks of the "last days" (2 Tim 3:1-5) as a time of greatly increased godlessness and overt wickedness in the world, and Jesus said it would be a time of great wickedness (Matt 24:9-14). These references seem to correspond to the "rebellion" of verse 3.

The other event that Paul says will precede the day of the Lord is that "the man of lawlessness" will be revealed (v. 3b). This person is called the Antichrist in 1 John 2:18, and refers to the beast in Revelation 13:1-8. *THE CHARACTER* of the man of lawlessness is revealed when he opposes God and exalts himself over God (v. 4). *HIS COMING* will be to do Satan's work, and he will perform (apparently) miraculous signs (v. 9), that will convince men and women he is divine. Note that the miracles, signs, and wonders are counterfeit; not really from God (v. 9). A counterfeit twenty-dollar bill can be seen and felt, and it appears genuine, but can be recognized as false by a person who is trained to see the difference. When Paul wrote the book, the man of lawlessness was restrained from his malicious intent (v. 7).

The restraint (v. 7) of the Antichrist is believed by many (but not by all) to be the Holy Spirit in the church. There will be a proper time for this evil person to be revealed, and it will be God's timing. Certainly, in one form or another, the hand of the sovereign Lord restrains this evil person, and will continue to do so until the moment of God's choosing.

The spiritual reality of evil and Satan's work in the world makes it crucial that we know and practice the truth from the Lord (vv. 13-15). Insight will come for the believer through knowledge of God's Word and discernment from the Holy Spirit. This exercise in reading the Bible builds what we need to tell truth from evil in today's world, and certainly in the days ahead.

JEREMIAH 21-22   King Zedekiah sent two officials to Jeremiah to ask for a word from the Lord, as Jerusalem was under siege (Ch. 21). Would the Lord again miraculously deliver the people and the city (vv. 1-2)? Jeremiah's answer from the Lord was not the one Zedekiah wanted to hear. Instead, God said He *would cause their own weapons of war to be directed against the city (vv. 3-5)*. It is an awesome thought that God's mighty arm that brought His people to the land would now be turned against them (v. 5).

There are three specific messages from the Lord. *First*, to ensure life, surrender to the enemy (vv. 8-10). This must have sounded like treason – but it came directly from the Lord. *Second*, even though time is short, see that justice is administered in the city. Address the inequities of oppression (vv. 11-12). *Third*, don't think for a moment that you can successfully survive the siege, for the Lord Himself will destroy the city (vv. 13-14).

The Lord's message, which Jeremiah gave outside the king's palace, is contained in Chapter 22. The heart of the message is in verse 3: Handle the problems of injustice, unrighteousness, and violence in the land! Three kings are mentioned: Shallum (v. 11; cf. 2 Kings 23:31-33), also known as Jehoahaz; Jehoiakim (v. 18; cf. 2 Kings 23:34-24:6; 2 Chron 36:5-8), Jehoahaz's brother; and Jehoiachin (v. 24; cf. 2 Kings 24:8-17), the son of Jehoiakim. All three of these kings were deposed and carried into exile! All had missed true righteousness. Read the chapter carefully with this in mind. Note verse 16. These comments refer to Jehoahaz' father Josiah. This is a remarkable definition of what it means to know God! How would you apply the principles of this message today? How does this fit with salvation by faith? (It does!)

PROVERBS 22:9-16   Once again, listen to the Lord's agenda! Those who are generous in sharing with the needy will be blessed (v. 9). This is a repeated truth in Proverbs (and in many other places in the Bible)! Note also the warning about oppression and bribery (v. 16).

OCTOBER 21

2 THESSALONIANS 3   Paul asked the Thessalonian church to remember him in prayer that the gospel would advance under his ministry (vv. 1-2). He also expressed confidence that God would protect

and continue His work in and through the Christians in that city (vv. 3-5).

Sometimes we speak of the "Christian work ethic." Verses 6-13 tell us what that work ethic ought to be. Certainly, Paul is saying loudly and clearly that God wants to see us do productive work that provides for our own needs. In addition to that, we know from 2 Corinthians 8 and 9 (and many other places in the Bible) that we should be willing to share with others in need. Note the advice about those who won't get busy and earn a living (vv. 14-15). Strong language, indeed.

JEREMIAH 23-24 It is a great responsibility to faithfully present God's word. This word from the Lord concerned the priests and prophets in Judah who were giving false assurances to the people. There are two parts to this message. ☑First, a time will come when a king of a completely different character will reign over a restored land (vv. 3-8). This will be a king of true righteousness: a descendant of David (vv. 5-6; cf. Isa 11:1-5). The people who have been exiled and scattered will be reclaimed and return to the land. It will be the time when Jesus the Messiah will return to care for His people and bring true righteousness to this world (cf. Mic 5:2-5).⇦

The second part concerns the priests and prophets who are falsely representing the Lord to the people. This remarkable section outlines what happens when spokesmen for the Lord are unfaithful (vv. 9-40). When the prophets themselves sin, the people do not repent (v. 14). They gave false assurance (v. 17) when, in contrast, the Lord had decreed disaster! Note carefully verses 28-29. We who have the word of the Lord need to declare it faithfully! The principle here is vital: If God's people are faithful to present His word, He will apply it to hearts appropriately. We do not need to hammer at people – but *the truth* can be as hard as a hammer (v. 29, Heb 4:12).

Two baskets of figs (Ch. 24) – this was the vision the Lord gave to Jeremiah. The good figs represented those who had gone into exile in 597 BC with Jehoiachin – the first exiles to Babylon. The bad figs represented the people who stayed in Jerusalem until the fall of the city in 586 BC.

God promised that the first exiles would return to their land (vv. 5-7). This promise was fulfilled under Ezra. Those who were left, however, would suffer great hardship when the city would be destroyed in 586 BC, and in a subsequent attempt to escape Babylon by going to Egypt.

PROVERBS 22:17-23 Note verses 22-23. Why is there so much emphasis on the poor? First of all, of course, because God is concerned. But also because the poor have no recourse. A wealthy person who is cheated has standing in the community and the financial means to make it uncomfortable for the one who has been dishonest. Not so with the poor – especially when this was written, but also today. The poor just don't have the time, energy (too busy attempting to stay alive), or finances to fight such a battle.

What about legal means? Even today, who hires skilled lawyers? It isn't unusual for a skilled attorney, through plea-bargaining, expert cross-examination, or other means, to obtain a minimal sentence or an undeserved not-guilty verdict. Justice, in God's eyes, is a level playing field (Deut 1:17).

OCTOBER 22

<u>1 TIMOTHY 1</u>   Timothy was a young believer in Lystra when Paul met him on his second missionary journey. His mother was Jewish and his father Greek. Paul and Silas took Timothy with them, and from that time onward, he was a fellow worker and companion to them (Acts 16:1-5). Paul sent him on special trips several times to encourage churches, and Timothy stayed in Ephesus to pastor the church there (v. 3). 1 and 2 Timothy are letters that Paul wrote to the younger pastor regarding leadership in the church – directed both to Timothy and the local church.

Paul was writing to Timothy while he served in Ephesus (v. 3), specifically about some who were teaching false doctrine in the church (vv. 3-7). These men were probably Jewish legalists who were caught in the Jewish traditions as well as the Mosaic law. Much of their teaching promoted controversy – missing the point of growth to maturity and the promotion of love in the fellowship. Paul comes down on them severely – charging that they didn't know what they were talking about (v. 7).

What, then, is the purpose of the law (v. 8)? It is given for lawbreakers and rebels (against God, which we all are), and will help us recognize our great need for redemption (vv. 9-11). Note carefully all acts the law addresses! Paul has given a catalogue of modern society!

It is possible to "shipwreck" one's faith (vv. 19-20). In this case, Hymenaeus and Alexander failed to "hold on to faith and a good conscience." Paul's comments about handing these men over to Satan to be taught the needed lesson is similar to his language in 1 Corinthians 5:5, 13. Remember, with the sinning man in Corinth, the church's "redemptive discipline" by putting him out of the fellowship led to repentance and reinstatement. Words as strong as these should make us diligent in our own Christian walk!

<u>JEREMIAH 25-26</u>   Jeremiah's message for the nation in Chapter 25 came in 605 BC, about nineteen years before the fall of Jerusalem in

586 BC. He had already been preaching repentance for twenty-three years (vv. 3-4). Several of his comments reflect basic principles from the Lord. After hearing over and over again the same message, it becomes easier to dismiss the truth and continue with the status quo ("Nothing has happened yet!"). They had done so for twenty-three years! Note also that repentance is an individual as well as a corporate act (v. 5). Any group of people, family, church, or nation is made up of individuals. Only individuals can personally repent of sin, but unless this happens, the group may suffer consequences as Judah did. Hardness of heart is self-destructive (vv. 7-11).

The cup of God's wrath was not optional for Judah or the other nations (vv. 15-38). The near-at-hand fulfillment came with Babylon's attack on Judah. ☑The latter portion of the chapter (vv. 30-38) seems to refer to the Lord's final judgment on all of the nations, or "the Day of the Lord."⇦

The Lord commanded Jeremiah to stand in the temple courtyard and review publicly all the prophecies the Lord had given him (Ch. 26). This "Temple courtyard" sermon evoked a hostile response, especially from the priests and the prophets. It is interesting that the religious leaders wanted to kill Jeremiah (vv. 7-8). The civil leaders, however, would not allow it (v. 16), calling upon the precedent of history during the days of Hezekiah when the king and the people listened to the Lord's prophet and changed their ways!

The prophet Uriah, however, who was saying the same things as Jeremiah, was threatened, fled to Egypt, and was hunted down and murdered (vv. 20-23). This is not to say that if Uriah had not fled he would not have been murdered, but the outcome *might* have been different. Remember the Lord's words in 1:17 to Jeremiah, and note Jeremiah's courage in 26:12-15. The charge against Jeremiah was treason (vv. 7-9). Jeremiah denied the treason by asserting that it was indeed the Lord who had sent him. Uriah may have seemed to admit guilt by fleeing.

PROVERBS 22:24-29   Bad company affects us (vv. 24-25). A person who is easily angered often evokes anger in others – and anger is destructive, both spiritually and physically. Don't choose as a close friend the kind of person described in verse 24. This doesn't mean we should not work with and help those who need to know God. That is our job description from the Lord. But when we do so, we must keep our eyes open and not fall into the same behavior.

Is it a good idea to strive for excellence? Read verse 29. A skilled individual will be in demand.

OCTOBER 23

1 TIMOTHY 2   This short chapter is packed with instruction for lifestyle, worship, and church life. Note the call to prayer in worship (vv. 1-2). There is specific instruction to pray for civil authorities so the church could function without harassment and carry on effective evangelism. Note the Lord's agenda in verses 3-4. God wants all to know the truth – and to be saved.

With regard to lifestyle, think about verses 9-10. The comments about women's dress and jewelry are just as applicable to men. Simple (not meaning shabby) clothing and accessories will free money for better uses. More important, it doesn't matter what we have on but what God has done on the inside!

Paul discusses authority in the church in verses 11-15, particularly in regard to women. In Chapter 3, Paul spells out the requirements for both elders and deacons, mentioning only men. All of the teaching in the church is subject to the authority of the leadership. The issue is not whether women can minister, but under what authority and in what capacity.

Notice that Paul makes his argument on two bases: first, on the order of creation and second, on the fall. Paul is not making a judgment about the worth of either sex – but only on their specific functions in the church.

This is controversial in the ecclesiastical world today. Each church body (grouping of churches and local church) must look carefully at what the Bible says and come to terms with its understanding of the biblical position.

JEREMIAH 27-28   Jeremiah was faithful in bringing God's warning to the people. Chapter 27 is a specific example of these warnings. The passage also shows what the false prophets were telling the people. If you have a choice, isn't it easier to listen to what you want to hear? *Here is where it is important to "test the spirits" (1 John 4:1-6) and use biblical truth to measure the message.*

Jeremiah was wearing a yoke on his neck and shoulders to illustrate the yoke of oppression that the Lord was bringing to the people through Nebuchadnezzar (27:2; Ch. 28). Imagine yourself in the courtyard listening to the conversation recorded in this chapter. Hananiah was saying just what the people wanted to hear. Jeremiah challenged him and, in fact, was told by the Lord to go back to Hananiah and give God's message to him personally. Note the result in verse 28:17.

PROVERBS 23:1-9   Verses 4-5 accurately describe how hard it is to hang on to wealth. The hazards of investment schemes make it difficult to be a winner in the money game. If that is what our life is about, we are likely headed for major disappointment. Even if we succeed in accumulating money, it will not bring contentment. Jesus goes so far as to say that too much emphasis on money is incompatible with life in the Spirit (cf. Matt 6:19-24). If we are living for money, we are not living for the Lord. *The principle behind what Jesus said is not whether a person has saved money but what that person is living for.* Think about it.

OCTOBER 24

1 TIMOTHY 3 Proper leadership is crucial to the life of the church, and it is qualification for leadership that Paul here addressed. The "overseer" (NIV), or "bishop" (KJV, RSV), refers to the office of spiritual leaders (plural) in the local church. The office of deacon was established in Acts 6, when seven men were chosen to assist in the administrative leadership of the church, freeing the Apostles for ministry.

Consider carefully the high qualifications expected of both the overseer (or elder, in our terms) and the deacon. Although many hold that the requirement of "husband of one wife" means a man who has been married only once, careful study has led many scholars to conclude that this means a faithful, monogamous marriage at the time of the office. Other qualifications included a high degree of maturity – a composite picture of a quiet, steady, gentle, and considerate person who knows how to use and teach the Bible and has allowed the Lord to work deeply in his own life. Compare these qualities with the fruit of the Spirit in Galatians 5:22-23. In considering qualifications church leaders, it is important not to look at superficial conformance to a few "key" things!

Certainly, this passage shows us that church leadership is a high calling with a high degree of accountability to the Lord and the church.

JEREMIAH 29-30 Jeremiah's letter to the exiles (Ch. 29) was a word from the Lord and also a warning not to listen to "prophets" who disagreed with Jeremiah. Certainly his message was not what they wanted to hear. They would much rather come back to their own land than settle in the foreign place and plan for long-term living there. *Further, Jeremiah tells them to pray for the city where they are living, for in so doing, they will be praying for themselves.* Note the word of grace from the Lord in verses 10-14. God had not forgotten them, but there would be no "quick fix" for their life in exile.

☑God, on the eve of their dispersal, promised the impossible – the preservation and future restoration of Israel (30:3-10, 18-24). Note that this restoration will be under "David their king" (v. 9). This tells us that what the prophet is predicting was not the return after the seventy-year exile – at that time there was no king and no nation! This refers rather to a future regathering under the Messiah. This was also the message of Ezekiel 36-37. (Ezekiel was a historical contemporary of Jeremiah, prophesying to the captive Israelites in Babylon while Jeremiah ministered in Jerusalem during its last days.)⇦ Discipline was coming, but it would be with justice (30:11b). Their condition made God's judgment inevitable (vv. 12, 15b).

PROVERBS 23:10-18   Children need the discipline of their parents (vv. 13-14).   Helping children, even young children, to respect people and property will keep them safe and be a great asset to them as they grow. The withholding of discipline is not a favor to a child.   None of us likes to be corrected, but each of us needs correction.   The values we build into the lives of our children are vital – and as the text states, will save the child's soul from death.

OCTOBER 25

1 TIMOTHY 4   The section begins with the term "in later times," which is not as specific in referring to end times as the term "the last days" used in 2 Timothy 3:1.   What Paul speaks of here (vv. 1-5) probably deals with some teachers who insisted that certain practices were necessary for salvation.   Paul combats these ideas aggressively: They were taught through the influence of demons (v. 1).   Anything that adds conditions to salvation by God's grace through faith in His Son is the work of Satan and is a direct attack on the church.   The protection from this kind of attack is in living close to the Lord and staying in His Word. In this regard, note verses 7-8 (requires discipline).   Real godliness will guard both the present and the future (v. 8).

Paul outlines important personal and ministry priorities for the pastor in verses 12-16.   The public reading of Scripture was prominent in the early church.   Perhaps this was because there were no printed Bibles; nevertheless early tradition emphasized public reading in worship, along with preaching and teaching.   Paul called Timothy to diligence in his walk with the Lord (vv. 14-16).   Good advice for each of us!

JEREMIAH 31-32   ☑The promise of return to the land that we saw in Chapter 30 is continued in Chapter 31, and is more than just a return under the same old conditions.   It promises a new faith and outlook. Note 31:3-14, 33-37.   God promises to put His law in their minds – to write it upon their hearts.   The result will be a totally new God-people relationship.   All will know the Lord (31:33-34; cf. Rom 11:25-27)! Compare these conditions with those Ezekiel described in Ezekiel 36:24-32.   Further, this promise is secured by God's character and power (31:35-37).   When the promise is fulfilled, Jerusalem will never again be destroyed (31:40b). Remember that these things will happen under the leadership of the Messiah (cf. 30:9). ⇦

The events in Chapter 32 took place a few months before the fall of the city. Jeremiah was confined to prison because of his message. The siege ramps were in place. In the midst of this, Jeremiah was directed to redeem a piece of land in the territory of Benjamin. Jeremiah did this, and directed Baruch to place the deed in a clay container where it would be safe for an extended period – for the Lord had promised that there would be a future for the land and the city.

Read Jeremiah's prayer in 32:17-25. Jeremiah looked to the Lord even though he was confused about the purchase. Then read the Lord's answer. It was true that the city would fall and the people go into captivity. The reason is clearly their sin (vv. 31-35). ☑Yet there is a future (vv. 36-41), and the Lord will perform the miracle of giving a new heart to His people (review once again Jer 31:31-34; Ezek 36:24-32). They will have a single-minded devotion to the Lord, and it will last (vv. 38-41). This, too, must be related to the restoration under the Messiah. ⇦

PROVERBS 23:19-28   The writer suggests healthy choices (vv. 20-21) that are tied to a wise heart (v. 19). Wisdom gives us the discipline to say "no" to what may be attractive but could hurt us.

Consider the message of verse 23. Study, obey God, allow God's word to permeate your life. Don't let the truth slip out of your grasp. Compare this with 24:14.

OCTOBER 26

1 TIMOTHY 5   Relationships structured as Paul suggests in verses 1-2 will avoid many problems in the church. Personal relationships, with these guidelines, honor the individuals involved and make people comfortable.

Widows in New Testament times often had no one to care for them (vv. 3-16). They had left the protection of their parental home and had lost the protection of a husband. This is why the Old Testament often speaks of the need to care for widows and orphans. Note that widows with genuine need should come under the protection and provision of the church. First of all, however, families should care for their own, and younger women who were widowed were encouraged to marry again. This last instruction was not a universal rule. Paul recognizes, however, that for a young widow, a family relationship in the faith is more fulfilling and practical than dependence on the church.

The ministry of an elder calls for care (vv. 17-20). He should be recognized for faithful ministry – including remuneration as necessary. Note also the responsibility of the elder to live carefully. If an elder falls into sin, Paul calls for a public rebuke to warn the church that such behavior is unacceptable.

The comment about wine in verse 23 probably was included because of the questionable water supply, especially when traveling.

JEREMIAH 33-34 The Lord's word to Jeremiah while he was confined in the courtyard had prophecies for both the immediate and the distant future (Ch. 33). Regarding what would soon come to the city, verses 4-5 predict defeat and death. ☑There is hope, however, for the future of the city and the nation (vv. 6-26). This will include healing, cleansing from sin, and awe throughout the world at what God does among His people (vv. 6-9). The promise that this restoration will take place under the Messiah is in verses 15-16. These predictions were not realized during the first advent – but will be when the Lord returns. If you read these verses without knowing what was accomplished at the cross, it is no wonder that the Jewish people at the time of Christ were looking for a Messiah to reestablish their political boundaries and free them from Roman rule. That is still to come! Look for the details of peace and faith in the lives of God's people (vv. 8, 16).⇦

The Lord sent Jeremiah to Zedekiah with the specific message that He, the Lord, would hand the city to the Babylonians (34:1-7). The king might live, but the city would fall! The king and the people had taken one step in the right direction by freeing their fellow Jews who were under bondage, but then enslaved them again (vv. 8-11). This violated God's law that every seven years all debts were to be forgiven and all indentured servants were to go free (Deut 15:1-2, 12-14). The Lord proclaimed "freedom" for the people because of this offense (freedom to fall by the sword! vv. 17-20). This occurred when there was temporary relief from the siege, after Nebuchadnezzar had withdrawn to meet a threat from Egypt's forces (v. 21b). The Lord, however, was clear that this was only temporary – that He would bring the army of Babylon back to conclude the siege (v. 22).

PROVERBS 23:29-35 Verses 29-35 describe the life of the alcoholic. First, the end result (v. 29): bloodshot eyes and bruises; woe, sorrow, and strife. The drug is deceptive; it has a beautiful color and taste (v. 31). But the results are poisoning (v. 32): the DT's (delirium tremens, v. 33), anesthesia (v. 35a), and addiction (v. 35b).

OCTOBER 27

1 TIMOTHY 6   The Bible recognized slavery as a fact of life in both the Old and New Testaments. In fact, God allowed the Israelites to become slaves of strong, ruthless, and pagan nations in order to bring them to their senses, repent, and trust Him. Today, although slavery is still widespread in the world, human rights are seen as paramount and receive a great deal of attention in our country and in the world. We should understand that basic human rights are not a modern invention, but from the Lord, and have been present since creation. We have the right even to choose wrong (albeit with consequences), and this liberty, too, is from the Lord.

Verses 1-2 look at freedom from a different perspective. Although it was better to be free than to be a slave (1 Cor 7:21), we demonstrate faithfulness to God by our relationships. *Our Christian testimony is more important than our freedom.* Perhaps the most difficult thing for a Christian slave would be to respect a master who treated him unfairly. From the perspective of Christian testimony, however, it was powerful.

Paul recognized that slavery was reprehensible. He placed slave traders alongside murderers, adulterers, perverts, liars, and perjurers (1 Tim 1:9-10). He also recognizes that the solution to slavery, as well as the other great sins of society, is change from within. In the church, the slave had the same recognition as the wealthy free (Col 3:11), and masters were called to treat slaves with respect and fairness (Col 4:1). These were absolutely radical concepts. They still are, for even though slavery is outlawed in many parts of the world, there remain many forms of slavery today that will be righted only by changed hearts. This is where the church needs to be salt as well as light in the world!

In contrast to trying to use godliness to get rich (absolutely reprehensible, v. 5), the state of godliness with contentment (in the Spirit) is a gift from God (v. 6). Hear the warning – some, caught in the desire for wealth, wander from the faith (v. 10)!

JEREMIAH 35-36   The events of Chapters 35-36 took place during the reign of Jehoiakim, son of Josiah. Josiah had been a godly man and led his people in the right direction. When he died, his son Jehoahaz assumed the throne and was deposed after three months by the king of Egypt, who made Johoahaz's brother Eliakim king. The king of Egypt changed Eliakim's name to Jehoiakim. Jehoiakim was evil and was deposed by the Babylonians and taken to Babylon in shackles after an eleven-year reign.

The descendants of Jonadab, son of Recab, had vowed to live a nomadic life and drink no wine at the command of their father (Ch. 35). They had carefully followed this vow, and the Lord used the Recabites as an object lesson for the people of Judah. They refused the wine that Jeremiah placed before them, explaining their vow. The Lord used them as an example of obedience – they kept the command of their forefather, but the people of Judah would not listen to the Lord (vv. 12-17)! As a result, judgment was coming!

The Lord instructed Jeremiah to commit to writing all of His prophecies for the people (Ch. 36). Baruch, Jeremiah's scribe and secretary, wrote the messages as Jeremiah dictated and then read the scroll at the temple (vv. 8-10). Some officials heard Jeremiah and asked for a private reading. As they heard the messages, they became afraid and took the scroll to the king to be read. In your mind, place yourself in the presence of the king as he cut the scroll and burned it as it was read (vv. 20-26). What arrogance! Baruch rewrote the messages, and this is probably the reason we have the book of Jeremiah today! Note the Lord's word to Jehoiakim after he burned the scroll (36:29-31).

PROVERBS 24:1-12   Verses 3-4 suggest how to build an impressive house. This doesn't necessarily refer to a house with four walls but could represent a life. A beautiful, meaningful, and productive life is built using wisdom, understanding, and knowledge – the knowledge and wisdom from God's Word and understanding from the Holy Spirit. Not in a day, but brick by brick. Not hastily, but with rare and beautiful things that are sought out and acquired one by one.

With today's society demanding instant results, this slow process of spiritual discipline is not popular. But can you find the biblical principle that contradicts the slow process? When God has His way with us, it may take longer than we would like, but God builds quality. Go for the gold!

A major theme in the Bible is justice. Justice and fairness are based on the character of God (review again Deut 1:16-17). Focus attention on verses 11-12, and compare these with Proverbs 31:8-9. There are times when we would rather fade into the background and say nothing. But there are also times when truth demands that we take action. When we see that justice is not being served or the system is taking advantage of people, it is time to speak up!

OCTOBER 28

2 TIMOTHY 1   The second letter to Timothy was written to encourage the younger pastor in his work and faith while Paul was imprisoned in Rome. The encouragement is not a "pat on the back," but rather a reminder of God's solid work in Timothy's life (vv. 6-7). The gift for ministry came from the Holy Spirit, and this spirit is one of power. The full potential, however, would be realized when Timothy himself fanned

the fire of the Spirit into flame (v. 6). The Spirit gives each of us a gift or gifts, and we must exercise faith and diligence to see resulting fruit.

Think of the truth of verse 7. Timidity in our testimony or in working out our faith is not from the Lord! Rather, from the Lord we have the spirit of power, with which comes love and discipline. It is the Lord's will that we have a selfless abandon in living for Jesus, allowing our testimony to be heard in our communities and in the marketplace.

Note verses 13-14. We must guard the gift and potential the Lord has given us, not by keeping it private, but by living it out boldly for Jesus' sake!

JEREMIAH 37-38   Zedekiah was the last king of Judah. Even though the king didn't take Jeremiah's advice, he still suspected that Jeremiah had an "open line" to the Lord. He asked Jeremiah to pray for them (37:3). But when Jeremiah tried to leave the city during a temporary respite from the Babylonian siege, Jeremiah was arrested and imprisoned, charged with treason (vv. 14-15). Notice that the king sent for him and responded to his plea for freedom, even though Jeremiah did not give the king hope from the Lord.

The king now found himself in a difficult position. Jeremiah was telling the people that the city would fall, and if they valued life, they should leave the city and give themselves up to the Babylonians (38:2-3). When some of the king's officials wanted to imprison Jeremiah, in fact wanted him dead, the king didn't oppose placing him in a cistern with mud on the bottom – leaving him to die (vv. 4-6). *Now notice what one man, Ebed-Melech, did in public.* He approached the king at the public gate and pleaded the injustice of Jeremiah's treatment (vv. 7-9). The accusation was true and the injustice real. Probably because it was made in public, the king gave the order to release Jeremiah. *One righteous man, armed with the truth, can accomplish much!*

A measure of how desperate the king was is the meeting that Zedekiah requested of Jeremiah (v. 14ff.). This was a private meeting, as the king was afraid of the people. Once again, he asked Jeremiah what was going to happen. Even though Jeremiah clearly told the king how to save lives in the city, the king could not bring himself to follow the advice from the Lord. This was the king's last meeting with Jeremiah.

PROVERBS 24:13-22   A principle that is seen several places in the Bible appears in verses 17-18. Compare these verses with Romans 12:17-21. The book of Obadiah, written to the nation of Edom, addresses the nation's pride and how Edom treated others in defeat (vv. 11-14). Because of this behavior, the Lord promised judgment for Edom.

It is easy to have a superior attitude – to secretly rejoice in another's difficulty. This is not from the Lord! A good dose of humility and mercy would be much closer to the heart of the Lord.

OCTOBER 29

2 TIMOTHY 2   Have you thought of yourself as a strong Christian? This chapter begins with the call to strength, and then shows how to develop that strength.

Be willing to endure hardships and be single-minded in motivation (vv. 3-7). The examples of the soldier, the athlete, and the farmer should help us understand the mind-set we need. Put aside peripheral matters to focus on the job at hand. In this process, remember Jesus (v. 8)!

Do your best to win approval from the Lord. Use the Word of God carefully and skillfully (v. 15). There are two aspects to practicing this skillful use of God's Word. First, grow continually in the *knowledge* of the Bible through ongoing Bible study and reading. This develops familiarity and the ability to move quickly from one part of the Bible to another, showing how the entire Bible is a unit that meets every need of the heart. In addition, to truly understand the Lord's intent in His Word, practice careful, growing, and continuing *obedience* in your life to apply the principles and specifics of the Bible. *It is a "life trip" not merely a "head trip!"*

Avoid what will throw you off track (vv. 16-18). Finally, heed the instruction and warning in verses 22-26: Don't be distracted and lose your best opportunities, or worse, dishonor the Lord.

Now go back to verse 2. Here is the basis of discipleship: multiplying the ministry potential of the church by teaching the Word of God and ministry skills! The program started with Moses in Exodus 18:21. Note that the qualifications were much the same in Moses' time as the time of Jesus and Paul. Jesus gave us this same model in training the twelve and sending them out.

JEREMIAH 39-40   Jerusalem fell to Nebuchadnezzar. Zedekiah's life was spared, but what an ending to his reign! The king watched as his family was killed before his eyes. This was the last thing he ever saw, for his eyes were then destroyed! The king was shackled and taken to Babylon. Review again the choice that Zedekiah had (38:20-23). Burned into his mind forever was the picture of his family killed before his eyes!

Chapter 40 begins the final episode of the people who were left in the land after the fall of Jerusalem. Jeremiah was given the freedom to go to Babylon or to stay in the land with Gedaliah, who had been placed in charge of those remaining (40:1-6). Even the Babylonian commander understood why Jerusalem fell (v. 3)! At this late hour, international intrigue was still taking place. There was a plot to kill Gedaliah, hatched by Baalis, king of the Ammonites (vv. 13-14). Perhaps the Ammonites hoped to profit in the vacuum left after the fall. To his harm, Gedaliah didn't believe the report.

LAMENTATIONS 1:1-9   The book of Lamentations was probably written by Jeremiah as he wept over the ruined city of Jerusalem. The city, which contained the temple, was the center of worship for God's people. This was the city of David. Jeremiah had seen it destroyed and its people killed or carried off to Babylon. He had watched during the siege, knowing the outcome. He tried over and over to impress upon the people the reality of their danger – to no avail.

The book should really be read at one sitting and read aloud. As you read for the large picture, the impact of the disaster and suffering will stand out uniquely.

The details are also important. Power had many friends. Now that power was gone, however, so were the friends (1:2). There was no real resting place for her sons and daughters (v. 3). The roads were empty (hear them mourn), the altars still and cold (v. 4). It was because of sin (vv. 5, 8). In the midst of this tragedy were memories of golden days of blessing – now gone (v. 7). No one was willing or even inclined to show mercy (v. 9).

OCTOBER 30

2 TIMOTHY 3   When we considered 1 Timothy 4, we looked at verses 1-5. Perhaps each generation since this was written might conclude that the conditions described in 1 Timothy 4 and here in 2 Timothy 3:1-5 were being fulfilled. It certainly seems true now as we review the last fifty years. There has been marked erosion of moral and family values. Contemporary rock music and the media are making a frontal assault upon the young. In many parts of the world we are losing a large part of a generation of young people to addiction. The Lord's return may be very near!

One of the most serious problems of these societal changes is the inroad they have made in the church. Think about this, and then consider Paul's further remarks in verses 10-16. Note how Paul applied the truth in his life and theology: teaching, lifestyle, motivation, relationships, and suffering (vv. 10-11). If we have a single-minded focus and apply God's Word thoroughly, the Lord will help us stay on track! Finally, note verses 16-17. *With the inroads of society in the church, there is less emphasis upon a deep knowledge and careful application of the Bible in our lives.* But remember, our tools for ministry are from the Bible (v. 17). Our discernment to keep on track in treacherous times will be from the same source!

JEREMIAH 41-43   The murder of Gedaliah by Ishmael took place as Johanan predicted (40:13; 41:1-3). This brought instability to the remnant left in Judah and Jerusalem. They not only feared Ishmael but were afraid that the Babylonians would return in anger because their man in charge (Gedaliah) had been killed. Flight to Egypt seemed the safest route to survival (41:16-18).

The people paused, however, to ask Jeremiah to inquire of the Lord what to do. Note that the people promised to do whatever the Lord directed (42:5-6). When the word came back for them to stay in Judah, however, they reneged on their promises, and despite the Lord's warnings through Jeremiah, they left for Egypt, taking Jeremiah with them.

Jeremiah's last word to his people from God came in Egypt (43:8-13). Nebuchadnezzar would come to Egypt bringing death with him. Obedience to the Lord would have avoided this last fatal encounter with Nebuchadnezzar. Babylon did, in fact, destroy Egypt, but there is no known historical record as to the fate of the Israelites who fled there.

LAMENTATIONS 1:10-22   You can almost feel the suffering of the people as you read the text. The treasures are gone (v. 10a). The privacy of the temple has been breached (v. 10b). There is hunger and starvation (v. 11). And the people are despised (v. 11b).

Note the metaphor: The sin of the nation has been woven into a yoke around the neck of the people (v. 14). Outside there is the sword – inside death (v. 20).

The moment of truth arrived when the price of sin and rebellion became apparent (v. 18). Jeremiah called on all who would listen to see the price and suffering of their sin.

OCTOBER 31

2 TIMOTHY 4   In the same theme as in Chapter 3, Paul says that in the last times, people will not tolerate sound teaching and preaching (vv. 3-4). *Note that the listeners will want to dictate the content of what they hear.* Paul's message is that the minister must be prepared to preach and teach the Word of God with all of the appropriate applications, even if it means opposition.

What a testimony Paul gives in verses 6-7. He saw that his life would soon be "poured out" as an offering! He had no regrets – he had been faithful since he saw Jesus on the road to Damascus. Yet he clearly saw beyond death to his meeting with his Master and the crown that awaited him (v. 8).

Place yourself in Paul's situation as you read the personal note at the end of the letter (vv. 9-18). Paul, the great apostle and preacher, faced personal hurts and difficulties. He also faced death from the Romans. Didn't he deserve better? He has indeed received better, but not in this world!

JEREMIAH 44-45   The Lord spoke to the people again, asking why they persisted in self-destructive behavior (44:7-10). Their answer was arrogant (vv. 15-19). They had a distorted perception, saying that when they were offering sacrifices to the Queen of Heaven (a fertility god) they had plenty – but now that they hadn't done so they had suffered. The truth was that previously, when they were worshiping foreign gods, only God's patience prevented their immediate destruction (vv. 20-23). Read the Lord's answer to them in the remainder of the chapter. Their condition – their future – was then fixed by their action and attitude (vv. 25b-28).

Baruch, son of Neriah, was Jeremiah's scribe who wrote down the messages Jeremiah received from the Lord (Ch. 45; cf. Jer 36). Several years previous to the fall of Jerusalem, during the reign of Jehoiakim, Baruch was apparently tempted to build his own "empire" or "estate," but Jeremiah had a word from the Lord – don't try it! (It isn't what is important, and it won't last.) The Lord promised that Baruch would escape with his life in the judgment coming, but that is all. Disaster was on the way.

LAMENTATIONS 2:1-10   Babylon and her army destroyed Jerusalem. But it was the Lord's doing! That is what these verses say over and over again. The Lord, through Habakkuk, told the people that He would do just that (Hab 1:5-11). And, of course, that is what Jeremiah had been saying for years before and during the lengthy siege.

The Lord covered Jerusalem with the cloud of His wrath (v. 1). He swallowed up the dwellings and tore down the strongholds (v. 2). He took away His protection (v. 3). The Lord Himself had become like an enemy: The palaces were gone, the strongholds were destroyed, the temple was destroyed, the altar was rejected (by the Lord), and the voice of the law was no more (vv. 5-9; cf. Amos 8:11). Truly, it was a terrible thing to fall into the wrathful hand of God!

November

Bible Reading Schedule
And Notes

ೞ

*This is the one I esteem: he who is humble
and contrite in spirit, and trembles at my word.
Isaiah 66:2b*

1	Titus 1	Jeremiah 46-47	Lam 2:11-22
2	Titus 2	Jeremiah 48-49	Lam 3:1-20
3	Titus 3	Jeremiah 50-51	Lam 3:21-39
4	Philemon	Jeremiah 52	Lam 3:40-66
5	Hebrews 1	Ezekiel 1-2	Lam 4
6	Hebrews 2	Ezekiel 3-5	Lam 5
7	Hebrews 3	Ezekiel 6-7	Proverbs 24:23-29
8	Hebrews 4	Ezekiel 8-9	Proverbs 24:30-34
9	Hebrews 5	Ezekiel 10-11	Proverbs 25:1-11
10	Hebrews 6	Ezekiel 12-13	Proverbs 25:12-20
11	Hebrews 7	Ezekiel 14-15	Proverbs 25:21-28
12	Hebrews 8	Ezekiel 16	Proverbs 26:1-12
13	Hebrews 9	Ezekiel 17-18	Proverbs 26:13-22
14	Hebrews 10	Ezekiel 19-20	Proverbs 26:23-28
15	Hebrews 11	Ezekiel 21-22	Proverbs 27:1-9
16	Hebrews 12	Ezekiel 23-24	Proverbs 27:10-18
17	Hebrews 13	Ezekiel 25-26	Proverbs 27:19-27
18	James 1	Ezekiel 27-28	Proverbs 28:1-10
19	James 2	Ezekiel 29-30	Proverbs 28:11-19
20	James 3	Ezekiel 31-32	Proverbs 28:20-28
21	James 4	Ezekiel 33-34	Proverbs 29:1-9
22	James 5	Ezekiel 35-36	Proverbs 29:10-18
23	1 Peter 1:1-12	Ezekiel 37-39	Proverbs 29:19-27
24	1 Peter 1:13-25	Ezekiel 40	Proverbs 30:1-10
25	1 Peter 2	Ezekiel 41-42	Proverbs 30:11-17
26	1 Peter 3	Ezekiel 43-44	Proverbs 30:18-20
27	1 Peter 4	Ezekiel 45-46	Proverbs 30:21-28
28	1 Peter 5	Ezekiel 47-48	Proverbs 30:29-33
29	2 Peter 1	Daniel 1-2	Proverbs 31:1-9
30	2 Peter 2	Daniel 3-4	Proverbs 31:10-31

NOVEMBER 1

TITUS 1   Titus remained on the Island of Crete to see that the converts on the island were properly settled in congregations and that leadership was established (v. 5). The qualifications for elders are similar to those in 1 Timothy 3. Note that leaders had responsibility to carry out the "trust" of God's work (v. 7) which touches matters of lifestyle and relationships (vv. 6-8). Further, note faithfulness to God's Word is crucial in carrying out these responsibilities (v. 9).

Crete was apparently a difficult place to apply the disciplines of the Christian life (vv. 10-12). This difficulty came both from the legalists (v. 10) and from the stubborn and rebellious (v. 12). Both the thinking (v. 15b) and the lifestyle (v. 16) of the latter were twisted. The answer was the application of God's Word (Ch. 2).

JEREMIAH 46-47   Not only Judah, but other nations, will also taste God's discipline. Egypt (Ch. 46) and the Philistines (Ch. 47) were due for judgment. It is of interest that Egypt would be God's instrument for Philistia, while Babylon would bring the discipline to Egypt. Egypt's judgment would be on their gods, their leadership including Pharaoh, and the people (46:25). Note the word of grace to Judah: God's discipline would bring down the land, but there was still a hope for the future (vv. 27-28).

These are the events of which Ezekiel spoke in Ezekiel 29:17-30:19, which we will read about on November 19. In the struggle to dominate the area, Egypt's army marched up the seacoast through Philistia and engaged Babylon's army in battle at Carchemish in Syria. Egypt defeated the Babylonians, but the next year Nebuchadnezzar returned to decimate the Egyptian army (46:2) at Carchemish, sending them fleeing southward. This was the beginning of the end for the Egyptians as a force in the area and finally led to the collapse of the country, as well as her neighbors (see notes for Nov. 19, Ezek 29-30).

Philistia (Ch. 47) was on the route used by both the Egyptians and the Babylonians as they engaged each other in battle. It is unclear which army brought the hardship described in this chapter – probably both contributed to the suffering.

LAMENTATIONS 2:11-22   Jeremiah had every reason to turn his back on his people after the way they had treated him. When he faithfully gave them the Lord's message, they had mistreated him, imprisoned him – almost killed him. Yet, read his testimony in verse 11. His eyes were full of tears and he was in torment.

As you read verse 14, remember Jeremiah's experience with Hananiah in Jeremiah 28. This false prophet told the people exactly what they wanted to hear – but it was entirely false!

Recall the words of the Lord in Deuteronomy 8:19-20 as you read verse 17. Over and over the Lord had warned the people that if they turned away from Him, He would not leave them in the land! Now that had been fulfilled! It is always easy to rationalize away the truth – to believe that such things really won't apply to me. That kind of thinking leads to disaster (v. 22b).

NOVEMBER 2

TITUS 2   If there is one theme that characterizes this chapter, it is "self-control." This term appears in verses 2, 5, 6, and 12. In spite of the opposition that Titus faced (v. 8b), Paul encouraged him to move on to appropriate instruction, with godly self-control as a needed element. Paul mentions in turn the older men, the older women, the younger women, and the young men, and the godly lifestyle that God desires for each.

Give special attention to verses 11-14. Count the ways the grace of God changes our lives. It teaches us to say "no" to wrong. It teaches us to live carefully now – and to look forward to the coming of Christ. These changes go deep in our lives, changing our behavior, motivation, lifestyle, and future. God's purpose is to purify a people who are His exclusively! This is the evidence of the kingdom that has invaded and infiltrated this present, evil world.

JEREMIAH 48-49   Jeremiah continued his message for the nations that surround Israel. Chapter 48 deals with Moab, warning that the eagle is swooping down to destroy the nation (v. 40). The reason: The nation defied the Lord (vv. 26, 42). Moab's national pride was bringing judgment (v. 29), and there would be no place to hide (vv. 43-44; see also Amos 5:19; Isa 24:17-18). In Chapter 49 Ammon, Edom, Syria (Damascus), Kedar (an Ishmaelite desert tribe), Hazor (probably a collection of Arabian settlements), and Elam (a nation about two hundred miles east of Babylon) are warned of coming judgment. No nation can snub God with impunity.

LAMENTATIONS 3:1-20   There has been disagreement as to whether Chapter 3 is the personal word of Jeremiah, or was written as a collective lament for Jerusalem. Modern scholarship is concluding that this is Jeremiah speaking – and speaking about his own feeling and experience.

The language is figurative, but gives a clear picture of the isolation that Jeremiah felt. Although he agreed with the Lord's message to the people, these were his people and his city, and he suffered personally with them. Humanly speaking, he had no reason for hope. All was truly "bitterness and gall" (v. 19), and Jeremiah was in emotional pain (v. 20).

NOVEMBER 3

TITUS 3   Note the reminders in verses 1-2: obedience to those in authority, readiness to do good, and humility in relationships. These characteristics mark God's person – actually, they are the mark of the Holy Spirit.

Salvation in practical terms is one way to read verses 3-11. We are saved *from* our old way of life (v. 3), saved *through* Christ's gracious work on our behalf (vv. 4-6), and saved *to* a totally new orientation and way of living (vv. 7-8). Think about the pervasive nature of this change. Every part of living is affected by the changes that come with salvation.

Compare verses 10-11 with Romans 16:17-18 and Proverbs 6:16-19. These references make it plain that divisive behavior does not come from the Lord.

JEREMIAH 50-51   Jeremiah now turned to Babylon. Of all the nations, Babylon would be the most important to the people of Jerusalem. Nebuchadnezzar had carried off Jehoiakim to Babylon (2 Chron 36:5-7), and later, Jehoiachin was also taken (2 Chron 36:9-10). Zedekiah was on the throne but would also fall to Nebuchadnezzar as Jerusalem fell.

These chapters predict the seemingly impossible. Babylon, too, would fall under the Lord's judgment (50:2-3) because it had sinned against the Lord (50:14b), opposed Him (50:24), defied Him (50:29), was a land full of idols (50:38), and did wrong in Israel (51:24). Habakkuk 1:6-11 also describes the sinful and violent nature of the Babylonians and how they sinned by worshipping their power as their god. Note the series of curses that God declares against Babylon in 50:35-38.

The Lord says that no matter how strong Babylon may be, the Lord will bring her down (51:53). God has His own methods. Jeremiah says that the Lord would make her officials, wise men, governors, officers, and warriors drunk (51:57). That is exactly what happened on the last night of Babylon's life as a nation (Dan 5). On that night, while the Babylonian officials were partying, the army of the Medes and Persians diverted the river, marched into the city on the dry waterbed of the river (under the barrier that blocked entrance to the city by boat), and took the city!

☑Embedded within this prophecy about Babylon is the promise that God will restore His people. The Lord promises a new heart among His people – one that will bind them to the Lord forever (50:4-5; cf. Ezek 36:24-33). Before that, however, seventy years after their exile to Babylon, God promised to bring them back and to forgive their sins (vv. 19-20; cf. Jer 29:10-14). Israel's God is strong, and He had not forgotten His people (50:34; 51:5). This first return to the land was accomplished under the Persian King Cyrus (Ezra 1:1-4; cf. Isa 44:28-45:13 written over two hundred years before the time of Cyrus). This passage, therefore, not only was fulfilled in the return to the land under Ezra and Nehemiah, but refers also to the final restoration when God will take away the sins of the people and give them a new heart (50:4-5, 19-20).⇦

LAMENTATIONS 3:21-39   Recall that, humanly speaking, Jeremiah had no hope (notes from Nov. 2). But there was another dimension, and Jeremiah knew where to look. He turned to the truth he knew about the Lord God. In that truth, he had hope – not pie in the sky, but hope based on God's purposes for His people.

It is true: God *does* love His people and He *does* have compassion on them; He *is* always faithful, and His blessings *are* new every morning. On this basis, Jeremiah could wait for the Lord (vv. 22-24). Through all that he had suffered, in his heart he knew that his hope and trust in God could allow him to wait for His deliverance (vv. 25-30). The present suffering would not be forever (vv. 31-36). Jeremiah himself had carried the message of restoration to the people from the Lord (Jer 33). He had also carried the message of destruction because of their sin, and the fulfillment of that message from the Lord was certain (vv. 37-39).

NOVEMBER 4

PHILEMON   Paul wrote this short letter while he was in prison in Rome to Philemon, probably a resident at Colosse. The subject of the letter was Onesimus, a runaway slave who belonged to Philemon. In the past, Onesimus had been a problem to Philemon (v. 11) but now had been converted and was assisting Paul in prison.

Paul also had been a blessing to Philemon, and he appealed to Philemon on this basis to forgive the slave and treat him like a brother in Christ. The letter implies that Paul would welcome a freed Onesimus back to assist him in his imprisonment (v. 13). At the least, he asks Philemon to welcome the returned slave into his household and treat him as a brother (vv. 15-16). This request tested the radical changes that the gospel demands in our lives. To welcome back a runaway slave – and to treat him as a brother – was consistent with the message of grace, but radically different from the society in which they lived.

JEREMIAH 52   While reading Chapter 52, imagine the carnage and the destroyed splendor. The palace was gone. The temple was gone. The treasures were taken to Babylon. The next mention of these treasures is in Daniel 5, when they were used to honor the gods of Babylon! The bronze pillars so carefully made were cut down and taken to Babylon. Verse 27b states, "So Judah went into captivity, away from her land." Verse 3 gives the reason. "It was because of the Lord's anger that all this happened to Jerusalem and Judah, and in the end he thrust them from his presence." Would it have been wise to obey God?

LAMENTATIONS 3:40-66   Based on the character, faithfulness, and blessing of the Lord – as well as God's promise of deliverance and restoration (3:21-39), Jeremiah calls for collective repentance before the Lord (vv. 41-42). As for Jeremiah, his tears would continue to flow until the Lord once again looked at His people (vv. 49-51).

While reading verses 52-58, remember what happened when Jeremiah was thrown into a cistern to die (Jer 38:1-13). The Lord delivered him in a remarkable way through the brave action of one man.

Finally, Jeremiah calls on the Lord to remember the unjust actions against him, and to punish those who had persecuted him (vv. 59-66).

NOVEMBER 5

HEBREWS 1   The book of Hebrews is thought to have been written rather early in the New Testament period, probably around 60-70 AD. It was long felt that Paul was the author of the book. However, the language and style are different from Paul's. The authorship of Hebrews is, therefore, uncertain. The recipients of the letter are thought to be Jewish Christians. The book is rich in material related to Jewish worship, and the author goes to considerable length to show how Jesus fulfilled Jewish expectations from the Old Testament.

The introduction of the book (vv. 1-4) magnificently describes Jesus as God's Son, the radiance of God's glory, who exactly represents God's being (cf. John 1:17-18). Jesus is the creator and the sustainer of the universe and all things in it by His powerful word. He is the redeemer who has provided the way for cleansing from sin. God appointed Jesus to be heir of all things (cf. Eph 1:20-22), and He now sits at God's right hand. There is scarcely another place in the New Testament that says so much in such little space about the Lord Jesus in His exalted position.

☑The text launches immediately after the introduction into the discussion of the person of Jesus. The remainder of the chapter is made up of quotations from the Old Testament to show how Jesus is God's Son (v. 5). As such, Jesus is now glorified at the right hand of the Father (v. 13), is unchanging (vv. 11-12), and has eternal authority (v. 8). He is the creator of the heavens and the earth (v. 10), and is worshipped by angels (v. 6). He will receive the nations as His inheritance (v. 13). All of this, documented by the use of Old Testament messianic prophecies, demonstrates to readers that Jesus is indeed the Messiah, the fulfillment of Old Testament prophecy.↩

EZEKIEL 1-2   Jehoiachin was eighteen years of age when he became king and reigned only three months.   He surrendered to Nebuchadnezzar and was taken to Babylon along with most of the significant people in the city (597 BC; 2 Chron 36:9-10).

Ezekiel, both a prophet and a priest, ministered to the Israelites who were brought to Babylon with Jehoiachin.   He gave his first prophecy about 592 BC, during the fifth year of captivity.

Ezekiel saw an awesome vision: four living creatures (1:4-14; cf. Rev 4:6-11), four flying vehicles (1:15-21; cf. Ezek 10:9-22), and the throne of God (1:25-28; cf. Rev 4:1-6). As you read this chapter, try to visualize what Ezekiel saw.   The flying vehicles may remind you of "flying saucers."   They were round, had "eyes" around the periphery, could hover in one place, moved swiftly, and changed directions abruptly.

Chapter 2 begins with Ezekiel before the Lord (1:25-28). The Lord gave Ezekiel specific instructions as his ministry began among the exiles in Babylon.   Judah was only a few years from total destruction; the best of the population had already come to Babylon in captivity, yet the Lord still had a message for the people.   The Lord's grace was still reaching out.

Ezekiel's assignment in Chapter 2 was not a pleasant one. The Lord described the people as obstinate, stubborn, and rebellious.   The Lord told Ezekiel four times that he must not be afraid of the people! This would imply that Ezekiel might face the same dangers as Jeremiah.

LAMENTATIONS 4   The description of the disaster continues, adding more details.   Once again, Jeremiah pinpointed the reason – the sin of the prophets, priests, and people (4:13).   Look for the descriptions of the people. *They had a delusive security that God would shelter them (through the false messages of their "prophets," v. 20).*   Sin demands a price, and the reality of its harsh consequences was too hard to bear. Note the glimmer of hope that the writer holds for the people (v. 22a).

NOVEMBER 6

HEBREWS 2   The message of Hebrews calls believers to careful living. *There are a number of warnings for believers in this book that are direct and provocative.* At first reading, they may seem to be more direct than in other parts of the New Testament, but they are much the same as the language of Jesus. The first of these warnings is found here (vv. 1-4). *Pay close attention to the truth that Jesus has given – it is possible to drift (v. 1)! Remember that God punished those who ignored the truth in the past (v. 2; cf. 1 Cor 10:1-12).* Compare this warning in Hebrews 2 with Jesus' words in Matthew 11:20-24. If those in the past couldn't get away with disobedience and careless living, why should we? Good question!

The author points out that at present, even though God has placed everything in Jesus' hands, all the prophecies of the Old Testament concerning the Messiah are not yet fully realized (vv. 8-9). The victory of the cross has been won – but the final and visible reign with the complete subjugation of Satan is still in the future. This is the meaning of the statement that "...at present we do not see everything subject to Him" (v. 8b).

Jesus bought freedom for those of the kingdom by sharing their humanity (v. 14). The text makes the remarkable statement that God made Jesus perfect through suffering (v. 10). This cannot refer to moral perfection – for He was already morally perfect and without sin. By assuming humanity, however, He was perfectly identified with the human condition and able to take our sin upon Himself – and understand our experience as human beings in an evil world (vv. 14-18). (See also John 1:14; Phil 2:6-8.) He has made us part of His family and is our brother (vv. 11-12). ☑Note that verses 12-13 use Old Testament messianic passages to validate Jesus as the Messiah.⇦

EZEKIEL 3-5   The book of Ezekiel is rich in symbolism and object lessons. Ezekiel was told to eat the scroll that the Lord gave him. This undoubtedly represented the message that Ezekiel was to take to the people. Symbolically, he was to digest the message and then speak it faithfully. It was sweet to the taste, perhaps meaning that Ezekiel agreed with the message.

Carrying the message to the Lord's people should not have been difficult, since he and the people spoke the same language (3:4-9). However, although their language was the same, the people's hearts were hardened and obstinate (v. 7). Note the warnings that the Lord had for Ezekiel, telling him to listen carefully to all that God told him. Then read the object lesson the Lord gave Ezekiel (vv. 24-27) to illustrate the difficulty he would have, but also how the Lord would enable him for the task (v. 27).

Think about God's warning to Ezekiel in verses 16-21. We are responsible to the Lord and to the people who should be hearing the message of grace. Consider this in relation to those around us.

Ezekiel's assignment in Chapter 4 was to dramatize the punishment that would come to the people of Judah and Jerusalem. The siege of Jerusalem and the meager food supply was part of the lesson. The assignment seems strange to us but must certainly have drawn attention. There is no indication that Ezekiel was required to lie down twenty-four hours a day. He received instructions for cooking that would have been impossible while lying down and tied up.

Another object lesson followed (Ch. 5). When the enactment of the siege was finished, Ezekiel was instructed to shave his hair, burning one-third within the city, scattering one-third with a sword around the outline of the city, and scattering the last one-third to the winds. Only a few strands of hair would remain, tucked in his garment. Look for the meaning of these symbolic acts (5:1-4, 11-12).

Note God's comments about the people in verses 5-7. They were worse than pagans (v. 7)! Then read what the Lord decreed about them (vv. 14-17).

LAMENTATIONS 5   Jeremiah's prayer to the Lord in Chapter 5 touches the heart. He had lived through the rebellion of the people. Nothing he had said reached them. Still, he prayed for his people, pleading for the Lord's mercy on their behalf. The present condition of the people was almost beyond imagining. In the midst of all that had happened, however, read Jeremiah's affirmation of God (v. 19). What a model of ministry!

NOVEMBER 7

HEBREWS 3   The chapter begins with the word "therefore," which calls attention to what has preceded. Based on Jesus' ability to understand the human condition and His victory as God's Son (Ch. 2), turn your attention to Him (vv. 1-6). In fact, it is stronger than that – the author tells us to "fix our thoughts" on Jesus. Get Him in your vision, and keep looking there! Hold on to courage and hope (v. 6b)!

Notice the strong warning in verses 7-19. As Paul does in 1 Corinthians 10, the author uses the Israelites to illustrate how *it is possible to have many of God's blessings, but miss out on a relationship with Him because of unbelief and disobedience.* As a result, many died in the desert after they had left Egypt instead of entering into the land that had been promised (v. 17).

The application for us individually, and for the church corporately, is in verses 12-15. We are each responsible to heed the warning and learn – and we as a church are to encourage one another to avoid sin and move forward in growth. In this sense we all share in being "our brother's keeper." *None of us – if we really know Christ – lives in isolation in the body of Christ.*

EZEKIEL 6-7   Many idols and places of heathen worship were in the countryside. The prophecies of Chapter 6 concern these places of worship that would be destroyed along with the people who worshipped there. Note too that there would be no escape (v. 12). When the Lord stretches out His hand in judgment, there will be no place to go (v. 14)!

A recurring phrase in Ezekiel is, "Then you will know that I am the Lord." In Chapter 7 the phrase appears in verses 4b, 9b, and 27b. The Lord's complaints against the people are arrogance (v. 10), violence (vv. 11, 23), idolatry (v. 20), and pride (v. 24). The message is that time has run out, and God will now deal with them according to their conduct. The grace of delay is gone.

Ezekiel points out that outside the city people will die by sword and inside by famine and plague (v. 15; cf. 5:12). Nothing they have will save them! Gold and silver will be useless (v. 19). And *they will know that it is the Lord* who has brought destruction.

PROVERBS 24:23-29   Once again we see the Lord's agenda with regard to justice (vv. 23-25). Money can talk in the courtroom, either through a smooth and skillful lawyer or through outright bribery. When this happens, society is eroded, and God is not pleased (cf. Deut 16:19-20).

The other side of injustice appears in verse 28. This warns against making an unjust accusation. Verse 24 warns against turning the eye when a person is guilty. Both are a miscarriage of truth (Isa 5:20, 23).

NOVEMBER 8

HEBREWS 4   Once again, the chapter begins with "therefore," calling attention to the warning of Chapter 3. Taking to heart the example of the Israelites who failed to find faith, we need to be careful not to follow their example (vv. 1-3)! The key to avoiding it is faith with a responsive heart (v. 11). Attention to the Word of God is primary, for it gets to the heart of the matter (v. 12). Further, God sees and we are responsible to Him (v. 13). "Therefore" (v. 14), hold firmly to faith in Jesus! We can approach Him with confidence because He understands us perfectly.

There is a paradox – a seeming contradiction – in verses 9-11. On the one hand, the author speaks of the rest and security that we have in the new life, which comes by faith. It is something we cannot work for. It is a gift, and not a result of our good deeds (Eph 2:8-9). Yet in verse 11 the text enjoins each of us to "make every effort to enter that rest." Jesus makes a similar statement in Luke 13:24 when He tells listeners to "make every effort to enter through the narrow door." In both instances, it means that we must be certain that what we are trusting – and how we are living (obedience to Jesus) – is the right way to a relationship with God. That way is faith in the person and work of the Lord Jesus and His redemption for us through the cross. That is how we "enter" His "rest" (v. 1).

The seeming paradox is that we cannot enter the relationship with God by presenting our good deeds (Eph 2:8-9), but the good deeds of obedience always accompany faith (v. 6; cf. 1 John 2:3-6).

EZEKIEL 8-9   Although Ezekiel was physically with the exiles in Babylon, in Chapter 8 he was taken, in a vision, to the temple in Jerusalem (v. 3). The temple had been desecrated with idols and idol worship, and this was what the Lord showed to Ezekiel. The idols were an abomination to the Lord (v. 6), but the subsequent vision of the elders of the nation participating in idol and pagan worship was even worse (vv. 9-13). The women participated in pagan worship (v. 14), and the elders worshipped the sun (v. 16). And if this were not enough, the land was filled with violence (v. 17). The result: Time was out. Judgment was coming (v. 18).

The vision of Chapter 9 is a continuation of the previous chapter. Having just seen the elders, each with their own idol, the Lord calls for guards. Six guards come, and a man with a writing kit. A special mark is placed on those in the city who mourned its evil practices (v. 4; cf. Matt 5:4), and the rest of the people were killed. The lesson for us is that the Lord *does see* the evil of society and is grieved and offended by the sin. The Lord also will protect the righteous (vv. 5-6).

PROVERBS 24:30-34   The lesson for the reader is the ethic of prudent work and study. Inattention to the disciplines of work and life leads to thorns, weeds, and broken walls. These may be figurative, or a real snapshot of our yard and home and how we are living. In either case, it isn't what the Lord desires for His child. *So* – keep working, and stay on a disciplined path. (And remember to mow your lawn!)

NOVEMBER 9

HEBREWS 5   A priest represents others before God. Aaron and his sons were appointed by the Lord, and so was Jesus. Jesus, however, was of a different order than the Aaronic priesthood. Melchizedek (v. 6) was the priest of ancient Salem (the city that became Jerusalem, Gen 14:18-20), who lived long before Aaron. Abraham – and Aaron through Abraham (7:4-10) – tithed to Melchizedek from the goods recovered by Abraham in his rescue of Lot and his family. Melchizedek blessed Abraham (and through him, the future priests of Aaron). Figuratively speaking, then, Melchizedek was of a higher order than Aaron, and so Jesus was (figuratively speaking) of the order of Melchizedek.

A problem in the church is identified in verses 11-14. There was lack of growth, and the church was made up of immature Christians who didn't understand righteousness (v. 13). Note carefully that the solid food of the Word is assimilated by the individuals who choose, by their discipline in the Christian life, to grow in spiritual morality (v. 14). There is a synergism between the Holy Spirit's application of God's truth and the individual's resolve to obedience. Jesus stated this in John 14:21. The Apostle John said the same thing in 1 John 2:5. The result of the discipline of obedience is genuine growth to maturity. We achieve this maturity not by only *knowing* the truth of the Bible, but by *applying* it!

EZEKIEL 10-11   After the temple had been defiled with the dead (Ch. 9), the glory of the Lord left the temple (10:4, 18; 11:23) with the four living creatures and the four "wheels" (cf. Ch. 1). It is interesting to think of this activity in the temple. Without question, there are spiritual dimensions of which we are not aware. The spiritual creatures that the prophet saw were not visible to the people of the city, but they were there. Remember that when Solomon dedicated the temple, and finished praying, the glory of the Lord had filled the temple (2 Chron 7:1-3). Now, the blessing of God's presence was gone!

The leaders of Jerusalem were giving false assurances to the people (11:1-4). The saying, "This city is a cooking pot, and we are the meat," meant they believed the city protected them. But the Lord turned their saying around, telling them He would drive them out of the "pot" (vv. 7-12).

☑Note God promises to care for His people in exile (11:16) and later, to restore them and give them a new heart (11:16-20). This could refer to the return under Nehemiah and Ezra, but probably also refers to the promised restoration under the coming Messiah. Included in this promise is an undivided heart with a new spirit, which seems to place this fulfillment at the time of the restoration of Israel when Jesus returns.⇐ (This promise will be much more detailed later in the book.) Finally, the glory of the Lord rose (v. 23), Ezekiel was returned to the exiles in Babylon, and the vision vanished (v. 24). Ezekiel reported to his fellow exiles all that he had seen.

PROVERBS 25:1-11   Compare verse 4 with 1 Peter 1:6-7. Contaminated silver isn't much good for making fine vessels. God sends us hardships to refine our faith to a purity that will bring praise and honor to the Lord Jesus. This is a form of discipline that is not punishment but His loving work to bring us to maturity. Difficulties build strength and help the Christian trust God – and to expect His hand in our lives. We should never grumble about what the Lord is doing in our lives (Heb 12:4-13).

NOVEMBER 10

HEBREWS 6   This chapter poses problems of interpretation. It seems to say that one can be lost after salvation, and that if this happens, salvation is not again possible (vv. 4-6).

Follow this simple outline for help with the theological question. *(1)* The problem of the church, and her individual Christians, was one of spiritual immaturity (5:11-14). *(2)* The immaturity led to faulty (unbiblical) practices in the church, which consisted of repeated repentance and baptism. People were repenting to be saved over (and, perhaps, over) again (6:1-3). *(3)* In verses 4-6, the author explains that this isn't possible! If Jesus' death wasn't sufficient, there is no sacrifice left. This practice (re-conversion) is saying, in effect, that Jesus is dying over and over, and this assertion is a disgrace! If Jesus' sacrifice was not enough, there is simply no other way. *(4)* An illustration (vv. 7-8) shows that when good seed is planted, (i.e., the new life in the believer) good crops come up. If the harvest is thorns and thistles, the ground was not tilled and the right seed not sown (cf. Matt 7:15-20)! *(5)* The application is that salvation brings good results, and the author is confident that in spite of immaturity, those results will come as believers continue diligently in the faith (vv. 9-12). *(6)* Finally, this hope and certainty of genuine life is anchored in the promises and oath of the Lord God (vv. 17-20).

We don't know the answer when we try to determine why someone who has seemed to be doing well in the faith has slipped away. The difficulty is that we cannot see the heart as the Lord can. We don't know all of the facts! The theology, as suggested above, would assert that when a person has been truly converted (good seed planted) it will show in life (good crops). Further, as developed above, *if* it were possible to be lost after conversion, it is correct that being converted again is not possible (vv. 4-6).

Having said this, note that the book of Hebrews, and the Bible as a whole, explicitly say that the *evidence* of salvation is obedience to Christ (Heb 4:1-2; 1 John 2:3-6) and perseverance (Matt 24:12-13). Walking in faith and obedience also contributes to the Christian's assurance in his relationship with Christ (1 John 2:3). Further, note the warnings to believers not to drift away and thus call in question their salvation (2:1-3; 3:7-19; 4:1-2, 11; 10:26-31; 12:15-17, 25). There is a balance between our confidence that Christ has saved us, and our responsibility to live out the faith as evidence of God's good work in our lives.

EZEKIEL 12-13   Principle: Rebellion blinds the mind (12:1-2). Because the people were so blinded they would not listen, the Lord used Ezekiel to bring them an object lesson.   The prophet packed his belongings, waited until dusk, and then dug through the wall and left (with his eyes shielded). Read the Lord's interpretation (vv. 12-14), and then read 2 Kings 25:1-7. The prophecy was fulfilled when Zedekiah attempted to leave Jerusalem as it fell to the Babylonians.

As you read the predictions of the rest of the chapter, listen to the people saying that it wouldn't happen for a long time (vv. 22, 27). How human to deceive ourselves! The fulfillment, however, was just around the corner (v. 28).

False prophets had been around for many years (Ch. 13). Recall that Micaiah was the only true prophet in the land when Jehoshaphat visited Ahab (1 Kings 22). All the other prophets had something to say – none of it true or from the Lord. These prophets in Ezekiel's day were willing to say what people wanted to hear, and were devoid of any contact with the Lord. It was actually worse than that, for they had made no effort to repair the damage in society and had given false assurances as well (13:5-7, 10).

During the trouble in Jerusalem, when it was threatened by Babylon, the people were anxious to hear that there would be peace and that the Lord would deliver them. The prophets were willing to deliver! Read verses 10-12 to understand God's evaluation. By their actions, they were putting the people at great risk! The Lord declared that He would take action against such teachers (vv. 13-16).

Another great evil that the Lord addresses through Ezekiel is sorcery (vv. 17-23).   Sorcery, witchcraft, and any involvement with spirits were expressly forbidden in the Mosaic law.   These practices involved Satan's spirit world.

PROVERBS 25:12-20   Have you thought of necessary correction from another person as a gift of gold (v. 12)? It is built into our human nature not to be pleased with criticism – even when needed.   Our immediate reaction is often defensive. We would be wise to get beyond the defensiveness to consider the appropriateness of rebuke or criticism. If needed, and if we will listen, corrective action will bring blessing to us!

Note the principle in verses 16-17. Don't overdo! Don't be a glutton, and don't make a nuisance of yourself!

NOVEMBER 11

HEBREWS 7   The author adds more detail about Melchizedek, pointing out that there is no record of his ancestors or his progeny. Figuratively, he was without beginning or end of days. Jesus is like him in this way as well: He has lived from the beginning of time, lives now, and lives forever.

Because Jesus is eternal, He meets our needs as human beings (vv. 23-28)! He saves us completely (v. 25). He prays for us, representing our needs before the Father (v. 25). He was sinless and is the sacrifice for our sins (vv. 26-27). The priests under the law died and were gone, but Jesus lives on forever (v. 28)!

EZEKIEL 14-15   We often think of idols as images or statues to which we bow and worship. And they are that. But there are also desires of the heart that are just as much idols as what we can see and touch. When the elders of Israel came to Ezekiel, *the Lord knew their heart* (14:1-6). Note carefully the word from the Lord in verses 7-8. Don't presume on God – and don't play games with Him. It simply won't work.

As you read 14:12-23, understand that there comes a time in a nation's history when god's punishment will come. When God spoke to Abraham about the Amorites, they still had four hundred years before God would judge them, but by then their sin would reach its full measure (Gen 15:13-16). The Lord is patient and forbearing with people, but time does run out. Any time we meddle with sin, believing that it is a small thing, we are presumptuous. We don't understand the nature of sin or the character of the Lord.

Chapter 15 compares Jerusalem to a useless vine. If a vine doesn't produce fruit, it isn't good for much, even for fuel. Particularly note verse 7. *The people came out of the fire (Egypt) through God's deliverance – but now would be consigned to the fire – through God's judgment!* What an awesome truth!

PROVERBS 25:21-28   In Hong Kong, in the old Central Post Office, the text of verse 25 was cut into stone. When a new post office replaced the old building in about 1975, the text in stone was transferred to the new building. We don't understand this verse in its real meaning today when we have instant communication. But in the time when Proverbs was written, and when the old post office was built in Hong Kong about 1900, news from a distant land could take weeks. Further, in the heat of the Middle East, or the sweltering humidity of Hong Kong, cold water has a special meaning. Perhaps we could give fresh meaning to this verse. Do you know of anyone to whom you should write a note of encouragement? A Christian brother or sister who may need a spiritual or emotional lift? "Cold water to a weary soul."

NOVEMBER 12

HEBREWS 8   The writer continues to contrast Jesus' ministry as high priest with the priesthood established under Moses, which continued until the time of Jesus. Review the last verses of Chapter 7 to lead into this chapter.

The covenant of the Old Testament priesthood is here called the "old" covenant (v. 6). The tabernacle, when the plans were given to Moses, was to be a "copy and shadow" of the real thing in heaven, which Jesus would fulfill (vv. 5-6). Jesus, as high priest, has completed the law's requirements and is in heaven in God's presence in the "true tabernacle" (vv. 1-2). Saying that the details of the tabernacle given to Moses were important implies that each part of that tabernacle and its furnishings was significant – foreshadowing the perfect fulfillment that would come in Christ.

The text says Jesus is the perfect high priest (7:26-8:2). The Jews, steeped in their traditions, were in tune with this concept, while we today do not think in these terms. We do, however, have a need of which we should be aware. A priest stands before God on behalf of another person. We need that – for we cannot approach God in our sinful condition. Jesus, the perfect answer to that problem, took our place at the cross and now continues to represent us before the Father (7:25; 9:24; 1 John 2:1). Jesus secures the New Covenant with His own blood, and brings all believers into a new and intimate relationship through Him with the Father.

EZEKIEL 16   Chapter 16 uses another allegory to bring home truth to the people. The Lord compared the nation (Judah) to a helpless newborn whom the Lord cared for and nourished (vv. 6-14), only to have the young woman turn to sin as she matured (v. 15ff.). To make matters worse, she used the Lord's gifts to attract lovers (vv. 17-19). She engaged in human sacrifice (vv. 20-22), public idolatry (vv. 23-24), and prostitution (v. 25ff.). ☑Yet God's promises hold; the covenant between God and the people will be honored (vv. 59-62), and atonement will be made for sin (Jesus' atonement, v. 63).⇦

PROVERBS 26:1-12   The chapter begins with eleven proverbs about the fool (v. 2 being the exception). A word about verses 4-5 may help. Verse 4 says trying to seriously answer a foolish question makes one foolish. Verse 5 implies that trying to answer a foolish question, gives legitimacy to it, and to the foolish man as well; the question should be ignored.

Don't trust a fool to carry an important message; it is like cutting off your own feet (v. 6). A fool cannot learn from mistakes (v. 11). There is, however, a surprising gem of wisdom here: Pride is worse than foolishness (v. 12). There is more hope for the fool than for the proud. Think about it.

NOVEMBER 13

HEBREWS 9   The contrast continues between the old and the new covenants. Note in verses 1-5 how the details of the tabernacle plan and furnishings are outlined (cf. 8:5). It is a disappointment that the author didn't explain how each of these things pointed to the new covenant (v. 5b). A time is coming, however, when all of these details will be crystal clear to each of God's children – in glory!

As you read verses 6-10, note that the ceremonies of the tabernacle had to be done repeatedly, but still were not able to clear the consciences of the worshippers (nor were they able to take away sins, vv. 13-14; cf. 10:4). They were temporary "external regulations" used until the coming of Christ (v. 10).

Jesus, however, with His own blood, accomplished what the animal sacrifices could not do. He paid the price for eternal redemption that has cleansed the consciences and forgiven the sins of those who come to God through Christ (vv. 11-14). He has also, through this cleansing, made us able to serve the living God (v. 14; cf. Col 1:13-14).

This raises a serious question. *What about the sins of those who died before the time of Christ?*   If the sacrifices were "external regulations" (v. 10), unable to clear the conscience (v. 9) and unable to take away sin (10:4), what was the status of the millions who died before Christ?   Verse 15 shows that Christ, as mediator of the "new covenant," died to set free from sin *those who had died under the "first covenant,"* i.e., before Jesus came and paid for sin. These people are the ones who brought their sacrifices in the faith of obedience to the regulations given by the Lord (and even those who lived before the regulations, such as Abraham).   Romans 3:25 makes this same point.

God left sins unpunished until Jesus died. Romans 4 emphasizes that it was the faith of Abraham that brought forgiveness. *All who have come to God have come by faith through the sacrifice of Christ.*

Finally, note that Jesus' sacrifice is a "once for all" event, not to be repeated as sacrifices were over and over under the first covenant (v. 26). All of us will die, and all of us will stand before God (v. 27). Those who have been forgiven through Christ will not face judgment for sin, for Christ has taken away their sin (v. 28).

These things may seem technical, but they are the basis of God's plan for handling sin. This wonderful plan was in the mind of the eternal God from before He created the world, and should lead us to careful living (1 Peter 1:17-21).

EZEKIEL 17-18   The allegory in Chapter 17 of two eagles is about the Babylonian captivity. The first eagle represents Babylon, and the top of the cedar that the eagle took was Jehoiachin and the exiles who were taken to "a city of traders" (Babylon, vv. 1-4). The planted seed represents the people left in Judah under oath to the king of Babylon (vv. 5, 13). Zedekiah was placed on the throne by Nebuchadnezzar, but turned to Egypt, breaking his oath to Babylon (2 Chron 36:11-13). Egypt, then, is the second eagle, and the vine turned toward the second eagle (vv. 7, 15). Notice the result. The growth would wither (v. 9). Read the Lord's explanation of the allegory (vv. 11-15) and the results to Zedekiah and the people (vv. 16-21).

☑But there is a note of hope. The top of the cedar would yield a "tender sprig" that would grow large and bring blessing (v. 22). This tender sprig will bring new life and hope for God's people, and will become a home for "birds of every kind" (v. 23b). The illustration refers to the universal blessing that will come through David's line (the Messiah). It is a different "sprig" from that mentioned in verses 3-4 (Jehoiachin, or Jeconiah), for Jeremiah 22:28-30 declared that Jehoiachin would never have a descendant on the throne of David. See the notes on Luke 3:21-38 for January 6 for the genealogy of Jesus, which lists Jeconiah (Jehoiachin) who came through Solomon in Matthew's genealogy. In contrast, David's son Nathan is the line through which Jesus came in Luke's genealogy.⇦

Read Chapter 18 carefully, as it sets out the principle of personal responsibility to the Lord for behavior. There is forgiveness for the repentant, whatever the past (vv. 21-23). There is death for the rebel, despite a history of apparent righteous living (v. 24). *It is essential to finish life well!* If we do not, there is no one to blame but ourselves.

The Lord wants us to have life (vv. 30-32). He takes no pleasure in the death of even one person. Take to heart the call for repentance.

PROVERBS 26:13-22   A sluggard is defined as habitually lazy. The sluggard doesn't leave his dwelling because "it's dangerous out there" (v. 13). He loves the recumbent position, turns back and forth like a door on a hinge – and goes nowhere (v. 14). He eats until he is too lazy to put more in his mouth (v. 15), and he is deceived by his supposed wisdom to the point that he can't accept advice or another's wisdom (v. 16). The lesson here is to take the opposite tack. Avoid laziness!

NOVEMBER 14

HEBREWS 10   The law of the Old Testament is a symbol of what Jesus would do (vv. 1-4), and in fulfillment, Jesus' lasting sacrifice cleanses from sin (the blood of bulls and goats could not do this), and thus permanently changes our lives (vv. 10, 14). In this regard, note that verse 10 speaks of having been made holy. This makes each believer ready to meet God through cleansing from sin when we place faith in Jesus. Verse 14 speaks of the sacrifice that has made us perfect forever (the same idea as verse 10), but also of the *process* of "being made holy." This is the ongoing work of God as we learn to align our lives with God's agenda. Both aspects of this (the event of salvation and the process of holiness) are the work of God through the Holy Spirit and through His grace.

Notice the word "therefore" again appears (v. 19). *Because* of what Jesus has done, we must exhibit personal holiness and encourage one another. Note each of the ways in this section (vv. 19-25) in which we are called to action: Each follows "let us..." Jesus is coming again, and His coming is added incentive for holiness (v. 25).

Now look at the warning that follows (vv. 26-31, 35-39). These are some of the strongest in the New Testament, but consistent with many warnings Jesus gave His listeners. Compare these verses with 1 John 2:3-6. This whole section (vv. 19-39) calls us to a level of Christian commitment that extends to every part of our lives! This section should show us that we must not treat God lightly. *We cannot play games with the living God!*

EZEKIEL 19-20   Ezekiel again uses allegories, or word pictures, to explain the truth to those listening (Ch. 19). The first allegory concerned two young lions (vv. 1-9). One of these was taken to Egypt and represents Jehoahaz (2 Kings 23:31-34). Jehoahaz was on the throne only three months, and even the allegorical account is short. The second young lion was violent, but was trapped in a net and carried to Babylon. This represented Jehoiachin (2 Kings 24:8-16).

The vine (vv. 10-14) is a symbol of Judah. Although it was healthy and well-watered, it was uprooted and then withered under the blast of the east wind. It portrays the devastated land after the fall to the Babylonians.

Chapter 20 begins with some elders of the nation in exile coming to the prophet to inquire of the Lord. The Lord gave a long answer, chronicling His dealings in grace with the nation. Over and over, the Lord deferred deserved judgment. But time did run out, and the Lord's judgment did come. The Lord declares that without repentance, the people may not come to Him to inquire about their welfare (vv. 30-31).

There are two principles and a promise in the remainder of the chapter. *First*, God expects more from those who promise allegiance to Him. Judah had made promises to the Lord, and although they wanted to be like the rest of the world, the Lord would not allow it (vv. 32-33). What the pagan may get away with, the child of God cannot! *Second*, the Lord wants to use His mighty hand to deliver His people (Ps 77:13-15), but He can also use it to bring His wrath when it is needed (vv. 33-38). ☑*Finally*, look at God's gracious promise (vv. 39-44). "But afterward..." (v. 39) points to the future when the Lord will, under the Messiah, reestablish His people in the land with a completely new heart to serve Him (vv. 41-43; cf. Zech 12:10).⇦ The overriding principle of the chapter is God's good and fair hand in and on His people – both in judgment and in grace.

PROVERBS 26:23-28   A malicious person is not to be trusted. He (or she) looks fine and sounds good, but there is injury in the smooth talk (v. 23). With smooth talk, such a person disguises himself as someone who cares (vv. 24-25). The wickedness behind the mask needs to be exposed – and will be when enough people have been hurt (v. 26). The lesson is to stay away from such a person. A second lesson is not to allow this behavior to slip into our own lives!

NOVEMBER 15

HEBREWS 11   This great chapter of faith brings us face to face with the heroes of the Bible. As you read and are reminded of their lives, allow their fidelity of trust to challenge your own life. All of them lived in the Old Testament era (under the "former covenant"). None had the Bible in hand. Each was deeply touched by God's grace. They were persons of spiritual life and depth (without the information we have). They invested their lives in the kingdom, and now wait for the coming of Christ in glory (9:28b).

Look for the action words that describe their decisions of faith and courage. Note that they considered themselves strangers on earth (v.

13). A higher vision drove their actions – one of God and His glory. As a result, God has prepared a city for them (v. 16). Their glory awaits them!

Note too that many of them suffered for their stand (vv. 32-38). They were misunderstood and rejected. Many, unnamed, lost their lives. God's evaluation was that the world was not worthy of them (v. 38a)!

Allow this inspiring chapter to speak to your own heart. The people chronicled in this chapter have all died. Their race has been run. *At this point, are they better off than the countless other people who drifted through life with worthless concerns?* The answer is obvious. Where is it that the Lord is speaking to you about your life? Will you respond? Remember your extraordinary position in the kingdom (Col 1:13) and the power of the Holy Spirit in your life (2 Tim 1:7-8a)! The Lord will give us all that we need to respond in the right way. *The opportunity is now – the final exam is still ahead (Heb 9:27; 2 Cor 5:10).*

EZEKIEL 21-22   The Lord's message to Ezekiel for the people was not good news (Ch. 21). He was to preach against the land and publicly mourn because of the disaster that was to come. It had been determined and would not be turned away (v. 7b). The illustration was that of a sword in hand – polished and ready for use. It would bring judgment to the whole land, and there would be no place to hide (v. 14b). The sword belonged to the king of Babylon, who would come to the land. On the way, he might be undecided whether to go to Ammon or to Judah, but it was certain that he would go to Jerusalem (vv. 18-23). The people's open rebellion had brought this judgment from the Lord (v. 24). ☑Note the special message to King Zedekiah (vv. 25-27). Note also that no son of David will sit on the throne after the coming disaster until "he comes to whom it rightfully belongs; to him I will give it" (v. 27; cf. Gen 49:10). This is a reference to the Messiah – still to come!⇦

In Chapter 22, read the list of sins that were bringing the nation down (vv. 1-12). At least ten sins of society are listed. Sins are committed by individuals, but the composite made the city guilty (v. 3)! The religious leaders were part of the problem (v. 26). The political leadership was guilty (v. 27). The prophets were deceiving the people with lies (v. 28), and the common people participated (v. 29). Feel the sadness of vv. 30-31. *At this very time, Jeremiah was in the city preaching, but no one would listen!*

The picture that Ezekiel draws with the pen in verses 17-22 should be noted. The Lord said He would draw the people into Jerusalem, and treat them like metal in a foundry furnace – that which was left after refining silver – to be thrown away. The people of the countryside did come into the city during the siege of Jerusalem, and this prophecy was fulfilled!

PROVERBS 27:1-9   What would you rather feel: kisses or wounds (v. 6)? The obvious answer isn't always the correct one. It depends on from whom and why we receive the kisses or the wounds. Strokes and flattery may be pleasant, but when an enemy gives them, the motivation is to cut us down. On the other hand, the hard words of a friend are meant to steer us to a safer and better course. We need wisdom to assess the source and the motivation behind both the praise and the criticism.

NOVEMBER 16

HEBREWS 12   "Therefore," i.e., based on the example of those who have gone before –the giants of faith – *get with the program* (v. 1)! Get rid of every single thing that will hinder your walk with Christ. Take Jesus' example as your own. He endured suffering because it was God's will for Him, and He understood the result. Fix your attention on Him (v. 2). *Resist sin!* Listen to the Lord (vv. 5-11).

This is a strong mandate to resist sin and to fight the battle as if it were real. The words used here have an unusual urgency: to resist to the point of shedding our own blood (v. 4)! Because He loves His children, the Lord may (and will) discipline us (vv. 5-6). A pure life is the Lord's agenda for each of His children.

Discipline, however, isn't always for sin. The Lord may use hardship in our lives to help us to grow (vv. 7-8). Think about it. We need to be stretched to develop. God brings us what we need to help us trust Him. A basic question should always be close at hand: "Is God in control of what's happening in my life?" *If so, we have no liberty to grumble about what comes to us!* God is at work! Allow God to shape your trust and understanding of Him.

Beginning with verse 14, there is both a personal mandate and a corporate responsibility to holy living, to ensure that no one in the fellowship goes astray (vv. 15-16). Explicit here is responsibility for one another. This is similar to Deuteronomy 29:18, which also outlines the corporate obligation. The church in action, caring for one another, is a powerful force for good!

Further, think about whom you are dealing with! This is not some earthly authority but the Lord God Himself (vv. 18-27). Therefore, worship the Lord with awe (v. 28).

EZEKIEL 23-24   Chapter 23 is a sad story of two sisters. Oholah represents Samaria (Israel), and Oholibah Jerusalem (Judah). The Lord had explicitly told the people what to do with the nations of Canaan and their worship practices when they came into the land (Deut 7; Josh 23:6-13). They were to be separate and avoid the sinful worship of the other nations. Further, they were to trust God (Josh 23:8)! Instead, Israel went to the Assyrians for help and took their worship for her own (23:5-8). Judah also looked to the nations around her for help (vv. 11-21). The Lord called this spiritual prostitution. Read the Lord's specific complaints against the people (vv. 35-39). The city had the noise of a carefree crowd (v. 42), but it was the noise of false freedom! Sin demands a price!

The time had come. Jerusalem was under siege (Ch. 24), and the judgment that the Lord had promised was under way. The Lord likened the city to a large cooking pot on a fire with the meat inside.

God used a severe object lesson to instruct the exiles. Ezekiel's wife died, and the Lord told Ezekiel not to mourn in the usual way. When his strange response to his wife's death raised questions, he was to tell the exiles that this was how they too would mourn for those left behind in Jerusalem (vv. 20-24). Jerusalem, as they knew it, would be only a memory, the news reaching them by a fugitive (vv. 25-27). And this is what happened! Look ahead to 33:21.

PROVERBS 27:10-18   Be wise enough to change course when necessary (v. 12). Whatever our project – whatever our plan, it is prudent to keep asking, "Are we on the right course; is the plan still viable?" Sometimes a minor change is all it takes. Sometimes, however, a radical change is needed. A wise person keeps his eyes open and is willing to adjust course. That is the application of godly wisdom.

Have you found someone with whom you can discuss – and even debate – issues of life? Such a person is a gift from the Lord (v. 17). Who you spend time with will inevitably make a difference in your thinking and perspective. Choose wisely, and reap the blessing.

NOVEMBER 17

HEBREWS 13   These concluding words of Hebrews offer some short reminders to keep us on track in the Christian life. They are a "short course" on what we should remember and observe. Each deserves emphasis, for it contributes to the whole of the Christian life. Highlight the comments on hospitality (v. 2, a largely lost art in the modern Christian community?), those who suffer for the Lord (v. 3), purity in marriage (v. 4), and secularism (v. 5). Note that contentment with what we have is tied to the presence of the Lord (v. 5b).

Verses 15-16 speak of praising the Lord and doing good – looking for needs to meet among those around us (cf. Isa 1:16-17). These are "sacrifices" with which God is pleased! Finally, understand the grace of God's work in our lives: He equips us for doing His will – and He works in us to help us do His will (vv. 20-21; cf. Phil 2:13).

EZEKIEL 25-26   Although the Lord may discipline a nation such as Judah, He is not pleased when other nations take advantage of those in difficulty. Ammon, Moab, Edom, Philistia, and Tyre surrounded Judah and took advantage of Judah's trouble for their own ends. Their sins against God were malice (25:6), revenge (v. 12), revenge and malice (v. 15), and gloating over the destruction of Jerusalem (26:2). *Principle: Don't rejoice in another's difficulty, or take advantage of their situation.* Read Amos 1:3-2:3 and Obadiah 1:11-15. It is more prudent to extend mercy to the disadvantaged person, people, or nation. God brings discipline. He doesn't need our help. And He is the one who keeps the books (Obad 1:15).

PROVERBS 27:19-27   The biblical work ethic is spelled out in verses 23-27. Carelessness in work responsibility (especially in an agrarian society) may jeopardize your family and future. Whatever you have in the bank now will not ensure the future (vv. 23-24). Careful attention to family responsibilities and vocation will guard your ability to meet ongoing needs. You may be acquainted with someone who has taken a tangent and whose ability to make a living has suffered. Allow these five verses to speak to your own heart.

NOVEMBER 18

JAMES 1   Most Bible scholars feel that the author of this epistle is James, the brother of Jesus, and that it was one of the first NT books to be written. The letter was written to the twelve tribes (Jewish) "scattered abroad," perhaps by the persecution after the martyrdom of Stephen (cf. Acts 7:59-8:1). The book addresses intensely practical subjects of Christian living. As you read this first chapter, focus on trust in God, temptation, and obedience.

In Hebrews 12, we saw that the Lord uses circumstances – even hard ones – to help our faith grow. James picks up on this theme in verses 2-12. Specifically, James makes it clear that as we trust God in difficulty, persevering in obedience to Him, our spiritual lives mature. Is God in charge of our circumstances? If so, we can move through hard times, trusting that God is in control. There is method in God's sending trials to His children, and there is blessing for the Christian who responds properly (v. 12).

There is a difference between trials (allowed by God and used for His purpose) and temptation (vv. 13-15). God never tempts us to sin! Notice how temptation turns into sin in these verses. *Remember: As a Christian, you are never helpless in the face of temptation (1 Cor 10:13).*

James makes a practical distinction between knowing God's Word and doing God's will (vv. 22-25). Applying the truth leads to real freedom!

Finally, think about how practical real faith is (vv. 26-27). Self-control in what we say (think how often this is necessary!) and our response to the needy are at the top of God's agenda.

EZEKIEL 27-28   In Chapter 27, Ezekiel describes Tyre as a beautiful ship. This was appropriate, since Tyre was a city-state on the eastern end of the Mediterranean Sea, and accumulated its wealth and reputation by sea commerce. The vessel Ezekiel described was made from the best materials, all imported. Further, the cities and states around Tyre contributed men and materials to its functioning and defense. The cities listed, which did business with Tyre, extended from as far west as Spain, and surrounded the seaport of Tyre (vv. 2-25). The list of the commercial products that were traded is impressive. It was a very busy place!

There will, however, be a problem. The heavily laden vessel at sea will be buffeted by an east wind (v. 26, Babylon) and will sink (v. 27). Those who traded with Tyre will be appalled (vv. 28-35), but this will quickly turn to derision (v. 36), perhaps out of fear of Babylon.

In the first verses of Chapter 28, we learn the reason for the Lord's judgment on Tyre. The wealth and influence of the city had led to pride – the city's ruler had even asserted that he was a god (v. 2). Actually, it was the Lord who established Tyre (v. 14a). And the Lord ordered her downfall. Along with pride, there was dishonest trade (v. 18). As you read the chapter, understand that national pride is wrong, and even though these people were not specifically the Lord's, yet the Lord was watching them and disciplined them for their sins. Tyre's sister city Sidon also was ripe for God's discipline (vv. 20-23).

☑Finally, God promises to restore His people from the nations, and they will live in safety (28:25-26). This will be a testimony to all nations and to the Israelites. There was, of course, a remnant who returned after the seventy years of exile. This promise, however, reaches beyond that to a time of safety and prosperity under the Lord Himself. This will happen when the Lord judges the nations, and will only be finally realized when the Messiah comes at the end of time.⇔

<u>PROVERBS 28:1-10</u>   Several of the proverbs in this chapter have to do with God's law. Verse 4, shows the result of forsaking the law. When one forsakes the law of God, he, in effect, supports the lawless (the wicked). Conversely, the practical effect of keeping the law is to rebuke and resist the wicked. By our decisions, we choose sides.

Verse 5 says that evil men do not understand justice. On the other hand, those who seek the Lord *do* understand justice, and understand it fully.   Why would the writer make such a blanket statement? Deuteronomy 1:17 says that judgment belongs to God. Justice is related to truth and its application.   Evil is connected to untruth, and thus cannot understand or promote justice. When ungodly judges sit in the courts, we cannot expect their judgments to reflect the justice God would want.   This is why Paul rebuked the Christians in Corinth for going to secular courts to settle disputes (1 Cor 6:1-6). *Those who have allowed God's Word to permeate their lives may not be trained in law, but the principles of God's Word can lead to judgments based on the truth.*

Note also verse 9 with regard to the law. If we disobey the Lord, we can't expect God to hear us when we pray. Proverbs 1:22-33 makes this argument very effectively.

<u>NOVEMBER 19</u>

<u>JAMES 2</u>   Even though we are Christians, we are still tempted to do wrong. Look at the discussion about the rich and the poor (vv. 1-7). It is sadly true that often, even in the church, "money talks." Deference is given to those who are wealthy, even though, as James points out, this financial power is often used against those in the church (v. 6). This deference to wealth breaks God's law.   James says one principle often repeated in the Old Testament is that of equity – closely related to justice. The dignity God has given to each individual calls for equal and fair treatment.   Otherwise we break God's law (vv. 8-13). *Think carefully: How we show mercy will have a bearing on how God deals with us (vv. 12-13)!*

In James' comments on faith and works (vv. 14-26), understand that you cannot be saved by works, but you cannot be a Christian unless you live out salvation with good works. The horse comes before the cart, but where there is a horse with an attached cart, the cart moves with the horse! James might have said, "Show me a moving cart (works), and I'll show you a horse (faith) that is pulling it." Jesus spoke the same truth in John 14:21a. If you love the Lord, it will show in obedience!

<u>EZEKIEL 29-30</u>   When the Lord called Egypt's king a "monster" (v. 3), He used the imagery of the crocodile. This animal was important in the

lore of Egypt, and although it was feared, it was significant. In addressing the king of Egypt, God intends to speak to the entire country. The prophecy came as Judah was under siege and had been for about one year.

Read the Lord's reason for punishing the Egyptians in verses 6-9. Egypt had proved to be a poor help to Judah (vv. 6-7), but perhaps more important was her pride (v. 9).

The prophecy of 29:17-30:19 came in approximately 571 BC, about fifteen years after the fall of Jerusalem. The political and military struggle between Babylon and Egypt for a number of years had included the strategic desire of each to dominate Israel. In the last years of Judah, Josiah lost his life intervening in a battle that was not his own as Egypt marched through Israel to face the Babylonians (2 Kings 23:29-30; 2 Chron 35:20-24).

Tyre (the Phoenician city on the Mediterranean) also had been the object of Babylon's military drive in the region (Ezek 29:18), but by the time the city fell to Babylon, Egypt had assisted the city by carrying off Tyre's wealth in ships to avoid loss to Babylon. For this, God promised that Babylon's payment would come in the military destruction and plunder of Egypt (29:19-20). This occurred about 568 BC, eighteen years after the fall of Jerusalem under Nebuchadnezzar in 586 BC.

Usually, but not always, the term "the Day of the Lord" refers to the last great judgment that will occur at the end of time. Here (30:3) it refers to the Lord's severe judgment on Egypt under Nebuchadnezzar. The judgment would involve the entire region from north to south (v. 6) and the surrounding countries (v. 5).

As you read Chapter 30, note the Lord's plans for Egypt. He intended to use Babylon to humble Egypt. The Lord indeed is sovereign over the affairs of men!

PROVERBS 28:11-19   Sin that is confessed looses its power and grip on an individual (v. 13). On the other hand, concealed sin exacts a heavy price in guilt. These principles have several applications. If you have sinned, and have confessed it, there is nothing left to talk about. The small talk and gossip loses its power. More important, cleanness of heart comes with forgiveness.

Concealed sin, on the other hand, has power. You are afraid the sin will be found out, leading to more untruths to cover your tracks. More important, if you are a believer, is the pain and suffering from disrupted relationships, both with people and with the Lord. Review David's heart and testimony over concealed sin in his life (Ps 32:3-4). The answer is, no matter what the fallout may be, the best course is to confess the sin and restore relationships with others and with the Lord.

NOVEMBER 20

JAMES 3   It is a great responsibility to be a spiritual teacher in the church (v. 1). Does that mean it would be better not to teach others even if you have the gift of teaching? Not at all. But it does mean it is terribly important that our own lives line up with the truth that we are teaching! Remember Jesus' comments about hypocrisy (Matt 23:1-33)! Teaching is a high calling. The ability to help another understand the truth and respond to it, whether in the primary department of Sunday school or with older youth or adults, is the work of the kingdom. This warning, however, is real. God will hold the teacher to the truth that he or she knows and teaches.

According to this chapter, control of what we say is the most difficult discipline of all (v. 2). Note the three illustrations showing that relatively small things can exert great influence (vv. 3-5). This is true about what we say (v. 6). Words poorly chosen, or untrue (even shades of untruth) or unkind, have the power to change the course of life. Notice also how our speech is inconsistent if we praise God and curse other men (vv. 9-10). James questions the praise given in these circumstances (v. 11).

In reading verses 13-18, think of your own life. Use these wise words to shape your attitudes and relationships. Take special note of the characteristics of godly wisdom (vv. 17-18; cf. Isa 32:17). Memorize verses 17-18. They are a road map for spiritual effectiveness! They are like a compass that will keep us headed true north.

EZEKIEL 31-32   The fall of Assyria is an example of what the Lord has planned for Egypt (Ch. 31). Assyria is like one of the majestic cedars of Lebanon (v. 3) but was destroyed by "the most ruthless of foreign nations" (Babylon, v. 12) because of the nation's pride (vv. 10-11). Although Assyria had been central in international commerce and politics ("All the nations... came out from under its shade and left it," v. 12), the Lord brought the nation down, using the Babylonians as His arm in judgment. The message concludes by saying this also will happen to Egypt (v. 18).

Almost two years after the prophecy of Chapter 31, and about twenty months after the fall of Jerusalem, Ezekiel had another message that concerned Egypt. The imagery of the crocodile is again used (monster, 32:2). The message describes the death of Egypt (vv. 4-8), which will cause a ripple of fear among the nations of the world (vv. 9-

10). The destruction of the country, however, will be effective and complete (vv. 11-16).

The remainder of the chapter is a remarkable warning to the nations of the world (vv. 17-32). Although it was meant specifically for the Egyptians, it applies also to the international community then and now. It is a list of the countries that the Lord has judged and broken because of their sins of violence and terror. National pride, as we have seen in the previous chapters, ranks alongside violence as an affront to the Lord. God is sovereign, and God watches the affairs of men.

PROVERBS 28:20-28   It is convenient to prosper financially. It is wise to seek prosperity for the inner man (vv. 25-26). The key to the second kind of prosperity is to trust God! This verse is not saying that by trusting God we will prosper as the world counts prosperity (although that conviction is heard in church circles). What it *will* mean, however, is a peaceful, quiet, and joyful heart. What is that worth? Can you buy that with dollars?

Another facet of this truth is safety (v. 26). Again, this does not mean that "bad" things cannot happen to the believer. What it *does* mean is that nothing can touch the believer but what the Father deems is best. Is that enough for us? Our problem is that we lose sight of this important fact. We are indeed safe in His care!

NOVEMBER 21

JAMES 4   In contrast to the roadmap to peace and righteousness in 3:17-18, 4:1-6 describes spiritual ineffectiveness! Personal ambition, lack of prayer, and sinful motives get in the way of the peace that should characterize the church. These sinful attitudes are the "world" invading the church!

Verse 4 is thought-provoking! What does it mean to love the world? Read 1 John 2:15-17 for insight. The word "world" here refers to the "world system" way of doing things and looking at life. It is the world of ambition, entertainment, doing things "my way," getting ahead, and getting competitors out of the way. It is the world of valuing things. In contrast, living the Christian life is submitting to the will of God – choosing to do what God desires (v. 7; 2 Cor 5:15). The question we ask should not be, "How close can I get to worldly things and still be safe in the Christian fold?" but "How close can I get to God and His will?" While reading this chapter, observe how many of Satan's pitfalls can be avoided with this perspective.

Finally, understanding our lives from an eternal perspective (life is like a mist that will soon dissipate, v. 14b) gives us great incentive to love and serve God – in the practical sense of doing what we know to be right (vv. 7-10, 13-17).

EZEKIEL 33-34   The responsibility of someone with a message from the Lord is specific and firm (Ch. 33). Ezekiel was responsible to the Lord to accurately convey His message to the people. The people, in turn, were responsible to obey God. Think carefully about this in relation to the Lord's message we have for the world. Review 2 Corinthians 5:14-6:2.

Eighteen months after the fall of Jerusalem, a refugee arrived from Jerusalem and told the exiles what had happened (v. 21; cf. 24:26). The Lord spoke through Ezekiel, helping the exiles understand the reality of the fall. Their sin had brought it about. Still, read the Lord's insight about the exiles – even those who gathered around Ezekiel to listen (vv. 30-33).

The shepherds of Chapter 34 are the priests, and the sheep are the people. The Lord has harsh words for the shepherds who were supposed to care for the sheep. The problem: an uncaring attitude about the welfare of the sheep and selfishness that turned their attention inward (vv. 2-4). There is obvious application for any in the church who have responsibility for the care of others!

Read what God will do for His people (vv. 11-31). ☑The Lord Himself will intervene, gathering and caring for the sheep and placing a shepherd (Messiah, identified as [the seed of] David, v. 24) over them. This is the promise of the restoration of Israel and Christ's earthly reign. For us today, the lesson is the Lord's concern for His sheep and our responsibility to take ownership of those concerns.⇦

PROVERBS 29:1-9   Consider verse 6. Anyone who weaves a web of lies and deception finds it harder and harder to support the deception. Such a person often implicates himself simply by what he says! Read again the advice to the reader in Proverbs 1:10-19. To choose sin is to waylay one's self.

On the other hand, truth brings freedom (v. 6b). There is nothing to hide, no tracks to cover, no fear. Who would choose the former of the two? Yet many do. That is the deception of the Evil One.

NOVEMBER 22

JAMES 5   As you read the warning to the wealthy in verses 1-6, find the specific reasons for the Lord's complaint. Money, as such, was not the problem, but the method of acquiring it and the way it was used were significant problems. Note the failure to fairly compensate workers (v. 4), and the silenced criticism (violently) of those who questioned such practices (v. 4b). These two problems called out to the Lord! Note, too, the use of the money – inappropriately hoarded and used for excessive luxury and self-indulgence.

James urges patience in difficult circumstances (vv. 7-12) and prevailing prayer (vv. 13-18). His statement that prayer is powerful when offered by the righteous should encourage Christians to do what is important – to pray! Both sections of this last chapter should significantly shape our attitudes and lives.

EZEKIEL 35-36   We again see in this message to Edom (descendants of Esau) that the Lord is not pleased when a nation takes advantage of another nation's calamity (Ch. 35). Refer again to the message of Obadiah (notes for Oct. 8), which was also directed to Edom. The plans and words of the Edomites were contemptible to the Lord (v. 12).

Even though Jerusalem had fallen and the people were in exile, the Lord had not forgotten about them. The Lord intended to punish the nations who reacted gleefully to Judah's calamity. But more than that, the Lord had deep concern for the land (promised to Abraham) and the people (the descendants of Abraham) of the covenant.

Chapter 36 is a remarkable message of grace. The Lord had punished the people because of their sin (vv. 16-21). ☑Yet for the sake of His name, God will do a new thing for His people (vv. 22-38). *They will be regathered, cleansed, given a new heart and God's Spirit, and receive His blessing.* Notice where God states, "I will" followed by His specific work in His people. This is a spectacular work of the living God. What is described goes far beyond the return to the land under Zerubbabel after the seventy-year exile. Along with regathering the people "from the nations" (v. 24) and repopulating the cities (more than before, v. 11b), the people will know that the Lord really is their God (v. 38). They will have cleansed hearts – and the Holy Spirit (vv. 26-27). It will be a time of unprecedented prosperity (vv. 29-30). All the nations will know that this is a work of the sovereign God (vv. 23, 36; cf. Isa 2:1-5). Remember the promise of Romans 11:25-27, for here is the picture of its fulfillment.

When will this happen? Paul places the time after "the full number of the Gentiles has come in" (Rom 11:25). It will be the beginning of Christ's messianic reign at His return and after the judgments of the Day of the Lord (cf. Zech 12:10; 14:1-5, 9, 16). What a wonderful time to anticipate!⇦

PROVERBS 29:10-18   Justice in civil government is the subject of verses 4 and 14. Stability in government and in the nation comes with justice; i.e., the equal application of righteous laws. When this is compromised, as with bribery, respect for the law is damaged, as is the entire system.

Restraint in society is lost when there is no consistent and clear presentation of truth (v. 18). The church must be the means to get the truth to as many corners of the world as possible. That is what Jesus meant when He said that believers are God's light and salt in the world (Matt 5:13-16). If we are faithful, the Holy Spirit will use the church. As God's ambassadors, we have the opportunity and responsibility to be light in society – to illumine the truth so it can be applied to the problems that individuals and society face.

NOVEMBER 23

1 PETER 1:1-12   Is the Christian life and hope for the future "pie in the sky," or is it real? This is the question Peter answers for his readers in verses 3-5.   He is unequivocal about the certainty of the heavenly promise. This perspective gives God's child the ability to keep spiritual equilibrium as trials come (vv. 6-9). *Note that God allows the hard times to come for a purpose.* We learn God's faithfulness at such times!

We live in a time of great privilege.   From a spiritual perspective, we understand God's plan in bringing salvation and how that plan has unfolded.   Think of what it would have been like to live in the time of Abraham – or Joshua – or even Isaiah.   They had some information – enough to place their faith in the living God, to be sure – but such an incomplete picture. We are able to see it all in Christ (vv. 10-12). Think about it! Even angels long to understand what we have.

EZEKIEL 37-39   Ezekiel's vision of the valley filled with dry bones (the remains of people dead for a long time) delivers in a different way the same message of the previous chapter. ☑The Lord promised to bring His people back to the land, cleanse them, give them a new heart, and prosper them. (From the "dry bones" of unbelief to genuine faith and a living relationship with their God and Messiah.)   In this vision, the prophet sees the dry bones that are commanded to reassemble into persons with flesh (vv. 7-8). Then they were brought to life (v. 10).

Read the Lord's interpretation of this vision (vv. 11-14).   The "graves" (v. 12) may be the many nations that held the Israelites during the dispersion.   As the Lord calls the people back to the land, they will have new life and a new heart for the Lord.   Further, Israel and Judah will be united (vv. 15-17) for the first time since King Rehoboam's reign when ten tribes left Judah and became known as Israel in about 920 BC (cf. 1 Kings 12). They will be united under one king, the Messiah (David, v. 24), during the Millennium.

Chapters 38 and 39 prophesy that Gog of the land of Magog will attack Israel with other nations (vv. 3-6). This will trigger God's judgment on these nations (vv. 17-23). Gog and Magog are mentioned in only one other place in the Bible, in Revelation 20:7-10, in Satan's final effort to overthrow the forces of the Lord *after* the Millennium. The result is that Satan is finally destroyed, along with the forces he has mustered for the battle, and *all the nations will know that the Lord God is who He has said He is.*

Chapter 39 continues the vision of Gog and Magog of Chapter 38. The prophecy is clear that there will be a great battle that will break the strength of the nations. The battle will be in Israel (v. 4). There will be so many dead from the foreign armies that it will take seven months to bury them. Regular burial details will take care of the dead (vv. 12-16). The debris of war will serve as fuel for months.

This destruction of the armies that came to defeat Israel must be the result of a sudden cataclysmic event for there is no mention of Israel's casualties. The Lord has His own methods. (Remember the demise of the Assyrian army in Isa 37:36.) It could represent a nuclear attack targeting the foreign armies.

The result will be the permanent acknowledgment of the Lord by Israel (v. 22). The Lord will be zealous for His holy name (v. 25) and will pour out His Spirit on His people (v. 29).

What is the timing of these events of Ezekiel 38-39? Before the Millennium, the battle of Armageddon occurs, which is probably the battle described in Revelation 19:11-21, and immediately precedes the Millennium (cf. Rev 16:13-16). After the Millennium, Satan will gather the nations and surround Israel (Rev 20:7-10). Gog and Magog are specifically mentioned in this context. If this battle follows the Millennium, the gathering and restoration of Israel (Ezek 36-37) most likely occurs just as the Millennium is beginning.⇔

PROVERBS 29:19-27   Too often, we human beings find ourselves concerned – and even afraid – of what other people think of us (v. 25). Fear may hinder our testimony of the Lord Jesus as Savior. Fear can even make it difficult to admit to being a believer! It should not be so! Think carefully of the second part of verse 25. True safety lies in a firm trust in the Lord. Review Jesus' words in Mark 8:34-38. Failure to acknowledge Jesus as Lord may indicate a flawed faith. Further, the Holy Spirit has not given a spirit of fear but a spirit of power (2 Tim 1:7). With the Lord's help, step out of the box of fear that restricts your freedom and joy, and claim the spirit of power that the Holy Spirit gives. And believe our text that safety comes from trusting the Lord.

NOVEMBER 24

1 PETER 1:13-25   Based on the revealed plan of salvation (vv. 10-12), Peter calls for action (vv. 13-25). As you read and consider verses 13-16, note the specific ways our lives should be molded to please the living God. This is no life of idleness. Rather, it is an alert, controlled, motivated (v. 13), purposeful (v. 14), and focused life set apart for the Lord (v. 15). Allow these action words to speak to your heart. The lifestyle described here has little to do with drifting, "going with the flow" of current thought. Rather, it is a life of holiness – separation from the world's thinking to that of the living God (v. 16). Think about it!

The truth that leads to this is the price that God paid for our redemption. This was nothing less than the blood of Jesus (vv. 18-19). Note the mind-stretching truth that the death of Jesus has been in God's plan since before the creation of the world (v. 20)! Further, God chose you before the creation of the world (Eph 1:4). Can you do less than respond with your whole heart? Note too that although human life is transient (v. 24), our life in the Lord Jesus is indestructible – imperishable (v. 23)!

EZEKIEL 40   Ezekiel 40 begins the last section of the book, which is concerned with the temple, the filling of the temple with God's glory, the temple area, the division of the land of Israel, and the reestablished sacrifices. This is one of the most difficult portions of the Bible. The difficulties concern the time when the temple will be restored (historical, millennial, or the eternal state after the Millennium), and what is the place of the sacrificial system if the time is the Millennium (or after), since the death of Jesus made the sacrifices unnecessary.

Because of the nature of Chapters 40-48, the notes for this section will be inserted here for some background on the chapters to come.

The question as to where this temple, with its people and rituals, fits into the timeline of biblical events is not immediately clear.

There are similarities between Ezekiel's vision and the vision that John received, as recorded in Revelation 21-22. Both Ezekiel and John were carried to a high mountain for the vision (Ezek 40:1-3; Rev 21:9-10). Both were taken by a heavenly messenger, and in both visions, the heavenly messenger measured the city that was seen in the vision (Ezek 40:5ff.; Rev 21:15ff.). Yet there are also differences. The dimensions of the two cities are very different, and the description of them is different as well. John's vision described the eternal city, but this is not how the city that Ezekiel saw looked like.

It is significant that Ezekiel 47 describes water as coming from the threshold of the temple toward the east. Revelation 22:1-2 tells of a river flowing from the throne of God, identifying this temple as that of the eternal city. Ezekiel 47:12 and Revelation 22:2 both describe trees growing beside the river that give fruit to eat, and whose leaves are used for healing. Joel 3:18b and Zechariah 14:8 also describe a river that seems to be in the millennial period. Psalm 46:4 (an apocalyptic psalm) speaks of such a river flowing from God's dwelling place after a time of terrible judgment on the nations. Remember that in Eden a river watered the garden (Gen 2:10). It would appear that a river of blessing like the one in the Garden of Eden will be in the Millennium (if this temple is placed in the millennial period), and will also be present in the heavenly city. *In all three instances, this river of provision and blessing is present when God rules.*

With regard to the time that Ezekiel's vision represents, recall that the temple of Solomon had just been destroyed a few years earlier by Nebuchadnezzar's army. The temple was later rebuilt under Zerubbabel (Ezra 3:7ff.) and again in the time of Herod just before Christ. The latter temple was destroyed in 70 AD and has not existed since then. In fact, the temple described in Ezekiel does not correspond with any of these. As noted above, it does not correspond to the heavenly city either. If the temple does not seem to be historical (Solomon, Zerubbabel, or Herod), and is different from the heavenly city, then Ezekiel's vision may represent the millennial temple.

But how would the sacrificial system fit into the Millennium? Jesus, after all, has completely paid the penalty for sin and has done away with the necessity of the Mosaic sacrificial system. Hebrews 9-10 are instructive in this regard. The sacrifices of the Old Testament never did take away sin (cf. Heb 10:4)! The sacrifices were carried out in response to the command given to Moses, but were, in reality, a symbol of what Jesus *would do* on the cross (cf. 1 Peter 1:18-20). This being so, millennial sacrifices, if present, may be a remembrance of what Jesus *has done* on the cross. It is significant that in the sacrificial system of Ezekiel there is no Day of Atonement (no need)! There is also no ark of the covenant and no high priest.

Today we commemorate the Lord's death in the grape juice and the broken bread. Jesus commanded us to remember Him in this way *until He comes again.* It is possible we will continue to observe His death this way in the Millennium *after He comes again.* Other cultures may remember His death through the sacrifices – or perhaps we all will do so!

The central event of Chapters 40-48 is the return of the glory of the Lord (Ezek 43:1-5). The glory of the Lord came to the tabernacle when it was dedicated (Exod 40:34-35), to the temple of Solomon when it was dedicated (2 Chron 7:1-3), and left the temple as Ezekiel watched (Ezek 10). Now, in his vision, Ezekiel had the privilege of seeing God return in His glory.

The entire book of Ezekiel emphasizes the holiness of God, and this is especially so in Chapters 40-48. Some details of the dimensions of the temple, courts, and surrounding areas may strike us as irrelevant. *Ezekiel, however, was admonished to correctly get every detail,* and someday we will understand their import!

Read these chapters thoughtfully. They are an important section of the Bible: In spite of difficulties, they deserve our attention.

PROVERBS 30:1-10   Read and take to heart verse 5. We need to know and understand – and do God's word. A zealous heart without knowing God's Word will lead to wrong practice and conviction. Knowing God's Word (even in detail) but not applying it in obedience and changed behavior will lead to a cold heart (fatal!). Real and genuine faith always results in action and obedience. Read verse 5 again. Take refuge in God. That can only mean paying attention to God's Word and doing what He desires in our lives.

NOVEMBER 25

1 PETER 2   Each of us has a significant place in the kingdom. *We are individual stones* in the building (v. 5), built on the cornerstone, Christ (v. 6). *We are a chosen people*, chosen by the Lord for His own purpose (v. 4). *We are a called people*, called from darkness to His light (v. 9). *We are an alien people*, alien to this world, but citizens of heaven (v. 11). And it should show in our lives and behavior (v. 12).

Read the section on submission (vv. 13-25) for its significance in your life. Notice that Jesus is the model and example.

EZEKIEL 41-42   See notes for November 24.

PROVERBS 30:11-17   Self-deception makes a person a hazard to himself and to others. As you read verses 11-14, note how self-deception is apparent: unwillingness to listen to the wisdom of fathers and mothers (v. 11);   inability to see our uncleanness and sin – which will inevitably keep the individual from God (v. 12);   pride, arrogance, and a cutting tongue (vv. 13-14a); and a lack of compassion for the needy (v. 14b).

Self-deception is part and parcel of the sinful nature we all share. The only way to get rid of this fatal flaw is to allow God to show us our true selves and what we need. This is the reason it is so important to be in God's Word every day. As we do so, we are challenged daily with the truth. As we ask Him, God will further reveal to us how we need help (Ps 139:23-24; cf. Rom 12:1-2).

NOVEMBER 26

1 PETER 3   In the section about husbands and wives, note what the Lord sees as beauty – and what Peter commends to his readers. This is a real comfort, for all of us become older, and the beauty prized by the world inevitably fades. The Lord's beauty is available to all and will be enhanced instead of eroded as time passes. A gentle and quiet spirit (v. 4) is "of great worth in God's sight," and is a powerful attribute in the home and community.   Husbands, mark verse 7 in your Bible. Consideration and respect from husbands would be a breath of fresh air for many women.

It is God's will that there be harmony in the community of Christ (vv. 8-12). Note the specific ways in which we should work this out (vv. 8-9). Then think about the quotation from Psalm 34:12-16, which calls us to disciplined speech (v. 10b), godly action (v. 11a), and goals (v. 11b). Is it worth the bother? Check verse 12!

Verse 15 offers a focus for life. Keep Christ as Lord central in your vision. The text ties this to our witness to the unsaved. If we have this mind-set, the witness flows naturally. If our mind-set is to follow Jesus, and we are rubbing shoulders with the unsaved, we will share what is on our minds!   Peter also suggests how to share the faith – with gentleness and respect for the other person.

The section regarding Christ preaching to the spirits after His death is one of the most difficult in the New Testament to interpret.   The questions that arise from these verses are generally as follows: (1) Who are the "spirits"? (2) When did this happen? (3) What did He say? Without going into the technicalities of Greek, one paraphrase is as follows: "He was put to death in the human sphere of existence but was made alive in the resurrection sphere of existence, in which state of existence he made a proclamation of His victory to the fallen angels."*

---

*This summary paraphrase as well as the supporting technical reasons for the conclusions are found in Ewdin A. Blum's commentary on 1 Peter. Taken from the book, *The*

EZEKIEL 43-44   See notes for November 24.

PROVERBS 30:18-20   Verses 18 and 19 are instructive. The eagle, the snake on a rock, and the ship have this in common: they leave no trail. They have been present, but there is no way to track them. *The same thing is true of the man who seduces a young woman and then leaves her* (v. 19b).

Habitual immorality requires rationalization and causes hardness of heart (v. 20). The rationalization allows self-deception. A hardened conscience is the result of willfully turning from the standards of God (cf. Rom 1:21-32).

NOVEMBER 27

1 PETER 4   *Peter says, "Give it up!"* Give up living like the pagans do (their accounting before God is coming, v. 5), and allow your life to count for the Lord. Jesus is coming! Clear your mind, and live with this in view (v. 7). Work at the really important things, such as exercising your spiritual gifts (vv. 7b-11). In short, make a difference for the kingdom with your life.

Think of suffering in the same context (vv. 12-19). Christ suffered, and it is no surprise that we will also endure hard times. But be sure that you suffer for the things that count! Verse 17 says judgment will begin with the family of God, which may mean that the beginning of the end times will be especially hard for the people of God. Jesus says this in Matthew 24:4-13 and Paul in 2 Timothy 3:1ff. When sin is widely prevalent, all of society suffers. We must be sure that hard times lead us closer to the Lord and to a more careful walk in the Spirit. Therefore, keep on doing good (v. 19).

EZEKIEL 45-46   See notes for November 24.

PROVERBS 30:21-28   Learn a lesson from little creatures. We have all watched the industry of the ant. They bustle about, gathering food and carrying it back to their storage spot. And they then make it through the winter to reappear the next year (v. 25). Those who have visited the mountains have watched the marmot (larger than the coney) scamper between the rocks and survive where there seems to be nothing to eat (v. 26). Consider the locusts, singly no threat but a scourge when they swarm (v. 27), and the tiny lizard that can live in tropical lands on the walls of even a king (v. 28).

Expositor's Bible Commentary, Volume 12 edited by Frank E. Gaebelein. Copyright 1976 by The Zondervan Corporation. Used by permission of Zondervan Publishing House.

The Lord has built into each of these the ability to survive: the industrious ant that prepares for the future; the rock badger that can hide and survive in a very hostile environment; the locusts that swarm in a coordinated attack on fields; and the lizard, appreciated for its ability to eat insects in the home. Apply the example of these small creatures. We should be as industrious as they are in planning for the future and making do with what we have. We should be working together as a group (what could the church do if all pulled together like a swarm of locusts?), contributing what is needed in our world.

NOVEMBER 28

1 PETER 5   The last chapter of the book has several important mandates for living. Peter's appeal to the elders was to serve faithfully, with the needs of those under their care foremost in their hearts. He urged a servant attitude in this responsibility – not for position, money, or by compulsion, but for the Lord (vv. 1-4).

Peter also urged the younger men to honor the older, and for all to have an attitude of submission. As we compare our station to the Lord, humbleness is the only response we can have (vv. 5-6). This is humility before men and God.

God cares – and we can give all of our cares and anxious thoughts to Him (v. 7).

Pay special attention to the truth of verses 8-9. *Satan is real and is a strong adversary.* There is no question that the power of the living God is sufficient to meet the devil, but the believer needs something as well: an acute awareness of the danger and self-control to stay away from his schemes. To resist is to exercise self-control. To stand firm in faith is to exercise self-control. As we turn to God, His power is ours!

EZEKIEL 47-48   *See notes for November 24.* As we finish the book of Ezekiel, note the last verse in the book (48:35). The name of the city will be, *"THE LORD IS THERE."* If we assume that this is the millennial city of God, it will be the precursor of the eternal city where God will dwell with His people!

PROVERBS 30:29-33   Consider the wisdom of verses 32-33. Even when we have embarked upon a course of action, if we see that it is unwise or wrong, it is time to change course. Never mind that others may think us weak and indecisive. Do the right thing and what will please God. Better to "eat crow" and pursue a righteous course than continue on a wrong path.

NOVEMBER 29

<u>2 PETER 1</u> *FACT*: The Lord has provided all that we need to live a holy and godly life (v. 3). God's divine power, glory, goodness, and promises enable us to share in the divine nature and to avoid the world's evil. If this is true, and the text says it is, we undermine God's will for us by living marginally or carelessly. There will be no excuses we can legitimately give the Lord for careless living. He has made the needed provision.

FACT: We do need some disciplined actions to make holiness and godliness a reality in our lives. These personal initiatives are listed in verses 5-7. Don't be blind to reality by neglecting them (v. 9). *If we are willing to take on these initiatives, our spiritual effectiveness is guaranteed (v. 8).* That is worth going for!

FACT: Each of us must be sure that our lives prove our faith (v. 10; cf. 2 Cor 13:5). Review the notes on Luke 13:22-35 (Jan. 26).

Peter's testimony is powerful because it is an eyewitness affirmation of the truth of the gospel (vv. 16-18). Peter and the other apostles who were with Jesus actually saw Jesus' glory on the Mount of Transfiguration (Mark 9:2-7), the power of His earthly ministry, and, even more powerful, the resurrection. The gospel accounts are not "cleverly invented stories" (v. 16)!

Finally, understand that Peter is speaking about the Old Testament Scriptures in verses 19-21. He calls us to pay attention to what they say. They are from the Lord, and are light shining in a dark place – and will be "until the day dawns" when Jesus comes.

<u>DANIEL 1-2</u> Jehoiakim and his army fell to Nebuchadnezzar in 605 BC, and some of the Israelites were taken to Babylon nineteen years before the fall of Jerusalem. Daniel and his three compatriots, who were chosen to be trained for royal service, were part of this exile to Babylon.

Observe the faith of these four young men and the results of their resolve to serve God. God honored their faith and allowed them to continue training without compromising their godly convictions by eating a Babylonian diet (vv. 8-16). Theirs was a remarkable commitment to what they knew to be truth. Without intervention from the Lord, it would have led to their deaths!

Their faith didn't end there. Their collective faith and prayer led to Daniel's ability to narrate and explain the dream that Nebuchadnezzar had (Ch. 2). In addition, note Daniel's courage in the king's presence (vv. 27-28, 45b).

The world governments from Nebuchadnezzar to the second coming of Christ are represented in the king's dream. These great world powers are identified later in the book as Babylon, the Empire of the Medes and the Persians, the Greek Empire, and the Roman Empire. Thus, we today still live in the extension of the Roman Empire. ☑The rock that smashes the world kingdoms (vv. 34, 44-45) is the Lord Jesus at His second coming.

How does the present kingdom of Christ fit into this picture of world government? The disciples expected a political kingdom during Jesus' first advent. Jesus told them that the kingdom was within them (Luke 17:20-21). When Jesus cast out demons, He said the kingdom of God was affecting the kingdom of the Evil One (Matt 12:28). In fact, the kingdom of God in this age is working within the realm of Satan (cf. Eph 2:1-2; Matt 13:33), and someone who comes to know Christ is brought *from* the kingdom of darkness *into* the kingdom of the Son (Col 1:13; Eph 2:1-5). The sons and daughters of Christ live physically in a hostile kingdom, but spiritually in the kingdom of God, and under the protection of the King of Heaven! *When Jesus comes again, the kingdom will be visible, powerful, and permanent (Dan 2:44)!*⇦

PROVERBS 31:1-9   There is a word for kings – and all others who are responsible for other people – in verses 4-5. Keep your mind clear! Not many of you readers will be kings, but all who are in the kingdom are responsible for others and need a clear head. We need to think of people's needs and how to represent the truth to those around us. This is a high calling, and we need a clear mind.

The message of verses 8-9 again highlights the Lord's agenda for justice and equity. We can never say that it wasn't "my business." If there is something we can do to help, it is our business. And it is kingdom business.

NOVEMBER 30

2 PETER 2   The warning in this portion is about false teachers. This may be subtle, however, *because the teachers arise from within the church* (cf. Acts 20:29-31; Jude 4). It is dangerous to vary from the truth while teaching the Bible; false teachers will reap God's judgment. The Lord is concerned for the purity of the church!

Note the examples of judgment for this kind of behavior in verses 4-10. Angels were banished from the presence of God when they embraced falsehood, and they now await the final judgment from God (v. 4). The flood came because of prevalent sin in the world (v. 5). Sodom and Gomorrah were destroyed along with all of their people because of their gross sin (v. 6). *And God will judge false teachers just as surely as He has judged sin in the past* (vv. 9b-10a). Although these persons have an exterior of religion, read about their character and end (vv. 10b-22). Although they are in the organized church, they are not of the Lord!

It should give pause to the church and its leadership that such subtle heresies can creep into the church and cause serious problems. The answer is to be aware that this can happen, to walk closely with the Lord – and to measure what is taught by the standard of God's Word.

DANIEL 3-4   If you think office or court politics are a new phenomenon, read Chapter 3! We don't know how much time has passed since the previous chapter, but after Daniel had interpreted Nebuchadnezzar's dream, the king acknowledged that Daniel's God was indeed the God of heaven. Now the king had issued the order for all to worship an image he had built! Further, the astrologers who had been superseded by Daniel and his friends (2:48-49, but whose lives had been saved by Daniel's narration of the dream) brought charges that Shadrach, Meshach, and Abednego had refused to worship the image (vv. 8-12)!

The straightforward and courageous testimony of Shadrach, Meshach, and Abednego is an outstanding model of godly conduct (3:16-18). Moreover, when the king saw how God delivered the men, he was again impressed with the power of God (vv. 28-29).

Chapter 4 in its entirety is a court document of Babylon. It is the testimony – after the fact of God's discipline in the king's life – that there is a God in heaven! Read the preamble to the account in verses 1-3.

The Lord graciously gave Nebuchadnezzar time to repent after his vision and Daniel's explanation of it (vv. 8ff., 19-27). But when the time ran out, the execution of the judgment on the king was swift (vv. 28-33). Yet the Lord did not intend to remove him completely, but to make the king acknowledge Him. Perhaps the real miracle in this account is the fact that the kingdom "waited" for him for seven years while he was insane. Remember that Daniel was in a position to help the king (2:48). Just as the preamble gave glory to the Lord, so does the conclusion (vv. 36-37).

PROVERBS 31:10-31   Choose well, young man, for a great deal hangs on the decision of whom to marry. This advice could well be given to every young man who contemplates marriage. The portrait of the wonderful wife in this chapter demonstrates the wisdom of thoughtful foresight. As you read verses 10-31, find the qualities that make this woman of the ancient world an exemplary wife – qualities such as planning ahead, managing the household, and supporting her husband.

The bad news is that many marriages are far from this picture. The good news is that God is in the business of changing people! This model should not be a cause for discouragement, but a model for change. One of the by-products of living out this model is that in the end it brings great honor not only to the family but also to the wife and mother.

December

Bible Reading Schedule
And Notes

ᘓ

Blessed is the one who reads the words of this prophecy, and blessed are those who hear it and take to heart what is written in it, because the time is near. Revelation 1:3

DISCOVERING THE BIBLE
READING SCHEDULE
DECEMBER

1	2 Peter 3	Daniel 5-6	1 Peter 1:10-12
2	1 John 1	Daniel 7-8	Genesis 3:15
3	1 John 2	Daniel 9-10	Genesis 12:1-7
4	1 John 3	Daniel 11-12	Genesis 15:1-6
5	1 John 4	Ezra 1-2	Genesis 49:10
6	1 John 5	Ezra 3-4	Num 24:15-19
7	2 John	Haggai 1-2	Job 19:23-27
8	3 John	Zechariah 1-2	2 Samuel 7:8-16
9	Jude	Zechariah 3-4	Isaiah 9:6-7
10	Revelation 1	Zechariah 5-6	Isaiah 11:1-5
11	Revelation 2	Zechariah 7	Isaiah 40:1-11
12	Revelation 3	Zechariah 8-9	Isaiah 42:1-9
13	Revelation 4	Zechariah 10-11	Isaiah 50:4-9
14	Revelation 5	Zechariah 12-13	Isa 52:13-53:12
15	Revelation 6	Zechariah 14	Psalm 22
16	Revelation 7	Ezra 5-6	Isaiah 61:1-3
17	Revelation 8	Ezra 7-8	Daniel 2:31-45
18	Revelation 9	Ezra 9-10	Psalm 110
19	Revelation 10	Esther 1-3	Micah 5:2, Jer 31:15
20	Revelation 11	Esther 4-6	Luke 1:5-25
21	Revelation 12	Esther 7-10	Luke 1:26-38
22	Revelation 13	Nehemiah 1-2	Luke 1:46-55
23	Revelation 14	Nehemiah 3-4	Luke 1:57-79
24	Revelation 15	Nehemiah 5-6	Luke 2:1-20
25	Revelation 16	Nehemiah 7-8	Luke 2:21-40
26	Revelation 17	Nehemiah 9-10	Luke 9:18-27
27	Revelation 18	Nehemiah 11-12	Matt 27:32-56
28	Revelation 19	Nehemiah 13	Matt 28:1-10
29	Revelation 20	Malachi 1	Luke 24:13-35
30	Revelation 21	Malachi 2	Matt 28:18-20; Acts 1:1-11
31	Revelation 22	Malachi 3-4	Titus 2:11-14

DECEMBER 1

2 PETER 3   In this last portion of his letter, Peter speaks of end times. Society will be anti-Christian, with men and women scoffing at the standards of the Lord (v. 3). Further, they will suggest that the Lord will not come and will not judge sin (v. 4). The prophecies, however, are valid (v. 7). The Lord's timetable may be different from ours (vv. 8-9), but His Word is sure; cataclysmic judgment *will* come (v. 10).

How, then, should we respond (v. 11)? With careful living, looking forward to Jesus' coming, and choosing to live a holy life (v. 14). Note the warning of verse 17 (the false teachers of Ch. 2) and the encouragement of verse 18.

DANIEL 5-6   Belshazzar was the son of Nabonidus – the son-in-law of Nebuchadnezzar. The year was 539 BC, some sixty-six years after Daniel and his fellow Jews were brought to Babylon. Nebuchadnezzar died twenty-four years earlier.

The banquet was a celebration of the Babylonian gods whom Belshazzar assumed had defeated Judah. This is probably why the gold and silver goblets from the temple in Jerusalem were brought for the dinner. As the people at the dinner drank from the goblets, they praised their gods (v. 4). But enough was enough! The prophecy concerning Babylon in Isaiah 13:19 was about to be fulfilled.

The hand that wrote on the wall terrified those at the banquet. The queen mother knew about Daniel and suggested that he be called to tell its meaning. Again we see Daniel's courage as he faithfully delivered God's message to the crowd of subdued, confused, and frightened guests and to the king. That very night Darius took the city by diverting the Euphrates River and marching into the fortified city on the dry riverbed under the gates that guarded the course of the river in and out of the city.

Daniel not only survived the change but came into one of the top three administrative positions in the nation (6:1-3)! As you read Chapter 6, follow the king's consternation over the trap laid for Daniel. Even when Daniel understood the implications of the edict, he continued to pray as he usually did – and left the windows open for anyone to observe. The testimony that resulted from God's intervention on Daniel's behalf was one more opportunity for Daniel to demonstrate the power of his God. Note Darius' praise to God (vv. 25b-27).

1 PETER 1:10-12   This last month of the year we will highlight some prophecies of both the first and second advents of our Savior. As you become aware of the references to the Messiah in the Old Testament, it is clear that the Bible has one message: redemption.   Without a Redeemer, there would be no redemption! In the advent season, take the time to appreciate these selected portions from the Old and New Testaments.

From today's reading, it is clear that the prophets understood part of what they wrote – but not the whole picture. They wrote about salvation (v. 10), and that they had some idea about Christ's suffering and His future glory (v. 11). But, and mark this, it was for us who have lived since the death and resurrection of Christ that they wrote (v. 12). It is a tremendous privilege to have the entire Bible in our hand, and to understand the prophecies from a backward look! From our vantage point, it all fits together.

DECEMBER 2

1 JOHN 1   John the Apostle wrote the gospel of John, the three epistles of John, and the book of Revelation. John is sometimes known as the Apostle of Love, for he emphasizes over and over the need for those in the church to love one another.

Jesus, as the Word of Life (v. 1), is a historical figure to which eyewitnesses could testify. John was one such eyewitness, and asserted that he had seen, heard, and touched the Lord Jesus. He documented what he had seen and heard (v. 3). Our fellowship as Christians is based upon common faith in the Father and with Jesus His Son (v. 3).

John's message was about God's holiness (v. 5). With God there is no darkness. *Truth is always related to light and all untruth to darkness (John 8:44). Our claim to fellowship with God must be based upon our walk in the light (V. 7).* Anything less gives the lie to our claim (v. 6). Further, walking in the light puts us in fellowship with the rest of the body of Christ and brings forgiveness through the blood of Christ (v. 7).

Walking in the light is not a claim to a sinless life. Rather, it is a lifestyle concerned with God's agendas and obedience to Him. All of us sin (vv. 8, 10), but confession brings forgiveness (v. 9).

DANIEL 7-8   As you read Chapter 7, look again at 2:31-35. Both of these visions cover the same time period: from Nebuchadnezzar and the Babylonian Empire to the coming of Christ in glory and power. Chapter 2 is the vision of an imposing man, while Chapter 7 is the vision of fearsome beasts. The first is history from man's point of view, the latter from a spiritual perspective. Note that in Chapter 2, the lowest part of the vision (the end of dream's time period) is the toes – ten parts. In Chapter 7, the final beast has ten horns (7:7).

Just before Daniel saw the judgment throne of God (vv. 9-10), he saw another horn that spoke boastfully (v. 8), oppressed the saints (vv. 24b-25), and will be destroyed by the Ancient of Days (vv. 21-22).

This final horn, coming at the end of time, is the Antichrist, who will attempt to seize the power that belongs to the Lord and destroy His people (vv. 24-25; cf. Rev 13:5-8). ☑This vile but powerful person will be destroyed by the Lord at His coming (vv. 26-27; cf. 2 Thess 2:8).⇦

Chapter 8 is a vision from the Lord about the kingdoms of Medo-Persia and Greece. The two horns of the ram represent the shared power of the Medes and the Persians. The goat with the prominent horn, which shattered the ram, is Greece, and the horn is Alexander the Great. After Alexander died, four of his generals (v. 8) assumed power. Verses 9-12 and 23-25 speak of an evil person thought to represent Antiochus Epiphanes, a Seleucid king who descended from one of the four generals, and who came into power between the last writings of the Old Testament and the New Testament period. The text states that he is destroyed by the Lord (v. 25b), and his character and actions are similar to the Antichrist.

GENESIS 3:15   In this verse at the very beginning of the Bible, we have the first promise of the coming Redeemer. After Satan had tempted the couple in the Garden of Eden and they had sinned by disobeying God, the Lord spoke to Adam and Eve and also to Satan. There were consequences to Adam and Eve that extend to each of us. We all are sinners through our nature as human beings (Rom 5:12).

☑In the verse that we consider today, however, there is hope. The Lord cursed Satan and told him that there would be hostility between Eve and him, and between her progeny and him. At that point in what the Lord said, the gender becomes masculine and singular. The "he" in verse 15b refers to a single man – one whom Satan would bruise – but who would crush Satan's head. This refers to the coming Savior – the Son of God who would defeat Satan at the cross (Col 2:14-15).⇦

We should not be surprised that this promise came so early. 1 Peter 1:18-21 tells us that redemption was in the mind of the Father long before the creation and fall. Praise God for the promise of Genesis 3:15, and praise God for the fulfillment in the Lord Jesus!

DECEMBER 3

1 JOHN 2   One of God's benevolent provisions is to furnish legal counsel when we are accused by Satan (vv. 1-2). Satan is still active

and ready to accuse us in our own minds, planting seeds of doubt about the effectiveness of Christ's work. The Lord Jesus represents us before the Father, based on His sacrifice for sin. Remember that Job was maligned by Satan when Satan suggested to God that Job was righteous only because it was to his own advantage (Job 1:9-11; 2:4-5). Joshua, the high priest in the time of Zechariah, was accused by Satan before the Lord (Zech 3:1). In Revelation 12:10 there is rejoicing because the "accuser of our brothers, who accuses them before our God day and night, has been hurled down." *The work of Satan against Christians is real. Jesus defends us before the Father.*

Note the straightforward truth in verses 3-6. Spiritual life is reflected in lifestyle! Look at the lifestyle described. We have referred to these verses in the past – they should be burned into our consciousness! Obeying Christ is of prime importance. There is no ambivalence here. Further, verse 6 says we must adopt the lifestyle of Jesus. *His was a life of obedience to the Father and concern for others: a life consumed with the kingdom.* Directly related to the truth of verses 3-6 is that of verses 15-17. We must not try to "straddle the fence," but to stay away from the "world" and its lifestyle. We march to a different drummer than people of the world!

DANIEL 9-10   In the first year of Darius (9:1), Daniel had been in Babylon about fifty-eight years. He had obtained a copy of Jeremiah's writings and learned that the captivity would last for seventy years (v. 2; cf. Jer 25:11; 29:10). If the fall of Jerusalem in 586 BC was the starting point, there were about twenty-three years left to complete Jeremiah's prediction.

Read Daniel's prayer, and feel his deep love for God and his identification with the sins of his people. Daniel was a man of spiritual depth. The seventy "sevens" of verse 24 represent seventy seven-year periods. This is "Jewish" history (v. 24). The starting point is the decree to rebuild Jerusalem (Ezra 1:1-4). Those who have calculated the time from Cyrus' decree to the time of Christ's death have found that it was 483 years, or sixty-nine sevens. ☑The "Anointed One" who is cut off after the sixty-nine sevens (v. 26) is the Lord Jesus at His first advent.⇔ From the end of the sixty-ninth seven until the final seven-year period before Christ's second coming is not primarily Jewish history, but the "times of the Gentiles" (Luke 21:24). Then the final "week," split into two three-and-a-half-year periods (9:27), will complete the final chapter in world – and Jewish – history until Christ's reign. ☑Most believe that this final seven-year period (or the last half of it, cf. Rev 13:5-8) will be the "great tribulation" that will end with Christ's second advent (Matt 24:15-31). The comment in 9:27b," until the end that is decreed is poured out on him," refers to Christ's coming to bring judgment on the Antichrist and the nations – the same end-point that Jesus speaks of in Matthew 24:30-31.⇦

The vision of 10:1 probably occurred around 535 BC (Cyrus' third year) when Daniel was about eighty-five years of age. The vision came after three weeks of fasting and prayer (vv. 2-3). As you read the description of the "man" (vv. 5-6), read also Revelation 1:13-15 and note the similarity between the man Daniel saw and the vision of Jesus that John saw in exile on Patmos.

This vision is significant in what it tells about the spiritual battle behind the scenes. As Daniel prayed, there was conflict on an angelic level (vv. 12-13, 20; cf. Eph 6:12)!

GENESIS 12:1-7   The call and the promise to Abraham set in motion God's plan to have a people for His own purposes. Abraham received a promise that God would make him great, and that through him a great nation would come. And that is what happened.

Abraham, in his old age, received his promised son Isaac, and to Isaac were born Jacob and Esau. God made it clear that the promise to Abraham would be realized through Isaac and then through Jacob. Jacob's twelve sons became the Patriarchs who were the fathers of the twelve tribes of Israel. When Jacob was elderly, sixty-six members of the family traveled to Egypt, where the family grew into a nation. When God brought them out of Egypt to the desert and Mount Sinai, God revealed Himself to them through the Ten Commandments and the other regulations that came through Moses. And through this chosen people the Lord Jesus came (Rom 9:1-5).

With that in mind, note Genesis 12:3b. ☑This blessing that would come through Abraham to the entire world is the promise of the Savior. God loved His people Israel and used them for His redemptive purposes. Through them we have the Scriptures, the revelation of God, which record His dealings with men. Ultimately it is in the Lord Jesus Christ that God's promise to Abraham was and is being fulfilled. That blessing has come through Jesus' death and the redemption that He brought through His sacrifice on the cross.⇦

DECEMBER 4

1 JOHN 3   Sometimes the "world" has negative feelings about the Christian (v. 1). This may happen when God's person refuses to play the same games as the "worldlings," spoiling their ability to "work the system" (cheat). The world cannot understand integrity – but it should not surprise us. It didn't understand Jesus either (v. 1). It is when the Christian's righteousness brings conviction that he is most resented.

We look and wait for the coming of Christ, and that expectation helps us to pursue holiness (v. 3) – no matter what the world thinks about it.

And this life is just the beginning! The miracle of life in the Spirit is that when Jesus returns, we will be like Him – perfect as He is perfect (v. 2). Think about verse 3. If being like Jesus is God's will for each of His children, then we should begin to live like Him now, as well as we are able, and with His help. What God will do in us at Jesus' return should be a strong incentive to holy living now.

There is a difference between committing a sin (of which we all are guilty, 1 John 1:8) and living carelessly in sin. The message of verses 4-10 is that the Christian life is incompatible with a casual attitude about sin, or habitual sinning. Compare verse 9 with Matthew 7:15-23. Note how this relates to what the apostle has been saying in verses 1-3.

Love is a central focus of the faith (v. 11). Jesus told us to love even our enemies (Matt 5:43-44). He calls us to the standard of love that He demonstrated in the world (John 13:34). Then note the intensely practical nature of love as we relate to one another and the world (vv. 16-18).

DANIEL 11-12   Chapters 10 through 12 are a unit, which covers the period from the vision (10:4 ff.) to the second coming of Christ. Much of Chapter 11 concerns the struggle for power in the Middle East. Chapter 11:3 refers to Alexander the Great and the division of his kingdom after his death (v. 4). As you read, look for character descriptions. Verses 21-35 describe the evil reign of Antiochus Epiphanes, who tried to stamp out Jewish religious practice (cf. 8:9-12, 23-25). Although some believe that the final verses of the chapter (11:36-45) also refer to Antiochus Epiphanes, many others believe they predict the Antichrist at the end of the age. For another description of the Antichrist, see Revelation 13:1-10.

Chapter 12:1-4 describe the end times, both the great tribulation (12:1; cf. Matt 24:21) and the resurrection of the righteous and the unrighteous. Notice that the scroll was closed and sealed until the end of time, and we are given only a part of what Daniel received (v. 4). Note in verse 4b the suggestion that at the end of time travel and learning will increase.

The "time, times and half a time" (v. 7) is generally believed to represent three-and-a-half years, the last half of the seventieth "seven" (9:27). At the beginning of this final period, the agreement between the Antichrist with Israel will be broken (9:27), and the period will end with the battle at Armageddon and the second coming of Christ. The 1,290 days (v. 11) are three-and-a-half years plus twelve days. For those who survive the terrible days, it will be a comfort to know when the final deliverance will come.

One final word. In these days of uncertainty, it is more than prudent to seek wisdom from the Lord (v. 10b) by looking seriously to God's Word and walking in obedience!

GENESIS 15:1-6 Abraham had a real problem. God had promised that he would become the father of a great nation, but he had no sons or daughters. When the Lord told him that He, the Lord God, was his great reward, Abraham asked about the promise of progeny he had received – since he could not realize that promise without children (vv. 2-3).

The Lord then promised Abraham a son, not an adoptive son, but one born to him (v. 4). ☑In 15:6 is a wonderful statement that because Abraham had faith in God, he received the gift of righteousness! For this he is known as the father of all men and women of faith (Rom 4:9-12). His righteousness was not through the law – the law had not yet been given (Rom 4:13). In fact, the gift of righteousness comes only by faith! The basis of that righteousness is the sinless life, substitutionary death and resurrection of the Lord Jesus Christ, and in no other way! God paid the price for sin in the person of His Son.

There is one more important thing to note in these verses. Abraham had received promises when God first spoke to him (Gen 12:1-3), including one that through him all the nations of the earth would be blessed. That was the universal promise that would be realized in salvation through Christ. Now in 15:4, God specifically promised Abraham a son through whom the previous promises would be realized. Through Isaac came the family and nation that would bring the law and the prophets (God's revelation to us), and finally the person of the Messiah. This moment looked forward to all that God would do. Revelation 5:9-10 looks back on the finished work of Christ that redeemed men from every tribe, language, people, and nation!↩

DECEMBER 5

1 JOHN 4 We need discernment in a world of hostile spirits (v. 1). John gives guidelines to test whether a spirit is really from the Lord. If the spirit acknowledges that Jesus Christ (God's Son) has lived here on earth, that is evidence that the spirit is from the Lord. That is an impossible admission for a false spirit to make. That question is really the watershed of truth. If someone answers that question in the affirmative, his lifestyle should show it (1 John 2:3-6).

There is a comforting truth in verse 4. The power of Jesus is greater than the power of any other spirit. That is our overcoming power.

Notice that the child of God has a different viewpoint than the world (vv. 5-6), and *because of this the world cannot understand him.*

Carefully note the Apostle's comments on the place of love in the life of the believer (vv. 7-21). The Lord's standard for His children in this regard is quite different than we often see, even in the church (vv. 10-11).

EZRA 1-2   An astonishing thing happened. Cyrus, the king of Persia ruling over the Israelites in Babylon, ordered that those exiles who were willing should return to Jerusalem and rebuild the temple as Jeremiah had prophesied (Jer 25:11; 29:10; cf. Isa 44:28 - 45:13). Two short phrases in Chapter 1 hold the key to these events. Verse 1 states, "the Lord moved the heart of Cyrus, king of Persia..." (The sovereign Lord of the Nations was at work!) Then in verse 5, "everyone whose heart God had moved" prepared to leave their homes in exile and return to Jerusalem. God moved in the heart of the king and in His people!

This was not as easy as it would first appear. These people had become acclimated to Babylon and had homes, families, and businesses. To go was an act of devotion to the Lord and to their homeland. Over fifty thousand people made that decision (2:64). Note also that Cyrus sent the implements of worship from the temple back with the people (1:7-11; cf. 2 Kings 24:13; Dan 5:2).

GENESIS 49:10   Jacob, Abraham's grandson, was nearing his death at age 147. He and the family clan were in Egypt, where they had come because of the famine in Canaan. Remember that the Lord had told Abraham that his descendants would be slaves in a foreign country for four hundred years, and then come back to Canaan (Gen 15:13-16). The family was at the beginning of that period. During the next four hundred years, God would be with the family as it grew into a strong nation, and protect them from assimilation into the Egyptian culture. In this way they would be ready to be the channel through which God would give the law, the prophets, and as mentioned in yesterday's reading, the Savior.

☑As Jacob blessed his sons before his death, note his words in the blessing to Judah (Gen 49:8-12; especially v. 10). Now the "promise," given to Abraham (Gen 12:1-7), confirmed to Isaac (Gen 17:19; 26:2-4) and then to Jacob (Gen 28:10-15), was channeled through Judah, where it would remain until "he comes to whom it belongs, and the obedience of the nations is his." This is the promise that the Messiah would come through the tribe of Judah, and that is precisely through whom Jesus came.

With regard to the nations (Gen 49:10), read once again how the Messiah will rule the nations in Psalm 2:7-9. Then note the same truth in Revelation 11:15 – how Jesus will rule over the nations of the world! All of this is contained in capsule form in Genesis 49:10!⇦

DECEMBER 6

1 JOHN 5   It is impressive how many times the Bible says that we demonstrate our love for the Lord by our obedience to Him (vv. 2-3). That is what Jesus asserted in John 14:21 and what John the Apostle says in 1 John 2:3-6. There is no way we can earn salvation, *but there is also no way to avoid showing that we love the Lord if we have genuine spiritual life.* John reminds us that this faith enables us to overcome the world (v. 4). We are part of the kingdom of Christ, living within a hostile kingdom of the Evil One – and challenging Satan's authority through the power of Jesus (vv. 19-20).

In the Apostle's concluding remarks, he says that he has written so that believers may *know* they have eternal life – *then lists six facts that believers know and can be sure about.* *(1)* As we pray in His will, we know that He hears us (v. 14). *(2)* We know that we have what we asked for (v. 15). *(3)* We know that believers do not continue in sin (v. 18). *(4)* We know that we are God's children (v. 19). *(5)* We know that the Son of God has given us understanding so that we can know Christ (v. 20). *(6)* We know Him who is true – and are in Him (v. 20).

Tucked within those six "we knows" are comments about the ministry of prayer (vv. 16-17). Note that these verses follow immediately what the Apostle has said about our confidence in prayer (vv. 14-15). John seems to make a distinction between sins that trap the believer, or are committed unintentionally, and sins of those who rebel against God's will. He speaks of praying for the brother (an act of love and our direct responsibility). In contrast, some even in the church have the spirit of the Antichrist (2:18-19). Their sin leads to death. Jude also speaks about scoffers who don't have the Spirit (Jude 18-19). They are outside the kingdom – not brothers for whom we have direct responsibility. Does this mean we have no reason to pray for the unbeliever? Not at all, but we pray for unbelievers differently – that God will give them the grace of repentance from their sin and that they will turn to the Savior.

EZRA 3-4   The altar was rebuilt, but in fear (v. 3). The return of the people of Judah and Benjamin disrupted the status quo. The people who had been living in the land had been brought there to displace the Judean exiles (cf. 2 Kings 17:24 ff.). They considered the people who had returned as "newcomers," who, in their minds, had no right to displace them. The work went on, however, and the people offered sacrifices and began rebuilding the temple.

Behind the scenes, the conflict was spiritual. Jeshua, the priest (3:1-2), called Joshua in Zechariah, was accused by Satan in the presence of God (Zech 3:1-5). It is clear from Zechariah 3 that the rebuilding of Jerusalem was the Lord's will, and that He was equipping Jeshua for the task.

Note how the opposition worked (Ch. 4). They tried to join with God's people and be part of the process (v. 2). When rebuffed, they hired lawyers and started legal action (v. 5). They sent a document to King Artaxerxes (Cyrus was now gone), asking for official action to stop the building (vv. 11-16). When the reply came, God's people were compelled to stop (vv. 17-24).

NUMBERS 24:15-19   When Balak, the king of Moab, hired Balaam to curse Israel, God intervened. Balaam could not curse the Israelites! ☑Instead, after the third time Balak asked for a curse, Balaam looked into the future with a specific reference to the coming Messiah – a "star" who would come out of Jacob with a scepter – and His victory over the nations around Israel. Zechariah 14:1-9 tells of such a victory at the second coming of Christ.

What is so amazing about this passage in Numbers is that God chose a man skilled in sorcery to bring His message to the king of Moab. The message came through the mouth of a sorcerer but was not sorcery. Rather it was from the Lord God. Further, the message is recorded in the Bible for all generations since that time to read and consider. It is the promise of the coming Messiah.⇦

DECEMBER 7

2 JOHN   The Apostle identifies himself as "the elder," and it is thought John was, in fact, quite old when he wrote this. Some language needs clarification. The "chosen lady" refers to the church, and the "children" are the members. "Your house" in verse 10 is probably the church assembly.

Note the two-pronged message of verses 5-6. The Apostle of love calls on church members to love one another, but then ties this to our love for Christ in obedience. *If we love God, we will obey Him. To obey God is to love one another.*

The warning against false teachers in verses 7-11 is still timely for us today. During the first century, the threat was from the Gnostics who believed that knowledge was the key to salvation and not Christ. Today, the threat is from those who assert that man is everything, and enjoyment and fulfillment our highest end. "He who has the most toys wins!" The answer from the Apostle is tied to "the teaching" (v. 9), which is the sound doctrine of the Scriptures. He also warns against letting the false teacher into "your house" – the church – to take people away from the truth.

HAGGAI 1-2   Haggai prophesied among the returned exiles in Jerusalem. His message related to the work on the temple that had been stopped by the letter from Artaxerxes (Ezra 4:18-24). The challenge from the Lord was to get to work on the temple. That was God's plan. It wasn't right to neglect the temple while the people lived in fine houses (1:2-4).

A key phrase of the book is, "Give careful thought..." (1:5, 7; 2:15-19), which calls attention to an important concept. Note that the Lord tied their economic success to their obedience (1:5-11). The people's unsatisfied expectations (1:6, 9) and failed crops (1:10-11) were caused by their disobedience and wrong priorities.

The people responded to the Lord's call (1:12), and the Lord energized them in the work (1:13-14; 2:4-5) and promised His presence (2:4). Things changed, and the Lord told them to remember *that their obedience affected their economic condition (2:15-19)*. ☑In the context of this message from the Lord, the text looks forward to a time when God will "shake the heavens, the earth, the sea, the dry land, and the nations – and the desired of all nations will come" (2:6-7, 20-22). This refers to when the Lord will come and bring a new level of glory to the land with His presence at His second advent.⇔

Haggai is a real success story. Leaders were in place who responded to the Lord's message. As you read, note the Lord's leading and energizing of the people – even though the legal injunction still stood in the way. Then preview Ezra 5-6 to see how the legal problem was solved.

JOB 19:23-27   Job was a man of faith. Because of that faith, the Lord entrusted him with the difficult task of remaining faithful under suffering. He was a man who knew God.

Job uttered the words in today's reading after months of terrible suffering and pain. He had lost all of his possessions and his children, and he could not understand the reason for his condition. His friends repeatedly told him that it was because of his sin.

☑We don't know how much of the Bible existed at the time Job lived or whether Job had read it. But it is absolutely striking to see how Job looked forward to seeing his redeemer. He was looking beyond the grave to the resurrection! He held to his faith in the living God, and looked to the time when he would see God, his defender, his redeemer, with his own eyes (vv. 26-27). Here is the promise of redemption and of the resurrection. It is the promise of the second coming of Christ (v. 25).

Job's theology may not have been systematic in the sense that we know it, but it was practical and gave Job a vibrant faith!↩

DECEMBER 8

3 JOHN   We can assume that Gaius was a faithful friend of the Apostle, perhaps an elder of the church. The phrase "you will do well" (v. 6) is another way of saying "please."   These words encourage hospitality to traveling kingdom-workers (vv. 5-8).

The Apostle also addresses a problem in the church. Diotrephes wanted to be the top leader in the church, and his ambition was hurting the church. That kind of ambition is never from the Lord (see the words of Jesus in Matt 20:25-28). John's comments are restrained, but it is clear that he intends to address the problem when he visits the church once again (v. 10). Would you rather have the reputation of Diotrephes (vv. 9-10) or Demetrius (v. 12)? Reputation is built on behavior that is driven from the heart. We need the Spirit of God to drive the heart.

ZECHARIAH 1-2   Zechariah was written to the Jews who had returned to Jerusalem after Cyrus's decree.   Haggai and Zechariah were contemporaries, and this book was written during the time of Ezra and Nehemiah.   It is one of several apocalyptic books in the Bible. Apocalyptic material speaks about the end times, uses symbols and symbolic language, and usually requires an interpretation. Daniel and Revelation as well as Zechariah are apocalyptic books, and other biblical books have apocalyptic sections.

The book begins with a call to repentance (1:2-6). Note the Lord's logic.   Those who had the message of the previous prophets were rebellious – they have come and gone (v. 5), but the truth of Lord's message to them has been fulfilled in judgment (v. 6).

In Chapters 1 and 2, there are three visions that the prophet received from the Lord. *The first vision* (1:7-17) was of a man on a horse among trees, with three other horses of different colors, perhaps with riders upon them, since they report to the horseman. The message of the vision concerns the welfare of Jerusalem. God will show His mercy to the city, and it once again will "overflow with prosperity." *The second vision* is of four horns and four craftsmen (1:18-21).   The horns represent the power or powers that took Judah into exile, while the craftsmen bring judgment upon the horns and deal with those powers. ☑*The third vision* of the man with the measuring line (Ch. 2) concerns the future of Jerusalem and the land. It refers to a time when there will be so many people that there will be no walls – when the Lord Himself will be a protecting wall of fire around the city (vv. 4-5). Note the Lord's promise to "live among you" (v. 10), and the promise that the nations

(Gentiles) will also be joined to the Lord (v. 11). The vision is one of promise and hope – the Lord is at work (v. 13). The kingdom is coming. This quite obviously has messianic overtones. The immediate fulfillment was the restoration of the temple. The more distant fulfillment is Christ's coming at the end of the age (God living among His people, the Messiah receiving Judah as His inheritance, v. 12, and the selection of Jerusalem to be His dwelling place, cf. Isa 2:1-5).⇦

2 SAMUEL 7:8-16 God's promise to David was a personal promise, but one that extended far beyond his own life. The Lord Himself would see that the promise was fulfilled (vv. 11b, 16). ☑Note God's remarkable promise that David's throne would be established *forever* (7:11b-16)! David, of course, was from the tribe of Judah. The lineage of Jesus is traced directly from Judah to David and from David to Jesus.

The nation expected that the Messiah would be a descendent of David – because of this promise. The promise that had come to Abraham, then to Isaac, and to Jacob, and through Jacob to Judah now was channeled through David. The Pharisees acknowledged this in response to a question Jesus posed (Matt 22:42). Jesus used their response to demonstrate that the Messiah would be more than just another man (Matt 22:43-46). David himself had referred to the Messiah as his own Lord (Ps 110:1)!⇦

DECEMBER 9

JUDE Jude identifies himself as the brother of James – probably the leader in Jerusalem and the half-brother of Jesus. The error that Jude addressed is antinomianism, or inappropriate and undisciplined behavior in the life of the professing Christian. It is a call to "contend for the faith" (v. 3). *The problem: teaching from within the church was leading to immorality and careless living* (v. 4).

To show that sinful behavior is dangerous, Jude gives three examples (vv. 5-7): the Israelites who came out of Egypt but who later died along the way because of their unbelief; angels who sinned and were cast from God's presence, and now await eternal punishment; and Sodom and Gomorrah, which were destroyed for their ungodliness, sin, and perversion. *The message: sin demands a price!*

Jude mentions three sins of the false teachers (v. 8), and gives examples of their behavior (v. 11): Cain's sin in Genesis 4 – jealousy and murder; Balaam's error in Numbers 25:1-3 (cf. 31:16); and Korah's sin (Num 16:1-35). Five striking illustrations describe these men's activity and character in verses 12-13. Four of these illustrations point to unfulfilled expectation: (1) shepherds who don't care for the sheep, (2) clouds that have no rain, (3) trees that do not produce fruit, and (4) stars that wander (not in their assigned place and are useless for navigation). The fifth illustration is wild waves of the sea. Notice the character of these men's work, methods and speech (v. 15), and five identifying marks (v. 16). You might think they should have been obvious to the church. False teaching, however, can be very subtle. Working from within, these men were able to lead people in the church astray.

Finally, find Jude's commands in verses 20-23. Rejoice in the power of God available on our behalf (vv. 24-25). This book is worth careful thought for the church today.

ZECHARIAH 3-4 As mentioned in the notes for Ezra, the "Joshua" in Zechariah is "Jeshua" in Ezra. Chapter 3 gives us a glimpse of the spiritual dimensions of rebuilding the temple and the political pressure the builders faced. Satan accused Joshua, the high priest, of being unworthy (vv. 1-5). The Lord cleansed Joshua and rebuked Satan. Note the promise to Joshua (v. 7).

☑Joshua and Zerubbabel were symbolic of the coming Messiah (the Branch, v. 8). The stone is Messiah, the building block of the kingdom. The seven (the perfect number) eyes on the stone may symbolize the Messiah's perfect knowledge and understanding. Sin will be gone in a single day (review Ezek 36:24-29 and Rom 11:25-27). There will be true peace in the land (v. 10).⇦

The prophet then received a vision of a lampstand with seven lights, and two olive trees (Ch. 4). The vision was to encourage Joshua and Zerubbabel to move ahead with rebuilding the temple. God is in the project (vv. 6-9)! The work would not be done with human might or power but by the Spirit of The Lord (v. 6). Note verse 7. The "mighty mountain" (of opposition) that they faced was nothing to the Lord. What does the lampstand represent? Probably the light of witness that God is great. The two olive trees (vv. 3, 14), representing Joshua and Zerubbabel, are anointed to serve the Lord.

ISAIAH 9:6-7 ☑One of the most beautiful messianic promises in Scripture is found in these verses. In this advent season we will hear these verses both read in services and sung in choral music. Notice that these words tie the coming Messiah to the throne of David, as we saw in our reading for yesterday. It will be an eternal reign – characterized by peace, righteousness, and justice.

We must note as well the character of the king (v. 6). He is at once the Wonderful Counselor, the Mighty God, and the Prince of Peace! Remembering the promise of Messiah and salvation that has developed from Genesis, Numbers, Job, and 2 Samuel, think of what has been added from this reading for today. We now can see the Messiah as God

Himself, reigning forever, bringing peace, justice, and righteousness to the world. ⇦

DECEMBER 10

REVELATION 1   The book of Revelation was written by the Apostle John after he was exiled for his faith and testimony to the Island of Patmos. We know very little about what happened to him in exile. Revelation is an apocalyptic book, with visions that foretell the future and require explanation.   Don't expect definite answers to every question you may have about end times. It is a message that must be compared with the rest of Scripture. If you read the book repeatedly, principles and insights become apparent that are worth the time spent in study. As you become familiar with the book, other parts of the Bible will fit with this message, helping you understand both this book and the rest of Scripture. Read with an open mind and heart. Understand and act upon what is clear.   Pray for insight for what you do not understand, and trust God to give you every truth you need for today and to prepare you for the future.

The prologue (vv. 1-3) says the book records the revelation of Jesus Christ from an eyewitness account. The events that are prophesied are "coming soon" (from God's perspective), now about nineteen hundred years closer than when they were written. There is a promise attached to reading the book and taking it to heart: *the only promise of this kind attached to a specific book of the Bible.*

Read verses 4-8 for the theology concerning Jesus: existent from eternity to eternity; the sovereign Lord over death and over the nations; the minister of salvation and the God of glory and power; the One who is coming!

John's vision of Jesus (vv. 12-18) is remarkable. Remember that John was the Beloved Disciple, perhaps the closest human companion Jesus had. When John saw Him in His glory, he fell at Jesus' feet as though dead (v. 17)! If there was any doubt in John's mind about the identity of the person he saw in the vision, it was answered by what the Lord said (vv. 17-18). Compare John's description of Jesus with Daniel 10:5-6 and Matthew 17:2.

John also saw golden lampstands beside Jesus and stars in His right hand. The lampstands symbolize the seven churches (vv. 4a, 20b), and the stars stand for the angels of the churches (v. 20). John's assignment was to write down the visions for the churches (vv. 11, 19).

ZECHARIAH 5-6   The flying scroll (5:1-4) illustrates that the law of God will find those who disregard its truth or rebel against it. It will be impossible to avoid, since it will enter the home of the disobedient and bring destruction.

The woman in a basket (5:5-11; cf. Rev 17:3-5) represents evil and is taken to Babylon, probably not the historic country, but the evil "world system," that will finally be destroyed (Rev 18).

The vision of the four chariots (6:1-8) represents the work that spirits (angels) from the Lord would do in the world. The horses remind us of Zechariah 1, but also of Revelation 6:1-8, where horsemen on similarly colored horses were sent for conquest, and to bring death, famine, and war to the world. The mission of the heavenly emissaries was carried out, for it brought rest to the Spirit of the Lord (v. 8). This vision may represent the Lord's destruction of world governments during the day of His wrath (The Day of The Lord). The fact that the chariots go out from two mountains (probably representing Mount Zion and the Mount of Olives) ties the events to Jerusalem.

☑The vision of the crown for Joshua is messianic. Joshua was the high priest, but a high priest was never the king. He is identified as the "Branch" who will build the temple of the Lord (cf. Isa 11:1-5 where the Messiah is the King). In Ezra, Zerubbabel was building the temple as the leader in civil government. The two positions of king and priest are thus combined in the "Branch." (This also appears in the messianic Psalm 110: cf. vv. 1-3 as king, v. 4 as priest.) This can only be the Messiah (v. 13, priest and king), and the vision refers to the setting up of the messianic kingdom. In this regard, note that in 3:8, Joshua and Zerubbabel symbolize things to come, and the verse also speaks to "my servant the Branch" (the Messiah) who would come.

Note the progression in these visions: the cleansing of the land and the people of Israel (Ch. 5; cf. Ezek 36:24-32); judgment on the nations (the Day of the Lord, 6:1-8); and the reign of the priest-king, the Messiah, 6:9-15.⇦

ISAIAH 11:1-5   ☑This too, is one of the most loved advent scripture passages. These verses also identify the Messiah as coming from David. Mark the words in your Bible that describe the character of the Messiah (vv. 2-3a) and of His reign (3b-5). Imagine, if you are able, a civil government that operated on these principles of righteousness, justice, and concern for all citizens. If we think about these matters, we must stand with those who "love His appearing" (2 Tim 4:8; Titus 2:13).⇦

DECEMBER 11

REVELATION 2   Chapters 2 and 3 contain letters to the seven churches in Asia. These were actual churches that started in the first century. The letters are personal – from the Lord Himself. They show us how the Lord Jesus views the church with its problems and imperfections. The messages are for the church at large and not just for the seven congregations. The problems are characteristic of those that the church has faced through history. Thus, there was a message to the specific church with specific application, but to the larger church throughout the ages as well.

Each of the letters begins by identifying the Lord in a particular way. Each ends with encouragement to listen and act – and with a blessing for those who do so.

Read the letters to the churches at Ephesus, Smyrna, Pergamum, and Thyatira, looking for God's concern for that particular church. Smyrna is one of only two of the churches for which the Lord had no criticism or correction (watch also for Philadelphia). Do you see any areas where your church needs to take action?

Note the deficiency that Jesus (the Lord of the church, v. 1) identified in the church at Ephesus (v. 4) and His warning to the church (v. 5). *A church's heart is more important to the Lord than the appearance of performance!* The church at Smyrna lived under great duress – yet was faithful (vv. 8-11). With regard to the church at Pergamum, we know little about the Nicolaitans, but Balaam had suggested sexual immorality to the Moabites to entice the Israelites to idolatry (Num 25; 31:16). This same thinking had crept into the church at Pergamum (v. 14). Idolatry and sexual immorality were also a problem at Thyatira (v. 20).

If we define idolatry as substitutes that take us away from the wholehearted devotion to the Lord God, and if we define sexual immorality the way Jesus did in Matthew 5:27-30, the church today has much to think about!

ZECHARIAH 7 In exile, it had been the people's practice to fast on the anniversary of the temple's destruction when Jerusalem fell (Jer 52:12-13). Now that the new temple was a reality, the people wondered if they should continue that practice (7:2-3). The Lord answered through Zechariah that their motives in fasting had been mixed, and to truly please the Lord, they should have other concerns (vv. 8-10). The Lord was far more interested in justice, mercy, and compassion than in their fasting. Learn, He suggests, from the past (vv. 11-14). If their fathers had been concerned about these things, they would not have been exiled!

Note carefully the message of verse 13. If we are coldhearted to the message of the Lord and unresponsive to the principles of His Word, He will also be unresponsive when we call in need! Compare this to Proverbs 1:23-33.

ISAIAH 40:1-11 ☑The comfort that Isaiah brings to his people and to Jerusalem is based on the coming of Messiah. The preparation by John the Baptist is seen in verses 3-4. The rough places that are smoothed in preparation of Christ's coming are hearts softened by repentance preached by John.

In the verses that follow the reference to John the Baptist, some could refer either to the first or the second advent. This is quite common when the coming of the Lord is addressed in the Old Testament. Verse 5, however, speaks about the universal recognition of the Messiah as the King (cf. Matt 24:30; Rev 1:7). This will be when all recognize Jesus as the Messiah at His coming in glory – some with sorrow, having rejected Him, and others with the joy of faith fulfilled.

On the other hand, verses 6-9, 11 could apply to either Jesus' first ministry on earth or when He comes again. Verse 10 refers to the second coming and Christ's powerful rule.⇦

DECEMBER 12

REVELATION 3   To the churches at Sardis, Philadelphia and Laodicea, the Lord Jesus says, "I know your deeds" (vv. 1, 8, 15). The church at Sardis appeared to be alive – but Jesus said it was dead (v. 1b)! His message to Sardis: Obey what you have received, and repent. If not, Jesus' coming would catch them unawares (v. 3).

It is significant that a few in Sardis were faithful to the Lord Jesus (v. 4). All the rest had soiled clothing, a reference to contamination with the things of this world (James 1:27). This should give us pause to think. *Adherence to the standards of those around us, even those in the church, does not mean our lives please God!* It is individually before the Lord that we will stand (2 Cor 5:10).

Jesus' salutation to each church was different. In relation to the church at Sardis, He was the Lord of the Church (v. 1). In the salutation to Philadelphia, Jesus is the Lord of truth – the Lord of the kingdom and the promise (v. 7; cf. Isa 22:22). Philadelphia was the church of little strength, but with an open door (of ministry) from the Lord that no one could close. Philadelphia was the obedient church and would be protected from the "hour of trial" coming to the earth (the Day of the Lord?). To Laodicea, Jesus appeared as the Lord of truth and sovereignty (v. 14). Laodicea was a church with much self-satisfaction, but had no fire for the Lord and His work.

The most needy of all of the churches was the church at Laodicea for it was self-deceived, felt self-sufficient, and was self-satisfied. It believed it was doing well (v. 17), but was, in fact, impoverished in the extreme (v. 17b; cf. Matt 22:11-13; Matt 25:1-13). The Lord's solution was that the church must repent (v. 19)! Note Jesus' gracious invitation in v. 20. This church was in grave danger.

The message to Laodicea points to the danger of our own ideas of success. *We must evaluate the church always against the standard of God's Word, never against our own idea of success.*

To each of the churches is appended a note to "him who overcomes." Seven churches, seven times! This must be important! One overcomes when one wins in conflict. In this context, it means victory through Christ in our conflict with "the world" and the enemy, Satan. How does one overcome? *Walk in the Spirit, obey God's Word* (get with God's agenda), and *continue in prayer* (cf. Rev 12:11). If we do these things, we will inevitably be in conflict with the enemy, but will have the tools to overcome.

ZECHARIAH 8-9   ☑Chapter 8 is about the coming messianic reign and millennial kingdom. It is the restored country living with the Lord's presence and blessing. Count the blessings and the ways things will be different. Consider the Lord's standard for behavior (vv. 16-17). Compare verses 20-23 with Isaiah 2:1-5.⇔

The prophecy of God's judgment on the nations surrounding Judah from the north, around the west on the coast, and down through the Philistine territory to the southwest is found in 9:1-8. Notice that verse 8 exempts Judah from this judgment through the Lord's intervention and protection. These kingdoms were destroyed when Alexander the Great marched through the territory in 333 BC, doing exactly as the text describes, sparing Judah and Jerusalem.

☑Beginning with 9:9 there is a prophecy of the coming Messiah, both the first and the second advents. The call is to rejoice over the coming of the king with righteousness, gentleness, and salvation (v. 9, first advent; cf. Matt 21:4-5). But verse 10 says His rule will extend throughout the world. The Lord will be with His people in battle and the victory will be sure and complete, for the Lord will appear (vv. 14-15; cf. Zech 14:3-4). The end will be God's hand of victory and blessing on His people (vv. 16-17).⇔

ISAIAH 42:1-9   ☑This wonderful passage describes Christ's ministry and reign. Again, the first and second advents are intertwined. Note that Messiah is the Lord's chosen and the Lord God's delight (v. 1a). The Messiah's agenda is the Lord's will! The universal rule of Christ is seen in verses 1b, 4 (second advent), but His ministry here on earth during His first advent appears in verses 2-3. Both advents are apparent in verses 6-9. Note the quiet gentleness of Jesus prophesied in verses 2-3. He encouraged those who had only a little faith (v. 3a). Note His liberating ministry (v. 7).

Jesus the Messiah has come as the Redeemer and Savior, opened blind eyes and set free those in bondage. And He is coming again as King to extend His rule to the whole earth, and will do so with faithfulness and justice! ⇦

DECEMBER 13

REVELATION 4   Remember the drama on the stage. John had been standing before the risen and glorified Lord, who dictated letters to the seven churches. Now the scene changed and *the same voice of the risen Lord (v. 1; cf. 1:10) called John into the throne room of heaven.* Picture the awesome scene. Compare this with Ezekiel 1:26-28 and Daniel 7:9-10 (the Daniel description includes God's throne in judgment). Meditate on the glory and majesty of the throne room. Note the seven blazing lamps (v. 5; cf. 1:20) and the four living creatures (v. 6bff.; cf. Ezek 1:5ff.) and listen to their message. Picture the twenty-four elders; watch their part in the scene. Listen to what they say.

What are we to learn? *God is a God of awesome wonder and glory.* Remember that when Isaiah (Isa 6:5), Ezekiel (1:25-28), Daniel (10:7-8), Saul (Acts 9:3-9), and now John (Rev 1:17) had visions of God or Jesus, they were profoundly affected physically and spiritually. We tend to think of God with a familiarity that is unbiblical. Keep in mind that we are welcomed into God's presence through the blood of Christ (Heb 10:19-22), but we should always feel awe and wonder. God is not an object that we can pick off the shelf at our convenience, but the great God of glory whom we worship. To do His will must be our soul's passion – and indeed will be if we see Him in His glory!

ZECHARIAH 10-11   The beginning of Chapter 10 returns to problems in Israel. Zechariah warns about the deceit of the idols (v. 2) and shepherds who lead people astray (v. 3a). ☑Observe what the Lord will do at His coming (vv. 3b-12). The cornerstone (Messiah) will come from Judah (v. 4). Israel (Ephraim) and Judah together will be restored from exile among the nations (vv. 6-10), and although they will pass through hard times (v. 11; see also 9:14-15), they will be established in the land.

The account of the sheep and the shepherds (Ch. 11) is an allegorical prophecy of the people's rejection of Jesus. It is directed to Zechariah and is thought to have been acted out by the prophet. The condition of the people at the time of Jesus is in verses 4-6: religious leaders interested in their own ends, not caring for the sheep. The Messiah cared for the flock (vv. 7-8), but was rejected (detested) by the people (v. 8b). The relationship between the shepherd and the people is broken, finally, by payment of the thirty pieces of silver, thrown into the house of the Lord (v. 13; cf. Matt 27:3-10), which then went to the potter. The two staffs of favor (from the Lord) and union (between Israel and Judah) were broken, as the people rejected God's shepherd. ⇦

The second shepherd, one who would not care for the sheep (vv. 15-17), is in contrast to the Messiah. The identification of this shepherd is unclear.

ISAIAH 50:4-9 ☑In this section we are able to see how the Lord Jesus depended upon the strength of His Father. There was a reason Jesus left the twelve to be alone to pray (Mark 1:35). The Father set His agenda and planned His time (v. 4). God gave Him ears to hear (v. 5). With this heart of obedience He suffered at the hands of men (vv. 6-7). With the Lord's help, He set His face toward Jerusalem and the reality of His death (v. 7; cf. Matt 16:21; Mark 14:32-36; Luke 18:31-34). ⇦

DECEMBER 14

REVELATION 5 Once again, remember the scene. *We are still in the throne room of heaven.* Review the throne, the vision of God, the rainbow, and the sea of glass. Remember the lightning and the peals of thunder (4:1-6).

The focus changes in verses 1-5 to a scroll, and then to a lamb (v. 6ff). The scroll had seven seals that could not be opened. This was a cause of great concern to John – until the spotlight illuminated the lamb – with the marks of death – in the center of God's throne! There is no question about the identity of the lamb. He is the Lion of the tribe of Judah, and the Root of David, and has triumphed (v. 5). This is the risen Lord!

Stop to read the text of the song that the elders sing (vv. 9-10). Jesus is the Holy One. He is the sacrifice. He has paid the price, and He has elevated the place of God's people.

What is the meaning of the sealed scroll? Why was it locked so tightly that no one could open the seals? This is a symbol of how God planned redemption for man long ago, but the plan was hidden until Jesus paid the price of blood (1 Peter 1:10-12, 18-20). *The Lord Jesus, crucified and risen, is the key that unlocks the mystery of salvation* (Eph 1:9-10). Specifically, in this context, He is the key that unlocks the mystery of the events at the end of time. Because He is holy (Rev 5:9a), He opened the way through His sacrifice for all people to come to God (v. 9b). He is indeed worthy of all praise!

ZECHARIAH 12-13 ☑Chapter 12 tells of events that surround the second coming of Christ. The term "on that day" occurs several times in this and the succeeding chapters. Jerusalem will be the center of conflict (v. 3). The nations will be gathered for a confrontation with

Israel (vv. 2-3). But the Lord will make Jerusalem a cup (of wine?) that makes the nations reel, and an immovable rock on which the nations will be injured. This will be an attack on Jerusalem and the surrounding countryside (vv. 2-3; cf. Joel 3:9-16). The Lord will protect Israel and confound the other nations. Through this, the leaders of the nation (Israel) will recognize that the Lord is working on their behalf (v. 5). Following this, the Lord will pour out His Spirit on the people (v. 10). They will recognize Jesus with the "marks of the cross" as the Messiah (v. 10b) and will repent with genuine contrition. Not with an emotional national outburst, but quietly, individually, there will be mourning and repentance (vv. 11-13). The Apostle John records the piercing of Jesus' side and relates this to verse 10b (cf. John 19:37). If we understand the context correctly, as noted above, this will occur at the time of Christ's second coming.

The first portion of Chapter 13 is a continuation of the previous chapter. The cleansing of the land that follows the repentance will be as thorough as the repentance. Idols will be gone (v. 2). Compare these verses with the new heart and the cleansing that are promised in Ezekiel 36:22-36. False prophets will be banished and will be afraid to prophesy (vv. 2b-6). Some believe that verse 6 refers to Jesus, but this is difficult to support. Rather, it probably refers to wounds inflicted during pagan worship that the priest now does not want to admit. ⇦

The scattering of the sheep (vv. 7-9) refers to the final scattering of the people of Judah and Jerusalem after the rejection of the Savior. This was fulfilled in 70 AD when Jerusalem was sacked and burned by the Romans. ☑The passage also refers to the scattering of the disciples at the time of Jesus' death (cf. Matt 26:31 where Jesus tied this prophecy to the time surrounding His death). ⇦

ISAIAH 52:13-53:12   ☑These verses, which tell of the suffering of the Lamb of God on our behalf, are situated exactly in the center of chapters 40-66, the second major section of the book of Isaiah.

As you read this section once again, you may refer to the notes for September 14. Be reminded again of the sacrifice of the Lord Jesus. He took our sin and our punishment (vv. 4-7). He did so willingly when He had no reason to die except to please the Father and to open the way for us to know God. Our hearts must fill with thankfulness and praise for Him. Without Him, we are absolutely lost and without hope. Read again 1 Peter 1:18-20. ⇦

DECEMBER 15

REVELATION 6   The scene is still the throne room of heaven. The seven seals that were opened by the Lamb (six this chapter) begin a series of "sevens" that we will follow for several chapters. There are seven seals, seven trumpets, seven thunders, and seven bowls of God's wrath. Much of the book's message is presented through these successive revelations.

Think of the throne room as the main stage. As the "sevens" are brought to our attention, imagine the spotlight shifting to illuminate a secondary stage, where we visualize the messages that the Lord has for us.

"The Four Horsemen of the Apocalypse" are now revealed as Jesus opened the first four seals (vv. 1-8). Each of these horsemen bring human suffering – the consequence of sin. The living creatures around the throne called these horsemen out (v. 1; cf. 4:6-8). The horsemen were released into the world to accomplish conquest, war, disease, famine, and death. Compare this with Jesus' words in Matthew 24:6-8, where He spoke about "the beginning of birth pains" at the time of the end; i.e., the events leading to His coming in glory.

The opening of the fifth seal revealed the souls of men and women who had died for their faith in the Lord and their testimony to the truth (vv. 9-11). Their vindication would still wait for "a little longer." Others would join them first. Note Jesus' comments in Matthew 24:9 as He told the disciples that at the time of the end His followers would face persecution and death.

Opening the sixth seal triggers cataclysmic events that shake the world. (vv. 12-17; see also Isa 13:9-11; Isa 34:1-4; Isa 51:6; Joel 3:14-16; Matt 24:29). As Jesus speaks about these events (the celestial signs) as recorded in Matthew 24:29-31 and Luke 21:25-27, they coincide with the coming of Christ in glory. *These events accompany (or introduce) the Day of the Lord, when God will judge the nations for their sin and rebellion.* Notice how the levels of society are made equal. The position of the powerful or the money of the rich do not protect from this time of judgment (vv. 15-17).

ZECHARIAH 14   ☑Chapter 14 deals with the deliverance of Jerusalem by the appearing of the Lord and the beginning of His millennial reign. The final battle (v. 2) is the time when the Lord Jesus returns to fight the nations, accompanied by cataclysmic events. This is the Day of the Lord. The Mount of Olives east of Jerusalem will be split (v. 4), and the usual lights of the day and the night will be altered (vv. 6-7). Water will flow from Jerusalem (v. 8; cf. Ezek 47; Joel 3:18; Ps 46:4; Rev 22:1-2).

With regard to the final battle, note verses 12-15. This sounds remarkably like a nuclear event, with the flesh of warriors rotting while they stand on their feet. This same battle is described in Revelation 19:11-21 from a spiritual perspective.

Note that the Lord will be king over the whole earth (v. 9), thus ushering in His millennial reign. Only one Lord! Righteousness will reign. Survivors will go year after year to worship the Lord in Jerusalem (v. 16; cf. Isa 2:2-3).

Finally, the term *HOLY TO THE LORD* will characterize Christ's reign (v. 20). This will be more than a jingle or trite term – it will be true. *Even so come, Lord Jesus!*⇦

PSALM 22 ☑Read this messianic psalm looking for references to the Lord Jesus. Note the striking images of Christ's crucifixion: the taunts of those who passed by (vv. 7-8; cf. Luke 23:35-39); the suffering of the Lord (vv. 12-17); casting lots for Jesus' clothing (v. 18; cf. Luke 23:34b). Added here to the gospel accounts are the Lord's emotions during His passion (vv. 1-6). In humble gratitude, thank God for His way of salvation, opened by our Lord Jesus.⇦

DECEMBER 16

REVELATION 7 Events now take place between the sixth and seventh seal. Shift the spotlight to four angels holding the wind from blowing on the earth (bringing judgment). An angel sealed the faithful on the forehead – 144,000 people from the twelve tribes of Israel. (The number 144,000 may symbolize a great number of people or a "complete number.") The seal signifies ownership by the Lamb and protects from the plagues that are God's judgments (cf. 9:4), but possibly not from persecution from the Antichrist and his human agencies.

Shift the spotlight once again (v. 9ff.), this time to the main stage in the throne room, and observe a great multitude from all nations and languages of the world gathered around the throne and the Lamb. Listen to what they say. Listen to what the elders and the four living creatures say. These are people who have come through the great tribulation (Matt 24:15-22; Rev 13:5-8) and are saved through the blood of the Lamb (v. 14). Perhaps these are the martyred saints who would join those under the fifth seal (6:9-11). Take special note of the intimate relationship that these people in white robes have with the Lord Jesus (vv. 15-17).

EZRA 5-6 In response to the challenge of Haggai's message, the returned exiles went back to building the temple. Nothing had changed – the former prohibition to build was still in place, but they obeyed the Lord. As might be predicted, those who opposed them took steps to stop them by intimidation (vv. 3-4). Note God's protection (v. 5).

The Medo-Persian governor of the area sent a fair report to King Darius, outlining the position of the Jews and asking for his direction (vv. 6-17). In response, a most amazing thing happened. →Cyrus's previous decree authorizing the building of the temple was "found" – not in the capital – but in a different city (6:1-2). With this "find," the situation turned around. Not only were the Jews allowed to proceed with the building, but the king ordered that their expenses be paid out of the government treasury and animals be provided for sacrifices (vv. 8-10)! And woe to the person who stood in their way (vv. 11-12).←

This is a remarkable example of how obeying the Lord in a seemingly impossible situation brought God's protection and intervention in the politics of a pagan government that allowed His work to go on. God is sovereign! Obedience is the way to blessing.

Under the preaching of Haggai and Zechariah (the prophets who wrote the books bearing their names) the work was completed (6:14-15). Finally, the Passover was observed in the rebuilt temple (v. 19). This was the first time since the exile that the Passover had been observed – and it was commemorated with joy as the people understood how the Lord's protection and intervention had made it all possible (v. 22).

ISAIAH 61:1-3 ☑When Jesus went to the synagogue in Nazareth early in His ministry, he stood, read from this portion of Isaiah, and applied the prophecy to Himself (Luke 4:16-21). But He stopped reading in the middle of a sentence, declaring that what He had read was then being fulfilled before their eyes!

This is one of the prophecies where it is difficult to separate the first and the second advents – unless we have the advantage of retrospection. When Jesus stopped in the middle of verse 2, it was because that was as far as His ministry extended during the first advent. Jesus understood that clearly. He came with the good news of the kingdom, to heal the sick, and to liberate the prisoners of evil and sin. His message proclaimed the year of God's favor!

Note what was still unfulfilled: judgment on sinners, and God's blessing on His people at His second coming (vv. 2b-3). Compare these promises with Ezekiel 36:24-32. God is not finished with His people yet!⇦

DECEMBER 17

REVELATION 8 Scene: the throne room in heaven as Jesus opens the seals. When Jesus opens the seventh seal, there is silence for thirty minutes – different from the other seals. Look at the offering of prayers of the saints (vv. 3-4, see also 5:8). Do the prayers of believers reach the Lord? Emphatically, yes!

The opening of the seventh seal introduces the seven angels with the trumpets. The sounding of the first four trumpets affects *the earth, the salt seas, the fresh water, and the celestial bodies,* respectively. Keep this sequence in mind, for we shall see it again. After the first four trumpets, a flying eagle warns of the woes associated with the last three trumpets.

EZRA 7-8   Ezra, the priest, had remained in Babylon when the first exiles returned to Jerusalem. Now, several years later he, and several hundred others, came to Jerusalem. Ezra traced his ancestry in the priesthood back through the priests who served King David (five hundred years), and to Aaron (one thousand years). Notice his commitment to God's Word (7:10).

The group came with the blessing and endorsement of the king of Persia, and with a considerable store of treasures. God had moved the king to the generous conditions of his decree (7:27-28). Traveling with valuables was hazardous; the text implies that the king would have sent a contingent of troops with Ezra. Because Ezra had already told the king that God would protect them, the group spent time in fasting and prayer before setting out and went without the soldiers (8:21-23). *At that point the reputation of the God of Israel was at stake!* This was faith put to the test.

For the trip Ezra prudently inventoried and weighed the silver and gold implements they took with them. These were then distributed among the people and were again checked against their list when they arrived. The gold and the silver were the Lord's!

DANIEL 2:31-45   ☑When Nebuchadnezzar had a strange dream, the Lord was telling the king (and Daniel, and us) what the future held until the second advent of Christ. The imposing statue that Nebuchadnezzar saw represented the great Gentile dynasties from his time until the second coming of Christ. These four governments are Babylon, the Medo-Persian Empire, Greece, and the Roman Empire. We now live in the last days – the extension of the Roman Empire.

Note the interpretation of the dream's final event in verses 34-35, 44-45. The God of Heaven will set up a kingdom that will crush the kingdoms of men – and the kingdom that God sets up will endure.

At the time of God's choosing (Matt 24:36) the Lord will return in power and glory with judgment for the godless, bringing righteousness for the whole world. This is the appearing of Christ in Matthew 24:30 and the judgment of Revelation 18. When we think of the first advent of Christ, we must also think of His second coming! The caution that Jesus gave His disciples and others was to be ready for this. Live with the future (His coming) in view!⇔

DECEMBER 18

REVELATION 9   In the throne room the fifth trumpet sounds, releasing the *first of the three woes.* In the vision, a "star that had fallen from the sky to the earth" opens the Abyss, releasing billows of smoke that obscure the sun and locusts who torment those that did not worship God (those without the seal 7:3). Suffering will be so severe that people will seek death but be unable to find it.

The description of the locusts is amazing (vv. 7-11). The locusts are similar to the locusts of Joel 2:1-11 (also speaking of the Day of the Lord), but those of Revelation 9 do not harm vegetation. Both, however, had a dreadful appearance, and the coming of both was accompanied by a darkened sun.

The identification of the "star" who was given the key to the Abyss is not certain. Is this a fallen angel or an angel of the Lord who has come down to open the Abyss? If this is the same angel as in Revelation 20:1, it would most certainly be angel of the Lord. The angel mentioned in verse 11 – the king of the locusts whose name is destroyer – is a highly placed demonic being, or Satan himself. The locusts from the Abyss could be imprisoned demons, released for this attack upon men. Why would Satan's minions torment people who are already under Satan's control? Remember: Satan has no love for men. His object is to keep them under his authority.

The sixth trumpet (bringing the second woe) brings us back to the throne room and the altar before God (v. 13ff.). Horns (v. 13) are a symbol of strength in the Old Testament, and God's strength has restrained the four angels who had been ready for this very time: *the second woe.* At the sounding of the trumpet, mounted troops numbering two hundred million are released (v. 16)! As you read the description of these troops, look again at Joel 2:2b-9. These are most probably demonic hordes loosed against mankind.

Most amazing is the attitude of those men and women left alive (vv. 20-21). This indicates the depth of wickedness in mankind and the hold that sin has on people. *When a person is released from sin and brought into the kingdom of the Lord Jesus (Col 1:13-14), it is an act of God's power and grace.*

EZRA 9-10   As Ezra arrived and settled, an enormous problem became apparent among those who had previously returned to Jerusalem. They had intermarried with the local people, disobeying God's instruction (9:1-2, cf. Deut 7:1-6). This was a problem because intermarriage mixed true worship with the local religious practices. Further, the leaders and officials of the people modeled this sinful practice (9:2b, 10:18-24).

Read carefully Ezra's reaction. He approached this situation differently than most would have done. He knew the Word of God and was devoted to observing it (7:6, 10). *God's Word had truly captured his heart!* His reaction was dramatic, but his bold stance attracted others with similar convictions (10:2-4). His prayer reflects God's will and dealings with His people (9:6-15). Notice that he identified with the people in their collective sin.

Read about the solution they agreed to (10:2-4). It is always more difficult to correct sin than to avoid it. The Israelites' action seems radical, but many of their problems came from such intermarriages, which introduced them to pagan worship. The leadership of this godly man made a difference!

PSALM 110   ☑This messianic psalm refers almost exclusively to the rule of Christ at His second coming. This portion was recognized as referring to the coming Messiah in Jesus' time, and Jesus quoted verse 1 to the Pharisees to show them, from the Scriptures, that the Messiah would be the Son of God (Matt 22:41-46). Jesus traced His lineage through David, through whom the Messiah would come, and validated that He was the Messiah by the miracles He performed (Luke 7:21-23; cf. Isa 42:6-7).

The universal rule of the Messiah (vv. 1, 2, 6) and His great power (vv. 3, 5, 6) are noted here. The victory in verses 3, 5, and 6 appears in John's vision in Revelation 19:11-21. Christ's everlasting priesthood is clearly present in verse 4. This role of priest previsions Jesus' central and personal part in redemption.⇦

DECEMBER 19

REVELATION 10   We are still in the throne room of heaven, between the sixth and seventh trumpet. Now the spotlight shifts to a mighty angel, huge, robed in a cloud, and with legs like fiery pillars. Visualize him with a face like the sun and a rainbow above his head. Altogether imposing! He has a little scroll in his hand. One foot is in the sea and one on land. As he gives a mighty shout, John hears seven thunders speak. They are intelligible, and the Apostle is about to record the message – but is prevented: The message is sealed. We do have the mighty angel's verbal message, however. *He announces that with the sounding of the seventh trumpet, the mystery of God will be completed!*

What can we say about the meaning of the thunders? Some things about God's dealings with us are still to be revealed (v. 4). Daniel had a similar experience when he attempted to understand the message the angel Michael brought him (Dan 12:7-10). That angel, too, raised his right hand and also swore by the Living God about the events of the end. But they also were sealed from Daniel's understanding.

John now is commanded to eat the scroll the angel is holding (vv. 8-9; cf. v. 2). It tastes sweet, but upsets his stomach. The little scroll is similar to that in Ezekiel 2:9-3:3. That scroll, and this one, symbolize the Lord's message to sinful man. While God's messenger agrees with the truth of God's will and work (sweet to the taste), the proclamation of that message is never easy or pleasant (bitter in the stomach).

ESTHER 1-3   The events recorded in Esther are in the capital of the Persian Empire – a vast power, as recorded in Esther 1:1-3. The king, Xerxes, is probably Artaxerxes of Ezra 4:6ff. The book is a glimpse into court life and politics of the ancient power, but more importantly, it reveals God's care for His people. As pernicious forces moved to destroy God's people (and thus the Promise), the Lord was also working, and this is the central message of the book.

Can you even imagine the banquet the king gave to demonstrate his power and wealth? Other existing accounts of the wealth of the court confirm the opulence of the furnishings recorded in Chapter 1. A crisis in the court occurred when the queen refused the king's request to appear before his guests in a way that to her was degrading (vv. 10-12). Her act of courage opened the way for Esther to become a candidate for queen.

As you read Chapters 1 and 2, remember Esther was a young Jewish girl, orphaned early in life and brought up by an older cousin (Mordecai), who was a devout Jew. Mordecai's grandfather Kish (the antecedent of "who" in 2:6) was taken to Babylon in 593 BC when Jehoiachin was carried into exile. When the events of this book took place over one hundred years later (Xerxes reigned from 486-465 BC), God would show His hand of deliverance on behalf of His people. Follow the account as Esther is brought to the center of court life through God's working.

In fact, the various threads of the account, seemingly unrelated all finally fit into God's plan. An example of this is Mordecai's knowledge of the conspiracy to kill the king and reporting the plot through Esther (2:19-23).

The evil plan to annihilate all Jews in the empire was conceived and made a legal requirement by Haman in the king's court. He understood that the Jews would not bow down to any person or false god and was piqued because Mordecai would not bow to him. Mordecai's response was that he was a Jew – to him it would be idolatry (3:3-4). How extraordinary that such a reason would lead to the mass killing of thousands of individuals.

MICAH 5:2; JEREMIAH 31:15 ☑The place of the Messiah's birth is identified only in Micah 5:2. The section 5:1-5a was recognized as referring to the coming Messiah. Note that the coming one would rule over Israel and that His origins were from ancient times. He was the one promised in Genesis 3:15, and 1 Peter 1:18-20 says this plan had been in place from before the foundations of the world. Except for the notation about the place of Christ's birth, the rest of this section refers to Christ's rule at His second coming (vv. 3b-5a).

As you contemplate the work of God in bringing every detail of prophecy into place, think about the order of Caesar Augustus that brought Mary and Joseph to Bethlehem from Nazareth (Luke 2:1-7). The timing, at God's hand, was exquisite!

When the wise men came from the east and inquired where to find the newborn king of the Jews, Herod heard about it. Upon asking the chief priests and the teachers of the law where the Messiah would be born, he learned that it would be in Bethlehem (Matt 2:1-6, from Micah 5:2). When the wise men didn't return to tell him of the child who would be king as he requested, he ordered all the male children in the area of Bethlehem killed (Matt 2:16-18). Matthew quotes Jeremiah 31:15, showing that this slaughter fulfilled that prophecy! Herod was actually intimidated by the birth of someone who could be the Messiah.⇦

DECEMBER 20

REVELATION 11 We are still in the interlude between the sixth and seventh trumpet. The spotlight shifts to the temple of God. The events occur as the holy city is trampled for forty-two months. This seems to correspond to the time in Daniel 9:26-27, perhaps after the Antichrist breaks the covenant with Israel following an initial forty-two months of peace (cf. 13:5-8).

Two witnesses are identified in verse 4, called the two olive trees and the two lampstands (cf. Zech 4:1-14, where the lampstand represented the truth, and the olive trees represented Joshua the high priest and Zerubbabel the governor). These two witnesses have the task of speaking the truth during forty-two months, the time that the Antichrist will have authority (13:5-8). Their job is most difficult, as they witness to God's truth when all seems to be in the hands of the Evil One.

Note their extraordinary power: power to prevent rainfall and power to turn water into blood. In addition, fire comes out of their mouths and destroys those who try to harm them. Historically, Moses turned water into blood and brought plagues to Egypt (Exod 7:19-21).

Historically, Elijah was God's messenger to Ahab, telling him there would be no rain except at his word (1 Kings 17:1), and who sent fire to destroy the soldiers who had come to arrest him (2 Kings 1:9-12). And significantly, it was Moses (representing the law) and Elijah (representing the prophets) who appeared with Jesus at His transfiguration (Luke 9:30-31) where they talked about the coming death (and resurrection, and second coming?) of Jesus. Notice that when these two witnesses are killed, there is worldwide rejoicing (on-the-spot coverage with worldwide transmission, vv. 7-12?). As people continue to watch, however, the two witnesses are raised to life and called up into heaven. What a demonstration of the power of God!

Are these actually Moses and Elijah? We cannot say, but they will speak god's truth in a time of great darkness. Even the most powerful voices of darkness cannot silence the voice of God!

Turn the spotlight back to the throne as the seventh trumpet is sounded (v. 15). The message of the loud voices and the elders is that now the Lord Jesus takes the authority that is rightfully His and begins to exercise it. The Ark of the Covenant is seen in the temple of the Lord in heaven (v. 19, the lost ark!). This will be the time for judging the dead (v. 18; cf. 20:11-15) and rewarding the saints (v. 18).

ESTHER 4-6   When he learned of the plot to kill all the Jews, Mordecai got Esther's attention by wearing sackcloth. Consider the message he sent to Esther. There are times when silence does not buy peace (4:13-14)! Mordecai also had a deep sense of God's working (4:14b). Although speaking out had its own grave dangers for Esther, *she approached the problem with prayer and fasting*, and courageously planned to try to intervene.

Chapters 5 and 6 are the turning point in the book. Queen Esther made her move to see the king and was invited into his presence. She invited the king and Haman to her apartments for dinner. Haman viewed this as a deep honor and boasted of it to his family and friends (5:9-13). The one cloud in his sky was Mordecai, who wouldn't bow to him. To solve this problem once and for all, he took the advice of his wife and friends and had a gallows built upon which he intended to hang Mordecai (5:14).

The suspense of Esther's request that the king and Haman come to her apartments for a meal was heightened by a second invitation, which they also accepted. Now some of the seemingly unrelated threads of God's working come together. Watch how the Lord elevated Mordecai and humbled Haman. *It was no happenstance that the king could not sleep (6:1), or that he read the particular place in the official chronicles where the record told how Mordecai reported a treasonous plan to kill the king (6:2).* The following morning, Haman's assignment was to bring recognition to Mordecai with the very honors he presumed would be his! This was seen by his friends and family (correctly) as a dire prediction. Events were out of his control – but in God's hand!

LUKE 1:5-25   ☑About eight hundred years before the events of this account, Isaiah wrote about the coming of John the Baptist (Isa 40:3-4). Matthew's gospel tied this prophecy to John the Baptist (Matt 3:3). The angel Gabriel appeared to Zechariah while he was performing his priestly duties to tell him that he and his wife Elizabeth would have a special child. The child was to be named John and would be influential among his people, preparing the way for the Messiah (vv. 11-20; especially v. 17).

God was in the events. Gabriel appeared to Zechariah just months before he also appeared to Mary to tell her she would be the mother of the Messiah (Luke 1:26ff.). The timing of the birth of John the Baptist as it related to the birth of Christ was absolutely in the Lord's hand.⇦

DECEMBER 21

REVELATION 12   There is now an interlude between the trumpets and the bowls of God's wrath. We will see the spotlight shift several times in Chapters 12-14 as we receive insights about the unseen (by human eyes) spiritual battle.

Turn from the main stage (the throne room of heaven) to see the drama of the woman, the dragon, and the child under the spotlight. This is a symbolic representation of the intense spiritual battle that has been and is being fought around the realization of redemption. Who is the woman clothed with the sun, with the moon under her feet, and a crown of twelve stars? Probably not a single person such as Mary, the mother of Jesus, but rather the plan of redemption. Or the woman may represent God's faithful people through the ages. Note that the woman is clothed with the brightness of God's glory and seems to be related to the twelve tribes of Israel (v. 1).

There is no question about the identity of the dragon. It is Satan, and his agenda is to destroy the male child who will rule the nations (v. 5, the Messiah; cf. Ps 2:9). Historically this attempt to disrupt God's plan was made several times in the history of God's people. Think of Haman's attack on the Jews in the Persian Empire. Herod's attempt to kill Jesus was one of these times. *The cross itself was an attempt to do away with Jesus, but the genius of God's holy plan turned this into the battle that won the spiritual war (Col 2:14-15)!*

Through history, with our limited human scope of vision, we see only a part of the battle. In verses 7-12, *understand that this is an intense spiritual battle.* In this vision we see the results of the battle won at the cross – the dragon cast from heaven (v. 10). Note particularly what is said about the "overcoming" brothers (v. 11). Is it important to be part of the army that helps win the battle? Does our personal behavior make a difference? Most emphatically! We are not playing games in this war.

Look also at the agenda of the dragon after being cast from heaven (vv. 13-17). If we understand the meaning of the chapter correctly to this point, then it is the church that the dragon is waging war against now. The Messiah is out of reach. As the dragon turns in rage and defeat from pursuing the child who was born, he turns to attack God's people (v. 17). Review Ephesians 6:10-18; this speaks of the same battle and gives tools to use in the conflict. The picture of an enraged dragon makes it especially important to use God's implements of warfare and His protection.

ESTHER 7-10   Follow God's continued and specific direction in this affair. Esther placed her life on the line when she boldly pointed to Haman as the person responsible for her people's danger (7:3-6a). Haman's fate was sealed, but made more sure when he pled for his life in close proximity to the queen.

With Haman hanged (7:10) and Mordecai promoted (8:1-2), Esther again pled for her people (8:3-6). The king authorized Mordecai to issue a decree that would nullify the previous edict by giving Jews the right to protect themselves and attack their enemies throughout the empire on the same day as the previous edict. Fast horsemen (8:14) sent the official documents with these directives through the kingdom. Imagine the transformed Mordecai as he left the presence of the king wearing royal robes (8:15).

The Jews in the empire had official permission to protect themselves from their enemies, and did so. Here is the origin of the observance of Purim. Think about Mordecai. Daniel was second in the kingdom of the Medes and Persians early in their reign after they defeated Babylon. Now another devout Jew was second in the country under a different king (Ch. 10)!

There is a deep significance to the book of Esther. Although they were dispersed among the nations, the Jews, God's people, were vital to God's unfolding plan of redemption. At the right time, Jesus the Savior would be born and would bear the sins of the world in His death (Gal 4:4-5). Haman's plan to wipe out the Jews in the world would have frustrated God's plan for the Messiah to come through a descendant of David (Isa 11). Mordecai believed God would not allow the destruction of the Jews (4:14, he understood the scriptures), and he also believed that God may have placed Esther in the king's court to prevent this from happening. The struggle was a spiritual one, and the bedrock issue was salvation. Herod's attempt to destroy the newborn King four hundred years later was part of the same battle (Matt 2:1-18). Satan's attempts to destroy Jesus by tempting Him in the desert and later at His death were attempts to destroy Jesus' mission and ministry.

Both Mordecai and Esther took actions that were humanly dangerous. Mordecai refused to bow to Haman. Esther came uninvited into the king's presence. As they acted on what they understood to be God's will, God blessed them and used them at that moment in Jewish history. We may not always be delivered in this way, but *we will always know God's blessing!*

LUKE 1:26-38 ☑The message that Gabriel brought Mary was at the same time disturbing, thrilling, and full of hope. Disturbing because of the unexpected presence of an angel (would you have been disturbed?). Thrilling in the context of Scripture because this would be the birth of the promised Messiah. Full of hope for the fulfillment of Scripture and God's plan of redemption.⇦

Think for a moment of this young woman receiving the message. She was likely not more than eighteen – perhaps younger. She was a pure, godly young woman looking forward to marriage. The implications of a pregnancy before her marriage would not be lost on the community. Yet see her response to Gabriel (v. 38). She was ready for God's will to be done in her life.

DECEMBER 22

REVELATION 13 Watch the same stage, but notice that the scene is changed – although it is a continuation of the previous vision. Before viewing this scene, a word of explanation is in order. *We are here to see the organizational plan of the enemy* – the hierarchy of top leadership dedicated to leading men to worship Satan. Satan uses clever counterfeits to lead men away from God. *What we see in this chapter is a counterfeit of the Trinity.*

Observe the dragon on the shore, and a beast coming out of the sea (v. 1). This beast is distinct from the dragon, for the dragon gives his power, throne, and authority to the beast (v. 2). *The identity of the dragon remains Satan. The beast is the Antichrist and is the counterfeit of the Lord Jesus.* The character of the beast is understood from the blasphemous names and the similarities to wild animals – the very parts that make them dangerous. Notice that one mark of the beast is that one of his heads had received a fatal wound, but now was again living. This beast, speaking with the authority of the dragon (Satan), blasphemes God and slanders His followers (vv. 5-6). Note also that the beast receives power (from the dragon) to make war on the saints and to conquer them (humanly). To understand the counterfeit nature of this beast, recall that Jesus came with the power and authority of His Father and that He died and was raised from the dead..

The authority of the Antichrist extends for forty-two months (v. 5; cf. 11:2). This matches the prophecy regarding the last half of the seventieth week in Daniel (Dan 9:24-27); after the wicked ruler breaks the agreement with God's people and country in the middle of the "seven" (forty-two months), he will disrupt the worship of God (Dan 9:27). This is the period that Jesus spoke of in Matthew 24:15ff. It is just before Christ comes to judge the nations (Matt 24:29-30). Note again the agenda of the beast: to make war on the saints (v. 7) and to make all people on the earth worship him (v. 8).

But there is yet another beast (vv. 11-18). This second beast, also called the false prophet (cf. Rev 19:20), acts on behalf of the Antichrist with miraculous signs (vv. 13-15). *The false prophet is the counterfeit of the Holy Spirit.* Remember that the Holy Spirit, working on behalf of the Lord Jesus, came with miraculous signs, and He seals God's people for final redemption (Eph 1:13b). The false prophet deceives people who believe his signs (v. 14). He sees to the execution of all who will not worship the Antichrist (v. 15), and forces all people, on threat of death, to receive a mark on the head or right hand in order to buy or sell (vv. 16-17, analogous to the Holy Spirit's seal of ownership).

Take special note of verse 10b and verse 18. The Lord has given us this information so we will not be deceived. We need wisdom, endurance, and faithfulness. Chapters 12 and 13 help us understand the nature of the spiritual conflict in which we are involved. There is no room for complacency! Recall that Jesus repeatedly told His followers to be prepared and alert when He spoke of end-time events (Matt 24)!

NEHEMIAH 1-2 Artaxerxes had another pious Jew near him (besides Esther)! Nehemiah was the cupbearer to the king. The time is several years after the first wave of exiles had gone to Jerusalem during Cyrus's reign. When word from them came back to the capital of Susa and reached Nehemiah, he was saddened to hear of the condition of the people and the city of Jerusalem, where the wall and gates of the city were broken.

After prayer (1:5-11; 2:4), and in answer to the king's question, Nehemiah told the king what had saddened him and requested a leave of absence to visit Jerusalem and rebuild the city. This was a courageous step, for such a request could just as likely have resulted in the loss of his head! God, faithful to His people, moved the king's heart, and Nehemiah's request was granted. Nehemiah pushed his request a step further by asking for letters to the governors of Israel's territory outlining Nehemiah's authority from the king and asking for materials to do the reconstruction (2:7-9).

Note the reaction of Sanballat and Tobiah when they learned that someone had come to work on behalf of the Jews (2:10). Follow Nehemiah as he made his secretive inspection of the wall and then proposed to the Jews that they rebuild the wall and the gates (2:11-18).

LUKE 1:46-55   Mary's beautiful expression of worship and praise to God was in response to meeting her cousin Elizabeth when both were expecting their babies. ☑Note that she links the coming of her child to the promise to Abraham and "our fathers." This makes it clear that she understood the import of Jesus as the coming Messiah (vv. 54-55).⇦ Think of Mary's prediction that all generations would call her blessed (v. 48) and how that has been literally fulfilled.

DECEMBER 23

REVELATION 14   Turn the spotlight back to center stage in the heavenly throne room. There is reference to Mount Zion with a voice and music coming from the throne (vv. 1-3). Is this Mount Zion, the heavenly Jerusalem (cf. Heb 12:22), or the earthly Jerusalem? We cannot say for certain. It is here that the 144,000 previously sealed have gathered in the presence of the Lamb. These are Jesus' followers – redeemed, pure, and truthful (vv. 3-5). When we read of the 144,000 who were sealed in Chapter 7, this was a sign of God's ownership. Now they have completed the course and are with the Lamb.

Next, pay attention to the three angels and their special messages (vv. 6-12). All people will have the opportunity to hear these messages of warning and truth (vv. 6-7). Trust God. Worship God. Judgment is imminent, calls the first angel. The second angel announces that Babylon is fallen – judgment has come – the world system has collapsed (v. 8). All that people trusted in is gone! The implication is that this world system, with all its allure, is not worth trusting. *Trust God!* The third angel announces the unmistakable consequence of allegiance to the beast (Antichrist) (vv. 9-12). Avoid the mark on the forehead or right hand at all cost! Judgment is coming and is sure to all followers of the beast.

Take note of the message of verse 13. This implies that there are still those who will die for their faith in God, perhaps as a result of the word from the heavenly messengers. Avoid the mark of the beast at all costs – even life itself.

Turn the spotlight to the scene of harvest (vv. 14-20). There seem to be two parts to the harvest – the first by one "like a son of man" whom we may identify as the Risen Lord. In this harvest (vv. 14-16; cf. Dan 7:13-14) there is no mention of judgment, and this seems to be the Lord coming for His faithful. Note that this follows immediately after the blessing of those who are faithful (vv. 12-13; cf. Matt 24:30-31). There is no question that the harvest of verses 17-20 is one of judgment. This last event does not seem to be a resurrection of the lost dead but the harvest of judgment for the ungodly on earth.

What should we learn from this chapter? Certainly that our choices are important, and that to dabble with the enemy in any way is dangerous in the extreme. Some choices (the mark on the hand or forehead, for instance) are irrevocable. The battle is very real. *Each one of us is a part of the battle in some way.* To be faithful, and to overcome, is to follow hard after Jesus!

NEHEMIAH 3-4   Under Nehemiah's direction, the people made rapid progress in repairing the wall (Ch. 3).

Again there was concerted opposition to restoring the city (previously opposition to the rebuilding of the temple). Sanballat and Tobiah were the leaders in organizing the opposition. They used intimidation (2:19), ridicule (4:1-3), and threats of violence (vv. 7-8). Nehemiah's strategy, on the other hand, was prayer (v. 9), encouragement (v. 14), prudent precaution (vv. 16-18), and practical hard work (vv. 16-23). He is an excellent model for our work in the church.

LUKE 1:57-79   ☑With the birth of John the Baptist, Zechariah's ability to speak was restored. His song of praise recognizes Jesus as the redeemer (v. 69, he was not speaking about John the Baptist, since he was a Levite and not from the Tribe of Judah). He saw these events as fulfillment of the promises to Abraham and those given through the prophets, and he recognized that liberty, holiness, and righteousness would be the result (vv. 72-75).

After referring to Jesus, he spoke about his own son (vv. 76ff.). Note that Zechariah understood that John would prepare the way for the Savior (v. 76b; cf. Isa 40:3), and that this would lead to forgiveness through Jesus' ministry (vv. 77-79).⇔

DECEMBER 24

REVELATION 15   Back to center stage in the throne room. John sees seven angels holding the seven last judgments in bowls, ready to be poured out on the earth.

Before pouring out the wrath, however, John notes people standing beside the sea of glass (vv. 2-4) who had prevailed in the time of the beast and his image (Ch. 13). They had refused the mark on their body, and had probably been killed because of it. They, as the 144,000 (14:2-3), had harps and sang an ancient song of Moses (cf. Exod 15:1-18).

As you read their song, think of two places and two perspectives. The perspective of these victorious saints is firm. The truth that God would rule the nations, and that all would worship Him, is firm. But go to earth for a moment and consider the dragon, the beast, and the false prophet, spewing out their lies, with people caught in the web of their falsehoods. True, these people allowed themselves to be deceived, but consider what is happening. *They are subjected to slavery of pure evil.* Thank God for redemption with all of your heart!

Focus on the seven angels (vv. 5-8). Clean, shining white clothing with golden sashes. Then notice the temple, filled with smoke. The temple will remain so until the judgments of wrath are completed. Note that this smoke is from God's glory and power (cf. 1 Kings 8:10-11). Stand in awe!

NEHEMIAH 5-6   When the injustice of the powerful and wealthy Jews came to his attention (5:1-5), Nehemiah faced the problem head-on, appealing to the people on biblical principles (vv. 6-11; cf. Exod 22:25-27). He followed through, making sure that the problems were corrected. Further, he did not demand or take what was rightfully his (vv. 15-16). Standing on biblical principle, it is amazing what one person can do!

As the work went forward, there were further attempts to frustrate its progress. First, Sanballat and his friends tried to get Nehemiah to meet them on their own territory so they could harm him (6:2). Note Nehemiah's answer to them – his work was too important to take time to meet them (v. 3). When Nehemiah would not talk, they tried lies and intimidation (vv. 6-7). *The discernment that Nehemiah demonstrated is remarkable.* He wouldn't talk with the opposition because he knew they were scheming against him. Even when they accused him falsely, he refused to talk with them. When one of the confederates of Sanballat tried to get Nehemiah to shut himself up in the temple by telling him that men were coming to kill him, Nehemiah again refused (vv. 10-13). Because of his single-minded purpose, the wall was finished in less than two months, and the enemies were themselves discouraged (vv. 15-16). Note the opposition from within the community of God's people (vv. 17-19)!

LUKE 2:1-20   Rejoice in Luke's beautiful account of the birth of Jesus. Even though the words are familiar, they are still moving. Here is the beginning of the literal fulfillment of the promise! Here is the hope of the ages past and future from that moment forward. Consider again the timing of the events. Mary and Joseph were in Bethlehem. The time had fully come (Gal 4:4-5).

Think too about how God chose to fulfill His promises. Mary had spoken of herself as humble (Luke 1:48a). There is no reason to believe that either Joseph or Mary was anything of note in the world's estimation. Yet both were godly individuals and God's own people. Certainly the circumstances of the Messiah's birth were humble. As the most significant person ever born spent His first minutes and hours, the world bustled on – except for the other humble people from the field who had heard the heralding choir (vv. 8-15)!

DECEMBER 25

REVELATION 16   The scene is still before the throne of God in heaven. As with the other dreadful judgments, we read here about the Day of the Lord. It is here in the presence of the throne that the angels appear. Watch the shifting scene, however, as they pour the bowls of wrath. The spotlight shifts to the devastation they bring. We look with a zoom lens, first at the entire earth, then at people individually cursing God.

As with the trumpets (8:6-12), the first four bowls touched *the earth, the seas, the fresh water of the earth, and the celestial bodies* in order. In contrast with the fourth trumpet, which darkened a third of the light of the sun, moon and stars, the fourth bowl increased the intensity of the sun, causing great suffering on earth. Still, men and women would not repent (vv. 9, 11; cf. 9:20-21). Sin and evil have a tenacious hold. This also demonstrates the power of redemption!

As the fifth bowl is poured, think of the darkness of Satan's evil rule (vv. 10-11). With this judgment from God, the kingdom of the beast becomes literally dark, as well as spiritually black (cf. Exod 10:21-23). With the sixth bowl, note the power of deception in the world (three evil spirits, v. 13). In fact, God Himself is preparing the way for the final battle that will bring the Heavenly King, while at the same time Satan calls out the troops.

Carefully note verse 15 (cf.1 Thess 5:4). Note that the warning comes here between the sixth and seventh bowls of wrath. It is the announcement of Christ's coming with the battle of Armageddon (v. 16). That battle must be occurring at the time of the seventh bowl. Compare this portion with Matthew 24:29-31. Compare verse 15 with Matthew 25:1-13 with regard to being prepared for Christ's appearing. Look again at Zechariah 14:1-6. Here too is the battle, the earthquake, the splitting of the city. What awesome events! *If ever there has been a time to be sure of our clothing of righteousness from the Lord, it is now (v. 15).* Surely, the coming of Christ must be soon!

NEHEMIAH 7-8   One of Nehemiah's first rules was that the gates of the city would be shut at night and not opened until the sun was high (7:1-3). At last there was some sense of safety for the residents of the city.

Ezra the priest (scribe), who traced his ancestry back to Aaron (Ezra 7:1-5), was asked to read the Law of Moses. He read from a raised platform so all could see and hear him (8:4a). Note especially 8:8. This was careful reading, giving expression and meaning for the people: It was so powerful it made people weep. After the reading, Nehemiah (the governor), with Ezra and the Levites, encouraged the people to enjoy themselves with food (vv. 9-10). It was a special day; this was probably the first time the Word had been read in such a way since the exile. It was worth celebrating! In God's Word, they found the portion outlining the Feast of Tabernacles, so they celebrated for seven days by making temporary booths in which to live (Lev 23:33-43). Ezra read from the Scriptures every day during the celebration.

LUKE 2:21-40   When Jesus was circumcised, his parents brought the requisite offering to the Lord. They brought doves and pigeons, the sacrifice reserved for those who could not afford the usual animal sacrifice (v. 24; cf. Lev 12:6-8). This further indicates their economic status.

Two special people were at the temple when Jesus was brought for the circumcision. These were people in communion with the Lord – each understood from God Himself who Jesus was. Think of what they felt as they saw in real life this Savior for whom they had been waiting. ☑Note how Simeon tied the birth of Jesus to the prophecies of the Scriptures (vv. 29-32).⇦ Consider the impact of their words on Mary and Joseph. Both Mary and Joseph had heard independently from the Lord's messenger that Jesus was from God. They had heard the shepherd's testimony as they came from the fields to worship Jesus. Now, the message was again confirmed.

DECEMBER 26

REVELATION 17   As the chapter begins, we are back at center stage – the temple where we saw the angels with the bowls. One of these angels invites our attention to another vision, and the spotlight shifts to highlight that vision.

It is a strange sight, indeed – a woman expensively dressed is sitting on a red beast, the one with seven heads and ten horns. This identifies the beast as the Antichrist (13:1-10). The woman, too, is easily identified. She is Babylon, the world system in step with Satan and his program of seducing everyone to follow him. We are seeing her as God sees her: a vile person, still drinking from the cup of iniquity. She is drunk with the blood of the saints – those who died for their godly testimonies. Keep in mind the agenda of the Antichrist who is working with the authority of the dragon, and assisted by the false prophet (Ch. 13).

The seven hills (vv. 9-11) have been thought by many to refer to the city of Rome, since there are seven hills in the ancient city. However, it is difficult to fit the seven kings into this idea – five who have been, one that "is" at the time of the writing, and one yet to come. Alternately, the kings, or kingdoms that they represent, could be the successive kingdoms that were problems to the Israelites: the Egyptians, the Assyrians, the Babylonians, the Persians, the Greeks, the Romans (now is, v. 10), and the coming kingdom of the Antichrist. The ten horns (v. 12) would refer to the confederation of ten nations at the time of the end (Dan 2:41-45).

Note that at the end of time, the conflict with the Lamb will be from this beast and the nations aligned with it (vv. 12-14). Actually, the conflict will be with the spiritual powers of evil (Eph 6:10-18), with the nations and their kings merely as "front men." Note also that as the end approaches, Satan's forces are divided. The nations turn on the woman, bring her to ruin, and leave her naked! The system of excessive luxuries (18:3) and wickedness (17:2) seems to have been repudiated by the nations and destroyed.

NEHEMIAH 9-10   The reading of the Scriptures led to conviction and confession of sin (Ch. 9)! Levites who had been cleansed and purified were ready to lead the people in worship and confession. Read carefully the praise and prayer to the Lord, which remembers God's goodness to the people in the past, and confesses how they and their forefathers had offended the Lord. God has been more than just, they said (9:33). They were, in effect, casting themselves upon the Lord's mercy. But they also acted. Civil and religious leaders, and representatives of the people publicly signed an agreement to follow the Lord (9:38-10:27).

The substance of the agreement was significant. They resolved to follow God's Word (10:29). They promised not to allow intermarriage with the pagan residents of the land (v. 30). They promised not to do business on the Sabbath (*that* touched their pocketbooks), and to observe the seventh year of rest for the land (v. 31, cf. Lev 25:1-7). They assumed financial responsibility for God's work (vv. 32-33), and took responsibility for the worship of the whole company (v. 34). They promised to observe the regulations regarding tithing, thus supporting the priests and the Levites (vv. 35-39). These were far-reaching reforms, indicating that they were indeed serious about following the Lord.

LUKE 9:18-27   The tender days of infancy and early childhood were behind. Jesus was now close to His last journey to Jerusalem – the path that would lead to the crucifixion. While Jesus and the disciples were alone in Caesarea Philippi, He asked them who they thought He was. Peter was quick to confess that He was the Christ – and Jesus did not dispute this. ⊃His lack of denial affirmed that it was true. Further, He revealed to the disciples that He would be killed and be raised from the dead on the third day (v. 22).⊂

This information seemed to go right past the disciples. Either they didn't understand or didn't believe that such an event would happen. Not until after his death and resurrection did they remember that Jesus had told them these things would happen.

Read once again the conditions of discipleship (vv. 23-27). Are you a disciple – by Jesus' definition? *Remember that there are no other valid definitions!*

DECEMBER 27

REVELATION 18   John sees another angel, so glorious that the earth is illuminated. The message of the heavenly messenger is that Babylon has fallen (v. 2). The reasons for the fall are obvious in verses 2-3. This is the judgment announced in 14:8 and 17:1. The proclaimed calamity refers to the world system of evil represented by the ancient city of Babylon. This is God's judgment on the deceptive and seductive system that has drawn men away from the living God since the Garden of Eden. Another voice from heaven calls God's people to leave the city and its evil (v. 4). *This is a call for all Christians to separate themselves from all parts of this evil system* – from its mind-set (see Rom 8:5-8), thinking patterns, and practices (cf. 1 John 2:15-16). As you read verses 4-8, understand why God's final judgment will come to this system.

Notice that this great catastrophe will affect all classes: the kings of the earth (vv. 9-10), the business tycoons of the world (vv. 11-17), and those who transport the goods produced by the system (vv. 17b-19), to name but a few.

Understand that this act of God will affect the fabric of society. The cabarets and nightclubs will be closed and the orchestras will be gone (v. 22a). The trades will be destroyed, industry will be totally disrupted (v. 22b), energy will be unavailable (v. 23a), and times of rejoicing will be only a memory (see comments about the bridegroom and bride in v. 23). Society as we know it will be unveiled, revealing its true character (vv. 23b-24).

Now read what the attitude of God's people should be (v. 20). This can be only the reaction of those who have, through the discernment of the Word of God and the application of truth by the Holy Spirit, understood the true nature of evil in the world and separated themselves from it. Now is the time for you and me to act on the call of verse 4. Read again 1:3.

NEHEMIAH 11-12   Picture the rejoicing as people poured into Jerusalem for the dedication of the wall (12:27ff.). Imagine the choirs marching on the top of the wall and the service of dedication. This was truly a time to praise God, for He had seen the project to completion in spite of opposition.

MATTHEW 27:32-56   Jesus came to the world to save sinners. He came to die for you and me. Perhaps it seems a bit hard to go directly from the birth of our Lord to His confession that He was God's Son and then to His death. Yet they must be seen together, or the story of salvation and redemption would be incomplete. As we are celebrating the birth of Christ in this season, we must keep in mind the purpose of it all. Jesus pointed out that it was for this reason that He had come (John 12:27). Don't let the whimsy of the world's Christmas celebration rob you of its real significance – redemption.

Remember that Simeon told Mary in Luke 2:34-35 that a sword would pierce her soul. Her heart was breaking as she watched her own son die this cruel death. The sword had indeed pierced her soul. In that process, however, Jesus paid for her sin!

DECEMBER 28

REVELATION 19   Remember how the earth mourned the destruction of the system that brought them wealth and luxury (Ch. 18). Contrast this reaction with that of the saints and heavenly beings (19:1-10), who understand sin and righteousness, and God's agenda! Our deep need is to also understand God's agenda and work actively to see it fulfilled. This, in fact, is what we ask in the Lord's Prayer (Matt 6:10) – for God's will (in the same way) on earth *as it is realized in heaven*. Note that the righteous acts of God's people are remembered (v. 8).

Now, as you read verses 11-21, see how Jesus (the rider) finally fulfills the promise of Psalm 2:9 (v. 15) and destroys the beast (Antichrist) and the false prophet (v. 20; cf. Rev 13).

NEHEMIAH 13   Despite the promises and the blessings, after Nehemiah returned to the Persian capital, the people returned to sins of the past (13:6). Tobiah, who had opposed the plan to rebuild the wall, had connections with top Israelites (6:17-18) and had obtained a room for his own use in the storerooms of the temple (13:4-5). As an

Ammonite, he should not have been in the temple at all. Further, the people had not been giving their tithes to the Levites, and the Sabbath was being broken (vv. 10, 15). Nehemiah immediately took decisive action (vv. 8-9, 11-13). And, even after the reforms under Ezra (Ezra 9-10), the people, including some among the priests, had married pagan residents of the land (13:23-28). Nehemiah also faced this directly and got results.

We should learn that society has a bent to sin that we must deal with in our own lives. *Whatever someone else is doing, it is our own responsibility to walk before the Lord in righteousness.* The lesson to leaders is that when truth slips, it is time to act (Acts 20:28-31).

MATTHEW 28:1-10   The words describing the resurrection are eloquent in their simplicity. The fact of the resurrection is the proof of the divinity of our Lord (Rom 1:4). God accomplished the impossible – making a way for men to truly know Him. Now there could be forgiveness and mercy within the context of God's holy justice. Even in these days of remembering the birth of Jesus, remember that Easter is the highest and most holy day on the Christian calendar. Rejoice in the complete work of the Lord Jesus.

DECEMBER 29

REVELATION 20   Remember that the Antichrist and the false prophet were destroyed in the lake of fire (19:20). Satan was bound with a chain and shut up in the Abyss, making him unable to deceive the nations for one thousand years. *This opens the way for Jesus to demonstrate that a righteous rule, based upon God's Word and with His agenda, will bring satisfaction and joy to the world.* For a picture of what this will look like, review Isaiah 2:2-4. It will be a time of peace, justice, and honesty. There will be no military establishment and no munitions industry. Despite all the plans for peace through the years, *there has never been peace. JESUS WILL BRING REAL PEACE!*

Notice that the faithful will reign with the Lord (v. 4). Does it pay to stand firm and faithful for our Lord? Indeed it does. The second death, the lake of fire, has no hold on these who are God's faithful (v. 6).

The "last stand" of Satan and evil is described in verses 7-10. Once again, deception is Satan's signature as he rallies the nations for the last battle with the Lord. It is amazing that after one thousand years of peace and justice, he is able to deceive the people of the world. But this demonstrates the hold of evil on the human heart, and Satan's power to deceive. For a description of this battle, review Ezekiel 38:14-39:6. With the defeat of Satan, he is destroyed forever in the lake of fire.

Turn the spotlight to God's throne in heaven. All the people of the earth – all who have ever lived and died, and who were not brought to life when Jesus returned for the church (1 Thess 4:13-18) – now stand before the Lord to be judged. Note that the book of life contains the names of God's faithful. All whose names were not found in the book of life were judged by God's record, and were thrown into the lake of fire. This is a solemn picture – the moment when Jesus said there would be weeping and gnashing of teeth (Matt 25:30; Luke 13:22-30). It is the moment when there is no retreat, no argument with God, no further chance to rectify wrong. No wonder that Paul urged the Corinthians to receive God's grace, telling them that "now is the time of God's favor, now is the day of salvation" (2 Cor 6:2b). Our opportunity to receive grace will not last forever, and our chance to share that grace with those who don't know the Lord will not last forever either.

MALACHI 1   Malachi was the last book of the Old Testament to be written, probably about 430 BC. The book is directed to the people of Judah who have returned to their land from Babylon. Jerusalem had fallen some 150 years earlier, and the exiles had returned to Israel about eighty years earlier.

Malachi delivered a series of statements from the Lord, listened to the people's questions in response, then answered their questions. It is as if the people said to God, "What? What are you talking about? How did we do that?"

God said, "I have loved you" (1:2). The people asked, "How have you loved us?" The Lord answered He had loved them by choosing and caring for them (vv. 2-5). The evidence was unmistakable!

God said to the priests, "You despise my name" (v. 6). The people ask, "How have we done that?" Read how the Israelites had compromised God's name. They hadn't cared enough for God to even bring sacrifices that met the standard of the Mosaic Law (v. 7; cf. Lev 1:1-3). The Lord pointed out that they wouldn't dare do such a thing to a political official (v. 8), yet they approached God casually with second-rate gifts. The Lord told them He would rather they closed the doors of the temple than to defile the altar with that kind of disrespect. ☑Note God's statement that His name would be honored among all of the peoples of the world and that people in every place will worship Him (v. 11; cf. Phil 2:5-11).⇦

The lesson is that our worship must be genuine and from the heart. God sees and knows how we come to Him. A "ho-hum" approach is not acceptable when coming before the God of the universe (nor would it be an acceptable way to approach the governor for an audience).

LUKE 24:13-35   When Jesus opened the Scriptures to those with Him on the road to Emmaus, their hearts burned within them (v. 32). ➲He explained that the promises of the Old Testament Scriptures pointed to Him and were being fulfilled before their eyes (v. 27).◓ These two disciples carried their new knowledge to the rest of the company of believers – and perhaps Jesus also opened the Scriptures to them as well. The Bible is one book with one message – the good news of God's intervention in human life, bringing redemption. It is the message of Christmas. It is the message of Good Friday. It is the message of Easter. It is the message of Jesus' coming again. It is the message of both the Old Testament and the New.

Today we have the privilege of easy access to God's word. The printing press has made this possible. Do justice to this privilege by continuing in your reading and study of this most significant book in existence. It will pay great dividends, and prepare you for life and eternity!

DECEMBER 30

REVELATION 21   John was privileged to see the New Jerusalem coming down from heaven (v. 2) and heard the proclamation that God would thenceforth live with men. Read how glorious it will be (vv. 3-4).

Those who "overcome" are again mentioned (v. 7). There will be no room in the city for the wicked and unbelieving (v. 8). The opportunity to know God's grace and become an overcomer is in the present!

Read the description of the New Jerusalem. Is this an exact representation or a metaphor to describe something wonderful and beautiful? We will know when we get there! Note the description of the city in verses 22-27. God is with His people; His glory is the light of the city; there is no room for impurity. It is true: This heritage is guaranteed for those who have placed their faith in the Savior.

MALACHI 2   Chapter 2 continues the message from Chapter 1. The people had not worshipped the Lord with their heart, and the priests had compromised their teaching so that people stumbled in their walk with God (2:7-8).

God said to the people, "You flood the Lord's altar with tears. You weep and wail because He no longer pays attention to your offerings or accepts them with pleasure from your hands" (2:13). The people ask, "Why (don't you, God, accept them)?" Note carefully the Lord's answer (2:14). It is because of the broken marriage promises of the people! Pay attention to the Lord's statement in verses 15-16.

Chapter 2 ends with God telling the people that they have wearied Him with their words (v. 17). When they ask "How?" the Lord tells them they have twisted the truth, putting words into the Lord's mouth that He has never uttered, and then asking "Where is the God of justice?"

This message to the Israelites who had returned to their land is very contemporary and applies to the church today. In one degree or another, we are guilty of the same offenses. We *must* be willing to hear the message from the Lord and apply its truth appropriately to our own lives. Reading God's Word must not be just from curiosity; we must allow God to speak to our need.

MATTHEW 28:18-20; ACTS 1:1-11   Before Jesus left the disciples, He gave them direction for the future – and for all who would come after them in the church. Our job description is to represent Jesus and His kingdom in a broken world: give people the good news, teach them the truth about the world and their need before God, and bring believers into the kingdom. We must never lose sight of this basic assignment that has eternal implications for those with whom we rub shoulders – and it is a world-wide assignment.

We are sent with the authority of the Lord Jesus (see also Matt 10:1), and we are not alone (v. 20). The Lord promises His presence to each of us in this assignment. And just before Jesus ascended into heaven, He also promised power for the task ahead (Acts 1:8). After this promise, the Lord went up to heaven before their eyes. As Jesus was ascending, two heavenly messengers told those watching that Jesus would return again as they had seen Him ascend.

In these two short passages, we have the assignment and mission as individuals and the church, the promise of power for the task – and the promise of Jesus' return.

DECEMBER 31

REVELATION 22   As we come to the end of this powerful book, we have a glimpse of life in the heavenly kingdom (vv. 1-5). The river of pure water is previsioned in the Old Testament in Psalm 46:4, Joel 3:18b, and Ezekiel 47:1ff. The tree of life is again available (v. 2). (Remember the tree in the Garden of Eden.) Most exciting is that God will be there, face to face, with His people (vv. 3-4)! *And this is true (v. 6)!*

Three times in this chapter, Jesus tells us that He is coming soon (vv. 7, 12, 20). This emphasis is meant to get and hold our attention! *Jesus is coming soon!* Note the words immediately following it in verses

7 and 12. Read the book, think about it, and take appropriate action to be prepared.

MALACHI 3-4   ☑As Chapter 3 begins, the Lord answers the people's question in 2:17b, wondering where the God of justice was. God's answer is not what the people had in mind. The people are not ready for His coming, but He will come in judgment when they are not expecting Him (vv. 1-4). That this refers to the coming of Christ is obvious in verse 1 with the announcement of the messenger who would come before Him. Jesus quoted the reference in 3:1 and identified the messenger as John the Baptist (Matt 11:10). Malachi does not differentiate between the first and second advents. He speaks of His first advent with the coming of John the Baptist, and then moves immediately into the second advent, The Day of the Lord (vv. 2, 5; cf. Isa 61:1-2). Why judgment? God enumerates the reasons in verse 5. This covers all dealings with evil spirits, immorality, all untruth, those who cheat, those who oppress, those who deny justice, and the arrogant; i.e., all those who do not know God through faith, expressed in obedience.⇔ Look carefully at these reasons to be sure that today we are addressing the Lord's list of concerns.

When the Lord called the people to return to Him, they again asked how (v. 7b). "Stop robbing me," God replied. "How do we rob you?" they asked (v. 8). By not obeying in giving the tithes, God answered (vv. 8-10). As you follow these exchanges, consider how practical God is. His requirements are not hidden! Then look at the promise God gave these people (v. 10).

One more exchange takes place. God accused the people of speaking against Him (3:13). When they asked how, He reminded them they had said it was useless to serve God. Even when they did serve Him, it seemed that evil people did well in spite of their sin (vv. 14-15). It is encouraging to see that the people listened and turned to the Lord (v. 16). See the Lord's response in verse 17, and how this action would protect them and turn to their blessing in the Day of the Lord (4:1-4).

☑Finally, these last words of the Old Testament bring us to the Day of the Lord (v. 1). The second coming will not mean judgment for those who love God. For them it will be a day of healing, joy, and liberation (vv. 2-3). How can we be ready? Remember the message of the Bible, and honor God with actions and obedience (v. 4).⇔ What a way to conclude God's Word before Christ comes!

TITUS 2:11-14   An agenda for life – that is what these verses contain. They tell us of God's agenda for His people – a fitting way to end our reading for the year.

The grace of God accomplishes God's work in our lives. We sometimes believe that we are doing it all. In fact, although our will is involved in our growth, the Lord accomplishes the task (vv. 11-12). Note the need for discipline and how this is linked with God's work. Grace teaches us to say no to the temptations that the world puts in our way, and it equips us to do His will. God's grace enables us to say yes to a disciplined, upright, and godly lifestyle. With God's help, we must choose the Lord's will and way.

We have an anticipation that also helps us live the right way. The term "blessed hope" refers to the Lord's return (v. 13; cf. 1 John 3:3). There is no way we can look for the Lord's return and be careless about life.

Finally, think carefully about Christ's purpose for believers (v. 14). This is the result of redemption: people of spiritual maturity, avoiding evil, pure, ready to be at the Savior's work in a broken world. *May God grant that grace to each one who has embarked on this discovery of the Bible and the Christian life!*

A POSTSCRIPT
AS THE YEAR ENDS

If you have followed the reading plan, you have read the entire Bible during the year. There is nothing that will so shape your thinking as the Word of God, combined with obedience to what you read.

For some, this may be your first time to read the entire Bible. Begin to read the Bible through again tomorrow. If you have appreciated the plan we have used, use it again. It will not be stale or "old hat." In fact, as you start again, you will be surprised at how the second – and third – time through, the Bible continues to bring new insights and identifies new areas in life that the Lord wants you to deal with. Regular reading will continue to be a discovery for as long as you live! Those who have read the Bible many times continue to be blessed, and blessed in greater measure, as they continue to read. God is at work in His children, and He uses His Word through the Holy Spirit to accomplish His purposes.

About the Author

Gordon L. Addington is a graduate of the Univ. of Minnesota, (BCE '48, BS '58, and MD '58), and also studied at Trinity Evangelical Divinity School, earning a BD in '53, and later a DMin in '87. He is a Diplomat of the American Board of Surgery and a Fellow in the American College of Surgeons. Addington, with his wife Bonnie and children, spent eleven years as a medical missionary in Hong Kong under the Evangelical Free Church of America, and from 1974 to 1990, practiced general surgery in St. Paul, MN. Since then he has carried out educational and administrative responsibilities in the area of surgery, as well as teaching in the local church.

He has written a Bible reading guide – <u>Discovering the Bible</u> – that leads a reader through the entire Bible in one year. Notes are given for each day's reading to give background and help the reader to see the development of God's plan of Redemption in the entire Bible.

Gordon and Bonnie have been married 52 years, have ten grown children, and live in White Bear Lake, MN. They are members of the First Evangelical Free Church in Maplewood, MN.